Hidden Coast of California

The Adventurer's Guide

Hidden Coast of California

The Adventurer's Guide

Ray Riegert

Production Director:
Leslie Henriques

Illustrator:
Victor Ichioka

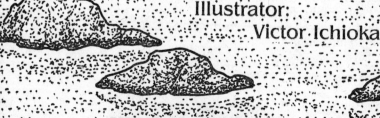

ULYSSES PRESS
Berkeley, CA

Published by: Ulysses Press
Sather Gate Station
Box 4000–H
Berkeley, CA 94704

Library of Congress Catalog Card Number 87-050719
ISBN 0-915233-06-1

Printed in the U.S.A. by the George Banta Company

10 9 8 7 6 5 4 3 2 1

Managing Editor: Lindsay Mugglestone
Cover Designer: Bonnie Smetts
San Diego Area Editor: Dave Houser
Research Assistance: Claire Chun, Jan Butchofsky, Tom McElheney
Map Design: Rob Hunter
Typesetting: Miki Demarest, Boyd Hunter, Cindy Scott
Cover Photography: front cover photo by Woody Woodworth/
Four By Five; back cover photos by Ed Simpson
Paste-up: Phil Gardner
Index: Sayre Van Young

For Keith and Alice

Acknowledgments

Despite all the road trips and research, writing represents only a fraction of the effort that went into this book. It's the folks back home who carried it through to completion. My wife and co-publisher Leslie worked on every phase of the project—planning, designing, coordinating, correcting, overseeing, and polishing the prose. The volume is a testimonial to her talents. I owe her a world of gratitude for her diligence and devotion.

Lindsay Mugglestone, a very capable managing editor, also served in numerous roles, working impossible hours. She prepared the manuscript, designed maps, kept the computer in line (and *on* line), offered invaluable advice, and performed countless other tasks which I cannot remember and she would probably prefer to forget.

Claire Chun did a brilliant job preparing my notes and assisted with everything from research to helping rear my children. Victor Ichioka added his artistic talents, contributing fine drawings throughout the book; and Bonnie Smetts, as always, designed a beautiful cover. Dave Houser did outstanding work in researching and preparing the San Diego Coast chapter. Professionals all, they each deserve a special thank you.

I also want to thank Jan Butchofsky and Tom McElheney for their research assistance; Phil Gardner for paste-up; Miki Demarest, Boyd Hunter and Cindy Scott for typesetting; Sayre Van Young for her comprehensive but accessible index; Rob Harper for mapmaking; as well as Woody Woodworth and Ed Simpson for their cover photography.

Peter Beren, that maven of marketing, offered many excellent suggestions. I want to convey a special thanks to those other people in the publishing industry who rarely receive credit for their vital work. Foremost are the distributors. Charlie Winton, Julie Bennett, Randy Fleming, Mike Winton, Bill Hurst, Bonnie Beren, and all the other folks at Publishers Group West have assisted in nearly every phase of publishing and marketing. Randy Beek at Bookpeople, the folks at Quality Books and Raincoast, and Bill Julius and Pat Nowell at Banta Company have also been particularly helpful over the years. And a tip of the hat to Robert Sheldon for his friendly advice and charming smile.

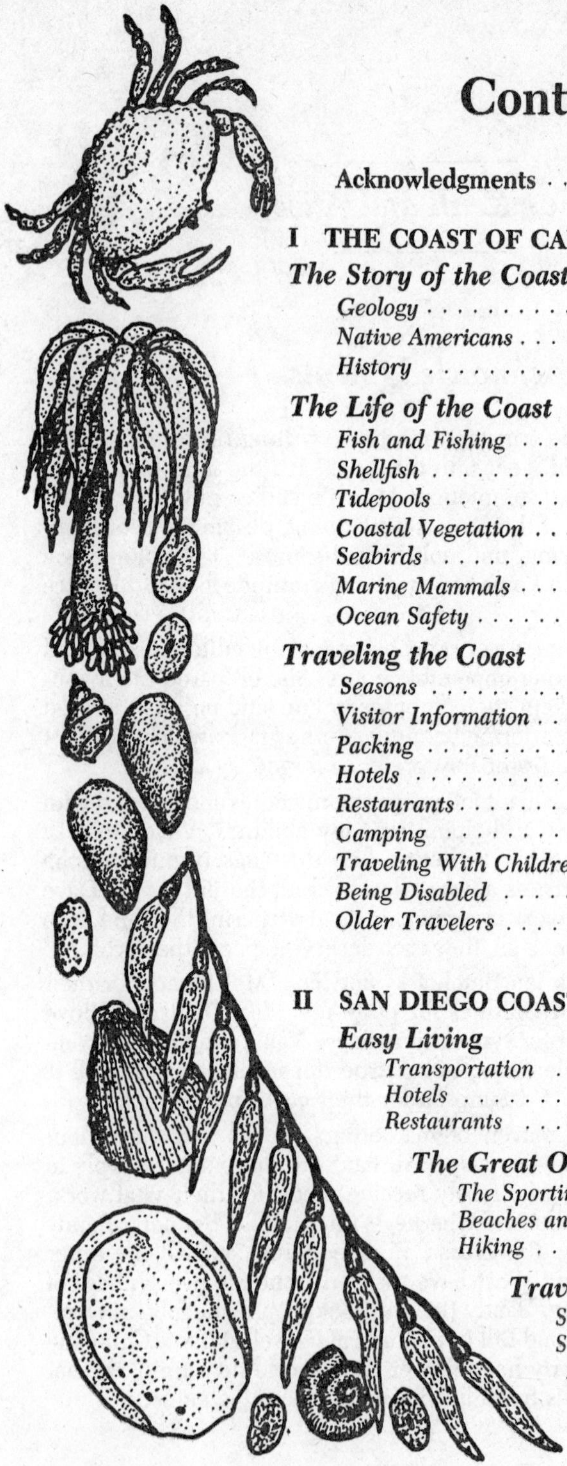

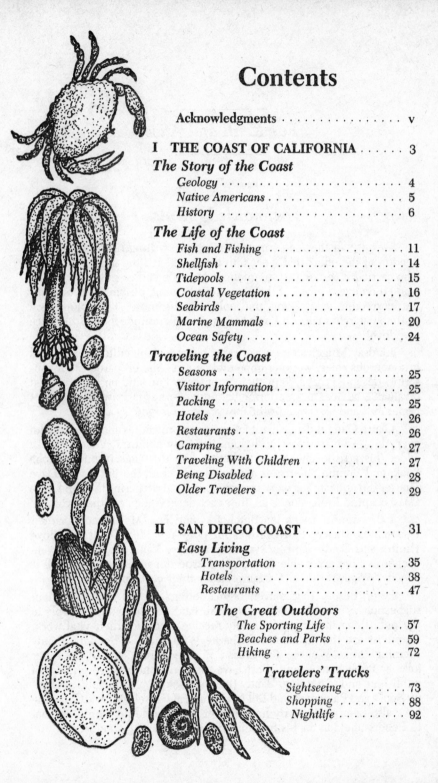

Contents

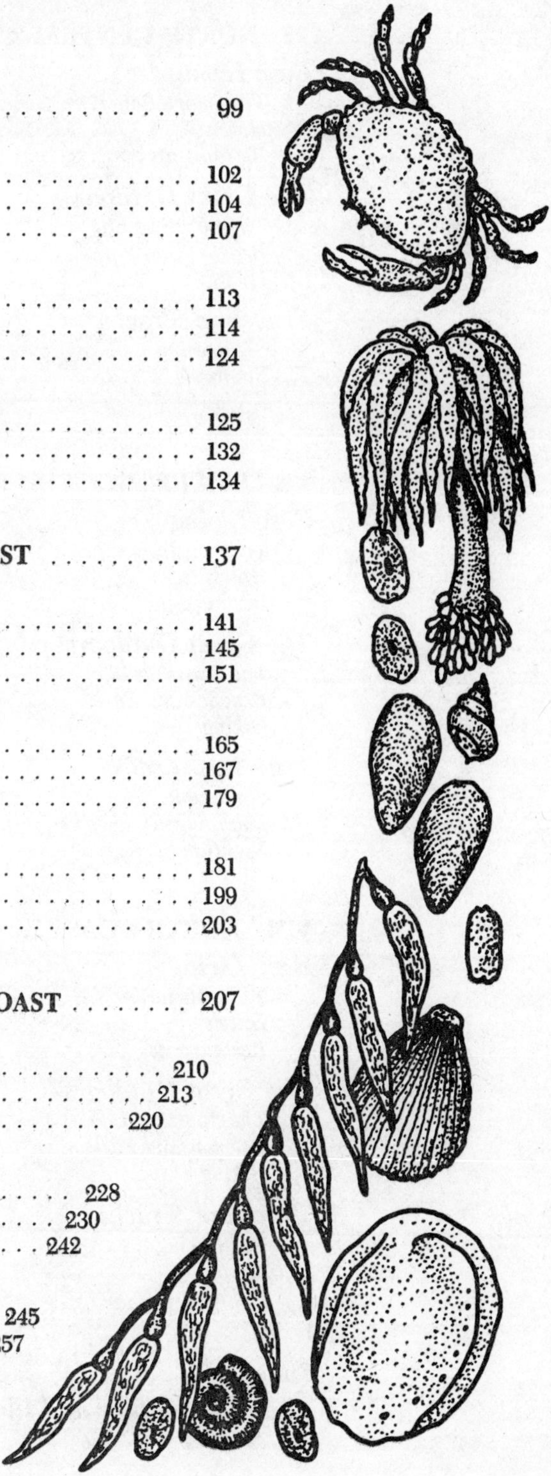

MAPS

SPECIAL FEATURES

Throughout the text, hidden locales, remote regions, and little- known spots are marked with a star (★).

CHAPTER ONE

The Coast of California

California. The word comes from an old Spanish novel about a mythic island populated by Amazons and filled with gold. It was, according to the author, "very near to the terrestrial paradise." The first part of this magical land to be explored, and the area which still symbolizes the California dream, is the coast.

Stretching 1100 miles along the rim of the Pacific, it is a wildly varied region with sharp mountains and velvet beaches, barren sand dunes and rich estuaries. Los Angeles, San Francisco, and San Diego, three of the nation's largest cities, are here, together with the old mission centers of Santa Barbara and Monterey. There are small fishing towns and international shipping ports, Victorian neighborhoods and oceanfront mansions.

Powerfully influenced by early Spanish culture, the coast today is responding to a fresh influx of Mexican immigrants as well as a growing Asian population. It is a region both at the edge of the continent and at the cutting edge of the global shift toward Asia and the Pacific Rim.

The California shore is also one of the most popular travel destinations in the world. Tens of millions of visitors explore its byways and beaches every year. *Hidden Coast of California*, the only guidebook to deal exclusively with this amazing territory, is an attempt to make the entire area accessible to everyone.

For those seeking the good life, each chapter describes the hotels, restaurants, shopping places, and night-owl roosts that dot every town along the coast. There is information on transportation, bicycling, and water sports. Then, when the spirit of adventure takes hold, there are descriptions of secluded beaches, remote hiking trails, and sightseeing spots both famous and unknown.

Beginning at the Mexican border and proceeding north toward Oregon, *Hidden Coast of California* takes in the sparkling bays and historic neighborhoods of San Diego, sweeps through Laguna Beach and Newport Beach, then scopes out the surfing scene at Huntington Beach.

The many faces of Los Angeles are uncovered to reveal Long Beach with its island neighborhood and industrial complex, the tumbling Palos Verdes Peninsula, the blond-haired surf cultures of the South Bay, bohemian Venice, and ultra-chic Malibu.

Venturing up the Central Coast past Ventura, a chain of mission towns including Santa Barbara, San Luis Obispo, Monterey, and Santa Cruz are separated by the adze-like peaks and flower-filled gorges of Big Sur. San Francisco is described as a port city, with special emphasis on its Pacific shoreline and magnificent bay. Along the Northern California coast, the book ranges through redwood forests, along twisting country roads, and high above sharp ocean cliffs.

It is a land of rare opportunity, where visitors can stay in art deco hotels or quaint country inns, bivouac on the beach or dine on fresh California cuisine. A multicultural extravaganza as well as a region of extraordinary beauty, the California Coast is a place for creative travelers, those anxious to combine the easy life of cities with the challenges of the open ocean in a place very near indeed to "the terrestrial paradise."

The Story of the Coast

GEOLOGY

Things are never what they seem. Trite though that adage might be, it perfectly fits the California Coast. Lined with softly rolling hills and bounded by a pacific sea, the shoreline is actually a head-on collision between the edge of the ocean and the rim of North America.

Two tectonic plates, those rafts of land that float upon the earth's core, meet in California. Here the North American Plate and the Pacific Plate push against each other in a kind of international arm wrestle. Between them, under colossal pressure from both sides, subject at any moment to catastrophic forces, lies the San Andreas fault, villain of the 1906 San Francisco earthquake.

Things were not always as they are. About 150 million years ago, the coast rested where the Sierra Nevada mountains reside today. Then the North American Plate shifted west, riding roughshod over the Pacific Plate, compressing and folding the earth upward to create the Coast Ranges, and moving the continent 100 miles westward.

Just 25 million years ago, a blink of the eye in geologic time, the Pacific Plate shifted north along the San Andreas fault, creating the Central Coast from what had been part of Baja. This northerly movement continued, building pressures of unimaginable magnitude, and formed the Transverse Range five million years ago.

As a result of this continental shoving match, modern day California comprises three distinct regions. In the south, the Peninsular Range, built of granite, runs from the tip of Baja to the Los Angeles basin.

After a journey of a thousand miles along the Pacific coast, the chain is broken by the Transverse Ranges, those unusual mountain formations which run east and west rather than north to south. Formed of 1.7 billion year old gneiss, among the oldest rock in North America, the mountains reach to Point Concepcion, the geographic dividing point between Northern and Southern California.

To the north rise the Coast Ranges, a series of sharp mountains which resume the march from south to north. Built of shale, sandstone, and other sedimentary rocks, the Coast Ranges extend up the San Francisco peninsula, through Northern California to Oregon.

Today the San Andreas fault reaches the coast just south of San Francisco, then cuts north through Stinson Beach, Bodega Bay, and Point Arena, before heading seaward from Shelter Cove. Meanwhile the Pacific Plate, carrying Los Angeles, is shifting north along the North American Plate, which holds San Francisco, at a pace that should position the rival cities next to each other in about ten million years. Anyone planning to hitch a ride north should pack extra sandwiches and prepare for a long wait at the side of the road.

NATIVE AMERICANS

Before the advent of Westerners as many as 300,000 Native Americans inhabited California. Of the 50 groups present, 16 lived along the coast and on offshore islands. Far to the south were the Diegueño; the Chumash occupied the South Central Coast while Costanoan Indians dominated the North Central Coast. North of San Francisco the coast Miwok, Pomo, and Athabascan language groups held sway. In the northwest corner of the state the Wiyot, Yurok, and Tolowa fished offshore waters.

They were hunter-gatherers, exploiting the boundless resources of the ocean, picking wild plants, and stalking indigenous animals. Primitive by comparison with the agricultural tribes of the American Southwest, coastal tribes chipped obsidian points for arrows, fished with hooks and nets, and used harpoons to spear migrating salmon.

Dwellings were basic, dome-shaped, and fashioned from woven grasses and wooden poles. Each village included storehouses, a ceremonial lodge, burial grounds, and individual quarters, as well as a *temescal*, or sweat lodge, that served as a kind of Native American men's club.

Men did the hunting, women gathered and cooked, and everywhere village life centered around the family. Polygamy was practiced and wives were purchased. The religious life of the community was conducted by shamans, who "cured" diseases by sucking out the illness. In some places jimsonweed was used to induce visions and became the basis of a cult.

Richer and more sophisticated than inland tribes, the coastal Indians themselves varied greatly. Language barriers were all but insurmountable. There were 21 different language families in California, further divided into dialects, often mutually unintelligible. Natives of San Diego could not understand Indians a few miles away in San Luis Rey.

Yet they fought less than Native Americans elsewhere on the continent and went to battle for revenge rather than plunder. When they did war—fighting with clubs, bows, and rocks—they were known to torture enemies and slaughter women and children.

Among the more advanced coastal tribes were the Chumash, who established an elaborate system of trade. Sailing in wood-planked canoes called *tomols,* they commuted to the Channel Islands and bartered with neighbor tribes. Other Indians used tule balsa canoes built from rushes; and along the open, rocky coast around Humboldt Bay, the northwestern California tribes hollowed canoes from redwood trunks.

These northerly tribes, greatly influenced by the rich cultures of the Pacific Northwest, hunted sea lions, spearing them with harpoons that carried barbed points of bone and antler. They also developed social classes and, like the Chumash, established a more elaborate social system.

Otherwise they were much like the tribes all along the California Coast, weaving beautiful baskets, making ceramics, and fashioning jewelry from shell and coral. They gambled, smoked tobacco, and used beads as currency. And everywhere they looked to the sea as provider and destroyer, drawing their livelihoods from its waters. They fished, canoed, dove, and gathered shellfish—rich, plentiful quantities of shellfish, which archaeologists later found in refuse mounds thirty feet deep, mounds that represented thousands of years of simple life along the California Coast.

HISTORY

DISCOVERY AND EXPLORATION

If the story of the world starts at the creation, the history of California begins with Juan Rodriguez Cabrillo. The year was 1542 and Cabrillo, a Portuguese navigator in the employ of the Spanish crown, sailed north from Mexico, pressing forward the boundaries of empire. Seeking the elusive Northwest Passage, he tacked up the coast of Baja, landing in San Diego, then pushed on to Santa Catalina Island, Point Concepcion, Monterey, and Point Reyes.

For years Spanish conquistadors in Mexico had pursued El Dorado, a mythic land ruled by a king whose people covered him in gold dust. Francisco Vasquez de Coronado trekked off seeking the Seven Cities of Cibola while from his base in Mexico City Hernan Cortes sent expeditions north from Mexico City in pursuit of untold wealth. Though they found neither fabulous kings nor gilded cities, Cabrillo had discovered a new land, Alta California, which he promptly claimed for the Spanish crown.

To world powers, even unpromising land is a prize to be coveted. The British, determined to thwart Spanish conquests in the New World, harried the Spanish and encouraged privateers to plunder their galleons. Sir Francis Drake, the most famous of these adventurers, happened upon the coast in 1579, possibly landing at Point Reyes and, naturally, claiming the territory for England.

This outpost of empire, known to the British as Nova Albion, proved more significant to the Spanish. Since their ships, laden with luxurious goods from the Philippines, passed California en route to Mexico, they began seeking ports of call. In 1587 Pedro de Unamuno anchored at Morro Bay. Eight years later Sebastian Rodriguez Cermeño, a daring seaman, swept down the coast past Cape Mendocino, lost his ship to a ferocious storm in Drake's Bay, then pressed on with 70 men in an open launch.

The next *adelantado*, or merchant-adventurer, to take up the challenge of the coast was Sebastian Vizcaino, who charted and named much of the shoreline, and so grossly exaggerated the harbor of Monterey that his mapmaker was eventually hanged. Vizcaino's 1602 story of this perfect port proved so distorted that when Juan Gaspar de Portola, exploring California by land in 1769, saw Monterey, he failed entirely to recognize it.

THE MISSIONS

In fact, all California was one grand disappointment. It was a region that promised rich gold discoveries, but delivered none, was rumored to contain a Northwest Passage, but did not, and which was desolate, dangerous, and difficult to reach. The British virtually ignored it and the Spanish took more than two centuries to even begin colonizing the place.

Then in 1769, as Portola and Padre Junipero Serra ventured north to establish the first mission in San Diego, the California dream began. Portola continued on to Los Angeles, and following a route which would become the fabled El Camino Real, reached San Francisco Bay, perhaps the first explorer to discover the site. Later Captain Juan Bautista de Anza opened the territory further north.

But it was Father Serra, the hard-driving Franciscan missionary, who wrote the early chapter in the history of the coast. Between 1769 and 1823, he and his successor, Padre Fermin Francisco de Lasuen, established a chain of 21 missions from San Diego to Sonoma. Fortified with presidios, they became the backbone of Spain's colonial empire.

Serra's dream of a New World became a nightmare for Native Americans. Devastated by European diseases, they were forcibly converted to Catholicism and pressed into laboring on the missions. While their slaves were dying in terrible numbers, the Spanish, dangerously overextended, were plagued with other problems throughout the empire. In 1821 Mexico declared its independence and Alta California, still numbering only 3000 Westerners, was lost.

MANIFEST DESTINY

Abandoned and ignored for centuries, the California Coast was becoming an increasingly vital area. British ships had reentered the Pacific in force and by 1812 the Russians, lured by the region's rich fur trade, built Fort Ross on the Sonoma coast. More importantly, the United States, asserting itself as a commercial power, was despatching New England harpooners in pursuit of California gray whales. Whaling stations were built in San Diego, Palos Verdes, and further up the coast in Monterey and Bolinas.

Meanwhile the Mexican government secularized the missions in 1833, distributed the land to early settlers and Native Americans, and ushered in the era of the *ranchos*. These generous land grants, often measuring 75 square miles and lining the narrow coastal strip once occupied by the missions, became huge cattle ranches. Merchants from New England traded pewter, copper, and jewels for animal skins as a lucrative trade developed. Hides became known as "California banknotes," and Richard Henry Dana, sailing along the coast in 1834, immortalized the industry in *Two Years Before the Mast*.

Gazing round him at the rich ocean and undeveloped shore, Dana remarked that "In the hands of an enterprising people, what a country this might be!" The thought was occurring increasingly among Americans, who tried unsuccessfully to buy California from Mexico. Manifest Destiny was on the march, wagon trains were crossing the Sierra Nevada with pioneers, and even the interior valleys were filling with Americans.

Finally in 1846 American settlers, with assistance from the United States government, fomented the Bear Flag Revolt. Colonel John Charles Fremont seized San Francisco while Commodore John D. Sloat took Monterey. Just two years before precious metal was finally found in Spain's fabled land of gold, the stars and stripes flew over California.

THE GOLD RUSH

On January 28, 1848 a hired hand named James Marshall discovered gold in the Sierra foothills, revealing how near the Spanish had come to their vision. But the yellow metal that lured and eluded the conquistadors proved to be located not along the coast they had settled but far to the interior.

The California Dream was realized. For anyone with courage and ambition, it represented a chance to blaze trails and become rich in the flash of a fortuitous find. Gold became the currency of Manifest Destiny, drawing 100,000 people across an implacable land and creating a civilization on the fringes of a continent.

San Francisco became the capital of that civilization. The town's population exploded with prospectors and a wild Barbary Coast ghetto grew along the Bay. Over 500 businesses sold liquor; gambling, drugs, and prostitution were rampant; gangs roamed the boom town and iron-fisted vigilance committees enforced law and order. Sailors were shanghaied and failed prospectors committed suicide at the rate of year. By 1850, about 500 ships, whose crews had deserted for the gold fields, lay abandoned in San Francisco Bay. Some were used as stores, hotels, even lunatic asylums; others became landfill. Speculators wildly divided the city into tiny plots.

The North Coast, filled with lumber needed in the gold mines, also flourished. Mills and settlements by the hundreds were established and every cove became a shipping port. Mendocino, Fort Bragg, Eureka, and other timber towns soon dominated the area.

The Gold Rush not only brought prospectors and loggers to Northern California: many of America's finest writers were soon mining literary material. Mark Twain arrived during the 1860s, as did local colorist Bret Harte. Ambrose Bierce excoriated everyone and everything in his column for William Randolph Hearst's *Examiner*. In 1879, Henry George published a book in San Francisco called *Progress and Poverty*, which propounded a revolutionary system of taxation. Robert Louis Stevenson explored the Bay Area a few years later, and Jack London used it as a setting for his adventure tales.

THE INDUSTRIAL AGE

By the time the continental railroad connected the California Coast with the rest of the country in 1869, Southern California trailed far behind its northern counterpart. Los Angeles, the largest town in the region, numbered 6000 people. During the 1870s the south began to rise. The Southern Pacific railroad linked San Pedro and Santa Monica with the interior valleys where citrus cultivation was flourishing. Southern California's rich agriculture and salubrious climate led to a "health rush." Magazines and newspapers romanticized the region's history and beauty, leading one writer to proclaim that "if the Pilgrim fathers had landed on the Pacific Coast instead of the Atlantic, little old New York wouldn't be on the map."

San Diego, Santa Monica, and Santa Barbara became fashionable resort towns, and the port of San Pedro expanded exponentially, making Los Angeles a major shipping point. Around the turn of the century Henry Huntington, nephew of railroad baron Collis P. Huntington, established the Pacific Electric Railway Company. Within a few years this ruthless and creative businessman revolutionized the beach towns of Los Angeles. Buying tracts along the coast, then extending his red trolley line to one coastal town after another, he became wealthier than even his uncle, creating in the process a land boom and population explosion up and down the coast.

The fishing industry, developed by the Chinese between 1860 and 1880, proved as lucrative as tourism and shipping. While Huntington was wresting control of the coast, local Portuguese, Japanese, Italians, and Yugoslavs were forcing the Chinese from the offshore fishing grounds.

When oil was discovered early in the 20th century, Southern California also became a prime drilling region. Oil wells sprang up along Huntington Beach, Long Beach, and San Pedro, adding to coastal coffers while destroying the aesthetics of the shore. The Signal Hill field in Long Beach, tapped by Shell Oil in the 1920s, became the richest oil deposit in the world and Los Angeles became the largest oil port. Little wonder that by 1925, flush with petroleum just as the age of the automobile shifted into gear, Los Angeles also became the most motor-conscious city in the world. The Pacific Coast Highway was completed during the 1930s, "auto camps" and "tourist cabins" mushroomed, and motorists began exploring the California Coast in unprecedented numbers.

MODERN TIMES

Meanwhile San Francisco, long since recovered from the horrific 1906 earthquake that shattered the San Andreas fault and rocked the coast, was becoming a strategic military area. During World War II the Navy also developed port facilities in San Diego. Coastal defense bases grew at Camp Pendleton, Point Mugu, Vandenberg, Fort Ord, and in Marin County.

This rush to protect the coast turned into a kind of social mania in 1942 when the United States government, in one of the most racist acts in its history, ordered the "relocation" of 93,000 Japanese Americans. Stripped of their rights, they were removed from coastal regions where, it was charged, they could aid the Japanese Empire. In fact the only attack on the coast occurred when a lone submarine lobbed a few shells at an oil field near Santa Barbara, doing minor damage to a wooden pier.

After the war, development of another sort became the order of the day. Homes and businesses sprouted up along the entire coastline. Los Angeles became the nation's second largest metropolis, and California, 80 percent of whose residents live within 30 miles of the coast, became the most populous state.

This unbridled development, combined with the 1969 Santa Barbara oil spill and plans for a controversial nuclear power plant in Diablo Canyon, led in 1972 to the creation of the California Coastal Commission.

Established by the voters, this watchdog agency has succeeded in slowing development and preserving the natural beauty of the shoreline. By the time the conservation movement began to flex its muscle, however, California had already demonstrated—through its tourism, ports, oil deposits, aircraft industry, construction trade, and fishing fleet—that the gold sought centuries before by Spanish explorers did not lie in the hills, but along the state's extraordinary coastline.

The Life of the Coast

FISH AND FISHING

The poet William Butler Yeats wrote of "the mackerel-crowded seas," oceans filled with a single species. Along California's lengthy coastline, in the shallow waters alone, over 250 kinds of fish thrive. Most are small, exotically colored creatures, which in an entire lifetime barely venture from their birthplace. Others, like the king salmon and steelhead trout, live off the Northern California coast until summer and fall, then run upstream for miles to spawn in freshwater.

Grunion actually climb onto land to lay their eggs. These small silvery fish come ashore between March and August after particularly high tides. The females anchor themselves in the sand and lay as many as 3000 eggs, which are hatched by surf action. During these grunion runs, popular from Morro Bay south, the fish are so plentiful they can be caught by hand.

Among California's other well-known species are halibut, surfperch, and rockfish, found along the entire coast, and gamefish like barracuda, yellowtail, and bonito, which inhabit the kelp beds of Southern California. There are also bluefin tuna, albacore, and Yeats' fabled mackerel.

Most famous of all is the shark, 30 species of which prowl California's coastal waters and bays. While none seem particularly to savor human flesh, all but a few are carnivores, and do periodically leave their teeth in divers and surfers. The great white shark, that fearful beast which grows to 25 feet in length, has become a common resident along the coast, where it feeds on sea lions, seals, and sea otters.

Methods for catching these different species are about as numerous as the fish themselves. There's surf casting, rock fishing, trolling, poke-pole fishing in tidepools, and deepsea fishing from party boats. Fishing licenses are required of everyone over 16 years old, except people fishing from public piers. Regulations and information can be obtained from the **Department of Fish and Game** (3211 S Street, Sacramento, CA 95816; 916-739-3380). The rest is a question of equipment, skill, and whether the fish are biting.

(Text continued on page 14.)

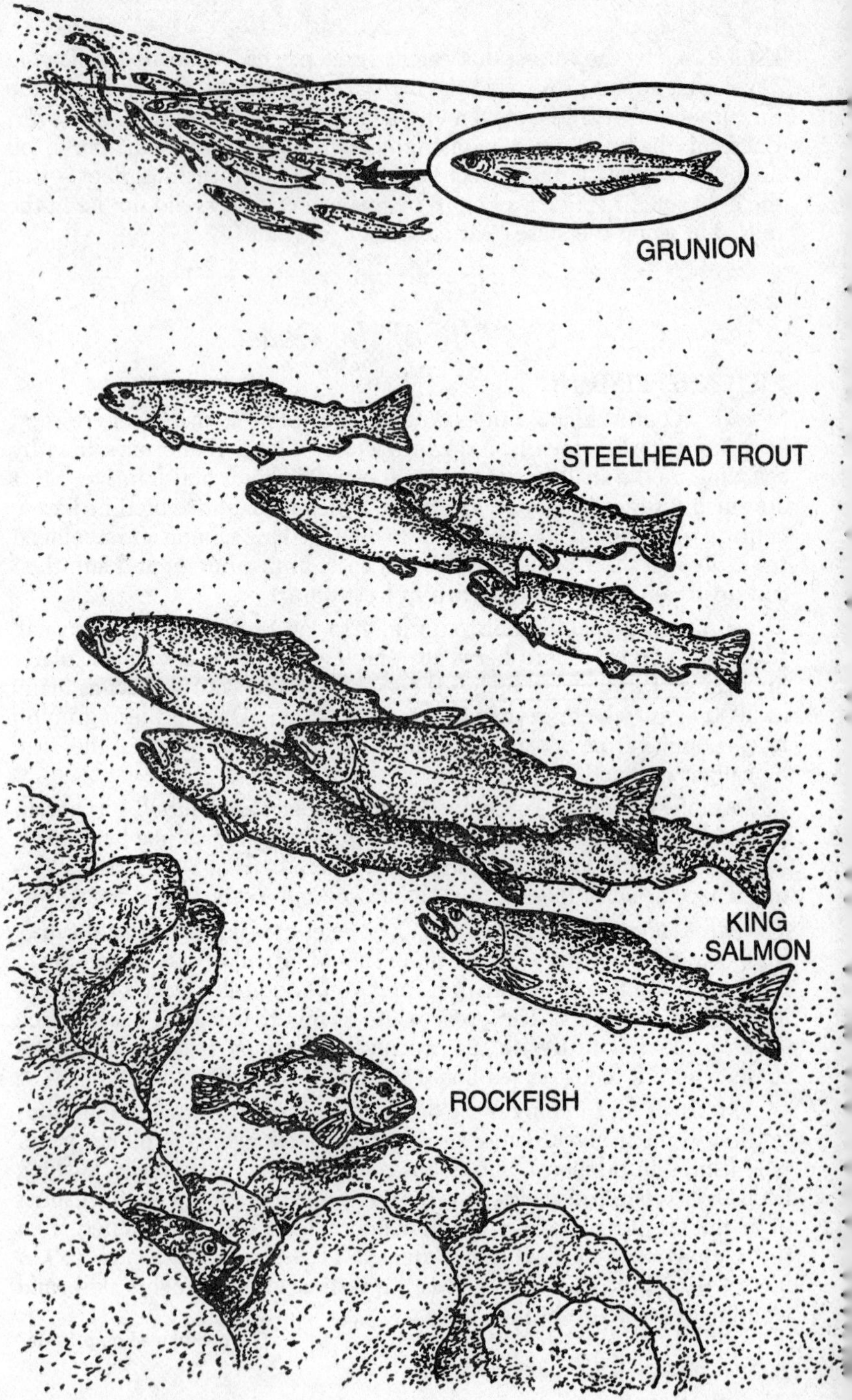
GRUNION
STEELHEAD TROUT
KING SALMON
ROCKFISH

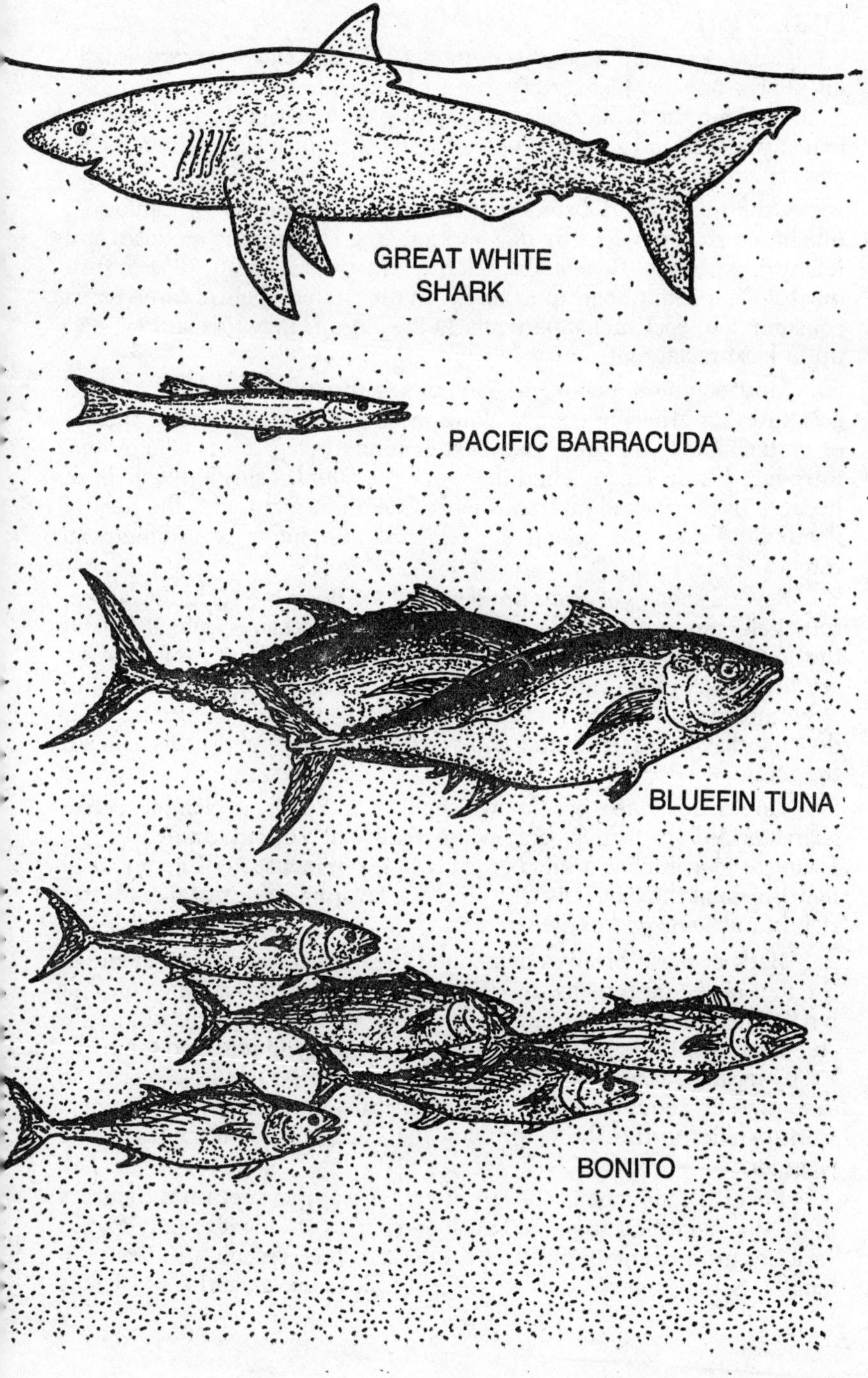
GREAT WHITE
SHARK
PACIFIC BARRACUDA
BLUEFIN TUNA
BONITO

SHELLFISH

Crustaceans and molluscs, those hard-shelled characters we usually encounter only in biology class and later in life on the dinner table, abound along the California coast. Among the crustaceans are lobsters, crabs, prawns, and shrimps, while the local molluscs include mussels, oysters, squid, clams, and abalone.

California spiny lobsters live on the coast of Southern California, inhabiting rock crevices by day and foraging at night for molluscs and fellow crustaceans. Rock crabs, another crusty crustacean, dine in turn on abalone, picking apart their shells. In the endless chain of carnivorous consumption, rock crabs, particularly the large Dungeness variety, end up in local restaurants.

Most common among the molluscs is the mussel, a black-shelled creature that grows in clumps along rocks and pilings. Several species of oyster inhabit the area, the most common being the Pacific oyster, introduced from Japan. Then there are the squid, considered shellfish because of their small internal shells. Caught at night with the help of floodlights, they are among the region's most important commercial catches.

Several species of clams proliferate along the coast, including gaper, soft-shell, geoduck, bent-nosed, and Washington clams, which inhabit the mud flats of bays and lagoons. Along the gravel areas of the bays are little-neck clams, also known as rock cockles. And on the beaches of Humboldt and Del Norte counties reside razor clams, known for their delicious flavor and frustrating ability to rapidly bury themselves beneath the sand.

One of the state's best known shellfish is the Pismo clam, a species characterized by a thick, gray-white shell marked with annual bands. Living as long as 35 years and growing to seven inches in diameter, they flourish along the San Luis Obispo coast, favoring cold, turbulent water rich in nutrients and oxygen.

Beds of these bivalves once lined the shore, serving as a staple in the diet of coastal Indians. In 1914 bag limits were 200 per person, but by 1947 commercial clamming was outlawed. Today sport clamming is still permitted though heavy storms have seriously diminished the beds. Easily located, Pismo clams reside no more than six inches beneath the sand in water about three feet deep at low tide. To catch them, clammers work parallel to the shore, probing the sand every two inches with a clam fork.

Favorite food among the sea otters, and at gourmet restaurants, is the red abalone. Of some 100 abalone species worldwide, only Pacific varieties grow to significant size; the red abalone, reaching 13 inches in length, is the largest. Marked by jet-black tentacles and a red fringe along the shell, they hold tenaciously to offshore rocks, many clinging to the same stone their entire lives.

Back in the 1930s abalone were harvested commercially in Northern California and great piles of their shells lined the road between Monterey and Castroville. In those days three million a year were taken, many processed in factories along Cannery Row. Today commercial harvesting occurs only in Southern California, but amateur divers still gather them everywhere along the coast.

Prized for their delicious meat, abalone also have beautiful shells with mother-of-pearl interiors that cast iridescent colors. Coastal Indians used the shells for barter and one tribe, the Ohlone, or abalone people, took their name from this valuable shellfish.

TIDEPOOLS

It's a climactic scene in that Hollywood classic, *Chinatown.* Jack Nicholson, portraying a 1930s-era private eye, is about to accuse John Huston of murdering his own partner. But Huston, a deceitful and powerful businessman playing the innocent, waxes sentimental about the dead friend. His partner, Hollis Mulrey, had been water commissioner, a great man who early in the century brought water to the Los Angeles basin, transforming a dusty town into a metropolis. Yet Hollis was a simple man, sensitive to nature, and loved the sea.

"Hollis was always fascinated by tidepools," Huston intones. "Do you know what he used to say? 'That's where life begins—sloughs, tidepools.' " As Huston knows, tidepools are also where life ends: he murdered Mulrey by drowning him in one.

Poor Hollis' fascination with tidepools is shared by everyone. These rocky pockets, exposed to view at low tide, are microcosms of the world. Delicately poised between land and sea, they are a frontier dividing two wildly varied environments.

Life flourishes here, but living is not easy. Denizens of tidepools are exposed to air twice a day during low tide. They must adapt to dehydration, the heat of the sun, and the effects of the atmosphere. Rain brings fresh water to a saline environment, disturbing the precious equilibrium. Waves, particularly during severe storms, wreak havoc with reefs. Exceptionally high or low tides upset the rhythm of air and water exposure.

It is this balance between time in the air and water that differentiates the tidal life forms. Tidepools, or intertidal areas, are divided into four zones, which parallel the beach and vary in their distance from shore.

The splash zone, dampened by mist and occasional large waves, rests far up along the beach and is inhabited by green algae and small snails. Below it lies the upper intertidal zone, an area covered only during high tide. Here barnacles, chitons, and limpets cling to rocks, closing tight during low tide to preserve moisture.

Covered by water twice a day, the middle intertidal zone is home to mussels and rock weed. Since mussels grow in clumps, they form a biological community in themselves, sheltering varieties of plants and animals, some of which spend their entire lives in a single clump.

Starfish, which generally inhabit the low intertidal zone, feed on these mussels, prying open the shells with their powerful suctioned tentacles. This fourth region, uncovered only when the ocean deeply recedes during minus tides, supports the most diverse life forms. Sea urchins, abalone, and anemones flourish here, as do crabs, octopus, and chitons, those oval-shaped molluscs that date back to before the age of dinosaurs.

When you go searching for these prehistoric creatures remember, even out here in the wild, there are a few rules of the road. Collecting plants and animals, including dead ones, is strongly discouraged and in some places entirely illegal. Follow the old adage and look but don't touch. If you do turn over a rock or move a shell, replace it in the original position; it may be someone's home. Also watch out for big waves and, unlike the erstwhile water commissioner, exercise caution, it can be dangerous out there.

COASTAL VEGETATION

From the rim of the sea to the peaks of surrounding mountains, the coastline is coated with a complex variety of plant life. Several plant communities flourish along the shore, each clinging to a particular niche in the environment. Blessed with a cooler, more moderate climate near the ocean, they are continually misted by sea spray and must contend with more salt in their veins.

On the beaches and along the dunes are the herbs, vines, and low shrubs of the coastal strand community. Among their numbers are beach primrose, sand verbena, beach morning glory, and sea figs, those tenacious succulents that run along the ground sprouting magenta flowers and literally carpeting the coast. Characterized by leathery leaves that retain large quantities of water, they are the plant world's answer to the camel.

Around the mud flats and river mouths grow rushes, pickleweed, tules, cord grass, and other members of the salt marsh community. Low, shrubby plants growing in clumps, these hearty fellows are inundated by tides and able to withstand tremendous concentrations of salt.

Coastal sage scrub inhabits a broad swath from above the waterline to about 3000 feet elevation. White and black sage, wild buckwheat, and California sagebrush belong to this community of short, tough plants.

The chaparral community grows in thick, often impenetrable stands along the hillsides and mountains. These scrub oak, manzanita, and Christmas holly bushes lend a distinct character to the fabled rolling hills of California. Down along the rivers and creeks resides the riparian community whose members range from willow, alder, and big-leaf maple to redwood and Douglas fir.

There are wildflowers everywhere—violets, lilies, irises, azaleas, wild roses, and of course California poppies, the state flower. Buttercups, with their shiny yellow petals, are abundant. Growing from the coast right out to the desert are the lupines, silky bushes with whorled flowers that stand straight as bottlebrushes.

The cactus family is represented by the prickly pear with its sharp spines and yellow blossoms; and there are nasty thickets of gorse, poison hemlock, and tenacious thistles. Several species of fern occupy coastal bluffs, descending to the very edge of the beach. In addition to serrated sword ferns and giant horsetails, these include California lace ferns and Saint Catherine's lace, with petals like finely woven textiles.

Then there are the trees—lofty Monterey pine; the rare Torrey pine that grows only in San Diego County and on an offshore island; oak, laurel, maple, and alder; fir, spruce, and cedar. The fabled Monterey cypress inhabits a picturesque region along the Monterey coast, the only place in the world it is found. Giant redwoods, the tallest trees on earth, grow in awesome groves along the coastal fog belt, living for centuries and reaching 350 foot heights.

And don't forget the tree that has no branches and sheds little shade, but is the foremost symbol of California—the palm tree. There are Pindo palms from Paraguay, European hair palms, plume palms from Brazil, blue palms, Washington palms, and the Erythea. Among the most common are the California palm, largest native palm in the continental United States, and the date palm, which lines many California streets and is nicknamed "pineapple palm" for its trunk's resemblance to the tropical fruit.

SEABIRDS

Somehow the mud flats of San Francisco Bay are the last place to go sightseeing, particularly at high tide, after the flood has stirred the ooze. But it is at such times that bird watchers gather to view flocks of as many as 60,000 birds.

The California shore is one of the richest bird habitats anywhere in North America. Over 500 species are found across the state, many along the coast and its offshore islands.

Coastal species fall into three general categories—near-shore birds like loons, grebes, cormorants, and scoters, that inhabit the shallow waters of bays and beaches; offshore birds, such as shearwaters, which feed several miles off the coast; and pelagic or open-ocean species like albatross and Arctic terns, that fly miles from land and live for up to 20 or 30 years.

(Text continued on page 20.)

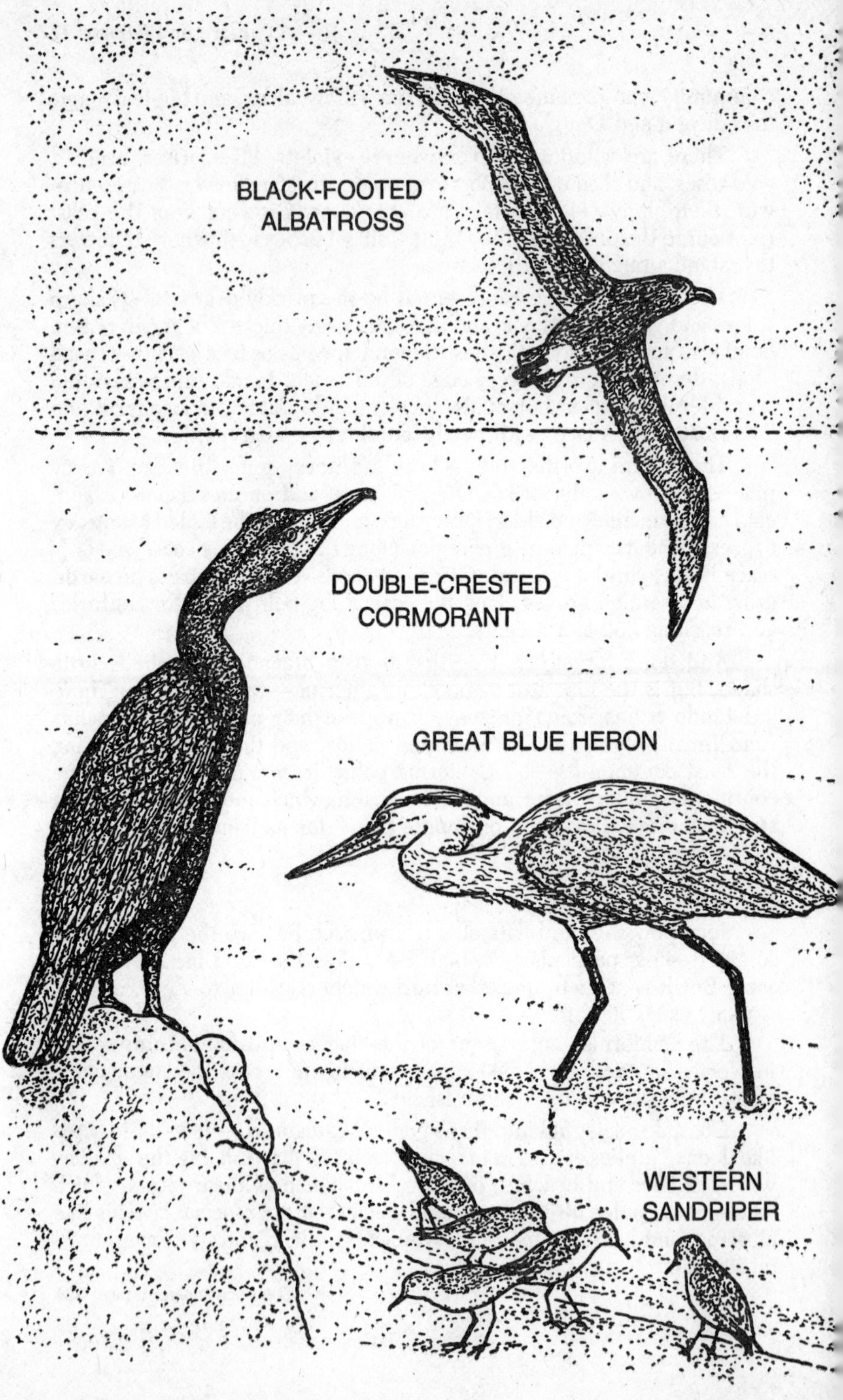
BLACK-FOOTED
ALBATROSS
DOUBLE-CRESTED
CORMORANT
GREAT BLUE HERON
WESTERN
SANDPIPER

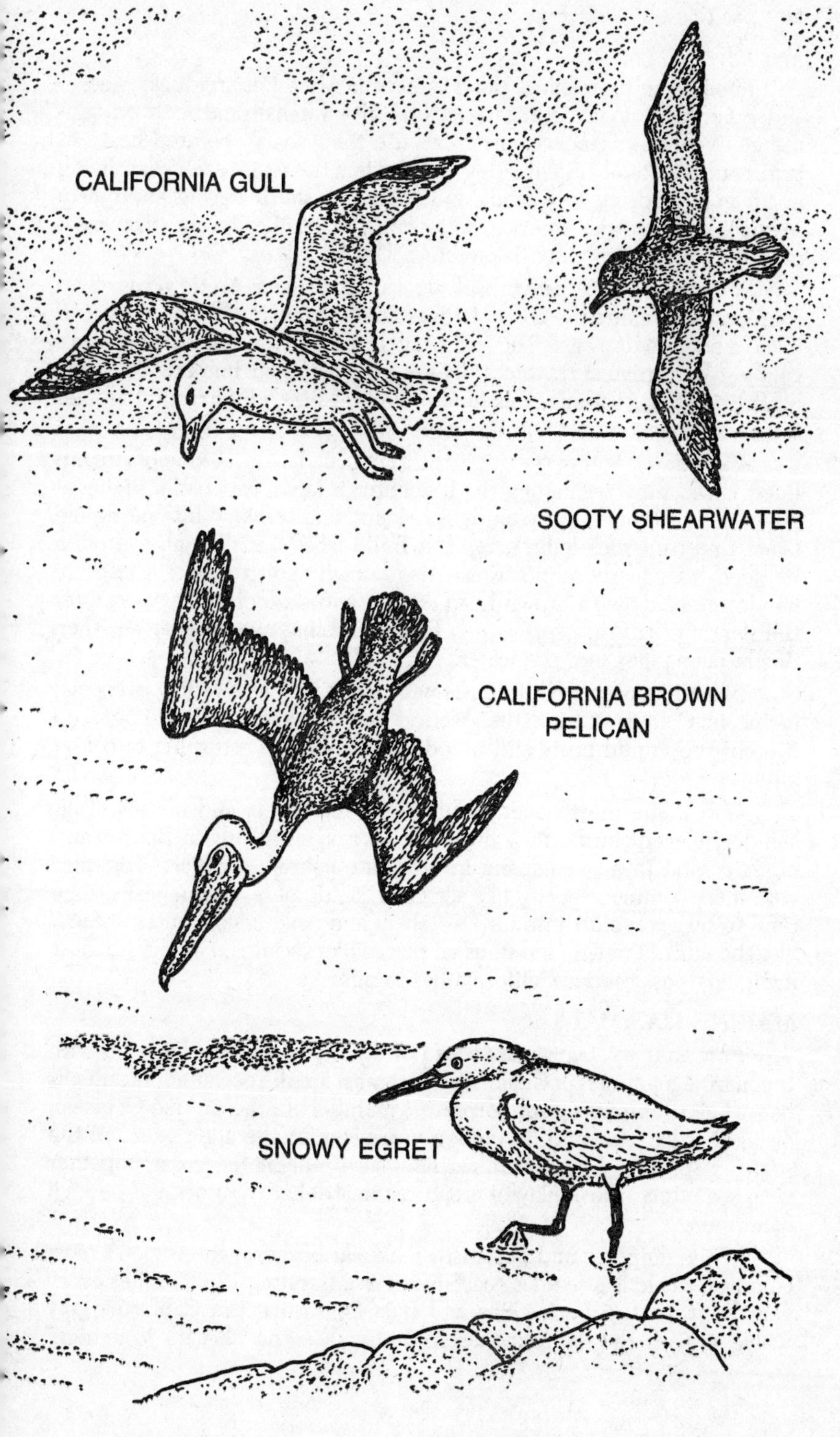
CALIFORNIA GULL
SOOTY SHEARWATER
CALIFORNIA BROWN
PELICAN
SNOWY EGRET

Joining the shore birds along California's beaches are ducks, geese, and other waterfowl. While waterfowl dive for fish and feed on submerged vegetation, near-shore birds use their sharp, pointed beaks to ferret out intertidal animals. Both groups flee the scene each year, flying north in the spring to Canada and Alaska or south during autumn to Mexico and Central America, following the Pacific flyway, that great migratory route spanning the western United States.

Some birds, like canvasback ducks, loons, and Arctic terns, fly a route entirely along the coast. Others finish wintering in California and make a beeline due east. The short-tailed shearwater, one of the world's smallest but greatest travelers, leaves everything far behind. Breeding off the coast of Australia, this incredible bird flies a figure eight around the Pacific, skirting California and covering 20,000 miles.

Another intriguing species is the peregrine falcon. A kind of streamlined hawk, they are among the fastest birds alive, capable of diving at 200 miles an hour to prey on ducks, coots, and terns. While peregrine falcons nest on rock ledges, ospreys build large nests which can often be seen high in shoreline trees. Also known as fish hawks, these are handsome birds with brown head crowns and six-foot wingspans. Ever the gentle creature, ospreys nab fish by circling over the ocean, then diving talons first into the water.

Whistling swans, white birds with black bills and yellow eyespots, arrive in California from the Arctic every November. Residing until March, they build nests and breed cygnets before returning to colder climes.

Among the most beautiful birds are the egrets and herons. Tall, slender, elegant birds, they live from January until July in Bolinas and other coastal towns, engaging in elaborate courtship rituals. Together with more common species like sea gulls, sandpipers, and pelicans, they tend to turn travelers into bird watchers and make inconvenient times, like the edge of dawn, and unusual places like swamps, among the most intriguing possibilities California has to offer.

MARINE MAMMALS

Few animals inspire the sense of myth and magic associated with the marine mammals of California. Foremost are the ocean-going animals like whales, dolphins, and porpoises, members of the unique Cetacean order that left the land 30 million years ago for the alien world of the sea. Six species of seals and sea lions also inhabit the coast, together with sea otters, those playful creatures that delight visitors and bedevil fishermen.

While dolphins and porpoises range far offshore, the region's most common whale is a regular coastal visitor. Migrating 12,000 miles every year between the Bering Sea and Baja Peninsula, the California gray whale cruises the shoreline each winter (see the "Whale Watching" section in Chapter 8). Measuring 50 feet and weighing 40 tons, these distinguished animals live to 50 years of age and commmunicate with sophisticated signalling systems.

The seals and sea lions that seem to loll about the shoreline are characterized by small ears and short flippers equipped for land travel. Fat and sassy, they have layers of blubber to keep them warm and loud barks to inform tourists who's king of the rookery.

Even people who never venture to the ocean have seen California sea lions, those talented circus performers. Occupying the entire coast, particularly around Santa Barbara, they stay offshore for months at a time, landing only during breeding season.

Harbor seals differ from these showmen in an inability to use their hind flippers for land travel. Not to be upstaged, they sport beautiful dark coats with silver and white spots from which they borrow their second name, leopard seals. Like other pinnipeds, harbor seals feed on fish, shellfish, and squid. Largest of all the pinnipeds are the Northern elephant seals, those ugly but lovable creatures that grow to 16 feet and weigh three tons. Characterized by a huge snout, they come ashore only to molt, mate, and give birth. Breeding season, beginning in December, is the best time to watch these waddling characters. The males wage fierce battles to establish who will be cock of the walk. A few weeks after the males finish their tournament the females arrive.

"Sentence first," said the Queen of Hearts in *Alice in Wonderland*, "verdict afterwards." In the upside-down world of the elephant seal, birth comes first, then breeding. Within days of arriving onshore, the females give birth to 75-pound pups. Three weeks later the mothers breed with their mates, conceiving pups that will be born eight months later.

Every California visitor's favorite animal is the sea otter. A kind of ocean-going teddy bear, they are actually members of the weasel family, weighing up to 85 pounds, measuring four feet, and characterized by thick fur, short paws used for feeding and grooming, and webbed hind feet that serve as flippers.

Smart critters, sea otters are capable of using tools, rocks with which they pry tenacious shellfish from the ocean bottom and hammer open shells. They are also voracious eaters, feeding on abalone, sea urchins, and crabs, and consuming 25 percent of their body weight daily.

Like most California marine mammals, sea otters were hunted to near extinction by 19th-century fur traders. Today they have made a remarkable recovery, populating the coast from the Channel Islands to Monterey. Inhabiting kelp beds where they are difficult to spot, these sleek animals can best be seen during feeding time in early morning and late afternoon. Watch for the sea gulls that circle kelp beds in search

(Text continued on page 24.)

COMMON
DOLPHIN
NORTHERN
ELEPHANT
SEAL
CALIFORNIA
SEA LION
HARBOR SEAL

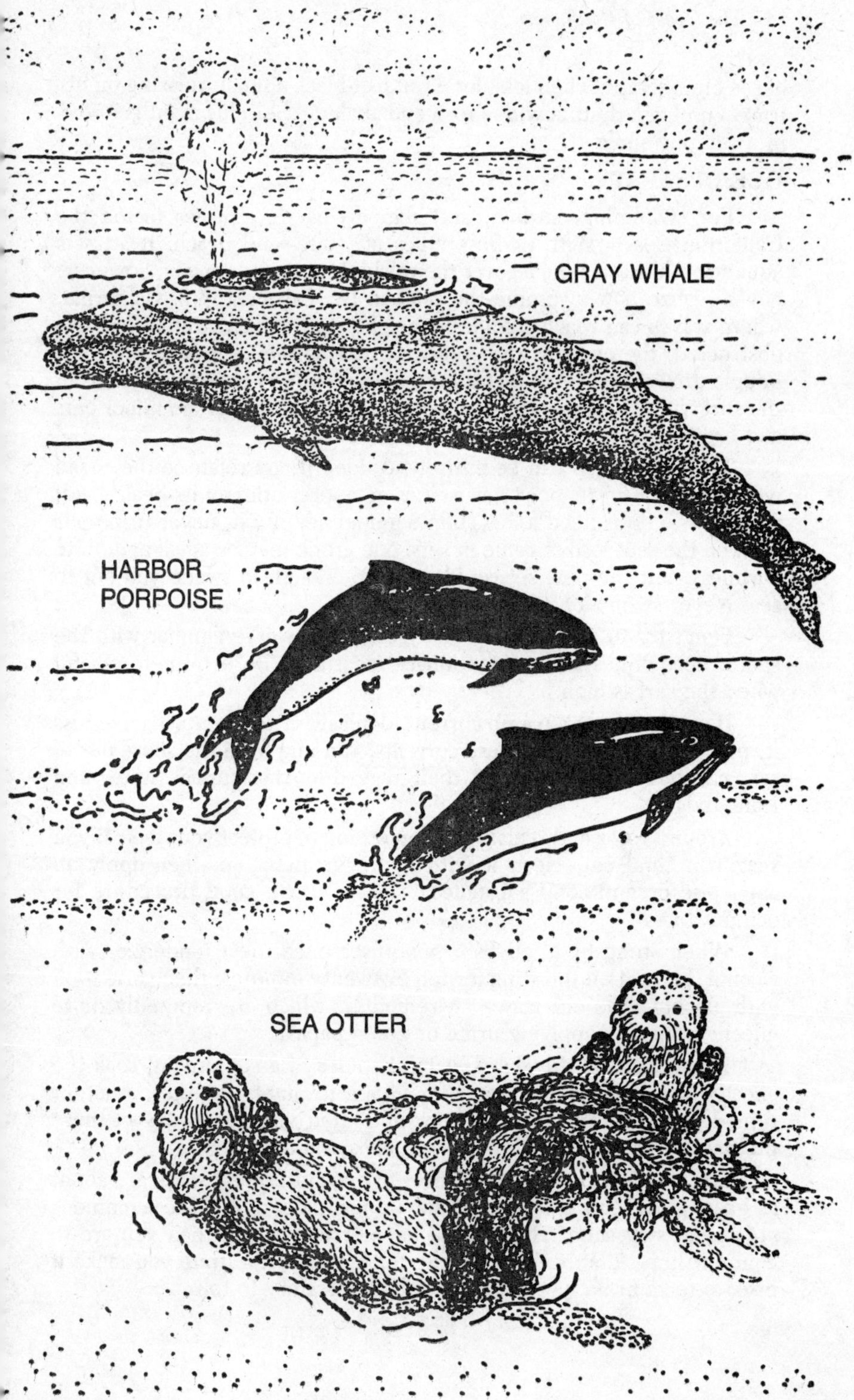
GRAY WHALE
HARBOR PORPOISE
SEA OTTER

of sea otter scraps. Then look for a reddish-black animal, relaxing on his back, tapping a rhythm with a rock and abalone shell, his mouth curved in a cunning smile.

OCEAN SAFETY

For swimming, surfing, and skin diving, few places match the California Coast. With endless miles of white-sand beach, it attracts aquatic enthusiasts from all over the world. Many water lovers, however, never realize how awesome the sea can be. Particularly in California, where waves can reach significant heights and currents often flow unobstructed, the ocean is sometimes as treacherous as it is spectacular. People drown every year on California beaches, others are dragged from the surf with serious injuries, and countless numbers sustain minor cuts and bruises.

These accidents can be entirely avoided if you relate to the ocean with a respect for its power as well as an appreciation of its beauty. All you have to do is heed a few simple guidelines. First, never turn your back on the sea. Waves come in sets: one group may be small and quite harmless, but the next set could be large enough to sweep you out to sea. Never swim alone.

Don't try to surf, or even bodysurf, until you're familiar with the sports' techniques and precautionary measures. Be extremely careful when the surf is high.

If you get caught in a rip current, don't swim *against* it: swim *across* it, parallel to the shore. These currents, running from the shore out to sea, can often be spotted by their ragged-looking surface water and foamy edges.

Around rocks and reefs, wear something to protect your feet. If you sustain a coral cut, clean it with hydrogen peroxide, then apply an antiseptic or antibiotic substance. This is also a good procedure for octopus bites.

When stung by a jellyfish, mix unseasoned meat tenderizer with alcohol, leave it on the sting for ten or twenty minutes, then rinse it off with alcohol. The old Hawaiian remedies, which are reputedly quite effective, involve applying urine or green papaya.

If you step on the sharp, painful spines of a sea urchin, soak the affected area in very hot water for fifteen to ninety minutes. Another remedy calls for applying urine or undiluted vinegar. If any of these preliminary treatments do not work, consult a doctor.

Oh, one last thing. The chances of encountering a shark are about as likely as sighting a UFO. But should you meet one of these ominous creatures, stay calm. He'll be no happier to see you than you are to confront him. Simply swim quietly to shore. By the time you make it back to terra firma, you'll have one hell of a story to tell.

Traveling the Coast

SEASONS

The California Coast extends all the way from Mexico to Oregon. Along this entire expanse the weather corresponds to a Mediterranean climate with mild temperatures year-round. Since the coastal fog creates a natural form of air conditioning and insulation, the mercury rarely drops below 40° or rises above 70°. September and October are the hottest months, and December and January the coolest.

Spring and particularly autumn are the ideal times to visit. During winter, the rainy season brings overcast days and frequent showers. Summer is the peak tourist season, when large crowds can present problems. Like Spring, it's also a period of frequent fog; during the morning and evening, fog banks from offshore blanket the coast, burning off around midday.

Since most winter storms sweep in from the north, rainfall averages and the length of the rainy season diminish as you go south. Crescent City receives 70 inches of rain annually, San Francisco averages about 20 inches, and San Diego receives only 12 inches. Inversely, temperatures vary from north to south: Eureka ranges from an average of 47° in January to 57° during August, while San Diego rises from 55° to 70° during the same months. The ocean air also creates significant moisture, keeping the average humidity around 65 percent and making some areas, particularly Northern California, seem colder than the thermometer would indicate.

VISITOR INFORMATION

Several agencies provide free information to travelers. The **California Office of Tourism** (1121 L Street, Suite 103, Sacramento, CA 95814; 916-322-1396) will help guide you to areas throughout the state. The **San Diego Convention and Visitors Bureau** (1200 3rd Avenue, Suite 824, San Diego, CA 92101; 619-232-3101), **Los Angeles Visitors and Convention Bureau** (515 South Figueroa Street, Los Angeles, CA 90071; 213-624-7300), and **San Francisco Convention and Visitors Bureau** (201 Third Street, Suite 900, San Francisco, CA 94103; 415-974-6900) are also excellent resources. For information on the North Coast counties between San Francisco and Oregon, contact the **Redwood Empire Association** (1 Market Plaza, Suite 1001, San Francisco; CA 94105; 415-543-8334). Also consult local chambers of commerce and information centers, which are mentioned in the various area chapters.

PACKING

There are two important guidelines when deciding what to take on a trip. The first is as true for the California Coast as anywhere in the world—pack light. Dress styles here are relatively informal and laundromats and dry cleaners are frequent. The airlines allow two suitcases and a carry-on bag; try to take one suitcase and perhaps a small accessory case.

The second rule is to prepare for cool weather, even if the closest you'll come to the mountains are the bluffs above the beach. While the coastal climate is temperate, temperatures sometimes descend below 50°. Even that might not seem chilly until the fog rolls in and the ocean breeze picks up. A warm sweater and jacket are absolute necessities. In addition to everyday garments, pack shorts year-round for Southern California, and remember, everywhere along the coast requires a raincoat between November and March.

HOTELS

Overnight accommodations along the California Coast are as varied as the region itself. They range from high-rise hotels and neon motels to hostels and bed and breakfast inns. One guideline to follow with all of them is to reserve well in advance. This is an extremely popular area, particularly in summer, and facilities fill up quickly.

Check through each chapter and you're bound to find something to fit your budget and personal taste. The neon motels offer bland facilities at low prices and are excellent if you're economizing or don't plan to spend much time in the room. Larger hotels often lack intimacy, but provide such conveniences as restaurants and shops in the lobby. My personal preference is for historic hotels, those slightly faded classics which offer charm and tradition at moderate cost. Bed and breakfast inns present an opportunity to stay in a home-like setting. Like hostels, they are an excellent way to meet fellow travelers; unlike hostels, California's country inns are quite expensive.

To help you decide on a place to stay, I've organized the accommodations not only by area but also according to price. *Budget* hotels are generally less than $40 per night for two people; the rooms are clean and comfortable, but lack luxury. The *moderate* price hotels run $40 to $70, and provide larger rooms, plusher furniture, and more attractive surroundings. At a *deluxe* hotel you can expect to spend between $70 and $120 double. You'll check into a spacious, well-appointed room with all modern facilities; the lobby will be a fashionable affair, and the hotel will usually include a restaurant, lounge, and cluster of small shops. If you want to spend your time (and money) at the very finest hotels, try an *ultra-deluxe* facility, which will include all the amenities and price above $120.

RESTAURANTS

It seems as if the California Coast has more restaurants than people. To establish a pattern for this parade of dining places, I've organized them according to location and cost.

Within a particular chapter, the restaurants are categorized geographically and each individual restaurant entry describes the establishment as budget, moderate, deluxe, or ultra-deluxe in price. Dinner entrees at *budget* restaurants usually cost $7 or less. The ambience is informal cafe-style and the crowd is often a local one. *Moderate* price restaurants range between $7 and $14 at dinner and offer pleasant surroundings, a more varied menu, and a slower pace. *Deluxe* establishments tab their entrees from $14 to $20, featuring sophisticated cuisines, plush decor, and more personalized service. *Ultra-deluxe* dining rooms, where $20 will only get you started, are gourmet gathering places where cooking (hopefully) is a fine art form and service a way of life.

Breakfast and lunch menus vary less in price from restaurant to restaurant. Even deluxe kitchens usually offer light breakfasts and lunch sandwiches, placing them within a few dollars of their budget-minded competitors. These early meals can be a good time to test expensive restaurants.

CAMPING

The state oversees more than 260 camping facilities. Amenities at each campground vary, but there is a standard day-use fee of $4 per vehicle, plus $10 per campsite ($12 in Southern California). For a complete listing of all state-run campgrounds, send $2 for the *Guide to California State Parks* to the **California Department of Parks and Recreation** (P.O. Box 2390, Sacramento, CA 94296; 916-445-6477). Reservations for campgrounds can be made by calling 800-446-7275.

For general information on Federal campgrounds, contact the **National Park Service** (Western Regional Office, Fort Mason, Building 201, San Francisco, CA 94123; 415-556-4122). To reserve campsites call **Ticketron** (800-952-5580 in California; 213-642-3888 elsewhere).

In addition to state and national campgrounds, the California Coast offers numerous municipal, county, and private facilities. See the "Beaches and Parks" section in each area chapter for the locations of these campgrounds.

TRAVELING WITH CHILDREN

Visiting California with kids can be a real adventure, and if properly planned, a truly enjoyable one. To ensure that your trip will feature the joy, rather than the strain, of parenthood, remember a few important guidelines.

Use a travel agent to help with arrangements; they can reserve spacious bulkhead seats on airlines and determine which flights are least crowded. Bring everything you need on board—diapers, food, toys, and extra clothes for kids and parents alike. If the trip to California involves a long journey, plan to relax and do very little during the first few days.

Always allow extra time for getting places. Book reservations well in advance and make sure the hotel has the extra crib, cot, or bed you require. It's smart to ask for a room at the end of the hall to cut down on noise. Also, many bed and breakfast inns do not allow children.

Even small towns have stores that carry diapers, food, and other essentials; in larger towns and cities, **7-11** stores are open all night (check the yellow pages for addresses).

Hotels often provide access to babysitters. Also check the yellow pages for state licensed and bonded babysitting agencies.

A first-aid kit is always a good idea. Ask your pediatrician for special medicines and dosages for colds and diarrhea.

BEING DISABLED

California stands at the forefront of social reform for the disabled. During the past decade, the state has responded to the needs of the blind, wheelchair-bound, and others with a series of progressive legislative measures.

The **Department of Motor Vehicles** provides special parking permits for the disabled. Many local bus lines and other public transit facilities are wheelchair accessible.

There are also agencies in California assisting disabled persons. For tips and information about the San Francisco Bay Area, contact the **Center for Independent Living** (2539 Telegraph Avenue, Berkeley; 415-841-4776), a self-help group that has led the way in reforming access laws in California. Other organizations on the coast include the **Westside Center for Independent Living** (12901 Venice Boulevard, Los Angeles; 213-390-3611) and the **Community Resource Center for the Disabled** (2864 University Avenue, San Diego; 619-293-3500).

Amtrak offers discount train fares to the disabled. For a pamphlet describing their services, call a local office or write to Amtrak (National Railroad Passenger Corporation, 400 North Capitol Street N.W., Washington, DC 20001).

Two federal brochures provide helpful information for disabled travelers. *Access Travel* and *Access to the National Parks* are available from the **U.S. Printing Office** (Washington, DC 20402) for a nominal fee. The **Society for the Advancement of Travel for the Handicapped** (26 Court Street, Brooklyn, NY 11242; 718-858-5483), **Travel Information Center** (Moss Rehabilitation Hospital, 12th Street and Tabor Road, Philadelphia, PA 19141; 215-329-5715); **Mobility International USA** (P.O. Box 3551, Eugene, OR 97403; 503-343-1284); or **Flying Wheels Travel** (143 West Bridge Street, P.O. Box 382, Owatonna, MN 55060; 800-533-0363) also offer information. Or consult the comprehensive guidebook, *Access to the World—A Travel Guide for the Handicapped*, by Louise Weiss (Holt, Rinehart & Winston).

Be sure to check in advance when making room reservations. Many hotels and motels feature facilities for those in wheelchairs.

OLDER TRAVELERS

The California Coast is an ideal spot for older vacationers. The mild climate makes traveling in the off-season possible, helping to cut down on expenses. Many museums, theaters, restaurants, and hotels offer senior discounts (requiring a driver's license, Medicare card, or other age-identifying card). Be sure to ask your travel agent when booking reservations.

The **American Association of Retired Persons**, or AARP, (1909 K Street Northwest, Washington D.C. 22049; 202-872-4700) offers members travel discounts and provides escorted tours. For those 60 or over, **Elderhostel** (80 Boylston Street, Suite 400, Boston, MA 02116; 617-426-7788) offers educational programs in California.

Be extra careful about health matters. Bring any medications you use, along with the prescriptions. Consider carrying a medical record with you—including your current medical status, and medical history, as well as your doctor's name, phone number, and address. Also be sure to confirm that your insurance covers you away from home.

CHAPTER TWO

San Diego Coast

San Diego County's 4261 square miles occupy a Connecticut-size chunk of real estate that forms the southwestern corner of the continental United States. Geographically, it is as varied a parcel of landscape as any in the world. Surely this spot is one of the few places on the planet where, in a matter of hours, you can journey from bluff-lined beaches up and over craggy, pine-clad mountain peaks and down again to sun-scorched desert sands.

But it is the coast—some 76 sparkling miles stretching from the Mexican border to San Mateo Point near San Clemente—that always has held the fascination of residents and visitors alike.

When Portuguese explorer Juan Rodriguez Cabrillo laid eyes on these shores in 1542, he discovered a prospering settlement of Kumeyaay Indians. For hundreds of years, these native peoples had been living in quiet contentment on lands overlooking the Pacific; they had harvested the rich estuaries and ventured only occasionally into the scrubby hills and canyons for firewood and game.

Sixty years passed before the next visitor, Spanish explorer Sebastian Vizcaino, came seeking a hideout for royal galleons beset by pirates. It was Vizcaino who named the bay for Saint San Diego de Acala.

In 1769, the Spanish came to stay. The doughty Franciscan missionary Junipero Serra marched north from Mexico with a company of other priests and soldiers and built Mission San Diego de Acala. It was the first of a chain of 21 missions and the earliest site in California to be settled by Europeans. Father Serra's mission, relocated a few miles inland in 1774, now sits incongruously amid the shopping centers and housing developments of Mission Valley.

California's earliest civilian settlement evolved in the 1820s on a dusty mesa beneath the hilltop presidio that protected the original mission. Pueblo San Diego quickly developed into a thriving trade and cattle ranching center after the ruling Spanish colonial regime was overthrown and replaced by the Republic of Mexico.

By the end of the century, new residents, spurred partly by land speculators, had taken root and developed the harbor and downtown business district. After the rails finally reached San Diego in 1885, the city flourished. Grand Victorian buildings lined 5th Avenue all the way from the harbor to Broadway, and 1400 barren acres were set aside uptown for a city park.

After its turn-of-the-century spurt of activity, the city languished until World War II, when the U.S. Navy invaded town en masse to establish the 11th Naval District headquarters and one of the world's largest Navy bases. San Diego's reputation as "Navytown USA" persisted well after the war-weary sailors went home. Some 140,000 Navy and Marine personnel are still based in San Diego and at Camp Pendleton to the north, but civilians now outnumber service types twenty to one and military influence has diminished accordingly.

The military has not been the only force to foster San Diego's growth. In the early 1960s, construction began on an important university that was to spawn a completely new industry. Many peg the emergence of the "new" San Diego to the opening of the University of California's La Jolla campus. Not only did the influx of 15,000 students help revive a floundering economy, it tended to liberalize an otherwise insular and conservative city.

Truth is, San Diego is no longer the sleepy, semitransparent little resort city it once was. Nowhere is the fact more evident than in the downtown district, where a building boom has brought new offices, condominiums, and hotels as well as a spectacular business and entertainment complex at Horton Plaza.

But for all the city's manmade appeal, it is nature's handiwork and an ideal Mediterranean climate that most delights San Diego visitors. With bays and beaches bathed in sunshine 75 percent of the time, less than ten inches of rainfall per year, and average temperatures that mirror a proverbial day in June, San Diego offers the casual outdoor lifestyle that fulfills vacation dreams. There's a beach for every taste, ranging from broad sweeps of white sand to slender scimitars beneath eroded sandstone bluffs.

Situated a smug 120 miles south of Los Angeles on Route 5, San Diego is not so much a city as a collection of communities hiding in canyons and gathered on small shoulders of land that shrug down to the sea. As a result, it hardly seems big enough (just over one million) to rank as America's seventh largest city. Total county population is two and a half million, and nine of ten residents live within 30 miles of the coast.

Linking downtown with the Mexican border city of Tijuana, 20 miles south, a string of seaside cities straddle Route 5. While thriving as manufacturing, commercial, and residential communities, Imperial

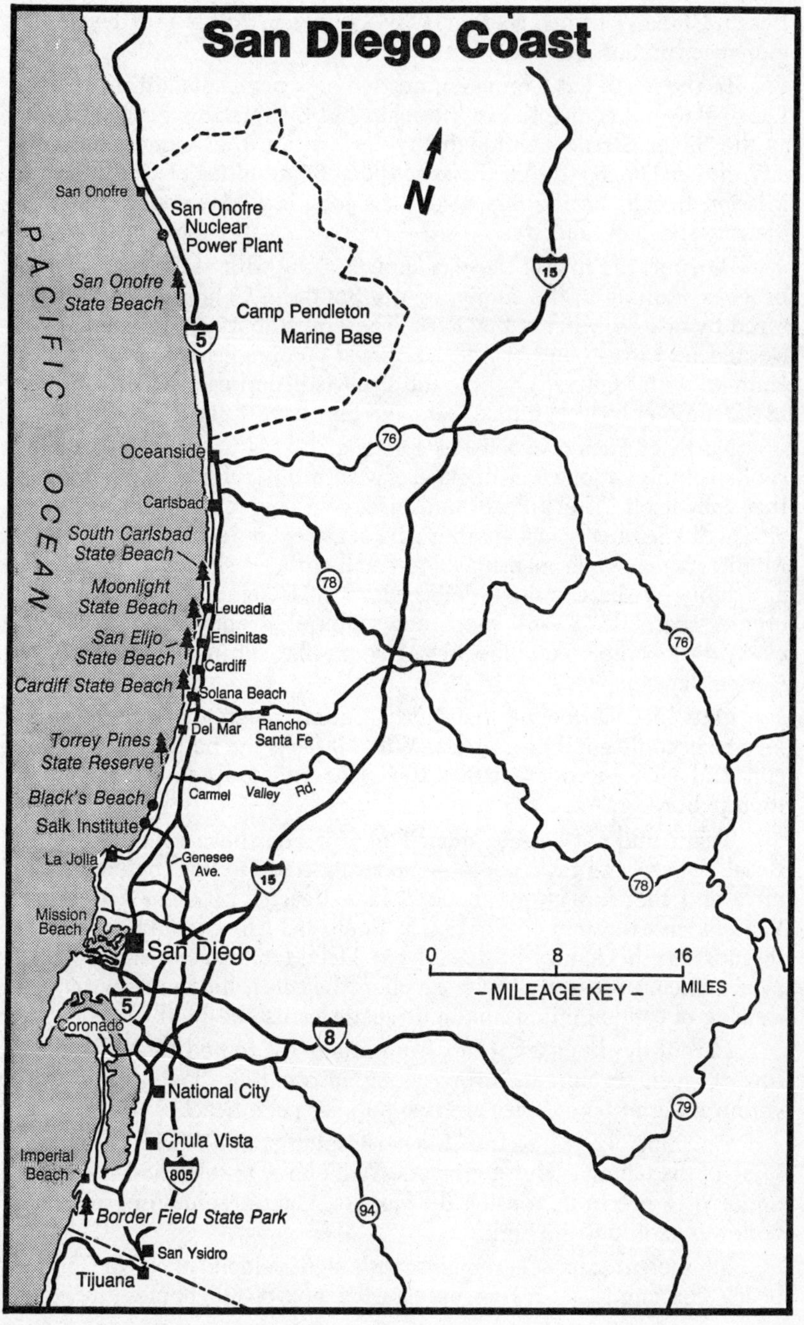
San Diego Coast
N
San Onofre
San Onofre Nuclear Power Plant
San Onofre State Beach
Camp Pendleton Marine Base
PACIFIC OCEAN
Oceanside
Carlsbad
South Carlsbad State Beach
Moonlight State Beach
Leucadia
San Elijo State Beach
Ensinitas
Cardiff
Cardiff State Beach
Solana Beach
Del Mar
Rancho Santa Fe
Torrey Pines State Reserve
Black's Beach
Carmel Valley Rd.
Salk Institute
La Jolla
Genesee Ave.
Mission Beach
San Diego
Coronado
National City
Chula Vista
Imperial Beach
Border Field State Park
San Ysidro
Tijuana
5
15
76
78
8
79
94
805
0 8 16
– MILEAGE KEY –
MILES

Beach, Chula Vista, and National City are only on the verge of developing tourist industries.

To the north lies Coronado, nestled on a peninsula jutting into San Diego Bay and connected to the mainland by a narrow sandbar known as the Silver Strand. Although they are within the boundaries of the city of San Diego, the northern seaside communities of Ocean Beach, Mission Beach, Pacific Beach, and La Jolla have developed their own identities, mood, and style.

"OB," as the first of these is known, along with Mission and Pacific beaches, exhults in the sunny, sporty Southern California lifestyle fostered by nearby Mission Bay Park. These neighboring communities are fronted by broad beaches and an almost continuous boardwalk that is jammed with joggers, skaters, and cyclists. The beaches are saturated in the summer by local sun-seekers, but they have much to offer visitors.

North of Pacific Beach lies La Jolla. Like a beautiful but slightly spoiled child, La Jolla is an enclave of wealth and stubborn independence that calls itself "The Village" and insists on having its own post office, although it's actually just another part of the extended San Diego family. Mediterranean-style mansions and small cottages shrouded by jasmine and hibiscus share million-dollar views of beaches, coves, and wild, eroded sea cliffs. Swank shops and galleries, trendy restaurants, and classy little hotels combine in a Riviera-like setting that rivals even Carmel for chicness.

One gets the feeling that North County neighbor Del Mar would love to become another La Jolla. While it lacks the natural attributes of cliff and cove, it does attract the rich, famous, and hopeful to its thoroughbred racetrack.

That could not be said about Del Mar's northern neighbor, Solana Beach. There's no town center—no real focus—to this coastal community, and that has always been Solana Beach's problem and charm. Visitors whiz through on Route 5 or Route 101 (the coastal highway that threads North County beaches from Del Mar to Oceanside) without even noticing the place or its excellent beaches, hidden from view by a string of condominiums and a dramatic sandstone bluff.

Cardiff-by-the-Sea appears from Route 101 to be little more than a row of chain restaurants strung along an otherwise lovely beach. But within its brief boundaries are two popular state beaches.

Encinitas, known as the "Flower Capital of the World," is home to some of the nation's largest growers. While they are slowly disappearing under pressure from housing developers, giant greenhouses and fields of flowers still dot the area.

Somnolent Leucadia remains the least developed of North County's beach communities. It's an uninspiring mix of old homes, new condominiums, and mom-and-pop commercial outlets, shaded by rows of towering eucalyptus. The place is a haven for artisans, musicians, vegetarians, triathletes (more of these iron types train in North County than anywhere else in the world), and others seeking lower rents and noise levels.

The city of Carlsbad has pushed to the front of the North County pack in terms of sprucing up its image and attracting visitors. Along with its redeveloped downtown area and oceanfront lodging, Carlsbad includes the community of La Costa, a labyrinth of luxury homes and parks built around prestigious La Costa Resort and Spa.

Often stereotyped because it is the home of Camp Pendleton, the nation's largest Marine Corps base, Oceanside is struggling to shed its reputation as a rough-and-tumble military town. Its greatest strides have come along the beachfront, where a concrete pier and five-block promenade have brightened the scene.

It is safe to say that San Diego is not as eccentric and sophisticated as San Francisco, nor as glamorous and fast-paced as Los Angeles. But those who still perceive it as a laid-back mecca for beach bums—or as a lunch stop en route to Mexico—are in for a huge surprise.

Easy Living

Transportation

ARRIVAL

Even though it is located in California's extreme southwest corner, San Diego is the hub of an elaborate highway network. The city is easily reached from north or south via Route 5; Route 8 serves drivers from the east; and Route 15 is the major inland freeway for travelers arriving from the mountain west.

BY AIR

San Diego International Airport (Lindbergh Field) lies just three miles northwest of downtown San Diego and is easily accessible from Routes 5 and 8. The airport is served by most major airlines, including **Alaska Airlines** (800-426-0333), **American Airlines** (800-433-7300), **American West Airlines** (800-278-5692), **Braniff** (800-272-6433), **Continental Airlines** (800-525-0280), **Delta Airlines** (800-221-1212), **Eastern Airlines** (800-327-8376), **Northwest Airlines** (800-225-2525), **Pacific Southwest Airlines** (800-435-9772), **Skywest Western Express** (800-453-9417), **Southwest Airlines** (800-531-5600), **Sunworld Airlines** (800-722-4111), **Trans World Airlines** (800-241-6522), and **USAir** (800-428-4322).

Taxis, limousines, and buses provide service from the airport. **San Diego Transit System** bus #2 (619-233-3004) carries passengers to downtown destinations. Or try the **Airporter Express** (619-231-1123) shuttles to major points in the city.

BY BUS

Greyhound Bus Lines (619-239-9171) services San Diego from around the country. The terminal is located in the downtown area at 120 West Broadway and 1st Avenue.

BY TRAIN

Chuffing to a stop at historic Santa Fe Depot, at Kettner Boulevard and Broadway downtown, is a nice and convenient way to arrive in San Diego. **Amtrak** (800-872-7245) offers several coast-hugging roundtrips daily between Los Angeles and San Diego, with stops at Oceanside and Del Mar.

CAR RENTALS

Much like the rest of Southern California, San Diego is spread out over a wide area and is best seen by car. Car rental companies abound. Most major rental agencies have franchises at the airport. These include **Avis Rent A Car** (619-231-7171), **Budget Rent A Car** (619-297-3851), **Hertz Rent A Car** (619-231-7023), **National Car Rental** (619-231-7103), and **Sears Rent A Car** (619-297-1917).

For better rates (but less convenient service) try agencies located near the airport that provide pick-up service: **Aztec Rent A Car** (619-232-6117), **Dollar Rent A Car** (619-234-3388), **Fuller Auto Rental** (619-232-3444), **Ladki International Rent A Car** (619-233-9333), **Rent A Wreck** (619-224-8235), and **Southwest Car Rental** (619-291-7368).

PUBLIC TRANSPORTATION

Several modern and efficient public transportation systems operate throughout San Diego. Information and schedules are available for *all* systems by calling **San Diego Transit** (619-233-3004).

The San Diego Transit (619-238-0100) bus system is the city's largest public transportation network, with lines linking all major points. All San Diego Transit stops are marked with a blue triangle.

National City Transit (619-474-7505) serves National City, and **Chula Vista Transit** (619-233-3004), or SCOOT, serves Bonita and the city of Chula Vista. **The Strand Route** (619-232-8505) runs from downtown San Diego to Coronado and along the Silver Strand to Imperial Beach. **North County Transit District** (619-743-6283), or NCTD, covers the general area from Del Mar to Camp Pendleton along the coast. NCTD operates numerous North County bus routes that service the communities of Del Mar, Solana Beach, Rancho Santa Fe, Cardiff, Leucadia, Encinitas, Carlsbad, and Oceanside.

The city's newest and most venturesome mode of public transportation is the **San Diego Trolley** (619-233-3004). The light rail system operates daily from the Santa Fe Depot to the Mexican border. Understandably, this line is known as the "Tijuana Trolley," but it also serves as a reliable, inexpensive commuter for the south bay cities of Imperial Beach, Chula Vista, and National City.

TAXIS

San Diego is not a taxi town in the usual big city sense, but there's a cab if you need it—just a telephone call away. Leading companies include **Checker Cab** (619-234-4477), **Co-op Cab** (619-280-2667), and **Yellow Cab** (619-234-6211). In Coronado there's **Coronado Cab** (619-435-6211). In North County (Del Mar to Encinitas), you can call **Bill's Cab** (619-755-6737) or **Oceanside Yellow Cab** (619-722-4217).

BICYCLING

Cycling has skyrocketed in popularity throughout San Diego County, especially in coastal areas. Balboa Park and Mission Bay Park both have excellent bike routes (see the "Sightseeing" section of this chapter).

North County's Old Route 101 provides almost 40 miles of scintillating cycling road along the coast from La Jolla to Oceanside. Traffic is heavy but bikes are almost as numerous as autos along this stretch. Bike lanes are designated along much of the route.

BIKE RENTALS

To rent a bike in San Diego, contact **Cruise Bicycle Rentals** (2453 5th Avenue, near Balboa Park; 619-235-8707), **Pennyfarthings** (520 5th Avenue in Old Town; 619-233-7696), and in the Mission Bay area, go to **Rent A Bike** (619-275-2644), with several locations. Another Rent A Bike outlet can be found in Mission Beach (4444 Mission Boulevard). Other bike outlets include **Holland's Bicycles** (977 Orange Avenue at 10th Street, Coronado; 619-435-3153), **Imperial Beach Schwinn Cyclery** (606 Palm Avenue, Imperial Beach; 619-429-9811), **Wind and Sea Cyclery** (325 Elm Avenue, Carlsbad; 619-434-5100), or **Carlsbad Surfside Bike Rental** (3136 Carlsbad Boulevard, Carlsbad; 619-729-7935).

WALKING TOURS

Several San Diego organizations and tour operators offer organized walks: **Gaslamp Foundation** (410 Island Avenue; 619-233-5227) conducts walking tours of the restored downtown historic district. **Offshootours** (1640 Monroe Avenue; 619-297-0289) has walking tours of Balboa Park and the zoo, while **Old Town Walking Tours** (3977 Twiggs Street; 619-296-1004) cover Old Town State Historical Park. **Promenade Tours** (751 7th Avenue; 619-239-5089) offer organized walks in the downtown area, Old Town, and La Jolla. Join **Coronado Touring** (1110 Isabella Avenue,

Coronado; 619-435-5993) for a leisurely guided stroll through quaint Coronado.

Hotels

Unlike San Francisco and Los Angeles, San Diego offers few grand hotels, bed and breakfast inns, small hotels, or even good budget accommodations. Nor are there many beachfront hotels. What there are tend to be moderately priced, rather ordinary chain-variety hotels and motels.

Nonetheless, I have scoured city and shore in an effort to provide a listing of the best and most interesting accommodations, covering a range of prices, always with the principle of good value as a guide. Unless you plan ahead, you will have difficulty finding a room anywhere on the water during the summer months, when many beachfront properties rent only by the week or month. Room rates at the beaches vary, usually going up ten percent or so during the peak summer season.

SOUTH SAN DIEGO COUNTY HOTELS

Beds at the **Imperial Beach Hostel** (170 Palm Avenue, Imperial Beach; 619-423-8039), tabbed in the low budget range, are the cheapest anywhere in San Diego County. Located in a former firehouse, the hostel features 36 bunk beds arranged none too privately in men's and women's dorms. There is a community kitchen and common room plus a rear courtyard with picnic tables and a basketball hoop.

For several decades now the **Surfside Motel** (800 Seacoast Drive; 619-424-5183) has been the only hostelry located directly on the sands of Imperial Beach. Recently modernized and decked out with a heated outdoor pool and hot tub, this 36-room complex looks good inside and out. Beachside units are especially nice and have full kitchens. Summer reservations should be made a year in advance; moderate.

It looks like an apartment complex, but **Hawaiian Gardens Suite-Hotel** (1031 Imperial Beach Boulevard, Imperial Beach; 619-429-5303) does put up overnight guests in 30 studio and one- and two-bedroom units. The hotel is situated about ten blocks from the beach. Palms and shrubbery surrounding the place create a garden atmosphere, but the Hawaiian theme somehow misses the mark. Rooms are reasonably well decorated and spacious. Extras include pool, sauna, clubhouse, laundry facilities, and color cable television. Moderate.

The closest you will come to a bed and breakfast in the South Bay area is the **Premier Hotel** (416 3rd Avenue, Chula Vista; 619-422-1877). Only a handful of the 22 rooms in this little pension are available for overnight guests. All are small and spartan, but go for a budget price and include continental breakfast.

Among all those identical motels grouped around the freeway exits in Chula Vista, **The Traveler Motel** (235 Woodlawn Avenue; 619-427-

9170) is your best bet. Conveniently located just a block from the highway, this family-owned 84-unit motel is early Holiday Inn throughout, but its rates hark back to 1960s. Not that you would really expect them, but extras include a pool, laundry facilities, and color cable television. Budget.

DOWNTOWN SAN DIEGO HOTELS

Among the few decent downtown budget overnight spots, **Hotel Churchill** (827 C Street; 619-234-5186) is about the cleanest and most livable. Billed as "small, quaint, and unique," this venerable seven-story, 100-room hotel is mostly quaint. Built in 1915, it was somewhat tastelessly remodeled to "depict an authentic medieval English castle." In an equally schmaltzy decorative scheme, 30 of the Churchill's better rooms are done up in different thematic motifs such as "Hawaiian Sunset" and "American Indian." Bedspreads and wall murals are the only difference. To really save money during a downtown stay, ask for one of the rooms with a shared bathroom.

If you are driving, you might try one of downtown's handiest budget-to-moderate priced accommodations, **Clarke's Lodge** (1765 Union Street; 619-234-6787). Conveniently situated, this decent but not very attractive 70-unit motel offers small, plainly furnished rooms plus a pool and coffee shop.

Chain hotels are normally not included in these listings, but because of the lack of good, low-cost lodgings downtown, I'm compelled to tell you about **Budget Hotels of America** (1835 Columbia Street; 619-544-0164). One of a chain including six other San Diego area motels, this 101-room property offers the nicest and newest rooms downtown in the budget-to-moderate range. Queen-sized beds complement a bright, functional, contemporary environment.

The best value for your dollar among moderately priced downtown hotels is the 67-room **Comfort Inn** (719 Ash Street; 619-232-2525). A million-dollar renovation has left the rooms looking very slick. They feature wood furniture, designer color schemes, and high-grade carpeting. The inn has a pool-sized jacuzzi and serves a continental breakfast. Conveniently located next to Balboa Park just a few blocks from the city center.

Highest marks for a midtown hotel in the moderate category go to **Best Western Columbia** (555 West Ash Street; 619-233-7500). Small enough (122 rooms) to offer some degree of personalized service, this modern highrise promises nearly all the niceties you would pay extra for at more prestigious downtown hotels, including a harbor view. Furnishings and amenities are virtually at par with those found in the typical Hilton or Sheraton. There is a pool and spa, plus a restaurant and cocktail lounge.

On the more charming side are San Diego's guesthouses, bed and breakfasts, and historic hotels. **Harbor Hill Guest House** (2330 Albatross Street; 619-233-0638) overlooks the harbor in a centrally located area known as "Banker's Hill." This elegant 1920 home once belonged to the city's mayor. Seven smartly decorated rooms and suites in the moderate price range are arranged on three levels, each with a kitchen-dining area, and sitting room. There is also a lovely garden and redwood deck where continental breakfast is served.

My vote for the prettiest and most hospitable of San Diego's bed and breakfasts goes to the **Keating House Inn** (2331 2nd Avenue; 619-239-8585). This historically designated 1888 Victorian home in a sunny hillside residential neighborhood between Balboa Park and downtown offers four comfy-cozy rooms in the moderate category. With its gabled roof, octagonal window turret, and conical peak, this beautifully restored Queen Anne is every bit as nice inside, where quality period furnishings and accessories round out the decor. A nice patio and garden and a friendly resident family of Irish setters complete the homey scene.

Looking much as it did when it was built in 1887, the majestic **Britt House** (406 Maple Street; 619-234-2926) stands three stories high and has space aplenty for ten rooms, all priced in the deluxe category. This immaculate Victorian, just steps from Balboa Park, is old lace and walnut and afternoon teas in the parlor. Just like staying at a rich aunt's. The innkeepers provide great care and attention, even preparing full breakfasts. San Diego's oldest and most popular bed and breakfast, it is also the most expensive.

No downtown hotel has a more colorful past than the **Horton Grand Hotel** (311 Island Avenue; 619-544-1888). This 110-room Victorian gem is actually two old hotels that were disassembled piece by piece and resurrected a few blocks away. The two were lavishly reconstructed and linked by an atrium-lobby and courtyard. The 1880s theme is faithfully executed, from the hotel's antique-furnished rooms (each with a fireplace) to its period-costumed staff. Room rates hover in deluxe territory, but such amenities as a concierge and afternoon tea combine with friendly service and perfect location to make it one of the city's best hotel values.

Built in 1910 in honor of the 18th president by his son Ulysses S. Grant, Jr., the **U.S. Grant Hotel** (326 Broadway; 619-232-3121) reigned as downtown San Diego's showcase hotel for decades. Now, after an extensive refurbishing, the U.S. Grant is once again a showcase, boasting 283 rooms and two restaurants. It is quite possibly the most elegant and certainly the most beautifully restored historic building in the city. There's a marble-floored lobby with cathedral-height ceilings and enormous crystal chandeliers. Rooms are richly furnished with mahogany poster beds, Queen Anne-style armoires, and wing-back chairs. Ultra-deluxe.

CORONADO HOTELS

Coronado has long been a playground of the rich and famous and the city's hotel rates reflect its ritzy heritage. The best deal on a nice, moderately priced room in the heart of Coronado seems to be at **El Cordova Hotel** (1351 Orange Avenue; 619-435-4131). Orginally built as a private mansion in 1902, El Cordova's moderate size (44 rooms) and lovely Spanish-hacienda architecture make it a relaxing getaway spot. A pool and patio restaurant are added niceties.

Nothing can detract from the glamor of the **Hotel del Coronado** (1500 Orange Avenue; 619-435-6611). With its turrets, cupolas, and gingerbread facade, it is one of the great hotels of California. The last in a proud line of extravagant seaside resorts, the Hotel del Coronado has long been the resting place of United States presidents and Hollywood stars. Remember, however, this celebrated 100-year-old Victorian landmark is a major tourist attraction, so in addition to guests, who usually fill its 700 rooms to capacity, thousands of visitors crowd the lobby and grounds every day. Be aware, too, that many rooms are in a highrise wing adjacent to the original building and though more comfortable are not the real thing. "Hotel Del" has two pools, a long stretch of beach, tennis courts, and a first-class health club. Ultra-deluxe.

Across the street rises the **Glorietta Bay Inn** (1630 Glorietta Boulevard; 619-435-3101), the 1908 Edwardian mansion of sugar king John D. Spreckels which has been transformed into an elegant 99-room hotel. Suites here reflect the grandeur of Spreckels' time, but ordinary rooms are, in fact, rather ordinary. Continental breakfast, ladies and gentlemen, is served on the mansion terrace. Deluxe.

POINT LOMA, SHELTER AND HARBOR ISLANDS HOTELS

Ensconced in a plain vanilla, two-story former church building, the **Point Loma Hostel** (3790 Udall Street; 619-223-4778) is filled with 60 to 70 budget-minded guests almost every night in the summer. Comfortable bunk beds are grouped in 18 rooms housing from two to ten people. Family rooms are also available and there is a common kitchen and dining area.

A rare beachfront find in residential Point Loma is the **Ocean Manor Hotel** (1370 Sunset Cliffs Boulevard; 619-222-7901). This trim, white, two-story, 25-room apartment hotel sits right on the seaside cliffs. Rooms are neat and clean but very basic. Rates for bachelor and studio apartments, including kitchen facilities, are moderate.

Manmade Shelter and Harbor Islands jut out into San Diego Bay, providing space for several large resorts. For a relaxing, offbeat alternative to these mammoth hotels try **Humphrey's Half Moon Inn** (2303 Shelter Island Drive; 619-224-3411). Surrounded by subtropical plants, this nautical-rustic 141-room complex overlooks the yacht harbor and gives the feeling of staying on an island. The rooms are tastefully but simply decorated using top-quality wood and rattan furnishings. There is a pool, spa, putting green, and restaurant. A good value at a deluxe price.

OLD TOWN HOTELS

Best bet in the budget category is the appropriately named **Old Town Budget Inn** (4444 Pacific Highway; 619-295-6444). Strolling distance from Old Town, this spiffy little 46-room family-owned motel has small rooms but adds amenities like a guest laundry. You couldn't expect much more for a budget price.

For the romantic, **Heritage Park Bed & Breakfast Inn** (2470 Heritage Park Row; 619-295-7088), a storybook 1889 Queen Anne mansion with a striking turret, is an enchanting bed and breakfast. Set on a grassy hillside, it provides a tranquil escape. Choose from nine distinctive chambers (four with private baths), each furnished with museum-quality antiques. Most feature ornate brass or four-poster canopy beds and old-fashioned quilts. Deluxe.

MISSION BAY AND THE BEACHES HOTELS

Most of the hotels within sprawling Mission Bay Park are upscale resorts in the deluxe to ultra-deluxe price range. But there's budget relief at the **Western Shores Motel** (4345 Mission Bay Drive; 619-273-1121), located just across the street from Mission Bay Golf Course. This is a quiet, neatly manicured 40-unit court that simply can't be matched for value anywhere in the area.

Only one Mission Bay resort stands out as unique—the **San Diego Princess** (1404 West Vacation Road; 619-274-4630). Over 40 acres of lush gardens, lagoons, and white-sand beach surround the villas and cottages of this 450-room resort. Except for some fancy suites, room decor is motel-modern, with quality furnishings. But guests don't spend much time in their rooms anyway. At the Princess there's more than a mile of beach, a children's playground, boat rentals, eight tennis courts, five pools, three restaurants, and two bars. A self-contained island paradise. Deluxe.

There aren't many beachfront facilities along Ocean Beach, Mission Beach, and Pacific Beach, except for condominiums. One particularly pretty four-unit condominium, **Ventanas al Mar** (3631 Ocean Front Walk; 619-459-7125), overlooks the ocean in Mission Beach. Its contemporary two- and three-bedroom units feature fireplaces, jacuzzi tubs, kitchens, and washer-dryers. They sleep as many as eight people and rent in the deluxe to ultra-deluxe range.

Just a few doors away is **Far Horizons** (3643-45 Ocean Front Walk; 619-459-7125), a rustic, two-story gray frame fourplex. Here two-bedroom apartments with views are deluxe-priced.

Pacific Beach boasts the San Diego County motel with the most character of all. **Crystal Pier Motel** (4500 Ocean Boulevard; 619-483-6983) is a throwback to the 1930s. Fittingly so, because that's when this tacky-looking assemblage of 19 cottages on Crystal Pier was built. This blue-and-white woodframe complex, perched over the waves, features little cottages that are hardly more than huts. Each comes with a kitchen and patio-over-the-sea, not to mention your own parking place on the pier. A unique discovery indeed. Deluxe in summer; moderate during the rest of the year.

LA JOLLA HOTELS

Like a Monopoly master, La Jolla possesses the lion's share of excellent accommodations in the San Diego area. Understandably, there are no budget hotels in this fashionable village by the sea; only a few, in fact, offer rooms in the moderate range. Among that scarce number, two stand out as the best values. **La Jolla Inn** (5445 La Jolla Boulevard; 619-454-2188) is a small 21-room motel on a busy thoroughfare. Rooms are not exactly designer showcases, but they are tastefully appointed and neatly maintained.

Tucked away on the north fringe of the village is **Andrea Villa Inn** (2402 Torrey Pines Road; 619-459-3311), a classy-looking 50-unit motel that packs more amenities than some resorts. There is a pool, spa, exercise room, valet, concierge, and continental breakfast sevice. The rooms are spacious and professionally decorated with quality furniture. Andrea Villa is one of La Jolla's best hotel buys; moderate to deluxe.

Small European-style hotels have always been popular in La Jolla, and the granddaddy of them all is the **Colonial Inn** (919 Prospect Street; 619-454-2181). Established in 1913, the 77-room establishment features lavishly redecorated rooms that beautifully blend antique and contemporary furnishings. Oceanfront rooms provide matchless views. Deluxe to ultra-deluxe.

More than just a hotel, **La Valencia** (1132 Prospect Street; 619-454-0771) is a La Jolla institution, the center of village life. The place simply thrives on attention, and it has received plenty as the "inn place" among stars and dignitaries. Casting aside the aura, "La V" is the loveliest hotel in San Diego, and the most idyllically located. Resplendent in pink stucco and Spanish tile, it is perched on a breezy promontory overlooking the coves and sea cliffs of La Jolla. From the moment guests enter via a trellis-covered tile loggia into a lobby that could pass for King Juan Carlos' living room, they are enveloped in elegance. The private accommodations, however, don't always measure up to the hotel's image. Some of the 100 rooms are rather small and furnished in reproduction antiques. Ah, but out back there's a beautiful garden terrace opening onto the sea and tumbling down to a freeform swimming pool edged with lawn. Facilities include a health club, putting green, and three distinctive restaurants. Deluxe to ultra-deluxe.

Just as the village boasts San Diego's finest selection of small hotels, it can also claim the best bed and breakfast. **The Bed and Breakfast Inn at La Jolla** (7753 Draper Avenue; 619-456-2066) is so nearly perfect it deserves five stars. Listed as an historical site, it was designed as a private home in 1913 by the renowned architect Irving Gill. The John Phillip Sousa family resided here in the 1920s. Faithfully restored by its present owners as a 16-room inn, it stands today as Gill's finest example of cubist-style architecture. Impeccably decorated and ideally situated a block from the ocean, this inn is the essence of La Jolla. Each room features an individual decorative theme carried out in period furnishings. Some have fireplaces and ocean views. All but one tiny sleeping room have private baths. Deluxe to ultra-deluxe.

La Jolla's only true beachfront hotel is **Sea Lodge** (8110 Camino del Oro; 619-459-8271). Designed and landscaped to resemble an old California hacienda, this 128-room retreat overlooks the Pacific on a mile-long beach. With its stuccoed arches, terra-cotta roofs, ceramic tilework, fountains, and flowers, Sea Lodge offers a relaxing south-of-the-border setting. Rooms are large and fittingly appointed with "rustic-Hispanic" furnishings. All feature balconies and the usual amenities; pool and tennis courts. Ultra-deluxe.

NORTH SAN DIEGO COUNTY HOTELS

Many of San Diego's best beaches lie to the north, from Del Mar to Oceanside. Sadly, most of the good hotels do not. But don't worry, among those listed below all but two are either oceanfront or oceanview properties.

It's all in the name when it comes to locating **Del Mar Hotel On The Beach** (1702 Coast Boulevard, Del Mar; 619-755-1534), the only hotel between La Jolla and Carlsbad on the beach. All 44 rooms in this plain stucco building are steps from the sand. That's undoubtedly where you'll spend your time because there is little about the rooms to enchant you. They are basic in design, equipped with stick furniture, and similar to motel accommodations. All rooms have refrigerators and color televisions. Because the hotel is at a right angle to the beach, only a few rooms have full views of the water. Nevertheless, summer rates are deluxe for an ocean view. Winter rates are moderate.

On a hill overlooking Del Mar's village center and coastline is the romantic little **Rock Haus** (410 15th Street, Del Mar; 619-481-3764). One of the region's finest bed and breakfasts, it would be hard to top this sprawling craftsman-style bungalow for location, charm, or quality. Built in 1906 and located two blocks from the beach, it saw action during Prohibition as a speakeasy and gambling den. Today its ten rooms, four with private baths, are thematically decorated and reflect considerable taste and talent. Rates range from deluxe for the little "Wren's Nest" with its ocean view and old-time iron twin beds to the ultra-deluxe "Huntsman's" suite, which features a fireplace. Guests assemble on a sunny veranda for light breakfast and sunset snacks.

There is really only one elegant country inn in all San Diego County. **The Inn at Rancho Santa Fe** (Paseo Delicias and Linea del Cielo, Del Mar; 619-756-1131), widely known among the world's genteel, is a secluded settlement of early California-style *casitas* on a wooded 20-acre site. Situated five miles inland from Solana Beach, the inn offers individually decorated guest rooms as well as two- and three-bedroom cottages. The latter generally feature private sun terraces, fireplaces, and kitchenettes. Furnishings, true to the understated theme, are old but durable, built from sturdy woods like chestnut and maple. Displayed in the homespun lobby is a priceless collection of antique hand-carved model ships. There are tennis courts, swimming pool, croquet, and two restaurants. Rooms are deluxe, suites and cottages ultra-deluxe.

Located on a lofty knoll above the Pacific, **Sandering Place** (85 Encinitas Boulevard, Encinitas; 619-942-7455) is one of the largest and best deluxe-priced hotels in North County. Built on three levels, the 94-room complex looks like a condominium. With a pool, spa, and putting green, it has many of the same features. The rooms are stylishly decorated in light pastel tones, with contemporary oak and bentwood furniture, and include private balconies overlooking the ocean. Continental breakfast is served at the poolside cabaña.

The best moderately priced lodging around the beach in Encinitas is **Moonlight Beach Motel** (233 2nd Street, Encinitas; 619-753-0623). This three-story, 24-unit family-run motel is tucked away in a residential neighborhood overlooking Moonlight Beach State Park. Rooms are a shade tacky and threadbare but contain everything you'll need, including kitchenettes. Accommodations on the upper two floors command ocean views. Service can be lackadaisical and even rude, but guests put up with it because rooms so near the beach are rare indeed.

Carlsbad offers several nice oceanfront facilities, including **Tamarack Beach Resort** (3200 Carlsbad Boulevard, Carlsbad; 619-729-3500), a Spanish contemporary-style condominium. Finished in peach and aqua hues, the Tamarack rents standard rooms as well as suites of all sizes. Most are smashingly decorated in upbeat tones and textures and incorporate sensitive touches like fresh flowers and photographic prints. Suites, though priced in the ultra-deluxe range, may be the best value on the North Coast. They have kitchens and private balconies. (Rooms are deluxe-priced.) All guests can make use of the oceanfront restaurant, clubhouse, fitness center, activities program, and concierge service as well as enjoying the adjacent beach.

Affordability and quietude are the order of the day at **Ocean Manor Motel** (2950 Ocean Street, Carlsbad; 619-729-2493). This tidy, 47-room mom-and-pop complex is so near the sea you can hear it, but a row of expensive beach houses blocks the view. Some sections of the rambling Ocean Manor date back to 1939, and "new" additions are 1950s vintage, so the general decor could best be described as Early-American Motel. An oldie but goodie in this case, however. The furniture may be oddly matched and a bit stodgy, but the place is clean and lovingly maintained and features a pretty garden. All rooms have fully equipped kitchens. Studios are moderate in summer, budget-priced the rest of the year. Larger units are deluxe and moderate, respectively.

For a place right on the sand consider **Beach Terrace Inn** (2775 Ocean Street, Carlsbad; 619-729-5951), which features three modern-style buildings grouped around a beachside terrace. The accommodations range from rooms to elaborate suites and generally include private balconies overlooking the sea. Quality furnishings and accessories are used throughout. Beach Terrace Inn is a first-class hotel with a deluxe to ultra-deluxe price structure.

Sporting a fresh look, the fabled **La Costa Hotel & Spa** (Costa del Mar Road, Carlsbad; 619-438-9111) can justly claim to be one of the world's great "total" resorts. This luxurious 1000-acre complex boasts 482 rooms, its own movie theater, two 18-hole championship golf courses, 27 tennis courts (hardcourt, clay, *and* grass), seven restaurants, and one of the country's largest and most respected spa and fitness centers. Simply put, the place is awesome. With rooms *starting* well up in the ultra-deluxe range, La Costa's appeal to the well-monied few is apparent.

The **Southern California Beach Club** (121 South Pacific, Oceanside; 619-722-6666) is a 44-suite Mediterranean-style facility situated on the beach near Oceanside Pier. Each suite is graciously appointed with quality furnishings in contemporary hues of peach, heather, and blue. Kitchens are standard; other extras include continental breakfast, a health club, rooftop jacuzzis, and laundry facilities; deluxe.

One good thing about the years of neglect along the Oceanside beachfront is that some of the 1940s-vintage tourist courts and cottages have survived. One, **The Blue Whale** (904 North Strand, Oceanside; 619-722-8849), has real possibilities for vacationers who don't mind the surrounding funkiness. This old-timer has been nicely refurbished and offers 12 oceanfront studios and apartments, tastefully decorated with rattan furnishings and soft blue fabrics. All have fully equipped kitchens. Rents run from deluxe to ultra-deluxe.

You are literally surrounded by water at **Villa Marina** (2008 Harbor Drive North, Oceanside; 619-722-1561), a 57-room resort motel situated on a jettylike peninsula at the mouth of Oceanside Harbor. Villa Marina's exterior is not inspiring, but its rooms belie the roadside-motel appearance. For starters, they are mostly large, deluxe-priced, family-sized, one- and two-bedroom suites smartly decorated and replete with fireplaces, full kitchens, and private balconies. There are saunas and swimming and therapy pools on the property. Best of all are the marvelous views of harbor and ocean.

Restaurants

Although panned by food critics since pioneer times, San Diego area restaurants have made great strides in recent years. The county is shackled with more than its share of fast food outlets and identical Mexican eateries, but there are dozens of excellent restaurants, too. Spurred by a wave of talented chefs from all over the world, San Diego is beginning to close the gourmet gap on San Francisco and Los Angeles.

SOUTH SAN DIEGO COUNTY RESTAURANTS

Among the few mentionable restaurants in Imperial Beach, the best is **Bryan's Landing** (285 Palm Avenue; 619-424-5373). Decorated around a nautical theme, the restaurant's atmosphere derives in part from rough-cut cedar paneling and a huge mounted marlin. The dinner menu features surf-n-turf fare with favorite choices being shrimp scampi and a big New York steak for two. Red snapper amandine is good, too, and always fresh. Soups, salads, and hot sandwiches make up the lunch menu. Moderate to deluxe.

La Bella Pizza Garden (373 3rd Avenue, Chula Vista; 619-426-8820) is like an annex to Chula Vista's town hall, and owner Kitty Raso is known as the "Mayor of Third Avenue." But the food will interest you far more than the latest political gossip. Besides pizza, there's great lasagna, rigatoni, and ravioli. La Bella features tender veal dishes, too, from a menu that amazingly never strays beyond budget prices. Best Italian food for the money in San Diego.

Another good bet for low-cost dining with an international twist lies just up the *strasse* at **House of Munich** (230 3rd Avenue, Chula Vista; 619-426-5172). Here the Austrian chef prepares such German dishes as *wienerschnitzel*, potato pancakes, *frikadellen*, and brats 'n kraut. Moderate.

DOWNTOWN SAN DIEGO RESTAURANTS

A couple of San Diego's better restaurant finds lie "uptown" just east of Route 5. **Jilly's** (5th Avenue and Hawthorn Street; 619-544-0940) is a neighborhood sensation, but not many tourists find their way to this chic little dining room. The owners present an array of tasty dishes ranging from marinated *tofu* and mandarin orange salad to grilled fresh salmon and Japanese eggplant. Their forte is Cajun dishes like blackened redfish and jambalaya. No breakfast; moderate.

Unless you happen to be looking for expensive European antiques, you will surely miss **Cafe des Beaux Arts** (2202 4th Avenue; 619-234-

0068). Tucked away in a wing of Galerie Bensoussan, behind the love seats and armoires, this is an undiscovered source of excellent, French country dishes. Lunch and dinner menus include homemade pâté, *poulet basquaise*, *boeuf bourguignon*, and creme caramel at prices ranging from budget to moderate. Antique furnishings (what else?) and a tree-shaded dining patio make for a delightful setting.

Attracting attention has never been a problem for the **Corvette Diner, Bar and Grill** (3946 5th Avenue; 619-542-1001). Cool 1950s music, a soda fountain (complete with resident jerks), rock-and-roll memorabilia, video replays of "Ozzie and Harriet," and a classy Corvette have proven a magnetic formula for this Hillcrest hotspot. The place is jammed for both lunch and dinner. Simple, budget-priced "blue-plate" diner fare features meat loaf, chicken fried steak, and hefty burgers named for '50s notables like as Annette, Eddie, and Kookie.

Everyone likes the warm, friendly atmosphere of a real family restaurant like **Hob Nob Hill** (2271 1st Avenue; 619-239-8176). Here's a place where the waitresses call you "hon" and remind you to finish your veggies. The owners have been serving breakfast, lunch, and dinner since 1946, and a gang of grandmas couldn't do it better. Favorites are waffles, homemade breads, chicken and dumplings, potatoes *avec* gravy, and corned beef cured in the restaurant's own vats. Wholesome, tasty food at budget prices.

Following a visit to Balboa Park or the zoo, there is nothing better than a plate of *poo ja* followed by a spicy serving of *gang ped*. Enjoy these and other wonderful Thai favorites at **Celedon** (3628 5th Avenue; 619-295-8800). Mild or spicy, Celedon's curried and stir-fried specialties are delicious. The stylish art nouveau surroundings, nicely appointed with original Thai brassworks and tapestries, add to the graceful flair of this excellent eatery. Moderate prices.

History, atmosphere, and great cooking combine to make dining at **Ida Bailey's Restaurant** (311 Island Avenue; 619-544-1886) a memorable experience. Located in the Horton Grand Hotel, Ida's was once a brothel, operated back in the 1890s by a madam of the same name. Things are tamer now, but the rich Victorian furnishings serve as a reminder of San Diego's opulent past. The chef serves primarily American fare, including Yankee pot roast and catfish, but wild game dishes are the real treat here. Ida's is the only place in town featuring consistently good venison, boar, buffalo, and pheasant. Moderate to deluxe.

Visitors to Horton Plaza are bombarded with dining opportunities. But for those who can resist the temptation to chow down on pizza, french fries, and enchiladas at nearby fast-food shops, there is a special culinary reward. On the plaza's top level sits **Panda Inn** (506 Horton Plaza; 619-233-7800), one of the city's finest Chinese restaurants. Here the plush, contemporary design alludes only subtly to the Orient with a scattering of classic artwork. But the menu is all-Asian. Three dishes stand out: orange-flavored beef with asparagus, lemon scallops, and chicken with garlic sauce. Lunch and dinner menus together present more than 100 dishes. Dine on the glassed-in veranda for a great view of the harbor. Moderate.

Established in 1907 and now the Gaslamp Quarter's landmark restaurant, the **Golden Lion Tavern** (801 4th Avenue; 619-233-1131) enjoyed a reputation in its early years as one of the finest restaurant-taverns in the West. While its current menu, featuring pasta and seafood, may not rate that kind of acclaim, the old building is truly a work of art. Original penny-tile floors, handsome crown molding, and a magnificent stained-glass dome add to the turn-of-the-century atmosphere. A Golden Lion favorite, and a dish invented here, is the "screw-up": fettucine Alfredo served with shrimp scampi. As the menu notes, "Some of the best things in life aren't planned." You can plan, however, on a moderate tab. No breakfast.

Fans of the late Jim Croce ("Bad Leroy Brown," "Time in a Bottle") will surely enjoy a visit to **Croce's** (802 5th Avenue; 619-233-4355). This new bar and restaurant in the heart of the Gaslamp Quarter is managed enthusiastically by Jim's widow, Ingrid Croce, and features an eclectic mix of dishes served in a friendly cabaret setting. Deli-style lunches

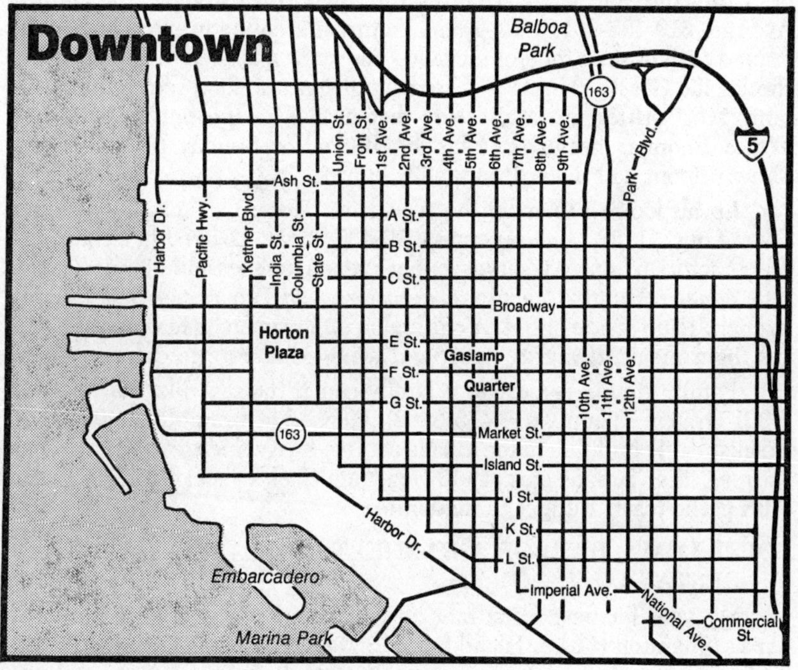

include the city's best blintzes, sandwiches, and exotic salads; dinner specialities are pastas, chicken, and seafood. Great bar, loaded with Croce memorabilia. Weekend brunch; budget to moderate prices.

You'd be remiss to visit San Diego without enjoying a fresh seafood feast at a spot overlooking the harbor. Why not go first class at **Anthony's Star of the Sea Room** (1360 North Harbor Drive; 619-232-7408)? This place wears more awards than a Navy admiral. Dramatically set over the water and elegantly decorated, Anthony's presents a remarkable menu including abalone, broad-bill swordfish, and Florida pompano. Prices range from deluxe to ultra-deluxe. Reservations and coat and tie are essential. If your budget can't handle the "Star," check out the other two Anthonys next door—the **Fish Grotto** (619-546-4443) and **Harborside** (619-232-6358). They're more moderately priced.

For decades, San Diegans have enjoyed the authentic Mexican dishes at **Chuey's** (1894 Main Street; 619-234-6937). Nestled in the shadow of Coronado Bridge, it draws crowds with its great tacos, made the authentic way, crammed with juicy string beef and heaped with grated Mexican cheese. No breakfast; budget.

CORONADO RESTAURANTS

Visitors crossing over to Coronado invariably tour the famous Hotel del Coronado, and many are lured into the **Crown Room** (1500 Orange Avenue; 619-435-6611). Its grand Victorian architecture and enormous domed ceiling set a tone of elegance and style unmatched anywhere on the Pacific Coast. The place is so magnificient the food seems unimportant. Most critics, in fact, assert that dinner in the hotel's **Prince of Wales Room** is better, but lunch, dinner, or Sunday brunch at the Crown Room will never disappoint; deluxe.

Locals looking to avoid the crowds at "Hotel Del" usually head for **Chez Loma** (1132 Loma Avenue; 619-435-0661). Located in a charming 1889 Victorian house, it serves lovely French lunches and dinners (excellent *canard Montmorency* and *crevettes à la Provençal*) plus Sunday brunch. Dine inside or out. A cozy salon *du vin* upstairs features appetizers, light meals, desserts, beer, and wine. Moderate to deluxe.

Family dining is best at a family-run restaurant like **La Avenida** (1301 Orange Avenue; 619-435-6262). Housed in a rambling, attractive, Spanish-style building in the village center, La Avenida features Mexican entrees, the "famous steak sandwich," and Jack's special romaine salad with garlic toast. Budget to moderate.

POINT LOMA, HARBOR AND SHELTER ISLANDS RESTAURANTS

My vote for best restaurant on San Diego's islands goes to **Sheppard's** (Sheraton Harbor Island East, 1380 Harbor Island Drive; 619-692-2225). This spectacular French-country-style dining room overlooking a marina offers gracious service and superb West Coast nouvelle cuisine. House specialties vary seasonally and include an array of fresh fish, game, and veal entrees in a variety of sauces. Classical music is performed live in this fine restaurant. Dinner only; deluxe to ultra-deluxe; jackets required.

At Fisherman's Village in Point Loma you'll find **The Blue Crab Restaurant** (4922 North Harbor Drive; 619-224-3000). Appealing Cape Cod decor and terrific bay views set the mood for fresh seafood, including Maryland blue and soft shell crabs. Great mesquite-broiled swordfish. No breakfast; moderate prices.

Critic's choice for the area's best omelettes is **Cafe Broken Yoke** (3350 Sports Arena Boulevard; 619-226-0442). Choose from nearly 30 of these eggy creations or invent your own. If you can eat it all within an hour, the iron-man/woman special—including a dozen eggs, mushrooms, onions, cheese, etc.—costs only $1.98. Faint or fail and you pay much more. Soups, sandwiches, and salads, too. Breakfast and lunch only; budget-priced.

The same Point Loma neighborhood boasts San Diego's best soup-and-salad bar and my personal favorite for healthy budget dining. **Souplantation** (3960 West Point Loma Boulevard; 619-222-7404) features two huge bars loaded with the prettiest produce this side of the farmer's market. Included are 50 items to heap on your plate. Six tasty soups are made from scratch daily, and a variety of muffins are served hot from the oven. Fresh fruit rounds out this wholesome fare. Comfy wood-paneled environment. Lunch and dinner only; budget.

OLD TOWN AND MISSION VALLEY RESTAURANTS

Mexican food and atmosphere abound in Old Town, especially in the popular Bazaar del Mundo. Here **Casa de Pico** (619-296-3267) lures a steady stream of diners into its festive, flowered courtyard. It's my favorite place to sit and munch cheese nachos and sip margaritas. Budget-to moderate-priced Mexican entrees are served outside or in one of the hacienda-style dining rooms. Mariachis perform regularly; lunch and dinner only.

Two Old Town charmers provide satisfying diversions from a Mexican diet. **Emil's** (3928 Twiggs Street; 619-295-2343) is a European country restaurant, pure and simple. Veal picatta, *wienerschnitzel*, seafood bisque, and hearty specials such as Hungarian goulash are wonderfully prepared and offered at a moderate price. Dinner only.

Cafe Pacifica (2414 San Diego Avenue; 619-291-6666) rates equally high marks for a creative menu of fresh fish specialties. Stylish but comfortable environs include a patio under a removable roof and a friendly wine bar. Lunch and dinner only; moderate prices.

Less than a mile from Old Town lies a pair of excellent ethnic take-out shops that few visitors ever find. **El Indio** (★) (3695 India Street;

619-299-0333) opened in 1940 as a family-operated *tortilleria*, then added an informal restaurant serving *quesadillas*, enchiladas, tostadas, burritos, tacos, and taquitos (or "little tacos"). Quality homemade Mexican food at Taco Bell prices; you can sit indoors, out on the patio, or order to go.

Another one-of-a-kind fast-food operation with an equally fervent following, **Saffron** (3731-B India Street; 619-574-0177) turns out zesty Thai-grilled chicken on a special rotisserie. The aroma is positively exquisite and so is the chicken served with jasmine rice, Cambodian salad, and the five tangy sauces. Eat on an adjacent patio or take a picnic to the beach. Budget.

MISSION BAY AND THE BEACHES RESTAURANTS

Hidden away in Ocean Beach is a cottage restaurant called **The Belgian Lion** (★) (2265 Bacon Street; 619-223-2700). Nobody in San Diego provides lustier, tastier European provincial fare than the folks here, who prepare French onion soup, roasted rabbit, crispy confit of duck, veal sweetbreads, turnip soufflé, and steaming cassoulets in the classic manner. Homegrown herbs and spices delight both the sauces and the senses. But go easy when you order; the portions are meant to satisfy a Flemmish farmer. Service here is especially personalized. Dinner only; deluxe-priced, and worth every franc.

Another European experience waits nearby in Mission Beach, where the **Blue Danube Hungarian Restaurant** (3861 Mission Boulevard; 619-488-1907) serves Hungarian goulash soup, chicken paprika, *spaetzel*, and stuffed cabbage. The Blue Danube does not regale you with recorded gypsy music and the simple decor won't remind you of Budapest, but huge portions of its hearty, spicy home-style food will put a hop back in your step. Dinner only; budget to moderate prices reflect an exceptional value.

A good breakfast is hard to find in the Pacific Beach area. So rather than punishing yourself with formula flapjacks, go straight to the Rack. The **Spice Rack** (4315 Mission Boulevard; 619-483-7666), that is. Locals know about it, so there is usually a crowd, and you'll also have the aroma of muffins fresh from the oven to keep you awake. Bakery items are the best buy here, but the herb-and-cheese omelettes are great, too. Wicker and garden greenery make for a relaxing atmosphere, and there is alfresco dining on the patio. Also serves lunch and dinner daily to mixed reviews. Moderate.

The most creative restaurant in Pacific Beach is **Chateau Orleans** (926 Turquoise Street; 619-488-6744), one of the city's finest Cajun restaurants. Cajun, that is, with a delightfully different, delicate nouvelle twist. Tasty appetizers fresh from the bayous include Lousiana frog legs and southern fried gator bites. Yes, indeed, they eat alligators down in Cajun country, and you should be brave enough to find out why. Seafood gumbo chocked with crawfish, pan-blackened prime rib, chicken sauce piquant, and gorgeous tiger-tail scampi fresh from the gulf are typical menu choices. Everything is authentic except the decor, which thankfully shuns board floors and bare bulbs in favor of carpets, classy furnishings, and a contemporary color scheme. Quality at a moderate to deluxe price; dinner only.

LA JOLLA RESTAURANTS

Just as it is blessed with many fine hotels, La Jolla is a restaurant paradise. **Gustaf Anders** (2812 Avenida de la Playa; 619-459-4499), possibly San Diego's finest restaurant, is here. A sleek arena in black, white, and gray, this is a place where dining is an aesthetic experience. Beautiful surroundings, superb service, and brilliant food combine to make this dining room everything a fine restaurant should be. Try the *carpaccio*-like *grave lox* garnished with lemon and dill. You'll need reservations, a jacket, and bundles of money. Lunch, dinner, and Sunday brunch; ultra-deluxe.

La Jolla's other great restaurant is **George's at the Cove** (1250 Prospect Street; 619-454-4244), which based its climb to success on a knockout view of the water, a casual, contemporary environment, fine service, and a trendsetting regional menu. Daily menus incorporate the freshest seafood, veal, beef, lamb, poultry, and pasta available. Smoked salmon *quesadilla* and shrimp and spinach with fettucine are two of my favorites. The food presentation alone is a work of art. Open for lunch, dinner, and Sunday brunch; there is also a cafe menu in the upstairs bar. Moderate to deluxe.

Manhattan (7766 Fay Avenue; 619-454-1182), which successfully replicates a New York City family-style Italian restaurant (despite the palms and pink stucco), features Neopolitan waiters who sing as they toss your salad. The most popular dishes include zesty shrimp *diavalo* over pasta, veal Marsala, and rack of lamb. Wonderful Caesar salads and *cannoli* desserts. Lunch, dinner, and Sunday brunch; moderate to deluxe.

La Jolla's most adventuresome dining is at **Pawinda** (1110 Torrey Pines Road; 619-454-9229), serving Afghan and Pakistani food. Here you'll find such dishes as *tikke* (marinated grilled lamb) and *kunar pulao* (chicken in yogurt sauce) prepared just as they are in the camps of Pawinda tribesmen. Dine at tables in this richly decorated restaurant or on cushy pillows for even more atmosphere. Lunch and dinner only; deluxe.

Jose's Court Room (1037 Prospect Street; 619-454-7655), a noisy, down-to-earth Mexican pub, is the best place in town for quick, casual snacks. Offers all the typical taco, tostada, and enchilada plates plus tasty sautéed shrimp and steak ranchero dinners. Lunch and dinner only; moderate.

John's Waffle Shop (7906 Girard Avenue; 619-454-7371) is a traditional La Jolla stopping place for old-fashioned, budget-priced, counter-style breakfasts or lunches. Locals start their day here with Belgian waffles and eggs Benedict. The best lunches are the country fried steak and grilled tuna melt on sourdough.

La Jolla's so-called "restaurant row" lies along La Jolla Boulevard south of the village. One Italian dining room here ranks among the city's best in that category. **Issimo** (5634 La Jolla Boulevard; 619-454-7004) is a tiny gourmet shop with a stone facade and devoted following. Sophisticated Northern Italian and French dishes are painstakingly prepared and beautifully presented. Favorites include canelloni, lasagna, gnocchi Parisienne, *agnolotti*, and antipasti as well as the wonderful desserts. Wall murals by internationally known Wing Howard create an artsy atmosphere. Lunch and dinner only; deluxe to ultra-deluxe.

NORTH SAN DIEGO COUNTY RESTAURANTS

Your favorite fish dish is comfortably priced in the budget to moderate range at **El Pescador Fish Market** (1342 Camino del Mar, Del Mar; 619-755-1919). This casual outdoor cafe adjoins a fish market, helping ensure freshness. Basic patio furniture and surrounding greenery make for a pleasant atmosphere. Great smoked fish sandwich and house salad in addition to daily fresh fish specials. Lunch and dinner only.

Remington's (2010 Jimmy Durante Boulevard, Del Mar; 619-755-5103), located near the Del Mar Race Track, has long reigned as a favorite among the gambling set. The surroundings are rather plain, but the owner bet on the kitchen rather than fancy furnishings. The payoff is high quality and large quantity. Traditional dishes such as steak, lamb, veal, and fresh Maine lobster are prepared to perfection. Definitely the place to go after a day at the races. Just be sure to bring a big appetite and all your winnings: Remington's runs in the ultra-deluxe range. Lunch and dinner only.

The place is mobbed all summer long, but **The Fish Market** (640 Via de la Valle; 619-755-2277) remains one of my favorite Del Mar restaurants. I like the noise, nautical atmosphere, oyster bar, budget-to-moderate prices, on-the-run service, and the dozen or so fresh fish items. Among the best dishes are the monkfish, yellowtail, orange roughie, and salmon, either sautéed or mesquite charbroiled.

Scalini (3790 Via de la Valle, Del Mar; 619-259-9944), housed in a classy new contemporary-style building with arched windows overlooking a polo field, is strictly star quality. The place has been decorated in a mix of modern and antique furnishings and wrapped in all the latest Southern California colors. But the brightest star of all is the menu. The Caesar salad and mesquite-broiled veal chops are exceptional, as is the duck with pear and raspberry sauce. There are many good homemade pasta dishes including lobster fettucine, lasagna, linguini, and tortellini. Dinner only; moderate to deluxe.

Mention the words "Mexican food" in Solana Beach and the reply is sure to be **Fidel's** (617 Valley Avenue; 619-755-5292). This favored spot has as many rooms and patios as a rambling hacienda. Given the good food and budget prices, all of them inevitably are crowded. Fidel's serves the best *tostada suprema* anywhere and the burritos, enchiladas, and *chimichangas* are always good. Lunch and dinner only.

Mille Fleurs (6009 Paseo Delicias, Rancho Santa Fe; 619-756-3085) tops everyone's list as San Diego's best French restaurant. The a la carte menu, which changes daily, provides exquisite appetizers, soup, and such entrees as veal chop stuffed with goat cheese, Norwegian salmon in pink grapefruit sauce, and whole Dover sole. A sophisticated interior features fireside dining, Portuguese tiles, and stunning *trompe l'oeil* paintings. There is also a Spanish courtyard for lunch as well as a smart cafe and bar that serves up light food and piano music. Lunch and dinner only; ultra-deluxe.

Best of the beachfront dining spots in Cardiff is **Charlie's Grill and Bar** (2526 South Route 101; 619-942-1300), where the surf rolls right up to the glass. Here you can choose from an innovative selection of fresh seafood items or an all-American menu of hickory-smoked ribs and chicken, steak, and prime rib. Charlie's has a smartly decorated contemporary setting with a full bar, but still creates an easy and informal atmosphere. Dinner and Sunday brunch only; moderate.

Most visitors to Encinitas never lay eyes on the **Potato Shack Cafe** (120 West I Street; 619-436-1282), hidden away on a side street. But locals start packing its pine-paneled walls at dawn to tackle North County's best and biggest breakfast for the buck. There are great three-egg omelettes, including a tasty cheese-and-tuna creation; but best of all are the home-style taters and the old-fashioned biscuits and gravy. Lunch is also served, but the Potato Shack is really a breakfast institution. Budget.

Another popular feeding spot is **Sakura Bana Sushi Bar** (1031 1st Street, Encinitas; 619-942 6414). The sushi here is heavenly, especially the sakura roll, crafted by Japanese masters from shrimp, crab, scallop, smelt egg, and avocado. The bar serves only sushi and *sashimi*, but table service will bring you such treats as teriyaki, tempura, shrimp *shumai*, beef *negima*, and *kushi katsu*. Lunch and dinner; budget to moderate.

Biarritz (1010 1st Street, Encinitas; 619-944-8490) is very L.A. with its neon-lit art deco interior and nouvelle cuisine. The decor may be a bit much, but we all can bow in prayer to the menu. It features a superb selection of dishes including *ahi* tuna sautéed with basil or grilled crispy duck topped with champagne grapes and accompanied by light corn crepes and sautéed potatoes. The pastas are great, too, especially the black-and-white angel hair in saffron sauce. Dinner only; reservations are a must; deluxe.

A Mexican restaurant called **El Cormal** (523 Encinitas Boulevard, Encinitas; 619-944-1575) outscores its competition largely on the merits of its design. At last someone has succeeded in creating an attractive Mexican eatery that doesn't look like an adobe casita or the Alamo. El Cormal also offers good food at budget prices. The *camarones rancheros* and *carne asada* are especially tasty. Mariachi entertainment; lunch, dinner, and Sunday brunch.

I'm always tempted to call it a vegetarian restaurant, but the **Basil St. Cafe** (576 North Route 101, Leucadia; 619-942-5145) is more than that. With its dual cuisines of gourmet seafood and "natural" dishes, it blends 1960s-era thinking with 1980-style sensibilities. It offers everything from Middle Eastern *tempe* to fresh opa, macrobiotic foods, calzone, and steamed vegetables. The cooking is imaginative, sprightly, and healthful. Dinner only; budget to moderate.

Pasta lovers should be sure to try the *penne* or *fusilli* in vodka-tomato sauce at **When In Rome** (828 North Route 101, Leucadia; 619-944-1771). High ceiling, arched windows, and an art-filled Roman decor provide the proper atmosphere, and the Italian owners certainly know their trade. All the breads and pastas are made fresh daily. Entrees include a variety of veal and seafood items. Dinner only; moderate.

British colonial meets California contemporary at the casual, convivial **Bombay Beach Club** (2777 Roosevelt Street, Carlsbad; 619-434-5515). Take a seat in a wicker peacock chair and dine in a mellow garden setting. Choose from an eclectic selection of fresh, tasty dishes including chicken curry *tandoori*, *feta spaghettini*, and stuffed sea bass. Moderate to deluxe.

Neiman's (2978 Carlsbad Boulevard, Carlsbad; 619-729-4131), an eye-catching Victorian landmark, houses both a dining room and cafe. Stick to the cafe, where LeRoy Neiman lithos hang on the walls and the menu includes trendy dishes such as orange-ginger chicken breast on spinach fettucine and smoked duck with Roquefort cheese *quesadillas*. It also has burgers, pasta, and salads. Lunch and dinner only; budget to moderate.

A cozy, old-world atmosphere is hard to find in Oceanside, so you'll appreciate the European flair and food at **Cafe Europa** (1733 South Hill Street; 619-433-5811). Such delights as veal Marsala, linguini with clam sauce, and chicken Swiss for lunch, plus continental dinner specialties like filet mignon Bernaise and chicken breast Normande, make this a worthwhile retreat. There's also a pasta bar. Lunch and dinner; moderate to deluxe.

Painted white and blue like an Aegean taverna, **Mykonos** (258 Harbor Drive South, Oceanside; 619-757-8757) adds dining diversity to

Oceanside's marina. Greek owned and operated, it features traditional dishes like *moussaka*, *souvlaki*, and chicken *salonika*, plus a variety of seafood specialties. Favorites are *kalamari Mykonos* (squid sautéed with bell peppers and wine) and scampi baked in tomato sauce and *feta* cheese. Complete with a patio dining area overlooking the harbor, Mykonos serves lunch and dinner at budget to moderate prices.

The Great Outdoors

The Sporting Life

FISHING

The lure of sports and bottom fishing attracts thousands of enthusiasts to San Diego every year. Albacore and snapper are the close-in favorites, with marlin and tuna the prime objectives for longer charters. For deep-sea charters, see **Chula Vista Boat Rentals** (Chula Vista Marina; 619-585-7245), **Chief Skis Charter** (836 Orange Avenue, Coronado; 619-437- 1983), **H & M Sportfishing Landing** (2803 Emerson Street, Point Loma; 619-222-1144), **Fish N' Cruise** (2731 Island Drive, Shelter Island; 619-244-2464), **Seaforth Sportfishing** (1717 Quivira Road, Mission Bay; 619-224-3383), **Islandia Sportfishing** (1551 West Mission Bay Drive, Mission Bay; 619-222-1164), or **Helgren's Sportsfishing** (315 Harbor Drive, Oceanside; 619-722-2133).

Spearfishing is very popular off La Jolla beaches, especially south of La Jolla Cove. Contact **San Diego Divers Supply** (7522 La Jolla Boulevard, La Jolla; 619-459-2691) for supplies, tours, and information. Note: Spearfishing is not allowed in protected reserves from La Jolla cove north.

WHALE WATCHING

For whale-watching tours contact **H & M Sportsfishing Landing** (Point Loma; 619-222-1144), **Point Loma Sportfishing Association** (Point Loma; 619-223-1627), **Fisherman's Landing** (Point Loma; 619-222-0391), or **Helgren's Sportfishing** (315 Harbor Drive, Oceanside; 619-722-2133).

Also, a free whale-watching station at Cabrillo National Monument on Point Loma offers a glassed-in observatory from which to spot whales.

SKIN DIVING

San Diego offers countless spots for skin diving. In Point Loma try the colorful tidepools at Cabrillo Underwater Reserve; at "No Surf Beach" (Sunset Cliff Boulevard) pools and reefs are for experienced divers only. The rocky La Jolla coves boast some of the best diving in San Diego. Bird Rock, La Jolla Underwater Park, and the underwater Scripp's Canyon are ideal havens for scuba and skin divers.

For diving rentals, sales, instruction, and dive tips contact **Buhrow Into Diving** (2434 Southport Street, Chula Vista; 619-477-5946), **National City Divers** (430 West 12th Street, National City; 619-477-5154), **San Diego Diver's Supply** (4004 Sports Arena Boulevard, San Diego; 619-437-1983), **New England Divers Incorporated** (3860 Rosecrans Street, San Diego; 619-298-0531), **Diving Locker** (1020 Grand Avenue, Pacific Beach; 619-272-1120), **San Diego Diver's Supply** (7522 La Jolla Boulevard, La Jolla; 619-459-2691), **Diving Locker** (405 North Route 101, Solana Beach; 619-755-6822), **Ocean Enterprises** (191 North El Camino Real, Encinitas; 619-942-3661), and **Underwater Schools of America** (707 Oceanside Boulevard, Oceanside; 619-722-7826).

SURFING AND WINDSURFING

Surf's up in the San Diego area. Ocean, Mission, and Pacific beaches, Tourmaline Surfing Park, Windansea Beach, La Jolla Shores, Swami and Moonlight beaches are well-known hangouts for surfers. Sailboarding is concentrated within Mission Bay. Oceanside is home to annual world-class boogie board and surfing competitions.

Insurance premiums have caused many surf shops to discontinue rentals.

BOATING AND SAILING

You can sail under the Coronado Bridge, skirt the gorgeous downtown skyline, and even get a taste of open ocean in this Southern California sailing mecca. Several sailing companies operate out of Harbor Island West in San Diego, including **San Diego Yacht Charters** (1880 Harbor Island Drive, 619-297-4555) and **San Diego Sailing Club and School** (1880 Harbor Island Drive, Harbor Island; 619-298-6623).

Other motor boat and sail rentals in the area can be found at **H & M Landing** (2803 Emerson Street, San Diego; 619-222-1144), **C.P. Sailing Sports** (Mission Bay; 619-270-3211), **Mission Bay Sportscenter** (1010 Santa Clara Place, Mission Bay; 619-488-1004), **Chula Vista Boat Rentals** (550 Tidelands Avenue, Chula Vista Marina; (619-585-7245), **Glorietta Bay Marina** (1715 Strand Way, Coronado; 619-435-5203), and **Hornblower Yacht Charters** (Glorietta Bay Marina; 619-435-2211).

HANG GLIDING

Torrey Pines Gliderport (La Jolla Village Farms Road, La Jolla; 619-457-9093) is an expert-rated hang gliding site, located atop a towering sandstone bluff overlooking Black's Beach. If you're not yet an expert, there is a great vantage point to watch from. Contact **The Hang Gliding Center** (4206 Sorrento Valley Center, Del Mar; 619-450-9008) for rentals, sales, and instruction.

OTHER SPORTS

GOLF

For the golfing set there's **Balboa Park Municipal Golf Course** (Golf Course Drive, Balboa Park; 619-232-2417), **Coronado Golf Course** (2000 Visalia Row, Coronado; 619-435-3121), **River Valley Golf Course** (2440 Hotel Circle North, Mission Valley; 619-297- 3391), **Mission Bay Golf Center** (2702 North Mission Bay Drive, Mission Bay; 619-273-1221), **Torrey Pines Municipal Golf Course** (11480 North Torrey Pines Road, La Jolla; 619-453-0380), **Whispering Palms Golf Course** (4000 Cancha de Golf, Rancho Santa Fe; 619-756-2471), **Rancho Carlsbad Golf Course** (5200 El Camino Real, Carlsbad; 619-438-1772), **Oceanside Golf Course** (825 Douglas Drive, Oceanside; 619-433-1360), and **Emerald Isle Golf Course** (660 El Camino Real, Oceanside; 619-721-4700).

TENNIS

San Diego has many private and public courts open to traveling tennis buffs. For information call **Balboa Tennis Club** (2221 Morley Field Drive, San Diego; 619-295-9278), **Cabrillo Recreation Center** (3051 Canon Street, Point Loma; 619-222-3536), **Mission Valley YMCA** (5505 Friars Road, Mission Valley; 619-298-3576), **Peninsula Tennis Club** (2525 Bacon Street, Ocean Beach; 619-226-3407), **La Jolla Recreation Center** (615 Prospect Street, La Jolla; 619-454-2071), and **Carlsbad Inn Beach and Tennis Club** (3001 Carlsbad Boulevard, Carlsbad; 619-434-7020).

In Coronado call 619-435-1616 for information on courts.

North County suffers from a lack of public tennis courts; however, Del Mar has two free courts located at Court and 21st streets. In Solana Beach courts are located at Earl Warren Junior High School (Stevens Street and Lomas Santa Fe Drive).

HORSEBACK RIDING

Imperial Beach is one of the few places in the county where you can ride on the beach. **Hilltop Stable** (2671 Monument Road, Imperial Beach; 619-428-5411) rents mounts for rides at Borderfield State Beach.

Beaches and Parks

SOUTH SAN DIEGO COUNTY BEACHES AND PARKS

Border Field State Park—True to its name, this oceanfront park actually borders on Mexico. It features a two-mile-long stretch of sandy beach, backed by dunes and salt marshes studded with daisies and chaparral. Equestrian and hiking trails crisscross this pristine wetlands area which adjoins a federal wildlife refuge at the mouth of the Tijuana River. Sounds idyllic except for the constant racket from Border Patrol helicopters and the ever-present threat of untreated sewage drifting north from Mexico.

Facilities: Picnic areas, restrooms, lifeguards; restaurants and groceries are several miles away in San Ysidro or Imperial Beach; information, 619-428-3034.

Fishing: Excellent from the surf.

Swimming: Very good.

Surfing: Good year round at "Tijuana Sloughs," a series of three peaks just north of the lagoon mouth.

Getting there: Take the Dairy Mart Road exit off Route 5 and go west. The name changes to Monument Road about a mile before reaching the park entrance.

Imperial Beach—A wide, sandy beach, popular at the south end with surfers; boogie-boarders and swimmers ply the waters between the two jetties farther north, just past the renovated fishing pier. The crowd is mostly young with many military personnel. Each July Imperial Beach hosts the annual U.S. Open Sandcastle Competition, attracting huge crowds.

Facilities: Picnic areas, restrooms, lifeguards, snack bars.

Fishing: Good from the surf.

Surfing: Very popular on both sides of the pier and rock jetties.

Getting there: Take Palm Avenue exit west off Route 5 all the way to the water.

Silver Strand State Beach—This two-mile strip of fluffy white sand fronts a narrow isthmus separating the Pacific Ocean and San Diego Bay. It was named for tiny silver sea shells found in abundance along the shore. The water is shallow and fairly calm on the ocean side, making it a good swimming beach. Things are even calmer and the water much warmer on the bay shore. The park also is popular for surf-fishing, clamming, and shell hunting.

Facilities: Picnic areas, restrooms, lifeguards, showers, equipment rentals; restaurants and groceries are several miles away in Imperial Beach; information, 619-435-5184.

Camping: Permitted for RVs and trailers only.

Getting there: Located on Route 75 (Silver Strand Boulevard) between Imperial Beach and Coronado.

DOWNTOWN AND CORONADO BEACHES AND PARKS

Coronado Shores Beach—It's the widest beach in the county but hardly atmospheric, backed up as it is by a row of towering condominiums. Still, crowds flock to this roomy expanse of clean, soft sand where gentle waves make for good swimming. The younger crowd gathers at the north end, just past the Hotel del Coronado.

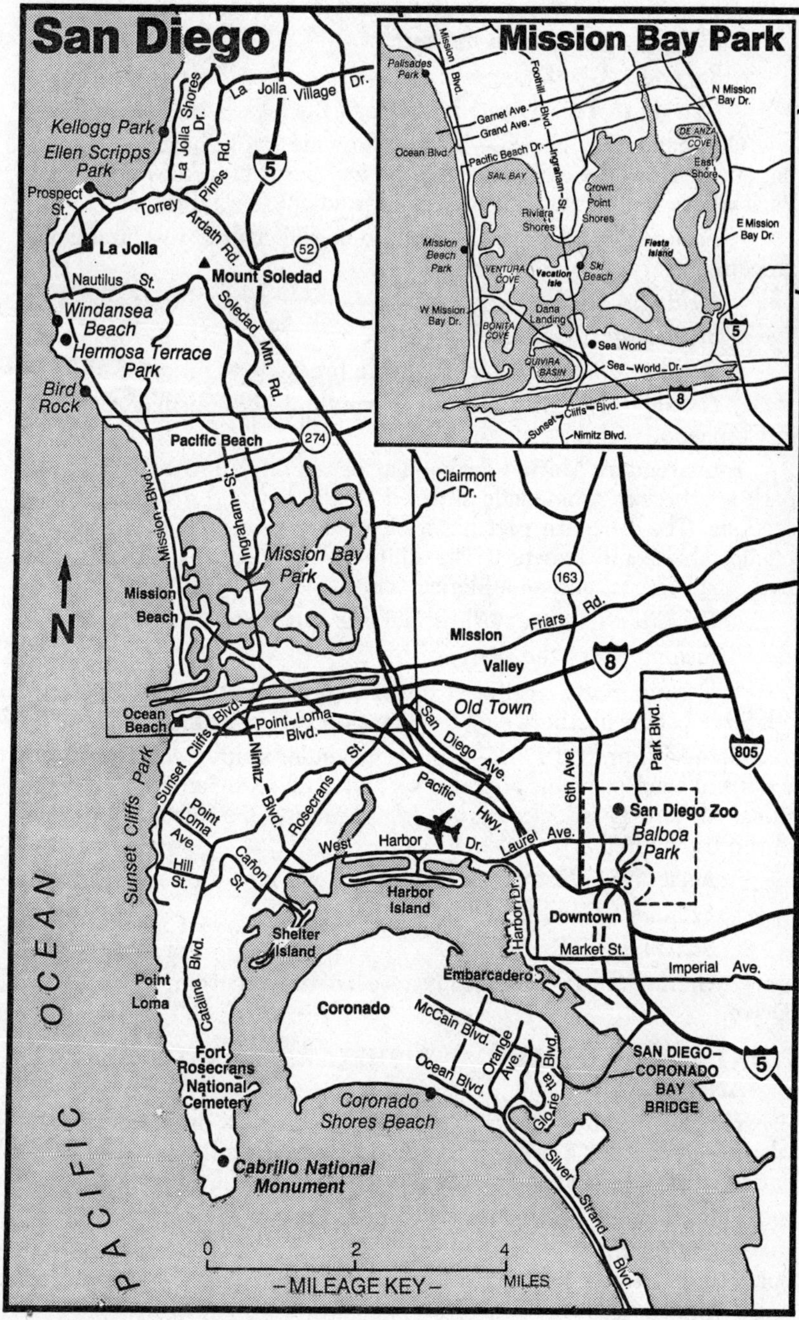
San Diego
Mission Bay Park
Palisades Park
Mission Blvd.
Foothill Blvd.
Garnet Ave.
Grand Ave.
Ocean Blvd
Pacific Beach Dr.
Ingraham St.
N Mission Bay Dr.
DE ANZA COVE
East Shore
SAIL BAY
Crown Point Shores
Riviera Shores
E Mission Bay Dr.
Mission Beach Park
Fiesta Island
VENTURA COVE
Vacation Isle
Ski Beach
W Mission Bay Dr.
BONITA COVE
Dana Landing
Sea World
QUIVIRA BASIN
Sea World Dr.
Sunset Cliffs Blvd.
Nimitz Blvd.
La Jolla Village Dr.
La Jolla Shores Dr.
Kellogg Park
Ellen Scripps Park
Pines Rd.
Prospect St.
Torrey Pines Rd.
Ardath Rd.
La Jolla
Mount Soledad
Nautilus St.
Soledad Mtn. Rd.
Windansea Beach
Hermosa Terrace Park
Bird Rock
Pacific Beach
Clairmont Dr.
Mission Bay Park
Mission Beach
N
Mission Valley
Friars Rd.
Ocean Beach
Old Town
Point Loma Blvd.
San Diego Ave.
Park Blvd.
6th Ave.
Sunset Cliffs Park
Rosecrans St.
Pacific Hwy.
San Diego Zoo
Balboa Park
Point Loma Ave.
Laurel Ave.
West Harbor Dr.
Hill St.
Cañon St.
Harbor Island
Harbor Dr.
Downtown
Shelter Island
Market St.
Imperial Ave.
Embarcadero
Point Loma
Catalina Blvd.
Coronado
McCain Blvd.
Orange Ave.
Glorietta Blvd.
Ocean Blvd.
SAN DIEGO-CORONADO BAY BRIDGE
Fort Rosecrans National Cemetery
Coronado Shores Beach
Cabrillo National Monument
Silver Strand Blvd.
PACIFIC OCEAN
0 2 4
–MILEAGE KEY–
MILES

Facilities: None. Restaurants and groceries nearby.

Fishing: Good from the surf.

Surfing: Good.

Getting there: Located off Ocean Boulevard in Coronado.

Coronado City Beach—That same wide sandy beach prevails to the north. Here the city has a large, grassy picnic area known as **Sunset Park** where frisbees and the aroma of fried chicken fill the air.

Facilities: Picnic areas, restrooms, lifeguards; restaurants and groceries nearby.

Fishing: Good.

Swimming: Good.

Surfing: Safe but unpredictable breaks.

Getting there: Located on Ocean Boulevard north of Avenue G in Coronado.

Embarcadero Marina Park—The center city's only real waterfront park is a breezy promenade situated on the bay and divided into two sections. The northern part has a nicely landscaped lawn and garden, picnic tables, and benches. The southern half features a fishing pier, basketball courts, and an athletic course.

Facilities: Restrooms; restaurants and groceries are nearby.

Fishing: Try the pier.

Getting there: Enter at the southern end at Harbor Drive and 5th Street; at the northern end, from Seaport Village Shopping Center.

Spanish Landing Park—This is a slender sandy beach with walkways and a grassy picnic area that's situated close to San Diego International Airport. Overlooks Harbor Island Marina and offers lovely views of the bay and city.

Facilities: Restrooms; restaurants and groceries are nearby.

Fishing: Good from the sea wall.

Swimming: Excellent.

Getting there: Located just west of the airport on North Harbor Drive.

POINT LOMA, HARBOR AND SHELTER ISLANDS BEACHES AND PARKS

Harbor Island—There are no sandy beaches on this manmade island, but there is a walkway bordered by lawn and benches along its entire length. Fabulous views of the city and great fishing.

Facilities: Restrooms, restaurants.

Getting there: South of San Diego International Airport on Harbor Island Drive.

Shelter Island—Like Harbor Island, its neighbor to the northeast, Shelter Island functions primarily as a boating center, but there's a beach facing the bay that is popular for swimming, fishing, waterskiing, and picnicking. A landscaped walkway runs the length of the island.

Facilities: Picnic areas, restrooms, fishing pier, restaurants.

Getting there: Located on Shelter Island Drive near Rosecrans Street.

Sunset Cliffs Park—The jagged cliffs and sandstone bluffs along Point Loma peninsula give this park a spectacular setting. High-cresting waves make it popular with expert surfers, who favor the rocky beach at the foot of Ladera Avenue. Tidepools evidence the rich marine life that attracts many divers. Winding staircases (at Bermuda and Santa Cruz avenues) and steep trails lead down to some nice pocket beaches.

Facilities: Hiking trails; restaurants and groceries nearby.

Getting there: Located off Sunset Cliffs Boulevard south of Ocean Beach.

Ocean Beach—Where you toss down your towel at "OB" will probably depend as much on your age as your interests. Surfers, sailors, and what's left of the hippie crowd hang out around the pier; farther north, where the surf is milder and the beach wider, families and retired folks can be found sunbathing and strolling.

Facilities: Picnic areas, restrooms, restaurants.

Fishing: Good from the surf.

Swimming: Good.

Surfing: Very popular.

Getting there: Take Ocean Beach Freeway (Route 8) west until it ends; turn left onto Sunset Cliffs Boulevard, then right on Voltaire Street.

MISSION BAY BEACHES AND PARKS

Mission Beach Park—The wide, sandy beach at the southern end is a favorite haunt of high schoolers and college students. The hot spot is at the foot of Capistrano Court. A paved boardwalk runs along the beach and is busy with bicyclists, joggers, and roller skaters. Farther north, up around the old Belmont Park roller coaster, the beach grows narrower and the surf rougher. The crowd tends to get that way, too, with heavy-metal teens, sailors, and bikers hanging out along the sea wall, ogling and sometimes harrassing the bikini set. This is the closest San Diego comes to Los Angeles' colorful but funky Venice Beach.

Facilities: Restrooms, lifeguards; boardwalk lined with restaurants and beach rentals.

Surfing: Good.

Getting there: Located along Mission Boulevard north of West Mission Bay Drive.

Mission Bay Park—As one of the nation's largest and most diverse city-owned aquatic parks, Mission Bay has something to suit just about everyone's recreational interest. Key areas and facilities are as follows: **Dana Landing** and **Quivira Basin** make up the southwest portion of this 4600-acre park. Most boating activities begin here, where port headquarters and a large marina are located. Adjacent is **Bonita Cove**, used for swimming, picnicking, softball, and volleyball. Mission Boulevard shops, restaurants, and recreational equipment rentals are within easy walking distance. **Ventura Cove** houses a large hotel complex but its sandy beach is open to the public. Calm waters make it a popular swimming spot for small children.

Vacation Isle and **Ski Beach** are easily reached via the bridge on Ingraham Street, which bisects the island. The west side contains public swimming areas, boat rentals, and a model yacht basin. Ski Beach is on the east side and is the favorite spot in the bay for waterskiing. **Fiesta Island** is situated on the southwest side of the park. It's ringed with soft sand swimming beaches and laced with jogging, cycling, and skating paths. A favorite spot for fishing from the quieter coves and for kite flying, softball, and those sometimes irritating jet skiers.

Over on the **East Shore** you'll find landscaped picnic areas, playgrounds, a physical fitness course, a sandy beach for swimming, and the park information center. **De Anza Cove**, at the extreme northeast corner of the park, has a sandy beach for swimming plus a large private campground. **Crown Point Shores** provides a sandy beach, picnic area, nature study area, physical fitness course, waterski landing, and a public boat dock.

Sail Bay and **Riviera Shores** make up the northwest portion of Mission Bay and back up against the apartments and condominiums of Pacific Beach. Sail Bay's beaches aren't the best in the park and are usually submerged during high tides. Riviera Shores has a better beach with waterski areas.

Santa Clara and **El Carmel Points** jut out into the westernmost side of the bay. Santa Clara Point is of interest to the visitor with its recreation center, tennis courts, and baseball field. A sandy beach fronts San Juan Cove between the two points.

Facilities: Just about every facility imaginable can be found somewhere in the park. Swimming beach; pool and jacuzzi; catamaran, windsurfer, and bike rentals; playgrounds and parks; frisbee and golf; restaurant and grocery. For further information contact the Mission Bay Aquatic Center (619-236-6652).

Camping: The finest and largest of San Diego's commercial campgrounds is **Campland On The Bay** (2211 Pacific Beach Drive; 619-274-6260), featuring hook-up sites for RVs, vans, tents, and boats.

Getting there: Located along Mission Boulevard and West Mission Bay Drive.

Pacific Beach Park—At its south end, "PB" is much like "OB," its boardwalk crowded with teens and assorted rowdies, but a few blocks north, just before Crystal Pier, the boardwalk becomes a quieter concrete promenade that follows scenic, sloping cliffs. The beach widens here and the crowd becomes more family oriented. The surf is moderate and fine for swimming and body surfing. North of the pier Ocean Boulevard becomes a pedestrian-only mall with a bike path, benches, and picnic tables.

Facilities: Restrooms, lifeguards, restaurants.

Getting there: Located near Grand Avenue and Pacific Beach Drive.

LA JOLLA BEACHES AND PARKS

Tourmaline Surfing Park—A year-round reef break and consistently big waves make La Jolla one of the best surfing areas on the West Coast. Because of its narrow, rocky strand, Tourmaline has been designated a surfing-only beach. Skin diving is permitted, too, but no swimming.

Facilities: Picnic areas, restrooms, lifeguards; restaurants and groceries are nearby in Pacific Beach.

Getting there: Located at the end of Tourmaline Street in La Jolla.

South Bird Rock—Tidepools and good fishing are the attractions along this rocky, cliff-lined beach.

Facilities: None. Restaurants and groceries are nearby.

Surfing: Best in summer.

Getting there: From Midway or Forward streets in La Jolla follow paths down to the beach.

Bird Rock—Named for a large sandstone boulder about 50 yards off the coast, this beach is rocky and thus favored by surfers and divers.

Facilities: None. Restaurants and groceries are nearby.

Fishing: Good.

Surfing: Rarely breaks but when it does this spot is primo.

Getting there: Located at the end of Bird Rock Avenue in La Jolla.

Hermosa Terrace Park—This beach is said to be "seasonally sandy" which is another way of saying its rocky at times. Best chance for sand is in the summer when this is a pretty good swimming and sunning beach.

Facilities: None. Restaurants and groceries are nearby.

Surfing: Good.

Getting there: Off Winamar Avenue in La Jolla; a paved path leads to the beach.

Windansea Beach—Also known as **Neptune Park**, this is surely one of the most picturesque beaches in the country. It has been protrayed in the movies and was immortalized in Tom Wolfe's 1968 nonfiction classic, *The Pumphouse Gang*, about the surfers who still hang around the old pumphouse (part of the city's sewer system), zealously protecting their famous surf from outsiders. Windansea is rated by experts as one of the best surfing locales on the West Coast. In the evenings, crowds line the Neptune Place sidewalk, which runs along the top of the cliffs, to watch the sunset. North of the pumphouse are several sandy nooks sandwiched between sandstone outcroppings. Romantic spot!

Facilities: None. Restaurants and groceries are nearby.

Getting there: Located at the end of Nautilus Street in La Jolla.

Marine Street Beach—Separated from Windandsea by towering sandstone bluffs, this is a much wider and more sandy strand, favored by sunbathers, swimmers, and frisbee-tossing youths. The rock-free shoreline is ideal for walking or jogging.

Facilities: None. Restaurants and groceries are nearby.

Fishing: Good from the surf.

Skindiving: Good.

Surfing: Good for board and body surfing; watch for rip currents.

Getting there: Turn west off La Jolla Boulevard on Marine Street.

Coast Boulevard Park—After about a half-mile of wide sandy beach, the bluffs and tiny pocket beaches that characterize Windansea reappear at what locals call "Coast Beach." The pounding waves are for surfers only, but savvy locals find the smooth sandstone boulders and sandy coves perfect for reading, sunbathing, and picnicking.

Facilities: Picnic area.

Getting there: Paths lead to the beach at several points along Coast Boulevard in La Jolla.

Children's Pool Beach—At the north end of Coast Beach a concrete breakwater loops around a small lagoon to provide relatively calm waters for the kids. Seasonal rip tides can be a hazard, however, so check with lifeguards on duty year-round at the site.

Facilities: Restrooms; restaurants and groceries are nearby.

Fishing: Good from the surf.

Getting there: Located off Coast Boulevard in La Jolla.

Ellen Scripps Park and **La Jolla Cove**—This grassy park sits on a bluff overlooking the cove and is the scenic focal point of La Jolla. The naturally formed cove is almost always free of breakers, has a small but sandy beach, and is a popular spot for swimmers and divers.

Facilities: Picnic areas, restrooms, shuffleboard, lifeguards; restaurants and groceries are nearby.

Fishing: Good from the surf.

Skindiving: Good.

Surfing: La Jolla's big wave action is right here.

Getting there: Located near Coast Boulevard and Girard Avenue in La Jolla.

Kellogg Park–La Jolla Shores Beach—The sand is wide and the swimming is easy at La Jolla Shores; so, naturally, the beach is covered with bodies whenever the sun appears. Just to the east is Kellogg Park, an ideal place for a picnic.

Facilities: Restrooms, lifeguards; restaurants and groceries are located nearby.

Fishing: Good from the surf.

Swimming: Good.

Surfing: Reliable beach surf.

Skindiving: Native American artifacts have been discovered off the north end of the beach.

Getting there: Located off Camino del Oro near Frescota Street in La Jolla.

Scripps Beach—With coastal bluffs above, narrow sand beach below, and rich tidepools offshore, this is a great strand for beachcombers. Two underwater reserves as well as museum displays at the Scripps Institute of Oceanography are among the attractions (see the "Sightseeing" section in this chapter).

Facilities: There are museum facilities at Scripps Institute.

Surfing: Good on north side of Scripps Pier.

Getting there: Scripps Institute is located at the 8600 block of La Jolla Shores Drive in La Jolla.

Black's Beach—One of the world's most famous nude beaches, on hot summer days it attracts bathers by the thousands, many in the buff. The sand is lovely and soft and the 300-foot cliffs rising up behind make for a spectacular setting. Hang-gliders soar from the glider port above to add even more enchantment.

Facilities: None.

Fishing: Good from the surf.

Swimming: Very good, but beware of currents.

Surfing: Excellent. One of the most awesome beach breaks in California.

Getting there: From Route 5 in La Jolla follow Genesee Avenue west; turn right on North Torrey Pines Road, then left at Torrey Pines Scenic Drive. There's a parking lot at the Torrey Pines Glider Port, but trails to the beach from here are very steep and often dangerous. If you're in doubt just park at the Torrey Pines State Reserve lot one mile north and walk back along the shore to Black's.

Torrey Pines State Beach—A long, wide, sandy stretch adjacent to Los Penasquitos Lagoon and Torrey Pines State Reserve, this beach is highly visible from the highway and therefore heavily used. It is popular for sunning, swimming, surf-fishing, volleyball, and sunset barbeques. Nearby trails lead through the reserves with their lagoons, rare trees, and abundant birdlife.

Facilities: Restrooms, picnic areas; restaurants and groceries are two miles away in Del Mar; information, 619-729-8947.

Fishing: Good.

Surfing: Powerful peaks; exercise caution.

Getting there: Located just north of Carmel Valley Road in Del Mar.

NORTH SAN DIEGO COUNTY BEACHES AND PARKS

Del Mar Beach—Rather narrow from Torrey Pines to about 15th Street, the beach widens further north. Seagrove Park, at the foot of 15th Street, is action central, with teens playing volleyball and frisbees while the elders read magazines beneath their umbrellas. Surfers congregate at the foot of 13th Street. Quintessential North County!

Facilities: Lifeguards; restaurants and groceries are nearby.

Fishing: Good from the surf; regular grunion runs.

Swimming: Good.

Surfing: Typical beach surf with smooth peaks, year round.

Getting there: Easiest beach access is at street ends from 15th to 29th streets off Coast Boulevard, one block below Old Route 101 in Del Mar.

Solana Beach County Park—Lined by cliffs and carpeted with sand, this is a popular spot for water sports. There's a natural break in the cliffs where the beach widens and the surf eases up to allow comfortable swimming. Surfers gather to the north and south of Plaza Street where the beach is narrow and the surf much bigger. It's also a prime area for surf-fishing, grunion runs, and skin diving.

Facilities: Restrooms, lifeguards, basketball, shuffleboard; restaurants and groceries are nearby; information, 619-565-3600.

Getting there: Located at the end of Plaza Street in Solana Beach.

Cardiff State Beach—This strand begins where the cliffs of Solana Beach end and where the town's most interesting feature, a network of tidepools, begins. Popular with surfers because of the interesting pitches off its reef break, this wide, sandy beach is part of a two-mile swath of state beaches.

Facilities: Picnic areas, restrooms, lifeguards; restaurants and groceries are nearby; information, 619-729-8947.

Fishing: Good from the surf.

Swimming: Good.

Getting there: Located off Old Route 101 in Cardiff directly west of San Elijo Lagoon.

San Elijo State Beach—Although the beach is wide and sandy, low tide reveals a mantle of rocks just offshore and there are reefs, too, making this one of North County's most popular surf-fishing and skin diving spots. Surfers brave big breakers at "Turtles" and "Pipes" reefs at the north end of the park. There is a campground atop the bluff overlooking the beach.

Facilities: Most amenities are located at the campground and include picnic areas, restrooms, showers, beach rentals, and grocery. Lifeguards; restaurants found nearby; information, 619-729-8947.

Camping: Permitted; information, 619-753-5091.

Swimming: Good.

Getting there: Located off Old Route 101 north of Chesterfield Drive in Cardiff.

Sea Cliff Roadside Park—North County's most famous surfing beach is locally known as "Swami's." It derives its nickname from an Indian guru who founded the Self-Realization Fellowship Temple here in the 1940s. The gold-domed compound is located on the clifftop just to the north of the park. A small, grassy picnic area gives way to stairs leading to a narrow, rocky beach favored almost exclusively by surfers, though divers and anglers like the spot as well. The reef point break here makes for spectacular waves.

Facilities: Restrooms, picnic areas, lifeguards, and a funky outdoor shower.

Getting there: Located off Old Route 101 in Encinitas about one mile south of Encinitas Boulevard.

Moonlight State Beach—A very popular beach, Moonlight boasts a big sandy cove flanked by sandstone bluffs. Surf is relatively tame at the center, entertaining swimmers and body surfers. Volleyball and tennis courts are added attractions. Surfers like the wave action to the south, particularly at the foot of D Street.

Facilities: Picnic areas, restrooms, lifeguards, snack bar, equipment rentals; information, 619-729-8947.

Fishing: Good from the surf.

Swimming: Good.

Getting there: Located in Encinitas near 4th Street and the end of B Street.

Seaside Gardens County Park—Locals, who go there to hide away from the tourists, call it "Stone Steps Beach." It is indeed stony and narrow to boot, but secluded and hard to find. Much like Moonlight to the south, its surf conditions are good for several types of water sports.

Facilities: Lifeguards.

Fishing: Good.

Swimming: Good.

Surfing: Good.

Getting there: The staircase to the beach is located at South El Portal Street, off Neptune Avenue, in Leucadia.

Leucadia State Beach—A broad sand corridor backdropped by coastal bluffs, this beach has appeal, though it's certainly not North County's finest. The strand is widest at the north end, but the breakers are bigger at the south end, an area local surfers call "Beacon's Beach."

Facilities: Picnic areas, restrooms; information, 619-729-8947.

Fishing: Good.

Swimming: Good.

Skindiving: Good.

Getting there: Located in Leucadia west of Neptune Avenue between Grandview Street and Leucadia Boulevard.

South Carlsbad State Beach—This is a big, bustling beachfront rimmed by bluffs. The pebbles strewn everywhere put towel space at a premium, but the water is gentle and super for swimming.

Facilities: Picnic area, restrooms, lifeguards, showers, grocery, beach rentals; restaurants nearby; information 619-729-8947.

Camping: Permitted.

Fishing: Good.

Swimming: Good.

Surfing: Good.

Skindiving: Good.

Getting there: Located west of Carlsbad Boulevard near Ponto Drive in Carlsbad.

Carlsbad State Beach—Conditions here are about the same as at South Carlsbad, a sand and rock beach bordered by bluffs. Rock and surf-fishing is quite good at this beach and even better at the adjoining

Encinas Fishing Area (at the San Diego Gas and Electric power plant), where Agua Hedionda Lagoon opens to the sea. **Carlsbad City Beach** connects to the north, extending another mile or so to the mouth of the Buena Vista Lagoon.

Facilities: Picnic areas, restrooms, lifeguards; restaurants and groceries are nearby; information, 619-729-8947.

Swimming: Good.

Surfing: Good.

Skindiving: Good.

Getting there: Park entrance is at Tamarack Avenue, west of Carlsbad Boulevard, in Carlsbad.

Oceanside Beaches—Two miles of clean, rock-free beaches front North County's largest city, stretching from Buena Vista Lagoon in the south to Oceanside Harbor in the north. Along the entire length the water is calm and shallow, ideal for swimming and body surfing. Lots of Marines from nearby Camp Pendleton favor this beach. The nicest section of all is around Oceanside Pier, a 1900-foot-long fishing pier. Nearby, palm trees line a grassy promenade dotted with picnickers; the sand is as clean as a pin. Added to the attractions is **Buena Vista Lagoon**, a bird sanctuary and nature reserve.

Facilities: Picnic areas, restrooms, lifeguards; restaurants and groceries are nearby.

Fishing: Try from the pier, rocks, or beach.

Swimming: Good.

Surfing: Reliable year round.

Getting there: Located along The Strand in Oceanside; the pier is at the foot of 3rd Street.

San Onofre State Beach—San Diego County's northernmost beach is about 16 miles north of Oceanside, uneasily sandwiched between Camp Pendleton and the San Onofre nuclear power plant. It's well worth a visit if you're not put off by the nearby presence of atomic energy. Technically, San Onofre is two parks, North and South, separated by the power plant and connected via a public walkway along the seawall. The southern beach features a superb campground with trailer spaces and primitive tent sites, the only primitive campsite anywhere on San Diego County beaches. Eroded bluffs rumple down to the beach creating a variety of sandy coves and pockets. Gentle surf, which picks up considerably to the north, makes this a good swimming and body surfing spot. It is more than a rumor that some discreet nude sunbathing takes place at the end of beach path #6. The north side of the park is a favorite with surfers who flock to "Surf Beach," not far from famous "Trestles Beach," which is just beyond the park boundary.

Facilities: Picnic areas, restrooms, lifeguards; hiking trails; restaurants and groceries are about five miles away in San Clemente; information 714-492-4872. The campground has showers, snack bar, and supply store.

Camping: Permitted.

Fishing: Good from the surf; also good clamming.

Swimming: Good.

Getting there: From Route 5, take Basilone Road exit and follow the signs.

Hiking

Most of the San Diego County coastline is developed for either residential or commercial purposes, limiting the hiking opportunities. There are some protected areas set aside to preserve remnants of the county's unique coastal chaparral communities and tidelands. These reserves offer short hiking trails.

Serious hikers might also consider taking on the San Diego section of the **California Coastal Trail.** It follows the shoreline, as much as possible, from the Mexican border all the way to San Onofre State Beach.

BORDER FIELD STATE PARK TRAILS

Hiking trails crisscross the dunes and marshes of this largely undeveloped park which forms the coastal border between the United States and Mexico. Trails lead through dunes anchored by salt grass, pickleweed, and sand verbena. The marshy areas, especially those in an adjacent federal wildlife refuge around the Tijuana River estuary provide feeding and nesting grounds for some 170 species of native and migratory birds, including hawks, pelicans, plovers, terns, and ducks.

Border Field to Tijuana River Trail (1.5 miles) is a level beach walk past sand dunes and the Tijuana River Estuary.

Border Field to Imperial Beach Trail (3 miles) covers the same ground, then continues past houses and low bluffs.

SILVER STRAND STATE BEACH TRAILS

Silver Strand Trail (3 miles) follows a lengthy sandspit en route from the Hotel del Coronado to Silver Strand State Beach. It passes the Navy Amphibious Base as well as some pretty beachfronts.

CABRILLO NATIONAL MONUMENT TRAILS

Bayside Trail (1 mile) begins at the Old Point Loma lighthouse, beautifully restored to its original 1855 condition, and meanders through the heart of a scenic coastal chaparral community. A wide variety of native plants including prickly pear cactus, yucca, buckwheat, and Indian paintbrush grow along the path. In addition to stunning views of San

Diego there are remnants of the coastal defense system built during World Wars I and II.

TORREY PINES STATE RESERVE TRAILS

Without a doubt, this 1750-acre sanctuary offers the county's best hiking. It was named for the world's rarest pine tree *(Pinus torreyana)* which the reserve was established to protect. An estimated 6000 of the gnarled and twisted trees cling to rugged cliffs and ravines, some growing as tall as 60 feet.

Several major trails offer hikers a variety of challenges and natural attractions. Most are easily walked loops through groves of pines, such as the **Parry Grove Trail** (.4 mile), which passes stands of manzanita, yucca, and other shrubs; and **Guy Fleming Trail** (.6 mile), which scans the coast at South Overlook. There are more strenuous treks such as **Broken Hill Trail** (1.3 mile), zigzaging to the coast past chamise and scrub oak; and **Razor Point Trail** (1.2 mile), which follows the Canyon of the Palisades and takes in eroded cliffs and ocean vistas.

Del Mar Beach Trail (3 miles) leads from the Del Mar Amtrak Station along the beach past flatrock tidepools and up to the bluffs of Torrey Pines State Reserve.

OTHER TRAILS

La Jolla Coastal Walk (1 mile), a dirt path atop La Jolla Bluffs, affords some of the most spectacular views anywhere on the San Diego County coastline. It begins on Coast Boulevard just up the hill from La Jolla Cove and continues past a sea cave accessible from the trail.

Three Lagoons Trail (5 miles) originates on the beach in Leucadia and heads north along the sand past three saltwater lagoons, ending in Carlsbad. Best place to begin is at the beach parking lot at Grandview Street in Leucadia.

Traveler's Tracks

Sightseeing

Thanks to its illustrious history, splendid natural setting, equable climate and quality visitor attractions, the once-sleepy seaside town of San Diego has blossmed into one of California's most popular year-round vacation destinations. The city itself is water-oriented, owing much of its beauty and appeal to a vast natural harbor that has been attracting enthusiastic visitors since the Spanish landed in 1542.

Intelligent city planning, evident since the boom years of the 1880s, has left San Diego a legacy of important, well-preserved historic sites and some fine parks, ranging from the cultured environs of Balboa Park to the aquatic excitement of Mission Bay Park. And, of course, there's the world famous zoo.

Up the coast are gemlike seaside villages, fronted by sandstone cliffs, grassy bluffs, and some of California's widest and sandiest beaches. Across the border lies the foreign fascination of Mexico.

SOUTH SAN DIEGO COUNTY

Border Field State Park (619-428-3034) and the adjoining **Tijuana Slough National Wildlife Refuge** comprise the county's largest and most pristine estuarine sanctuary. For nature lovers, this haven of salt marsh and sand dunes is a must-see diversion. Trails lead to the beach and wildlife refuge at this fascinating wetland (see the "Beaches and Parks" and "Hiking" sections of this chapter for more information).

SAN DIEGO HARBOR

San Diego's beautiful harbor is a notable exception to the rule that big-city waterfronts lack appeal. Here, the city embraces its bay and presents its finest profile along the water.

The best way to see it all is on a harbor excursion. A variety of vessels dock near Harbor Drive at the foot of Broadway. They provide leisurely trips around the 22-square-mile harbor, which is colorfully backdropped by commercial and naval vessels as well as the dramatic cityscape. My favorite harbor cruises are aboard the 151-foot schooner **Invader** (619-234-8687) and the 72-foot **Red Witch** (619-542-0646).

All along the cityside of the harbor from the Coast Guard Station opposite Lindbergh Field to Seaport Village is a lovely landscaped boardwalk called the **Embarcadero**. It offers parks where you can stroll and play, a floating maritime museum, and a thriving assortment of waterfront diversions.

The **Maritime Museum of San Diego** (1306 North Harbor Drive; 619-234-9153) is composed of three vintage ships: most familiar is the 1863 *Star of India*, the nation's oldest iron-hulled merchant ship still afloat. Visitors go aboard for a hint of what life was like on the high seas more than a century ago. You can also visit the 1898 ferry *Berkeley*, which helped in the evacuation of San Francisco during the 1906 earthquake, and the 1904 steam yacht *Medea*.

Nautical buffs or anyone concerned about American naval power will be interested in the huge **U.S. Navy** presence in San Diego harbor. As headquarters of the 11th Naval District, San Diego hosts one of the world's largest fleets of fighting ships—from aircraft carriers to nuclear submarines. Naval docks and yards are off-limits but you'll see the sprawling facilities and plenty of those distinctive gray-hulled ships during a harbor cruise. Naval vessels moored at the Broadway Pier hold open house on weekends.

Chances are you'll also see a cruise ship docked at the adjacent B Street Pier. The *Love Boat* of television fame home ports here together with the ships of several other major lines.

Near the south end of the Embarcardero sits the popular shopping and entertainment complex known as **Seaport Village** (Pacific Highway and Harbor Drive). Designed to replicate an early California seaport, it comprises more than 20 acres of bayfront parks and promenades, shops, and galleries. On the south side, overlooking the water, is the 45-foot-high Mulkilto Lighthouse, official symbol of the village, a re-creation of a famous lighthouse in Washington state. Nearby is the Broadway Flying Horses Carousel, a hand-carved, turn-of-the-century model that originally whirled around Coney Island.

DOWNTOWN SAN DIEGO

At one time downtown San Diego was a collection of porn shops, tattoo parlors, and strip-tease bars. Billions of dollars invested in a stunning array of new buildings and in the restoration of many old ones have changed all that.

Within the compact city center there's Horton Plaza, an exciting experiment in avant-garde urban architecture, and the adjacent Gaslamp Quarter, which reveals how San Diego looked at the peak of its Victorian-era boom in the 1880s. Together they are a study in contrasts which provides one of the most fascinating architectural tours of any American city.

Horton Plaza (bounded by Broadway and G Street and 1st and 4th avenues) is totally unlike any other shopping center or urban redevelopment project. It has transcended its genre in a whimsical, multilevel, open-air, pastel-hued concoction of ramps, escalators, rambling paths, bridges, towers, piazzas, sculptures, fountains, and live greenery. Mimes, minstrels, and fortune tellers meander about the six-block complex performing for patrons.

Horton Plaza was inspired by European shopping streets and districts such as the Plaka of Athens, the Ramblas of Barcelona, and Portobello Road in London. In all, 14 different styles, ranging from renaissance to post modern, are employed in the design.

The **Gaslamp Quarter** is one of America's largest national historic districts, covering a 16-block strip along 4th, 5th, and 6th avenues from Broadway to the waterfront. Architecturally, the Quarter reveals some of the finest Victorian-style commerical buildings constructed in San Diego during the 50 years between the Civil War and World War I. It was this area, along 5th Avenue, that became San Diego's first main street. The city's core began on the bay where Alonzo Horton first built a wharf in 1869.

It was this same area that later fell into disrepute as the heart of the business district moved north beyond Broadway. By the 1890s, prositution and gambling were rampant. Offices above the street level were converted into bordellos and opium dens. The area south of Market Street became known as the "Stingaree," an unflattering reference coined by the many who were stung by card sharks, con men and, of course, con ladies.

Rescued by the city and a dedicated group of preservationists, the area not only survived but played a major role in the massive redevelopment of downtown San Diego. The city has added wide brick sidewalks, period street lamps, trees, and benches. In all, more than 100 grand old Victorian buildings have been restored to their original splendor.

History buffs and lovers of antique buildings should promptly don their walking shoes for a tour of the Gaslamp Quarter. One way to do this is to join a walking tour (see the "Transportation" section in this chapter). Or head out on your own, accompanied by a map available at the **William Heath Davis House** (410 Island Avenue; 619-233-5227).

The Quarter includes 153 buildings so I couldn't hope to describe them all, but let me take you on a mini-tour of the most important structures. Begin at the aforementioned William Heath Davis House, a well-preserved example of a pre-fabricated "salt box" family home, dating to about 1850. Framed on the East Coast, it was shipped to San Diego by boat around Cape Horn and represents the oldest structure in the Quarter.

Just across the street is the **Royal Pie Bakery** (554 4th Avenue). Almost unbelievably, a bakery has been on this site since 1875. Around the turn of the century the bakery found itself in the middle of a red-light district. It never stopped turning out cakes and pies, though a notorious bordello operated on the second floor.

Go back down Island Avenue to 5th Avenue and turn left. Not only was this block part of the Stingaree, as hinted by the old 1887 hotel by the same name on your left, at 542 5th Avenue, but it was San Diego's Chinatown. **Wong's Nanking Cafe** (467 5th Avenue) was built in 1913 and retains the atmosphere of the past.

The nearby **Timken Building** (5th Avenue and Market Street), notable for its fancy arched brick facade, was erected in 1894. Across the street is the **Backesto Building**, beautifully remodeled to re-create an 1890s-era bank, complete with teller's cages.

The tall, Romanesque Revival **Keating Building** (5th Avenue and F Street) was one of the most prestigious office buildings in San Diego during the 1890s, complete with such modern conveniences as steam heat and an elevator. Next door is **The Mercantile** and ajoining **Ingersoll-Tutton Building** (832 5th Avenue). When this 90-foot-long structure was built in 1894 for $20,000 it was considered the most expensive building on the block!

Most of the block on the other side of 5th Avenue, from F up to E Street, represents the most architecturally significant row in the Gaslamp Quarter. From south to north, there's the **Marston Building** on the corner of F Street. Built in 1881, it was downtown San Diego's leading department store. Next is the 1887 **Hubbell Building**, originally a dry goods establishment. The **Nesmith-Greeley Building** next door is another example of the then-fashionable Romanesque Revival style with its ornamental brick coursing. With twin towers and intricate Baroque Revival architecture, the 1888 **Louis Bank of Commerce** is probably the most beautiful building in the Quarter. It originally housed a ground-floor oyster bar that was a favorite haunt of Wyatt Earp. The famous western lawman-cum-real-estate speculator resided in San Diego from 1886 to 1893. Be sure to go to the fourth floor to see the beautiful skylight.

While most of the Gaslamp Quarter's X-rated enterprises have fallen to the advance of gentrification, a few of the original denizens remain. At least one, the **Lux Adult Theater** (728 5th Avenue), has joined in the spirit of things, restoring its facade in authentic Victorian trim.

Though it's situated a few blocks east of the Gaslamp Quarter, make a point to visit **Villa Montezuma** (1925 K Street; 619-239-2211). This ornate, Queen Anne-style Victorian mansion, magnificently restored, was constructed by a wealthy group of San Diegans in 1887 as a gift to a visiting musician. Culture-hungry civic leaders actually "imported" world-famous troubadour Jesse Shepard to live in the opulent dwelling as something of a court musician to the city's upper crust. Shepard stayed only two years but decorated his villa to the hilt with dozens of stained-glass windows and elaborate hand-carved wood trim and decorations.

BALBOA PARK AND THE SAN DIEGO ZOO

History is unclear as to whether it was intelligent foresight or unbridled optimism that prompted the establishment of **Balboa Park**. Certain that a fine neighborhood would flourish around it, city fathers in 1868 set aside 1400 acres of rattlesnake-infested hillside above "New Town" as a public park. The park's eventual development, and most of its lovely Spanish Baroque buildings, came as the result of two world's fairs—The Panama–California Exposition of 1915–16 and the California–Pacific International Exposition of 1935–36.

Today Balboa Park ranks among the largest and finest of America's city parks. Wide avenues and walkways curve through luxurious subtropical foliage leading to nine major museums, three art galleries, four theaters, picnic groves, the world's largest zoo, a golf course, and countless other recreation facilities. Its verdant grounds teem with cyclists, joggers, skaters, picnickers, weekend artists, and museum mavens.

The main entrance is from 6th Avenue onto Laurel Street, which becomes El Prado as you cross Cabrillo Bridge. Begin your visit at the **House of Hospitality** at the southeast corner of Plaza de Panama. It houses the **Park Information Center** (619-239-0512) which has free pamphlets and maps on the park.

From here you can stroll about, taking in Balboa Park's main attractions. To the right, as you head east on the pedestrian-only section of El Prado, is the newly rebuilt Casa de Balboa. It houses the **San Diego Model Railroad Museum** (619-696-0199), which features the largest collection of mini-gauge trains in the world. Here, too, is the **San Diego Historical Society's** extensive collection of documents and photographs spanning the urban history of San Diego. Upstairs, the **Museum of Photographic Arts** (619-239-5262) features exhibits of internationally known photographers.

Sports fans will want to take in the **Hall of Champions** and **Hall of Fame**, both in Casa de Balboa. On display are exhibits featuring world-class San Diego athletes from more than 40 sports.

Continuing east to the fountain, you'll see the **Reuben H. Fleet Space Theater and Science Center** (619-238-1168) on your right. Among the park's finest attractions, it features one of the largest planetariums and most impressive multimedia theaters in the country. The hands-on Science Center features exhibits and displays dealing with modern phenomena.

Just across the courtyard is the **Natural History Museum** (619-232-3821) with displays devoted mostly to the Southern California environment.

Going back along El Prado, take a moment to admire your reflection in the **Lily Pond**. With the old, latticed **Botanical Building** in the background, the scene is a favorite among photographers. The fern collection inside is equally as striking.

Next is the **Timken Gallery** (619-239-5548), considered to have one of the West Coast's finest collections of European and Early American paintings. The displays include works by Rembrandt, Cezanne, and Monet, as well as an amazing collection of Russian icons.

Right next door on the plaza is the **San Diego Museum of Art** (619-232-7931), with an entrance facade patterned after the University of Salamanca in Spain. The museum treasures a permanent collection of Italian Renaissance, Dutch, and Spanish Baroque paintings and sculpture, a display of Asian art, and a gallery of Impressionist paintings.

The grandest of all Balboa Park structures, built as the centerpiece for the 1915 Panama–California Exposition, is the 200-foot Spanish Renaissance **California Tower**. The **Museum of Man** (619-239-2001), at the base of the tower, is a must for anthropology buffs and those interested in Native American cultures.

Another museum not to be missed is the **Aerospace Museum** (619-234-8291), several blocks south of the plaza. It contains a replica of Charles Lindbergh's famous "Spirit of St. Louis," the original of which was built in San Diego. En route you'll pass the **Spreckels Organ Pavil-**

ion. Those 3600 pipes make it the world's largest outdoor instrument of its kind.

You'll want to attend a play at the **Old Globe Theatre** (619-239-2255) to absorb the full greatness of this Tony Award-winning stage, but for starters you can stroll around the 581-seat theater, famed for its Shakespearean presentations. Located in a grove on the north side of California Tower, the Old Globe is part of the trio of theaters that includes the **Cassius Carter Centre Stage** and the outdoor **Festival Stage**.

North of the Balboa Park museum and theater complex is **San Diego Zoo** (619-234-3153; admission), which needs no introduction. It quite simply is the world's top-rated zoo. The numbers alone are mind-boggling: 3200 animals, representing 500 species, spread out over 128 acres. Most of these wild animals live in surroundings as natural as man can make them. Rather than cages there are many moated enclosures where lions roam free on grassy islands and exotic birds fly about in a tropical rain forest. All around is a manmade jungle forest overgrown with countless species of rare and exotic plants.

Best of the best is the zoo's state-of-the-art primate exhibit. Some of the world's rarest and most interesting primates can be viewed here. For a bird's eye view of the entire zoo, you can take the "Skyfari" aerial tramway.

Incidentally, the San Diego Zoo has a large collection of those cuddly koalas from Australia. You can pet one at the **Children's Zoo**. Don't let the name mislead you! There are as many adults in this enclosure as kids. There's even a hatchery where you can watch baby chicks peck out of their shells.

Balboa Park's museums charge a small admission fee but most of them can be visited free on the first Tuesday of the month.

CORONADO

Once known as the "Nickel Snatcher," the **Coronado Ferry** for years crossed the waters of San Diego Harbor between the Embarcadero and Coronado. All for five cents each way.

That's history, of course, but the 1940-vintage, double-deck *Silvergate* still plies the waters. The ferry leaves from the Bay Cafe on North Harbor Drive at the foot of Broadway and docks 15 minutes later at the Old Ferry landing on the Coronado side.

An islolated and exclusive community in San Diego Bay, Coronado is almost an island, connected to the mainland only by the graceful San Diego–Coronado Bay Bridge and by a long, narrow sandspit called the Silver Strand.

The town's main attraction is the **Hotel del Coronado** (1500 Orange Avenue; 619-435-6611), a red-roofed, Victorian-style, wooden wonder, a century-old National Historic landmark. Explore the old palace and its manicured grounds, discovering the intricate corridors and cavernous public rooms.

It was Elisha Babcock's dream, when he purchased 4100-acres of barren, windblown peninsula in 1885, to build a hotel that would be the "talk of the Western world." Realizing Babcock's dream from the beginning, it attracted such famous guests as Thomas Edison, Robert Todd Lincoln, Henry Ford, and more than a dozen United States presidents.

Although shadowed by its noted neighbor, the **Glorietta Bay Inn** (1630 Glorietta Boulevard; 619-435-3101) is a worthy landmark in its own right. It was built in 1908 as the private mansion of sugar scion John D. Spreckels. From here you can cruise the quiet neighborhood streets that radiate off Orange Avenue between the bay and the ocean, enjoying the town's handsome blend of cottages and historic homes.

POINT LOMA, SHELTER AND HARBOR ISLANDS

The Point Loma peninsula forms a high promontory that shelters San Diego Bay from the Pacific. It also provided Juan Rodriquez Cabrillo an excellent place from which to contemplate his 16th-century discovery of California. Naturally, **Cabrillo National Monument** (Cabrillo Memorial Drive; 619-557-5450), featuring a statue of the navigator, stands facing his landing site at Ballast Point. The sculpture itself, a gift from Cabrillo's native Portugal, isn't very impressive but the view is outstanding. With the bay and city spread below, you can often see all the way from Mexico to the La Jolla mesa.

The visitor's center includes a small museum. The nearby **Old Point Loma Lighthouse** guided shipping from 1855 to 1891.

On the ocean side of the peninsula is **Whale Watch Lookout Point** where, during winter months, you can observe the southward migration of California gray whales. Close by is a superb network of tidepools where rangers lead daily tours during low tide periods. Call 619-557-5450 for schedules and information.

To reach Point Loma from San Diego, go southwest on Rosecrans Street and follow the signs. You'll enter the monument through the U.S. Navy's Fort Rosecrans, home to a variety of sophisticated military facilities and the haunting **Fort Rosecrans National Cemetery**. Here, thousands of trim, white markers march down a grassy hillside in mute testimony to San Diego's fallen troops and deep military roots.

When you leave the monument, follow Catalina Boulevard to Hill Street and go left. At water's edge turn right onto Sunset Cliffs Boulevard and enjoy one of San Diego County's most dramatic coastlines. Continue north a bit to **Ocean Beach**, whose reputation as a haven for hippie hold-outs is not entirely undeserved.

OLD TOWN AND MISSION VALLEY

Back in 1769, Franciscan missionary Junipero Serra selected a hilltop site overlooking the bay for a mission that began the European settlement of California. A town soon spread out at the foot of the hill, complete with plaza, church, and the tile-roofed adobe casas of California's first families. Through the years, Spanish, Mexican, and American settlements thrived until an 1872 fire destroyed much of the town, prompting developers to relocate the commercial district nearer the bay.

Some of the buildings and relics of the early era survived, however, and have been brought back to life at **Old Town San Diego State Historic Park** (park headquarters, Mason Street and San Diego Avenue; 619-237-6770). Lined with abode restorations and brightened with colorful shops, the six blocks of Old Town provide a lively and interesting opportunity to stroll, shop, and sightsee.

As it has for over a century, everything focuses on **Old Town Plaza** (sometimes called Washington Square). This was the social and recreational center of the town: political meetings, barbeques, dances, shootouts, and bullfights all happened here.

Casa de Estudillo, at the Mason Street corner of the plaza, is the finest of the original adobe buildings. It was a mansion in its time, built in 1827 for the commander of the Spanish Presido.

Casa de Bandini (Mason and Calhoun streets) was built in 1829 as a one-story adobe but gained a second level when it became a stagecoach station in the 1860s. **Seeley Stables** next door is a replica of the barns and stables of Albert Seeley, who operated the stage line. Nowadays it houses a collection of horse-drawn vehicles and Western memorabilia.

Casa de Altamirano (San Diego Avenue and Twiggs Street) was Old Town's first frame building and the site where the *San Diego Union* was first printed in 1868. It has been restored as a 19th-century printing office. Adjacent to the old newspaper office is **Squibob Square**, a collection of shops finished with Old West-style falsefronts.

Shoppers seem to gravitate in large numbers toward the north side of the plaza to browse the unusual shops comprising **Bazaar del Mundo.** Built in circular fashion around a tropical courtyard, this complex also houses several restaurants.

On the outskirts of Old Town lies **Heritage Park** (Juan and Harney streets), an area dedicated to the preservation of the city's Victorian past. Seven historic 1880-era houses and an old Jewish temple have been moved to the hillside site and beautifully restored.

The original mission and Spanish Presidio once stood high on a hill behind Old Town. This site of California's birthplace now houses **Serra Museum** (2727 Presidio Drive; 619-297-3258), a handsome Spanish Colonial structure containing an excellent collection of research data, relics, and artifacts from the state's pioneer days.

Within five years after Father Serra dedicated the first of California's 21 missions, the site had become too small for the growing numbers it served. So **Mission San Diego de Alcala** (10818 San Diego Mission Road; 619-281-8449) was moved from Presidio Hill six miles east into Mission Valley. Surrounded now by shopping centers and suburban homes, the "Mother of Missions" retains its simple but striking white adobe facade topped by a graceful campanile. There's a museum containing mission records in Junipero Serra's handwriting and a lovely courtyard with olive trees from the mission's original grove. Services have been held each Sunday in the chapel since 1774.

MISSION BAY PARK AND THE BEACHES

Dredged from a shallow, mosquito-infested tidal bay, 4600-acre **Mission Bay Park** is the largest municipal aquatic park in the world. For San Diego's athletic set it is Mecca, a recreational paradise dotted with islands and lagoons and ringed by 27 miles of sandy beaches.

Here, visitors join with residents to enjoy swimming, sailing, windsurfing, waterskiing, fishing, jogging, cycling, golf, and tennis. Or perhaps a relaxing day of kite flying and sunbathing.

More than just a playground, Mission Bay Park features a shopping complex, resort hotels, restaurants, and the popular marine park, **Sea World** (Sea World Drive; 619-226-3901; admission). This 135-acre park-within-a-park has rapidly developed into the world's largest oceanarium, known for its killer whale shows and Penguin Encounter, an icy habitat for the largest colony of penguins north of Antarctica.

The trained killer whales perform in a flashy stadium; world-class high divers execute both daring and comical stunts; singers, dancers, and street entertainers perform; there are hydrofoil rides, an aerial tram, and a Sky Tower ride that lifts visitors in a capsule 320 feet above Mission Bay. It's quality material, but much of it is wasted on me. I prefer simply to watch the penguins waddling about on a simulated iceberg and zipping around after fish in their glass-contained ocean. Or to peer in at the fearsome makos at the shark exhibit. The park's magnificent marine creatures are all the entertainment I need.

Down along the oceanfront, **Mission Beach** is strung out along a narrow jetty of sand protecting Mission Bay from the sea. Mission Boulevard threads its way through this eclectic, wall-to-wall mix of shingled beach shanties, condominiums, and luxury homes.

Pacific Beach which picks up at the northern edge of the bay, is the liveliest of the city beaches, an area packed with high school and college students. Designer shorts, a garish Hawaiian shirt, strapped-on sunglasses, and a skateboard are all you need to fit in perfectly along the frenetic boardwalk at "PB." Stop and see the 1920s **Crystal Pier** (end of Garnet Avenue) with its tacky little motel built out over the waves. Or take a stroll along the boardwalk, checking out the sunbathers, skaters, joggers, and cyclists.

LA JOLLA

A certain fascination centers around the origins of the name La Jolla. It means "jewel" in Spanish, but according to Indian legend it means "hole" or "caves." Both are fairly apt interpretations: this Mediterranean-style enclave perched on a bluff above the Pacific is indeed a jewel; and its dramatic coves and cliffs are pocked with sea caves. Choose your favorite interpretation but for goodness sake don't pronounce the name phonetically—it's "La Hoya."

La Jolla is a community within the city of San Diego, though it considers itself something more on the order of a principality—like Monaco. Locals call it "The Village" and boast that it's an ideal walking town, which is another way of saying La Jolla is a frustrating place to drive around. Narrow, curvy 1930-era streets are jammed with traffic and hard to follow. A parking place in The Village is truly a jewel within the jewel.

The beauty of its seven miles of cliff-lined sea coast is La Jolla's *raison d'être*. Spectacular homes, posh hotels, chic boutiques, and gourmet restaurants crowd shoulder to shoulder for a better view of the ocean. Each of the area's many beaches has its own particular character and flock of local devotees. Though most beaches are narrow, rocky, and not really suitable for swimming or sunbathing, they are the best in the county for surfing and skin diving.

To get the lay of the land, wind your way up **Mount Soledad** (east on Nautilus Street from La Jolla Boulevard), where the view extends across the city skyline and out over the ocean. That large white cross at the summit is a memorial to the war dead and the setting for sunrise services every Easter Sunday.

Ah, but exploring The Village is the reason you're here, so head back down Nautilus Street, go right on La Jolla Boulevard, and continue until it leads into **Prospect Street**. This is La Jolla's hottest thoroughfare and where it intersects **Girard Avenue**, the town's traditional "main street," is the town epicenter. Here, in the heart of La Jolla, you are surrounded by the elite and elegant.

Although Girard Avenue features as wide a selection of shops as anyplace in San Diego, Prospect Street is much more interesting and stylish. By all means, walk Prospect's curving mile from the cottage shops and galleries on the north to the **Museum of Contemporary Art** (700 Prospect Street; 619-454-3541; admission) on the south. The museum, by the way, is a piece of art in itself. Its modern lines belie the fact it was designed as a private villa back in 1915, one of many striking contemporary structures in La Jolla by noted architect Irving

(Text continued on page 86.)

South of the Border

Tijuana, a favorite day-trip destination for San Diego visitors, has been amazingly transformed in recent years from a bawdy border-town to a modern, bustling city of almost two million people. Gone, or very well hidden, are the borderline attractions which once lured sailors and marines. In their place is a colorful center of tourism suitable for the entire family.

A major revitalization effort brought high-rise buildings, broad boulevards, huge shopping centers, and classy shops and restaurants. But don't get the idea Tijuana has become completely Americanized. It still retains much of its traditional Mexican flavor and offers visitors an exciting outing and some surprising cultural experiences.

Perhaps the most impressive attraction, ideal for learning about Mexico, is the **Tijuana Cultural Center** (Paseo de los Héroes y Calle Mina; 706-684-1111). Here the striking 85-foot-high Omnimax Space Theater is a silvery sphere held up by a stylized hand that symbolizes the earth housing a world of culture. Inside, the giant 180° screen carries viewers on a journey through Mexico. The complex, designed by Pedro Ramírez Váquez, architect of Mexico City's famous Anthropological Museum, houses six exhibit halls and a multilevel cultural and historical museum.

Spectator sports are an exciting and popular pastime for Tijuana visitors, including year round thoroughbred and greyhound racing at **Caliente Race Track** (Boulevard Agua Caliente; 706-685-2001 in Tijuana; 619-421-0378 from San Diego), and colorful bullfights in two separate rings, **El Toreo** (Boulevard Agua Caliente) and **Plaza Monumental** (six miles west via Highway 1D). Call Ticketron for tickets and information, 619-565-9949.

Jai Alai fans crowd the newly refurbished **Frontón Palacio** (Avenida Revolución and Calle 7a; 706-685-1612 in Tijuana; 619-282-3636 in San Diego) for the fastest moving sport in the world (the ball travels at speeds in excess of 160 miles per hour). Call the **Tijuana Visitors Bureau** at 619-298-4105 for information about all events.

No doubt a major reason to visit "TJ" is to shop. The central shopping district is downtown, along Avenida Revolución, where arcades, stalls, and hawkers line the boulevard promoting the usual selection of tourist trinkets, piñatas, colorful flowers, serapes, pottery, and lace. There are numerous shops featuring quality merchandise such as leather goods, designer clothes, perfumes, artwork, and jewelery at incredible savings. **Sara's** (Avenida Revolución at Calle 4a) has ladies designer fashions and perfumes; **Fernández Leather Fashions** (Avenida Revolución No. 8 in Gómez Arcade) carries fine leather goods; **Jorge Espinosa** (Avenida Revolución No. 918-B1) features a beautiful selection of custom jewelery; and **Tolan-Arte de México** (Avenida Revolución No. 1111) offers authentic Mexican folk art and fashions.

American currency is accepted everywhere but small bills are recommended since getting change can sometimes be a problem. U.S. residents receive a duty and federal tax exemption on the first $400 in personal goods purchased in Mexico. One liter of alcoholic beverage is allowed for those 21 years and older.

Tijuana has some exceptional restaurants. **Perin's** (Avenida Revolución No. 1115; 706-685-4052) serves succulent seafood in a quiet, comfortable atmosphere. **Le Chateau** (Calle 7a No. 1940; 706-685-0744) has an interesting and enticing menu of French and Mexican cuisine. **Tía Juana Tilly's** (Avenida Revolución and Calle 7a; 706-685-2524) is a great spot to sit on the patio, sip margaritas, munch on tacos, and listen to mariachis.

Should you decide to stay longer than a day, enjoy Tijuana's stylish hotel, **Fiesta Americana Tijuana** (Boulevard Agua Caliente No. 4500; 706-668-1700). This 430-room luxury complex boasts dramatic city views from its 24-story glass towers and offers such amenities as golf, tennis, a health club, and a gallery of shops.

Just a little further south of Tijuana, along the coast, the small towns of Rosarito Beach and Ensenada provide a less commercial glimpse of Mexico. A modern highway makes the trip easy and comfortable.

See **Hidden Mexico: Adventurer's Guide to the Beaches and Coasts**, also from Ulysses Press, for more detailed information about Mexico.

Gill. The museum's highly regarded collection focuses on minimal, California, pop, and other avant garde developments in painting, sculpture, and photography. A fascinating design collection features the evolution of the modern chair.

During this stroll along Prospect Street, also visit the lovely **La Valencia Hotel** (1132 Prospect Street; 619-454-0771), a very pink, very prominent resting place nicknamed "La V." This pink lady is a La Jolla landmark and a local institution, serving as both village pub and town meeting hall. You can feel the charm and sense the rich tradition of the place the moment you enter. While La V. has always been a haven for the gods and goddesses of Hollywood, the Gregory Peck, Mel Ferrer, and Olivia de Haviland gang of old has been replaced by a client roster of current stars like Liza Minelli and Dustin Hoffman.

Another center of interest lies at the northern end of La Jolla. The best beaches are here, stretching from the ritzy La Jolla Shores to the scientific sands at Scripps Beach. The latter strand fronts Scripps Institute of Oceanography, the oldest institution in the nation devoted to oceanography and the home of the **Thomas Wayland Vaughn Aquarium Museum** (8602 La Jolla Shores Drive; 619-452-6933). Here you'll find two dozen marine life tanks, a manmade tidepool, breathtaking exhibits of coastal underwater habitats, and displays illustrating recent advances in oceanographic research.

Another research center, **The Salk Institute** (at the crest of North Torrey Pines Road just north of the University of California–San Diego campus), created by the man whose vaccine helped vanquish polio, is renowned not only for its research but its architecture as well. The surrealistic concrete structure was designed by Louis Kahn in 1960 to be an environment that would stimulate original thinking. It is a stunning site, perched on the lip of a high canyon overlooking the Pacific. For information on tours call 619-453-4100.

Next to the institute is the **Torrey Pines Glider Port** (Torrey Pines Scenic Drive) where you can watch hang-gliding masters soar over the waves from atop a 360-foot cliff. Trails leading down to the notorious **Black's Beach** begin here. Black's is San Diego's unofficial, illegal, ever-loving nude beach. And a beautiful strip of natural landscape it is.

Bordering Black's on the north is **Torrey Pines State Beach and Reserve** (west of North Torrey Pines Road, two miles north of Genesee Avenue), whose 1750-acre preserve was established to protect the world's rarest pine tree, the Torrey Pine. The tree itself is a gnarled and twisted specimen. Centuries ago these pines covered the southern coast of California; today they are indigenous only to Santa Rosa Island, off the coast of Santa Barbara, and to the reserve. A network of trails through this bluff-top reserve makes hiking sheer pleasure. Among the rewards are the views, extending along the cliffs and ocean, and the chance to walk quietly among La Jolla's rare treasures.

NORTH SAN DIEGO COUNTY

Although **Del Mar** is inundated every summer by "beautiful people" who flock here for the horse racing, the town itself has retained a casual, small-town identity. Its trim, Tudor-style village center and luxurious oceanfront homes reflect the town's subtle efforts to "keep up with the Joneses" next door (i.e., La Jolla).

While seasonal, the **Del Mar Race Track** (Route 5 and Via de la Valle; 619-481-1207; admission) and companion **Fairgrounds** are the main attractions here. The track was financed back in the 1930s by such stars as Bing Crosby, Pat O'Brien, and Jimmy Durante to bring thoroughbred racing to the fairgrounds. It was no coincidence that Del Mar, "where the turf meets the surf," became a second home for these and many other top Hollywood stars.

On the east side of Route 5, about five miles inland on either Via de la Valle or Lomas Santa Fe Drive, is **Rancho Santa Fe.** If La Jolla is a jewel, then this stylish enclave is the crown itself. Residing in hillside mansions and horse ranches parceled out from an old Spanish land grant are some of America's wealthiest folks. Rancho Santa Fe is like Beverly Hills gone country. The area became popular as a retreat for rich industrialists and movie stars in the 1920s when Douglas Fairbanks and Mary Pickford built their sprawling **Fairbanks Ranch.** To make a looping tour of this affluent community, drive in on Via de la Valle, then return to Route 5 via Linea del Cielo and Lomas Santa Fe Drive.

The best way to see the remainder of North County's fine beaches is to cruise along Old Route 101, which preceded Route 5 as the north–south coastal route. It changes names in each beach town along the way, but once you're on it you won't be easily sidetracked.

Yogis, as well as those of us still residing on terra firma, might want to make a stop at Paramahansa Yogananda's **Self Realization Fellowship Center** (Old Route 101 and K Street, Encinitas; 619-436-7220). The gold-domed towers of this monastic retreat were built by an Indian religious sect in the 1920s and are still used as a retreat. Yogananda's house and the gardens inside the compound and are beautifully maintained and open to the public. The views, overlooking the famous "Swami's" surfing beach, are spectacular.

Encinitas is popularly known as the "flower capital of the world" and the hillsides east of the beach are a riot of colors. A quick call to the friendly folks at the local Chamber of Commerce (619-753-6041) will net you information about what's blooming and how to get there as well as information on seasonal tours of farms and greenhouses.

Further north, **Carlsbad** is a friendly, sunny beachfront town that has been entirely redeveloped, complete with cobblestone streets and quaint shops. Originally the place established its reputation around the similarity of its mineral waters to the springs of the original Karlsbad in Czechoslovakia. But don't waste your time looking for the fountain of youth, the spring has long since dried up. Go to the beach instead.

Old Route 101 leads next into **Oceanside**, gateway to Camp Pendleton Marine Base. San Diego county's second largest city is busy renovating its beachfront and image. The refurbished fishing pier is a lengthy one, stretching almost 2000 feet into the Pacific.

Your final sightseeing opportunity in San Diego County is at **San Onofre State Beach**, about 16 miles north of Oceanside. Unique in that it's actually two beaches, North and South, this certainly is one of the county's most scenic beach parks. Its eroded sandstone bluffs hide a variety of secluded sandy coves and pocket beaches. But all this beauty is broken by an eerie and ungainly structure rising from the shoreline. Dividing the park's twin beaches is a mammoth facility, potent and ominous, the San Onofre nuclear power plant.

Shopping

To explore San Diego County's shopping opportunities is to embrace the particular personality of each town and city within the region. There's Horton Plaza, with its multilevel melange of shops, and Old Town's colorful Mexican bazaars. Sporty beach-town boutiques contrast with the sophisticated salons and galleries of La Jolla and Rancho Santa Fe.

SOUTH SAN DIEGO COUNTY SHOPPING

Chula Vista's newly renovated downtown is highlighted by **Park Plaza in the Village Shopping Plaza** (310 3rd Avenue). Here twenty stores, including fashion and specialty shops in English-Tudor style cottages, cluster around a central court. In addition, the shopping district on 3rd Avenue between E and H streets is a charming mix of long-standing family businesses and quality specialty shops.

Plaza Bonita (3330 Plaza Bonita Road) in National City is a modern mall with four department stores and a range of smaller outlets.

DOWNTOWN SAN DIEGO SHOPPING

No other shopping center in the county is quite like **Horton Plaza** (between Broadway and G Street, 5th and 4th avenues). More than 150 individually designed stores are situated here. Department stores occupy the four corners, and a flood of specialty and one-of-a-kind shops complete the picture. Along the tiled boulevard are shops offering whimsical items—everything from saltwater taffy to psychic readings.

Clever designs distinguish many of the shops, such as **Wild Horizons**, where a split-log cabin facade invites you in to shop for outdoor and adventure travel apparel, books, and accessories. Nearby on the same level, a full-size safari jeep emerges from the storefront at **Banana Republic**, a popular emporium for clothes, baggage, footwear, hats, and travel accessories.

There are men's apparel shops, shoe stores, jewelry shops, art galleries, and women's haute couture boutiques, dozens of stores in all. Worth a special visit is **Irvine Ranch Farmer's Market**, where 25,000 square feet of fresh produce and specialty food products are beautifully displayed.

The **Gaslamp Quarter** (along 5th Avenue) is a charming 16-block assemblage of shops, galleries, and sidewalk cafes in the downtown center. Faithfully replicated in the quarter are Victorian-era street lamps, red-brick sidewalks, and window displays thematic of turn-of-the-century San Diego. Stroll down the **G Street Arts Corrido** to the **Java Coffeehouse-Gallery** (837 G Street), where you can relax, browse, and enjoy a cup of fine-blend coffee. The gallery presents a constantly changing selection of contemporary art with a focus on works by Southern Californians. **MBS Studios** (744 G Street, #101) and **Spectrum Gallery** (#102) showcase San Diegans' prints and paintings.

The 19th-century Broker's Block has been renovated to house **San Diego International Shopping Bazaar** (corner of Market Street and 4th Avenue). This four-level marketplace offers exotic foods, unique import items, objets d'art, specialty shops, jewelry, handicrafts, and more.

A favorite spot for antique lovers is **The Olde Cracker Factory** (448 West Market Street), which offers a 40-store selection in the restored 1913 Bishop Cracker Factory. Legend has it that a resident ghost named "Crunch" shuffles through mounds of broken crackers here searching for a small brass cookie cutter.

A perfect place to stock up for a picnic is the **Farmers Bazaar** (205 7th Avenue), a down-to-earth produce market.

Kobey's Downtown (5th Avenue at Broadway) provides bargain shopping at its best. Inspired by the owner's famous swap meet at the Sports Arena, this clever merchandising setup consists of 80 stalls jammed full of merchandise.

Seaport Village (foot of Pacific Highway and Harbor Drive) was designed to capture the look and feel of an early California waterfront setting. Its 65 shops dot a 14-acre village and include the usual mix of boutiques, galleries, clothing stores, and gift shops.

CORONADO SHOPPING

Coronado's fancy Orange Avenue in the village center harbors six blocks of unusual shops and two mini-malls, **Coronado Plaza** (1330 Orange Avenue) and **El Cordova** (1351 Orange Avenue).

The **Old Ferry Landing** has been renovated to include a modern shopping area complete with boutiques, specialty shops, galleries, and eateries.

The Gallery at the Landing (137 Orange Avenue) has an interesting selection of framed historic photographs of Coronado "back when."

The **Hotel del Coronado** (1500 Orange Avenue) is a city within a city and home to several intriguing specialty shops, such as the **British Importing Company**, where you can locate your family's crest or coat of arms. Crests, plain or gold-plated, are available for purchase.

OLD TOWN AND MISSION VALLEY SHOPPING

Historic Old Town is blessed with several exciting bazaars and shopping squares. By far the grandest is **The Bazaar del Mundo** (Mason Street between Calhoun and Juan streets), Old Town's version of the famous marketplaces of Spain and Mexico. Adobe *casitas* house a variety of international shops. Here **Fabrics and Finery** unfurls cloth, beads, and craft accessories from around the world, **Ariana** features wearable art, and **Treasures** provides a marvelous selection of gifts and crafts from exotic lands.

Walk down San Diego Avenue and take a gander at **Squibob Square** (2611 San Diego Avenue). The cactus-lined courtyard and bougainvillea-laced cottages lend an authentic feel of yesteryear to the souvenir shops.

A haven for art lovers is **Spanish Village Arts and Crafts** (near the San Diego zoo entrance). Its open-air studios are staffed by artists displaying their work. For sale are original paintings, sculpture, photographs, jewelry, stained glass, lapidary, and pottery.

MISSION BAY AND THE BEACHES SHOPPING

Commercial enterprises in the beach communities cater primarily to sun worshipers. Beachie boutiques and rental shops are everywhere. **Cuchis** (3691 Mission Boulevard) and **Sand Pebbles Beach Wear** (3719 Mission Boulevard) are sportswear shops worthy of mention. Everything about **Art and Harmony** (3780 Mission Boulevard) is unique, especially the inventory, which includes beachwear, natural skin-care products, books, shells, jewerly, cards, posters, and toys.

The Promenade at Pacific Beach (Mission Boulevard between Pacific Beach Drive and Reed Street), a modern, Mediterranean-style shopping complex, houses dozens of smartly decorated specialty shops. Among them are the **Ivory Coast Safari Club**, a trendy men's and women's sportswear shop, **Tropical Nights**, a beachwear boutique, and **Side Orders**, which features a clever display of hats and bags.

LA JOLLA SHOPPING

Once a secluded seaside village, La Jolla has emerged as a world-famous resort community that offers style and substance. The shopping focuses on Girard Avenue (from Torrey Pines Road to Prospect Street) and along Prospect Street. Both are lined with designer boutiques, alluring specialty shops, and fabulous art galleries.

In La Jolla's many galleries, traditional art blends with contemporary paintings, and rare Oriental antiques complement 20th-century bronze sculpture. **Simic Galleries** (7925 Girard Avenue) offers a fine selection of seascapes and master impressionist work. At nearby **Bennett Sculpture** (7916 Girard Avenue), the remarkable style of Bob and Tom Bennett's works—sleek, fluid, highly polished bronze—captivates collectors.

The **Master's Gallery of La Jolla** (955 Prospect Street) hangs the paintings of such artists as Dali, Picasso, Chagall, and Miro alongside the work of an eclectic array of other artists. **Hanson Art Galleries** (1227 Prospect Street) features unique contemporary art exhibitions representing new graphic works and rare selections from important 20th-century artists.

Housed as it is in a landmark 1903 cottage covered with wisteria, **John Cole's Book Shop** (780 Prospect Street) provides a refuge from these slick, chic La Jolla shops. Its nooks and crannies are lined with books ranging from best sellers to rare editions.

Located some distance south of the village center, **Capriccio** (6919 La Jolla Boulevard) has made its mark in the world of women's fashions, having been numbered by *Women's Wear Daily* among the top three fashion stores in America.

One of the oldest and most unusual shops in La Jolla guards the entrance to a sea cave and can actually be entered from land or sea. Dating to 1903, the **La Jolla Cave and Shell Shop** (1325 Coast Boulevard) displays every kind of shell imaginable along with a variety of nautical gifts and tourist baubles. From inside the shop, 133 steps lead down a tunnel to the main chamber of Sunny Jim Cave.

NORTH SAN DIEGO COUNTY SHOPPING

A seacoast village atmosphere prevails along Del Mar's half-mile-long strip of shops. Tudor-style **Stratford Square**, the focal point, houses a number of shops in what once was a grand turn-of-the-century resort hotel. The most intriguing enterprises here are the adjoining **Ocean Song** (1438 Camino del Mar) and **Earth Song Books** (1440 Camino del Mar), which offer musical gifts and books, respectively.

Flower Hill Mall (2636 Via de la Valle), a rustic mini-mall, has the usual fashion and specialty shops. But the real draw here is the **Bookworks** and an adjoining coffeehouse called **Pannikin**. Together they're perfect for a relaxed bit of book browsing and a spot of tea.

If little else, Solana Beach harbors an enclave of good antique stores. Two of the best are the **Antique Warehouse** (212 South Cedros Avenue), with its collection of 101 small shops, and **Spinners Antiques**, (212 South Cedros Avenue), featuring 16,000 square feet devoted to furniture and collectibles.

Detouring, as every sophisticated shopper must, to Rancho Santa Fe, you'll find an assortment of chic shops and galleries along Paseo Delicias. My favorites are **Marilyn Mulloy Estate Jewelers**, with its stunning collection of old and new pieces, and **The Two Goats**, featuring designer fashions and exclusive gifts. There are lots of millionaires per acre here, but bargains can still be found: **Carolyn's** (La Flecha Avenue) is a consignment shop boasting designer fashions from the closets of the community's best-dressed women. Another place where the rich like to rummage is **Country Friends** (El Tordo and Avenida de Acacias), a charity-operated repository of antique furniture, silver, glass, and china priced well below local antique shops.

The very best of the new North County shopping malls are in Encinitas. Conveniently situated on the east side of Route 101 between I and E streets, **The Lumberyard** is an attractive woodframe shopping village on the former site of an old lumber mill.

Carlsbad, too, has blossomed with a variety of trendy shops. You'll see many beach-and-surf-type shops, including **Kathmandu Trading Company** (3076 Carlsbad Avenue), which has nearly anything you might need for enjoying the sand and sea. **Alt Karlsbad Hanse Gift Shop** (2802 Carlsbad Boulevard), ensconced in a hundred-year-old, German-style stone house, sells European art and collectibles, including steins, Hummels, and crystal pieces.

Old World Center (Roosevelt Street and Grand Avenue) in Carlsbad has some little shops tucked away in its arcade. The best shopping in Oceanside is around the harbor at **Cape Cod Village**, a mock whaling port with a few interesting shops.

Nightlife

The sun is certainly the main attraction in San Diego, but the city also features a rich and varied nightlife, offering the night owl everything from traditional folk music to high-energy discos. There are piano bars, singles bars, a few gay bars, and a growing number of jazz clubs.

If you're a culture vulture with a limited pocketbook, try **Artsticks** (619-238-3810), a 24-hour recorded announcement listing half-priced theater, music, and dance tickets. **The Arts and Entertainment Hotline** (San Diego, 619-234-2787; North County, 619-942-3515) offers a 24-hour public service announcement providing up-to-the-minute listings. KIFM Radio (98.1 FM) hosts the 24-hour **Lights Out Jazz Hotline** (619-492-9898), which provides the latest in jazz happenings.

SOUTH SAN DIEGO COUNTY NIGHTLIFE

If you're looking for nighttime entertainment in these areas, you'll probably want to consider a trip to the city. Otherwise be content with scattered restaurant bars and local pubs. There's one notable exception: **Dance Machine/Country Bumpkin** (1862 Palm Avenue, Imperial Beach; 619-429-1161). Advertised as San Diego's largest nightclub, it houses two dance clubs. A pair of live bands, rock and country, appears nightly. Cover.

DOWNTOWN SAN DIEGO NIGHTLIFE

THE BEST BARS

An elegant old world setting of marble, brass, and leather makes **Grant Grill Lounge** (U.S. Grant Hotel, 326 Broadway; 619-232-3121) *the* place for the elite to meet. Pianists play a mix of contemporary tunes, popular standards, and jazz.

Golden Lion Tavern (801 4th Avenue; 619-233-1131) is a Gaslamp Quarter landmark and a favored place to bend an elbow.

At **Croce's** (802 4th Avenue; 619-233-4355) fans of the immortal Jim Croce will love the bar built as a memorial to the late singer-songwriter by his wife, Ingrid. Family mementos line the walls in tribute to a talented recording artist.

There's no hotel at **Hotel Bar** (203 5th Avenue; 619-232-2272), but there is a grand 50-foot-long bar. This hot spot carries its Mexican theme to the hilt with decorative exotica such as piñatas, stuffed wildcats, and a giant Chihuahua beer bottle chandelier.

Smedley's Baseball Inn (510 5th Avenue; 619-233-8519) is dedicated to the San Diego Padres but is loaded with early baseball memorabilia as well. Bag it on one of the baseball-bat bar stools and slug down a few. Nothing fancy, but a great character bar.

It's easy to spot the shocking pink, neon-lit facade of **Fat City** (2137 Pacific Highway; 619-232-0686). Art deco styling marks the exterior, but the bar features an authentic Victorian decor. It's not a meat market, but Fat City is a favorite among friendly young singles and hosts a good jazz and light rock lineup every Thursday, Friday, and Saturday.

Plaza Bar (1055 2nd Avenue; 619-238-1818), at the distinctive Westgate Hotel, is a graceful period French lounge where prominent locals and visitors enjoy classy piano entertainment nightly.

Mr. A's (5th Avenue and Laurel Street; 619-239-1377) is the critics' choice for "best drinking with a view." The atmosphere at this piano bar is one of monied luxury, and gentlemen are expected to wear jackets.

The **Sunset Lounge** (1355 North Harbor Drive; 619-232-6358), built out over the water, attracts a younger business crowd and lots of visitors with its panoramic bay views.

Featuring views of San Diego Bay and one of the largest dancefloors in town, **Harbor House** (831 West Harbor Drive, Seaport Village; 619-232-1141) dishes up everything from Top-40 disco to big band music nightly.

THEATER

The **Old Globe Theater** (Balboa Park; 619-239-2255), a critically acclaimed dramatic organization, includes three different theaters, which produce all types of performances.

The **Gaslamp Quarter Theatre** (547 4th Avenue; 619-234-9583) and the **New Deane Theatre** (494 4th Avenue; 619-234-9583) offer productions of classic and contemporary works.

In addition to performances of the San Diego Opera, the **San Diego Civic Theater** (202 C Street; 619-232-7636) presents a variety of entertainment ranging from pop artists to plays to dance performances.

The **San Diego Repertory Theatre** (79 Horton Plaza; 619-235-8025), performs dramas, comedies, and musicals.

Just north of the downtown theater district, **The Bowery Theatre** (480 Elm Street; 619-232-4088) presents contemporary and often controversial theater. Many works are original and/or San Diego premieres of powerful national plays.

The Marquis Public Theatre (3717 India Street; 619-295-5654) is noted for its original scripts and unique productions as well as classic dramas.

OPERA, SYMPHONY AND DANCE

The **San Diego Opera** (202 C Street; 619-236-6510 or 619-232-7636) presents such international stars as Luciano Pavarotti, Joan Sutherland, and Kiri Te Kanawa. The season begins in October and runs through March.

Performing in the historic 1929 Spanish Renaissance-style Fox Theatre, the **San Diego Symphony Orchestra** (770 B Street; 619-699-4200) presents an array of guest conductors and artists.

California Ballet (619-560-5676) presents a diverse repertoire of contemporary and traditional ballets.

THE GAY SCENE

West Coast Production Company (1845 Hancock Street; 619-295-3724) is a high-energy gay club featuring deejay disco dancing nightly and special events such as the Green Groves Drag Show. Four large bars, a game room, and a patio are housed in this artfully decorated, extravagant spot. Located near Old Town. Cover.

CORONADO NIGHTLIFE

If you're out Coronado way, stop for a cocktail in the famed Hotel del Coronado's **Ocean Terrace Room and Bar** (1550 Orange Avenue;

619-435-6611). The Del's latest addition is the **Palm Court**, offering live piano music in a palm-studded lounge.

Mexican Village (120 Orange Avenue; 619-435-1822) is a Mexican-theme nightclub, but the music isn't Mexican at all. Solo performers play classics and contemporaries on the piano from Sunday through Thursday, then disco dancing charges up the weekends.

POINT LOMA, SHELTER AND HARBOR ISLANDS NIGHTLIFE

Victor's (1403 Rosecrans Street; 619-266-1871) is an intimate, European-style, split-level lounge featuring solo crooners and attracting a melting-pot of singles and professionals; Thursday through Saturday. Downstairs, live Top-40 sounds mixed with comedy and dancing get the house rockin' from Wednesday through Saturday.

For the mellow crowd interested in enjoying cocktails with conversation or some light dancing overlooking a picturesque marina, there's **Dock Masters** (2051 Shelter Island Drive; 619-223-2572). Some of the city's finest contemporary groups and jazz bands perform nightly. Cover.

Even musicians head outdoors during San Diego summers. **Humphrey's** (2241 Shelter Island Drive; 619-224-3577) hosts the city's most ambitious series of jazz and mellow rock shows, which include an impressive lineup of name artists in a beautiful bayside lawn setting.

Aside from being a popular restaurant and lounge, **Tom Ham's Lighthouse** (2150 Harbor Island Drive; 619-291-9110) is a real lighthouse and the official Coast Guard-sanctioned beacon of Harbor Island. This scrimshaw-filled nautical lounge is a great place to relax and take in easy-listening duos nightly.

OLD TOWN AND MISSION VALLEY NIGHTLIFE

A musician's nightclub, **Our Place** (2424 5th Avenue; 619-232-1773) is a '40s-style cabaret where many of San Diego's most respected jazz musicians perform.

If it's '50s fun you're seeking, go to **The Corvette Bar and Grill** (3946 5th Avenue; 619-542-1001). Great oldies keep this joint jumpin'.

The roof at **Mandolin Wind** (308 University Avenue; 619-297-3017) is supported by tree trunks charred in a Northern California forest fire. This cozy mountain ski lodge-type nightclub has hosted King Biscuit Blues Band for nearly a decade. Cover.

If you want to dance disco, **Confetti's** (5373 Mission Center Road; 619-291-8635) has a multilevel dancefloor and, of course, confetti spewing from the ceilings. All three bars are packed nightly. Cover.

The prevailing culture in Old Town is Mexican, as in mariachis and margaritas. The **Old Town Mexican Cafe y Cantina** (2489 San Diego Avenue; 619-297-4330), a festive, friendly establishment, has a patio bar.

O'Hungry's (2547 San Diego Avenue; 619-298-0133), a nearby folk club, features folk singers and guitarists nightly.

MISSION BAY AND THE BEACHES NIGHTLIFE

Texas Teahouse (4970 Voltaire Street; 619-222-6895) should be listed under "Dives" in the yellow pages. This musty, Ocean Beach hole-in-the-wall is the home of Tom "Cat" Courtney, a real-life legend who's been singin' and playin' the blues every Thursday night for some 15 years here. He's strummed guitar with the likes of T-Bone Walker, Lightnin' Hopkins, and Freddie King. More blues bands play on weekends.

The Pennent (2893 Mission Boulevard; 619-488-1671) is a landmark where local writers and beachies congregate en masse on the deck to get rowdy and watch the sunset. The entertainment here is the clientele.

Mary's By The Pier (710 Garnet Avenue, Pacific Beach; 619-483-7844), on Crystal Pier, is a homey, casual, cedar-paneled bar, with oldies and Top-40 bands playing nightly.

Catamaran Resort Hotel Lounge (3999 Mission Boulevard; 619-488-1081) features live pop and jazz bands every Wednesday and Thursday, and rock and oldies bands during the rest of the week. Cover.

Atlantis (2595 Ingraham Street; 619-226-3888) has a floor-to-ceiling aquarium and a classy lounge. Live jazz and pop music nightly.

Pacific Beach has one of San Diego's trendiest nightlife districts, offering a wide range of entertainment options from jazz to rock, comedy to blues. **Steamers** (1165 Garnet Avenue; 619-274-2323) is a slick art deco nightclub where a piano and brass duo play soft jazz nightly to a mellow crowd.

The undisputed king of beach area nightlife is **Club Diego's** (860 Garnet Avenue; 619-272-1241). Modeled after the high-tech video discos of New York and London, it features black-and-white checkered dance-floors and video screens monitoring the "beautiful people" who pack the place to capacity nightly. Cover.

Just next door, the **Improv** (832 Garnet Avenue; 619-483-4521), a 1930s-style cabaret, showcases many local and East Coast comedians. Cover.

Standing-room-only crowds are attracted to the **Old Pacific Beach Cafe** (4287 Mission Boulevard; 619-270-7522), where a steady stream of pop and jazz acts plays Thursday through Sunday, while rock bands perform the rest of the week. Cover.

LA JOLLA NIGHTLIFE

Among the most romantic restaurants in town, **Top O' The Cove** (1216 Prospect Street; 619-454-7779) features a piano bar.

A panoramic view of the ocean makes **Elarios** (7955 La Jolla Shores Drive; 619-459-0541) the perfect place to enjoy a mix of local and national jazz acts nightly.

The Comedy Store (916 Pearl Street; 619-454-9176) features comedians exclusively, many with national reputations. Cover plus minimum.

Hidden inside a nondescript building, **D.G. Wills Books and Coffeehouse** (7527 La Jolla Boulevard; 619-456-1800) is a tiny literary haven featuring workshops and readings and serving desserts and coffees.

San Diego Toujours (828 Prospect Street; 619-456-2944) offers jazz and new age music in a patio setting.

The La Jolla Chamber Music Society (619-459-3724) hosts summer and fall performances by such notables as the Vienna Boy's Choir, flautist James Galway, and the Stuttgart Chamber Orchestra. The prestigious **La Jolla Playhouse** (619-534-3960), located on the University of California's San Diego campus, produces innovative dramas and spotlights famous actors.

NORTH SAN DIEGO COUNTY NIGHTLIFE

There's not much nighttime action in laid-back Del Mar, but signs of life stir around the beachfront **Poseidon Restaurant** (1670 Coast Boulevard, Del Mar; 619-755-9345), where solo singers and guitarists entertain on weekends.

The **Old Del Mar Cafe** (2730 Via del la Valle; 619-755-6614), a nightclub of the oak-and-brass genre, features live rock, two bars, a dancefloor, and a lot of action. Cover.

Tucked away in the Flower Hill Mall, the **Bookworks-Pannikin Coffeehouse** (2670 Via de la Valle, Del Mar; 619-481-8007) brings a true taste of culture in the form of live jazz and poetry readings.

Solana Beach's low-profile daytime image shifts gears at night when the-little-town-that-could spotlights two of North County's hottest clubs. **Club Diego's** (635 South Route 101; 619-755-4813) is an opulent nightclub, while the **Belly Up Tavern** (143 South Cedros Avenue; 619-481-9022) is a converted quonset hut that now houses a concert club and sometimes draws big name rock and blues stars. Cover.

Bella Via (2591 North Route 101, Cardiff; 619-942-1487) is a real find, a fashionable club that hosts national and local jazz bands nightly.

Ireland's Own (656 1st Street, Encinitas; 619-944-0233) is an Irish pub complete with shamrocks, Guinness on tap, genuine Irish whiskey, and traditional Irish folk music every Thursday through Sunday.

A cozy coffeehouse called the **Old Time Cafe** (1464 North Route 101, Leucadia; 619-436-4030) brings live folk music favorites from around the world. Cover.

There's a terrific view of Oceanside Harbor from **Monterey Bay Canners** (1325 Harbor Drive, Oceanside; 619-722-3474), a nautical theme bar where contemporary bands play every Thursday through Saturday.

CHAPTER THREE
Orange Coast

Places are known through their nicknames. More than official titles or proper names, sobriquets reveal the real identity of a region. "Orange Coast" can never describe the 42 miles of cobalt blue ocean and whitewashed sand from San Clemente to Seal Beach. That moniker derives from the days when Orange County was row on row with orchards of plump citrus. Today prestigious homes and marinas sprout from the shoreline. This is the "Gold Coast," habitat of beachboys, yachtsmen, and tennis buffs, the "American Riviera."

The theme which ties the territory together, and gives rise to these nicknames, is money. Money and the trappings that attend it—glamor, celebrity, elegance, power. The Orange Coast is a sun-blessed realm of beautiful people, where politics is right wing and real estate sells by the square foot.

Ever since Walt Disney founded his fantasy empire nearby in the 1950s, the place has exploded with population and profits. In Disney's wake came the crowds, and as they arrived they developed—housing projects and condominium complexes, mini-malls and business centers. To the interior, towns now look alike and Orange County, once an empire of orange groves, has become a cookie-cutter civilization.

Along the coast progress also levied a tremendous toll but has left intact some of the natural beauty, the deep canyons and curving hills, soft sand beaches and sharp escarpments. The towns too have retained their separate styles, each projecting its own identifying image.

San Clemente, which served as President Nixon's Western White House, is a trim, strait-laced residential community. San Juan Capistrano, a small town surrounding an old mission, is closer to its roots than any place in this futuristic area. Dana Point represents a marina development in search of a soul; while Laguna Beach is an artist colony so *in* that real estate prices have driven the artists *out*. Nearby Corona del Mar is a model community with quiet streets and a placid waterfront.

The capital of this beachside society is Newport Beach, fashion conscious center for celebrities, business mavens, and those to whom God granted little patience and a lot of money. To the north lies Huntington Beach, working-class counterpoint to Newport and a place that claims the nickname "Surfing Capital of the World." Just beyond the oil derricks of Huntington rests Seal Beach, Orange County's answer to small-town America, a pretty community with a sense of serenity. Linking this string of beach towns together is Route 1, the Pacific Coast Highway, which runs from Capistrano Beach north along the entire coast.

The geography throughout is varied and unpredictable. To the south, particularly around Laguna Beach, a series of uplifted marine terraces creates bold headlands, coastal bluffs, and pocket coves. Further north, around Newport Beach and Huntington Beach, rugged heights give way to low-lying terrain cut by rivers and opening into estuaries. These northerly towns, together with Dana Point, are manmade harbors carved from swamps and surrounded by landfill islands and peninsulas. Huntington Harbor, the first of its kind, consists of eight islands weighted down with luxury homes and bordered by a mazework of marinas.

Land here is so highly prized that it's not surprising the city fathers chose to create more by dredging it from river bottoms. The Gabrieleño and Juañero Indians who originally inhabited the area considered the ground sacred, while the Spanish who conquered them divided it into two immense land grants, the San Joaquin and Niguel ranchos.

Establishing themselves at the San Juan Capistrano mission in 1776, the Spanish padres held sway until the 19th century. By the 1830s American merchants from the East Coast were sending tall-masted trading ships up from Cape Horn. Richard Henry Dana, who sailed the shoreline, giving his name to Dana Point, described the area in *Two Years Before the Mast* as "the most romantic spot along the coast."

By the 1860s, after Americans seized California, the Spanish ranchos were joined into the Irvine Ranch, a land parcel extending ten miles along the coast and 22 miles inland, and controlled with a steel fist by a single family.

They held in their sway all but Laguna Beach, which was settled in the 1870s by pioneers developing 160-acre government land grants. A freestyle community, Laguna developed into an artist colony filled with galleries and renowned for its cliff-rimmed beaches. Over the years artists and individualists—including LSD guru Timothy Leary and a retinue of hippies, who arrived during the 1960s—have been lured by the simple beauty of the place.

Just as Laguna Beach has always relied on natural beauty, Newport Beach has worked for its reputation. During the 1870s the harbor was built; channels were dredged, marshes filled, and stone jetties constructed as sternwheelers began frequenting the "new port" between

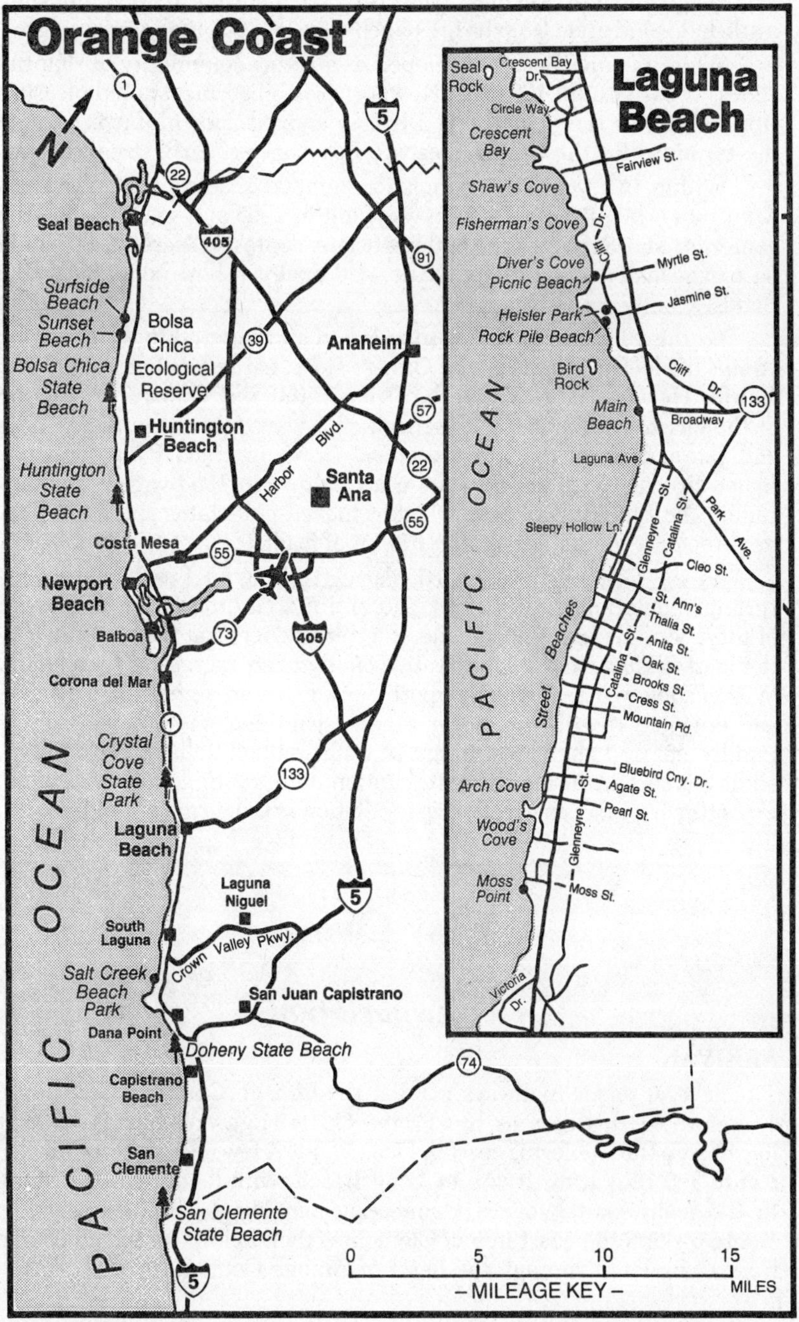
Orange Coast
Laguna Beach
Seal Rock
Crescent Bay Dr.
Circle Way
Crescent Bay
Fairview St.
Shaw's Cove
Fisherman's Cove
Cliff Dr.
Diver's Cove
Picnic Beach
Myrtle St.
Jasmine St.
Heisler Park
Rock Pile Beach
Bird Rock
Cliff Dr.
Main Beach
Broadway
Laguna Ave.
Glenneyre St.
Catalina St.
Park Ave.
Sleepy Hollow Ln.
Cleo St.
St. Ann's
Thalia St.
Anita St.
Oak St.
Brooks St.
Cress St.
Mountain Rd.
Street Beaches
Bluebird Cny. Dr.
Agate St.
Pearl St.
Arch Cove
Wood's Cove
Moss Point
Moss St.
Victoria Dr.
PACIFIC OCEAN
Seal Beach
Surfside Beach
Sunset Beach
Bolsa Chica State Beach
Bolsa Chica Ecological Reserve
Huntington Beach
Huntington State Beach
Anaheim
Harbor Blvd.
Santa Ana
Costa Mesa
Newport Beach
Balboa
Corona del Mar
Crystal Cove State Park
Laguna Beach
Laguna Niguel
South Laguna
Crown Valley Pkwy.
Salt Creek Beach Park
San Juan Capistrano
Dana Point
Doheny State Beach
Capistrano Beach
San Clemente
San Clemente State Beach
1
22
405
5
91
39
57
55
73
133
74
0
5
10
15
– MILEAGE KEY –
MILES

San Diego and Los Angeles. Newport Pier followed in 1888, allowing cattle hides and grain from Irvine Ranch to be loaded onto waiting ships.

While Laguna Beach developed as a resort community during the 1880s, it wasn't until 1904 that Newport Beach became a noted pleasure stop. That was the year the red trolley arrived and the town became the terminus for the Pacific Electric, Los Angeles' early streetcar line.

Within two years the population jumped sixfold and land values went into orbit. Balboa Pavilion was built in 1905 and soon became the center for Max Sennett-type bathing beauty contests. Years later it would be a dancehall and gambling casino, and finally a showroom for the Big Bands.

By the 1960s those brassy sounds had surrendered to the twanging strains of electric guitars as the Orange Coast earned its final nickname, "Surfer Heaven." Dick Dale, the "King of the Surf Guitar," hit the top of the charts with "Pipeline," setting off a wave which the Beach Boys and Jan and Dean rode to the crest. Down in Dana Point local boy Bruce Brown contributed to the coast culture in 1964 with a surf flick called *The Endless Summer*, which achieved cult status and earned for its director a reputation as "the Fellini of foam."

As the Orange Coast, particularly Huntington Beach, earned its surfing reputation in the 1960s, the entire area broke from the power of the Irvine Ranch. The suicide of a third generation scion resulted in the land passing from a conservative family to an aggressive foundation. Within a few years it built Newport Center, the area's high-rise district, and crowned it with the chic Fashion Island enclave. Orange County rapidly entered the modern age of multi-million-dollar development, adding a certain luster to its reputation and granting to its shoreline, for better or worse, an everlasting reputation as California's "Gold Coast."

Easy Living

Transportation

ARRIVAL

Several major highways parallel the Orange County coast. **Route 1**, known in this area as the Pacific Coast Highway, begins its long journey up the California coast in Dana Point. A few miles further inland, **Route 405** runs from Irvine to Long Beach, with feeder roads leading to the main coastal towns. Connecting San Diego and Los Angeles, **Route 5** skirts the coast in San Clemente, then follows an inland course from Dana Point through the heart of Orange County.

BY AIR

John Wayne International Airport, located in Irvine, is the main terminal in these parts. Major carriers presently serving it include **American Airlines** (800-433-7300), **America West** (800-247-5692), **Continental Airlines** (800-525-0280), **Delta Airlines** (800-221-1212), **Jet America** (800-255-0565), **Pacific Southwest Airlines** (800-435-9772), **Trans World Airlines** (800-221-2000), and **United Airlines** (800-241-6522).

BY BUS

Greyhound Bus Lines serves the Orange Coast, stopping in San Clemente, Laguna Beach, Dana Point, Corona del Mar, Newport Beach, Huntington Beach, and Seal Beach. Most stops are flag stops; depots are located in San Clemente (510 North Avenida de la Estrella; 714-492-1187) and Laguna Beach (375 Broadway; 714-494-8642).

BY TRAIN

Amtrak's "San Diegan" (800-872-7245) travels between San Diego and Los Angeles, stopping along the Orange Coast in San Clemente and San Juan Capistrano.

CAR RENTALS

Arriving at John Wayne International Airport, you'll find the following car rental agencies: **Avis Rent A Car** (714-852-8608), **Budget Rent A Car** (714-955-3700), and **Hertz Rent A Car** (714-756-8161). For less expensive (and less convenient) service, try the outfits providing free airport pick-up: **Alamo Rent A Car** (714-852-0403), **American International** (714-951-5333), **Cal American Car Rentals** (714-756-8313), **Dollar Rent A Car** (714-756-1444), **Enterprise Car Rentals** (714-851-7701), **National Car Rental** (714-852-1284), and **Thrifty Rent A Car** (714-852-8222).

PUBLIC TRANSPORTATION

Orange County Transit District (714-636-7433), or OCTD, carries passengers the length of the coast with stops in San Clemente, San Juan Capistrano, Laguna Beach, Corona del Mar, Newport Beach, Huntington Beach, and Seal Beach.

BICYCLING

Route 1, the Pacific Coast Highway, offers cyclists an opportunity to explore the Orange County coastline. The problem, of course, is the traffic. Along **Bolsa Chica State Beach,** however, a special pathway runs the length of the beach. Other interesting areas to explore are Balboa Island and Balboa Peninsula in Newport Beach. Both offer quiet residential streets and are connected by a ferry which permits bicycles.

To rent bikes in Orange County try **Ernie's Pro Bikes** (24422 Del Prado Avenue, Dana Point; 714-493-8382), **Rainbow Bicycle Company**

(485 North Route 1, Laguna Beach; 714-494-5806), **Oceanfront Wheel Works** (Balboa Pier, Newport Beach; 714-675-6510), **Baldy's Tackle** (100 McFadden Place, Newport Beach; 714-673-4150), **Jack's Beach Concession** (on Huntington Beach; 714-536-8328), and **Bolsa Chica Bicycles** (4952 Warner Avenue, Huntington Beach; 714-846-6646).

Hotels

SOUTH ORANGE COUNTY HOTELS

Algodon Motel (135 Avenida Algodon, San Clemente; 714-492-3382), a standard type 28-unit facility several blocks from the beach, has rooms at budget prices. Accommodations with a kitchen rent in the moderate range. Not much to write home about, but it is clean and trim (and cheap!).

Cheaper still is the **San Clemente International Hostel** (233 Avenida Granada, San Clemente; 714-492-2848), an AYH facility located in a stucco building on a residential street. The accommodations consist of bunk beds in dormitory rooms; one family room is also available. Visitors share a television room, kitchen, and small patio. Budget.

Capistrano Country Bay Inn (34862 Pacific Coast Highway, Capistrano Beach; 714-496-6656), situated on the highway directly across from a beach, is a 1930s-era establishment on the grounds of an old estate. The 28 units are set in a long, low-slung building designed in Spanish style with a red tile roof. The narrow lawn is attractively landscaped and adorned with a fountain. Each guest room has a wet bar and woodburning stove. Most have tile floors, ceiling fans, and vintage wallhangings. Prices range from moderate to deluxe; jacuzzi; continental breakfast.

Most motels have a stream of traffic whizzing past outside, but the **Dana Marina Inn Motel** (34111 Route 1, Dana Point; 714-496-1300), situated on an island where the highway divides, manages to have traffic on both sides! The reason I'm mentioning it is not because I'm sadistic but because rooms in this 29-unit facility are priced on the cusp between budget and moderate. The accommodations are roadside-motel style.

The Ritz Carlton Laguna Niguel (33533 Shoreline Drive, Laguna Niguel; 714-240-2000), set on a cliff above the Pacific, is simply the finest resort hotel along the California coast. Built in the fashion of a Mediterranean villa, it dominates a broad sweep of coastline, a 393-room mansion replete with gourmet restaurants and dark-wood lounges. An Old World interior of arched windows and Italian marble is decorated with one of the finest hotel collections of 19th-century American and English art anywhere. The grounds are landscaped with willows, sycamores, and a spectrum of flowering plants. Tile courtyards lead to two swimming pools, a pair of jacuzzis, four tennis courts, and a fitness center. The guest rooms, equal in luxury to the rest of the resort, are priced at the etherial end of the ultra-deluxe range.

Tucked into a secluded canyon is **Aliso Creek Inn** (31106 Route 1, South Laguna; 714-499-2271), an appealing 87-acre resort complete with swimming pools, jacuzzi, restaurant, and 9-hole golf course. Particularly attractive for families, every unit includes a sitting area, patio, and kitchen. Removed from the highway but within 400 yards of a beach, the resort is surrounded by steep hillsides which are populated by deer and raccoon. Tying this easy rusticity together is a small creek that tumbles through the resort. Studios and one-bedroom suites are deluxe, two-bedroom complexes are ultra-deluxe.

LAGUNA BEACH HOTELS

Hotel Firenze (1289 South Route 1; 714-497-2446), like an old Italian hotel fallen on hard times, conveys a sense of faded elegance. The lobby boasts antique furnishings, brick fireplace, and tile floor, but needs painting and replastering. A vague odor of must prevails. Carpets show wear and furniture is damaged. But the place possesses character—the furniture was attractive in its day and the artwork was chosen by someone with a sense of aesthetics. Located a block from the beach, many rooms offer ocean views. The real allure is the cost: budget to moderate in the off-season, rising to moderate during summer months.

Even if you never stay there, you won't miss the **Hotel Laguna** (425 South Route 1; 714-494-1151). With its octagonal tower and Spanish motif, this huge whitewashed building dominates downtown Laguna Beach. The oldest hotel in Laguna, it sits in the center of town, adjacent to Main Beach. In addition to 70 guest rooms there are several restaurants, lounges, and a casual lobby. The place shows signs of age and suffers some of the ills characteristic of large old hotels. But for a place on the water *and* at the center of the action, it cannot be matched; deluxe.

The premier resting place in Laguna Beach is a sprawling 161-room establishment overhanging the sand. The **Surf & Sand Hotel** (1555 South Route 1; 714-497-4477) is a blocky 1950-era complex, an architectural melange of five buildings and a shopping mall. The accent here is on the ocean: nearly every room has a sea view and private balcony, the pool sits just above the sand, and the beach is a short step away. A full-service hotel, the Surf & Sand has two restaurants and an art deco lounge. Guest rooms are understated but attractive with raw silk furnishings, unfinished woods, and sand hue walls. Ultra-deluxe.

Casa Laguna Inn (2510 South Route 1; 714-494-2996), a hillside hacienda, has a dreamlike quality about it. The cottages and rooms are nestled into a garden setting complete with stone terraces and winding paths. Built in the 1930s, the Spanish-style complex features a courtyard, bell tower, and a swimming pool overlooking the ocean. The rooms are small, equipped with overhead fans, and furnished in antiques; many offer ocean views, though they also pick up noise from the highway.

Continental breakfast and afternoon tea are served in the library. Rooms price deluxe; suites and cottages with kitchens are ultra-deluxe.

It's not just the residential neighborhood that makes **The Carriage House** (1322 Catalina Street; 714-494-8945) unique. The colonial architecture of the "New Orleans style" bed and breakfast inn also sets it apart. Within this historic landmark structure are six suites, renting at deluxe prices, each with a sitting room and separate bedroom. All face a luxurious brick courtyard filled with flowering plants and adorned with a tiered fountain. Certainly the Carriage House is one of the prettiest and most peaceful inns along the entire Orange Coast.

NEWPORT BEACH HOTELS

You'd have a hell of a time docking your boat at the **Sail Inn Motel** (2627 Newport Boulevard; 714-675-1841). Actually it's on an island, but the island is a median strip dividing the two busiest streets on the Balboa Peninsula. Offering standard motel accommodations at moderate to deluxe prices, the Sail Inn is a block from the beach and walking distance from many restaurants.

The **Balboa Inn** (105 Main Street; 714-675-3412), next to the beach at Balboa Pier, is a Spanish-style hotel built in 1930. With its cream-colored walls and tile-roofed tower this 34-room hostelry is vintage Southern California. Adding to the ambience is a swimming pool that looks out on the water. The rooms, some of which have ocean views, are furnished in knotty pine, decorated with colorful prints, and equipped with added features like tile baths and brass fixtures. A Mediterranean atmosphere at a deluxe price.

Portofino Beach Hotel (2306 West Ocean Front; 714-673-7030), a 12-room bed and breakfast inn, rests on the beach in an early 20th-century building. Richly appointed with brass beds, armoires, and antique fixtures, the Portofino has a wine bar downstairs and an oceanfront parlor overlooking Newport Pier. Each room is decorated with wallpaper and equipped with a private bath; some have jacuzzis and ocean views. Room rates are deluxe and ultra-deluxe in the off-season, utlra-deluxe during summer months.

Hotels are as rare as unicorns on tiny Balboa Island. One, the **Balboa Island Hotel** (127 Agate Avenue; 714-675-3613), is a family-operated, three-bedroom affair. Set in a 1925 house, it's about one block from the water (of course on Balboa Island everything is one block from the water). Each room of this bed and breakfast inn has been decorated in period and furnished with antiques. The place has a small, intimate, homey feel. Guests share bathrooms and there are two porches which serve as sitting rooms; moderate.

By way of full-facility destinations, Southern California-style, few places match the **Newporter Resort** (1107 Jamboree Road; 714-644-

1700). Situated on a hillside above Upper Newport Bay, it sprawls across 26 acres and sports three swimming pools, three jacuzzis, a 9-hole pitch-and-putt course, and a tennis club. There are restaurants and lounges, a lavishly decorated lobby, and a series of terraced patios. Guest rooms are modern in design, comfortably furnished, and tastefully appointed. An inviting combination of elegance and amenities; ultra-deluxe.

NORTH ORANGE COUNTY HOTELS

The **Colonial Inn Youth Hostel** (421 8th Street, Huntington Beach; 714-536-3315) is a cavernous three-story house located four blocks from the beach. Capable of accommodating couples and families as well as individual travelers, its many rooms each contain two to eight beds. The house is in a residential neighborhood and offers a kitchen, dining room, television room, and yard. Chores are required and the hostel is closed during the day; budget.

Sunset Inn (16401 Route 1; 213-592-1666) is a tiny six-room hostelry right on the highway in Huntington Beach. Decorated in bed and breakfast fashion, it has individual rooms as well as accommodations with bedroom-sitting room combinations. Features like overhead fans, oak armoires, and handwrought headboards add to the ambience. Moderate.

It's only fitting that Seal Beach, Orange County's answer to a small town, houses the area's most appealing bed and breakfast. With its wrought-iron balcony, ornate fence, and garden ambience, the **Seal Beach Inn** (212 5th Street; 213-493-2416) has garnered a reputation for style and seclusion. Its 22 rooms, pricing from deluxe to ultra-deluxe, are furnished in hardwood antiques and appointed with period wallhangings. Guests breakfast in a cozy "tea room," then adjourn to the parlor with its upholstered armchairs and tile fireplace. The guest rooms are named for flowers, many of which grow on the grounds. Indeed the landscaping, which includes wrought-iron lawn furniture and early 20th-century lampposts, may be the most appealing feature of this fine old inn.

Restaurants

SOUTH ORANGE COUNTY RESTAURANTS

Center of the casual dining scene in San Clemente is along the beach at the foot of the municipal pier (end of Avenida del Mar). Several take-out stands and cafes are here. **The Fisherman's Restaurant** (714-498-6390), a knotty-pine and plate-glass establishment, sits right on the pier, affording views all along the beach. With a waterfront patio it's a good spot for seafood dishes at moderate prices.

One of San Juan Capistrano's many historic points, a 19th-century building, **El Adobe de Capistrano** (31891 Camino Capistrano; 714-493-1163) has been converted into a restaurant. The interior is a warren of whitewashed rooms, supported by *vegas* and displaying the flourishes of Spanish California. Stop by for a drink next to the old jail (today a wine cellar) or tour the building. (Counterpoint to all this dusty history is a display of Nixon memorabilia.) If you decide to dine, the menu inclues lunch, dinner, and Sunday brunch. Naturally the cuisine is Mexican, prices in the moderate range.

Just up the street, the 1895 railroad station has been reincarnated as the **Capistrano Depot Restaurant** (26701 Verdugo Street; 714-496-8181). Brick archways lead from the old waiting room and station master's office to the freight and pullman cars, all neatly transformed into a restaurant and lounge. The lunch, dinner, and Sunday brunch menus are a mix of neo-American dishes like chicken teriyaki, pork ribs, filet of sole, scallops, and braised veal shanks. Moderate.

Who can match the combination of intimacy and French-Belgian cuisine at **L'Hirondelle** (31631 Camino Capistrano, San Juan Capistrano; 714-661-0425)? Add a moderate price tag and you have a rare dining room indeed. It's quite small, about a dozen tables and banquettes and conveys a French country atmosphere. Serving dinner and Sunday brunch, the restaurant offers a varied menu beginning with escargots, garlic toast, and crab crepes. Entrees include roast duckling, rabbit in wine sauce, veal cordon bleu, bouillabaise, tournedos, sautéed sweetbreads, and daily fresh fish specials.

The **Harbor Grill** (34499 Golden Lantern, Dana Point; 714-240-1416), located in spiffy Dana Point Harbor, lacks the view and polish of its splashy neighbors. But this understated restaurant serves excellent seafood dishes at moderate rates. The menu includes brochettes of swordfish and prawns, fried calamari, steak, and grilled chicken, but the real attraction is the list of daily specials. This might include Cajun selections such as blackened sea bass, gumbo, and other fresh fish dishes. Lunch, dinner, and Sunday brunch are served in a light, bright dining room with contemporary posters.

If you'd prefer to dine alfresco overlooking the harbor, there's **Proud Mary's** (34689 Golden Lantern, Dana Point; 714-493-5853), a little hole in the wall where you can order sandwiches, hot dogs, hamburgers, and a few platters, then dine on picnic tables outside. Budget.

Japanese food in these parts is spelled **Gen Kai** (34143 Route 1, Dana Point; 714-240-2004). In addition to a trimly appointed dining room this chain restaurant features a sushi bar. The menu is comprehensive and moderately priced. When I ate here the food was quite good.

Monique French Restaurant (31727 Route 1, South Laguna; 714-499-5359) is a little jewel set on a coastal bluff. Situated in a former home it offers intimate dining indoors or outside on the patio. The restaurant is provincially decorated with patterned wallpaper and china plates. In addition to ocean views it offers a lunch and dinner menu that changes daily. On a typical evening they might be preparing scampi

Provençal, filet of pork à l'orange, tournedos, bouillabaise, and fresh seafood dishes. Highly recommended by local residents, Monique is deluxe in price.

LAGUNA BEACH RESTAURANTS

Laguna Beach is never at a loss for oceanfront restaurants. But somehow the sea seems closer and more intimate at **Laguna Village Cafe** (577 South Route 1; 714-494-6344). Probably because this informal eatery is entirely outdoors, with tables placed at the very edge of the coastal bluff. The menu is simple and budget-priced: egg dishes in the morning, and a single menu with salads, sandwiches, and smoothies during the rest of the day. There are also house specialties like calamari, scallops amandine, teriyaki chicken, skewered shrimp, and Chinese-style chicken dumplings.

The **Penguin Malt Shop** (981 South Route 1; 714-494-1353) is from another era entirely. The 1930s to be exact. A tiny cafe featuring counter juke boxes, swivel stools, and period posters, it's a time capsule with a kitchen. Breakfast, lunch, and dinner are all-American affairs from ham and eggs to hamburgers to pork chops. It's budget-priced, so what have you got to lose. Step on in and order a chocolate malt with a side of fries.

Poor Richard's Kitchen (1198 South Route 1, Laguna Beach; 714-497-1667) combines two seemingly insoluble ingredients—budget prices and ocean views. Granted, you'll have to be early, late, or lucky to snag one of the few tables that overlook the boundless blue. But anywhere you sit you'll be able to partake of the family-style dishes. In addition to a full array of breakfast servings and sandwiches, the menu includes steak, gumbo, broiled cod, chicken breast, and steamed vegetables.

Choose one place to symbolize the easy elegance of Laguna and it inevitably will be **Las Brisas** (361 Cliff Drive; 714-497-5434). Something about this whitewashed Spanish building with arched windows captures the natural-living-but-class-conscious style of the Southland. Its cliffside locale on the water is part of this ambience. Then there are the beautiful people who frequent the place. Plus a dual kitchen arrangement that permits formal dining in a white-tablecloth room or bistro dining on an outdoor patio. The deluxe-priced menu consists of Mexican seafood dishes and other specialties from south of the border. Out on the patio there are sandwiches, salads, and fajitas; moderate.

If any place in town can challenge Las Brisas in setting the style for Laguna Beach, it is **Ron's in Laguna** (1464 South Route 1; 714-497-4871). Rather than ocean vistas, here we are talking mirrored walls, upholstered booths, fireplaces, and potted palms everywhere, plus waiters in red shoes to match the dozens of photos of celebrities, also clad in red shoes. The continental cuisine includes duck, tournedos, rack of lamb, veal marsala, and fresh fish. Dinner, Saturday lunch, and Sunday brunch are served indoors or on the patio; deluxe.

Five Feet Restaurant (328 Glenneyre Street; 714-497-4955) prepares "Chinese cuisine European style." This "interpretation of modern Chinese cuisine" carries you from catfish to veal loin sautéed with sweet pepper. Also on the unique bill of fare is blackened venison, spring lamb in curry-cilantro sauce, and steak chinoise. Applying the principles of California cuisine to Chinese cooking and adding a few French flourishes, Five Feet has gained an impressive reputation. The decor is as avant garde as the food. Dinner only; deluxe.

Dizz's As Is (2794 South Route 1; 714-494-5250) represents one of those singular dining spots that should not be overlooked. Funk is elevated to an art form in this woodframe house. The tiny dining room is decorated with art deco pieces and 1930s-era tunes play throughout dinner. This studied informality ends at the kitchen door where a continental cuisine that includes veal piccata, Cornish game hen, chicken stuffed with cheese and shallots, halibut amandine, and cioppino is prepared by talented chefs. Deluxe; dinner only.

The most remarkable aspect of the **Cottage Restaurant** (308 North Route 1; 714-494-3023) is the cottage itself, an early 20th-century California bungalow. The place has been neatly decorated with stained glass and patterned wallpaper. Meal time in this historic house is a traditional American affair. Lunch consists of salads and sandwiches plus specials like Swiss steak, quiche, and steamed vegetables. At dinner there are sirloin tips, chicken alfredo, poached shrimp and scallops, plus daily specials like braised lamb shanks, honey-baked chicken, roast duck, and baby back ribs. Moderate.

North of town, you'll encounter a noted roadside stand called **Sunshine Cove** (7408 North Route 1; 714-494-5589). The specialty items here are the date shakes. They also offer smoothies, sandwiches, *quesadillas*, and other healthful morsels.

NEWPORT BEACH RESTAURANTS

A local favorite in Corona del Mar, the small town adjacent to Newport Beach, is **The Quiet Woman** (3224 East Route 1; 714-640-7440), a small, dark, friendly place serving mesquite-grilled food. Lunch and dinner are served, both featuring steak and seafood menus at deluxe prices.

Everything in Newport Beach was built last week. Everything, that is, except **The Cannery** (3010 Lafayette Avenue; 714-675-5777). This 1934 fish cannery is today much as it was way back when. The conveyor belts and pulleys are still here, their gears exposed; and there are fire wagons, a fierce-looking boiler, and more tin cans than you can imagine. All part of a waterfront seafood restaurant that serves lunch, dinner, and weekend brunch at deluxe prices, and that features dinner and weekend brunch cruises aboard a 54-foot boat.

Character is a quality in abundance at the **Bouzy Rouge Cafe** (3110 Newport Boulevard; 714-673-3440). A simple bistro decorated with a kind of controlled flamboyance, it's a cultural center where dinner might be combined with French lessons, a string quartet, or bossa nova vocalists. Welsh rarebit and cheese blintzes are among the breakfast specials, at lunch there are fondues and crepes, then dinner includes *tapas*, quiche, pasta, vegetable stir-fry, and roast chicken. Moderate.

Don't worry, you won't miss **The Crab Cooker** (2200 Newport Boulevard; 714-673-0100). First, it's painted bright red; secondly, it's located at a busy intersection near Newport Pier; lastly, the place has been a local institution since the 1950s. Actually, you don't *want* to miss The Crab Cooker. This informal eatery, where lunch and dinner are served on paper plates, has fish, scallops, shrimp, crab, and oysters at moderate price. There's a fish market attached to the restaurants, so freshness and quality are assured.

The Rex Restaurant (2100 West Ocean Front; 714-675-2566) is a gourmet seafood dining place that wins national awards annually. Located on the beach overlooking Newport Pier, the interior is done (or rather overdone) in a kind of shiny Victorian style with black trim and brass chandeliers. The secret is to close your eyes and surrender to the senses of taste and smell. At dinner the chef prepares *ono*, *opakapaka*, and other Hawaiian fish as well as abalone, Maine lobster, bouillabaise, and halibut. For those who miss the point there is rack of lamb, veal piccata, and filet mignon. No breakfast; ultra-deluxe.

Around **Balboa Pavilion** you'll find snack bars and amusement park food stands.

A place nearby that's worth recommending is **Newport Landing** (503 East Edgewater Avenue; 714-675-2373), a double-decker affair where you can lounge downstairs in a wood-paneled dining room or upstairs on a deck overlooking the harbor. Serving lunch, dinner, and Sunday brunch, it specializes in fresh fish selections and also features hickory-roasted prime rib, grilled duck, free-ranging chicken, and sausage with Cajun rice. While the restaurant is deluxe in price, a sister facility with alfresco seating on the water, the **Newport Landing Cafe**, serves budget-priced soups, sandwiches, and salads at lunch.

If this doesn't excite you, head over to **Jaco's** (105 Main Street; 714-675-0281), a Mexican restaurant in the courtyard of the venerable Balboa Inn. Nothing fancy, but the tile floor, potted plants, and complete menu make it well worth the budget tab.

Who could imagine that at the end of Balboa Pier there would be a vintage 1940s-era diner complete with art deco curves and red plastic booths. **Ruby's** (1 Balboa Pier; 714-675-7829) is a classic. Besides that it provides 180° views of the ocean at budget prices. Of course the menu, whether breakfast, lunch, or dinner, contains little more than omelettes, hamburgers, sandwiches, and salads. But who's hungry anyway with all that history and scenery to consider?

The top Thai restaurant hereabouts is **Bangkok 3** (101 Palm Street; 714-673-6521), a sparkling dining room painted in pastel hues and adorned with fabric paintings. The surroundings are ultramodern but the cuisine is traditional, a tasteful mix of curry and ginger dishes. Start off with chicken coconut soup or vegetable vermicelli, add a spicy beef salad, then move to the main courses. There is *ped op* (marinated baked duck), beef *satay, kai phad keng* (chicken with ginger), seafood kebab, and *pla nam lard prig* (fish in spice sauce). Be sure to try the avocado or coconut ice cream (sweetened with corn). A fine restaurant with a friendly staff; moderate.

The fact of the matter is that there are very few restaurants on Balboa Island. As a result, one place stands out. **Amelia's** (311 Marine Avenue; 714-673-6580), a family-run restaurant serving Italian-style seafood, is a local institution. At lunch you'll find them serving a half dozen pasta dishes, fresh fish entrees, sandwiches, and salads. Then in the evening the chef prepares calamari stuffed with crab, scallops, Icelandic cod, bouillabaise, veal piccata, and another round of pasta platters; moderate to deluxe; no breakfast, but they serve Sunday brunch.

If you were hoping to spend less money, **Wilma's Patio** (225 Marine Avenue; 714-675-5542) is just down the street. It's a family-style restaurant—open morning, noon, and night—that serves multicourse American meals at budget prices.

For a multicourse feast, Moroccan-style, reserve a tent at **Marrakesh** (1100 West Route 1; 714-645-8384). Decorated in the fashion of North Africa with tile floor and cloth drapes, this well-known dining room conveys a sense of Morocco. There are belly dancers on weekends and any night of the week you can experience *harira*, an aromatic soup; *jine fassi*, chicken with marinated lemon rinds; *couscous*; and a host of rabbit, lamb, quail, and chicken dishes. Deluxe.

NORTH ORANGE COUNTY RESTAURANTS

Everyone wants to eat on the water; at **The End Cafe** (Huntington Beach; 714-969-7437) you can dine out over it. This easy-going eatery sits at the end of Huntington Pier. It's an all-American establishment, serving omelettes in the morning, then hamburgers, hot dogs, and sandwiches the rest of the day. Stop in and enjoy what the cafe calls its "ten million dollar view." Budget.

Step down to the foot of the pier for more elaborate cuisine at **Maxwell's** (317 Route 1, Huntington Beach; 714-536-2555). This vintage 1924 building is done entirely in art deco fashion, a motif which nicely fits its beachfront locale. Specialty of the house is seafood; at dinner there are well over a dozen selections varying from fresh Hawaiian fish to halibut, stuffed trout, lobster, and Cajun-style shrimp. There are pasta dishes, vegetarian plates, plus veal and steak entrees. Also offering breakfast and lunch, Maxwell's is a choice spot for an oceanfront meal; deluxe.

Tibbie's Music Hall (16360 Route 1, Huntington Beach; 714-840-5661) is decidedly not the place to go for a quiet dinner on the water. If you're looking for a full-fledged musical revue with dessert, this *is* the spot. The waiters and waitresses at this popular supper club become performers later in the evening, putting together a variety show that could range from an 1890s musical medley to a tribute to the Beach Boys. Corny but fun; deluxe.

Harbor House Cafe (16341 Route 1, Huntington Beach; 213-592-5404) is one of those hole-in-the-wall places packed with local folks. In this case it's "open 24 hours, 365 days a year" and has been around since 1939. Add knotty-pine walls covered with orange-crate labels and you've got a coastal classic. The menu, as you have surmised, includes hamburgers and sandwiches. Actually it's pretty varied—in addition to croissant and pita bread sandwiches there are Mexican dishes, seafood platters, steaks, and chicken entrees, all budget-priced.

Dating back to 1930, the **Glide 'er Inn** (1400 Route 1, Seal Beach; 213-431-3022) is an unusual landmark indeed. The motif is aviation, as in model airplanes dangling from the ceiling and aeronautical pictures covering every inch of available wall space. The menu is covered with biplanes and, almost as an afterthought, includes an extensive list of seafood selections as well as European dishes like *wienerschnitzel* and veal *smetana* (sautéed in light cream and mushrooms). Dinner and Sunday brunch only; moderate to deluxe.

The Great Outdoors

The Sporting Life

FISHING AND WHALE WATCHING

Among the Orange County outfits offering sportfishing charters are: **Dana Wharf Sportfishing** (34675 Golden Lantern Road, Dana Point; 714-496-5794) and **Davey's Locker** (400 Main Street, Balboa; 714-673-1434). For those more interested in gazing at California's big grays, these companies also sponsor whale-watching cruises during the migratory season.

SKIN DIVING

The coastal waters abound in interesting kelp beds rich with sea life. To explore them contact **Black Bart's Aquatics** (34145 Route 1, Dana Point; 714-496-5891), **Ocean's Rhythms** (27601 Forbes Road, Laguna Niguel; 714-582-3883), **Mr. Scuba** (1031 South Coast Highway,

Laguna Beach; 714-494-4146), **Laguna Sea Sports** (925 North Coast Highway, Laguna Beach; 714-494-6965), and **Aquatic Center** (4537 West Coast Highway, Newport Beach; 714-650-5440).

SURFING AND WINDSURFING

Orange County is surfer heaven. So, grab a board from **Steward Sports** (2101 South El Camino Real, San Clemente; 714-492-1085), **Hobie Sports** (34195 Coast Highway, Dana Point; 714-496-1251), **Jack's Surf Ski and Sport** (34318 Coast Highway, Dana Point; 714-493-6100), or **The Fog House** (6908 West Coast Highway, Newport Beach; 714-642-5690) and head for the waves.

GOLF

The climate and terrain make for excellent golfing. Tee up at **San Clemente Municipal Golf Course** (150 Avenue Magdalena, San Clemente; 714-492-3943), **Shorecliffs Golf Course** (501 Avenida Vaquero, San Clemente; 714-492-1177), **The Links at Monarch Beach** (23841 Stonehill Drive, Laguna Niguel; 714-240-8247), **Aliso Creek Golf Course** (31106 Coast Highway, South Laguna; 714-499-1919), and **Newport Beach Golf Course** (3100 Irvine Avenue, Newport Beach; 714-852-8681).

TENNIS

Public courts are hard to find, except in San Clemente. Try, **Bonito Canyon Park** (El Camino Real and Calle Valle, San Clemente; 714-361-8264), **San Luis Rey Park** (San Luis Rey Street, San Clemente; 714-361-8264), **Verde Park** (Calle Escuela, San Clemente; 714-361-8264), **Ocean View Tennis Club** (635 Camino de los Mares, San Clemente; 714-661-1202), **Dana Hills Tennis Center** (24911 Calle de Tennis, Dana Point; 714-240-2104), and the **Marriott Hotel** (Newport Center Drive, Newport Beach; 714-640-4000).

SAILING

With elaborate marina complexes at Dana Point, Newport Beach, and Huntington Beach, this is a great area for boating. Sailboats and powerboats are available for rent at **Embarcadero Marina** (Embarcadero Place, Dana Point; 714-496-6177), **Balboa Boat Rentals** (Edgewater Avenue and Palm Street, Newport Beach; 714-673-1320), and **Balboa Pavilion** (400 Main Street, Newport Beach; 714-673-1434).

Beaches and Parks

SOUTH ORANGE COUNTY BEACHES AND PARKS

San Clemente State Beach—Walk down the deeply eroded cliffs guarding this coastline and you'll discover a long narrow strip of sand that curves north from San Diego County up to San Clemente City Beach. There are camping areas and picnic plots on top of the bluff.

Down below a railroad track parallels the beach and surfers paddle offshore. You can stroll north toward downtown San Clemente or south to former President Nixon's old home (see the "Sightseeing" section in this chapter).

Facilities: Lifeguards; picnic areas; restrooms; restaurants and groceries are nearby in San Clemente; information, 714-492-3156.

Camping: Permitted.

Swimming: Beware of rip currents.

Surfing: Year-round breaks at the north end of the beach.

Getting there: Located off Avenida Calafia in San Clemente.

San Clemente City Beach—Running nearly the length of town this silver strand is the pride of San Clemente. Landlubbers congregate near the municipal pier, anglers work its waters, and surfers blanket the beachfront. There are railroad tracks and coastal bluffs paralleling the entire beach. Eden this ain't, San Clemente is heavily developed, but the beach is a pleasant place to spend a day.

Facilities: There are restaurants and other amenities at the municipal pier; picnic areas, restrooms, lifeguard, playground, volleyball. The **Ole Hanson Beach Club** (105 Avenida Pico; 714-361-8207; admission), at the north end of the beach, is a public pool with dressing rooms.

Fishing: Try the pier.

Swimming: Good.

Surfing: Good on either side of the pier.

Getting there: The pier is at the foot of Avenida del Mar in San Clemente.

Capistrano Beach Park—This is a big rectangular sandbox facing the open ocean. Like many beaches in the area it offers ample facilities and is often quite crowded. Bounded by sedimentary cliffs and offering views of Dana Point Harbor, the beach is landscaped with palm and deciduous trees. The park is particularly popular with families and surfers.

Facilities: Picnic areas, restrooms, lifeguards, volleyball, basketball court; restaurants and groceries are nearby.

Swimming: Good.

Surfing: "Killer Capo" breaks are about 400 yards offshore along the northern fringes of the beach (near Doheny State Park). "Dody's Reef" breaks are about one half mile to the south but are not predictable.

Getting there: Located along the Coast Highway in Capistrano Beach.

Doheny State Beach—This park wrote the book on oceanside facilities. In addition to a broad swath of sandy beach there is a five-acre lawn complete with private picnic areas, beach rentals, and food concessions. The grassy area offers plenty of shade trees. Surfers work the north end of the beach and divers explore an underwater park just offshore. Dana Point Harbor, with complete marina facilities, borders the beach.

Facilities: In addition to the services above there are restrooms with changing areas, lifeguards, volleyball courts; restaurants and groceries are nearby; information, 714-496-6171.

Camping: Permitted.

Fishing: Try the jetty in Dana Point Harbor.

Swimming: Good.

Surfing: Comfortable for beginners, particularly on a south swell.

Getting there: Located off Dana Point Harbor Drive in Dana Point.

Salt Creek Beach Park—This marvelous locale consists of two half-mile sections of beach divided by a lofty point on which the Ritz Carlton Laguna Niguel Hotel stands. Each beach is a broad strip of white sand, backdropped by bluffs and looking out on Santa Catalina Island. The hotel above dominates the region like a palatial fortress on the Mediterranean. Though both beaches are part of Salt Creek, the strand to the south is also known as **Laguna Niguel Beach Park**. It's possible to walk from one beach to the other.

Facilities: Both beaches have restrooms and lifeguards; at Salt Creek (north) there is also a snack bar.

Fishing: Better at Laguna Niguel.

Swimming: Good.

Surfing: From Laguna Niguel you can surf "Dana Strand," located a short distance south. Salt Creek has two well-known breaks, "The Beach," just north of the outcropping that separates the two beaches, and at "The Point" itself.

Getting there: Laguna Niguel Beach Park is reached via a long stairway at the end of Selva Road. The staircase to Salt Creek is on Ritz Carlton Drive. Both lie off Route 1 in Laguna Niguel.

South Laguna coves (★)—Hidden by the hillsides that flank South Laguna's waterfront are a series of pocket beaches. Each is a crescent of white sand bounded by sharp cliffs of conglomerate rock. These in turn are crowned with plate-glass homes. Two particularly pretty inlets can be reached via accessways called **1000 Steps** and **West Street.**

Facilities: Both beaches have lifeguards; there are restrooms at 1000 Steps. Restaurants and groceries are nearby.

Swimming: Good.

Surfing: The bodysurfing is excellent in both coves.

Getting there: Both access ways are on Route 1 in South Laguna. 1000 Steps is at 9th Avenue; West Street is (surprise!) at West Street.

Aliso Creek Beach Park—Set in a wide cove and bounded by low coastal bluffs, this park is popular with local folks. The nearby highway buzzes past and the surrounding hills are adorned with houses. A sand scimitar with rocks guarding both ends, the beach is bisected by a fishing pier. To escape the crowds head over to the park's **southern cove** (★), a pretty beach with fluffy sand.

Facilities: Picnic areas, restrooms, showers, lifeguard, volleyball, snack bar. Restaurants and groceries are nearby.

Fishing: Good from the pier.

Swimming: Beware of strong shore breaks.

Surfing: Better for bodysurfing.

Getting there: Located along Route 1 in South Laguna; there is a public access way to the southern cove along the 31300 block of Route 1.

LAGUNA BEACH BEACHES AND PARKS

Victoria Beach (★)—Known primarily to locals, this quarter-mile sand corridor is flanked by homes and hills. The rocks on either side of the beach make for good exploring and provide excellent tidepooling opportunities. Amenities are few, but that is the price to pay for getting away from Laguna's crowds.

Facilities: Lifeguard, volleyball; restaurants and groceries are nearby.

Swimming: Okay, but watch for the strong shore break.

Surfing: Good bodysurfing.

Getting there: From Route 1 take Victoria Drive, then turn right on Dumond Street.

Moss Point (★)—This tiny gem is little more than 50 yards long, but for serenity and simple beauty it challenges the giant strands. Rocky points border both sides and sharp hills overlook the entire scene. The sea streams in through the mouth of a cove and debouches onto a fan-shaped beach.

Facilities: Lifeguard; restaurants and groceries nearby.

Swimming: The cove is well protected.

Skindiving: Surrounding rocks provide interesting areas.

Getting there: Located at the end of Moss Street.

Wood's Cove (★)—An S-shaped strand backed by Laguna's ever-loving shore bluff, this is another in the town's string of hidden wonders. Three rock peninsulas give the area its topography, creating a pair of sandy pocket beaches. The sea works in, around, and over the rocks, creating a tumultuous presence in an otherwise placid scene.

Facilities: Lifeguards; restaurants and groceries nearby.

Swimming: Well protected by rock outcroppings.

Skindiving: Good off the rocks.

Getting there: Steps from Diamond Street and Ocean Way lead down to the water.

Arch Cove—Stretching for more than a half mile, bordered by a palisade of luxury homes and resort hotels, this sandy swath is ideal for sunbathers. A sea arch and blowhole rise along the south end of the beach; the northern stretch is more populated and not as pretty.

Facilities: Lifeguards; restaurants and groceries nearby.

Swimming: Not as protected as the pocket beaches but still okay.

Surfing: There are sizeable breaks around Agate Street.

Getting there: Entrances to the beach are at the ends of Pearl Street, Agate Street, Bluebird Canyon Drive, Mountain Road, and Cress Street. As a result, you will hear sections of the strand referred to as "Pearl Beach," "Agate Beach," etc.

Street Beaches—Paralleling downtown Laguna for nearly a mile is a single slender strand known to locals by the streets that intersect it. Lined with luxury homes, it provides little privacy but affords easy access to the town's amenities.

Facilities: Lifeguards; everything you want, need, or couldn't care less about is within a couple blocks.

Swimming: Good.

Surfing: Excellent peaks are created by a submerged reef off Brooks Street, which is also a prime bodysurfing locale. The surf is also usually up around Thalia Street.

Getting there: Off Route 1 there are beach entrances at the ends of Brooks, Oak, Anita, Thalia, St. Ann's, and Cleo streets and Sleepy Hollow Lane.

Main Beach—You'll have to venture north to Muscle Beach in Venice to find a scene equal to this one. It's located at the very center of Laguna Beach, with shopping streets radiating in several directions. A sinuous boardwalk winds along the waterfront, past basketball players, sunbathers, volleyball aficionados, little kids on swings, and aging kids on rollerskates. Here and there an adventuresome soul has even dipped a toe in the wa-wa-water. In the midst of this humanity on holiday stands the lifeguard tower, an imposing glass-encased structure that looks more like a conning tower and has become a Laguna Beach icon.

Facilities: Unless someone has gotten to them first, the amenities I mentioned are all available to you. There are also restrooms, showers, picnic areas, a playground, and a grassy area.

Fishing: Try the rocks near the north end of the beach.

Swimming: Very good; well guarded.

Skindiving: The Laguna Beach Marine Life Refuge lies just offshore, making this a popular place for diving.

Getting there: Located at Route 1 and Broadway.

Heisler Park, Rock Pile Beach, and **Picnic Beach**—One of Laguna's prettiest stretches of shoreline lies along the clifftop in Heisler Park and below on the boulder-strewn sands of Rock Pile and Picnic beaches. The park provides a promenade with grassy areas and shade trees. You can scan the coastline from Laguna Beach south for miles, then meander down to the beach where sedimentary formations shatter the wave patterns and create marvelous tidepools. Rock Pile and Picnic form adjacent coves, both worthy of exploration.

Facilities: Picnic areas, restrooms, lifeguards, shuffleboard; restaurants and groceries are nearby.

Fishing: Excellent here and along most of the Laguna coast. Perch, cod, bass, and halibut inhabit these waters.

Swimming: Good at both beaches.

Skindiving: The rocks offer great places to explore.

Surfing: There is no surfing at Picnic, but Rock Pile has some of the biggest waves in Laguna Beach. The best spots are at the south end.

Getting there: Heisler Park is located along Cliff Drive. Rock Pile Beach is at the end of Jasmine Street; Picnic Beach lies to the north at the end of Myrtle Street.

Diver's Cove, Fisherman's Cove, and **Shaw's Cove**—These three miniature inlets sit adjacent to one another, creating one of Laguna Beach's most scenic and popular sections of shoreline. Each features a white-sand beach backdropped by a sharp bluff. Rock formations at either end are covered in spuming surf and honeycombed with tidepool pockets (particularly at the south end of Shaw's Cove). Well known to local residents, the beaches are sometimes crowded.

Facilities: Lifeguards; restaurants and groceries are nearby.

Fishing: Good.

Swimming: Generally good but can be hazardous at Fisherman's Cove because of rocks.

Skindiving: Excellent along this entire shoreline. Diver's Cove is often awash with scuba divers.

Getting there: All three rest along Cliff Drive. The entrances to Diver's and Fisherman's are within 50 feet of each other in the 600 block of Cliff Drive; the walkway to Shaw's Cove is at the end of Fairview Street.

Crescent Bay—This half-moon inlet is flanked by a curving cliff upon which the fortunate few have parked their palatial homes. Down on the beach, the sand is as soft and thick as the carpets in those houses. Offshore stands Seal Rock with barking denizens whose cries echo off the surrounding cliffs. This, to say the least, is a pretty place. You can swim, skin dive, sunbathe, explore the rocks and tidepools, or venture up to the vista point that overlooks this natural setting.

Facilities: Restrooms, lifeguards; restaurants and groceries are nearby.

Fishing: Good.

Swimming: A great place to take the plunge.

Surfing: Very good bodysurfing; occasionally good surfing.

Skindiving: Excellent.

Getting there: Entrances to the beach are located near the intersection of Cliff Drive and Circle Way.

Crystal Cove State Park—This outstanding facility has a long, winding sand beach which is sometimes sectioned into a series of coves by high tides. The park stretches for over three miles along the coast and extends up into the hills. Grassy terraces grace the sea cliffs and the offshore area is designated an underwater preserve. Providing long walks along an undeveloped coastline and on upland trails in El Moro Canyon, it's the perfect park when you're seeking solitude.

Facilities: Lifeguards, restrooms; restaurants and groceries are several miles away in Laguna Beach; information, 714-237-7411.

Swimming: Good.

Surfing: There are breaks north of Reef Point in Scotchman's Cove.

Getting there: Located along Route 1 between Laguna Beach and Corona del Mar. There are entrances at El Moro Canyon, Reef Point, Crystal Cove, and Pelican Point.

NEWPORT BEACH AREA BEACHES AND PARKS

Little Corona del Mar Beach—Another in the proud line of pocket beaches along the Orange Coast, this preserve features offshore rocks, tidepools, and a sea arch. The bluff to the north consists of sandstone that has been contorted into a myriad of magnificent lines. There's a marsh behind the beach thick with reeds and cattails. Unfortunately you won't be the first explorer to hit the sand; Little Corona is known to a big group of local people.

Facilities: Lifeguards; restaurants and groceries are nearby in Corona del Mar.

Fishing: Try from the rocks.

Swimming: Good.

Getting there: There is an entrance to the beach at Poppy Avenue and Ocean Boulevard in Corona del Mar.

Corona del Mar State Beach—Located at the mouth of Newport Harbor, this park offers an opportunity to watch sailboats tacking in and out from the bay. Bounded on one side by a jetty, on the other by homes, with a huge parking lot behind, it is less than idyllic. It is also inevitably crowded. Throngs congregate because of its easy access, landscaped lawn, and excellent facilities. (You will find one possible escape valve: there are a pair of pocket beaches on the other side of the rocks next to the jetty.)

Facilities: Restrooms, picnic areas, lifeguards, showers, concession stands, beach rentals, volleyball courts; information, 714-237-7411.

Fishing: Try the jetty bordering Newport Harbor.

Swimming: Very well protected.

Skindiving: Good around the jetty.

Getting there: Located at Jasmine Avenue and Ocean Boulevard in Corona del Mar.

Newport Dunes Aquatic Park—This private facility is a broad, horseshoe-shaped beach about one-half mile in length. It curves around the lake-like waters of Upper Newport Bay, one mile inland from the ocean. Very popular with families and campers, it offers a wide range of activities, including volleyball, playground activities, boat rentals, even a video arcade. There's ample opportunity for swimming, with diving rafts offshore and lifeguards on duty. The park is very popular, so plan to come for the attractions, not peace and quiet.

Facilities: In addition to the amenities mentioned there are restrooms, restaurants, groceries, picnic areas, beach rentals, and a kiddie pool. Information, 714-644-0510.

Getting there: Located at 1131 Backbay Drive in Newport Beach.

Jetty View Park—Set at the very end of the Balboa Peninsula, this triangle of sand is perfectly placed. From the tip extends a rock jetty that borders Newport Harbor. You can climb the rocks and watch boats in the bay, or turn your back on these trifles and wander across the broad sand carpet that rolls down to the ocean. There are wonderful views of Newport Beach and the coast. If you're daring enough you can challenge the waves at **The Wedge.** Known to body surfers around the world, the area between the jetty and beach is one of the finest and most dangerous shorebreaks anywhere, the "Mount Everest of bodysurfing."

Facilities: Lifeguards; restaurants and groceries are about a half mile away.

Fishing: Good from the jetty.

Swimming: The shorebreak here is fierce.

Surfing: Bodysurfing is the main sport; surfing is permitted further down the beach. But take heed, these breaks are only for veteran bodysurfers.

Getting there: Located at the end of Balboa and Ocean boulevards at the tip of the Balboa Peninsula.

Balboa Beach—This broad sandy strip forms the ocean side of Balboa Peninsula and extends along its entire length. There are entrances to the beach from numerous side streets, but the center of the facility is around Balboa Pier, a wooden fishing pier. With a palm-shaded lawn and many nearby amenities, this beach, together with neighboring Newport Beach, is the most popular spot in town.

Facilities: Restrooms, showers, lifeguards, playground, beach rentals; restaurants, groceries, etc. are near the pier.

Fishing: Good from the pier.

Swimming: Good.

Surfing: Good in different spots at different times.

Getting there: The beach parallels Balboa Boulevard. Balboa Pier is at the end of Main Street.

Newport Beach—Narrow at the northern end and widening to the south, this sandy strip extends for several miles along the base of the Balboa Peninsula. Newport Pier (also know as McFadden's Pier) and the surrounding facilities serve as the center of the strand. Here fishermen from the Newport Dory Fishing Fleet beach their boats and sell their daily catches. A wonderful beach, with entrances along its entire length, this is an important gathering place for the crowds that pour into town.

Facilities: Restrooms, lifeguards, beach rentals; restaurants, groceries, and all amenities imaginable are at the foot of the pier.

Fishing: Good from the pier.

Swimming: Good.

Surfing: Good in the morning around Newport Pier and then in the afternoon at the 30th Street section of the beach. There are year-round breaks near the Santa Ana River mouth at the far north end of the beach.

Getting there: The beach parallels Balboa Boulevard in Newport Beach. Newport Pier is between 20th and 21st streets.

NORTH ORANGE COUNTY BEACHES AND PARKS

Huntington State Beach—One of Southern California's broadest beaches, this strand extends for three miles. In addition to a desert of soft sand, it has those curling waves that surfer dreams (and movies) are made from. Pismo clams lie buried in the sand, a bike path parallels the water, and there is a five-acre preserve for endangered least terns.

Before you decide to move here permanently, take heed: these natural wonders are sandwiched between industrial plants and offshore oil derricks.

Facilities: Restrooms, picnic areas, lifeguards, showers, dressing rooms, snack bars, volleyball, beach rentals; restaurants and groceries are about two miles away in Huntington Beach; information, 714-536-3053.

Fishing: Good.

Swimming: Good when the surf is low.

Surfing: Excellent along most of the beach front.

Getting there: Located along Route 1 in Huntington Beach; entrances are at Magnolia Street, Newland Street, and Beach Boulevard.

Huntington City Beach—An urban continuation of the state beach to the south, this strand runs for several miles. One of the most famous surfing spots in the world, it is highlighted by Huntington Pier, a fishing pier with awesome surf breaks on either side. The surrounding waters are crowded with surfers in wet suits while the pier is lined with anglers. A great place for water sports and people watching. This surfer heaven gives way to an industrial inferno north of the pier where the oil derricks that plague offshore waters climb right up onto the beach, making it look more like the Texas coast than the blue Pacific.

Facilities: Picnic areas, restrooms, lifeguards, showers, volleyball courts, beach rentals; restaurants and fishing tackle shops are at the pier; information, 714-536-5281.

Fishing: Good from the pier.

Swimming: Good when the surf is flat.

Surfing: It pumps year round. There are international competitions in September.

Getting there: Located along Route 1 in Huntington Beach; the pier is at the end of Main Street.

Bolsa Chica State Beach—With six miles of fluffy sand, this is another in a series of broad, beautiful beaches. There are regular grunion runs and rich clam beds here; the beach is backdropped by the **Bolsa Chica Ecological Reserve**, an important wetlands area. Since the summer surf is gentler than at Huntington Beach, Bolsa Chica is ideal for swimmers and families.

Facilities: Picnic areas, restrooms, lifeguards, showers, snack bars, beach rentals; restaurants and groceries are nearby in Huntington Beach; information, 714-848-1566.

Camping: Permitted for self-contained vehicles only.

Fishing: Good.

Swimming: Good in summer.

Surfing: Small waves in summer, big breaks in winter.

Getting there: Located along Route 1 in Huntington Beach between Huntington Pier and Warner Avenue.

Sunset Beach and **Surfside Beach**—These contiguous strands extend over three miles along the ocean side of Huntington Harbor. Broad carpets of cushioning sand, they are lined with beach houses and lifeguard stands. Both are popular with local people, but Surfside is still a great beach to get away from the crowds.

Facilities: Sunset Beach has restrooms, lifeguards, and volleyball courts; Surfside fronts a private community and lacks facilities; restaurants and groceries are nearby.

Fishing: Good at Sunset.

Swimming: Good.

Surfing: There are reliable sandbar peaks along both beaches; spectacular winter breaks near the jetty at the end of Surfside Beach.

Getting there: Sunset extends from Warner Avenue to Anderson Street in Huntington Beach; Surfside runs north from Anderson Street, which provides the only public access to the beach.

Seal Beach—Rare find indeed, this is a local beach tucked between Huntington and Long Beach. In addition to a swath of fine-grain sand, there is a fishing pier from which you can take a **barge ride** (213-598-8677) to Long Beach. Oil derricks loom offshore and Long Beach rises in the misty distance.

Facilities: Restrooms, lifeguards; restaurants and groceries are nearby.

Fishing: Very popular from the pier.

Swimming: Good.

Surfing: Good breaks at the pier and around 13th Street.

Getting there: Located along Ocean Avenue in Seal Beach; the pier is at the intersection with Main Street.

Hiking

Though heavily developed, the Orange Coast still provides several outstanding trails. All are located near the beaches and offer views of private homes and open ocean.

The **California Coastal Trail** extends over 40 miles from San Mateo Point in San Clemente to the San Gabriel River in Seal Beach. Much of the route follows sandy beachfront and sedimentary bluffs. There are lagoons and tidepools, fishing piers, and marinas en route.

Aliso Beach Trail (1 mile) begins near the fishing pier at Aliso Beach County Park in South Laguna, leads north through a natural arch, and passes the ruins of an old boat landing.

Crown of the Sea Trail (3.5 miles) provides a seaside stroll south from Corona del Mar to Crystal Cove State Park. Starting from the East Jetty of Newport Harbor it travels one mile to Arch Rock, a natural sea arch, continues another mile to a cluster of cottages at Crystal Cove, then follows an undeveloped beach to Abalone Point, a 200-foot-high promontory.

Newport Trail (2.5 miles) traces the oceanside of Balboa Peninsula from Newport Pier south to Balboa Pier, then proceeds to the peninsula's end at Jetty View Park. Private homes run the length of this pretty beach walk.

Back Bay Trail (1.8 Miles) follows Back Bay Drive in Newport Beach along the shores of Upper Newport Bay. This fragile wetland, an important stop on the Pacific flyway, is an ideal bird-watching area.

Huntington Beach Trail (4 miles) parallels the ocean from Beach Boulevard in Huntington Beach to Bolsa Chica Lagoon. Along the way it takes in Huntington Pier, a haven for surfers, and passes an army of unspeakably ugly oil derricks.

At **Bolsa Chica Lagoon Loop Trail** (3 miles) you can say hello to some of the same birds you saw on Back Bay Trail. Another migratory rest stop, this lagoon features a loop trail which runs atop a levee past fields of cordgrass and pickleweed.

Traveler's Tracks

Sightseeing

SAN CLEMENTE

If any place is the capital of Republican politics, it is San Clemente, a seaside town which sets the standard for Southern California's notorious conservatism because of one man. Richard Milhous Nixon, President of the United States from 1969 until his ignominious resignation during the Watergate scandal in 1974, established the Western White House on a 25-acre site overlooking the ocean. **La Casa Pacifica**, a magnificent Spanish-style home, was famous not only during Nixon's presidency, but afterwards when he retreated to San Clemente to lick his wounds. There are stories of Nixon, ever the brooding, socially awkward man, pacing the beach in a business suit and leather shoes.

The Nixon house is located off Avenida del Presidente in a private enclave called Cypress Shore. You can see it, a grand white stucco home with red-tile roof, on the cliffs above San Clemente State Beach. Just walk south from the beach entrance about one half mile toward a point of land obscured by palms; the house is set back in the trees.

Another point of interest (quite literally) is **San Clemente Municipal Pier** (foot of Avenida del Mar; 714-492-1011), a popular fishing spot and centerpiece of the city beach. There are food concessions, bait and tackle shops, and local crowds galore.

SAN JUAN CAPISTRANO

When you're ready to flee Southern California's ultramodern coastline, Camino Capistrano is the perfect escape valve. Just north of San Clemente it leads from the Coast Highway up to **Mission San Juan Capistrano** (Camino Capistrano and Ortega Highway; 714-493-1111; admission). Seventh in the state's chain of 21 missions, the church was founded in 1776 by Father Junipero Serra. Considered "the jewel of the missions," it is a hauntingly beautiful site, placid and magical.

There are ponds and gardens here, archaeological sites, and the ruins of the original 1797 stone church, destroyed by an earthquake in 1812. The museum displays Native American crafts, early ecclesiastical artifacts, and Spanish weaponry, while an Indian cemetery memorializes the enslaved people who built this magnificent structure.

The highlight of the mission is not the swallows, which are vastly outnumbered by pigeons, but the chapel, a 1777 structure decorated with Indian designs and baroque *reredos*. The oldest building in California, it is the only remaining church used by Father Serra.

Of course the mission's claim to notoriety is a 1939 ditty, *When the Swallows Return to Capistrano*, a tune which, like many schmaltzy songs about California, seems to remain eternally lodged in the memory whether you want it there or not. The melody describes the return of flocks of swallows every March 19. And return they do, though in ever decreasing numbers and not always on March 19, only to depart in October for Argentina.

At the **O'Neill Museum** (31831 Los Rios Street; 714-493-8444), housed in a tiny 1870s Victorian, there are walking-tour maps of the town's old adobes. Within a few blocks you'll discover about a dozen 19th-century structures.

The **Capistrano Depot** (26701 Verdugo Street) appeared a little later in the century but is an equally vital part of the town's history. Still operating as a station, the 1895 depot has been beautifully preserved. Built of brick in a series of Spanish-style arches, the old structure houses railroad memorabilia. An antique pullman, a brightly colored freight car, and other vintage cars line the tracks.

Jolting you back to contemporary times are two nearby buildings, both constructed in the 1980s. The **New Church of Mission San Juan Capistrano** (31522 Camino Capistrano), a towering edifice next to the town's historic chapel, is a replica of the original structure. Spanish Renaissance in design, it even re-creates the brilliantly painted interior of the old mission.

Across the street rises the **San Juan Capistrano Regional Library** (31495 El Camino Real; 714-493-1752), an oddly eclectic building. Drawing heavily from the Moorish-style Alhambra in Spain, the architect also incorporated ideas from ancient Egypt and classical Greece.

DANA POINT

North on Route 1, called the Pacific Coast Highway in these parts, you'll pass through **Dana Point.** This ultramodern enclave, with its man-made port and 2500-boat marina, has a history dating back to the 1830s when Richard Henry Dana immortalized the place. Writing in *Two Years Before the Mast*, the Boston gentleman-turned-sailor described the surrounding countryside: "There was a grandeur in everything around."

Today much of the grandeur has been replaced with condominiums, leaving little for the sightseer. There is the **Orange County Marine Institute** (24200 Dana Point Harbor Drive; 714-496-2274) with a small sealife museum and a 121-foot replica of Dana's brig *The Pilgrim.*

The **Dana Point Lighthouse** (24532 Del Prado Avenue; 714-661-1001) has been converted into a nautical museum. You can tour the old beacon while viewing a collection of model sailing ships and other miniatures. Then, for a lighthouse keeper's view of the harbor and outlying coastline, take in either of the **lookout parks** at the ends of Old Golden Lantern and Blue Lantern streets.

LAGUNA BEACH

Next stop on this cavalcade of coastal cities is Laguna Beach. Framed by the San Joaquin hills, the place is an intaglio of coves and bluffs, sand beaches and rock outcroppings. It conjures images of the Mediterranean with deep bays and greenery that runs to the sea's edge.

Little wonder that Laguna, with its wealthy residents and restful beachfront, has become synonymous with the chic but informal style of Southern California. Its long tradition as an artist colony adds to this sense of beauty and bounty, aesthetics and aggrandizement.

Highlighting its artistic tradition is the **Festival of the Arts & Pageant of the Masters** (Irvine Bowl, 650 Laguna Canyon Road; 714-494-1145), staged during July and August. While the festival displays the work of local artists and craftspeople, the Pageant of the Masters is the highpoint, an event which you *must not miss.* It presents a series of *tableaux vivants* in which local residents, dressed to resemble figures from famous paintings, remain motionless against a frieze that re-creates the painting. Elaborate make-up and lighting techniques flatten the figures and create a sense of two-dimensionality. Also be sure to go **back stage** afterwards to see the friezes, and learn the techniques involved in this amazing production.

During the 1960s freelance artists, excluded from the more formal Festival of the Arts, founded the **Sawdust Festival** (935 Laguna Canyon Road; 714-494-3030) across the street. Over the years this fair too has become pretty established, but it still provides an opportunity to wander along sawdust-covered paths past hundreds of arts and crafts displays. It also runs during July and August.

Laguna Beach's artistic heritage is evident in the many galleries and studios around town. The **Laguna Beach Chamber of Commerce** (357 Glenneyre Street; 714-494-1018), with its maps and brochures, can help direct you. The **Laguna Art Museum** (307 Cliff Drive; 714-494-6531) has a wonderfully chosen collection of historic and contemporary California paintings.

Beauty in Laguna is not only found on canvases. The coastline too is particularly pretty (see the "Beaches and Parks" section in this chapter). One of the most enchanting areas is along **Heisler Park** (Cliff Drive), a winding promenade set atop seaside cliffs. Here you can relax on the lawn, sit beneath a palm tree, and take in the broad vistas of wave-whitened shoreline. Paths from the park descend to a series of coves with tidepools and sandy beaches. Here the rocks, twisted by geologic pressure into curving designs, rise in a series of protective headlands.

Cliff Drive streams along Heisler Park and then past sparkling coves and pocket beaches. At the north end of this shoreline street take a left onto Route 1, then another quick left onto Crescent Bay Drive, which leads to **Crescent Bay Point Park.** Seated high upon a coastal cliff, this landscaped facility offers views for miles along the Laguna shore.

When you're ready to leave the beach behind and head for the hills, take Park Avenue up from the center of Laguna Beach, turn right at the end onto Alta Laguna Boulevard, and right again to head back down on Temple Hills Drive and Thalia Street. This climbing course will carry you high into the **Laguna hills** with spectacular vistas along the entire coastline and into the interior valleys.

NEWPORT BEACH

Back on Route 1, head north through Corona del Mar en route to Newport Beach. A wealthy enclave with trim lawns and spacious homes, Corona del Mar offers a pretty **coastal drive** along residential Ocean Boulevard.

Also drop by the **Sherman Library and Gardens** (2647 East Route 1, Corona del Mar; 714-673-2261). Devoted to the culture and recent history of the "Pacific Southwest," this complex features a specialized library set in Early California-style buildings. Also inviting is the botanical garden, a kind of desert museum alive with cacti, succulents, and over 1000 tropical plant species.

Neighboring Newport Beach is a melange of manmade islands and peninsulas surrounding a small bay. For help finding your bearings

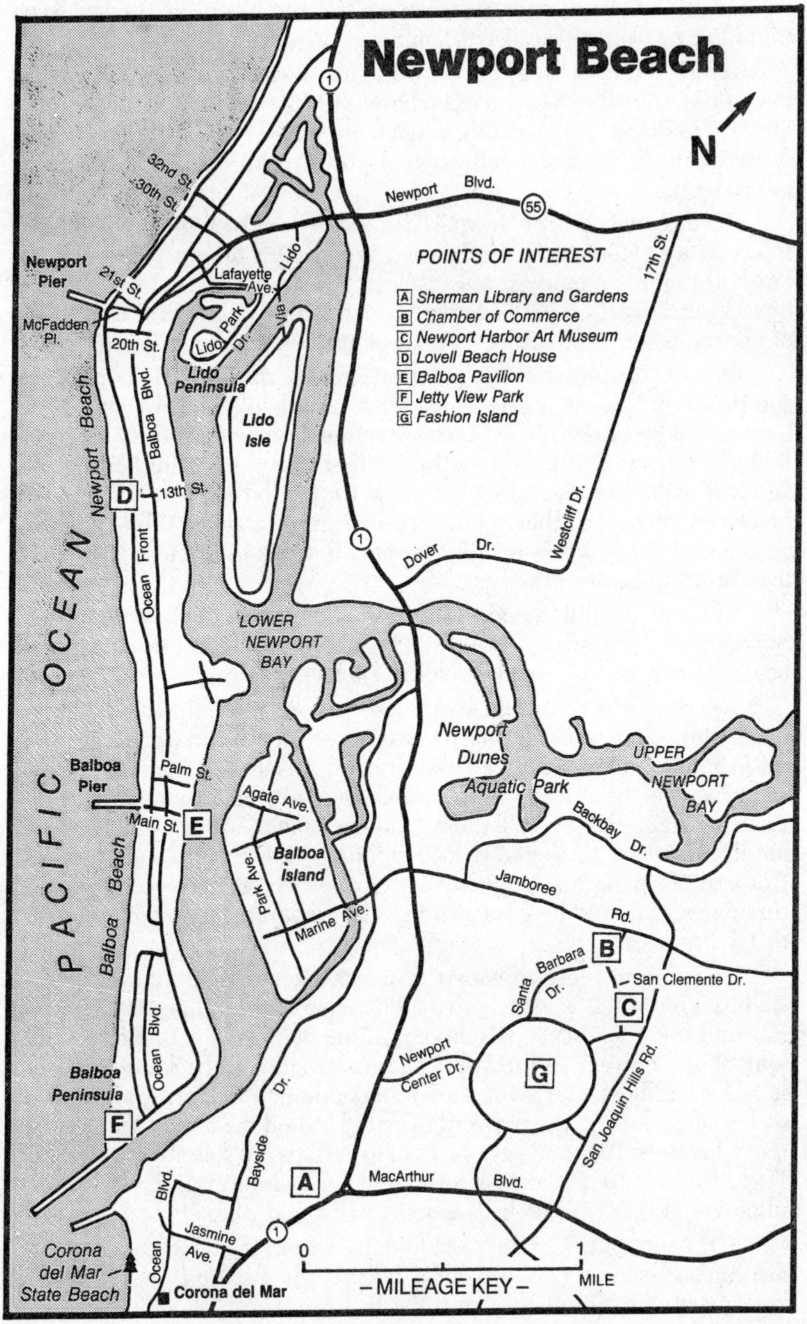

Newport Beach
N
POINTS OF INTEREST
A Sherman Library and Gardens
B Chamber of Commerce
C Newport Harbor Art Museum
D Lovell Beach House
E Balboa Pavilion
F Jetty View Park
G Fashion Island
PACIFIC OCEAN
Newport Pier
Newport Beach
Balboa Pier
Balboa Beach
Balboa Peninsula
Corona del Mar State Beach
Corona del Mar
McFadden Pl.
32nd St.
30th St.
21st St.
20th St.
13th St.
Palm St.
Main St.
Balboa Blvd.
Ocean Front
Ocean Blvd.
Lafayette Ave.
Via Lido
Lido Park Dr.
Lido
Lido Peninsula
Lido Isle
LOWER NEWPORT BAY
Agate Ave.
Park Ave.
Balboa Island
Marine Ave.
Bayside Dr.
Jasmine Ave.
Newport Blvd.
55
1
17th St.
Westcliff Dr.
Dover Dr.
Newport Dunes Aquatic Park
UPPER NEWPORT BAY
Backbay Dr.
Jamboree Rd.
Santa Barbara Dr.
San Clemente Dr.
Newport Center Dr.
San Joaquin Hills Rd.
MacArthur Blvd.
0
1
MILE
– MILEAGE KEY –

around this labyrinth of waterways, contact the **Newport Harbor Area Chamber of Commerce** (1470 Jamboree Road; 714-644-8211).

While it cannot compete with Laguna Beach as an art center, the town does offer the **Newport Harbor Art Museum** (850 San Clemente Drive; 714-759-1122). Specializing in contemporary art, this facility possesses perhaps the finest collection of post-World War II California art in existence.

Further evidence of Newport's creativity can be found at the **Lovell Beach House** (13th Street and Beach Walk). This private residence, set on the beach, is a modern masterpiece. Designed by Rudolf Schindler in 1926, it features a Bauhaus-like design with columns and cantilevers of poured concrete creating a series of striking geometric forms.

One of Newport Beach's prettiest neighborhoods is **Balboa Island**, comprised of two manmade islets in the middle of Newport Bay. It can be reached by bridge along Marine Avenue or via a short ferry ride from Balboa Peninsula. Walk the pathways that circumnavigate both islands and you will pass clapboard cottages, Cape Cod homes, and modern block-design houses that seem made entirely of glass. While sailboats sit moored along the waterfront, streets that are little more than alleys lead into the center of the island.

Another landfill island, **Lido Isle**, sits just off Balboa Peninsula. Surrounded by Newport Bay, lined with sprawling homes and pocket beaches, it is an imposingly wealthy enclave.

Nearby **Lido Peninsula** seems like yet one more upscale neighborhood. But wait a minute, doesn't that house have a corrugated roofline? And the one next to it is made entirely of metal. Far from an ordinary suburban neighborhood, Lido Peninsula is a trailer park. In Newport Beach? Granted they call them "mobile homes" here, and many are hardly mobile with their brick foundations, flower boxes, and shrubs. But a trailer park it is, probably one of the fanciest in the country, with tin homes disguised by false awnings and elaborate landscaping. Surreal to say the least.

The central piece in Newport Beach's geographic jigsaw puzzle is **Balboa Peninsula**, a long, narrow finger of land bounded by Newport Bay and the open ocean. Highpoint of the peninsula is **Balboa Pavilion** (end of Main Street), a Victorian landmark that dates back to 1905, when it was a bathhouse for swimmers in ankle-length outfits. Marked by its well-known cupola, the bayfront building hosted the nation's first surfing tournament in 1932 and gave birth to its own dance sensation, the Balboa Hop. Today it's a miniature amusement park with carousel, ferris wheel, photograph booths, skeeball, video games, and pinball machines.

Cruise ships to Catalina Island debark from the dock here and there are **harbor cruises** (714-673-5245) aboard the *Pavilion Queen*, a mock river boat which motors around the bay.

This is also home to the **Balboa Island Ferry** (714-673-1070), a kind of floating landmark that has shuttled between Balboa Peninsula and Balboa Island since 1919. A simple, single-deck ferry that carries three cars and sports a pilot house the size of a phone booth, it crosses the narrow waterway every few minutes.

The beach scene in this seaside city extends along the Pacific side of Balboa Peninsula. Here a broad white-sand beach, lined with lifeguard stands and houses, reaches for over five miles. The centers of attention and amenities are **Newport Pier** (Balboa Boulevard and McFadden Place) and **Balboa Pier** (Ocean Front Boulevard and Main Street). At Newport Pier, also known as McFadden's Pier, the skiffs of the **Newport Dory Fishing Fleet** are beached every day while local fishermen sell their catches. This flotilla of small wooden boats has been here so long it has achieved historic landmark status. At dawn the fishermen sail ten miles offshore, set trawl lines, and haul in the mackerel, flounder, rockfish, and halibut sold at the afternoon market.

To capture a sense of the beauty which still inheres in Newport Beach, take a walk out to **Jetty View Park** (end of Ocean Boulevard) at the tip of Balboa Peninsula. Here civilization meets the sea. To the left extend the rock jetties forming the mouth of Newport Harbor. Behind you are the plate-glass houses of the city. A wide beach, tufted with ice plants and occasional palm trees, forms another border. Before you, changing its hue with the phases of the sun and clouds, is the Pacific, a single sweep of water that makes those million-dollar homes seem fragile and tenuous.

Not all the wealth of Newport Beach is measured in finances. The richness of the natural environment is evident as well when you venture through **Upper Newport Bay Ecological Reserve** (Backbay Drive). Southern California's largest estuary, the bay is a vital stopping place for migrating birds on the Pacific flyway. Over 200 species can be seen here; and two endangered species, Belding's savannah sparrow and the light-footed clapper rail, live along the bay.

HUNTINGTON BEACH

Then leave this natural world behind and enter the surf capital of California. In the mythology of surfing, Huntington Beach rides with Hawaii's Waimea Bay and the great breaks of Australia. Since the 1920s boys with boards have been as much a part of the seascape as blue skies and billowing clouds. They paddle around **Huntington Pier** (end of Main Street), poised to catch the next wave that pounds the pilings. Anglers also work the pier, just past the point where the waves break. And at night Huntington's 500 fire rings blaze with light, making it one of Southern California's great party beaches.

Route 1 continues north, bordered on one side by broad beaches and on the other by **Bolsa Chica Ecological Reserve** (access ways across from the entrance to Bolsa Chica State Beach and at Warner Avenue). An important wetlands area dotted with islands and overgrown in cordgrass and pickleweed, this 530-acre preserve features a mile-long loop trail. Among the 100 animal species inhabiting the marsh are egrets, herons, and five endangered species. There are raucous seagulls as well as rare Belding's savannah sparrows and California terns.

Shopping

SAN JUAN CAPISTRANO SHOPPING

The mission town of San Juan Capistrano has a cluster of shops along its main thoroughfare, Camino Capistrano. Not surprisingly, the most common establishment in this two-century-old town is the antique store. In line with contemporary times, there are also pocket malls featuring boutiques, jewelers, and other outlets.

Particularly noteworthy are **The Old Barn** (31792 Camino Capistrano), a warehouse-size store filled to the rafters with antiques, and **El Peón** (26832 Ortega Highway), a modern emporium crowded with ironwood carvings, folk art, Peruvian wallhangings, Mexican tiles, and other Latin American imports. Also visit the **Latham Stevens Gallery** (31681 Camino Capistrano), a studio with a rotating collection of work by local artists.

LAGUNA BEACH SHOPPING

Given its long tradition as an artist colony, it's little wonder Laguna Beach is crowded with galleries and studios. In addition to painters and sculptors, the town claims to support more goldsmiths and jewelers than any place in the country. Add a few designer clothing shops plus antique stores and you have one very promising shopping spot. The center of all this action lies along Route 1 (Pacific Coast Highway) between Bluebird Canyon Drive and Laguna Canyon Road.

There are several art galleries clustered together which I found particularly interesting. Foremost is **Redfern Gallery** (1540 South Route 1); the others include **Vladimir Sokolov Studio Gallery** (1540 South Route 1), and **The Esther Wells Collection** (1930 South Route 1). All feature carefully chosen selections of contemporary California art.

At **Sherwood Gallery** (460 South Route 1), on the other hand, they have a hilarious collection of soft sculptures portraying an odd assortment of frumpy people.

Fine fashion is taken for granted at **Shebue** (540 South Route 1). This plush shop houses beautiful designer clothing for women. *Très chic* (and *très cher*).

Chicken Little's (574 South Route 1) bills itself as "The Museum of Modern Retail." Translation: they stock New Wave knickknacks like inflatable dinosaurs, ceramic fish, and Betty Boop cups. Similar in spirit, though not in age, is **Tippe Canoes** (648 South Route 1), a used clothing store with a collection of antique knickknacks.

Bookstores are as rare as radicals in Orange County. One notable exception is **Farenheit 451** (509 South Route 1), a pocket-sized pocketbook store. You won't miss it, that's for sure: the outside wall is decorated with a huge whale mural. Unfortunately, the store is much smaller than the artwork, but within its limited space is a connoisseur's collection of newspapers, magazines, hardcovers, and page turners.

Laguna Beach's other shopping strip is Forest Avenue, a three-block promenade wall-to-wall with specialty stores. **From Laguna** (241 Forest Avenue) is here, a clothing store specializing in upscale, sportswear as well as jewelry by local designers.

For imported goods there's **Khyber Pass** (263 Forest Avenue), dealing in rugs, statuary, and lapis lazuli pieces from Afghanistan, and **A Touch of Latin** (265 Forest Avenue), which carries clothing, and handcrafts from Latin and South America. **Thee Foxes Trot** (264 Forest Avenue) has an unpredictable inventory, a kind of cultural hodgepodge ranging from American Indian jewelry to African masks. For contemporary painting I particularly recommend **Diane Sassone Gallery** (278 Forest Avenue), which displays the work of modern day impressionist Marco Sassone and other artists.

There are also two rustic, raw wood malls, **Forest Avenue Mall** (332 Forest Avenue) and **Lumberyard Plaza** (384 Forest Avenue), which blend neatly into the background. The former features a pair of intriguing stores: **Kristalle Natural History Gallery** specializes in fine minerals and natural crystals, while **Aqua Classics** carries everything from jewelry and pottery to paintings and statuary, all with an aquatic theme.

NEWPORT BEACH SHOPPING

The streets radiating out from **Balboa Pavilion** (end of Main Street) are lined with beachwear stores, sundries shops, and souvenir stands. While there's little of value here, it is a good place to shop for knickknacks. The scene is much the same around **Newport Pier** (Balboa Avenue and McFadden Place).

For more upscale shopping, cast anchor at **Lido Marina Village** (Via Oporto). This well-heeled complex features a host of shops lining a brick courtyard and adjacent boardwalk.

Another Newport Beach shopping enclave lies along Marine Avenue on Balboa Island. This consumer strip is door-to-door with card shops, gift shops, and sundries stores. Without exaggerating, I would estimate that more than half the outlets here sell beachwear.

After all is said and done, but hopefully before the money is all spent, the center for Newport Beach shopping is Fashion Island (Newport Center Drive). Situated at the heart of Newport Center, the town's high-rise financial district, it is also the best place for beautiful-people watching. Every self-respecting department store is here. **Neiman Marcus**, **Buffums'**, **Bullock's Wilshire**, **Robinson's**, and **The Broadway** are all represented.

There's an outdoor plaza filled with fashion outlets and an atrium displaying three floors of designer dreams. If you don't believe Newport Beach is a match for Beverly Hills in flash and cash, take a tour of the parking lot. It's a showplace for Rolls Royces, Jaguars, and Mercedes, as well as plebian models like Volvos and Audis.

Nightlife

SOUTH ORANGE COUNTY NIGHTLIFE

The sounds are live every Thursday through Saturday evening at **Tecate Grill & Bar** (1814 North El Camino Real, San Clemente; 714-492-1710). This hacienda-style Mexican restaurant has a tile patio as well as an indoor dining area.

Swallows Inn (31786 Camino Capistrano, San Juan Capistrano; 714-493-3188) is a hellbent Western bar with sawdust on the floors and ranch tools tacked to the walls. As you've already guessed, the music is country and western. A band kicks into action every evening.

More appealing is the **Capistrano Depot Restaurant** (26701 Verdugo Street, San Juan Capistrano; 714-496-8181), a converted station house where you can lounge in an old pullman car while listening to a duo perform nightly. They also feature jazz on Sunday afternoon.

The **Wind & Sea Restaurant** (34699 Golden Lantern Street, Dana Point; 714-496-6500), on the waterfront in Dana Point Harbor, features sparkling views and solo entertainers nightly.

The ultimate evening destinations are at the ultra-posh Ritz Carlton Laguna Niguel (33533 Shoreline Drive, Laguna Niguel; 714-240-2000). Here, along corridors of polished stone, is the **Club Grill and Bar**, a wood-paneled rendezvous decorated with 19th-century paintings of sporting scenes, and an elegant dark-wood lounge called **The Bar.** The first offers a combo nightly and the latter features a solo pianist. Dinner jackets, gentlemen.

LAGUNA BEACH NIGHTLIFE

Admirers of art deco are bound to fall in love with the **Towers Lounge** in the Surf & Sand Hotel (1555 South Route 1; 714-497-4477). This softly lit piano bar combines the ambience of the 1930s with wide-angle views of the ocean.

The White House (340 South Route 1; 714-494-8088) is a landmark 1918 building in downtown Laguna Beach. A long, narrow lounge with dark-wood paneling and mirrored walls, it turns tradition upside down every night with live rock, reggae, and Motown; cover.

One of Laguna Beach's hottest nightspots is also its most funky. **The Sandpiper** (1183 South Route 1; 714-494-4694) is a rundown club filled with dart boards and pinball machines. Often it is also filled with some of the finest sounds around. Rock, reggae, and other music is live nightly, sometimes performed by well-known groups.

Las Brisas (361 Cliff Drive; 714-497-5434), a sleek, clifftop restaurant overlooking the ocean, is a gathering place for the fast and fashionable. A wonderful place to enjoy a quiet cocktail, it features a tile bar as well as an open-air patio.

Cabaret entertainment is the order of the evening, every evening, at **Ron's in Laguna** (1464 South Route 1; 714-497-4871). This plush supper club is *the* place to be seen in fashionable Laguna.

Laguna Beach's gay scene centers around the **Boom Boom Room** (1401 South Route 1; 714-494-9071) at the Coast Inn. A three-tiered discotheque one-half block from the beach, it contains a dancefloor, pinball machines, and two bars. Weekend cover.

NEWPORT BEACH NIGHTLIFE

For an evening on Newport Bay, climb aboard the *Pavilion Queen*, a double-deck boat which departs from the Balboa Pavilion on a **harbor cruise** (end of Main Street; 714-673-6245).

There's live jazz nightly at the **Studio Cafe** (100 Main Street; 714-675-7760), a waterfront watering hole near Balboa Pier.

Even if you don't care for 1930s-era sounds, stop by **Bubbles Balboa Club** (111 Palm Street; 714-675-9615). This art deco club is trimly decorated with vintage accouterments and highpointed by a translucent "bubble column." The music fits the period motif, ranging from the Ink Spots to a 14-piece band; live nightly.

Rumplestiltskin's (114 McFadden Place; 714-673-5025) has rock music and dancing seven nights a week. The rhythms range from hard rock to New Wave; very popular with locals; a good party bar.

The Cannery (3010 Lafayette Avenue; 714-675-5777), an old fish cannery that's been converted into a restaurant-cum-museum (and a fascinating one at that), has entertainment nightly. During the week a duo performs mellow music, then on weekends a full-bore band pounds out rock rhythms.

NORTH ORANGE COUNTY NIGHTLIFE

The after-dark scene in Huntington Beach centers around the pier, where beach fires and parties rage long into the night. At the foot of the pier, **Maxwell's** (317 Route 1; 714-536-2555), an art deco lounge, offers groups playing Top-40 music Wednesday through Saturday.

CHAPTER FOUR

Los Angeles Coast

L.A., according to a popular song, is a great big freeway. Actually this sprawling metropolis by the sea is a great big beach. From Long Beach north to Malibu is a 74-mile stretch of sand that attracts visitors in the tens of millions every year. Life here reflects the culture of the beach, a freewheeling, pleasure-seeking philosophy that combines hedonism with healthfulness.

Perfectly fitted to this philosophy is the weather. The coastal climatic zone, called a maritime fringe, is characterized by cooler summers, warmer winters, and higher humidity than elsewhere in California. Sea breezes and salt air keep the beaches relatively free from smog. During summer months the thermometer hovers around 75° or 80° and water temperatures average 67°. Winter carries intermittent rain and brings the ocean down to a chilly 55°.

Add a broadly ranging coastal topography and Los Angeles has an urban escape valve just minutes from downtown. The shoreline lies along the lip of the Los Angeles basin, a flat expanse interrupted by the sharp cliffs of the Palos Verdes Peninsula and the rocky heights of the Santa Monica Mountains. There are broad strands lapped by gentle waves and pocket beaches exploding with surf. Though most of the coast is built up, some sections remain raw and undeveloped.

Route 1, the Pacific Coast Highway, parallels the coast the entire length of Los Angeles County, tying its beach communities together. To the south lie Long Beach and San Pedro, industrial enclaves which form the port of Los Angeles, a world center for commerce and shipping. Embodying 50 miles of heavily developed waterfront, the port is a maze of inlets, islets, and channels protected by a six-mile breakwater. It is a region of technological superlatives—the largest manmade harbor in the world, center of the seafood canning industry, the most productive port in the country. Despite all this hubbub, the waterfront supports 100 fish species and over 80 types of birds, including several endangered species.

The great port dates to 1835 when a small landing was built on the shore. Following the Civil War an imaginative entrepreneur named Phineas Banning developed the area, brought in the railroad, and launched Los Angeles into the 20th century. Now Long Beach wears several hats. In addition to being a major port and manufacturing center, it is the site of a naval base and a revitalized tourist center. Home to the retired ocean liner *Queen Mary* and financier Howard Hughes' dream plane, the *Spruce Goose*, Long Beach also contains the neighborhood of Naples, a system of islands, canals, and footbridges reminiscent of Italy's gondola cities.

Once an amusement center complete with airship, carousel, and sword swallowers, the city became one big oil field during the 1920s. That's when wildcat wells struck rich deposits and the region was transformed into a two-square-mile maze of derricks. Even today the offshore "islands" hide hundreds of oil wells.

Commercial fishing, another vital industry in Long Beach and San Pedro, supports an international collection of sailors. Mariners from Portugal, Yugoslavia, Greece, and elsewhere work the waterfront and add to the ethnic ambience.

Just a few miles north, along the Palos Verdes Peninsula, blue collar gives way to white collar and the urban surrenders to the exotic. A region of exclusive neighborhoods and striking geologic contrasts, Palos Verdes possesses Los Angeles' prettiest seascapes. A series of 13 marine terraces, interrupted by sheer cliffs, descend to a rocky shoreline. For 15 miles the roadway rides high above the surf past tidepools, rocky points, a lighthouse, and secluded coves.

This wealthy suburban environment is replaced in turn by another type of culture, typified by blond-haired surfers. Santa Monica Bay, the predominant feature of the Los Angeles Coast, is a single broad crescent of sand extending 30 miles from Redondo Beach through Venice and Santa Monica to Point Dume. South Bay—comprising the towns of Redondo Beach, Hermosa Beach, and Manhattan Beach—is the surfing center of Southern California, where the sport was first imported from Hawaii. This strip of coast is also home to Los Angeles International Airport and is considered the world's top aerospace research center.

Like most of the coastal communities, South Bay didn't take off as a beach resort until the turn of the century, after railroad lines were extended from the city center to the shore and several decades after downtown Los Angeles experienced its 1880s population boom.

It was well into the 20th century, 1962 to be exact, that neighboring Marina Del Rey, the largest manmade small boat harbor in the world, was developed. Nearby Venice, on the other hand, was an early 1900s attempt to re-create its Italian namesake. Built around plazas and grand canals, Venice originally was a fashionable resort town with oceanfront

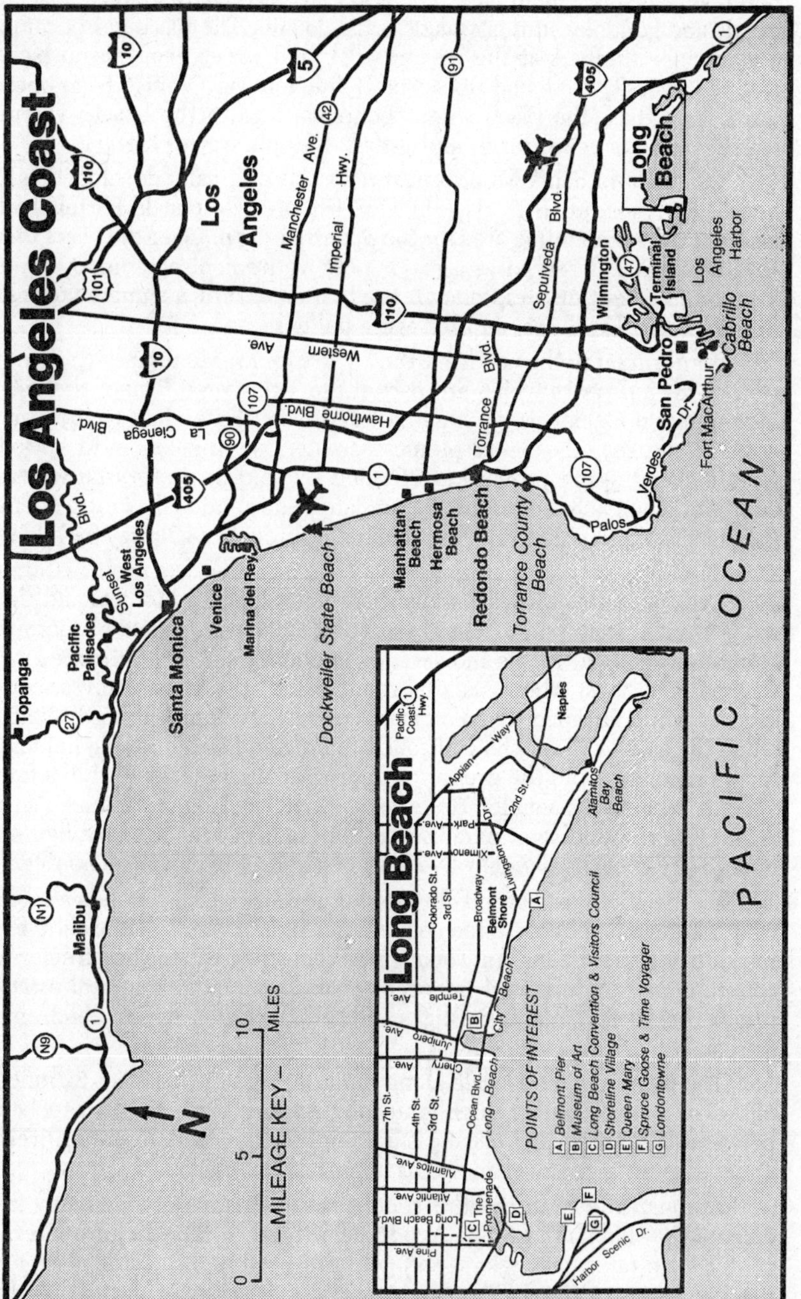

Los Angeles Coast
Topanga
Pacific Palisades
Malibu
Santa Monica
West Los Angeles
Sunset Blvd.
Venice
Marina del Rey
Dockweiler State Beach
Manhattan Beach
Hermosa Beach
Redondo Beach
Torrance County Beach
Palos Verdes Dr.
San Pedro
Fort MacArthur
Cabrillo Beach
Los Angeles Harbor
Terminal Island
Wilmington
Long Beach
Los Angeles
La Cienega Blvd.
Hawthorne Blvd.
Western Ave.
Manchester Ave.
Imperial Hwy.
Sepulveda Blvd.
Torrance Blvd.
PACIFIC OCEAN
N
0
5
10
MILEAGE KEY
MILES
Long Beach
Pacific Coast Hwy.
Naples
Appian Way
2nd St.
Park Ave.
Ximeno Ave.
Livingston Dr.
Colorado St.
3rd St.
Broadway
Belmont Shore
Alamitos Bay Beach
Temple Ave.
Juniper Ave.
Cherry Ave.
7th St.
4th St.
3rd St.
Ocean Blvd.
Long Beach City Beach
Alamitos Ave.
Atlantic Ave.
Long Beach Blvd.
Pine Ave.
The Promenade
Harbor Scenic Dr.
POINTS OF INTEREST
A Belmont Pier
B Museum of Art
C Long Beach Convention & Visitors Council
D Shoreline Village
E Queen Mary
F Spruce Goose & Time Voyager
G Londontowne

hotels and an amusement park. Today studios and galleries have replaced canals and gondolas in this seaside artist colony. The place has become a center for thinkers at the cutting edge and street people who have stepped over it. Zany and unchartable, modern-day Venice is an open ward for artists, the place where bohemians go to the beach, where roller skating is an art form, and weight lifting a way of life.

The town of Santa Monica next door was originally developed as a beachside resort in 1875. Back in 1769 explorer Gaspar de Portola had claimed the surrounding area for the Spanish crown. Over the years this royal domain has served as a major port, retirement community, and location for silent movies; today it is a bastion of brown-shingle houses, flower-covered trellises, and left-wing politics.

Bordering it to the north are the Santa Monica Mountains, a succession of rugged peaks which are part of the Transverse Range, the only mountains in California running east and west. Extending to the very edge of the sea, the Santa Monicas create Los Angeles' most varied terrain. White-sand beaches are framed by bald peaks, crystal waters and flourishing kelp beds attract abundant sealife and make for excellent fishing and skindiving, while the mountains provide a getaway for hikers and campers.

Lying along a narrow corridor between the Santa Monicas and the sea is Malibu, that quintessential symbol of California, a rich, glamorous community known for its movie stars and surfers. Once inhabited by Chumash Indians, whose skeletal remains are still occasionally uncovered, Malibu escaped Los Angeles' coastal development until 1928, when the aging widow who controlled the region like a personal fiefdom finally succumbed to the pressures of progress and profit. Within a few years it became a haven for Hollywood. Stars like Ronald Coleman and John Gilbert found their paradise on the sands of Malibu. Like figures out of *The Great Gatsby*, they lived insouciant lives in movie-set houses.

By the 1960s artists and counterculturalists, seeking to flee a town which in turn had become too commercial and crowded, left Malibu for the outlying mountains. In Topanga Canyon they established freeform communities, undermined in recent years by breathtaking real estate prices, but still retaining vestiges of their days as a flower children's retreat.

The most romantic locale along the Los Angeles Coast lies 22 miles offshore. Santa Catalina, highlighted by Avalon, a resort town tucked between mountains and ocean, is a 28-mile-long island almost entirely undeveloped, given over to cactus and grazing buffalo.

Through the centuries this solitary island has undergone many incarnations—habitat for Stone Age Indians; base for Russian fur hunters; center for pirates, smugglers, and gold prospectors; gathering place for the big bands of the 1930s; and strategic military base during World

War II. Today it's a singular spot where visitors enjoy the amenities of Avalon and the seclusion of the island's outback. If Avalon, with its art deco waterfront, provides a picture of Los Angeles circa 1933, the rest of the island is a window on Los Angeles in its natural state, wild and alluring, long before freighters embarked from Long Beach, surfers worked the South Bay, and movie moguls uncovered Malibu.

Easy Living

Transportation

ARRIVAL

Route 1, which parallels the coast throughout Los Angeles County, undergoing several name changes during its course, is the main coastal route. **Route 101** shadows the coast further inland, while **Route 405** provides access to the Los Angeles basin from San Diego and **Route 10** arrives from the east.

BY AIR

Two airports bring visitors to the Los Angeles coast area: the small **Long Beach Airport** and the very big, very busy **Los Angeles International Airport.**

Presently, carriers into Long Beach are **American Airlines** (800-433-7300), **Alaska Airlines** (800-426-0333), **America West** (800-247-5692), **Delta Airlines** (800-523-7777), **Jet America** (800-255-0565), **Pacific Southwest Airlines** (800-435-9772), and **United Airlines** (800-241-6522).

Los Angeles International Airport, better known as LAX, is served by many domestic and foreign carriers. Currently (and this seems to change daily) the following airlines fly into LAX: **Alaska Airlines** (800-426-0333), **American Airlines** (800-433-7300), **Braniff Airlines** (800-272-6433), **Continental Airlines** (800-525-0280), **Delta Air Lines** (800-221-1212), **Eastern Airlines** (800-327-8376), **Hawaiian Airlines** (800-367-5320), **Horizon Airlines** (800-547-9308), **Northwest Orient Airlines** (800-225-2525), **Pan American World Airways** (800-221-1111), **Piedmont Airlines** (800-251-5720), **Pacific Southwest Airlines** (800-435-9772), **Southwest Airlines** (415-885-1221), **Trans World Airlines** (800-221-2000), **United Airlines** (800-241-6522), **USAir** (800-428-4322), and **WestAir Airlines** (800-225-9993).

International carriers are also numerous: **Air Canada** (800-422-6232), **British Airways** (800-247-9297), **CAAC** (415-392-2156), **China Airlines** (800-227-5118), **Canadian Airlines International** (800-426-7000), **Japan Airlines** (800-525-3663), **Lufthansa German Airlines** (800-645-

3880), **Mexicana Airlines** (800-531-7921), **Philippine Airlines** (800-435-9725), **Qantas Airways** (800-227-4500), **Singapore Airlines** (800-742-3333), and **TACA International Airlines** (800-535-8780).

The Airport in the Sky (213-510-0143), set at 1600-foot elevation in the mountains of Santa Catalina, may be the prettiest landing strip anywhere. The small terminal building conveys a mountain lodge atmosphere with a stone fireplace adorned by a trophy bison head. **Allied Air Charter** (213-510-1163) and **Resort Commuter Airlines** (714-546-2444) service the airport from the mainland.

Another means of transportation to Catalina is **Island Express** (800-228-2566), a helicopter service from Long Beach and San Pedro. (They also offer around-the-Island tours.) Or try **Helitrans** (800-262-1472), a commuter jet helicopter service from San Pedro to Avalon.

BY BOAT

Several companies provide regular transportation to Catalina by boat. The island is just "26 miles across the sea," but it's still necessary to make advance reservations. **Catalina Express** (P.O. Box 1391, San Pedro; 213-519-1212) has service to Avalon and Two Harbors from the Catalina Terminal in San Pedro; **Catalina Cruises** (P.O. Box 1948, San Pedro; 213-775-6111) travels from the Catalina Landing in Long Beach and the Catalina Terminal in San Pedro to Two Harbors and Avalon; and **Catalina Passenger Service** (400 Main Street, Newport Beach; 714-673-5245) has service from Orange County. (Catalina Passenger Service provides transportation only from Easter through October with weekend service December 26 to Easter.)

BY BUS

Greyhound Bus Lines has service to the Los Angeles area from all around the country. The Long Beach terminal is located at 6601 Atlantic Avenue (213-428-7777); the main Los Angeles station is at 208 6th Street (213-620-1200); the Santa Monica terminal is at 1433 5th Street (213-394-5433).

Green Tortoise (P.O. Box 24459, San Francisco, CA 94124; 415-821-0803), is an alternative New Age bus company that runs funky buses equipped with sleeping platforms. It stops at unusual sightseeing spots and offers an experience in group living. The bus leaves San Francisco for Los Angeles once a week.

BY TRAIN

Amtrak (Union Station, 800 North Alameda Street, Los Angeles; 800-872-7245) will bring you into Los Angeles via the "Coast Starlight" from the Northwest, the "San Diegan" from San Diego, the "Desert Wind" and "Southwest Chief" from Chicago, the "Eagle" from Chicago by way of Texas, and the "Sunset Limited" from New Orleans.

CAR RENTALS

Having a car in Los Angeles is practically a must. Distances are great and public transportation leaves much to be desired. As you can imagine, it's not difficult to find a car rental agency. The challenge is to find the best deal. Be sure to request a mileage-free rental, or one with at least some free mileage. One thing is certain in the Los Angeles area, you'll be putting many miles on the car.

If you arrive by air, consider renting a car at the airport. These cost a little more but eliminate the hassles of getting to the less expensive agencies.

At the Long Beach Airport you'll find **Avis Rent A Car** (213-421-3767), **Budget Rent A Car** (213-421-7172), **Dollar Rent A Car** (213-421-8841), **Hertz Rent A Car** (213-420-2322), **Sears Rent A Car** (213-432-9917), and **National Car Rental** (213-421-8877).

Some outfits outside the airport provide free pick-up and will be less expensive than agencies located at the airport. In Long Beach these include **Agency Rent A Car** (213-426-8126), **Amerex Rent A Car** (213-498-8663), **Avon Rent A Car** (213-420-1007), **Don Kott Extra Car Rent A Car** (213-498-7816), **Altra Auto Rental** (714-534-1702), **Thrifty Rent A Car** (213-494-5054), and **Snappy Car Rental** (213-425-1271).

To save even more money, try agencies that rent used cars. In the Long Beach area these include **Ugly Duckling Rent A Car** (213-212-6144), **ABC U Save Rent A Car** (213-599-5444), **Rent A Dent Car Rental** (213-804-1453), and **Rent a Car Cheep** (213-436-7900).

Looking for a car at Los Angeles International Airport will bring you to **Avis Rent A Car** (213-646-5600), **Budget Rent A Car** (213-645-4500), **Hertz Rent A Car** (213-646-4861), and **National Rent A Car** (213-670-4950).

Agencies providing free airport pick-up service include **Ajax Rent A Car** (213-746-1626), **Altra Auto Rental** (213-534-5296), **Avon Rent A Car** (213-568-9991), **Dollar Rent A Car** (213-645-9333), **Enterprise Rent A Car** (213-649-5400), **Rent Rite** (213-673-0300), **Snappy Car Rental** (213-670-2660), **Sunset Car Rental** (213-823-3327), and **Thrifty Rent A Car** (213-645-1880).

Used-car rentals in the Los Angeles area can be found at **Rent A Car Cheep** (213-678-9146), **Rent A Wreck** (213-478-0676), or **Ugly Duckling Rent A Car** (in West Los Angeles, 213-478-4208; Marina Del Rey, 213-827-9666).

In Catalina, golf carts are the only vehicles permitted for sightseeing Avalon. Check with **Cartopia Cart Rentals** (213-510-2493) or **Island Rentals** (125 Pebbly Beach Road; 213-510-1456). For further information on vehicle rentals on Santa Catalina Island see the "Sightseeing" section in this chapter.

PUBLIC TRANSPORTATION

Long Beach Transit (1300 Gardenia Avenue, Long Beach; 213-591-2301) transports riders throughout the Long Beach area.

RTD Bus Line (425 South Main Street, Los Angeles; 213-273-0910) serves the Los Angeles area from Topanga Beach south; disabled riders can call a hotline for information, 213-972-3509.

In Santa Monica, call the **Big Blue Bus** (Santa Monica Municipal Bus Lines, 1660 Seventh Street; 213-451-5444).

In Catalina, **Catalina Island Shuttle** (213 Catalina Street, Avalon; 213-510-2078) has daily inland safari excursions and service to all campgrounds. **Catalina Safari Bus** (213-510-2800) provides daily buses from Avalon to Two Harbors, Little Fishermans Campground, Black Jack, Little Harbor, and The Airport in the Sky.

TAXIS

From Long Beach Airport **Long Beach Yellow Cab** (213-435-6111) provides taxi service.

Several cab companies serve Los Angeles International Airport, including **Airport Taxi Service** (213-837-7252), **Blue & Yellow Cab** (213-204-4833), and **LA Taxi** (213-412-8000).

In Catalina you will find the **Catalina Cab Company** (213-510-0025).

BICYCLING

Though Los Angeles might seem like one giant freeway, there are scores of bike trails and routes for scenic excursions. Foremost is the **South Bay Bike Trail**, with over 19 miles of coastal vistas. The trail, an easy ride, extends from King Harbor in Redondo Beach to the Santa Monica Pier and is extremely popular and crowded. It passes the Venice Boardwalk, as well as piers and marinas along the way.

Naples, a Venice-like neighborhood in Long Beach, provides a charming area for freeform bike rides. There are no designated paths but you can cycle with ease past beautiful homes, parks, and canals.

Of moderate difficulty is the **Palos Verdes Peninsula** coastline trail. Offering wonderful scenery, the 14-mile round trip ride goes from Malaga Cove Plaza in Palos Verdes Estates to the Wayfarers Chapel. (Part of the trail is a bike path, the rest follows city streets.)

The **Santa Monica Loop** is an easy ride starting at Ocean Avenue and going up San Vicente Boulevard, past Palisades Park and the Santa Monica Pier. Most of the trail is on bike lanes and paths; ten miles round trip.

In **Catalina** bikes are permitted only in Avalon. Permits are required (free) and may be obtained at the Los Angeles County Parks Office (213 Catalina Street; 213-510-0688). Cross-channel carriers have special requirements for transporting bicycles and must be contacted in advance for complete details.

For additional information on bike routes in Los Angeles contact the Department of Transportation (City of Los Angeles Room 1200, City Hall, Los Angeles, CA 90012; 213-485-3051) for maps and brochures.

BIKE RENTALS

To rent bikes in coastal Los Angeles try **Fun Bunns** (1106 Manhattan Avenue, Manhattan Beach; 213-379-4898), **Jeffers** (1338 Strand, Hermosa Beach; 213-372-9492), **RPM Rent A Car** (36 Washington Street, Marina del Rey; 213-399-6331), **Rollerskates of America** (64 Windward Avenue, Venice; 213-399-4481), **Spokes 'n Stuff** (Venice Boardwalk; 213-306-3332), and **Sea Mist Skate Rentals** (1619 Ocean Front Walk, Santa Monica; 213-395-7076).

In Catalina try **Brown's Bikes** (107 Pebbly Beach Road, Avalon; 213-510-0986).

Hotels

LONG BEACH AND SAN PEDRO HOTELS

Beach Terrace Manor Motel (1700 East Ocean Boulevard, Long Beach; 213-436-8204) is a 44-unit complex which occupies both sides of a side street off Long Beach's main drag. Mock-Tudor in design, the facility has some units fronting the beach; many others are equipped with kitchen facilities. Guest rooms are comfortable if undistinguished. At moderate price for a room with a kitchen, the Beach Terrace provides a fair bargain.

The **Surf Motel** (2010 East Ocean Boulevard, Long Beach; 213-437-0771), a similar layout, has 40 units, some with ocean views, many offering kitchens and all with easy access to the beach. Each room is furnished in contemporary fashion. There's a pool and jacuzzi. Prices are moderate, deluxe for ocean front.

Granted I'm a fool for gimmicks, but somehow the opportunity to stay aboard an historic ocean liner seems overwhelming. Where else but at the **Hotel Queen Mary** (Pier J, Long Beach; 213-435-3511) can you recapture the magic of British gentility before World War II. What other hotel offers guests a "sunning deck?" Staying in the original state rooms of this grand old ship, permanently docked on the Long Beach waterfront, you are surrounded by the art deco designs for which the Queen Mary is famous. Some guest rooms are small (this *is* a ship!) and dimly illuminated through portholes, but the decor is classic. There are also restaurants, lounges, and shops onboard. Prices begin in the deluxe range.

The **Los Angeles International Hostel** (3601 South Gaffey Street, San Pedro; 213-831-2836) is located in the army barracks of old Fort MacArthur. Set in Angel's Gate Park on a hilltop overlooking the ocean, it's a pretty site with easy access to beaches. Men and women are housed separately in dorms; kitchen facilities are provided; guests can not occupy rooms during the day; budget.

SOUTH BAY HOTELS

Route 1 barrels through Los Angeles' beach towns and serves as the commercial strip for generic motels. As elsewhere, these facilities are characterized by clean, sterile rooms and comfortable, if unimaginative surroundings. **Starlite Motel** (716 South Route 1, Redondo Beach; 213-540-2406) and **East West Motel** (625 South Route 1, Redondo Beach; 213-316-1184), for instance, each with about two dozen units, have accommodations at budget prices. Or try the **Hi View Motel** (100 South Route 1, Manhattan Beach; 213-374-4608).

The **Portofino Inn** (260 Portofino Way, Redondo Beach; 213-379-8481) is a big, brassy hotel set on King Harbor. Many of the 133 units are decorated with textured wallpaper, colorful furnishings, and shag carpets. Some of these squeaky clean rooms face the ocean while others look out on the adjoining marina. There is a decorous lobby facing the waterside swimming pool; restaurants and other facilities are nearby in the marina. Very comfortable if a little sterile, the hotel has rooms in the deluxe to ultra-deluxe range.

The best bargain on lodging in South Bay is found at **Sea Sprite Apartment Motel** (1016 Strand, Hermosa Beach; 213-376-6933). Located right on Hermosa Beach, this multibuilding complex offers oceanview rooms with kitchenettes at moderate price. The accommodations are tidy, well furnished, and fairly attractive. There is a swimming pool and sundeck overlooking the beach. The central shopping district is just one block away, making the location hard to match. You can also rent suites at deluxe prices or a turn-of-the-century, two-bedroom beach cottage (ultra-deluxe). Be sure to ask for an oceanview room in one of the beachfront buildings.

The **Sea View Inn** (3400 Highland Avenue, Manhattan Beach; 213-545-1504) is an eight-unit stucco hotel a block up from the beach. There's a tiny swimming pool, plus two floors of guest rooms, equally as cramped. You'll find nicked furniture, wall-to-wall carpeting, refrigerator, and cable television in accommodations that are tidy if undistinguished. But it is close to the surf and lodging is rare in these parts, so. . . . Moderate.

Manhattan Motel (4017 Highland Avenue, Manhattan Beach; 213-545-9020), located on the same busy street and with similar partial ocean views, has small, non-descript rooms at moderate prices. Again, the appeal is location rather than ambience.

Far from the South Bay beach scene, though only a mile inland, is **Barnabey's Hotel** (3501 North Route 1, Manhattan Beach; 213-545-8466), a sprawling 128-room Edwardian-style hostelry. Re-creating turn-of-the-century England, Barnabey's provides stylish guest rooms with antique furnishings, floral-pattern carpets, and vintage wallpaper. The lobby is finished in dark woods and appointed with gilded clocks and crystal light fixtures. There's a restaurant and British pub and guests also enjoy a pool and jacuzzi. Deluxe.

VENICE, SANTA MONICA, AND MALIBU HOTELS

There's nothing quite like **The Venice Beach House** (15 30th Avenue, Venice; 213-823-1966). That may well be because there are so few bed and breakfast inns in the Los Angeles area. But it's also that this is such a charming house, an elegant and spacious California bunglow-style home built early in the century. The living room, with its beam ceiling, dark-wood paneling, and brick fireplace, is a masterwork. Guests also enjoy a sunny alcove, patio, and yard. The stroll to the Venice boardwalk and beach is only one-half block. The nine guest rooms are beautifully appointed and furnished with antiques; each features patterned wallpaper and period artwork. Add to this the fact that rooms with shared bath are moderate in price (deluxe for private bath) and I can't recommend the place highly enough.

Also consider the **Marina Pacific Hotel** (1697 Pacific Avenue, Venice; 213-452-1111). Located in the commercial center of Venice only 100 yards from the sand, this three-story hostelry has a small lobby and cafe downstairs. The guest rooms are spacious, nicely furnished, and well maintained; very large one-bedroom suites, complete with kitchen and fireplace, are also available. All rooms have small patios; standard accommodations are moderately priced, suites are deluxe.

Ocean Avenue, which runs the length of Santa Monica, paralleling the ocean one block above the beach, boasts the most hotels and the best location in town. Among its varied facilities are several generic motels. These are all-American type places furnished in veneer, carpeted wall-to-wall, and equipped with telephones and color televisions. If you book a room in one, ask for quiet accommodations since Ocean Avenue is a busy, noisy street.

One such establishment, the **Breakers Motel** (1501 Ocean Avenue, Santa Monica; 213-451-4811), a 34-unit facility, features a small swimming pool. Rooms are moderately priced; accommodations with kitchenettes are deluxe in price. Or save a few dollars and step next door to the **Pacific Sands Motel** (1515 Ocean Avenue, Santa Monica; 213-395-6133). The furniture is nicked and there are paint spots at this 68-unit facility, but there is a pool; moderate. **Auto Motel** (1447 Ocean Avenue, Santa Monica; 213-393-9854) lacks the pool, but otherwise is a 31-unit carbon copy; moderate.

A better bargain by far is the **Bayside Hotel** (2001 Ocean Avenue, Santa Monica; 213-396-6000). Laid out in motel fashion, this two-story complex offers plusher carpets and plumper furniture than motels hereabouts and is decorated with patterned wallpaper. More important, it's just 50 yards from the beach across a palm-studded park. Many rooms have ocean views; no pool; moderate.

If location, location, and location are the three most important factors in real estate, then the **Hotel Drake** (33 Pico Boulevard, Santa Monica; 213-394-9354) is truly a find. This 12-unit resting place is perhaps 100 yards from the water and has several rooms overlooking the beach. Since the building is old, the accommodations are timeworn, but each room is tidy and neatly furnished. Carpeting, wallhangings, and color television are among the accouterments. Each room has a kitchenette and is priced in the budget to moderate range, making the Drake one of the best deals in Santa Monica. Ask for a room with a view.

The **Pacific Shore Hotel** (1819 Ocean Avenue, Santa Monica; 213-451-8711) looks the part of a contemporary Southern California hotel. One block from the beach, this sprawling 168-room facility boasts a pool, sauna, jacuzzi, and sundeck. There's a restaurant off the lobby as well as a lounge and gift shop. Guests are whisked to their rooms in a glass elevator. The accommodations are furnished with modular pieces painted in brilliant enamels; the appointments are art deco and the wallpaper has been roughed to resemble raw fabric; private balconies. Slightly plastic, but what the hell.

The Sovereign (205 Washington Avenue, Santa Monica; 213-395-9921) on the other hand is the classic Southern California hostelry. Constructed during the 1920s, it's a massive whitewashed building. The style is Mediterranean and the sheer size of the structure lends grandeur to the place. The lobby is filled with antiques and designed with a series of archways leading in all directions. Each guest room is furnished differently—some in art deco fashion, others with Oriental pieces or antiques. Despite the remodeling you're liable to find a carpet stain here or a paint nick there, but the rooms are very large and attractively appointed. Matter of fact, the moderate price on standard rooms, and deluxe tab on the huge "superior" rooms with kitchens and terraces, make this one of the best hotel bargains in town; three blocks from the beach.

Now forget everything I've said. Never mind the variety and quality of accommodations here, there's only one place to stay in Santa Monica. Just ask Cybil Shepherd, Diane Keaton, Bill Murray, or Gene Hackman. They all stay at the **Hotel Shangri-La** (1301 Ocean Avenue, Santa Monica; 213-394-2791). The place is private, stylish, and nothing short of beautiful. A 1939 art deco building with a facade like the prow of a steamship, the 55-room home-away-from-papparazzi is entirely remodeled. The art moderne-era furniture has been laminated and lacquered and each appointment is a perfect expression of the period. Randy Newman filmed his "I Love L.A." rock video here, but it seems more likely that you'll see detective Philip Marlowe saunter in with liquor on his lips and a bulge beneath his jacket. Located on the palisades one block above Santa Monica Beach, every room sports an ocean view. Rooms (with kitchens) price in the deluxe range. There's no pool or restaurant, but the hotel has a sundeck, serves continental breakfast and afternoon tea, and is close to the beach, shops, and pier.

There are several motels scattered along the coastal highway in Malibu, two of which I particularly recommend. **Topanga Ranch Motel** (18711 Route 1, Malibu; 213-456-5486) is a 30-unit complex that dates back to the 1920s. Here are cute little cottages painted white with red trim and clustered around a circular drive. Granted they're somewhat timeworn, but each is kept neat and trim with plain furnishings and little decoration. A few have kitchens and all of them, including some two-room suites, are moderately priced. A good deal for a location right across the highway from the beach.

At **Casa Malibu Motel** (22752 Route 1, Malibu; 213-456-2219) you'll be in a 21-room facility that actually overhangs the sand. Located smack in the center of Malibu, the building features a central courtyard with lawn furniture and ocean view plus a balcony dripping with flowering plants. The deluxe-priced rooms are decorated in an attractive but casual fashion; some have private balconies, kitchens, and/or ocean views.

SANTA CATALINA ISLAND HOTELS

One fact about lodging in Catalina everyone seems to agree upon is that it is overpriced. Particularly during summer months, when Avalon's population swells from under 3000 to over 10,000, hotels charge stiff rates for rooms. But what's a traveler to do? The island is both pretty and popular, so you have no recourse but to pay the piper.

It's also a fact that rates jump seasonally more than on the mainland. Summer is the most expensive period, winter the cheapest, with spring and fall somewhere in between. Weekend rates are also sometimes higher than weekday room tabs.

The last fact of life for lodgers to remember is that since most of the island is a nature preserve, the hotels, with one lone exception, are located in Avalon.

Low price lodgings are as rare as snow in Avalon. But at the **Hotel Atwater** (127 Sumner Street; 213-510-1788) you'll find accommodations priced in the moderate category. What that buys is a room with a veneer dresser, nicked night tables, soft mattress, spotty carpet, postage stamp bathroom, and, if it's like the room I saw, a hole in the wall. But, hey, the place *is* clean and this *is* Catalina. Besides it has a friendly lobby with oak trim and naugahyde furniture plus 152 rooms to choose from. Good luck.

One of Santa Catalina's most popular hotels is the **Pavilion Lodge** (513 Crescent Avenue; 213-510-1788), a 72-room facility on Avalon's waterfront street. Designed around a central courtyard, it offers guests a lawn and patio for sunbathing. The rooms contain modern furniture, wall-to-wall carpeting, and stall showers. For decoration there are vintage Catalina prints. If you want to be at the heart of downtown in a comfortable if undistinguished establishment, this is the place. Rates are moderate in winter, deluxe during the rest of the year.

Further along the same street is **Hotel Villa Portofino** (111 Crescent Avenue; 213-510-0508) with 34 rooms situated around a split-level brick patio. The accommodations are small but have been stylishly decorated with art deco furniture, dressing tables, and wallpaper in pastel shades. There are tile baths with stall showers. A small lobby downstairs has been finished with potted plants and antique pieces. Deluxe rates are in effect year-round on weekends and during the week from May through October; on weekdays during the rest of the year moderate rates apply.

It's a big, bold, blue-and-white structure rising for five levels above the hillside. **Hotel Catalina** (129 Whittley Avenue; 213-510-0027) has been a fixture on the Avalon skyline since 1892. The 32-unit facility features a comfortable lobby complete with overhead fans, plus a sundeck and jacuzzi. There's even a private movie theater here. The sleeping rooms are small but comfy with standard furnishings; many offer ocean views. There are also trim little cottages that are warmly decorated. A bright, summer atmosphere pervades the place. Deluxe.

La Paloma Cottages (top of Sunny Lane; 213-510-0737), a rambling complex consisting of several buildings, features a string of contiguous cottages at deluxe prices. These are cozy units with original decor and comfortable furnishings. There are also larger family units (with kitchens) available at similar cost in a nearby building. Set on a terraced street in a quiet part of town, La Paloma is attractively landscaped. No daily maid service.

Catalina Canyon Hotel (888 Country Club Drive; 213-510-0325) is a chic, modern 80-room complex complete with pool, jacuzzi, sauna, weight room, restaurant, bar, and room service. This Mediterranean-style hotel sits on a hillside in Avalon Canyon. The grounds are nicely landscaped with banana plants and palm trees. Each guest room is furnished in white oak, adorned with art prints, and decorated in a motif of soft hues. This jet set landing ground requires an ultra-deluxe ticket from May through October, deluxe during the rest of the year.

Rare and incredible is the only way to describe **The Inn on Mt. Ada** (P.O. Box 6560, Avalon, CA 90704; 213-510-2030). Nothing on the island, and few places along the California coast, compare. Perched on a hillside overlooking Avalon and its emerald shoreline, this stately hostelry resides in the old Wrigley mansion, a 7000-square-foot Georgian

Colonial home built by the chewing gum baron in 1921. A masterwork of french doors and elegant columns, curved ceilings, and ornamental molding, the grande dame is beautifully appointed with antiques, curios, and plush furnishings. The entire ground floor—with rattan sitting room, oceanfront veranda, formal dining room, and spacious living room—is for the benefit of visitors. Wine is served in the afternoon and there's a full breakfast every morning. The wonder of the place is that all this luxury serves just six guest rooms, guaranteeing personal service and an atmosphere of intimacy. The private rooms are stylishly furnished in period pieces and adorned with a creative selection of artwork. Ultra-deluxe.

Banning House Lodge (Two Harbors; 213-510-0303), the only hotel on the island located outside Avalon, serves as a hunting lodge during the winter months and a remote resort in the summer. Set in the isthmus that connects the two sections of Santa Catalina, it's a low-slung shingle building with a dining facility and a mountain lodge atmosphere. The living room boasts a brick fireplace and is adorned with a dozen trophy heads. Staring out dolefully from the wood-paneled walls are deer, bison, fox, wild turkey, boar, and mountain goats. The guest rooms are bland but comfortable with formica floors, chipped furniture, no wall decorations, and shared baths. A bit rustic, it nevertheless provides an excellent opportunity to experience the island's outback. Moderate.

Restaurants

LONG BEACH AND SAN PEDRO RESTAURANTS

If you don't like hamburgers, you are fated never to set foot in **Hamburger Henry** (4700 East 2nd Street, Long Beach; 213-433-7070). It's a cosmic center for burger lovers everywhere, a diner decorated in neon and painted with murals of 50s-era convertibles. The counter has swivel stools and there are individual jukeboxes in the booths. Get the picture? We're talking vintage cuisine in a local hotspot that's open 24 hours a day. There are hamburgers served with pineapple or peanut butter, blue cheese or deep-fried bananas, caviar or ice cream, eggs or apples. They also serve breakfast dishes, salads, chili, and special dinner platters. Definitely a scene; patio dining; moderate. Hamburgers with ice cream?

Crab Shell Restaurant (5374 2nd Street, Long Beach; 213-434-1856) dishes out fresh seafood at moderate prices. The decor, not surprisingly, is nautical. Fish nets, glass balls, trophy fish, etc. The menu is similarly dedicated to salmon, trout, scallops, shrimp, crab, shark, and sea bass. Other than that you'll find a few steaks in the evening and hamburgers at lunch. No breakfast.

Lebanese cuisine is the order of the day at **Sahara Restaurant** (5333 East 2nd Street, Long Beach; 213-439-1518). Open evenings only, they offer the obligatory shish kebab as well as leg of lamb with Lebanese potato stew, grape leaves, "Sahara chicken" (baked with garlic and spices), falafel, and kafta kebab (ground beef and lamb broiled with tomato and green chile). This small, simple restaurant has a mural running the entire length of one wall. Moderate.

Southern cooking at the **Shenandoah Cafe** (4722 East 2nd Street, Long Beach; 213-434-3469) is becoming a tradition among savvy shore residents. The quilts and baskets decorating this understated establishment lend a country air to the place. Add waitresses in aprons dishing out hot apple fritters and it gets downright homey. Dinner is all she wrote here, but it's a special event occasioned with "riverwalk steak" (flank steak in mustard caper sauce), shrimp in beer batter, country-style sausage, gumbo, "granny's fried chicken," and Texas-style beef brisket. Moderate. Try it!

The Reef (880 Harbor Scenic Drive, Long Beach; 213-435-7096) is rambling, ramshackle, and wonderful. Built of tin, old planks, and spare parts, it sits along the waterfront on a dizzying series of levels. Don't be deceived by the slapdash look; it's just for effect at this deluxe-priced Cajun and Creole restaurant. The walls may be decorated with rusty signs and old farm implements, but the cuisine specializes in Southern gourmet selections. There's blackened red fish, halibut in pecan sauce, jambalaya, and bayou-style red snapper. For the Yankees, there are steaks, swordfish, and rack of lamb. Lunch and dinner only.

What more elegant a setting in which to dine than aboard the Queen Mary (Pier J, Long Beach; 213-435-3511). A boarding fee is charged on weekends, but during the week you're permitted on the ship's restaurant deck for free. There you will find everything from snack kiosks to coffee shops to first class dining rooms.

The **Promenade Cafe** offers a moderately priced menu of chicken teriyaki, steak, seafood, and vegetarian dishes. They also have salads, sandwiches, and hamburgers. The coffee shop is a lovely art deco room with wicker furnishings and period lamps.

For a true taste of regal life aboard the old ship, cast anchor at **Sir Winston's.** The continental cuisine in this deluxe-priced dining emporium includes rack of lamb, breast of capon, beef medallions, roast duckling with raspberry sauce, sautéed scallops, and broiled swordfish with caviar. Open at lunch and dinner, Sir Winston's is a wood-paneled dining room with copper-rimmed mirrors, white tablecloths, and upholstered armchairs. The walls are adorned with photos of the great Prime Minister and every window opens onto a full view of Long Beach.

The vintage shopping mall at **Ports O' Call Village** (entrance at the foot of 6th Street, San Pedro) is Los Angeles Harbor's prime tourist center. It's situated right on the San Pedro waterfront and houses numerous restaurants. Try to avoid the high ticket dining rooms, as they are overpriced and serve mediocre food to out-of-town hordes. But there are a number of take-out stands and ethnic eateries, priced in the budget and moderate ranges, which provide an opportunity to dine inexpensively on the water.

Of course local fishermen rarely frequent Ports O' Call. The old salts are over at **Canetti's Seafood Grotto** (309 22nd Street, San Pedro; 213-831-4036). It ain't on the waterfront, but it is within casting distance of the fishing fleet. Which means it's the right spot for fresh fish platters at moderate prices. Dinner on Friday and Saturday; breakfast and lunch all week.

For ethnic cuisine, why not go Yugoslavian or Greek. **Cigo's** (915 South Pacific Avenue, San Pedro; 213-833-0949) will fill the former bill with an Adriatic menu that includes *pljeskavica* (minced steak), *burek* (cheese, meat, and onions rolled in thin dough leaves), and *cevapcici* (Yugoslav sausage). Regional murals and waitresses in local dress add to the atmosphere. Moderate; lunch and dinner.

Trade the Adriatic for the Aegean and set anchor at **Papadakis Taverna** (301 West 6th Street, San Pedro; 213-548-1186). It's dinner only with a menu that features *moussaka,* Greek-style cheese dishes, and daily specials like stuffed eggplant, fresh seafood, and regional delicacies. Moderate.

The Grand House (809 South Grand Avenue, San Pedro; 213-548-1240), the finest restaurant hereabouts, sits in a 50-year-old Mediterranean home decorated with an ever-changing art exhibit. The house is warm and intimate and the cuisine provides a culinary adventure. Call ahead to reserve the private dining room upstairs (a snug hideaway for two with a private balcony adjoining), then order from a Continental-cum-California cuisine menu that changes daily. Perhaps they'll be serving sweetbreads flambéed with cognac, tenderloin of pork with white wine, tournedos topped with truffles and pâté, or swordfish à l'orange. Regardless of the day's fare, it's bound to be delicious. Lunch, dinner, and Sunday brunch; deluxe.

PALOS VERDES PENINSULA RESTAURANTS

Restaurants are a rare commodity along the Palos Verdes Peninsula. You'll find a cluster of them, however, in the Golden Cove Shopping Center. Granted, a mall is not the most appetizing spot to dine, but in this case who's complaining.

There's **Francesco's Italian Gourmet** (31218 Palos Verdes Drive West, Rancho Palos Verdes; 213-541-3350), a homey little cafe with congenial staff. Here you can order pizza, sandwiches, and a variety of pasta dishes at budget prices; lunch and dinner.

Then there's **The Admiral Risty** (31250 Palos Verdes Drive West, Rancho Palos Verdes; 213-377-0050). It's one of those nautical cliche restaurants decorated along the outside with ropes and pilings and on the interior with brass fixtures. Know the type? Normally I wouldn't mention it, but the place has a full bar, a knockout view of the ocean, and happens to be the only member of its species in the entire area. My advice is to play it safe and order fresh fish (or never leave the bar). It's dinner and Sunday brunch only, ladies and gentlemen. The menu is a surf-and-turf inventory of local fish (prepared four ways), steaks, chicken dishes, and so on. Deluxe.

For genuine elegance, make lunch or dinner reservations at **La Rive Gauche** (320 Tejon Place, Palos Verdes Estates; 213-378-0267), an attractively appointed French restaurant. With its upholstered chairs, brass wall sconces, and vintage travel posters, this cozy dining room is unique to the peninsula. The dinner menu is a study in classic French cooking including veal loin sautéed with cream sauce, duck à l'orange, stuffed quail, frog's legs Provençal, filet mignon bernaise, and rack of lamb. The lunch offerings, while more modest, follow a similar theme. In sum, excellent gourmet cuisine, warm ambience, and ultra-deluxe tabs.

SOUTH BAY RESTAURANTS

In downtown Redondo Beach, just a couple blocks from the water, are several small restaurants serving ethnic cuisines. **Village Cafe** (247 Avenida del Norte, Redondo Beach; 213-316-9806) specializes in Thai dishes and seafood. Open for lunch and dinner; moderate. **Petit Casino** (1767 South Elena Avenue, Redondo Beach; 213-543-5585), a French bakery, serves quiche, *croque monsieur*, soups, salads, and sandwiches. At **Kikusui** (1809 Catalina Avenue; 213-375-1244) there is a sushi bar as well as a menu featuring other Japanese dishes.

In addition to serving good Asian food, **Thai Thani** (1109 South Route 1, Redondo Beach; 213-316-1580) is an extremely attractive restaurant. Black trim and pastel shades set off the blond-wood furniture and etched glass. There are fresh flowers all around plus a few well placed wall prints. The lunch and dinner selections include dozens of pork, beef, vegetable, poultry, and seafood dishes. Unusual choices like spicy shrimp coconut soup, whole pompano smothered in pork, and whole baby hen make this a dining adventure. Budget to moderate.

One wall of **Millie Riera's Seafood Grotto** (1700 Esplanade, Redondo Beach; 213-375-1483) is entirely filled with a plate-glass view of the ocean. The rest of this family-run restaurant is decorated with flowers and traditional walllhangings. Open for lunch, dinner, and Sunday brunch, the "grotto," true to its title, specializes in seafood. Expect to find bouillabaise, cracked crab, lobster newburg, sea bass, and a few steak entrees at deluxe prices.

The Strand, a pedestrian byway paralleling the waterfront in Hermosa Beach, is lined with small restaurants. **La Playita By The Sea** (Strand and 14th Street, Hermosa Beach; 213-374-9542) has a complete

Mexican menu at budget prices. They offer a take-out stand if you're headed for the beach or an oceanview patio for leisurely dining. **Good Stuff On The Strand** (Strand and 13th Street, Hermosa Beach; 213-374-2334) has hamburgers, pita-bread sandwiches, and, in the evening, entrees like ratatouille, teriyaki steak, calamari, and quiche; budget.

Albanian cuisine? Albania, in case you've forgotten, is that tiny Balkan country that went communist after World War II and hasn't been heard from since. But its culinary tradition lives on at **Ajeti's Restaurant** (425 Pier Avenue, Hermosa Beach; 213-379-9012). Open for dinner only, this small dining room with the oversized chandelier serves lamb dishes, excellent salads, and a host of Balkan-style platters. Priced moderate to deluxe.

For a taste of elegance consider **Jeanette's** (807 21st Street, Hermosa Beach; 213-376-9838), a Cajun-and-American restaurant. There's a mirrored dining room and brick fireplace plus a garden patio with a canvas roof that rolls back to reveal a brilliant sky. Open for lunch and dinner, this comfortable restaurant features painted platters like almond crusted roughy; they also offer blackened prime rib, gumbo, jambalaya, and Cajun barbeque shrimp. More traditional fare includes rack of lamb, duckling, filet mignon, and stuffed chicken breast. Add a host of appetizers and salads for a filling and fulfilling dining experience. Deluxe.

Gourmet cuisine at moderate price is the order of the day at **El Rio** (1128 Hermosa Avenue, Hermosa Beach; 213-374-8884). This postage stamp eatery features "authenic cuisines of Mexico and the Southwest," charbroiled or lightly sautéed. Entrees include papaya chicken, steak picado, shrimps in salsa, and *pescado Vera Cruz* (red snapper with salsa), plus black beans and rice. Open for lunch and dinner daily, breakfast on weekends, it serves high-quality fresh food.

Cafe Pierre (317 Manhattan Beach Boulevard, Manhattan Beach; 213-545-5252) is another excellent choice for budget-minded gourmets. This fashionable French bistro—with pastel walls, art prints, and skylight—offers the same moderate-priced menu at lunch and dinner. You can feast on veal sweetbreads cognac, boneless saddle of lamb, marinated chicken on a bed of spinach, roast duckling, rainbow trout, and scallops Provençal. There are different daily specials at lunch and dinner, which in the evening may include stuffed swordfish, venison, or pheasant.

No restaurants line the strand in Manhattan Beach, so you'll have to make do with the pier's snack shop or trot a half-block uphill to **Hibachi** (120 Manhattan Beach Boulevard, Manhattan Beach; 213-374-9493). Here is a take-out stand and a patio crowded with sawed-off picnic tables. Beach-goers chow down on hamburgers and hot dogs while table diners feast on stir-fry, seafood platters, teriyaki dishes, and other Japanese entrees. Lunch and dinner only; budget.

From the outside it's certainly unassuming. A diminutive dining room in a suburban shopping mall. The furniture is blond wood. The decor consists of oil paintings from the American Southwest. But behind the simple surfaces lies one of the region's finest, most innovative restaurants. **St. Estephe** (2640 Route 1 North, Manhattan Beach; 213-545-1334) is a pioneer in modern Southwestern cuisine. Blending American Indian foods with Southwestern herbs and spices, then preparing them in a French nouvelle style, the restaurant has created a series of unique dishes. Lamb, veal, poultry, fish, and scallops are part of the fare, and so is rattlesnake. Sauces are painted onto the plate, creating swirling, multihued designs reminiscent of New Mexico landscapes. Highly recommended by friends and critics alike, it is open for lunch and dinner, priced ultra-deluxe, and well worth a visit.

VENICE RESTAURANTS

The best place for finger food and junk food in all Southern California might well be the *boardwalk* in Venice. Along Ocean Front Walk are vendor stands galore serving pizza, yogurt, hamburgers, falafels, submarine sandwiches, corn dogs, etc., etc.

Regardless, there's really only one spot in Venice to consider for dining. It simply *is* Venice, an oceanfront cafe right on the boardwalk, **The Sidewalk Cafe** (1401 Ocean Front Walk; 213-399-5547). Skaters whiz past, drummers beat rhythms in the distance, and the sun stands like a big orange wafer above the ocean. Food is really a second thought here, but eventually they are going to want you to spend some money. So, on to the menu. . . Breakfast, lunch, and dinner are what you'd expect—omelettes, sandwiches, hamburgers, pizza, and pasta. There are also fresh fish dishes plus platters of wok-fried vegetables, steak, spicy chicken, and fried shrimp. Budget.

For a step uptown take a walk down the boardwalk to **Land's End Restaurant** (323 Ocean Front Walk; 213-392-7472). This beachfront establishment is a white-tablecloth dining room with tile floor, brick walls, and a baby grand piano. Cozy and spiffy, it features a varied menu including swordfish *grenobloise*, Lake Superior white fish, scampi, veal piccata, duck à l'orange, and tournedos. There's also an extensive wine list; the lunch menu offers burgers, sandwiches, egg dishes, quiche, and fresh oysters; deluxe.

The landing ground for Venetians is a warehouse dining place called **The Rose Cafe** (220 Rose Avenue; 213-399-0711). There's a full-scale deli, bakery counter, and a restaurant offering indoor and patio service. The last serves three meals daily, including moderately priced dinners like angel hair pasta with flaked salmon, sea scallops with mango purée, roast duck, sautéed sweetbreads, and a couple vegetarian dishes. A good spot for pasta and salad, The Rose Cafe, with its wall murals and paintings, is also a place to appreciate the vital culture of Venice.

"A New Age of humankind has evolved," and the folks at **The Comeback Inn** (1633 West Washington Boulevard; 213-396-7255) are intent on nourishing it. This vegetarian restaurant, serving dinner only, has an exotic menu ranging from pizza with sunflower cheese to *tempe* to raw fruit pie. The dining room is slightly austere with wooden booths and a small counter, but as an alternative there's a large patio surrounded by palms and succulents. Budget.

Even in avant garde Venice people still yearn for mom's apple pie. Hence the popularity of **Merchant of Venice** (1349 West Washington Boulevard; 213-396-3105), where breakfast sticks to your ribs and dinner includes pan-fried pork chops, vegetable casserole, chicken with cornbread stuffing, and bread pudding for dessert. A light, airy dining room, Merchant of Venice has a touch of the early West about it. Perhaps it's the wooden booths, vintage circus posters, and rambling atmosphere; moderate.

In the mood for Asian cuisine? **Hama** (213 Windward Avenue; 213-396-8783) is a well-respected Japanese restaurant in the center of Venice. The place features an angular sushi bar, a long, narrow dining room, and a patio out back. The crowd is young and the place is decorated to reflect Venice's vital culture. There are paintings on display representing many of the area's artists. In addition to scrumptious sushi, Hama offers a complete selection of Japanese dishes including tempura, teriyaki, and *sashimi*. Dinner only; moderate.

For a gourmet restaurant tabbed in the ultra-deluxe price range, **West Beach Cafe** (60 North Venice Boulevard; 213-823-5396) is quite understated. The walls are cinderblock, adorned by contemporary artworks, and the chairs are metal-and-plastic. But track lighting and skylights add flourish while the menu demolishes any doubts about the standing of this trendy eating place. Open for breakfast, lunch, and dinner, the restaurant serves unusual dishes like *penne* with eggplant and sausage, Norwegian king salmon on marinated salt cod, and chicken with *foie gras*. The lunch menu is equally creative and in the evening after 11:30 they serve gourmet pizza. *Très chic, très* California.

72 Market Street (72 Market Street; 213-392-8720) could be the last word in modern art restaurants. The place is a warren of brick, mirrors, opaque glass, and studio lights. It's adorned with striking art pieces and equipped with a sound system that seems to be vibrating from the inner ear. Moderne to the max, the restaurant serves Cajun-style catfish, grilled Louisiana sausages, and other regional dishes. Open for lunch, dinner, and Sunday brunch, it also hosts an oyster bar; deluxe.

SANTA MONICA RESTAURANTS

Santa Monica is a restaurant town. Its long tradition of seafood establishments has been expanded in recent years by a wave of ethnic

(Text continued on page 160.)

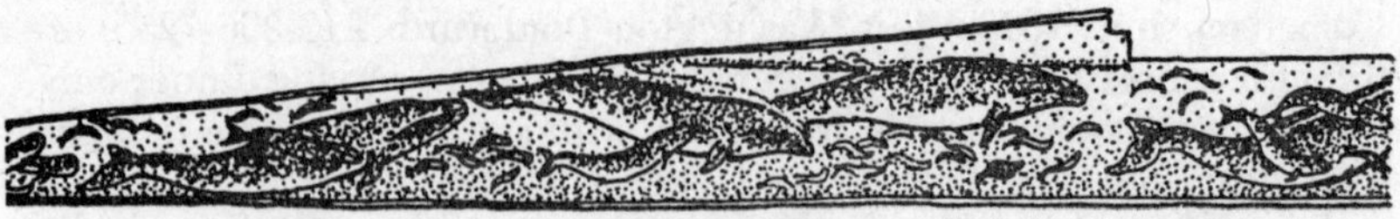

The Murals of Venice and Santa Monica

Nowhere is the spirit of Venice and Santa Monica more evident than in the murals adorning their walls. Both seaside cities house major art colonies and the numerous galleries and studios make them important centers for contemporary art.

The region's free-wheeling, individualistic lifestyle has long been a magnet for painters and sculptors. Over the years, as more and more artists made their homes here, they began decorating the twin towns with their art. The product of this creative energy lives along street corners and alleyways, on storefronts and roadways.

Crowded with contemporary and historic images, these murals express the inner life of the city. Some are officially commissioned and appear on major thoroughfares, others represent guerrilla art and are found in out-of-the-way spots.

Murals adorn nooks and crannies all over Venice. You'll find a cluster of them around Windward Avenue between Main Street and Ocean Front Walk. The interior of the **Post Office** (Main Street and Windward Avenue) is adorned with public art. There's a *trompe l'oeil* mural nearby that beautifully reflects the street (Windward Avenue)

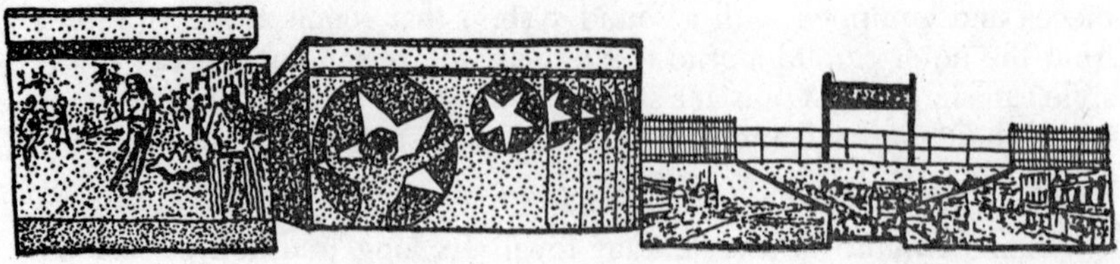

along which you are gazing. The Venice Pavilion down the street near the beach features a brilliant **parody** of Botticelli's "Venus Rising from the Foam," with Venus on roller skates.

At last count Santa Monica boasted about two dozen outdoor murals. Route 1, or Lincoln Boulevard, is a corridor decorated with local artworks. **John Muir Woods** (Lincoln and Ocean Park boulevards) portrays a redwood forest; **Early Ocean Park and Venice Scenes** (two blocks west of Lincoln Boulevard along Kensington Road in Joslyn Park) captures the seaside at the turn of the century. Nearby Marine Park (Marine and Frederick streets) features **Birthday Party,** with a Noah's ark full of celebratory animals, and **Underwater Mural,** which pictures the world of the deep.

Ocean Park Boulevard is another locus of creativity. At its intersection with the 4th Street underpass you'll encounter **Whale Mural,** illustrating whales and underwater life common to California waters, and **Unbridled,** which pictures a herd of horses fleeing from the Santa Monica Pier carousel. One of the area's most famous murals awaits you at Ocean Park Boulevard and Main street, where **Early Ocean Park** vividly re-creates scenes from the past.

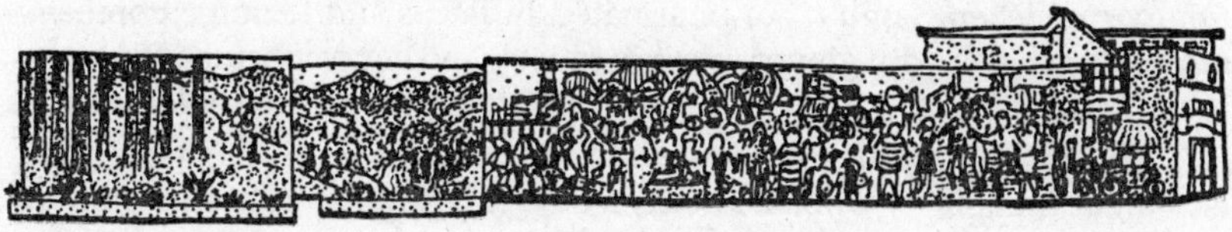

and California cuisine restaurants. While some of the most fashionable and expensive dining rooms in Los Angeles are right here, there are also many excellent and inexpensive cafes. Generally you'll find everything from the sublime to the reasonable located within several commercial clusters—near the beach along Ocean Avenue, downtown on Wilshire and Santa Monica boulevards, and in the chic, gentrified corridors of Main Street and Montana Avenue.

One of the best places in Southern California for stuffing yourself with junk food while soaking up sun and having a whale of a good time is the **Santa Monica Pier** (foot of Colorado Avenue). There are taco stands, fish and chips shops, hot dog vendors, oyster bars, snack shops, pizzerias, and all those good things guaranteed to leave you clutching your stomach. The prices are low to modest and the food is amusement park quality.

There's a sense of the Mediterranean at the sidewalk cafes lining Santa Monica's Ocean Avenue: palm trees along the boulevard, ocean views in the distance, and (usually) a warm breeze blowing. Any of these bistros will do (since it's atmosphere we're seeking), so try **Cafe Club** (1551 Ocean Avenue; 213-395-5596). It features a full bar, serves espresso, and, if you want to get serious about it, has a full menu with pizza, pasta, grilled dishes, and sandwiches. Open for lunch, dinner, and weekend brunch; moderate.

Every type of cuisine imaginable is found on the bottom level of **Santa Monica Place** (Broadway between 2nd and 4th streets). This multi-tiered shopping mall has an entire floor of take-out food stands. It's like the United Nations of dining, where everything is budget priced.

If steak-and-kidney pie, bangers and mash, or shepherds pie sound appetizing, head over to **Ye Olde King's Head** (116 Santa Monica Boulevard; 213-451-1402). You won't see a king's head on the wall of this British pub, but there are several trophy animals adorning the place. You'll find them beside photographs of the celebrities who inhabit the place. Like you, they are drawn here by the cozy ambience, lively crowd, and budget prices. Open for lunch and dinner.

For Indian cuisine the best-known restaurant is **Shanta** (502 Santa Monica Boulevard; 213-451-5191), a plush, pink-tablecloth dining room. Trimly decorated with Asian chandeliers and carved wood screens, the place is small enough to convey intimacy. The dinner menu includes *tandoori* chicken, lamb *tikka* (marinated in herbs and lemon), Bombay *machli* (fresh fish with ginger in curry sauce), and curry lobster. At lunch there is a similar selection of dishes from the subcontinent. Moderate.

Zucky's (431 Wilshire Boulevard; 213-393-0551) is the place for late-night munchies. Open 24 hours a day, this popular delicatessen has an endless assortment of hot platters, kosher sandwiches, and delicious pastries. It's a sprawling formica-counter-and-plastic-booth establishment that has been around since 1946. Budget priced to boot!

Tampico Tilly's (1025 Wilshire Boulevard; 213-451-1769) is long on atmosphere. Laid out in courtyard style, the dining room is surrounded by a wrought-iron balcony and illuminated through a skylight. Potted ferns and palms decorate the place and the floor is inlaid with brick. The menu is similarly inspired. Rather than simply serving the standard Mexican dishes, Tampico Tilly's offers specialties like *carne ornelas* (filet mignon with chile peppers), skewered meat dishes, ranchero-style chicken, and seafood flautas. Open for lunch, dinner, and Sunday brunch and featuring a full bar, it's well worth the moderate meal tab.

The taste of Italy combines with the sights and sounds of the old country to create an original ambience at **Verdi Ristorante Di Musica** (1519 Wilshire Boulevard; 213-393-0706). This attractive dinner club prepares a variety of Northern Italian dishes that reflect special skill and care. In addition to shopping for fresh fish and other ingredients, the chef prepares his own pasta and pastries. The true talent here resides in the repertory group which presents hourly shows each evening. The theatrical revues vary from opera to Broadway musical routines to audience sing-along sessions. It's a marvelous way to soak up culture with your chianti. Deluxe (no extra charge for the entertainment and no minimum).

Hiro Sushi (1621 Wilshire Boulevard; 213-395-3570), a Japanese restaurant with sushi bar, is one of the area's prime choices for Asian cuisine. In addition to raw-fish specialties they feature sukiyaki, teriyaki, *yosenabe*, and tempura dishes. Simple in decor, the dining room is lined with bamboo mats and adorned with bright cloth hangings. Open for dinner nightly, lunch during the week.

Pioneer Boulangerie (2012 Main Street; 213-399-7771) is a sprawling, multiroom establishment with an ample dining room, separate patio, and a full-fledged bakery. Out on the patio they serve cafeteria-style meals at budget to moderate prices. The bakery features all kinds of breads and yummy sweets. In the dining room there is a traditional Basque country dinner which includes a tureen of soup, salad, beans, marinated tomatoes, starch dish, pickled tongue, a roasted meat entree, wine, cheese, fruit, and coffee. An incredible deal at a moderate price. They also offer a complete steak and seafood menu. From 4:30 to 7 p.m. there are early bird specials at budget prices; otherwise the menu is in the moderate range. Patio open all day; dining room for lunch and dinner only.

In the world of high chic, **Chinois on Main** (2709 Main Street; 213-392-9025) stands taller than most. Owned by famous restauranteur Wolfgang Puck, the fashionable dining room is done in nouveau art deco-style with track lights, pastel colors, and a central skylight. The curved bar is hand-painted; contemporary artworks adorn the walls. Once you drink in the glamourous surroundings, move on to the menu, which includes roasted Maine lobster, sizzling catfish, grilled Szechuan beef, sautéed quail, and wok-charred fish. The appetizers and other entrees are equal in originality, a medley of French, Chinese, and California cuisine. Open for lunch and dinner, this is an excellent restaurant, ultra-deluxe in price, with high standards of quality.

There are vegetarian-style dinners at **Meyera** (3009 Main Street; 213-399-1010). A small, modest restaurant with pastel walls, contemporary paintings, and art deco light fixtures, it is open evenings only. That's when the cook whips up favored dishes—"Wellington Lentille" (lentils, mushrooms, and gruyere cheese in puff pastry), sautéed vegetables, and stuffed zucchini. If you'd prefer, there are pizzas, pastas, and several seafood and poultry dishes; moderate.

The spot for breakfast in Santa Monica is **Rae's Restaurant** (2901 Pico Boulevard; 213-828-7937), a diner on the edge of town several miles from the beach. With its formica counter and naugahyde booths, Rae's is a local institution, always packed. The breakfasts are hearty American-style feasts complete with buttermilk biscuits and country-style gravy. At lunch they serve the usual selection of sandwiches and side orders. Come dinner time they have fried shrimp, pork chops, veal, liver, fried chicken, and other hot platters at prices that haven't changed since the place opened in 1958. Budget.

There are many who believe the dining experience at **Michael's** (1147 Third Street; 213-451-0843) to be the finest in all Los Angeles. Set in a restored stucco structure and decorated with original artworks by David Hockney and Jasper Johns, it is certainly one of the region's prettiest dining rooms. The menu is a nouvelle cuisine affair with original entrees like squab on duck liver, duck with Grand Marnier sauce, and scallops on watercress purée. At lunch there is charbroiled salmon, chicken on watercress, and several elaborate salads. Haute cuisine is the order of the evening here. The artistry that has gone into the restaurant's cuisine and design have permanently established Michael's stellar reputation. Open for lunch and dinner only, there is a cozy lounge and a garden terrace; ultra-deluxe.

MALIBU RESTAURANTS

Malibu's best-known eating spot sits at the foot of Malibu Pier. **Alice's Restaurant** (23000 Route 1; 213-456-6646) is a trim, glass-encased dining room with views extending across the beach and out over the ocean. A gathering place for locals in the know and visitors on the make, it serves a lunch and dinner menu of seafood and pasta dishes. Salads—including roasted goat cheese and warm lamb salads—are another specialty. The good food, friendly bar, and lively crowd make it a great place for carousing. Lunch and dinner; moderate to deluxe.

The **Reel Inn** (18661 Route 1; 213-456-8221) is my idea of heaven—a moderately priced seafood restaurant. Located across the highway from the beach, it's an oilcloth restaurant with an outdoor patio and a flair for serving good, healthful food at low prices. Among the fresh fish dinners are shark, salmon, snapper, lobster, and swordfish. Open for lunch on weekends only.

There's nothing fancy about **Malibu Fish & Seafood** (25653 Route 1; 213-456-3430). It's just a take-out stand with a few picnic tables outside. But there's nothing costly about it either. The fresh fish, oyster, lobster, and other seafood dishes are budget priced. Hard to beat when you add the ocean view.

When you're out at the beaches around Point Dume or elsewhere in northern Malibu, there are two adjacent roadside restaurants worth checking out. **Coral Beach Cantina** (29350 Route 1; 213-457-5503) is a simple Mexican restaurant with a small patio shaded by umbrellas. The menu contains standard south-of-the-border fare and prices in the budget category.

Over at **I Love Sushi** (29350 Route 1; 213-457-3604) they have a sushi bar and table service. In addition to the house specialty there are tempura and teriyaki dishes, all at moderate prices. Like its neighbor this is a small, unassuming cafe.

The quintessential Malibu dining experience is **Geoffrey's** (27400 Route 1; 213-457-1519), a cliff-top restaurant overlooking the ocean. The marble bar, whitewashed stucco walls, and fresh-cut flowers exude wealth and elegance. The entire hillside has been landscaped and beautifully terraced, creating a Mediterranean atmosphere. The menu features "Malibu fare," a variation on California cuisine, and includes veal *medaillons* in shallot sauce, *ahi* marinated in pineapple juice, and salmon with angel hair pasta. The lunch and dinner menus are almost identical and on weekends they serve brunch. The setting, cuisine, and ultra-deluxe prices make Geoffrey's a prime place for celebrity gazing.

Beau Rivage Mediterranean Restaurant (26025 Route 1; 213-456-5733), another gourmet gathering place, located across the highway from the ocean, is a cozy dining room. With exposed-beam ceiling, brick trim, and copper pots along the wall, it has the feel of a French country inn. But the lunch and dinner menus are strictly Mediterranean. In addition to several fettuccine and linguine dishes there is white fish in meuniere sauce, baby lamb chops, Spanish-style scampi, and daily specials that range from grilled shark with persimmon sauce to ragout of wild boar. Deluxe.

Up in the Santa Monica Mountains, high above the clamor of Los Angeles, rests **The Inn of the Seventh Ray** (128 Old Topanga Canyon Road; 213-455-1311). A throwback to the days when Topanga Canyon was a hippie enclave, this mellow dining spot serves "energized" foods to "raise your body's light vibrations." These auricly charged entrees include "artichoke queen of light" (artichokes stuffed with *tofu*) and "gold chalice" (squash filled with millet, almonds, and raisins). Open for every meal, the restaurant features dining indoors or outside on a pretty, tree-shaded patio. Far out (and priced deluxe).

SANTA CATALINA ISLAND RESTAURANTS

As with Catalina hotels, there are a few points to remember when shopping for a restaurant. Prices are higher than on the mainland. With very few exceptions the dining spots are concentrated in Avalon; services around the rest of the island are minimal. Also, business is seasonal, so restaurants may vary their schedules, serving three meals daily during summer and weekends but dinner only during winter. The wisest course is to check beforehand.

Antonio's Pizzeria (114 Sumner Avenue; 213-510-0060) is a hole-in-the-wall, but a hole-in-the-wall with panache. It's chockablock with junk—old pin-up pictures, record covers, dolls, trophies, fish nets. There's sawdust on the floor and a vague '50s theme to the place. The food—pizza, pasta, and hot sandwiches—is good, filling, and served daily at lunch and dinner. "Come on in," as the sign suggests, "and bask in the ambience of the decaying 1950s." Moderate.

The Busy Bee (306 Crescent Avenue; 213-510-1983), established in 1923, is a local gathering place located right on the beach. It's hard to match the views from the patio of this simple cafe. Every day at lunch you can dine on vegetable platters, tacos, tostadas, salads, and sandwiches while gazing out at the pier and harbor. During peak season they are open for breakfast and feature a dinner menu with prime rib, swordfish, teriyaki chicken, and steak. Moderate.

The other half of the vintage stucco-and-red-tile building housing the Busy Bee is the site of **Armstrong's Seafood Restaurant** (306 Crescent Avenue; 213-510-0113). The interior is trimly finished in knotty pine and white tile with mounted gamefish on the walls. Since the establishment doubles as a fish market you can count on fresh seafood. The menu is the same at lunch and dinner with only the portions and prices changing. Mesquite-grilled dishes include *mahimahi*, scallops, swordfish, skewered shrimp, and steak. They also feature lobster, abalone, and orange roughy. You can dine indoors or on the patio right along the waterfront, making Armstrong's moderate prices a bargain.

Cafe Prego (609 Crescent Avenue; 213-510-1218), a small Italian bistro complete with oilcloth tables and stucco arches, comes highly recommended. The specialties are seafood and pasta; you'll find a menu offering fresh swordfish, sea bass, halibut, snapper, and sand dabs, plus manicotti, rigatoni, lasagna, and fettucine. There are also steak and veal dishes at this waterfront nook. Open for dinner only, it features good food at moderate to deluxe prices.

For a step upscale head down the street to **Ristorante Villa Portofino** (111 Crescent Avenue; 213-510-0508). Here a white piano is set off by pink stucco walls and the candlelit tables are decorated with flowers. With art deco curves and colorful art prints the place has an easy Mediterranean feel about it. The Italian cuisine includes several veal scallopine dishes, scallops in butter and wine sauce, cioppino, chicken marsala, tournedos with artichoke hearts and lobster stuffing, beef *medaillons* with mozzarella, and a selection of pasta dishes. Romance in the deluxe league.

The **Runway Cafe** (213-510-2196), situated up in the mountains at 1600 feet, is part of Catalina's Airport in the Sky complex. This breakfast-and-lunch facility serves egg dishes, hot cakes, buffalo burgers, and a variety of sandwiches. There's not much to the self-service restaurant itself, but it adjoins a lobby with stone fireplace and a tile patio that overlooks the surrounding mountains. Budget.

Catalina's remotest dining place is **Doug's Harbor Reef Restaurant** (Two Harbors, 213-510-0303), located way out in the Two Harbors area. This rambling establishment has a dining room done in nautical motif with fish nets, shell lamps, and woven lauhala mats. There's also an adjoining patio for enjoying the soft breezes that blow through this isthmus area. Serving lunch, dinner, and Sunday brunch, Doug's offers pork loin back ribs, beef kebab, chicken teriyaki, and a steamed vegetable platter. Prime rib and swordfish are local favorites and at lunch there are buffalo burgers. Moderate to deluxe. There's also an adjoining **snack bar** serving three meals daily. Budget priced, it offers egg dishes, sandwiches, burgers, and burritos.

The Great Outdoors

The Sporting Life

SPORTFISHING

Fish the waters around Los Angeles and you can try your hand at landing a barracuda or maybe a white croaker, halibut, calico bass, or a relative of Jaws. For sportfishing outfits call, **Annie's Barge, Inc.** (Belmont Pier, 213-434-6781; and Seal Beach Pier, 213-598-8677), **Belmont Pier Sportfishing** (Ocean Avenue and 39th Place, Belmont Shore; 213-434-6781), **Ports O' Call Sportfishing** (Berth 79, San Pedro; 213-547-9916), **Queen's Wharf Sportfishing** (555 Pico Avenue, Long Beach; 213-432-8993), **Redondo Sportfishing** (233 North Harbor Drive, Redondo Beach; 213-372-2111), **Marina del Rey Sportfishing** (13759 Fiji Way, Marina del Rey; 213-822-3625), **Malibu Pier Sportfishing** (23000 Route 1, Malibu; 213-456-8030).

In Catalina contact the **Catalina Visitors Bureau** (213-510-2000) for listings of private boat owners who outfit sportsfishing expeditions.

SKIN DIVING

To explore Los Angeles' submerged depths, call **Pacific Sporting Goods** (11 39th Place, Long Beach, 213-434-1604; or 1719 South Pacific Avenue, San Pedro, 213-833-2422), **New England Divers, Inc.** (4148 Viking Way, Long Beach; 213-421-8939), **Marina del Rey Divers** (2539 Lincoln Boulevard, Marina del Rey; 213-827-1131), **Dive n' Surf** (504 North Broadway, Redondo Beach; 213-372-8423), **Sea D Sea** (1911 South Catalina Avenue, Redondo Beach; 213-373-6355), **New England Divers, Inc.** (11830 West Pico Boulevard, West Los Angeles; 213-477-5021), **Blue Cheer Ocean Water Sports** (1731 Wilshire Blvd, Santa Monica; 213-828-4289), **Scuba Haus** (2501 Wilshire Boulevard, Santa Monica; 213-828-2916), or **Malibu Divers** (21231 Route 1, Malibu; 213-456-2396) to rent gear and/or take a tour.

Without doubt Santa Catalina Island offers some of the finest skin diving anywhere in the world. Perfectly positioned to attract fish from both the northern and southern Pacific, it teems with sea life. Large fish ascend from the deep waters surrounding the island while small colorful species inhabit rich kelp forests along the coast. There are caves and caverns to explore as well as the wrecks of rusting ships.

Several outfits rent skin diving and scuba equipment and/or sponsor tours. In Avalon, call **Catalina Divers Supply** (213-510-0330), **Island Charters, Inc.** (213-510-0600), **Argo Diving Service** (213-510-2208), and **Catalina Adventure Tours** (213-510-1811). In Two Harbors try **Catalina Safari Tours** (213-510-2800).

WHALE WATCHING

During the annual migration the following outfits offer whale-watching trips: **Mickey's Belmont, Inc.** (Belmont Pier, Long Beach; 213-434-6781), **Queen's Wharf Sportfishing** (555 Pico Avenue, Long Beach; 213-432-8993), **Los Angeles Harbor Cruise** (Berth 77, San Pedro; 213-831-0996), **Pilgrim Sailing Cruise** (Berth 76, San Pedro; 213-547-0941), **Spirit Adventures** (Berth 75, San Pedro; 213-831-1073), **Catalina Cruises** (P.O. Box 1948, San Pedro; 213-514-3838), and **Pacific Charter Company** (555 North Harbor Drive, Redondo Beach; 213-374-4015).

WINDSURFING AND SURFING

"Surfing is the only life," so grab a board from **Fun Bunns** (1106 Manhattan Avenue, Manhattan Beach; 213-379-4898), **Jeffers** (1338 Strand, Hermosa Beach; 213-372-9492), **Rollerskates of America** (64 Windward Avenue, Venice; 213-399-4481), **La Planche** (2619 Main Street, Santa Monica; 213-392-5254), **Zuma Jay Surfboards** (Route 1, Malibu; 213-456-8044), or **Catalina Adventure Tours** (the Mole, Avalon; 213-510-2888).

SKATING AND SKATE BOARDING

Los Angeles may well be the roller skating capital of California. To rent skates or maybe even a skateboard call, **Fun Bunns** (1106 Manhattan Avenue, Manhattan Beach; 213-379-4898), **Pacific Strand** (1328 Strand, Hermosa Beach; 213-372-8812), **RPM Rent A Car** (36 Washington Street, Marina del Rey; 213-399-6331), **Rollerskates of America** (64 Windward Avenue, Venice; 213-399-4481), **Spokes 'n Stuff** (three kiosks in Venice along Ocean Front Walk at Washington Street, Venice Boulevard, and Rose Avenue; 213-306-3332), or **Sea Mist Skate Rentals** (1619 Ocean Front Walk, Santa Monica Pier, Santa Monica).

OTHER SPORTS

GOLF

For the golfers in the crowd, try **El Dorado Park Municipal Golf Course** (2400 Studebaker Road, Long Beach; 213-430-5411), **Skylink Golf Course** (4800 East Wardlow Road, Long Beach; 213-421-3388), **Recreation Park** (5000 Federation Drive, Long Beach; 213-494-5000), **Los Verdes Golf Course** (7000 West Los Verdes Drive, Rancho Palos Verdes; 213-377-7370), **Penmar Golf Course** (1233 Rose Avenue, Venice; 213-396-6228), or **Westchester Golf Course** (6900 West Manchester, Los Angeles; 213-670-5110). In Catalina call **Catalina Visitors Golf Club** (1 Country Club Drive, Avalon; 213-510-0530).

TENNIS

There are public tennis courts available in **El Dorado Park** (2800 Studebaker Road, Long Beach; 213-425-0553), **Alta Vista Tennis Courts** (715 Julia Avenue, Redondo Beach; 213-376-7117), **The Sport Center at King Harbor** (819 North Harbor Drive, Redondo Beach; 213-372-8868), **Marina Tennis World** (13199 Mindanao Way, Marina del Rey; 213-822-2255), **Lincoln Park** (1155 7th Street, Santa Monica; 213-394-6011), and **Douglas Park** (1155 Wilshire Boulevard, Santa Monica; 213-828-9912).

Beaches and Parks

LONG BEACH AND SAN PEDRO BEACHES AND PARKS

Alamitos Peninsula—The ocean side of this slender salient offers a pretty sand beach looking out on a tiny island. Paralleling the beach is an endless string of woodframe houses. The sand corridor extends all the way to the entrance of Alamitos Bay where a stone jetty provides recreation for anglers, surfers, and strollers.

Facilities: Picnic areas, restrooms, lifeguards, volleyball courts; restaurants and groceries nearby.

Fishing: Try your luck from the jetty.

Swimming: Good.

Surfing: Best bet is the jetty.

Getting there: Located along Ocean Boulevard between 54th Place and 72nd Place in Long Beach; park at the end of the road.

Alamitos Bay Beach—This hook-shaped strand curves along the eastern and southern shores of a narrow inlet. Houses line the beach along most of its length. Protected from the ocean by a peninsula and breakwater, the beach faces the lovely waterfront community of Naples.

Facilities: Restrooms; restaurants and groceries nearby; information, 213-594-0951.

Fishing: Good.

Swimming: Protected from surf and tide, this is a safe, outstanding spot.

Surfing: There's no surf, but the bay presents perfect conditions for windsurfing.

Getting there: Located along Bayshore Avenue and Ocean Boulevard in Long Beach.

Long Beach City Beach—They don't call it Long Beach for nothing. This strand is broad and boundless, a silvery swath traveling much the length of the town. There are several islets parked offshore. Along the miles of beachfront you'll find numerous facilities and good size crowds. **Belmont Pier,** a 1300-foot-long, hammerhead-shaped walkway, bisects the beach and offers boat tours and fishing services.

Facilities: Restrooms, lifeguards, snack bar, playground, volleyball.

Fishing: Good from Belmont Pier.

Swimming: The beach is protected by the harbor breakwater making for safe swimming.

Getting there: Located along Ocean Boulevard between 1st and 72nd places in Long Beach. Belmont Pier is at Ocean Boulevard and 39th Place.

Cabrillo Beach—The edge of Los Angeles harbor is an unappealing locale for a beach, but here it is, a two-part strand, covered with pewter-gray sand and bisected by a fishing pier. One half faces the shipping facility; the other looks out on the glorious Pacific and abuts on the **Point Fermin Marine Life Refuge,** a rocky corridor filled with outstanding tidepools and backdropped by dramatic cliffs. If you like tidepooling, beeline to Cabrillo, if not—there are hundreds of other beaches in the Golden State.

Facilities: Restrooms, picnic areas, lifeguards, snack bar, museum, playground, volleyball courts; restaurants and groceries nearby in San Pedro; information, 213-372-2166.

Camping: Not permitted here, but there is camping in **Harbor Regional Park** (25820 Vermont Avenue, Harbor City; 213-548-7515), a 231-acre urban park inland from Cabrillo.

Fishing: From pier.

Swimming: People do it, but I saw a lot of refuse from the nearby shipping harbor.

Surfing: Try in front of the beach and near the jetty.

Getting there: Located at 3720 Stephen M. White Drive in San Pedro.

Royal Palms State Beach—Situated at the base of a sedimentary cliff, this boulder-strewn beach gains its name from a grove of elegant palm trees. Before it was swallowed by a 1920s storm, the Royal Palms Hotel was located here. Today the guests of honor are surfers and tidepoolers. While the location is quite extraordinary, I prefer another beach, Point Fermin Park's **Wilder Annex**, located to the south. This little gem also lacks sand, but is built on three tiers of a cliff. The upper level is decorated with palm trees, the middle tier has a grassy plot studded with shady magnolias, and the bottom floor is a rocky beach with promising tidepools and camera-eye views of Point Fermin.

Facilities: Restrooms at both parks, lifeguards at Royal Palms; restaurants and groceries nearby in San Pedro; information, 213-372-2166.

Fishing: Good at both parks.

Swimming: Try Royal Palms since there are lifeguards.

Surfing: Very popular at Royal Palms and off White Point, a peninsula separating the two parks.

Getting there: Both parks are located along Paseo del Mar in San Pedro. Royal Palms is near the intersection with Western Avenue and Wilder Annex is around the intersection with Meyler Street.

PALOS VERDES PENINSULA BEACHES AND PARKS

Smuggler's Cove (★)—This nude beach is an unheralded beauty. A world to itself, it offers a swath of pewter sand, outlying tidepools, and a backdrop of dramatic cliffs. Known to skinnydippers everywhere, this horseshoe inlet is protected from the wind by headlands that stand like bookends on each side. It's a great spot for watersports, tidepooling, and sunbathing.

Facilities: None; restaurants and groceries are several miles away in San Pedro.

Swimming: Good.

Getting there: Listening? Follow Palos Verdes Drive South in Rancho Palos Verdes to a spot about 50 yards north of Peppertree Drive and eight-tenths of a mile south of the Abalone Cove County Beach parking lot. There you'll find an opening in the chain-link fence leading to a path down to the beach.

Abalone Cove County Beach—The Palos Verdes Peninsula is so rugged and inaccessible that any beach by definition will be secluded. This gray-sand hideaway is no exception. It sits in a natural amphitheater guarded by sedimentary rock formations and looks out on Catalina Island. There are tidepools to ponder and an ecological reserve to explore.

Facilities: Picnic areas, restrooms, lifeguards; restaurants and groceries several miles away in San Pedro; information, 213-372-2166.

Fishing: Good.

Swimming: Good.

Surfing: Try around the south point of the cove.

Getting there: Located off Palos Verdes Drive South in Rancho Palos Verdes. From the parking lot a path leads down to the beach.

Torrance County Beach—This is a lengthy stretch of bleach-blond sand guarded on one flank by the stately Palos Verdes Peninsula and on the other by an industrial complex and colony of smokestacks. Just your average middle class beach, it's not one of my favorites, but it has the only white sand hereabouts. Also consider adjacent **Malaga Cove** (nicknamed "RAT" beach because it's "right after Torrance"), a continuation of the strand, which is noted for tidepools, shells, and rock-hounding. Prettier than its pedestrian partner, Malaga Cove is framed by rocky bluffs.

Facilities: At Torrance there are restrooms and lifeguards; restaurants and groceries are located downtown. Around Malaga Cove you're on your own; information, 213-372-2166.

Fishing: Good at both beaches.

Swimming: Recommended at Torrance where lifeguards are on duty.

Surfing: Very good at Malaga Cove.

Getting there: Paseo de la Playa in Torrance parallels the beach. To reach Malaga Cove, walk south from Torrance toward the cliffs.

SOUTH BAY BEACHES AND PARKS

Redondo State Beach—Surfers know this strand and so should you. Together with neighboring Hermosa and Manhattan beaches, it symbolizes the Southern California beach scene. You'll find a long strip of white sand bordered by a hillside carpeted with ice plants. In addition to surfers, the area is populated by bicyclists and joggers, while anglers cast from the nearby piers.

Facilities: Restrooms, lifeguards, volleyball courts; restaurants and groceries nearby; information, 213-372-2166.

Fishing: Good from nearby Fisherman's Wharf.

Swimming: Good.

Surfing: Very good.

Getting there: Located along the Esplanade in Redondo Beach.

Hermosa City Beach—One of the great beaches of Southern California, this is a very, very wide (and very, very white) sand beach extending the entire length of Hermosa Beach. Two miles of pearly sand is only part of the attraction. There's also The Strand, a pedestrian lane that runs the length of the beach; Pier Avenue, an adjacent street lined with interesting shops; a quarter-mile fishing pier; and a local community know for its artistic creativity. Personally, if I were headed to the beach, I would head in this direction.

Facilities: Restrooms, lifeguards, volleyball courts, pier, playground; restaurants and groceries nearby; information, 213-372-2166.

Fishing: Good from the Municipal Pier.

Swimming: Good.

Surfing: Very good around the pier and all along the beach.

Getting there: Located at the foot of Pier Avenue in Hermosa Beach.

Manhattan State Beach—Back in those halcyon days when their first songs were climbing the charts, the Beach Boys were regular fixtures at this silvery strand. They came to surf, swim, and check out the scene along The Strand, the walkway that extends the length of Manhattan Beach. What can you say, the gentlemen had good taste. This sand corridor is wide as a desert, fronted by an aquamarine ocean and backed by the beautiful homes of the very lucky. If that's not enough, there's a fishing pier and an adjacent commercial area door-to-door with excellent restaurants.

Facilities: Restrooms, lifeguards, volleyball courts; restaurants and groceries nearby; information, 213-372-2166.

Fishing: Try Manhattan Beach Pier.

Swimming: Good.

Surfing: Good, especially around the pier.

Getting there: Located at the foot of Manhattan Beach Boulevard in Manhattan Beach.

Dockweiler State Beach—It's long, wide, and has fluffy white sand—what more could you ask? Rather, it's what less can you request. Dockweiler suffers a minor problem. It's right next to Los Angeles International Airport, one of the world's busiest terminals. Every minute planes are taking off, thundering, reverberating, right over the beach. To add insult to infamy, there is a sewage treatment plant nearby.

Facilities: Picnic areas, restrooms, playground; restaurant and groceries nearby in Playa del Rey; information, 213-322-5008.

Fishing: Good.

Swimming: Good.

Surfing: Good.

Getting there: Located along Vista del Mar Boulevard in Playa del Rey.

VENICE AND SANTA MONICA BEACHES AND PARKS

Venice City Beach—If you visit only a single Southern California beach, this should be the one. It's a broad white-sand corridor that runs the entire length of Venice and features Venice Pier. But the real attraction—and the reason you'll find the beach described in the "Restaurants," "Sightseeing," and "Shopping" sections—is the boardwalk. A center of culture, street artistry, and excitement, the boardwalk parallels Venice City Beach for two miles.

Facilities: Picnic areas, restrooms, showers, pavilion, lifeguards, playgrounds, fishing pier, basketball courts, and paddle ball courts; restaurants, groceries, and vendors line the boardwalk; information, 213-394-3266.

Fishing: Good from Venice Pier.

Swimming: Good.

Surfing: Good.

Getting there: Ocean Front Walk in Venice parallels the beach; Venice Pier is located at the foot of Washington Street.

Santa Monica State Beach—If the pop song is right and "L.A. is a great big freeway," then truly Santa Monica is a great big beach. Face it, the sand is very white, the water is very blue, the beach is very broad, and they all continue for miles. From Venice to Pacific Palisades, it's a sandbox gone wild. Skaters, strollers, and bicyclists pass along the promenade, sunbathers lie moribund in the sand, and volleyball players perform acrobatic shots. At the center of all this stands the Santa Monica Pier with its amusement park atmosphere. If it wasn't right next door to Venice this would be the hottest beach around.

Facilities: Picnic areas, restrooms, lifeguards, snackbars, volleyball courts, pier; restaurants and groceries nearby; information, 213-394-3266.

Fishing: From Santa Monica Pier.

Swimming: Good.

Surfing: Good.

Getting there: Located at the foot of Colorado Avenue in Santa Monica.

Will Rogers State Beach—Simple and homespun he might have been, but humorist Will Rogers was also a canny businessman with a passion for real estate. He bought up two miles of beachfront property which eventually became his namesake park. It's a wide, sandy strand with an equally expansive parking lot running the length of the beach. Route 1 parallels the parking area and beyond that rise the sharp cliffs that lend Pacific Palisades its name.

Facilities: Restrooms, lifeguard; restaurants, and groceries nearby; information, 213-394-3266.

Swimming: Good.

Surfing: Good where Sunset Boulevard meets the ocean.

Getting there: Located along Route 1 at Sunset Boulevard in Pacific Palisades.

Will Rogers State Historic Park—The former ranch of humorist Will Rogers, this 187-acre spread sits in the hills of Pacific Palisades. The late cowboy's home is open to visitors and there are hiking trails leading around the property and out into adjacent Topanga Canyon State Park.

Facilities: Picnic areas, museum, restrooms; restaurants and groceries nearby in Pacific Palisades; information, 213-454-8212.

Getting there: Located at 14253 Sunset Boulevard in Pacific Palisades.

Santa Monica Mountains National Recreation Area—One of the few mountain ranges in the United States to run transversely (from east to west), the Santa Monicas reach for fifty miles to form the northwestern boundary of the Los Angeles basin. This federal preserve, which covers part of the mountain range, encompasses about 150,000 acres between Routes 1 and 101; in addition to high country, it includes a coastal stretch from Santa Monica to Point Mugu. Considered a "botanical island," the mountains support chaparral, coastal sage, and oak forests; mountain lions, golden eagles, and many of California's early animal species still survive here.

Facilities: Information center located at 23018 Ventura Boulevard, Woodland Hills, CA 91364 (213-888-3770); hiking trails.

Camping: Permitted.

Getting there: Several access roads lead into the area; Mulholland Drive and Mulholland Highway follow the crest of the Santa Monica Mountains for about 50 miles from Hollywood to Malibu.

MALIBU BEACHES AND PARKS

Topanga Canyon State Park—Not much sand here, but you will find forests of oak and fields of rye. This 9000-acre hideaway nestles in the Santa Monica Mountains above Malibu. Along the 35 miles of hiking trails and fire roads are views of the ocean, San Gabriel Mountains, and San Fernando Valley. There are meadows and a stream to explore. The park climbs from 200 to 2100 feet in elevation, providing an introduction to one of Los Angeles' few remaining natural areas.

Facilities: Picnic areas, restrooms; restaurants and groceries are several miles away; information, 213-455-2465.

Getting there: Located at 20825 Entrada Road; from Route 1 in Malibu take Topanga Canyon Road up to Entrada Road.

Topanga State Beach—This narrow sand corridor extends for over a mile. The adjacent highway breaks the quietude, but the strand is still popular with surfers and those wanting to be close to Malibu services.

Facilities: Restrooms, lifeguards; restaurants and groceries nearby; information, 213-451-2906.

Swimming: Good.

Surfing: Good around Topanga Creek.

Getting there: Located along Route 1 near Topanga Canyon Road in Malibu.

Malibu Creek State Park—Once a Twentieth Century Fox movie set, this 4000-acre facility spreads through rugged, virgin country in the Santa Monica Mountains. Among its features are 15 miles of hiking trails, four-acre Century Lake, and Malibu Creek, which is lined with willow and cottonwood. In spring the meadows explode with wildflowers; at other times of the year you'll encounter squirrels, rabbits, mule deer, and bobcats. The bird life ranges from aquatic species like ducks and great blue herons along the lake to hawks, woodpeckers, and golden eagles. The lava hills, sloping grasslands, and twisted sedimentary rock formations make it an intriguing escape from the city.

Facilities: Picnic areas, restrooms; restaurants and groceries several miles away; information, 213-991-1827.

Getting there: Located off Mulholland Highway and Las Virgenes Road above Malibu.

Malibu Lagoon State Beach—Not only is there a pretty beach here but an estuary and wetlands area as well. You can stroll the white sands past an unending succession of lavish beachfront homes, or study a different species entirely in the park's salt marsh. Here Malibu Creek feeds into the ocean, creating a rich tidal area busy with marine life and shorebirds.

Facilities: Picnic area, restrooms, lifeguards; restaurants and groceries nearby; information, 213-706-1310.

Fishing: Excellent. Surf perch are caught here. There's also fishing from adjacent Malibu Pier.

Swimming: Very popular.

Surfing: Engineering work around the channel has diminished the waves at what once was one of California's greatest surfing beaches.

Getting there: Located along Route 1 at Cross Creek Road in Malibu.

Robert H. Meyer Memorial State Beaches—This unusual facility consists of three separate pocket beaches—**El Pescador, La Piedra,** and **El Matador.** Each is a pretty strand with sandy beach and eroded bluffs. Together they are among the nicest beaches in Malibu. My favorite is El Matador with its rock formations, sea stacks, and adjacent Malibu mansions.

Facilities: Picnic areas, toilets, lifeguards; restaurants and groceries several miles away; information, 213-706-1310.

Swimming: Good.

Getting there: Located on Route 1 about 11 miles north of Malibu.

Westward Beach Point Dume State Park—This long narrow stretch is really a southerly continuation of Zuma Beach. Unlike its neighbor, it is conveniently located away from the highway and bordered by lofty sandstone cliffs. There are tidepools here and trails leading up along the bluffs. For white-sand serenity this is a choice spot. Matter of fact, on the far side of Point Dume you'll encounter a nude beach in **Pirate's Cove** (★).

Facilities: Restrooms, lifeguards; restaurants and groceries nearby; information, 213-457-9891.

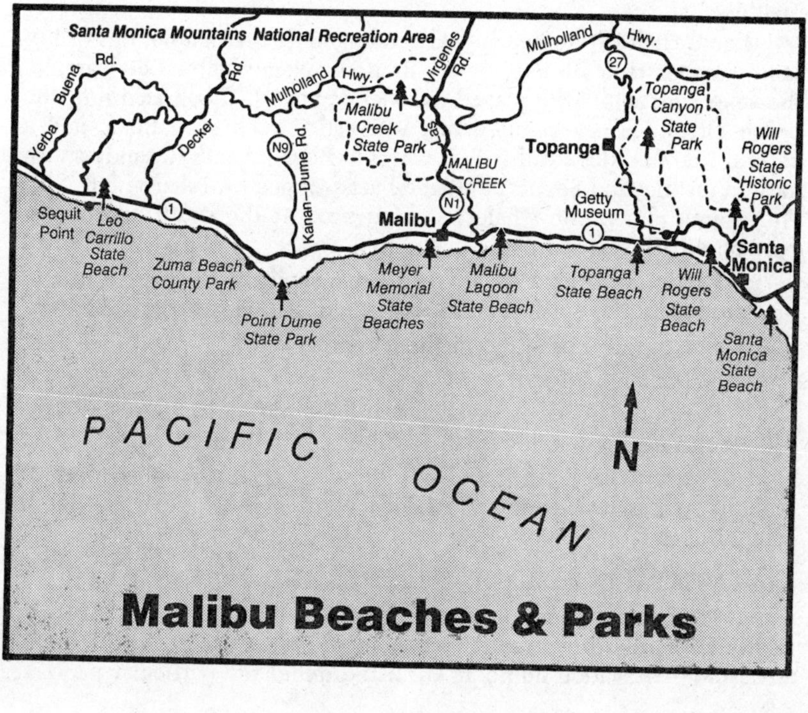

Swimming: Good.

Surfing: Good along Westward Beach and off Point Dume.

Getting there: The park entrance is adjacent to the southern entrance to Zuma Beach County Park, just off Route 1 about six miles north of Malibu. To reach the nude beach, park at Paradise Cove, on Route 1 two miles further south, and hike back toward Point Dume; or you can take the trail over the Point Dume Headlands and down to Pirate's Cove.

Zuma Beach County Park—This long, broad beach is a study in the territorial instincts of the species. Los Angeles County's largest beach park, it is frequented in one area by Chicanos; "Vals," young residents of the San Fernando Valley, have staked claim to another section, while families and students inhabit another stretch (Zuma 3 and 4). Not as pretty as other Malibu beaches, it offers more space and better facilities, making Zuma a popular spot.

Facilities: Picnic areas, restrooms, lifeguards, playgrounds; restaurants and groceries nearby; information, 213-457-9891.

Swimming: Good.

Surfing: Good.

Getting there: Located along Route 1 about six miles north of Malibu.

Leo Carrillo State Beach—Extending more than a mile, this white-sand corridor rests directly below Route 1. Named after Leo Carrillo, the television actor who played sidekick Pancho in *The Cisco Kid*, the beach offers sea caves, tidepools, interesting rock formations, and a natural tunnel. Nicer still is **Leo Carrillo Beach North,** a sandy swath located just beyond Sequit Point and backdropped by a sharp bluff. This entire area is a prime whale-watching site. At the south end of this 1600-acre park you can bathe in the buff.

Facilities: Picnic areas, restrooms, showers, lifeguards; restaurants and groceries several miles away; information, 213-706-1310.

Camping: Permitted in three campgrounds.

Swimming: Good.

Surfing: Good, especially around Sequit Point. There's also excellent surfing a few miles north at **County Line Beach.**

Getting there: Located on Route 1 about 14 miles north of Malibu. Access to Leo Carrillo Beach North is from a parking lot at 40000 Route 1.

SANTA CATALINA ISLAND BEACHES AND PARKS

If you are planning to camp on Catalina, there are a few things to know. First, there is a fee for camping and reservations are generally advisable (reservation numbers are listed under the particular park).

In addition to designated beaches, camping is permitted in many of the island's coves. These are undeveloped sites with no facilities and are most readily accessible by boat. Patrolling rangers collect the fees here.

For more information on camping, contact the **Los Angeles County Department of Parks and Recreation** (213 Catalina Street, Avalon; 213-510-0688), the **Santa Catalina Island Conservancy** (206 Metropole Avenue, P.O. Box 2739, Avalon; 213-510-1421), or the **Catalina Cove and Camp Agency** (P.O. Box 5044, Two Harbors; 213-510-0303).

For information on transportation to campgrounds and on hiking permits (which are required of everyone venturing beyond Avalon) see the "Sightseeing" section in this chapter.

Crescent Beach—About as relaxing as Coney Island, this beach is at the center of the action. Avalon's main drag parallels the beach and a pier divides it into two separate strips of sand. Facing Avalon Harbor, the strand is flanked on one side with a ferry dock and along the other by the famous Avalon Casino.

Facilities: Full service facilities are available on the street adjacent to the beach.

Fishing: Good from the pier.

Swimming: The harbor provides protection from the surf, making it an excellent swimming area.

Getting there: Located along Crescent Avenue in Avalon.

Descanso Beach—Somehow the appeal of this private enclave escapes me. A rock-strewn beach on the far side of the Avalon Casino, it seconds as a mooring facility for sailboats. Granted, there is a rolling lawn dotted with palm trees and the complex is nicely surrounded by hills. But with all the commotion at the bar, cafe, shuffleboard, and volleyball courts it's more like being on an amusement pier than a beach. Besides that you have to pay to get in.

Facilities: Restrooms, playground, showers; information, 213-510-0484.

Swimming: Good.

Getting there: Located off Crescent Avenue just past the Avalon Casino.

Bird Park Campground—Once the site of the Wrigley Bird Park, this grassy field is dotted with palm and pine trees. Located up in Avalon Canyon inland from the beach, it provides a convenient and inexpensive way to visit Avalon and utilize its many services. There are pretty views of the surrounding hills.

Facilities: Picnic areas, restrooms, showers; restaurants and groceries nearby in Avalon; information, 213-510-0688.

Camping: Permitted.

Getting there: Located on Avalon Canyon Road about one mile from downtown Avalon.

Black Jack Campground—Situated at 1500 feet elevation, this facility sits on a plateau below Mt. Black Jack, the island's second highest peak. It's a lovely spot shaded by pine and eucalyptus trees and affording views across the rolling hills and out along the ocean. The old Black Jack silver mine is nearby. Among backcountry facilities this is about the most popular on the island.

Facilities: Picnic areas, toilets; restaurants and groceries are way back in Avalon; information, 213-510-0688.

Camping: Permitted.

Getting there: Located south of The Airport in the Sky off Airport Road.

Ben Weston Beach—A favorite among locals, this pewter-colored beach is surrounded by rocky hills. Located at the end of a long canyon road, it is serene and secluded. Avalon residents come here to flee the tourists, so you might consider making it your hideaway.

Facilities: Toilet.

Camping: Permitted, but there is no water.

Fishing: Good.

Swimming: Good when the surf is low.

Surfing: One of the island's best spots.

Getting there: Located about eight miles south of Two Harbors off Middle Ranch Road.

Little Harbor Campground—On the Pacific side of the island, this camp sits near a sandy beach between rocky headlands. It's studded with palm trees and often filled with grazing bison. A good base camp for hikers, it is one of the island's prettiest facilities. In addition, **Shark Harbor,** an adjacent strand, is excellent for shell collecting and body surfing.

Facilities: Picnic areas, toilets, showers, lifeguards; restaurants and groceries about six miles away in Two Harbors; information, 213-510-0688.

Camping: Permitted.

Fishing: Good.

Swimming: Good.

Skindiving: Good.

Getting there: Located about six miles south of Two Harbors along Little Harbor Road.

Little Fisherman's Cove Campground—Set along a series of terraces above a brown-sand beach, this facility is adjacent to the services at Two Harbors. It's also a convenient base camp from which to hike out along the island's west end.

Facilities: Picnic areas, restrooms, showers, lockers, laundry, volleyball; restaurants and groceries nearby; information, 213-510-0303.

Camping: Permitted.

Fishing: Good.

Swimming: Good.

Skindiving: Very good; the waters here are particularly colorful.

Getting there: Located next to Two Harbors.

Parson's Landing—The most remote of Catalina's campgrounds, this isolated facility sits along a small brown-sand beach with heavily eroded hills in the background.

Facilities: Picnic areas, toilets; restaurants and groceries are several miles away in Two Harbors; information 213-510-0303.

Camping: Permitted.

Fishing: Good.

Swimming: Good.

Skindiving: Good.

Getting there: Located several miles west of Two Harbors along West End Road.

Hiking

COASTAL TRAILS

The Los Angeles portion of the **California Coastal Trail** begins on Naples Island in Long Beach. From here the trail is a varied journey across open bluffs, boat basins, rocky outcroppings accessible only at low tide, along beachwalks filled with roller skaters, jugglers, and skate boarders, and up goat trails with stunning views of the Pacific Ocean.

Set beneath wave-carved bluffs, the **Palos Verdes Peninsula Trail** (5 miles) takes you along a rocky beachside trail past coves and teeming tidepools. The trail begins at Malaga Cove and ends at Point Vicente Lighthouse.

If you're interested in exploring a shipwreck, head out to Palos Verdes Estate Shoreline Preserve, near Malaga Cove, and hike along the **Seashore–Shipwreck Trail** (2.25 miles). The trail hugs the shoreline (and requires an ability to jump boulders), skirting tidepools and coves, until it arrives at what is left of an old Greek ship, the *Dominator*.

Zuma–Dume Trail (1 mile) in Malibu takes you from Zuma Beach County Park, along Pirate's Cove (a nude beach) to the Point Dume headlands and Paradise Cove, a popular diving spot.

For a pleasant hike along part of the Malibu coast dotted with coves and caves, and providing terrific swimming, surfing and skindiving, head out the **Leo Carrillo Trail** (1.5 miles), located at Leo Carrillo State Beach. Or to hike up a gently sloping hill for a view of the coastline, take the nearby **Ocean View Loop Trail** (2 miles).

SANTA MONICA MOUNTAINS TRAILS

It is difficult to imagine, but Los Angeles does have undeveloped mountain wilderness areas prime for trekking. The Santa Monica Mountains offer chaparral-covered landscapes, grassy knolls, mountain streams, and dark canyons.

When visiting Will Roger's State Historic Park, take a walk down **Inspiration Point Trail** (1 mile) for a view overlooking West Los Angeles.

Topanga Canyon State Park has over 32 miles of trails. The **Musch Ranch Loop Trail** (4 miles) passes through five different types of plant communities. Or try the **Santa Ynez Canyon Trail** (6.6 miles), which guides you along the Palisades Highlands with views of the ocean and Santa Ynez Canyon. In spring wildflowers add to the already spectacular scenery.

Several trails trace the "backbone" of the Santa Monica Mountains. In fact, conservationists are trying to secure a trail that extends from Will Rogers State Historic Park to Point Mugu State Park. Presently, you will have to be happy with routes that hop, skip, and jump through the area.

Eagle Rock to Eagle Springs Loop Trail (6.5 miles), for instance, begins in Topanga State Park and traverses oak and chapparral countryside on its way to Eagle Spring. Another section of the "Backbone Trail," **Tapia Park–Malibu Creek State Park Loop** (12 miles) begins near Tapia Park, just off of Malibu Canyon Road. The trail follows fire roads and offers choice views of the ocean and Channel Islands before it winds into Malibu Creek Canyon.

For a nostalgic visit to the location of many movie and television shows, including *MASH* and *Love Is A Many Splendored Thing*, check out the **Century Ranch Trail** (2.3 miles) in Malibu Creek State Park. The trail travels along Malibu Creek to Rock Pool, the Gorge, and Malibu Lake.

An easy climb up **Zuma Ridge Trail** (6.3 miles) brings you to the center of the Santa Monica Mountains and affords otherworldly views of the Pacific. The trail begins off Encinal Canyon Road, 1.5 miles from Mulholland Highway.

SANTA CATALINA ISLAND TRAILS

For a true adventure in hiking, gather your gear and head for Santa Catalina. A network of spectacular trails crisscrosses this largely undeveloped island. Bring plenty of water and beware of rattlesnakes and poison oak. You'll also need a hiking permit (see the "Sightseeing" section in this chapter).

Catalina Trail (8 miles) begins at Black Jack Junction and ends up at Two Harbors. The path passes a lot of interesting terrain and provides glimpses of island wildlife, especially buffalo. (You can arrange with the ferry service to ride back to the mainland from Two Harbors.)

If you are an experienced hiker and ready for a good workout, hike **Silver Peak Trail** (10.1 miles). There are wonderful views of mountains and ocean along the way.

Other routes you might consider are **Sheep Chute Trail** (3.3 miles), a moderate hike between Little Harbor and Empire Landing; **Empire Landing Road Trail** (6.2 miles), another moderate hike from Two Harbors; and **Boushey Road** (2.1 miles), a strenuous trek between Silver Peak Trail and Parsons Landing.

Travelers' Tracks

Sightseeing

LONG BEACH

Anchoring the southern end of Los Angeles County is Long Beach, one of California's largest cities. Back in the Roaring Twenties, after oil was discoverd and the area experienced a tremendous building boom, Long Beach become known as "The Coney Island of the West." Boasting five miles of beachfront and a grand amusement park, it was a favorite spot for daytripping Angelenos.

Several decades of decline followed, but recently the metropolis began a $1.5 billion redevelopment plan. Today it ranks together with neighboring San Pedro as the largest manmade harbor in the world and is becoming an increasingly popular tourist destination. Ignoring the Chamber of Commerce hoopla about the city's refurbishment, you should find Long Beach a revealing place, a kind of social studies lesson in modern American life. Travel Ocean Boulevard as it parallels the sea and you'll pass from quaint homes to downtown skyscrapers to fire-breathing smokestacks.

For a dynamic example of what I mean, visit the enclave of **Naples** near the south end of town. Conceived early in the century, modeled on Italy's fabled canal towns, it's a tiny community of three islands separated by canals and linked with walkways. Waterfront greenswards gaze out on Alamitos Bay and its fleet of sloops and motorboats. You can wander along bayside paths past comfortable homes, contemporary condos, and humble cottages. Fountains and miniature traffic circles, alleyways and boulevards, all form an incredible labyrinth along which you undoubtedly will become lost.

Adding to the sense of old Italia is the **Gondola Getaway** (5437 East Ocean Boulevard, Long Beach; 213-433-9595), a romantic hour-long cruise through the canals of Naples. For a hefty price (less, however, than a ticket to Italy), you can climb aboard a gondola, dine on hors d'oeuvres, and be serenaded with Italian music.

The **Long Beach Museum of Art** (2300 East Ocean Boulevard; 213-439-2119) is a must. Dedicated to 20th-century art, this avant garde museum has ever-changing exhibitions ranging from German Expressionism to contemporary Southern California work. Particularly noted for its video presentations, the museum is a window on modern culture.

For a touch of early Spanish culture, plan on visiting the region's old adobes. **Rancho Los Alamitos** (6400 Bixby Hill Road; 213-431-2511), built in 1806 with walls four feet thick, is Southern California's oldest remaining house. Among its gardens, brick walkways, and majestic magnolias, you can tour old barns, a blacksmith shop, and feed shed. There's also a restored chuck wagon with a coffee pot still resting on the wood-burning stove.

Rancho Los Cerritos (4600 Virginia Road; 213-424-9423), a two-story Spanish colonial home, once served as headquarters for a 28,000-acre ranch. Now the 19th-century adobe is filled with Victorian furniture and surrounded by gardens.

The Pacific Ocean may be Long Beach's biggest natural attraction, but many birds in the area prefer the **El Dorado Nature Center** (7550 East Spring Street; 213-425-8569). Part of the 800-acre El Dorado Park complex, this wildlife sanctuary offers one- and two-mile hikes past a lake and creek. About 150 bird species as well as numerous land animals can be sighted. Though located in a heavily urbanized area, the facility encompasses several ecological zones.

Chapter Two in the Long Beach civics lesson is the steel-and-glass downtown area, where high-rise hotels vie for dominance. The best way to tour this crowded commercial district is to stroll **The Promenade,** a six-block brick walkway leading from 3rd Street to the waterfront. There's a **tile mosaic** (Promenade and 3rd Street) at the near end portraying an idyllic day at the beach complete with sailboats, sunbathers, and lifeguards. Midway along the landscaped thoroughfare sits the **Long Beach Convention & Visitors Council** (180 East Ocean Boulevard, #150; 213-436-3645), home to maps, brochures, and other bits of information. Then you'll arrive at a park shaded with palm trees and adjacent to **Shoreline Village** (407 Shoreline Village Drive) a marina and shopping center disguised as a 19th-century fishing village.

Long Beach Part III rises in the form of oil derricks and industrial complexes just across the water. To view the freighters, tankers, and warships lining the city's piers, climb aboard the **Long Beach Harbor Cruise** (213-514-3838), which departs from Shoreline Village or the *Queen Mary* for hour-long narrated tours of blue-collar Long Beach.

Fittingly, the climax of a Long Beach tour comes at the very end, after you have experienced the three phases of urban existence. Just across the Los Angeles River, along Harbor Scenic Drive ("scenic" in this case meaning construction cranes and cargo containers), lies one of the strangest sights I've ever encountered. The first time I saw it, peering through the steel filigree of a suspension bridge, with harbor lights emblazoning the scene, I thought something had gone colossally wrong with the world. An old style ocean liner, gleaming eerily in the false light, appeared to be parked on the ground. Next to it an overgrown geodesic dome, a kind of giant polyethelene tit, was swelling up out of the earth.

Unwittingly I had happened upon Long Beach's two top tourist attractions, the *Queen Mary* and the *Spruce Goose*, respectively the world's largest ocean liner and airplane. Making her maiden voyage in 1936, the **Queen Mary** (Pier J; 213-435-3511) was the pride of Great Britain. Winston Churchill, the Duke and Duchess of Windsor, Greta Garbo, and Fred Astaire sailed on her, and during World War II, converted to military service, she carried so many troops across the Atlantic that Adolf Hitler offered $250,000 and the Iron Cross to the U-boat captain who sank her.

Today she is the pride of Long Beach, a 1000-foot-long "city at sea" transformed into a floating museum which brilliantly re-creates shipboard life. An elaborate walking tour carries you down into the engine room (a world of pumps and propellers), out along the decks, and up to each level of this multistage behemoth.

The grand lady is a masterpiece of art deco architecture. Dioramas throughout the ship realistically portray every aspect of sailing life during the great age of ocean liners.

The *Queen Mary* is expertly refurbished and wonderfully laid out, an important addition to the Long Beach seafront. Her neighbor in the geodesic dome, on the other hand, is an absurdity capped by an absurdity. The **Spruce Goose** (Pier J; 213-435-3511), the largest plane ever built, resides in the world's biggest free-standing dome.

In case you've forgotten, the *Spruce Goose* was built by Howard Hughes, the bizarre billionaire who ended his life hiding in a hotel room, addicted to drugs, imprisoned by his own employees. His plane, with a 320-foot wing span and a tail section eight stories high, is the biggest white elephant in history.

Built to ferry World War II troops and materiel across the Atlanic, the 200-ton behemoth was deemed "a half-baked" idea by critics. It was. The monster cost millions to build, wasn't completed until after the war, and then flew only once, for one mile. Why anyone would memorialize this monument to waste and excess is a question to ponder. Happily, the admission you pay to see this eighth wonder includes tours of the *Queen Mary*, a space-age complex called the **Time Voyager**, and **Londontowne,** an ersatz-shopping-mall-cum-19th-century-English-village.

SAN PEDRO

San Pedro is home to **Los Angeles Harbor,** a region of creosote and rust, marked by 28 miles of busy waterfront. This landscape of oil tanks and cargo containers services thousands of ships every year and houses the country's largest commercial fishing fleet.

Head over to the **22nd Street Landing** (foot of 22nd Street) and watch the boats unload their hauls of tuna, mackerel, bass, and halibut. You can buy crab and fish fresh from the nets. Then wander the waterfront and survey this frontier of steel and oil. Here awkward, unattractive ships glide as gracefully as figure skaters and the machinery of civilization goes about the world's work with a clatter and boom. The most populous shorebirds are cargo cranes.

Ports O' Call Village (entrance at foot of 6th Street) a shopping mall in the form of a 19th-century port town, houses several outfits conducting harbor cruises. The boats sail around the San Pedro waterfront and venture out for glimpses of the surrounding shoreline; for information, contact **Buccaneer Cruises** (Ports O' Call Village, San Pedro; 213-548-1085).

For a view of how it used to be, stop by the **Los Angeles Maritime Museum** (Berth 84; 213-548-7618). This dock-side showplace displays models of ships ranging from fully rigged brigs to 19th-century steam sloops to World War II battleships. There's even an 18-foot re-creation of the ill-starred *Titanic* and the ocean liner model used to film *The Poseidon Adventure*.

Another piece in the port's historic puzzle is placed several miles inland at the **Phineas Banning Residence Museum** (401 East M Street, Wilmington; 213-548-7777). This imposing Greek Revival house, built in 1864, was home to the man who dreamed, dredged, and developed Los Angeles harbor. Today Phineas Banning's Mansion, complete with a cupola from which he watched ships navigate his port, is furnished in period pieces and open for guided tours.

By definition any shipping center is of strategic importance. Head up to **Fort MacArthur** (Angel's Gate Park, 3601 South Gaffey Street; 213-548-7705) and discover the batteries with which World War II generals planned to protect Los Angeles Harbor. From this cement-and-steel compound you can inspect the bunkers and a small museum, then survey the coast. Once a site of gun turrets and grisly prospects, today it is a testimonial to the invasion that never came.

Another war, the Korean, will be commemorated in a monument being built nearby, but until it's completed you can visit the **Bell of Friendship**, which the people of South Korea presented to the United States during its 1976 bicentennial. Housed in a multicolor pagoda and cast with floral and symbolic images, it rests on a hilltop looking out on Los Angeles Harbor and the region's sharply profiled coastline.

Down the hill at the **Cabrillo Marine Museum** (3720 Stephen M. White Drive; 213-548-7562) there is a modest collection of display cases with samples of shells, coral, and shorebirds. Several dozen aquariums demonstate local fish and marine plants. Nearby stretches 1200-foot **Cabrillo Fishing Pier.**

Of greater interest is **Point Fermin Park** (807 Paseo del Mar), a 37-acre blufftop facility resting above spectacular tidepools and a marine preserve. The tidepools are accessible from the Cabrillo Marine Museum, which sponsors exploratory tours, and via steep trails from the park. Also of note is the **Point Fermin Lighthouse,** a unique 19th-century clapboard house with a beacon set in a rooftop crow's nest. From the park plateau, like lighthouse keepers of old, you'll have open vistas of the cliff-fringed coastline and a perfect perch for sighting whales during their winter migration.

Then drive along Paseo del Mar through arcades of stately palm trees and along sharp sea cliffs until it meets 25th Street. The sedimentary rocks throughout this region have been twisted and contorted into grotesque shapes by tremendous geologic pressures.

PALOS VERDES PENINSULA

The forces of nature seem entirely in control as you proceed out along the **Palos Verdes Peninsula** from San Pedro. Follow 25th Street, then Palos Verdes Drive South and encounter a tumbling region where terraced hills fall away to sharp coastal bluffs.

As you turn **Portuguese Bend,** the geology of this tumultuous area becomes startlingly evident when the road begins undulating through landslide zones. The earthquake faults which underlie the Los Angeles basin periodically fold and collapse the ground here. To one side you'll see the old road, fractured and useless. Even the present highway, with more patches than your favorite dungarees, is in a state of constant repair.

Of course the terrible power of nature has not dissuaded people from building here. Along the ridgetops and curving hills below are colonies of stately homes. With its rocky headlands, tidepool beaches and sun-spangled views, the place is simply so magnificent no one can resist.

Most lordly of all these structures is **The Wayfarer's Chapel** (5755 Palos Verdes Drive South, Rancho Palos Verdes; 213-377-1650), a simple but extraordinary center designed by the son of Frank Lloyd Wright. Nestled neatly into the surrounding landscape, the sunlit chapel is built entirely of glass and commands broad views of the terrain and ocean. With its stone altar and easy repose the temple was built to honor Emanuel Swedenborg, the 18th-century Swedish philosopher and mystic.

The **Point Vicente Lighthouse** rises further down the coast, casting an antique aura upon the area. While the beacon is not open to the public, the nearby **Point Vicente Interpretive Center** (31501 Palos Verdes Drive West, Rancho Palos Verdes; 213-377-5370) offers a small regional museum. This is a prime whale-watching spot in the winter when onlookers gather in the adjacent park to catch glimpses of migrating gray whales.

For a vision of how truly beautiful this region is, turn off Palos Verdes Drive West in Palos Verdes Estates and follow Paseo Lunado until it meets the sea at **Lunada Bay.** This half-moon inlet, backdropped by the jagged face of a rocky cliff, looks out upon an unending expanse of ocean. Steep paths lead down to a rocky shoreline rich in tidepools.

The road changes names to Paseo del Mar but continues past equally extraordinary coastline. There is a series of open fields and vista points along this **shoreline preserve** where you can gaze down from the blufftop to beaches and tidepools. Below, surfers ride the curl of frothing breaks and a few hardy hikers pick their way goat-like along precipitous slopes.

The setting is decidedly more demure at the **South Coast Botanic Gardens** (26300 South Crenshaw Boulevard, Palos Verdes; 213-377-0468; admission). This 87-acre garden is planted with exotic vegetation from Africa and New Zealand as well as species from other parts of the world.

SOUTH BAY

The birthplace of California's beach culture lies in a string of towns on the southern skirt of Santa Monica Bay—Redondo Beach, Hermosa Beach, and Manhattan Beach. It all began here in the South Bay with George Freeth, "the man who can walk on water." It seems that while growing up in Hawaii, Freeth resurrected the ancient Polynesian sport of surfing and transplanted it to California. Equipped with a 200-pound, solid-wood board, he introduced surfing to fascinated onlookers at a 1907 event in Redondo Beach.

It wasn't until the 1950s that the surfing wave crested. That's when a group of local kids called The Beach Boys spent their days catching waves at Manhattan Beach and their nights recording classic surfing songs. The surrounding towns became synonymous with the sport and a new culture was born, symbolized by blond-haired, blue-eyed surfers committed to sun, sand, and the personal freedom to ride the last wave.

Sightseeing spots are rather scarce in these beach towns. As you can imagine, the interesting places are inevitably along the waterfront. Each town sports a municipal pier, with rows of knickknack shops, cafes, and oceanview lounges, either along the pier or on the nearby waterfront.

In Redondo Beach, **Fisherman's Wharf** (Municipal Pier) is home to surfcasters and hungry seagulls. Walk out past the shops, salt breeze in your face, and you can gaze along the waterfront to open ocean. Waves wash against the pilings. Beneath the wood-plank walkway, seabirds dive for fish. These sights and sounds are repeated again and again on the countless piers that line the California coast.

In fact you'll find them recurring right up in Hermosa Beach at the **Municipal Pier** (foot of Pier Avenue). Less grandiose than its neighbor, this 1320-foot concrete corridor is simply equipped with a snack bar and bait shop. From the end you'll have a sweeping view back along Hermosa Beach's low skyline.

Similarly, the **Manhattan Beach Pier** (foot of Manhattan Beach Boulevard) extends 900 feet from the beach and offers the generic bait store and take-out stand. Not so generic are the ocean vistas and views of Manhattan Beach's pretty neighborhoods.

The other sightseeing diversion in these parts is the stroll. The stroll, that is, along the beach. **Esplanade** in Redondo Beach is a wide boulevard paralleling the waterfront. Wander its length and take in the surfers, sunbathers, and swimmers who keep this resort town on the map. Or walk down to the waterline and let the cool Pacific bathe your feet.

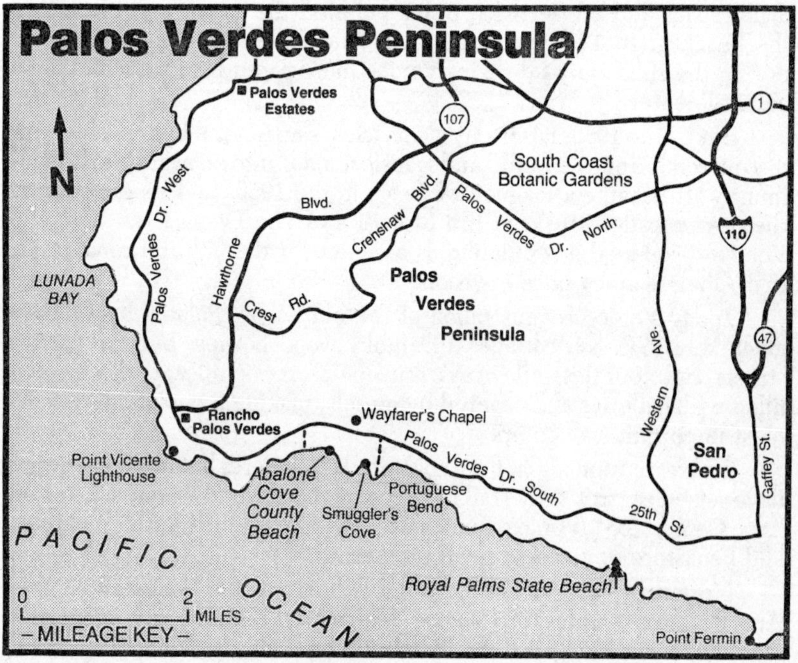

In Hermosa Beach you can saunter along **The Strand.** This pedestrian thoroughfare borders a broad beach and passes an endless row of bungalows, cottages, and condominiums. It's a pleasant walk with shops and restaurants along the way.

The Strand in Manhattan Beach lacks the commercial storefronts but parallels a silver strand. Wide and wonderful, the beach is lined by beautiful homes with plate-glass windows that reflect the blue hues of sea and sky. Together, these oceanfront walkways link the South Bay towns in a course that bicyclists can follow for miles.

VENICE

Venice, California was the dream of one man, a tobacco magnate named Albert Kinney. He envisioned a "Venice of America," a Renaissance town of gondoliers and single-lane bridges, connected by 16 miles of canals.

After convincing railroad barons and city fathers, Kinney dredged swampland along Santa Monica Bay, carved a network of canals, and founded this dream city in 1905. The place was an early 20th-century answer to Disneyland with gondola rides and amusement parks. The canals were lined with vaulted arches and rococo-style hotels.

Oil spelled the doom of Kinney's dream. Once black gold was discovered beneath the sands of Venice, the region became a landscape of drilling rigs and oil derricks. Spills polluted the canals and blackened the beaches. In 1929 the city of Los Angeles filled in the canals and during the subsequent decades Venice more resembled a tar pit than a cultural center.

But by the 1950s latter-day visionaries—artists and bohemians—rediscovered "Kinney's Folly" and transformed it into an avant garde community. It became a magnet for Beats in the 1950s and hippies during the next decade. Musician Jim Morrison of The Doors lived here and Venice developed a reputation as a center for the cultural renaissance that Albert Kinney once envisioned.

Today Venice retains much of the old flavor. Palatial hotels have given way to beach cottages and funky wood houses, but the narrow streets and countless alleyways remain. More significant, the town is filled with galleries and covered by murals, making it one of the region's most important art centers.

The revolution might have sputtered elsewhere, but in Venice artists have seized control. City Hall has become the **Beyond Baroque Literary Arts Center** (681 Venice Boulevard; 213-822-3006), housing a library and bookstore devoted to small presses.

Next door, the Venice City Jail is home to the **Social and Public Arts Resource Center** (685 Venice Boulevard; 213-822-9560). The prison is an imposing 1923 art deco-style building with a cell block converted into an art gallery. Many of the cells are intact and you'll walk through an iron door to view contemporary paintings by local artists. The center also sponsors lectures, poetry workshops, performance art events, and video screenings.

Both the Venice City Hall and Jail are great places to learn about what's going on in the community. Matter of fact, the **Venice Chamber of Commerce** (213-827-2366) resides in City Hall. If you can find someone in (which is not always easy) they will provide maps, brochures, and answers.

The commercial center of Venice rests at the intersection of Windward Avenue and Main street. Windward was the central boulevard of Kinney's dream city and the **Traffic Circle,** marked today by a small sculpture, was to be an equally grand lagoon. Continue along Windward Avenue to the **arcades,** a series of Italian-style colonnades which represent one of the few surviving elements of old Venice.

The heart of modern-day Venice pulses along the **boardwalk,** a two-mile strip that follows Ocean Front Walk from Washington Street to Ozone Avenue. **Venice Pier** (Ocean Front Walk and Washington Street), an 1100-foot fishing pier, anchors one end. Between Washington Street and Windward Avenue, the promenade is bordered by a palisades of beachfront homes, two- and three-story houses with plate-glass facades.

Walking north, the real action begins around 18th Avenue, at **Muscle Beach,** where rope-armed heavies work out in the weight pen, smacking punching bags and flexing their pecs, while gawking onlookers dream of oiling their bodies and walking with a muscle-bound strut.

The rest of the boardwalk is a grand open-air carnival which you should try to visit on the weekend. It is a world of artists and anarchists, derelicts and dreamers, a vision of what life would be if heaven was an insane asylum. Guitarists, jugglers, conga drummers, and clowns perform for the crowds. Kids on roller skates and bicycles whiz past rickshaws and unicycles. Street hawkers and panhandlers work the unwary while singers with scratchy voices pass the hat. Vendors dispense everything from corn dogs to cotton candy, T-shirts to wind-up toys. Venice, to quote Bob Dylan, represents "life and life only," but a rarefied form of life, slightly, beautifully askew.

Up the coast, **Marina del Rey** represents the largest manmade small boat harbor in the world. Over 6000 pleasure boats and yachts dock here. Harbor cruises are provided aboard a mock Mississippi riverboat by the **Marina Cruise Line** (13727 Fiji Way; 213-822-1151).

The entire region was once a marsh inhabited by a variety of waterfowl. Personally I think they should have left it to the birds. Marina del Rey is an ersatz community, a completely fabricated place where the main shopping area, **Fisherman's Village** (13763 Fiji Way; 213-823-5411), resembles a New England whaling town, and everything else attempts to portray something it's not. With its endless condominiums, pretentious homes, and overpriced restaurants, Marina del Rey is an artificial limb appended to the coast of Los Angeles.

SANTA MONICA

Pass from Venice into Santa Monica and you'll trade the boardwalk for a **promenade.** It's possible to walk for miles along Santa Monica's fluffy beach, past pastel-colored condominiums and funky woodframe houses. Roller skaters and bicyclists galore crowd the byways and chess players congregate at the picnic tables.

A middle-class answer to mod Malibu, Santa Monica started as a seaside resort in the 1870s when visitors bumped over long, dusty roads by stagecoach from Los Angeles. After flirting with the film industry in the age of silent movies, Santa Monica reverted in the 1930s to a quiet beach town which nevertheless was notorious for the gambling ships moored offshore. It was during this period that detective writer Raymond Chandler immortalized the place as "Bay City" in his brilliant Philip Marlowe novels.

Today Santa Monica is *in*. Its clean air, pretty beaches, and attractive homes have made it one of the most popular places to live in Los Angeles. As real estate prices have skyrocketed, liberal politics have ascended. Former Chicago Seven activist Tom Hayden is the state assemblyman here, working on local causes with his wife, actress Jane Fonda. Santa Monica, it seems, has become Southern California's answer to Berkeley.

Highlight of the beach promenade (and perhaps all Santa Monica) is the **Santa Monica Pier** (foot of Colorado Avenue). No doubt about it, the place is a scene. Acrobats work out on the playground below, surfers catch waves offshore, and street musicians strum guitars. And I haven't even mentioned the official attractions. There's a turn-of-the-century carousel with hand-painted horses that was featured in that cinematic classic, *The Sting*. There are shooting galleries, peep shows, video parlors, pinball machines, skee ball, and bumper cars.

From here it's a jaunt up to the **Santa Monica Convention & Visitors' Bureau** information kiosk (1430 Ocean Avenue; 213-392-9631). Here are maps, brochures, and helpful workers.

The booth is located in **Palisades Park,** a pretty, palm-lined greensward that extends north from Colorado Avenue more than a mile along the sandstone cliffs fronting Santa Monica beach. One of the park's stranger attractions here is the **Camera Obscura** (located in the Senior Recreation Center, 1450 Ocean Avenue), a periscope of sorts through which you can view the pier, beach, and surrounding streets.

For a glimpse into Santa Monica's past, take in the **Heritage Square Museum** (2612 Main Street; 213-392-8537). Heirlooms and antiques are housed in a grand American Colonial Revival-style home. The mansion dates to 1894 and is furnished entirely in period pieces. There are photo archives and historic knickknacks galore.

Angels' Attic (516 Colorado Avenue; 213-394-8331) is more than a great name. Contained in this 1894 Victorian is a unique museum of antique playthings for children. Toy trains run along the ceiling and dollhouses in every shape from Tudor home to crennelated castle adorn the rooms. There's a Noah's ark worth of miniature animals plus a gallery of precious dolls. In keeping with the spirit of the museum, they serve tea on the front porch.

Sympathetic as it is to liberal politics, Santa Monica is nonetheless an extremely wealthy town. In fact it's an fusion of two very different neighbors, mixing the bohemian strains of Venice with the monied elements of Malibu. For a look at the latter influence, take a drive from Ocean Avenue out along **San Vicente Boulevard.** This fashionable avenue, with its arcade of magnolias, is lined on either side with lovely homes. But they pale by comparison with the estates you will see by turning left on **La Mesa Drive.** This quiet suburban street boasts a series of marvelous Spanish Colonial, Tudor, and contemporary-style houses.

At first glance, the **Self Realization Fellowship Lake Shrine** (17190 Sunset Boulevard; 213-454-4114) in nearby Pacific Palisades is an odd amalgam of pretty things. Gathered along the shore of a placid pond are a Dutch windmill, a houseboat, and a shrine topped with something resembling a giant artichoke. A waterfall tumbles here, bamboo stalks rise there, a highway hums in the background. In fact, the windmill is a chapel welcoming all religions, the houseboat is a former stopping place of yogi and Self Realization Fellowship founder Paramahansa Yogananda, and the oversized artichoke is a golden lotus archway near which some of Indian leader Mahatma Gandhi's ashes are enshrined. A strange but potent collection of icons in an evocative setting.

Several miles inland at **Will Rogers State Historic Park** (14253 Sunset Boulevard, Pacific Palisades; 213-454-8212), on a hillside overlooking the Pacific, you can tour the ranch and home of America's greatest cowboy philosopher. Will Rogers, who started as a trick roper in traveling rodeos, hit the big time in Hollywood during the 1920s as a kind of cerebral comedian whose humorous wisdom plucked a chord in the American psyche.

From 1928 until his tragic death in 1935, the lariat laureate occupied this 31-room home with his family. The house is deceptively large but not grand; the woodframe design is basic and unassuming, true to Will Rogers' Oklahoma roots. Similarly the interior is decorated with Indian rugs and ranch tools. Western knickknacks adorn the tables and one room is dominated by a full-sized stuffed calf which Rogers utilized for roping practice. Well worth visiting, the "house that jokes built" is a simple expression of a vital personality.

MALIBU

Continuing north, Los Angeles County's final fling is **Malibu,** a 27-mile long ribbon lined on one side with pearly beaches and on the other by the Santa Monica Mountains. Famed as a movie star retreat and surfer's heaven, Malibu is one of America's mythic communities.

It has been a favored spot among Hollywood celebrities since the 1920s when a new highway opened the region and film stars like Clara Bow and John Gilbert publicized the idyllic community. By the 1950s Malibu was rapidly developing and becoming nationally known for its rolling surf and freewheeling lifestyle. The 1959 movie *Gidget* cast Sandra Dee and James Darren as Malibu beach bums and the seaside community was on its way to surfing immortality.

Today blond-mopped surfers still line the shore and celebrities continue to congregate in beachfront bungalows. Matter of fact, the most popular sightseeing in Malibu consists of ogling the homes of the very rich. **Malibu Road,** which parallels the waterfront, is a prime strip. To make it as difficult as possible for common riffraff to reach the beach, the homes are built townhouse-style with no space between them. It's possible to drive for miles along the water without seeing the beach, only the backsides of baronial estates. Happily there are a few access ways to the beach, so it's possible to wander along the sand enjoying views of both the ocean and the picture-window palaces. Among the access ways is one which local wags named after "Doonesbury" character Zonker Harris.

What's amazing about these beachfront colonies is not the houses, which really can't compare to the estates in Beverly Hills, but the fact that people insist on building them so close to the ocean that every few years several are demolished by high surf while others sink into the sand.

One of Malibu's loveliest houses is open to the public. The **Adamson Home,** located at Malibu Lagoon State Beach (23000 Route 1; 213-456-8432), is a stately Mediterranean-style structure adorned with ceramic tiles. With its bare-beam ceilings and inlaid floors, the house is a study in early 20th-century elegance. Outstanding as it is, the building is upstaged by the landscaped grounds, which border the beach at Malibu and overlook a lagoon alive with waterfowl.

The town's most prestigious address is the **J. Paul Getty Museum** (17985 Route 1; 213-459-8402), one of the wealthiest art museums in the world. Set on a hillside overlooking the sea, the building re-creates a 2000-year old Roman villa in the most splendid manner imaginable.

The colonnaded entranceway, which greets the visitor with a reflecting pool and fountains, is nothing short of magnificent. This grand passage is adorned by bronze sculptures and lined with hedgerows. The floors are inlaid with tile, the walls are painted fresco style.

The galleries are equally as beautiful. Focusing on Greek and Roman antiquities, Renaissance and Baroque art, and French furniture, the museum reflects the taste of founder J. Paul Getty. Some of the world's finest artworks are displayed here and the relatively young museum has already established an awesome reputation in the art world.

Another seafront attraction is **Malibu Pier** (23000 Route 1) where you can walk out over the water, cast for fish, or gaze back along Malibu's heavily developed coastline. If you're in a sporting mood, they rent fishing tackle here; if you prefer less strenuous sports, there's a bar at the foot of the pier.

When you tire of Malibu's sand and surf, take a drive along one of the canyon roads which lead from Route 1 up into the Santa Monica Mountains. This chapparal country is filled with oak and sycamore forests and offers sweeping views back along the coast. Topanga Canyon Boulevard, perhaps the best known of these mountain roads, curves up to the rustic town of **Topanga.** Back in the 60s it was a fabled retreat for flower children. Even today vestiges of the hip era remain in the form of health food stores, New Age shops, and natural restaurants. Many of the woodframe houses are handcrafted and the community still vibrates to a slower rhythm than coastal Malibu and cosmopolitan Los Angeles.

To reach the top of the world (while making a mountain loop of this uphill jaunt), take Old Topanga Canyon Road from town and turn left out on **Mulholland Highway.** With its panoramic views of the ocean, Los Angeles Basin, and San Fernando Valley, Mulholland is justifiably famous. The road rides the ridgetop of the Santa Monica Mountains for almost fifty miles from Hollywood down to the Malibu shore. Late on weekend nights it's a rendezvous for lovers and a drag strip for daredevil drivers, but the rest of the time you'll find it a sinuous country road far from the madding mobs. (To complete the circle follow Kanan–Dume Road back down to the ocean.)

SANTA CATALINA ISLAND

Twenty-six miles across the sea,
You know the song.
Santa Catalina is a'waitin' for me,
Everyone has heard it.
Santa Catalina, the island of
Romance, romance, romance, romance.

Actually this Mediterranean hideaway is parked just 22 miles off the Los Angeles coastline. But for romance, the song portrays it perfectly. Along its 54 miles of shoreline Catalina offers sheer cliffs, pocket beaches, hidden coves, and some of the finest skin diving anywhere. To the interior mountains rise sharply to over 2000 feet elevation. Island fox, black antelope, mountain goats, and over 400 bison range the island while its waters teem with marlin, swordfish, and barracuda.

Happily, this unique habitat is preserved for posterity and adventurous travelers by an arrangement under which 86 percent of the island lies undeveloped, protected by the Santa Catalina Conservancy. Avalon, the famous coastal resort enclave, is the only town on the island. The rest is given over to mountain wilderness and pristine shoreline.

As romantic as its setting is the history of the island. Originally part of the Baja coastline, it broke off from the mainland eons ago and drifted 100 miles to the northwest. Its earliest inhabitants arrived perhaps 4000 or 5000 years ago, leaving scattered evidence of their presence before being supplanted by the Gabrielino Indians around 500 B.C. A society of sun worshippers, the Gabrielinos constructed a sacrificial temple, fished island waters, and traded ceramics and soapstone carvings with mainland tribes, crossing the channel in canoes.

Juan Rodriguez Cabrillo discovered Catalina in 1542, but the place proved of such little interest to the Spanish that other than Sebastian Vizcaino's exploration in 1602 they virtually ignored it.

By the 19th century Russian fur traders, attracted by the rich colonies of sea otters, succeeded in exterminating both the otters and the indigenous natives. Cattle and sheep herders took over the Gabrielinos' land while pirates and smugglers, hiding in Catalina's secluded coves, menanced the coast.

Later in the century Chinese coolies were secretly landed on the island before being illegally carried to the mainland. Even during Prohibition it proved a favorite place among rumrunners and bootleggers. Gold fever swept Santa Catalina in 1863 as miners swept onto the island, but the rush never panned out.

Other visionaries, seeing in Catalina a major resort area, took control. After changing hands several times the island was purchased in 1919 by William Wrigley, Jr. The Wrigley family—better known for their ownership of a chewing gum company and the Chicago Cubs baseball team—developed Avalon for tourism and left the rest of the island to nature.

Attracting big-name entertainers and providing an escape from urban Los Angeles, Avalon soon captured the fancy of movie stars and wealthy Californians. Today **Avalon** is the port of entry for the island. Set in a luxurious amphitheater of green mountains, the town is like a time warp of Southern California early in the century. The architecture is a blend of Mediterranean and Victorian homes as well as vernacular structures designed by creative locals who captured both the beautiful and whimsical.

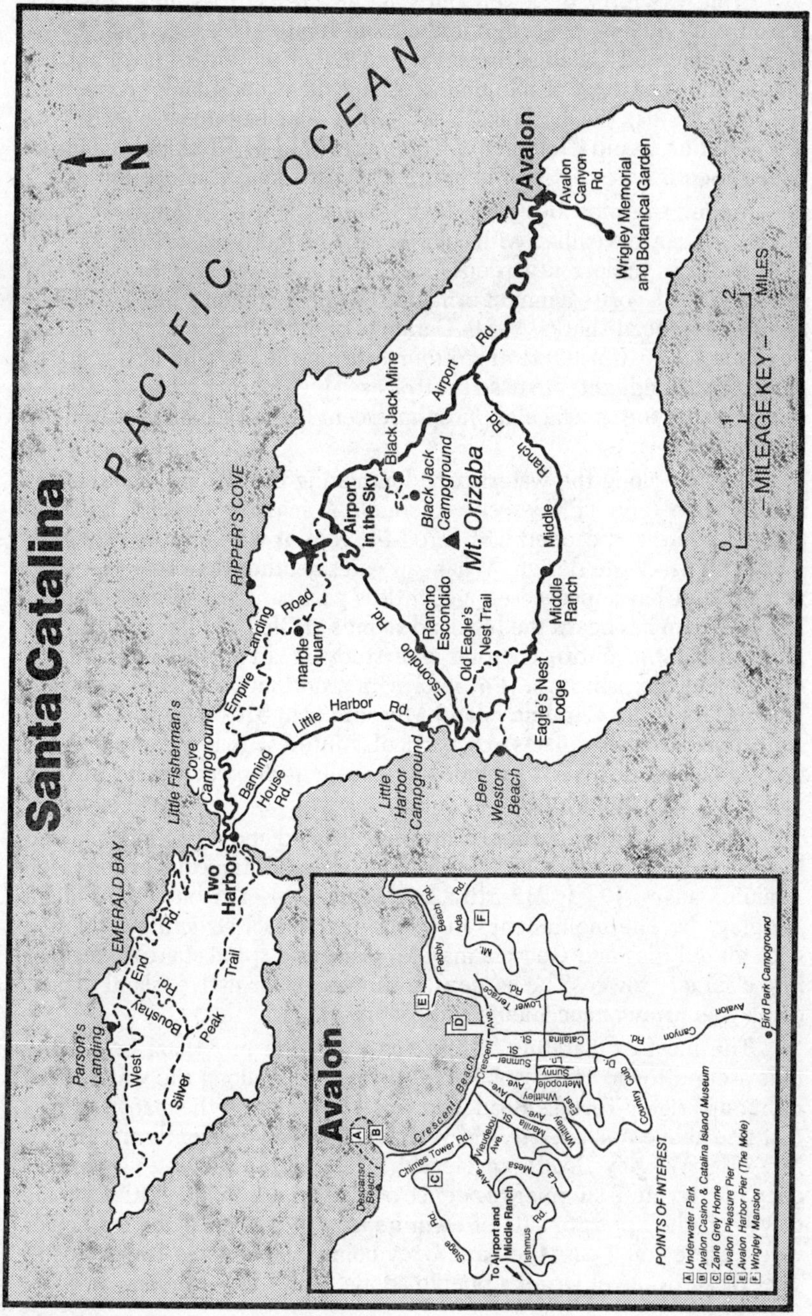
Santa Catalina
N
PACIFIC OCEAN
Parson's Landing
EMERALD BAY
West End Rd.
Boushay Rd.
Silver Peak Trail
West
Two Harbors
Little Fisherman's Cove Campground
Banning House Rd.
Empire Landing Road
marble quarry
RIPPER'S COVE
Little Harbor Rd.
Little Harbor Campground
Ben Weston Beach
Eagle's Nest Lodge
Old Eagle's Nest Trail
Escondido Rd.
Rancho Escondido
Airport in the Sky
Black Jack Campground
Black Jack Mine
Mt. Orizaba
Middle Ranch
Middle Ranch Rd.
Airport Rd.
Avalon
Avalon Canyon Rd.
Wrigley Memorial and Botanical Garden
0 1 2
— MILEAGE KEY — MILES
Avalon
Descanso Beach
Chimes Tower Rd.
Crescent Beach
Crescent Ave.
Vieudelou Ave.
Marilla St.
Whitley Ave.
East Whitley
Metropole
Sunny Ln.
Sumner St.
Catalina St.
Lower Terrace Rd.
Pebbly Beach Rd.
Ada Rd.
Mt.
Country Club Dr.
Canyon Rd.
Avalon
Bird Park Campground
Mesa Ave.
La Mesa
Isthmus Rd.
Stage Rd.
To Airport and Middle Ranch
POINTS OF INTEREST
A Underwater Park
B Avalon Casino & Catalina Island Museum
C Zane Grey Home
D Avalon Pleasure Pier
E Avalon Harbor Pier (The Mole)
F Wrigley Mansion

From the ferry dock you can wander **Crescent Avenue,** Avalon's oceanfront boulevard. Stroll out along the **Avalon Pleasure Pier** (Crescent Avenue and Catalina Street) for a view of the entire town and its surrounding crescent of mountains. Along this wood-plank promenade are food stands, the harbormaster's office, and bait-and-tackle shops. The **Catalina Island Chamber of Commerce** (213-510-1520) has an information booth here that will help orient you to Avalon and the island.

Among the pier kiosks are some offering **glass bottom boat tours** out to a nearby cove filled with colorful fish and marine plant life. Known as Catalina's "undersea gardens," the area is crowded with rich kelp beds and is a favorite haunt of brilliant red goby, golden adult Garibaldi, and hammerhead sharks. **Santa Catalina Island Company** (Avalon Harbor Pier; 213-510-2000) features tours during the day and also at night when huge floodlights are used to attract sea life. During summer months they seek out the spectacular phosphorescent flying fish which seasonally inhabit these waters.

Further along the waterfront, dominating the skyline, sits the **Avalon Casino** (end of Crescent Avenue). A massive circular building painted white and capped with a red-tile roof, it was built in 1929 after a Spanish Moderne design. What can you say other than that the place is famous: it has appeared on a countless post cards and travel posters. The ballroom has heard the big band sounds of Glenn Miller and Tommy Dorsey and the entire complex is a study in art deco with fabulous murals and tile paintings. (For information on tours call 213-510-2000.) Downstairs is the **Catalina Island Museum** (213-510-2414) with a small collection of local artifacts. Of particular interest is the contour relief map of the island which provides an excellent perspective for anyone venturing into the interior.

Another point of particular interest, located about two miles inland in Avalon Canyon, is the **Wrigley Memorial and Botanical Garden** (1400 Avalon Canyon Road; 213-510-2288; admission), a tribute to William Wrigley, Jr. The monument, an imposing 130-foot structure fashioned with glazed tiles and Georgia marble, features a spiral staircase leading into a solitary tower. The gardens, a showplace for native island plants, display an array of succulents and cactus.

The most exhilarating sightseeing excursion in Avalon lies in the hills around town. Head out Pebbly Beach Road along the water, turn right on Wrigley Terrace Road, and you'll be on one of the many terraces that rise above Avalon. The **old Wrigley Mansion** (currently the Inn on Mt. Ada, Wrigley Road), an elegant estate with sweeping views, was once the (ho hum) summer residence of the Wrigley family. Other scenic drives on the opposite side of town lie along Stage and Chimes Tower roads. Here you'll pass the **Zane Grey home** (199 Chimes Tower Road). The Western novel writer's pueblo adobe is also now a hotel.

Both routes snake into the hills past rocky outcroppings and patches of cactus. The slopes are steep and unrelenting. Below you blocks of houses run in rows out to a fringe of palm trees and undergrowth. Gaze around from this precarious perch and you'll see that Avalon rests in a green bowl surrounded by mountains.

When it comes time to venture further afield, you'll find that traveling around Santa Catalina Island is more complicated than it first seems. You can hike or bicycle anywhere on the island. **Brown's Bikes** (107 Pebbly Beach Road; 213-510-0986) rents bicycles, tandems, and mountain bikes. In Avalon proper it's possible to rent golf carts from outfits like **Avalon's Cartopia Cars** (615 Crescent Avenue; 213-510-2493) or **Catalina Auto Rental** (301 Crescent Avenue; 213-510-0111). There are also taxis in town.

No rental cars operate on the island and visitors are not permitted to drive. **Santa Catalina Island Company** (213-510-2000), which has a visitor information center at 420 Crescent Avenue, conducts tours around the island. They offer coastal cruises and inland motor tours and will drop off hikers and campers en route.

Catalina Safari Bus (213-510-2800) provides tours and drop-offs and **Catalina Island Conservancy** (206 Metropole Avenue; 213-510-1421), the agency charged with overseeing the island, shuttles visitors into the interior and provides drop-off services. To hike independently outside Avalon you will need a permit from the **Los Angeles County Department of Parks and Recreation** (213 Catalina Street; 213-510-0688). Permits are also available at The Airport in the Sky (213-510-0143) and from the Catalina Cove and Camp Agency (P.O. Box 5044, Two Harbors; 213-510-0303).

The other thing to remember about Catalina is that perhaps more than any other spot along the California coast, its tourism is seasonal. The season, of course, is summer when mobs of people descend on the island. During winter everything slows down, storms wash through intermittently, and some facilities close. Spring and fall, when the crowds have subsided, the weather is good, and everything is still open, may be the best seasons of all.

Regardless of how you journey into Catalina's outback, there's only one way to get there, Airport Road. This paved thoroughfare climbs steadily from Avalon, offering views of the rugged coast and surrounding hills. Oak, pine, and eucalyptus dot the hillsides as the road follows a ridgetop with steep canyons falling away on either side. **Mt. Orizaba**, a flat-topped peak which represents the highest point on the island, rises in the distance.

A side road out to Black Jack Campground leads past **Black Jack Mine,** a silver mine closed since early in the century. Today little remains except tailing piles and a 520-foot shaft. Then the main road climbs to

Catalina's **Airport in the Sky,** a small landing facility located at 1600-feet elevation.

From the airport you might want to follow a figure eight course in your route around the island, covering most of the island's roads and taking in as much of the landscape as possible (beyond the airport all the roads are dirt). Just follow Empire Landing Road, a curving, bumping track with side roads that lead down past an **old marble quarry** to **Ripper's Cove.** Characteristic of the many inlets dotting the island, the cove is framed by sharply rising hills. There's a boulder-and-sand beach here and a coastline bordered by interesting rock formations.

Two Harbors, at the intersection of the figure eight's loops, is a half-mile wide isthmus connecting the two sections of Catalina Island. A small fishing pier, several tourist facilities, and a boat harbor, make this modest enclave the only developed area outside Avalon.

From here West End Road curves and climbs, bends and descends along a rocky coast pocked with cactus and covered by scrub growth. There are Catalina cherry trees along the route and numerous coves at the bottom of steep cliffs. Not for the faint-hearted, West End Road is a narrow, bumpy course that winds high above the shore.

Anchored off **Emerald Bay** are several rock islets crowded with sea birds. From **Parsons' Landing,** a small inlet with a gray-sand beach, dirt roads continue in a long loop out to the west end of the island, then back to Two Harbors.

Catalina possesses about 400 species of flora, some unique to the island, and is rich in wildlife. Anywhere along its slopes you are likely to spy quail, wild turkey, mountain goats, island fox, mule deer, and wild boar. Bison, placed on the island by a movie company filming a Western way back in the 1920s, graze seemingly everywhere. En route back toward Avalon, Little Harbor Road climbs into the mountains. From the hilltops around **Little Harbor** you can see a series of ridges which drop along sheer rockfaces to the frothing surf below.

Take a detour up to **Rancho Escondido,** a working ranch that breeds champion Arabian horses. There's an arena here where trainers work these exquisite animals through their paces, and a "saddle and trophy room" filled with handcrafted riding gear as well as prizes from major horse shows.

Back at Little Harbor, Middle Ranch Road cuts through a mountain canyon past **Middle Ranch,** a small spread with livestock and oat fields. En route lies **Eagles' Nest Lodge,** a stagecoach stop dating to 1890. Numbered among the antique effects of this simple woodframe house are wagon wheels and a split-rail fence. Carry on to Airport Road then back to Avalon, completing this easy-eight route around an extraordinary island.

Shopping

LONG BEACH AND SAN PEDRO SHOPPING

The best street shopping in Long Beach is located near the Naples neighborhood along **East 2nd Street.** This 15-block strip between Livingston Drive and Bayshore Avenue is a gentrified row. Either side is lined with art galleries, book shops, boutiques, jewelers, and import stores.

Shoreline Village (Shoreline Drive, Long Beach) is one of those waterfront malls Southern California specializes in. With a marina on one side, the buildings are New England-style shingle and clapboard structures designed to re-create an Atlantic Coast port town. My favorite spot here is not a shop at all but the carousel, a vintage turn-of-the-century beauty awhirl with colorful animals.

There are more than a dozen stores onboard the **Queen Mary** (Pier J, Long Beach). Shoppers are permitted to board the shopping deck freely during the week and for a special fee on weekends. Concentrated in the Piccadilly Circus section of the old ship are several souvenir shops as well as stores specializing in articles and artifacts from Great Britain. Perhaps the prettiest shopping arcade you'll ever enter, it is an art deco masterpiece with etched glass, dentil molding, and brass appointments.

Los Angeles Harbor's answer to the theme shopping mall craze is **Ports O' Call Village** (entrance at the foot of 6th Street, San Pedro), a mock 19th-century fishing village. There are clapboard stores with shutter windows, New England-style homes with gable roofs, and storehouses of corrugated metal. Dozens of shops here are located right on the water, giving you a chance to view the harbor while browsing the stores. It's one of those hokey but inevitable places that I swear to avoid but always seem to end up visiting.

SOUTH BAY SHOPPING

If they weren't famous Pacific beach communities, the South Bay enclaves of Redondo, Hermosa, and Manhattan beaches would seem like small-town America. Their central shopping districts are filled with pharmacies, supply shops, and shoe stores.

There are a few places of interest to folks from out of town. In Redondo Beach, scout out Catalina Avenue, particularly along its southern stretches. Shops in Hermosa Beach concentrate along Pier and Hermosa avenues, especially where they intersect. Likewise in Manhattan Beach, Manhattan Beach Boulevard is traversed by Highland and Manhattan avenues.

Be sure to stop in at **The Either/Or Bookstore** (124 Pier Avenue, Hermosa Beach). Situated on a hillside above the ocean, it's a multilevel affair built in a series of terraces. With an outstanding inventory of books and magazines, the store is also endowed with an intriguing history. It seems that years ago Thomas Pynchon—the brilliant, reclusive, rarely photographed author of *V* and *Gravity's Rainbow*—stopped in regularly to buy books and talk contemporary literature.

VENICE SHOPPING

To combine slumming with shopping, be sure to wander the **boardwalk** in Venice. Ocean Front Walk between Windward and Ozone avenues is lined with low-rent stalls selling beach hats, cheap jewelry, sunglasses, beach bags, and souvenirs. You'll also encounter **Small World Books** (1405 Ocean Front Walk, Venice; 213-399-2360), a marvelous beach-side shop with new books, used books, and magazines.

L.A. Louver (55 North Venice Boulevard and 77 Market Street), with two locations, is one of Venice's many vital and original galleries. It represents David Hockney and other famous painters as well as up-and-coming Los Angeles artists. There is also a covey of **art galleries** and **antique shops** along the 1200 to 1500 blocks of West Washington Boulevard.

The **Native American Art Gallery** (215 Windward Avenue) offers a fascinating collection of pottery, masks, woven baskets, turquoise jewelry, and Kachina dolls.

The **Beyond Baroque Library Arts Center** (681 Venice Boulevard), a clearinghouse for local talent, sponsors poetry readings, dramatic revues, lectures, and concerts. It's located in the old Venice City Hall. Next door, in the town's erstwhile jail, the **Social and Public Arts Resource Center** (685 Venice Boulevard) also organizes cultural events.

SANTA MONICA SHOPPING

Montana Avenue is Santa Monica's version of designer heaven, making it an interesting, if inflationary, strip to shop. From 7th to 17th Street chic shops and upscale establishments line either side of the thoroughfare.

Artcessories (704 Montana Avenue) has a stunning assortment of handwrought jewelry and other decorative pieces fashioned by regional and national artists. There's **Tess** (908 Montana Avenue) for women's wear and accessories or **Weathervane For Men** (1132 Montana Avenue) when shopping for men's clothing.

Sara (1324 Montana Avenue) up the street is like a miniature department store with fashions, jewelry, art pieces, and distinctive gifts. **The Quilt Gallery** (1611 Montana Avenue) has folk art, handwoven quilts, and other items of Americana.

Browse Main Street and you'll realize that Montana Avenue is only a practice round in the gentrification of Santa Monica. Block after block of this thoroughfare has been made over in trendy fashion and filled with stylish shops. Main Street was even the focus of a civic campaign which highlighted its upscale amenities.

The shopper's parade stretches most of the length of Main Street, but the center of action resides around the 2700 block. **Galleria Di Maio** (2525 Main Street) is an art deco mall with several spiffy shops. The **Gallery of Eskimo Art** (2665 Main Street), set in a beautifully refurbished brick building, has wonderful examples of Alaskan carving.

Main Street Gallery (2803 Main Street) specializes in Japanese folk art and antiques; the collection here is extraordinary. Even closer to museum status is the array of crystals, shells, and fossils at **Nature's Own** (2736 Main Street). The **B-1 Gallery** (2730 Main Street) displays strikingly original paintings by contemporary California artists; and **Colors of the Wind** (2900 Main Street), more than just a pretty name, has kites, pennants, flags, and banners.

Venture out Wilshire Boulevard and you'll uncover several specialty locations. **I. M. Chait Gallery** (2409 Wilshire Boulevard) features a very exclusive selection of Oriental artworks. Next door at **Wounded Knee** (2413 Wilshire Boulevard) there is an assortment of Native American crafts including sand paintings, jewelry, Kachina dolls, and Southwestern pottery.

Tortue Gallery (2917 Santa Monica Boulevard) could be better described as a museum of contemporary California art than a shop selling art. The canvases hanging here are brilliant and the gallery provides a singular insight into the local art scene.

The last of Santa Monica's several shopping enclaves is located in the center of town. Here you'll find **Santa Monica Place** (Broadway between 2nd and 4th streets), a mammoth triple-tiered complex with about 150 shops. This flashy atrium mall has everything from clothes to books to sporting goods to luggage to leather work, jewelry, toys, hats, and shoes.

Step out from this glittery gathering place and you'll immediately encounter **Santa Monica Mall** (between Broadway and Wilshire Boulevard), a three-block pedestrian promenade lined on either side with shops. The stores here are more functional, less expensive, and serve the surrounding community. There is one in particular that exemplifies Santa Monica's liberal politics. **Midnight Special Bookstore** (1350 Santa Monica Mall) specializes in politics and social sciences. Rather than current best sellers, the window displays will feature books on Latin America, world hunger, Africa, or disarmament.

It might be just around the corner from Santa Monica's chic shops but the 100 block of Broadway is the center of local funk. **Muskrat Clothing** (109 Broadway) specializes in secondhand items like *aloha* shirts, bowling shirts, velour jackets, and silk coats with maps of Japan embroidered on the backs. (Thought you'd never find one, eh?) **Out of**

the Past (130 Broadway) has more hand-me-downs. At **Na Na** (120 Broadway) the past is dead, but the future is happening in the form of New Wave accouterments like skull-and-crossbone earrings and Virgin Mary watches.

MALIBU SHOPPING

Over in Malibu, the **Tidepool Gallery** (22762 Route 1) is a beachcomber's dream. There are hundreds of varieties of seashells here as well as coral and shell jewelry. They also feature cards, wood carvings, and artwork, all reflecting the shop's oceanic motif.

Another singular store is **Cheryl Wilson's Doll Works** (22774 Route 1). Specializing in soft sculpture, the owner-artist creates lifelike (and sometimes life-size) dolls. Matter of fact they are so true to detail that she is often commissioned to make portrait dolls. So if you were thinking of giving your loved one something special, why not a stuffed version of yourself?

Somehow the name **Malibu Country Mart** (3835 Cross Creek Road) doesn't quite describe this plaza shopping mall. There's not much of the "country" about the pricey boutiques and galleries here. The parking lot numbers more Porsches than pickup trucks. But these two dozen stores will provide a sense of the Malibu lifestyle and give you a chance to shop (or window shop) for quality.

Up in the secluded reaches of Topanga Canyon there are numerous artists and craftspeople who have traded the chaos of the city for the serenity of the Santa Monica Mountains. **The Topanga Carver** (1944 Topanga Canyon Boulevard, Topanga) is one such urban exile. His sign welcomes you "to drop in to either bullshit or commission a piece;" or you might want to watch him "butcher wood" into anything from figureheads to carousel horses.

White Horse (1944 Topanga Canyon Boulevard, Topanga), an American Indian gift shop, is next door. Here you'll find Native American artifacts as well as handmade pottery, jewelry, and Kachina dolls.

SANTA CATALINA ISLAND SHOPPING

No one sails to Santa Catalina Island searching for bargains. Everything here has been shipped from the mainland and is that much more expensive as a result. The town of Avalon has a row of shops lining its main thoroughfare, Crescent Avenue, and other stores along the streets running up from the waterfront. Within this commercial checkerboard are also several mini-malls, one of which, **Metropole Market Place** (Crescent and Sumner avenues), is a nicely designed, modern complex. Half the stores in town are either souvenir or curio shops. I'd wait until you return to that shopping metropolis 26 miles across the sea.

Nightlife

LONG BEACH AND SAN PEDRO NIGHTLIFE

Panama Joe's (5100 East 2nd Street, Long Beach; 213-434-7417) cooks seven nights a week. The bands are jazz ensembles, rock groups, and assorted others, which create an eclectic blend of music. Your average tiffany-lamp-and-hanging-plant nightspot, the place is lined with sports photos and proudly displays an old oak bar.

Over at **The Reef** (880 Harbor Scenic Drive, Long Beach; 213-435-7096), a sprawling waterfront establishment, there's soft rock every weekend in the Mardi Gras ballroom.

No matter how grand, regardless of how much money went into its design, despite the care taken to assure quality, any Long Beach nightspot is hard pressed to match the elegance of the **Observation Bar** aboard the *Queen Mary* (Pier J, Long Beach; 213-435-3511). Once the first class bar for this grand old ship, the room commands a 180° view across the bow and out to the Long Beach skyline. The walls are lined with fine woods, a mural decorates the bar, and art deco appointments appear everywhere. Besides that, they feature live music every night (unfortunately in this Glenn Miller setting, the tunes are Top-40). For soft sounds you can always adjourn aft to **Sir Winston's Piano Bar,** a cozy and elegant setting decorated with memorabilia of the World War II British leader.

Buccaneer Cruises (Ports O' Call Village, San Pedro; 213-548-1085) hosts sunset dinner cruises around Los Angeles Harbor. These feature dining and dancing.

Landlubbers can enjoy a quiet drink on the waterfront at **Ports O' Call Restaurant** (Ports O' Call Village, San Pedro; 213-833-3553). In addition to a spiffy oak bar, they have a dockside patio.

Better yet, climb aboard the **S.S. Princess Louise** (Berth 94, San Pedro; 213-831-2351), a stately old yacht permanently moored in the harbor. It's a multideck affair with varnished wood trim and elegant appointments. For entertainment there's usually a pianist or small ensemble.

SOUTH BAY NIGHTLIFE

The folks at **Annabelle's** (1700 South Route 1, Redondo Beach; 213-316-1434) dance to Top-40 deejay music every night. Cover on weekends.

Concerts By The Sea (100 Fisherman's Wharf, Redondo Beach; 213-379-4998) is an important showcase for jazz musicians. Considered one of Los Angeles' most popular jazz clubs, it is located near the waterfront; cover.

The Comedy & Magic Club (1018 Hermosa Avenue, Hermosa Beach; 213-372-1193) features name acts nightly. Many of the comedians are television personalities with a regional, if not national, following. The supper club atmosphere is upscale and appealing. Cover.

One of Los Angeles' finest jazz clubs sits just a half-block from the beach. In appearance **The Lighthouse** (30 Pier Avenue, Hermosa Beach; 213-372-6911) is just a bar. But what a bar! Outstanding jazz and blues groups pass through regularly and there's live entertainment every night.

Brennan's (3600 Highland Avenue, Manhattan Beach; 213-545-4446) is a good old-fashioned Irish pub with a four-sided bar and lively crowd. Just a block up from the beach, it features live rock on weekends.

Orville & Wilbur's Restaurant (401 Rosecrans Boulevard, Manhattan Beach; 213-545-6639) is a lush, wood-paneled establishment with an upstairs bar that looks out over the ocean. The music, usually Top-40 or vintage rock, is live every night.

VENICE, SANTA MONICA, AND MALIBU NIGHTLIFE

The Townhouse (52 Windward Avenue, Venice; 213-392-4040), set in a '20s-era speakeasy, has live entertainment every weekend. The sound is mostly rock, but they also headline blues and country groups.

The Comeback Inn (1633 West Washington Boulevard, Venice; 213-396-7255), an informal restaurant-club, has jazz nightly. It's a small place, so you can usually count on a duo or trio performance; cover.

Merlin McFly's (2702 Main Street, Santa Monica; 213-392-8468) is a must. Magic is the password here: every evening magicians wander from table to table performing sleight-of-hand tricks. Even more unique is the wildly baroque interior. There's an elaborate carved wood bar guarded on either end by menacing griffins and highlighted by a stained-glass image of the great Merlin himself. Even the bar stools are decorated with molded figures while the walls are adorned with old show biz posters.

At My Place (1026 Wilshire Boulevard, Santa Monica; 213-451-8596), a spacious dinner club with live acts nightly, offers an eclectic blend of jazz, rhythm-and-blues, pop music, and comedy; cover.

Ye Olde King's Head (116 Santa Monica Boulevard, Santa Monica; 213-451-1402) might be the most popular British pub this side of the Thames. From dart boards to dark-wood walls, trophy heads to draft beer, it's a classic English watering hole. Known throughout the area, it draws crowds of local folks and expatriate Britishers.

Vaudeville is alive and well at the **Mayfair Theatre** (214 Santa Monica Boulevard, Santa Monica; 213-451-0621). This vintage 1911 building, with its gaslight decor, features a classic show that includes singers, dancers, magicians, comics, and a band. If variety is the spice of life, this is the main course. Cover.

McCabe's Guitar Shop (3101 Pico Boulevard, Santa Monica; 213-828-4497) is a folksy spot with live entertainment on weekends. The sounds are all acoustic and range from Scottish folk bands to jazz to blues to country. The concert hall is a room in back lined with guitars. Get down. Cover.

For a raucous good time try **The Oar House** and **Buffalo Chips** (2941 Main Street, Santa Monica; 213-396-4725). These adjoining bars are loud, brash places that draw hearty crowds. The music is recorded and the decor is Early Insanity—sawdust floors, mannekins and wagon wheels on the ceiling, alligator skins on the wall.

The **Screaming Clam Dance Club** (21150 Route 1, Malibu; 213-459-7866), located on the beach at Malibu, has dancing to deejay music every night. If you get tired hoofing it, you can lean back and watch the moon over the ocean.

SANTA CATALINA ISLAND NIGHTLIFE

Like all other Catalina amenities, nightspots are concentrated in Avalon. During summer months the **Santa Catalina Island Company** (420 Crescent Avenue; 213-510-2000) conducts buffet cruises along the coastline in an old paddlewheeler. There are splendid sunsets, pretty views of the shore, music, and dancing.

The **Chi Chi Club** (107 Sumner Avenue; 213-510-1441) is one of the hottest dance clubs on the island with live music and a lively crowd.

There's also dancing to deejay records or live sounds at **Solomon's Landing** (101 Marilla Avenue; 213-510-1474). The bar here is outdoors and the motif decidedly Mexican.

Also check the schedule for **Avalon Casino** (end of Crescent Avenue; 213-510-2000). This fabulous vintage ballroom still hosts big bands and most of the island's major events.

CHAPTER FIVE
South Central Coast

To call any one section of the California Coast the most alluring is to embark upon uncertain waters. Surely the South Central Coast, that 200-mile swath from Ventura to San Simeon, is a region of rare beauty. Stretching across Ventura, Santa Barbara, and San Luis Obispo counties, it embraces many of the West's finest beaches.

Five of California's 21 missions—in Ventura, Santa Barbara, Lompoc, San Luis Obispo, and further inland in Solvang—lie along this stretch. Chosen by the Spanish in the 1780s for their fertile pastures, natural harbors, and placid surroundings, they are an historic testimonial to the varied richness of the landscape.

The towns that grew up around these missions, evocative of old Spanish traditions, are emblems of California's singular culture. Santa Barbara, perhaps the state's prettiest town, is a warren of whitewashed buildings and red tile roofs, backdropped by rocky peaks and bounded by a five-mile palm-fringed beach.

Ventura and San Luis Obispo represent two of California's most underrated towns. In addition to a wealthy heritage, Ventura possesses beautiful beaches and San Luis Obispo is set amid velvet hills and rich agricultural areas. Both are less expensive than elsewhere and offer many of the same features without the pretensions.

Offshore are the Channel Islands, a 25-million-year-old chain and vital wildlife preserve. Sandblasted by fierce storms, pristine in their magnificence, they are a China shop of endangered species and unique life forms. While the nearby reefs are headstones for the many ships that have crashed here, the surrounding waters are crowded with sealife.

Together with the rest of the coast, the islands were discovered by Juan Rodriguez Cabrillo in 1542. The noted explorer found them inhabited by Chumash Indians, a collection of tribes occupying the coast from Malibu to Morro Bay. Hunters and gatherers, the Chumash were master mariners who built wood-plank canoes called *tomols*, capable of carrying ten people across treacherous waters to the Channel Islands. They in turn were preceded by the Oak Grove Tribes, which inhabited the region from 7000 to 3000 B.C.

Once Gaspar de Portola opened the coast to Spanish colonialists with his 1769 explorations, few Indians from any California tribes survived. Forced into servitude and religious conversion by the padres, the Chumash revolted at Santa Barbara Mission and Mission de la Purisima Concepcion in 1824. They held Purisima for a month before troops from Monterey overwhelmed them. By 1910 the Westerners who had come to save them had so decimated the Indians that their 30,000 population dwindled to 1250.

By the mid-1800s these lately arrived white men set out in pursuit of any sea mammal whose pelt would fetch a price. The Central Coast was a prime whale-hunting ground. Harpooners by the hundreds speared leviathans, seals, and sea lions, hunting them practically to extinction. Earlier in the century American merchants, immortalized in Richard Henry Dana's *Two Years Before the Mast*, had combed the coast trading for cattle hides.

The land that bore witness to this colonial carnage endured. Today the Central Coast and its offshore islands abound in sea lions, harbor seals, Northern fur seals, and elephant seals. Whales inhabit the deeper waters and game fish are plentiful. The only threats remaining are those from developers and the oil industry, whose offshore drilling resulted in the disastrous 1969 Santa Barbara spill.

The Central Coast traveler finds a Mediterranean climate, dry and hot in the summer, tempered by morning fog and winds off the ocean, then cool and rainy during winter months. Two highways, Routes 1 and 101, lead through this salubrious environment. The former hugs the coast much of the way, traveling inland to Lompoc and San Luis Obispo, and the latter, at times joining with Route 1 to form a single roadway, eventually diverges into the interior valleys.

Almost as much as the ocean, mountains play a vital part in the life of the coast. Along the southern stretches are the Santa Monica Mountains, which give way further north to the Santa Ynez Mountains. Below them, stretching along the coastal plain, are the towns of Oxnard, Ventura, Santa Barbara, and Goleta.

Both mountain systems are part of the unique Transverse Range, which unlike most North American mountains, travels from east to west rather than north and south. They are California's Great Divide, a point of demarcation between the chic, polished regions near Santa Barbara and the rough, wild territory around San Luis Obispo.

Arriving at the ocean around Point Concepcion, the Transverse Range separates the curving pocket beaches of the south and the endless sand dunes to the north. Here the continent takes a sharp right turn as

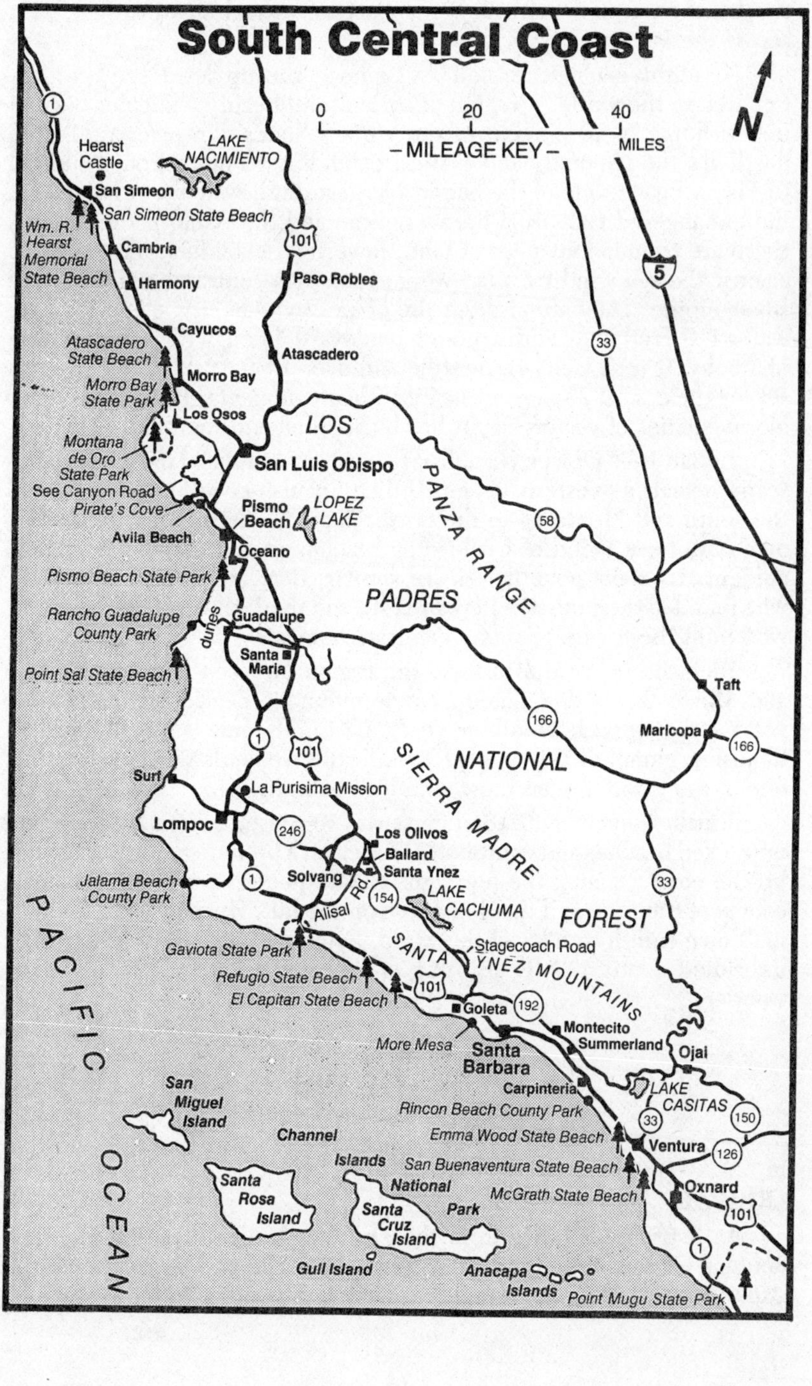
South Central Coast
0
20
40
– MILEAGE KEY –
MILES
N
1
Hearst Castle
LAKE NACIMIENTO
San Simeon
San Simeon State Beach
Wm. R. Hearst Memorial State Beach
101
Cambria
Paso Robles
Harmony
5
Cayucos
33
Atascadero State Beach
Atascadero
Morro Bay State Park
Morro Bay
Los Osos
LOS
Montana de Oro State Park
San Luis Obispo
See Canyon Road
Pirate's Cove
Pismo Beach
LOPEZ LAKE
PANZA RANGE
58
Avila Beach
Oceano
Pismo Beach State Park
PADRES
Rancho Guadalupe County Park
dunes
Guadalupe
Santa Maria
Point Sal State Beach
Taft
166
Maricopa
166
1
101
SIERRA MADRE
NATIONAL
Surf
La Purisima Mission
Lompoc
246
Los Olivos
Ballard
Santa Ynez
Jalama Beach County Park
1
Solvang
Rd.
154
LAKE CACHUMA
33
Alisal
FOREST
PACIFIC
Gaviota State Park
SANTA YNEZ MOUNTAINS
Stagecoach Road
Refugio State Beach
101
El Capitan State Beach
Goleta
192
Montecito
More Mesa
Santa Barbara
Summerland
Ojai
San Miguel Island
Carpinteria
LAKE CASITAS
Rincon Beach County Park
33
150
Channel
Emma Wood State Beach
Ventura
126
Islands
San Buenaventura State Beach
OCEAN
Santa Rosa Island
National
McGrath State Beach
Oxnard
Santa Cruz Island
Park
101
1
Gull Island
Anacapa Islands
Point Mugu State Park

the beaches, facing south in Santa Barbara, wheel about to look west across the Pacific.

Amid this geologic turmoil lies Lompoc, the top flower seed producing area in the world, a region of agricultural beauty and color beyond belief, home to 40 percent of the United States' flower crop. To the north are the Nipomo Sand Dunes, extending 18 miles from Point Sal to Pismo Beach, one of the nation's largest dune systems. A habitat for the endangered California brown pelican and the California least tern, these are tremendous piles of sand, towering to 450 feet, held in place against the sea wind by a lacework of ice plant, grasses, verbena, and silver lupine. They are also the site of an Egyptian city, complete with walls 110 feet high and a grand boulevard lined with sphinxes and pharaohs. It took Cecil B. deMille and over 1000 workers to build this set for the epic 1923 movie *The Ten Commandments*. Today, like other glorious cities of yesteryear, it lies buried beneath the sand.

In San Luis Obispo oceanfront gives way to ranch land as the landscape reveals a Western visage. Unlike Spanish-style Santa Barbara to the south and Monterey to the north, San Luis Obispo has defined its own culture, a blend of hard-riding ranchhand and easy-going college student. Its roots nonetheless are similar, deriving from the Spanish, who founded their mission here in 1772, and the 19th-century Americans who built the town's gracious Victorian homes.

Rich too in natural history, the region between San Luis Obispo and Morro Bay is dominated by nine mountain peaks, each an extinct volcano dating back 20 million years. Last in the line is Morro Rock, an imposing monolith surrounded by a fertile wetlands which represents one of the country's ten most vital bird habitats.

Further north civilization gives way to coastal quietude. There are untracked beaches and wind-honed sea cliffs, a prelude to Big Sur further up the coast. Among the few signs of the modern world are the artist colony of Cambria and that big house on the hill, Hearst Castle, California's own eighth wonder of the world. Symbol of boundless artistry and unbridled egotism, it is also one of the South Central Coast's many wonders.

Easy Living

Transportation

ARRIVAL

As it proceeds north from the Los Angeles area, coastal highway **Route 1** weaves in and out from **Route 101.** The two highways join in Oxnard and continue as a single roadway until a point 30 miles north of

Santa Barbara. Here they diverge, Route 1 heading toward the coast while Route 101 takes an inland route. The highways merge again near Pismo Beach and continue north to San Luis Obispo. Here Route 1 leaves Route 101 and begins its long, beautiful course up the coast past Morro Bay and San Simeon.

BY AIR

Santa Barbara and San Luis Obispo have small airports serving the South Central Coast. Several airlines stop at the **Santa Barbara Municipal Airport**, including **American Airlines** (800-433-7300), **United Airlines** (805-964-6863), **Delta Airlines** (800-221-1212), **Trans World Airlines** (800-221-2000), and **Continental Airlines** (800-525-0280). The **Airport Express** (805-965-1611) meets all scheduled arrivals and transports folks to Carpinteria, Montecito, Goleta, Santa Maria, and Lompoc as well as downtown Santa Barbara. There are also a number of taxi companies available. For the disabled, call **Easy Lift Transportation** (805-964-3554).

To get to and from **Los Angeles International Airport** from Santa Barbara take the **Santa Barbara Airbus** (805-964-7374).

San Luis Obispo Municipal Airport is serviced by **American Airlines** (800-433-7300) and **United Airlines** (800-241-6522). Ground transportation is provided by **Yellow Cab** (805-543-1234).

BY TRAIN

For those who want spectacular views of the coastline, try **Amtrak's** "Coast Starlight." This train hugs the shoreline, providing rare views of the Central Coast's cliffs, headlands, and untracked beaches. Amtrak (805-687-6648) stops in Oxnard, Santa Barbara, and San Luis Obispo on its way north to Oakland and Seattle.

BY BUS

Greyhound Bus Lines has continual service along the South Central Coast from Los Angeles or San Francisco. Terminals are located in Ventura (805-653-0164), Santa Barbara (805-966-3962), Pismo Beach (805-773-2144), and San Luis Obispo (805-543-2123).

For an alternative "trip" by bus, book reservations with **Green Tortoise** (805-569-1884). This New Age company has once-a-week service from Los Angeles or San Francisco.

CAR RENTALS

The larger towns in the South Central Coast have car rental agencies; check the yellow pages to find the best bargains. To pick up a car in the Oxnard–Ventura area, try **Avis Rent A Car** (805-652-2275), **Budget Rent A Car** (805-647-3536), **Hertz Rent A Car** (805-985-0911), **National Car Rental** (805-985-6100), **Sears Car Rental** (805-486-7702), **Snappy**

Car Rental (805-658-0866), and **Thrifty Rent A Car** (805-654-0101). For second-hand cars try **Cheap Wheels Rent A Car** (805-656-0866) or **Ugly Duckling Rent A Car** (805-485-0475).

At the airport in Santa Barbara try **Budget Rent A Car** (805-964-6791), **Hertz Rent A Car** (805-967-0411), or **National Car Rental** (805-967-1202). Agencies located outside the airport with free pick-up include **Airport Rent A Car** (805-964-6202), **Avis Rent A Car** (805-964-6202), **Community Rent A Car** (805-966-2235), **Dollar Rent A Car** (805-683-1468), **Coast Car Rental** (805-964-8620), and **Santa Barbara Rent A Car** (805-964-8774).

In San Luis Obispo, car rental agencies at the airport include **Budget Rent A Car** (805-541-2722) and **Hertz Rent A Car** (805-543-8843). Those with free pickup are **Sears Car Rental** (805-541-3978) and **Community Rent A Car** (805-541-4811).

PUBLIC TRANSPORTATION

Public transportation in the South Central Coast is fairly limited. In the Ventura area you'll find **South Coast Area Transit** (SCAT) (805-487-4222) which serves Oxnard, Port Hueneme, Ojai, and Ventura.

In the Santa Barbara area, the **Santa Barbara Metropolitan Transit** (Carrillo and Chapala streets; 805-683-3702) stops in Summerland, Carpinteria, Santa Barbara, Goleta, and Isla Vista.

The San Luis Obispo area has **San Luis Obispo Transit** (SLO) (805-541-2877) which operates on weekdays during daylight hours and even less frequently on weekends.

BICYCLING

Bicyling the Central Coast can be a rewarding experience. The coastal route, however, presents problems in populated areas during rush hour.

The town of Ventura offers an interesting bicycle tour through the historical section of town with a visit to the county historical museum and mission. Another interesting bike tour off of Harbor Boulevard leads to the Channel Islands National Monument and Wildlife Refuge Visitor Center.

Santa Barbara is chockful of beautiful bicycle paths. There are also several bike trails around the area: two notable beach excursions are the **Atascadero Recreation Trail**, which starts at the corner of Encore Drive and Modoc Road and ends over seven miles later at Goleta Beach; and **Cabrillo bikeway**, which takes you from Andree Clark Bird Refuge to Leadbetter Beach. The **Goleta Valley bikeway** travels from Santa Barbara to Goleta along Cathedral Oaks Road. Also, the University of California–Santa Barbara has many bike paths through the campus grounds and into Isla Vista.

BIKE RENTALS

In Santa Barbara, try **Beach Rentals** (8 West Cabrillo Boulevard; 805-963-2524) for tandems and ten-speeds as well as traditional bikes.

Hotels

Lodging facilities all along the South Central Coast run the gamut from budget to ultra-deluxe. Most are concentrated in Ventura, Santa Barbara, and San Luis Obispo, as well as the Pismo Beach and Morro Bay area. Room prices here fluctuate more than elsewhere along the California Coast and are often considerably cheaper during the winter and on weekdays.

VENTURA AREA HOTELS

For something spacious, plush and formal consider the **Bella Maggiore Inn** (67 South California Street, Ventura; 805-652-0277). Set in downtown Ventura, this 17-room hostelry follows the tradition of an Italian inn. There are European appointments and antique chandeliers in the lobby and a Roman-style fountain in the courtyard. The accommodations I saw were painted in soft hues and decorated with pastel prints. The furniture was a mixture of cane and washed pine. Moderate.

Up the hill, overlooking Ventura and the ocean, sits **La Mer European Bed & Breakfast** (411 Poli Street, Ventura; 805-643-3600). The flags decorating the facade of this 1890 house illustrate the inn's international theme. Each of the five guest rooms is decorated after the fashion of a European country—England, Austria, Norway, Germany, and France. They vary from the Norwegian "Captain's Coje," decorated nautically with a shared bath, to the French "Madame Pompadour," with its bay window and private bath. Deluxe.

Because of its excellent beach Carpinteria is very popular with families. Many spend their entire vacation here, so most facilities rent by the week or month. Among the less expensive spots for overnighters is **La Casa del Sol Motel** (5585 Carpinteria Avenue, Carpinteria; 805-684-4307). This multi-unit complex has rooms available at budget prices (moderate price with a kitchen). The one I saw was paneled in knotty pine and trimly furnished. Small pool.

SANTA BARBARA AREA HOTELS

Just south of Santa Barbara in Carpinteria, the **Eugenia Motel** (5277 Carpinteria Avenue, Carpinteria; 805-684-4416) has six rooms renting in the budget range. Each is small, uncarpeted, and clean. The furniture is comfortable though nicked. The baths have stall showers.

To provide an idea of the full range of accommodations available in the Santa Barbara area there are two centralized reservation agencies in town. **Accommodations in Santa Barbara** (1216 State Street; 805-963-

9518) and **D.B. Tourist Co.** (805-687-8605) can give information on prices and availability. Since room rates in Santa Barbara fluctuate by season and day of the week, it's advisable to check.

For modest-priced accommodations within a block or two of the beach, check out **Cabrillo Boulevard.** This artery skirts the shoreline for several miles. Establishments lining the boulevard are usually a little higher in price. But along the side streets leading from Cabrillo are numerous generic motels.

From these you can generally expect rooms which are small but tidy and clean. The wall-to-wall carpeting is industrial grade, the furniture consists of naugahyde chairs and formica tables, and the artworks make you appreciate minimalism. There's usually a swimming pool and surrounding terrace, plus a wall of ice machines and soda dispensers. One such place, **Pacific Crest Motel** (433 Corona Del Mar Drive; 805-966-3103) has 24 units renting at moderate prices during summer months, budget in winter. Next door, that generic generic facility, **Motel 6** (443 Corona Del Mar Drive; 805-564-1392), has budget-priced rooms. Both are a block from Santa Barbara's best all-around beach.

Over in the West Beach area, **Beach House Motel** (320 West Yanonali Street; 805-965-9275) has 12 units located three blocks from the beach. Rooms here are larger than usual and most have kitchens, but there's no pool. Budget. **L-Rancho Motel** (316 West Montecito Street; 805-962-0181), a block further away, has 22 units. Ask for a room with a kitchen. No pool. Budget. The **Tides Motel** (116 Castillo Street; 805-963-9772), one block from the water, has 24 units and a jacuzzi but no pool. Rates are moderate, with or without a kitchen.

The **Miramar Hotel-Resort** (1555 South Jameson Lane, Montecito; 805-969-2203) is billed as "the only hotel right on the beach" in the Santa Barbara area. Indeed there is 500 feet of beautiful beachfront. It also is right on noisy Route 101. Not to worry—the Miramar is still the best bargain around. Where else will you find dining facilities, room service, two swimming pools, tennis courts, health spa, and shuffleboard at moderate prices? Granted that will place you in a plainly appointed room closer to motor city than the beach, but you can be oceanfront for a deluxe price. Wherever you choose, you'll be in a lovely 15-acre resort inhabited by blue-roof cottages and tropical foliage.

For chic surroundings few spots compare with **Villa Rosa** (15 Chapala Street; 805-966-0851). Built during the 1930's in Spanish palazzo fashion, it was originally an apartment house. Today it is a shining 18-room inn with raw wood furnishings, pastel walls, and private baths. There's a pool and spa in the courtyard. Guests commingle over continental breakfast and afternoon wine-and-cheese, then settle into plump armchairs around a tile fireplace in the lobby. The spacious rooms are pleasingly understated and located a block from the beach. Deluxe.

The **California Hotel** (35 State Street; 805-966-7153) has one thing going for it—location. It sits on the main street in Santa Barbara just a block from the beach. The hotel is in a blocky, four-story building with a restaurant and lounge downstairs. The rooms are decently appointed though the furniture is nicked and the entire place shows its age. If you can get an oceanside room on the fourth floor it could be worth it, otherwise keep on reading. Moderate.

The Eagle Inn (232 Natoma Avenue; 805-965-3586) is an attractive Mediterranean-style apartment house converted into a 17-room hotel. Just two blocks from the beach, most of the rooms are studio units with living room and kitchen. Prices fluctuate but are generally pegged in the moderate to deluxe range.

Small and intimate as bed and breakfasts tend to be, the **Brinkerhoff Inn** (523 Brinkerhoff Avenue; 805-963-7844) is even more so. Close to downtown, it resides along a quiet block lined with single-story Victorians. The century-old inn features seven guest rooms, a cottage, and patio deck. Each room has its own theme: one has a canopied bed, another a pine armoire, darkwood furnishings, or brass fixtures. Plumed hats add to the elaborate decor. Room tabs begin in the moderate category with shared bath; deluxe with private bath.

The Old Yacht Club Inn (431 Corona Del Mar Drive; 805-962-1277) is two inns in one. The main facility is a 1912 California craftsman-style house with five rooms, priced moderately, and sharing baths. There's a parlor with piano downstairs and a decorative motif throughout that brings back cheery memories of grandmother's house. Next door, in a 1927-vintage stucco, are four rooms with private baths tabbed deluxe. Each has been decorated by a different family and features their personal photographs and other heirlooms. The inn is just one block from East Beach, serves a full breakfast and provides bicycles, beach chairs, and towels to guests.

The Glenborough Inn (1327 Bath Street; 805-966-0589) is laid out in similar fashion. The main house is a 1906 California craftsman design with moderate-priced rooms sharing baths; the second house is an 1880-era cottage with rooms and suites priced deluxe and enjoying private baths. The theme in both abodes is romance. The rooms are beautifully fashioned with embroidered curtains, inlaid French furniture, rocking chairs, canopied beds, crocheted coverlets, and needlepoint pieces. There's a garden and hot tub at the main house and a patio beside the cottage. Guests enjoy a full breakfast in bed and afternoon hors d'oeuvres; they also share a cozy living room with tile fireplace.

Down the road at the **Bath Street Inn** (1720 Bath Street; 805-682-9680) you'll encounter a Queen Anne Victorian constructed in 1873. It's an attractive house with an equally charming hostess, Nancy Stover. Enter along a garden walkway into a warm living room with marble-trimmed fireplace. The patio in back is set in another garden. Rooms on the second and third floor feature the hardwood floors and patterned wallpaper which are the hallmarks of California bed and breakfasts. They price in the deluxe category with private baths and include breakfast, afternoon snack, and use of the inn's bicycles. There is also a television lounge for guests.

Personally, I prefer the **Upham Hotel** (1404 De la Vina Street; 805-962-0058) to the nearby bed and breakfasts. Established in 1871, it shares a sense of history with the country inns, but enjoys the lobby and restaurant amenities of a hotel. Victorian in style, the two-story clapboard is marked by sweeping verandas and a cupola. Around the landscaped grounds are cottages, lawn chairs, and a gazebo. While not as personalized as the bed and breakfast guest rooms, the accommodations are nicely appointed with hardwood furnishings and period wall-hangings. Prices are in the deluxe range and include continental breakfast and evening wine. Not a bad price for a stay at "the oldest cosmopolitan hotel in continuous operation in Southern California."

Santa Barbara's two finest hotels dominate the town's two geographic locales, the ocean and the mountains. **Marriott's Santa Barbara Biltmore Hotel** (1260 Channel Drive; 805-969-2261) is a grand old Spanish-style hotel set on spacious grounds beside the beach. It's the kind of place where guests play croquet or practice putting on manicured lawns, then meander over to the hotel's Coral Casino Beach and Cabana Club. There are several dining rooms as well as tennis courts, swimming pools, and whirlpools. The rooms are quite large and handsomely appointed with floral prints and dark-wood furnishings. Many are located in multiplex cottages and are spotted around the magnificent grounds which have made the Biltmore one of California's most famous hotels since it opened back in 1927. Ultra-deluxe.

El Encanto (1900 Lasuen Road; 805-687-5000) sits back in the Santa Barbara hills and is a favorite hideaway among Hollywood stars. The hotel's 100 rooms are set in cottages and villas which dot this ten-acre retreat. The grounds are beautifully landscaped and feature a lily pond, tennis court, and swimming pool. The ocean views are simply spectacular. The rooms begin in the deluxe range and are very spacious: even the least expensive have a patio and fireplace, bedroom with attached sitting room, plus extra features like room service, refrigerator, and terry-cloth bathrobes. The decor is French country with a lot of brass and etched-glass fixtures. A very good buy for the money.

In the Santa Ynez foothills above Montecito sits another retreat where the rich and powerful mix with the merely talented. **San Ysidro Ranch** (900 San Ysidro Lane, Montecito; 805-969-5046) sprawls across 550 acres, most of which is wilderness traversed by hiking and horse trails. There are tennis courts, pool, bocci ball court, riding stables, and a nearby hot spring. The grounds vie with the Santa Barbara Botanical Gardens in the variety of plant life: there are meadows, mountain forests, and an orange grove. The restaurant serves gourmet dishes and there are two bars as well as sitting rooms and lounges. Privacy is the password: all these features are shared by guests occupying just 38 units. The accommodations are dotted around the property in cottages and small multiplexes. Rooms are ultra-deluxe in price. Even the simplest are trimly-appointed and spacious with hardwood furnishings, plump armchairs, wall-to-wall carpeting, and wood-burning fireplaces.

SAN LUIS OBISPO AREA HOTELS

Lodging in the Pismo Beach–Shell Beach–Avila Beach area generally means finding a motel. None of these seaside towns has expanded more than a few blocks from the waterfront, so wherever you book a room will be walking distance from the beach.

For budget accommodations there's **Cypress Motel** (541 Cypress Street, Pismo Beach; 805-773-5505), a small 7-unit establishment. The furniture and decoration is standard motel style, but each room has a kitchenette. **Adams Motel** (1000 Dolliver Street, Pismo Beach; 805-773-2065) is a 20-unit hostelry priced similarly.

It's a step up and a lot nearer the water at **Motel Seawall** (170 Main Street, Pismo Beach; 805-773-4706). This place is right above the beach (hence the name) and each of its 22 units has an ocean view. Moderate (deluxe for room with a kitchenette). **Surfside Motel & Apartments** (256 Front Street, Avila Beach; 805-595-2300) is directly across the street from lovely Avila Beach. Here rooms with or without kitchenette are moderate.

Sycamore Mineral Springs Resort (1215 Avila Beach Drive, Avila Beach; 805-595-7302) reposes on a hillside one mile inland from Avila Beach. Situated in a stand of oak and sycamore trees are 26 motel-style rooms. Each has a private spa; there are also redwood hot tubs scattered about in the surrounding forest; swimming pool. The rooms are decorated in contemporary style and rent for moderate to deluxe prices.

The premier resting place in these parts is **San Luis Bay Inn** (Avila Beach Drive, Avila Beach; 805-595-2333), a 76-room hotel on a hillside overlooking the ocean. Billed as a small resort, this excellent facility sports a heated swimming pool, four tennis courts, and an 18-hole golf course. There are also two restaurants and a lounge. The guest rooms are spacious accommodations, stylishly appointed, and feature private balconies and sunken tubs. Deluxe to ultra-deluxe.

Heritage Inn Bed & Breakfast (978 Olive Street, San Luis Obispo; 805-544-7440) is a San Luis Obispo anomaly. There aren't many country inns in town and this one is not even representative of the species. It sits in a neighborhood surrounded by motels and a nearby freeway.

What's more, the house was moved—lock, stock, and bay windows—to this odd location. Once inside, you'll be quite pleased. There's a warm, comfortable sitting parlor and nine guest rooms, all furnished with antiques. The beds are brass or oak; and some accommodations include window seats and terraces. All but one of the rooms in this 1902 home share baths and rent at a moderate price.

The motels that keep the Heritage Inn company are strung out along Monterey Street. This buzzing strip is the center for drive-in-and-sleep establishments; they line both sides of the street. But why stop at just anyplace when you can spend the night snoring in an historic building? The **Motel Inn** (2223 Monterey Street, San Luis Obispo; 805-543-4000) is the world's first motel. It's a Spanish-style complex fashioned from stucco and red tile. A courtyard surrounds the swimming pool and there is a restaurant and lounge. The establishment dates back to 1925 when the architect, playing with the idea of a "motor hotel," coined the term "motel." Budget to moderate.

The most outlandish place in town is a roadside confection called the **Madonna Inn** (100 Madonna Road, San Luis Obispo; 805-543-3000). Architecturally it's a cross between a castle and a gingerbread house, culturally it's somewhere between light opera and heavy metal. The lampposts are painted pink, the lounge looks like a cave, and the gift shop contains the biggest, gaudiest chandeliers you've ever seen. Personally, I wouldn't be caught dead staying in the place, but I would never miss an opportunity to visit. Where else does a waterfall serve as the men's room urinal? If you prove more daring than I, there are 109 rooms, each decorated in a different flamboyant style, renting at deluxe prices.

There are countless motels to choose from in Morro Bay, ranging across the entire spectrum in price and amenities. For information on availability contact the **Morro Bay Chamber of Commerce** (895 Napa Street, Morro Bay; 805-772-4467 or 800-231-0592).

Point Motel (3450 Toro Lane, Morro Bay; 805-772-2053) is an incredible find. It's a squat little five-room complex on the beach at the north end of Morro Bay. Route 1 rumbles outside but so does the ocean on the other side. The place offers great views of Morro Rock. Each room is tidy, but the furniture is 40 years old—not antique, just 40 years old. The rate structure is almost as ancient: rooms begin and end in the budget range, even some with kitchens and ocean views.

For deluxe accommodations at reasonable rates, check in to **The Inn at Morro Bay** (19 Country Club Road, Morro Bay; 805-772-5651). Fashionable but casual, this waterfront complex has the amenities of a small resort: restaurant, lounge, swimming pool, and an adjacent golf course. It sits on ten acres overlooking Morro Bay and contains 100

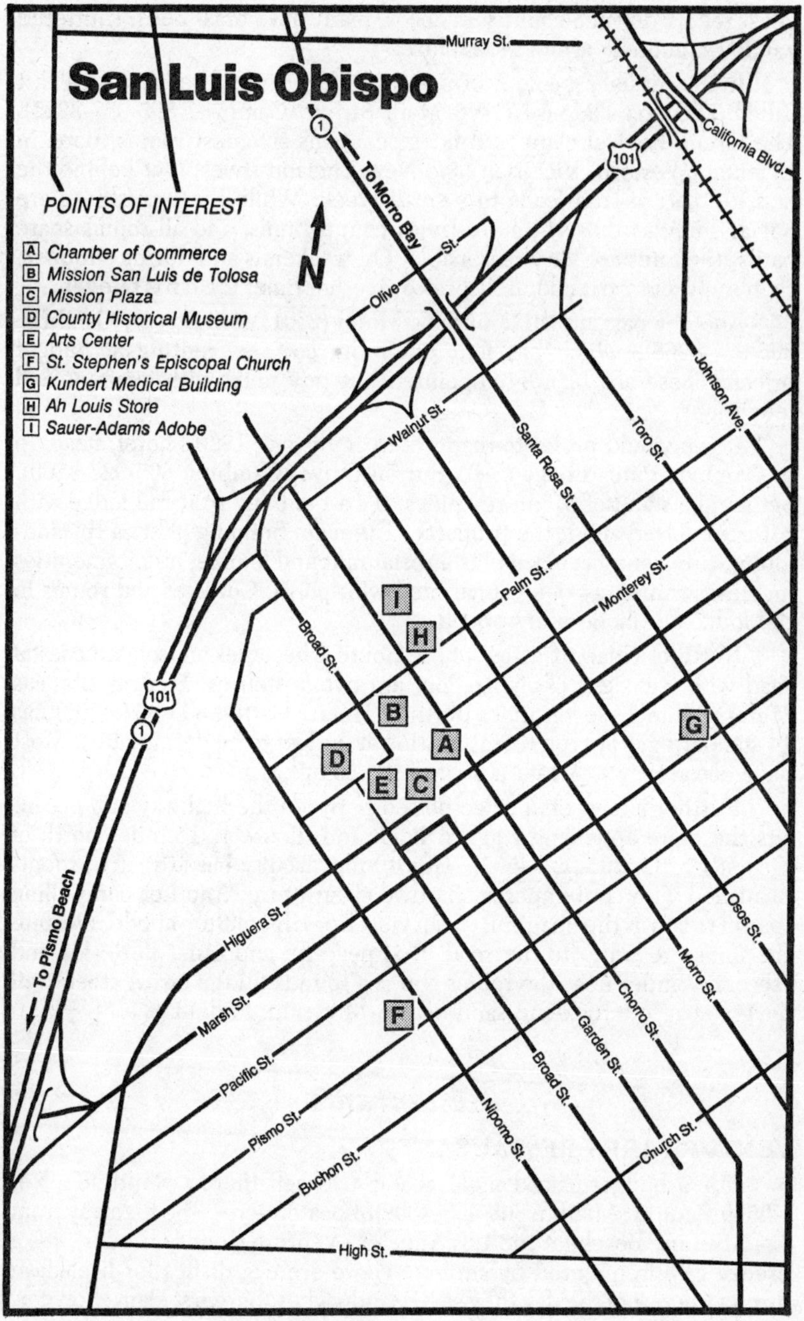
San Luis Obispo
POINTS OF INTEREST
A Chamber of Commerce
B Mission San Luis de Tolosa
C Mission Plaza
D County Historical Museum
E Arts Center
F St. Stephen's Episcopal Church
G Kundert Medical Building
H Ah Louis Store
I Sauer-Adams Adobe
N
Murray St.
To Morro Bay
California Blvd.
101
Olive St.
Walnut St.
Santa Rosa St.
Toro St.
Johnson Ave.
Palm St.
Monterey St.
Broad St.
Higuera St.
Marsh St.
Pacific St.
Pismo St.
Buchon St.
High St.
Nipomo St.
Broad St.
Garden St.
Chorro St.
Morro St.
Osos St.
Church St.
To Pismo Beach
1

guest rooms. French country in decor, many have brass beds, shuttered windows, and oak armoires. Deluxe.

In the coastal art colony of Cambria is an 1870-era bed and breakfast called **The Shaw House** (2476 Main Street, Cambria; 805-927-3222). The Greek Revival clapboard house contains six guest rooms, done in Oriental, Western, Victorian, and New England styles. Out behind the house a nature trail leads to a small creek. While the furnishings are not as spiffy as those in more lavish country inns, and all rooms share baths, the rates are very reasonable. On weekends and during summer, rooms upstairs are moderately priced; at other times the tab is budget.

Another bargain is **Hampton's Motel** (2601 Main Street, Cambria; 805-927-8968), which has four one-room cottages renting at budget prices. These are blandly appointed but tidy units with kitchens and televisions.

If you would prefer to rusticate in an historic 1920's hotel, head up to **Cambria Pines Lodge** (2905 Burton Drive, Cambria; 805-927-4200). Set amid a stand of Monterey pines, it's a rambling split-rail lodge with cottages dotted about the property. The main building offers a spacious lobby with stone fireplace plus a restaurant and lounge; other amenities include swimming pool, saunas, and whirlpools. Cottages and rooms in the lodge are moderately priced.

North of Hearst Castle, where Route 1 becomes an isolated coastal road with few signs of civilization, are two hostelries. **Piedras Blancas Motel** (Route 1, seven miles north of Hearst Castle; 805-927-4202) has 14 standard motel-type rooms renting at budget to moderate rates. Most have ocean views. A cafe is part of the complex.

Further along, on a ridge poised between the highway and ocean, sits the more appealing **Ragged Point Inn** (Route 1, 15 miles north of Hearst Castle; 805-927-4502). This 19-unit facility has attractive rooms furnished with contemporary hardwood furniture. Another compelling reason to stay is the beautiful ocean view from this clifftop abode. Despite the inn's proximity to the road, it is peaceful and quiet here; fox and raccoon wander near the rooms and sea sounds fill the air. A steep trail leads down to a rock-and-sand beach. Moderate to deluxe.

Restaurants

VENTURA AREA RESTAURANTS

For a budget-priced meal near the beach there's **Neptune's Net** (42505 Route 1, Malibu; 805-488-1302). Located across the highway from County Line Beach (at the Los Angeles–Ventura County border), it's a breezy cafe frequented by surfers. There are egg dishes for breakfast; during the rest of the day they serve sandwiches, burgers, clam chowder, as well as shrimp, oyster, clam, and scallop baskets. Ocean views at beach bum prices.

Up at the Fisherman's Wharf complex in Oxnard you'll find two more budget eateries. The **International Seafood Market** (3920 West Channel Islands Boulevard; 805-985-5374) has a take-out stand serving numerous charbroiled fresh fish dishes. Depending on the season, these can include halibut, swordfish, sole, red snapper, sea bass, shark, and on and on. They also serve oysters, shrimp, and scallops. Next door at the **Captain's Galley** (3900 West Channel Islands Boulevard; 805-985-7754) there are breakfast dishes as well as hamburgers, sandwiches, and salads.

For an elegant meal, head up the coast to the **Seafood and Beverage Co.** (211 East Santa Clara Street, Ventura; 805-643-3264) where the dinner entrees include Alaskan King crab legs, Australian lobster tails, and sirloin steak kebab. Housed in a 1914-vintage home, this comfortable dining place is painted in pastel shades and adorned with leaded-glass windows. Open for lunch, dinner, and weekend brunch, it features mesquite-broiled dishes and hosts a piano bar. Prices are moderate to deluxe, but there's a limited early bird menu from 4 to 5:30 p.m. with dinners tabbed in the budget range.

Or try **Eric Ericsson's Fish Company** (1140 South Seaward Avenue, Ventura; 805-643-4783), a small snuggery done in knotty pine with nautical appointments. At lunch they could be serving fish chowder, seafood pasta, poached shrimp, or fresh-fish burritos. Then for dinner they might charbroil *mahimahi*, salmon, swordfish, or sea bass, depending on the season. Located near the beach this understated restaurant is a good place for fresh fish. Deluxe.

Franky's Restaurant (456 East Main Street, Ventura; 805-648-6282) is a trip. The place resembles a mini-museum, decorated with paintings, mobiles, and statuary. All the artwork is for sale, so the decorative scheme is ever-changing. The interior is liable to be adorned with marble busts and Modernist canvases. Moving from palette to palate, the menu contains omelettes and salads, plus pita bread sandwiches and croissants stuffed with chicken salad, shrimp, or tuna. Breakfast and lunch only; moderate.

SANTA BARBARA AREA RESTAURANTS

There are two good, inexpensive restaurants next door to each other in the beach town of Carpinteria. **Villa Campos** (721 Linden Avenue; 805-684-4445) is a two-room Mexican eatery lined with books. The menu covers the gamut from tacos to tostadas, chili to *chorizo*, and includes innovations like Mexican pizza and *chile relleno* soup. Lunch, dinner, and Sunday brunch.

At The Palms (701 Linden Avenue, Carpinteria; 805-684-3811) you cook your own steak or shark dinner, or have them prepare a shrimp or scallop meal. A family-style restaurant with oak chairs and pseudo-Tiffany lamps, it hosts a salad bar and adjoining lounge. Not bad at all for the budget price. Lunch and dinner only.

A step upscale at **Clementine's Steak House** (4631 Carpinteria Avenue, Carpinteria; 805-684-5119) they feature filet mignon, fresh fish dishes, vegetarian casserole, steak teriyaki, and Danish-style liver. It's dinner only here, but the meal—which includes soup, salad, vegetable, starch dish, homemade bread, and pie—could hold you well into the next day. The interior has a beamed ceiling and patterned wallpaper. Lean back in a captain's chair and enjoy some home-style cooking. Moderate to deluxe.

For a scent of Santa Barbara salt air with your lunch or dinner, **Brophy Brothers Clam Bar & Restaurant** (119 Harbor Way; 805-966-4418) is the spot. Located out on the Breakwater, overlooking the marina, mountains, and open sea, it features a small dining room and patio. If you love seafood, it's heaven; if not, then fate has cast you in the wrong direction. The clam bar serves all manner of clam and oyster concoctions and the restaurant is so committed to fresh fish they print a new menu daily to tell you what the boats brought in. When I was there the daily fare included fresh snapper, shark, scampi, salmon, sea bass, halibut, *mahimahi*, red fish, and butter fish. No breakfast; moderate.

Best of Santa Barbara's budget restaurants is **La Tolteca** (614 East Haley Street; 805-963-0847). This tortilla factory contains an informal, self-order cafe serving delicious Mexican food. Almost everything is fresh, making it *the* place for tacos, tostadas, burritos, and enchiladas. You can sit at one of the few tables inside or out near the sidewalk.

Santa Barbara natives have been eating at **Joe's Cafe** (536 State Street; 805-966-4638) for sixty years. Crowds line the coal-black bar, pile into the booths, and fill the tables. They come for a moderately priced, meat-and-potatoes lunch and dinner menu that stars prime rib. This is where you go for pork chops, lamb, rainbow trout, and steak. The walls are loaded with mementos and faded photographs; bowling trophies, deer antlers, and a buffalo head decorate the place; and the noise level is the same as the Indy 500. Paradise for slummers.

Change the work jeans for something simple but chic when you cruise into **Gallagher's Bar & Grill** (633 State Street; 805-963-4424). Santa Barbara's answer to hip, it's an oak-bar-and-potted-plant establishment with flags of all nations overhanging the bar and plush booths out in the dining room. Nicely appointed with art photos and hanging rugs, Gallagher's is a popular gathering place. They serve lunch and dinner, featuring seafood specialties, poultry dishes, and lots of pasta. At lunch there is an array of grilled sandwiches and hamburgers. No breakfast; moderate.

Santa Barbara Shellfish Company (230 Stearns Wharf; 805-963-4415) ain't fancy: just a take-out stand with a few picnic tables. But they serve fresh crab and shrimp cocktails, chowder, crab louie, and hot seafood platters at budget prices. Even better, they're located way out on Stearns Wharf where you can enjoy the open waterfront. Lunch and early dinner only.

Suishin Sukiyaki (511 State Street; 805-962-1495) has that greatest of imports—a sushi bar. There are also private booths with Oriental screens at this very fine, very popular Japanese restaurant. In addition to sushi and *sashimi* selections, there are teriyaki, sukiyaki, and *shabu shabu* dinners. The surroundings, with bamboo partitions and intricate wooden trim, are relaxed and attractive. Open only for dinner and priced from moderate to deluxe.

Downey's (1305 State Street; 805-966-5006), a small, understated dining room, numbers among Santa Barbara's premiere restaurants. The dozen tables here are set in a conservatively appointed room with art prints and scattered plants. The food is renowned: specializing in California cuisine, Downey's has a menu which changes daily. A typical evening's entrees are salmon with forest mushrooms, lamb loin, sea bass with artichokes, veal sweetbreads, duck with wild rice, and scallops with dungeness crabs. There is a good wine list featuring California vintages. No breakfast, but the lunch menu is as carefully prepared as dinner; deluxe. Very highly recommended.

The graphics on the wall tell a story about the cuisine at **The Palace Cafe** (8 East Cota Street; 805-966-3133). Portrayed are jazz musicians, catfish, redfish, and New Orleans-style funerals. The message is Cajun and Creole, and this informal bistro is very good at delivering it. Serving dinner and Sunday brunch only, the moderate-to-deluxe priced restaurant prepares soft-shelled crab, blackened filet mignon, crawfish *étouffée*, and jambalaya. For dessert, honey, we we have key lime pie and bread pudding with pecan sauce.

If you prefer your bistros French, there's an excellent place a few doors up called **Mousse Odile** (18 East Cota Street; 805-962-5393). Plaid tablecloths, folk art, and a piano create an easy ambience here. Dinner includes couscous, mushrooms on pastry shell, and veal in basil cream; lunch features *ficelles*, those foot-long Parisian sandwiches, as well as quiche and stuffed croissants. Even the breakfasts have a French flair. Modest but well managed, Mousse Odile is quite popular with local residents.

If your mother is Italian you'll know what to expect at **Mom's Italian Village** (421 East Cota Street; 805-965-5588). If not you'll still be at home. This friendly, familiar eatery is a local institution. Mom has been cooking for more than 40 years, preparing the north Italian dishes that fill the lunch and dinner menus. Lasagna is a house specialty, but there's also chicken cacciatore, beef *spezzatini*, breaded veal cutlet, and a kitchenful of pasta dishes. Budget to moderate.

Hanging out in coffeehouses is my favorite avocation. There's no better spot in Santa Barbara than **Sojourner Coffeehouse** (134 East Canon Perdido; 805-965-7922). Not only do they serve espresso and cappucchino, but lunch and dinner as well. Everyone seems to know everyone else in this easy-going cafe. They come to kibbitz and enjoy the tostadas, rice-and-vegetable plates, and stuffed baked potatoes. The accent is vegetarian so expect daily specials like zucchini-mushroom quiche, ratatouille curry, and potato-leek pie. Budget.

Cafe del Sol (516 San Ysidro Road; 805-969-0448) is that rarest of creatures, an upscale Mexican restaurant. The dining room has been comfortably furnished and painted with bright-colored murals; out on the patio you can dine in a botanic setting. Open for lunch, dinner, and Sunday brunch, they feature a Mexican menu combined with dishes like chicken cordon bleu, tournedos, scallops, lobster, and shrimp. The tab is moderate if you order Mexican, slightly more for American fare.

Dining at **El Encanto** (1900 Lasuen Road; 805-687-5000) is pleasurable not only for the fine California and French cuisine but the sweeping vistas as well. The restaurant resides in a hillside resort overlooking Santa Barbara. There's a luxurious dining room and a terrace for dining outdoors. Dinner prepared by chef Renaud Defond, who trained in Lyon, France, is a gourmet experience. Changing daily according to harvest and catch, the menu could include *mahimahi* with champagne sauce, veal tenderloin in grapefruit sauce, Muscovy duck, rack of lamb, or monkfish with tarragon sauce. The appetizers and desserts are equally outrageous, as are the breakfast and lunch courses. Julia Child is reputed to love the place. I certainly do. Ultra-deluxe.

Located outside town, on the beach at Arroyo Burro Country Park, is the **Brown Pelican** (2981-1/2 Cliff Drive; 805-687-4550). It's a good restaurant with ocean views at a moderate price. What more need be said? They serve sandwiches, salads, hamburgers, and several fresh seafood dinners. Trimly appointed and fitted with a wall of plate glass, it looks out upon a sandy beach and tawny bluffs. A low-budget answer to waterfront tourist traps (with an espresso bar to boot!).

Timbers Restaurant (10 Winchester Canyon Road, Goleta; 805-968-2050), quite literally, is surrounded by history. The place is built entirely from the foot-thick timbers of the old Ellwood Pier. The pier, it seems, was attacked by a Japanese submarine during World War II and the detritus from that unique incident was fashioned into a sprawling, Western-style restaurant and bar. The raw wood interior is decorated with hunting trophies, sepia photographs, and frontier artifacts; a stone fireplace dominates the main dining room. Serving dinner only, the restaurant features a half-dozen steak dishes as well as teriyaki chicken, Australian lobster tail, Alaskan king crab, and coconut fried shrimp. A good place to chow down. Deluxe.

Nick's Place, Gaviota (Gaviota Village Complex, Route 101, Gaviota; 805-567-5113) is a multi-room complex with wooden lunch counter, rustic bare-beam dining room, and attached store. A way station in an area with few restaurants, it serves three meals daily. Lunch consists of sandwiches and burgers; in the evening they barbeque fresh meat by a slow-cook process. Budget.

SAN LUIS OBISPO AREA RESTAURANTS

For breakfast and lunch in Pismo Beach try the **All American Cafe** (1053 Price Street, Pismo Beach; 805-773-2764). The wallhangings make it look like we're still fighting World War II. But if you can handle the chauvinism, there's a good breakfast menu with over a dozen egg and omelette dishes. At lunch they have the usual assortment of sandwiches and salads. Moderate.

There's Japanese food at a cozy cafe called **Sukoshi Inn** (246 Pomeroy Street, Pismo Beach; 805-773-5044). Serving dinner only, they offer teriyaki and tempura plus an Oriental barbeque beef dish. You'll also find *tonkaisu*, rolled and breaded pork cutlets. Budget.

At **The Old Custom House Restaurant** (324 Front Street, Avila Beach; 805-595-7555) ask for a table out on the patio. It's a garden arrangement with umbrellas shading the tables. Quite nice, and besides, the indoor dining area is just a counter and a series of plain formica tables. Serving three meals daily, they specialize in seafood (what else?) and steak. Dinners are prepared on an oak pit barbeque and breakfast features 20 different omelettes. Moderate.

Avila Bay Seafood Co. (Pier 3, Avila Beach; 805-595-7808) has it all—cheap food, great views, and ocean breezes. What you won't get is a roof over your head, but there are a few tables with umbrellas at this pier-side take-out stand. You can order fresh fish, clam, scallop, shrimp, and oyster plates, or ask them to cook a hamburger. Then lean back and enjoy the easy life out on Avila Bay. Budget.

If you missed the swinging doors in the saloon you'll get the idea from the moose head trophies and branding irons. "Taste the Great American West" is the motto for **F. McLintock's Saloon & Dining House** (750 Mattie Road, Shell Beach; 805-773-1892). This is the place where you can get an 18-ounce steak for breakfast. At lunch there are buffalo burgers. And every evening, when the oak pit barbeque really gets going, there are a dozen kinds of steak, Cornish game hen, pan-fried rainbow trout, grilled veal liver, and scampi. If popularity means anything, this place is tops. It's always mobbed. So dust off the stetson and prepare to chow down. Moderate to deluxe.

Sick of seafood by now? Tired of saloons serving cowboy-sized steaks? Happily, San Luis Obispo has several ethnic restaurants. Two are located in The Creamery, a turn-of-the-century dairy plant that has been transformed into a shopping mall.

Tsurugi Japanese Restaurant (570 Higuera Street, San Luis Obispo; 805-543-8942) features a sushi bar and dining area decorated with Oriental screens and wallhangings. At lunch and dinner there are shrimp tempura, chicken teriyaki, *nigiri*, and other Asian specilties. The atmosphere is placid and the food quite good; moderate. Next door at **Tortilla Flats** (1051 Nipomo Street, San Luis Obispo; 805-544-7575) they have fashioned an attractive restaurant from the brick walls, bare ducts, and exposed rafters of the old dairy. It's lunch, dinner, and Sunday brunch at this Mexican eatery where the bar serves margaritas by the pitcherful; moderate.

If you can get past the garish red-and-yellow sign at **Golden China Restaurant** (675 Higuera Street, San Luis Obispo; 805-543-7576), there's an array of standard Chinese dishes printed on a menu that continues for pages. Budget to moderate.

The **Wine Street Inn** (774 Higuera Street, San Luis Obispo; 805-543-4488) draws from Swiss and French cuisine to create a half-dozen fondue dishes. This candlelit bistro also serves seafood dishes and has an ample wine list. At lunch there are fondues, salads, and sandwiches; no breakfast; moderate.

The British are represented at **The Rose and Crown** (1000 Higuera Street, San Luis Obispo; 805-541-1911), a pub serving bangers, Welsh rarebit, shepherd's pie, and Cornish pasties for lunch. At dinner you can order a roast beef dinner complete with roast potatoes and Yorkshire pudding. Budget to moderate; they also serve Sunday brunch.

Italy enters the picture with **Cafe Roma** (1819 Osos Street, San Luis Obispo; 805-541-6800), a delightful restaurant decorated in country inn style. Copper pots as well as portraits from the old country decorate the walls. Lunch and dinner include Italian sausage, veal marsala, steak *fiorentina*, and several daily specials. There are also assorted pasta and antipasta dishes, an extensive Italian wine list, and homemade ice cream for dessert. Run by an Italian family, it serves excellent food; highly recommended; moderate.

For a budget-priced meal in a white-tablecloth restaurant with views of the surrounding hills, beat a path to the California Polytechnic campus. **Vista Grande Restaurant** (Grand Avenue, San Luis Obispo; 805-546-1204) serves Cal Poly students as well as the public in a comfortable plate-glass dining room. Open for lunch, dinner, and Sunday brunch, it features filet mignon, veal parmesan, teriyaki chicken, and *pescado con queso* (fresh fish with salsa and mornay sauce). There are also several different salads and a host of sandwiches.

Outside town there's a particularly good Western-style restaurant. (You didn't think I'd let you off scott free, did you?). **This Old House** (740 West Foothill Boulevard, San Luis Obispo; one and one-half miles west of Route 1; 805-543-2690) is another oak pit grill serving steak and ribs, plus lobster, sweetbreads, barbequed chicken, and stuffed sole. The decor is early Western with oxen yokes, cowboy boots, and branding irons on the wall. With its unique barbeque sauce and rib-sticking meals, This Old House merits a visit. Moderate to deluxe.

You needn't cast far in Morro Bay to find a seafood restaurant. Sometimes they seem as frequent as fishing boats. One of the most venerable is **Dorn's Original Breakers Cafe** (801 Market Street, Morro Bay; 805-772-4415). It's a bright, airy place with a postcard view of the waterfront. While they serve all three meals, in the evening you better want seafood because there are about two dozen fish dishes and only a couple steak platters. Moderate.

The Fondue Pot Restaurant (213 Beach Street, Morro Bay; 805-772-8900) is an intimate little place decorated with art prints. At lunch and dinner they serve a variety of fondues as well as red snapper, stuffed shrimp, and sautéed chicken. Then on the weekend they prepare a special prime rib dinner; budget.

Fine California cuisine is the order of the day at **The Inn at Morro Bay** (19 Country Club Drive, Morro Bay; 805-772-5651). Situated in a waterfront resort, the dining room looks out over Morro Bay. In addition to great views and commodious surroundings, it features an enticing list of local and French entrees. All three meals are served, but the highlight is dinner. The menu might include cream-poached salmon, roast duckling, fresh fish in chive butter, sole stuffed with scallop mousse, and sautéed veal loin. Deluxe.

Further north, ethnic and vegetarian food lovers will fare well at **Robin's** (4286 Bridge Street, Cambria; 805-927-5007). Set in a pretty bungalow with picket fence and flower garden, it serves home-style lunches and dinners. Selections range from burritos to sweet-and-sour prawns to stir-fried *tofu*. It's an eclectic blend with the accent on Mexican and Asian cuisine. Budget.

For fine California cuisine try **Ian's Restaurant** (2150 Center Street, Cambria; 805-927-8649). The decor is contemporary, featuring floral prints on pastel-shaded walls, blond-wood furniture, and upholstered banquettes. Lunch and dinner menus draw upon local fresh produce, herbs, and seafood. Also among the specialties are duck, rabbit, and lamb. Dinner will include abalone, prawns in garlic and cream, plus beef dishes. For lunch there is veal cutlet with mustard butter, baby back ribs, and salmon filet. Deluxe.

The Great Outdoors

The Sporting Life

SPORTFISHING

Albacore, barracuda, bonito, bass, halibut, yellowtail, and marlin are just some of the fish that ply the waters off the South Central Coast and the Channel Islands. If you're interested in a fishing cruise, contact one of the following companies: **Cisco's Sportfishing** (Captain Jack's Landing, 4151 South Victoria Avenue, Oxnard; 805-985-8511), **Island Packers** (1867 Spinnaker Drive, Ventura; 805-642-1393), **Sea Landing Sportfishing** (The Breakwater, Santa Barbara; 805-963-3564), **Virg's Fish'n** (1215 Embarcadero, Morro Bay or across from Hearst Castle; 805-772-1222), or **Port San Luis Sportfishing** (San Luis Obispo; 805-595-7200).

WHALE WATCHING

If you're in the mood for a whale-watching excursion during the annual migration, contact **Cisco's Sportfishing** (Captain Jack's Landing, 4151 South Victoria Avenue, Oxnard; 805-985-8511), **Captain Dave's Channel Islands Tours** (4151 South Victoria, Ventura; 805-647-3161), **Sea Landing Aquatic Center** (The Breakwater, Santa Barbara; 805-963-3564), **Virg's Fish'n** (1215 Embarcadero, Morro Bay; 805-772-1222), or **Port San Luis Sportfishing** (Avila Beach; 805-595-7200).

SKIN DIVING

For those more interested in watching fish, there are several outfits in the South Central Coast area offering skin diving rentals and/or lessons. In the Oxnard–Ventura area try **Poncho's Bait & Tackle** (2840 South Harbor Boulevard, Oxnard; 805-985-4788), **Cisco's Sportfishing** (Captain Jack's Landing, 4151 South Victoria Avenue, Oxnard; 805-985-8511), or **Ventura Scuba Schools** (1559 Spinnaker Drive #108, Ventura; 805-656-0167).

In Santa Barbara call **Divers Den** (22 Anacapa Street, Santa Barbara; 805-963-8917) or **Sea Landing Aquatic Center** (The Breakwater, Santa Barbara; 805-963-3564).

Bill's Sporting Goods (Cayucos Pier, Cayucos; 805-995-1703) and **Sea Wink** (750 Price Street, Pismo Beach; 805-773-4794) serve the San Luis Obispo area.

SURFING AND WINDSURFING

Hang ten or catch the wind with board rentals from the following enterprises: **Pipe Line Surf Shop** (1124 South Seaward Avenue, Ventura; 805-652-1418; surfing only), **Sundance Windsurfing** (2026 Cliff Drive, Santa Barbara; 805-966-2474), **Mountain Air Sports** (731 State Street, Santa Barbara; 805-962-0049), **Windance** (6 West Anapamu Street, Santa Barbara; 805-962-4774), **Sea Wink** (750 Price Street, Pismo Beach; 805-773-4794), **Good Clean Fun** (136 Ocean Front, Cayucos; 805-995-1993), or **Wavelengths Surf Shop** (711 Morro Bay Boulevard, Morro Bay; 805-772-3904; surfing only).

OTHER SPORTS

GOLF

Golf enthusiasts will enjoy the weather as well as the courses along the South Central Coast. In the Oxnard–Ventura area try **River Ridge** (2401 West Vineyard Avenue, Oxnard; 805-984-4639), **Olivas Park** (3750 Olivas Park Drive, Ventura; 805-485-5712), or **San Buenaventura** (5882 Olivas Park Drive, Ventura; 805-485-3050). In the Santa Barbara area try **Santa Barbara Community Course** (Las Positas Road and McCaw Avenue, Santa Barbara; 805-687-7087), **Twin Lakes Golf Course** (6034 Hollister Avenue, Goleta; 805-964-1414), **Sandpiper Golf Course** (7925 Hollister Avenue, Goleta; 805-968-1541), or **Ocean Meadows Golf Course** (6925 Whittier Drive, Goleta; 805-968-6814). The San Luis Obispo area has **Pismo State Beach Golf Course** (Le Sage Drive, Grover City; 805-481-5215), **Laguna Lake Golf Course** (11175 Los Osos Valley Road, San Luis Obispo; 805-549-7309), **San Luis Bay Golf Course** (Avila Beach Road, Avila Beach; 805-595-2307), **Morro Bay Golf Course** (State Park Road, Morro Bay; 805-772-4560), and **Sea Pines Golf Course** (250 Howard Avenue, Los Osos; 805-528-1788).

TENNIS

Tennis anyone? Courts are available at the following sites: **Moranda Park** (200 Moranda Parkway, Port Hueneme; 805-488-0010), **Santa Barbara Municipal Courts** (contact the Santa Barbara Recreation Department; 805-963-0611), **Cuesta College** (Route 1, San Luis Obispo; 805-544-5356), **Sinshelmer Park** (990 Southwood Drive, San Luis Obispo; 805-549-7300), and **Pismo Beach Municipal Courts** (Wadsworth and Bello streets, Pismo Beach; 805-773-4657).

HORSEBACK RIDING

A variety of riding opportunites are available in the South Central Coast. Call **Gene O'Hagan Stables** (1900 Refugio Road, Goleta; 805-968-5929), **Circle Bar B Stables** 1800 Refugio Road, Goleta; 805-968-3901), or **The Livery Stable** (1207 Silverspur Place, San Luis Obispo; 805-489-8100).

SAILING

To sail the Pacific or visit the Channel Islands, contact **Navigators Channel Island Cruise** (1621 Posilipo Lane, Santa Barbara; 805-969-2393), **Santa Barbara Boat Rentals** (The Breakwater, Santa Barbara; 805-962-2826), **Santa Barbara Sailing Association** (The Breakwater, Santa Barbara; 805-962-2826), **Sea Landing Aquatic Center** (The Breakwater, Santa Barbara; 805-963-3564), or **Seahorse Charters** (1817 De la Vina Street, Santa Barbara; 805-569-0403).

Beaches and Parks

VENTURA AREA BEACHES AND PARKS

Point Mugu State Park—This outstanding facility extends along four miles of beachfront and reaches back six miles into the Santa Monica Mountains. The beaches—which include **Sycamore Cove Beach, La Jolla Beach,** and **Point Mugu Beach**—are wide and sandy, with rocky outcroppings and a spectacular sand dune. To the interior the park rises to 1266-foot Mugu Peak and to Tri-Peaks, 3010 feet in elevation. There are two large canyons as well as wide, forested valleys. Over 70 miles of hiking trails lace this diverse park.

Facilities: Picnic areas, restrooms; restaurants and groceries within a few miles; information center at Sycamore Cove, 805-987-3303.

Camping: Permitted inland at Sycamore Canyon (showers and flush toilets) and at La Jolla Beach (primitive facilities). There are hike-in campsites in La Jolla Valley.

Swimming: Good; also a prime spot for bodysurfing; but watch for rip currents.

Surfing: Good a few miles south of the park at **County Line Beach.**

Getting there: Located on Route 1 about five miles south of Oxnard.

McGrath State Beach—This long, narrow park extends for two miles along the water. The beach is broad and bounded by dunes. A lake and wildlife area attract over 200 bird species. The Santa Clara River, on the northern boundary, is home to tortoises, squirrels, musk-rats, weasels, and other wildlife. Together the lake and preserve make it a great spot for camping or daytripping at the beach.

Facilities: Picnic areas, restrooms, lifeguards; restaurants and groceries are nearby in Ventura; information, 805-985-1188.

Camping: Permitted.

Swimming: Good, but watch for rip currents.

Surfing: Good.

Getting there: Located at 2211 Harbor Boulevard in Oxnard.

San Buenaventura State Beach—In the world of urban parks this 114-acre facility ranks high. The broad sandy beach, bordered by dunes, extends for two miles to the Ventura pier. Since the pier is a short stroll from the city center, the beach provides a perfect escape hatch after you have toured the town.

Facilities: Picnic areas, restrooms, showers, dressing rooms, snack bar, lifeguards; groceries and restaurants nearby in Ventura; information, 805-654-4611.

Camping: Not permitted.

Swimming: The breakwaters here provide excellent swimming.

Surfing: Good at **Surfer's Point Park,** foot of Figueroa Street; and at **Peninsula Beach,** at the north end of Spinnaker Drive.

Fishing: From the 1700-foot pier anglers catch bass, shark, surf perch, corbina, and bonito. The rearby rock jetties are a haven for crabs and mussels.

Getting there: Located along Harbor Boulevard southeast of the Ventura Pier in Ventura.

Emma Wood State Beach—Sandwiched between the ocean and the Southern Pacific railroad tracks, this slender park measures only 116 acres. The beach consists almost entirely of rocks, making it undesirable for swimmers and sunbathers. There is a marsh at one end inhabited by songbirds and small mammals. Considering the fabulous beaches hereabouts, I rank this one pretty low.

Facilities: Restrooms, lifeguard; restaurants and groceries nearby in Ventura; information, 805-643-7532.

Camping: Permitted. Far from idyllic, the campsites are right below the freeway. There is also camping at **Faria County Park** and **Hobson County Park** (805-654-3974). These are small, rocky beaches north of Emma Wood on the Old Pacific Coast Highway. There is better surfing at **Rincon Parkway South,** immediately north of Emma Wood.

Fishing: Cabezon, perch, bass, and corbina are caught here.

Getting there: Located on the northwest boundary of Ventura just off Route 101.

SANTA BARBARA AREA BEACHES AND PARKS

Rincon Beach County Park—Wildly popular with nudists and surfers, this is a pretty white-sand beach backed by bluffs. At the bottom of the wooden stairway leading down to the beach, take a right along

(Text continued on page 234.)

The Channel Islands

Gaze out from the Ventura or Santa Barbara shoreline and you will spy a fleet of islands moored offshore. At times fringed with mist, on other occassions standing a hand's reach away in the crystal air, they are the Channel Islands, a group of eight volcanic islands.

Situated in the Santa Barbara Channel 11 to 40 miles from the coast, they are a place apart, a wild and storm-blown region of sharp cliffs, rocky coves, and curving grasslands. Five of the islands—Anacapa, Santa Cruz, Santa Rosa, San Miguel, and Santa Barbara—comprise Channel Islands National Park while the surrounding waters are a marine sanctuary.

Nicknamed "America's Galapagos," the chain teems with every imaginable form of life. Sea lions and harbor seals frequent the caves, blowholes, and offshore pillars. Brown pelicans and black oystercatchers roost on the sea arches and sandy beaches. There are tidepools crowded with brilliant purple hydrocorals and white-plumed sea anemones. Like the Galapapos, this isolated archipelago has given rise to many unique life forms, including 40 endemic plant species and the island fox, which grows only to the size of a house cat.

The northern islands were created about 14 million years ago by volcanic activity. Archaeological discoveries indicate that they could be among the oldest sites of human habitation in the Americas. When explorer Juan Cabrillo revealed them to the West in 1542 they were populated with thousands of Chumash Indians.

Today, long since the Chumash were removed and the islands given over to hunters, ranchers, and settlers, the Channel Islands are largely uninhabited. Several, however, are open to hikers and

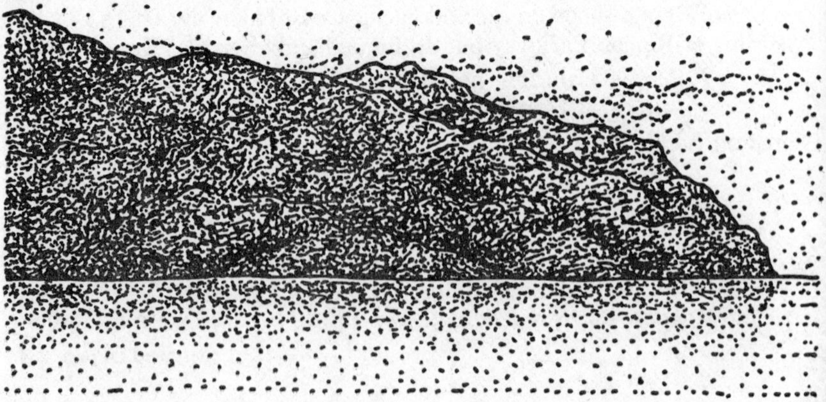

campers. At the mainland-based **Channel Islands National Park Visitor Center** (1901 Spinnaker Drive, Ventura; 805-644-8262) there are contemporary museum displays and an excellent 25-minute movie to familiarize you with the park.

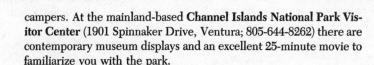

Next door at **Island Packers** (1867 Spinnaker Drive, Ventura, CA 93001; 805-642-1393) you can arrange transportation to the islands. This outfit schedules regular daytrips by boat to Anacapa, Santa Barbara, Santa Cruz, and San Juan Miguel islands. They can arrange camping trips on the first three islands or will book you into a room at the 19th-century Scorpion Ranch on Santa Cruz Island.

The Nature Conservancy (213 Stearns Wharf, Santa Barbara; 805-962-9111) also leads tours of Santa Cruz, the largest and most diverse of the islands. Here you will find an island just 24 miles long which supports 600 species of plants, 130 types of land birds, and several unique plant species. There are Indian middens, earthquake faults, and two mountain ranges to explore. To the center lies a pastoral valley while the shoreline is a rugged region of cliffs, tidepools, and offshore rocks.

Anacapa Island, the island closest to shore, is a series of three islets parked 11 miles southwest of Oxnard. There are tidepools here, a nature trail, and a 19th-century grounded steamer. Like the other islands, it is a prime whale-watching spot and is surrounded by the giant kelp forests which make the Channel Islands one of the nation's richest marine environments.

Whether you are a sailor, swimmer, daytripper, hiker, archaeologist, bird watcher, camper, tidepooler, scuba diver, seal lover, or simply an interested observer, you'll find this amazing island chain a place of singular beauty and serenity.

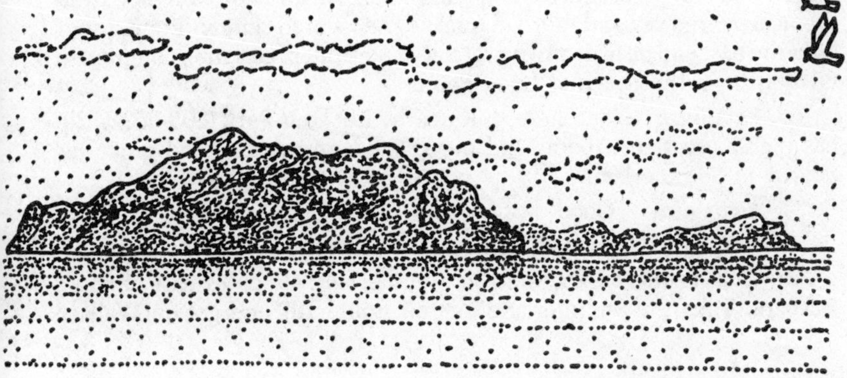

the strand and head over to the seawall. There will often be a bevy of nude sunbathers snuggled here between the hillside and the ocean. Surfers, on the other hand, turn left and paddle out to Rincon Point, one of the most popular surfing spots along the entire California coast.

Facilities: Picnic area, restrooms; restaurants and groceries are two miles away in Carpinteria.

Swimming: Good.

Surfing: Excellent.

Getting there: Located two miles southeast of Carpinteria; from Route 101 take the Bates Road exit.

Carpinteria State Beach—This ribbon-shaped park extends for nearly a mile along the coast. Bordered to the east by dunes and along the west by a bluff, the beach has an offshore shelf which shelters it from the surf. As a result, Carpinteria provides exceptionally good swimming and is nicknamed "the world's safest beach." Wildlife here consists of small mammals and reptiles as well as many seabirds. It's a good spot for tidepooling; there is also a lagoon here. The Santa Ynez Mountains rise in the background.

Facilities: Picnic areas, restrooms, dressing rooms, showers, lifeguards; restaurants and groceries nearby in Carpinteria; information, 805-684-2811.

Swimming: Excellent.

Skindiving: Good along the breakwater reef, a habitat for abalone and lobsters.

Surfing: Very good in the "tarpits" area near the east end of the park.

Fishing: Cabezone, corbina, and barred perch are caught here.

Getting there: Located at the end of Palm Avenue in Carpinteria.

Summerland Beach—This narrow strip of white sand is a popular nude beach. It's backed by low-lying hills, which afford privacy from the nearby freeway and railroad tracks. The favored skinny-dipping spot is on the east end between two protective rock piles. Gay men congregate further down the beach at Loon Point.

Facilities: None here, but nearby **Lookout Park** (805-969-1720) has picnic areas, restrooms and playground; restaurants and groceries nearby in Summerland.

Swimming: Good.

Surfing: Good bodysurfing.

Getting there: Located in Summerland six miles east of Santa Barbara. Take the Summerland exit off Route 101 and get on Wallace

Avenue, the frontage road between the freeway and ocean. Follow it east for three-tenths of a mile to Finley Road and the beach.

East Beach—Everyone's favorite Santa Barbara beach, this broad beauty stretches more than a mile from Montecito to Stearns Wharf. In addition to a fluffy-sand corridor there are grassy areas, palm trees, and a wealth of service facilities. Beyond Stearns Wharf the strand continues as **West Beach**. A nude beach, called **Butterfly Beach**, lies at the far east end.

Facilities: Picnic areas, restrooms, showers, lifeguards, playground, and volleyball courts. **Cabrillo Pavilion Bathhouse** (1118 East Cabrillo Boulevard, Santa Barbara; 805-965-0509) provides lockers, showers, and a weight room for a small daily fee; restaurant. Other facilities are at Stearns Wharf.

Swimming: Very good.

Fishing: Good.

Getting there: Located in Santa Barbara along East Cabrillo Boulevard between the Andree Clark Bird Refuge and Stearns Wharf. The nude beach can be reached by following East Cabrillo Boulevard east past the Cabrillo Pavilion Bathhouse until the road turns inland. From this juncture continue along the beach on foot. The clothing-optional area is just beyond the Clark Mansion.

Leadbetter Beach—A crescent of white sand, this beach rests along a shallow cove. While it is quite pretty here, with a headland bordering one end of the strand, it simply doesn't compare to nearby East Beach.

Facilities: Picnic areas, restrooms, lifeguards, snack bar; restaurants and groceries nearby.

Swimming: Good.

Surfing: Excellent west of the breakwater.

Fishing: Good.

Getting there: Located along the 800 block of Shoreline Drive in Santa Barbara.

Shoreline Park—The attraction here is not the park but the beach that lies below it. The park rests at the edge of a high bluff; at the bottom, secluded from view, is a narrow, curving length of white sand. It's a great spot to escape the Santa Barbara crowds while enjoying a pretty beach. Stairs from the park lead down to the shore.

Facilities: Topside in the park are picnic areas, restrooms, and a playground. Restaurants and groceries are within a mile in Santa Barbara.

Getting there: Located in Santa Barbara along Shoreline Drive.

Mesa Lane Beach (★)—This is the spot Santa Barbarans head when they want to escape the crowds at the better-known beaches. It's a meandering ribbon of sand backed by steep bluffs. You can walk long distances along this secluded strand.

Facilities: None. Restaurants and groceries several miles away in Santa Barbara.

Surfing: Good.

Getting there: There's a stairway to the beach at the end of Mesa Lane, off Cliff Drive in Santa Barbara.

Arroyo Burro County Park—This six-acre facility is a little gem. The sandy beach and surrounding hills are packed with locals on summer days. If you can arrive at an uncrowded time you'll find beautiful scenery along this lengthy strand.

Facilities: Picnic areas, restrooms, lifeguards, restaurant, snack bar; information, 805-687-3714.

Swimming: Good.

Surfing: Excellent west of the breakwater.

Fishing: Good.

Getting there: Located at 2981 Cliff Drive in Santa Barbara.

More Mesa (★)—According to nude beach aficionado Dave Patrick, this is the region's favorite bare-buns rendezvous. Thousands of sunbathers gather at this remote site on a single afternoon. "On a hot day," Patrick reports, "the beach almost takes on a carnival atmosphere, with jugglers, surfers, world-class frisbee experts, musicians, dancers, joggers, horseback riders, and volleyball champs." A scene that should not be missed.

Facilities: None.

Getting there: That's the trick. It's located between Hope Ranch and Goleta, three miles from Route 101. Take the Turnpike Road exit from Route 101; follow it south to Hollister Avenue, then go left; from Hollister turn right on Puente Drive, right again on Vieja Drive, then left on Mockingbird Lane. At the end of Mockingbird Lane a path leads about three-quarters of a mile to the beach.

El Capitan State Beach—Another of Southern California's sparkling beaches, it stretches along three miles of oceanfront. The park is 168 acres and features a nature trail, tidepools, and wonderful opportunities for hiking along the beach. El Capitan Creek, fringed by oak and sycamore trees, traverses the area. Seals and sea lions often romp offshore and in winter gray whales cruise by.

Facilities: Picnic areas, restrooms, showers, store, lifeguard; information center, 805-968-1411.

Camping: Permitted in the park near the beach. There is also a private campground, **El Capitan Ranch Park** (11560 Calle Real, Goleta; 805-685-3887), about one-half mile inland. It is a sprawling 100-acre complex with picnic areas, restrooms, showers, store, pool, playground, game areas, and outdoor theater.

Swimming: Good.

Surfing: Good off El Capitan Point.

Fishing: Good. Also a good place to catch grunnion.

Getting there: Located in Goleta off Route 101 about 20 miles north of Santa Barbara.

Refugio State Beach—This is a 39-acre park with over a mile of ocean frontage. You can bask on a sandy beach, lie under palm trees on the greensward, and hike or bicycle along the two-and-a-half-mile path that connects this park with El Capitan. There are also interesting tidepools.

Facilities: Picnic areas, restrooms, showers, lifeguard, store; information, 805-968-1350.

Swimming: Good.

Surfing: Good.

Fishing: Good.

Getting there: Located on Refugio Road in Goleta, off Route 101 about 23 miles north of Santa Barbara.

Gaviota Beach or **"Secret Spot"** (★)—This nude beach is a rare find indeed. Frequented by few people, it is a pretty white-sand beach that winds along rocky headlands. There's not much here except beautiful views, shore plant life, and savvy sun bathers. Wander for miles past cliffs and coves.

Facilities: None. Restaurants and groceries located about two miles away in Gaviota.

Getting there: Located off Route 101 about 30 miles north of Santa Barbara and two miles south of Gaviota. Driving north on Route 101 make a U-turn on Vista Del Mar Road; drive south on Route 101 for seven-tenths of a mile to a dirt parking area. Cross the railroad tracks; a path next to the railroad light signal leads to the beach.

Gaviota State Park—This mammoth 2776-acre facility stretches along both sides of Route 101. The beach rests in a sandy cove guarded on either side by dramatic sedimentary rock formations. A railroad trestle traverses the beach and a fishing pier extends offshore. On the inland side a hiking trail leads up to **Gaviota Hot Springs** and into Los Padre National Forest.

Facilities: Picnic areas, restrooms, showers, store, lifeguard, fishing pier, playground; information, 805-968-0019.

Camping: Permitted at the beach.

Swimming: Good.

Fishing: Good off the pier.

Getting there: The beach is located off Route 101 about 33 miles north of Santa Barbara. To get to the hot springs take Route 101 north from the beach park; get off at Route 1 exit; at the end of the exit ramp turn right; turn right on the frontage road and follow it a short distance to the parking lot. The trail from the parking lot leads several hundred yards to the hot springs.

Jalama Beach County Park—This remote park sits at the far end of a 15-mile long country road. Nevertheless, in summer there are likely to be many campers here. They come because the broad sandy beach is fringed by coastal bluffs and undulating hills. Jalama Creek cuts through the park, creating a wetland frequented by the endangered California brown pelican. Point Conception lies a few miles to the south, and the area all around is undeveloped and quite pretty (though Vandenberg Air Force Base is situated north of the beach). A good area for beachcombing as well as rock-hounding for chert, agate, travertine, and fossils.

Facilities: Picnic areas, restrooms, store, snack bar, playground; information, 805-734-1446.

Swimming: Dangerous rip currents.

Surfing: Good at Tarantula Point about one-half mile south of the park.

Fishing: You can surf-fish for perch or fish from the rocky points for cabizon and rock fish.

Getting there: From Lompoc take Route 1 south for five miles; turn onto Jalama Road and follow it 15 miles to the end.

Point Sal State Beach (★)—This is one of the most secluded and beautiful beaches along the entire Central Coast. Access is over a nine-mile country road, part of which is unpaved and impassable in wet weather. When you get to the end of this steep, serpentine monster there are no services available. But the scenery is magnificent. A long crescent beach curves out toward Point Sal, a bold headland with a rock island offshore. The Casmalia Hills rise sharply from the ocean, creating a natural amphitheater. Seabirds roost nearby and the beach is a habitat for harbor seals.

Facilities: None; information, 805-733-3713.

Fishing: There's surf-fishing from the beach and rocks.

Getting there: From Route 1 three miles south of Guadalupe turn west on Brown Road, then pick up Point Sal Road. Together they travel nine miles to a bluff-top overlook. Steep paths lead to the beach.

SAN LUIS OBISPO AREA BEACHES AND PARKS

Rancho Guadalupe County Park—Saudia Arabia has nothing on this place. The sand dunes throughout the area are spectacular, especially

450-foot Mussel Rock, the highest dune on the West Coast. The dunes provide a habitat for California brown pelicans, California least terns, and other endangered birds and plants. The Santa Maria River, which empties here, forms a pretty wetland area.

Facilities: None; restaurants and groceries are five miles away in Guadalupe; information, 805-937-1302.

Fishing: Very good.

Getting there: From Route 1 in Guadalupe, follow Main Street west for five miles to the beach. Wind-blown sand sometimes closes the road, so call beforehand.

Pismo Beach State Park—This spectacular beach runs for six miles from Pismo Beach south to the Santa Maria River. Along its oceanfront are some of the finest sand dunes in California, fluffy hills inhabited by shorebirds and tenacious plants. Also home to the pismo clam, it's a wonderful place to hike and explore.

Facilites: Picnic areas, restrooms, showers; restaurants and groceries nearby in Pismo Beach; information, 805-489-8655.

Camping: Permitted in two campgrounds near the beach. There is also camping at **Oceano Memorial County Park** (near Mendel Drive and Pier Avenue, Oceano; 805-549-5930).

Fishing: Good from the **Pismo Beach Pier** (end of Winds Avenue, Pismo Beach) for cod and red snapper. You can also dig for pismo clams along the beach (check local restrictions).

Getting there: The park parallels Route 1 in Pismo Beach.

Pirate's Cove or **Mallagh Landing** (★)—This crescent-shaped nude beach is a beauty. Protected by 100-foot cliffs, it curves for a half mile along a placid cove. At one end is a rocky headland pockmarked by caves.

Facilities: None. Restaurants and groceries are about a mile away in Avila Beach.

Swimming: Very good. The beach is in a sheltered area and the water is shallow.

Skindiving: Very good.

Getting there: Located ten miles south of San Luis Obispo in Avila Beach. From Route 101 take Avila Beach Drive west for two miles; turn left on Cave Landing Road (the road travels immediately uphill); go six-tenths of a mile to a dirt parking lot; crude stairs lead down to the beach.

Montana de Oro State Park—This 7000-acre facility is one of the finest parks along the entire Central Coast. It stretches over a mile along the shore, past a sandspit, tidepools, and sharp cliffs. There are remote coves for viewing seals, sea otters, and migrating whales and for sunbathing on hidden beaches. Monarch butterflies roost in the eucalyptus-filled canyons and a hiking trail leads to Valencia Peak, with views scanning almost 100 miles of coastline. Wildlife is abundant along 50 miles of hiking trails. Chapparal, Bishop pine, and coastal live oak cover the hillsides; in spring wildflowers riot, giving the park its name, "Mountain of Gold."

Facilities: Picnic areas, restrooms; restaurants and groceries are several miles away in Los Osos; information, 805-528-0513 or 805-772-2560.

Camping: Permitted above the beach and in several primitive sites.

Fishing: Good. There's also clamming here.

Surfing: Good around Hazard Canyon.

Getting there: Located on Pecho Valley Road about ten miles south of Morro Bay.

Morro Bay State Park—Located amid one of the biggest marshlands along the California coast, this 2435-acre domain is like an outdoor museum. The tidal basin attracts over 250 species of sea, land, and shore birds. Great blue herons roost in the eucalyptus trees. There's a marina where you can rent boats to explore the salt marsh and nearby sandspit, and a natural history museum with environmental displays. Camping is in an elevated area trimmed with pine and other trees. Since the park fronts the wetlands, there is no beach here; but you can reach the beach at **Morro Bay State Park Sand Spit** by private boat (see the "Sightseeing" section in this chapter).

Facilities: Picnic areas, restrooms, showers, snack bar; restaurants and groceries are one mile away in Morro Bay; information, 805-772-2560.

Camping: Permitted.

Fishing: Good from the sandspit.

Getting there: Located on Country Club Drive in Morro Bay.

Atascadero State Beach—Another of the Central Coast's long, skinny parks, this sandy beach stretches almost two miles along Morro Bay. Private homes border one side, but in the other direction there are great views of Morro Rock. It's a good place for beachcombing and clamming.

Facilities: Restrooms, showers; restaurants and groceries nearby in Morro Bay; information, 805-772-2560.

Camping: Permitted.

Fishing: Good.

Getting there: Located parallel to Route 1 in Morro Bay; park entrance is along Yerba Buena Street.

Los Padres National Forest—The southern section of this mammoth park parallels the coast from Ventura to San Luis Obispo. Rising from sea level to almost 9000 feet, it contains the Sierra Madre, San Rafael, Santa Ynez, and La Panza mountains. Characterized by sharp slopes and a dry climate, only one third of the preserve is forested. But there are coast redwoods, ancient bristlecone pines, and amazingly diverse plant life. Los Padres was formerly home to the rare California condor, which with its nine-foot wing-span is the largest land bird in North America. Among the animals still remaining are golden eagles, quail, owls, woodpeckers, wild pig, mule deer, black bear, and several species which escaped from the Hearst Ranch, including Barbary sheep and Rocky Mountain elk.

Facilities: The northern and southern sectors of the national forest contain over 1700 miles of hiking trails, almost 500 miles of streams, a ski trail on Mt. Pinos, and 88 campgrounds (14 with swimming facilities). For information and permits contact forest headquarters at 42 Aero Camino Street, Goleta, CA 93017; 805-968-1578.

Camping: Permitted.

Getting there: Route 33 cuts through the heart of Los Padres. Route 101 provides numerous access points.

CAMBRIA AREA BEACHES AND PARKS

San Simeon State Beach—This wide sand corridor reaches for about two miles from San Simeon Creek to Santa Rosa Creek. It's a wonderful place to wander and the streams, with their abundant wildlife, add to the enjoyment. Unfortunately, Route 1 divides the beach from the camping area and disturbs the quietude. Other parts of the park are very peaceful, especially the **Moonstone Beach** section opposite Cambria, known for its moonstone agates and otters.

Facilities: Picnic areas, restrooms; restaurants and groceries nearby in Cambia; information, 805-927-4621.

Getting there: Located on Route 1 in Cambria.

William R. Hearst Memorial State Beach—Located directly below Hearst Castle, this is a placid crescent-shaped beach. The facility measures only two acres, including a grassy area on a rise above the beach. There is a 1000-foot long fishing pier. Scenic San Simeon Point curves out from the shoreline, creating a pretty cove and protecting the beach from surf.

Facilities: Picnic areas and restrooms; restaurants and groceries nearby in San Simeon town; information, 805-927-4621.

Swimming: Very good.

Fishing: Good. Also, charter boats leave from the pier.

Getting there: Located on Route 1 opposite Hearst Castle.

Hiking

With its endless beaches and mountain backdrop, the South Central Coast is wide open for exploration. Shoreline paths and mountain trails crisscross the entire region.

First among equals in this hiker's dreamland is the **California Coastal Trail,** the 600-mile route that runs the entire length of the state. Here it begins at Point Mugu and travels along state beaches from Ventura County to Santa Barbara. In Santa Barbara the trail turns inland toward the Santa Ynez Mountains and Los Padres National Forest. It returns to the coast at Point Sal, then parallels sand dunes, passes the hot springs at Avila Beach, and continues up the coast to San Simeon.

VENTURA AREA TRAILS

Bounded by the Santa Monica and Santa Ynez mountains and bordered by 43 miles of shoreline, Ventura County offers a variety of hiking opportunities.

Sycamore Canyon Loop Trail (10 miles) starts at the Big Sycamore Canyon entrance to Point Mugu State Park and leads through a wooded canyon, dropping down sharply to Deer Camp Junction. The trail continues beside a stream lined with sycamores.

La Jolla Valley Loop Trail (4 miles) begins at a Route 1 turnoff north of Big Sycamore Canyon and heads up the steep right side of the canyon. En route to Mugu Peak, La Jolla Valley walk-in camp is a good spot for a picnic. From Mugu Peak an alternative trail leads back down through oak copses and open grassland. There are wonderful views of the ocean and Channel Islands along the way.

Emma Wood Trail (3 miles) is a lovely shoreline hike from the Emma Wood State Beach to Seaside Wilderness Park; popular with bird watchers.

SANTA BARBARA AREA TRAILS

What distinguishes Santa Barbara from most California coastal communities is the magnificent Santa Ynez mountain range, which forms a backdrop to the city and provides excellent hiking terrain.

A red steel gate marks the beginning of **Romero Canyon Trail** (5.75 miles) on Bella Vista Road in Santa Barbara. After joining a fire road at the 2350 foot elevation, the trail follows a stream shaded by oak, sycamore, and bay trees. From here you can keep climbing or return via the right fork, a fire road which offers an easier but longer return trip.

San Ysidro Trail (4.5 miles), beginning at Park Lane and Mountain Drive in Santa Barbara, follows a stream dotted with pools and waterfalls, then climbs to the top of Camino Cielo ridge. For a different loop back, it's only a short walk to Cold Springs Trail.

Cold Springs Trail, East Fork (4.5 miles) heads east from Mountain Drive in Santa Barbara. The trail takes you through a canyon covered with alder and along a creek punctuated by pools and waterfalls. It continues up into Hot Springs Canyon and crosses the flank of Montecito Peak.

Cold Springs Trail, West Fork (2 miles) leads off the better known East Fork. It climbs and descends along the left side of a lushly vegetated canyon before arriving at an open valley.

Tunnel Trail (4 miles) is named for the turn-of-the-century tunnel through the mountains which brought fresh water to Santa Barbara. The trail begins at the end of Tunnel Road in Santa Barbara and passes through various sandstone formations and crosses a creek before arriving at Mission Falls.

San Antonio Creek Trail (3.5 miles), an easy hike along a creek bed, starts from the far end of Tucker's Grove County Park in Goleta. In the morning or late afternoon you'll often catch glimpses of deer foraging in the woods.

Thirty-five miles of coastline stretches from Stearns Wharf in Santa Barbara to Gaviota State Beach. There are hiking opportunities galore along the entire span.

The **Summerland Trail** (2.5 miles), starting at Lookout Park in Summerland, takes you along Summerland Beach, past tiny coves, then along Montecito's coastline to the beach fronting the Biltmore Hotel.

Goleta Beach Trail (3.5 miles) begins at Goleta Beach County Park in Goleta and curves past tidepools and sand dunes en route to Goleta Point. Beyond the dunes is Devereux Slough, a reserve populated by egrets, herons, plovers, and sandpipers. The hike also passes the Ellwood Oil Field where a Japanese submarine fired shots at the mainland United States during World War II.

Gaviota Hot Springs and Peak Trail (2.5 miles) begins in Gaviota State Park. The first stop on this trek is the mineral pools at Gaviota Hot Springs (about a half mile from the trailhead). After a leisurely dip you can continue on a somewhat strenuous route into Los Padres National Forest, climbing to Gaviota Peak for a marvelous view of ranch land and the Pacific.

Point Conception Trail (6 miles) begins at Jalama County Park and heads southwards past Jalama Beach, a popular spot for surfing and fishing. It then turns inland up to the bluffs overlooking Point Conception lighthouse.

The **Point Sal Trail** (6 miles) offers an excellent opportunity to hike in a forgotten spot along the coast. (But beware, it's not for inexperienced hikers or those afraid of heights.) Alternating between cliffs and seashore, the trail takes you past tidepools, pelicans, cormorants, and basking seals. An excellent whale-watching area, the trail ends near the mouth of the Santa Maria River.

SAN LUIS OBISPO AREA TRAILS

The San Luis Obispo area, rich in wildlife, offers hikers everything from seaside strolls to mountain treks. Many of the trails in this area are in the Los Padres National Forest and often require a wilderness permit (for information, call 805-925-9538).

Nipomo Dunes Trail (4 miles) is especially rewarding for dune lovers. There's a multitude of dune flowers like magenta and yellow sand verbena, daisies, asters, and coreopsis. The trail begins at Oso Flaco Lake (in the dunes south of Oceano) and wends its way to the mouth of the Santa Maria River. This wetland area is a habitat for many endangered birds.

The golden mustard plants and poppies along the way give **Montana De Oro Bluffs Trail** (2 miles) its name ("Mountain of Gold"). This coastal trail takes you past Spooner's Cove (a mooring place for bootleggers during Prohibition). You'll pass clear tidepools, sea caves, basking seals, otters, and sandstone bluffs.

For an interesting hike along the sandspit which separates Morro Bay from Estero Bay, try the **Morro Bay Sandspit Trail** (5 miles). The trail leads past sand dunes and ancient Chumash shell mounds. Stay on the ocean side of the sandspit if you want to avoid the muck. To make this a one-way hike, arrange to take the Clam Taxi (805-772-8085) boat service.

LOPEZ LAKE TRAILS

Several trails in the vicinity of Lopez Lake Recreational Area offer opportunities to see the region's flora and fauna. Deer, raccoon, fox, and woodrats predominate, along with a variety of birds species (not to mention rattlesnakes and poison oak.)

At the entrance to the park, **Lopez Lake Trail** (3.5 miles) climbs steeply through oak and chapparal and offers splendid views of the lake and the Santa Lucia Mountains.

Two Waters Trail (1.5 miles) connects the Lopez and Wittenberg arms of Lopez Lake. It offers marvelous views, but requires a boat to reach the trailheads at Encinal or Miller's Cove.

Blackberry Spring Trail (1 mile) commences at upper Squirrel campground and passes many plant species used by the Chumash Indians. This is a moderate hike with a 260-foot climb which connects with High Ridge Trail.

Little Falls Creek Trail (2.75 miles) begins along Lopez Canyon Road and ascends 1350 feet up the canyon past a spectacular waterfall. Views of the Santa Lucia wilderness await you at the top of the mountain.

Travelers' Tracks

Sightseeing

VENTURA AREA

The serpentine highway and magnificent ocean views that have made Malibu famous continue as Route 1 wends north from Los Angeles into Ventura County. Backdropped by the Santa Monica Mountains, the road sweeps past a string of fluffy white beaches.

At **Point Mugu,** a talus-covered outcropping, a vista point overlooks miles of beaches to the south and a wildlife sanctuary to the north. Then, as nature gives way to civilization, Route 1 plunges through **Oxnard,** a fast-developing beach town, and continues into Ventura.

Situated 60 miles northwest of Los Angeles and 30 miles to the southeast of Santa Barbara, **Ventura** has generally been overlooked by travelers. History has not been so remiss. Long known to the Chumash Indians, who inhabited a nearby village named Shisholop, the place was revealed to Europeans in 1542 by the Portuguese explorer Juan Rodriguez Cabrillo. Father Junipero Serra founded a mission here in 1782 and the region soon became renowned for its fruit orchards.

Today the city preserves its heritage in a number of historic sites. Stop by the **Visitor and Convention Bureau** (785 South Seaward Avenue; 805-648-2075) for a booklet describing three walking tours through town.

The highlight of these urban strolls is **San Buenaventura Mission** (211 East Main Street; 805-643-4318), a whitewash and red-tile church flanked by a flowering garden. The dark, deep chapel is lined with Stations of the Cross paintings and features a Romanesque altar adorned with statues and pilasters. My favorite spot is the adjacent garden with its tile fountain and stately Norfolk pines.

Just down the street, the **Ventura County Historical Museum** (100 East Main Street; 805-653-0323; admission) traces the region's secular history with displays of Chumash Indian artifacts, cowboy spurs and saddles, oil industry photographs, and simple agricultural tools.

Then stroll across to the **Albinger Archaeological Museum** (113 East Main Street; 805-648-5823) and view an archaeological dig that dates back 3500 years. A small museum displays the arrowheads, shell beads, crucifixes, and pottery uncovered here. At the dig site itself you'll see the foundation of an 18th-century mission church, an ancient earth oven, and a remnant of the Spanish padres' elaborate aqueduct system.

Further along sits the **Ortega Adobe** (215 West Main Street; 805-654-7837), a small, squat home built in 1857. With its woodplank furniture and bare interior it provides a strong example of how hard and rudimentary life was in that early era.

Backtrack to San Buenaventura Mission and wander down **Figueroa Plaza**, a broad promenade decorated with tile fountains and flowerbeds. This is the site of the town's old Chinatown section, long since passed into myth and memory.

Figueroa Street continues to the waterfront, where a **promenade** parallels the beach. This is a prime area for water sports, and countless surfers, with their blond hair and black wetsuits, will be waiting offshore, poised for the perfect wave. Along the far end of the esplanade, at the **Ventura Pier**, you'll encounter one more Southern California species, the surf fisherman.

Another local wonder is the **Ventura County Courthouse** (501 Poli Street), a sprawling structure designed in Neo-Classical style. The place is a melange of Doric columns, bronze fixtures, and Roman flourishes. But forget the marble entranceway and grand staircase, what makes it memorable is the row of friars' heads adorning the facade. Where else but in Southern California would a dozen baroque priests stare out at you from the hall of justice?

By contrast, the **Olivas Adobe** (4200 Olivas Park Drive; 805-654-7837) is a spacious hacienda surrounded by flowering gardens. This two-story gem, with balconies running the full length of the upper floor, is a study in the Monterey-style architecture of 19th-century California. The rooms are furnished in period pieces and there is a museum adjacent to the house, providing a window on the world of California's prosperous Spanish settlers.

SANTA BARBARA AREA

From Ventura, Route 101 speeds north and west to Santa Barbara. For a slow-paced tour of the shoreline, take the **Old Pacific Coast Highway** instead. Paralleling the freeway and the Southern Pacific Railroad tracks, it rests on a narrow shelf between sharply rising hills and the ocean. The road glides for miles along sandy beaches and rocky shoreline, passing the woodframe communities of Solimar Beach and Seacliff Beach.

Past this last enclave the old road ends as you join Route 101 once more. With the Santa Ynez Mountains looming on one side and the Pacific extending along the other, you'll pass the resort town of Carpinteria. The temperature might be 80° with a blazing sun overhead and a soft breeze off the ocean. Certainly the furthest thing from your mind is the North Pole, but there it is, just past Carpinteria—the turnoff for Santa Claus Lane.

Santa Claus Lane? It's a block-long stretch of trinket shops and toy stores with a single theme. Frosty the Snow Man is here in the form of a huge rooftop statue and there's a Santa Claus replica with a waistline measuring maybe 30 feet. It's one of those places that are so tacky you feel like you've missed something if you pass them by. If nothing else, you can mail an early Christmas card. Just drop it in the mailbox at **Toyland** (3821 Santa Claus Lane, Carpinteria; 805-684-3515) and it will be postmarked (ready for this?) "Santa Claus, California."

Tucked between a curving bay and the Santa Ynez Mountains lies one of the prettiest places in all California. It's little wonder that the Spanish who settled **Santa Barbara**, establishing a presidio in 1782 and a mission several years later, called it *la tierra adorado,* the beloved land.

Discovered by a Portuguese navigator in 1542, it was an important center of Spanish culture until the Americans seized California in the 19th century. The town these Anglo interlopers built was a post-Victorian style community. But a monstrous earthquake leveled the downtown area in 1925 and created a *tabla rasa* for architects and city planners.

Faced with rebuilding Santa Barbara, they returned the place to its historic roots, combining Spanish and Mission architecture to create a Mediterranean metropolis. The result is modern day Santa Barbara with its adobe walls, red-tile roofs, rounded archways, and palm-lined boulevards.

Sightseeing Santa Barbara is as simple as it is rewarding. First stop at the **Santa Barbara Chamber of Commerce** (1330 State Street, 805-965-3021). The myriad materials here include more pamphlets, books, and booklets than you ever want to see. The most important piece is a brochure entitled "Santa Barbara" which outlines a "Red Tile Tour" for walkers as well as a lengthier "Scenic Drive." Together they form two concentric circles along whose perimeter lie nearly all the city's points of interest.

RED TILE TOUR

The 14-block **Red Tile Tour** begins at the **Santa Barbara County Courthouse** (1100 Block of Anacapa Street; 805-962-6464), the city's grandest building. This U-shaped Spanish-Moorish "palace" covers almost three sides of a city block. The interior is a masterwork of beamed ceilings, arched corridors, and palacio tile floors. On the second floor of this 1929 courthouse are murals depicting California history. The highlight of every visit is the sweeping view of Santa Barbara at the top of the clock tower. From the Santa Ynez Mountains down to the ocean all that meets the eye are palm trees and red-tile roofs.

Two blocks down, the **Hill Carrillo Adobe** (11 East Carrillo Street) is an 1826-vintage home built by a Massachusetts settler for his Spanish bride. Today the house is furnished with period pieces.

Along State Street, the heart of Santa Barbara's shopping district, many stores occupy antique buildings. **El Paseo** (814 State Street) represents one of the most unique malls in the entire country. It is a labyrinthine shopping arcade comprised of several historic complexes. Incorporated into the architectural motif is **Casa de la Guerra,** a spendid house built in 1827 for the commander of the Santa Barbara presidio and described by Richard Henry Dana in his classic *Two Years Before the Mast.*

Across the street rests **Plaza de la Guerra**, a palm-fringed park where the first city hall stood in 1875. Nearby, another series of historic structures has been converted into a warren of shops and offices. In the center of the mall is **Presidio Gardens** (de la Guerra Street between Anacapa and Santa Barbara streets), a tranquil park with a carp pond and elephant-shaped fountains which spray water through their trunks.

The **Santiago de la Guerra Adobe** (110 East de la Guerra Street) and the **Lugo Adobe,** set in a charming courtyard, are other 19th-century homes that have been converted to private use.

The **Santa Barbara Historical Society Museum** (136 East de la Guerra Street; 805-966-1601) certainly looks its part. Set in an adobe building with tile roof and wrought-iron window bars, the facility sits behind heavy wooden doors. Within are a series of displays depicting the Spanish and Mexican periods of Santa Barbara history, including memorabilia from author Richard Henry Dana's visits. There is a pleasant courtyard in back with a fountain and shade trees, a perfect place for a sightseer's siesta.

A right turn on Santa Barbara Street carries you to **Casa de Covarrubias** (715 Santa Barbara Street). Most places in Santa Barbara are a little too neatly refurbished to provide a dusty sense of history. But this L-shaped house, and the adjacent **Historic Fremont Adobe** (715 Santa Barbara Street), are sufficiently wind-blasted to evoke the early 19th century. The former structure, dating to 1817, was the site of the last Mexican assembly in 1846; the latter became headquarters for Colonel John C. Fremont after Americans captured the town later that year.

Turn back along Santa Barbara Street and pass the **Rochin Adobe** (820 Santa Barbara Street). This 1856 adobe, now covered with clapboard siding, is a private home.

It's a few steps over to **El Presidio de Santa Barbara State Historic Park** (123 East Canon Perdido Street; 805-966-9719), which occupies both sides of the street and incorporates some of the city's earliest buildings. Founded in 1782, the Presidio was one of four military fortresses built by the Spanish in California. Protecting settlers and missionaries from Indians, it also served as a seat of government and center of Western culture. Today only two original buildings survive. **El Cuartel,** the guards' house, served as the soldiers' quarters. The **La Caneda Adobe,** also built as a military residence, is now the offices of the Santa Barbara Trust for Historic Preservation. Most interesting of all is the **Santa**

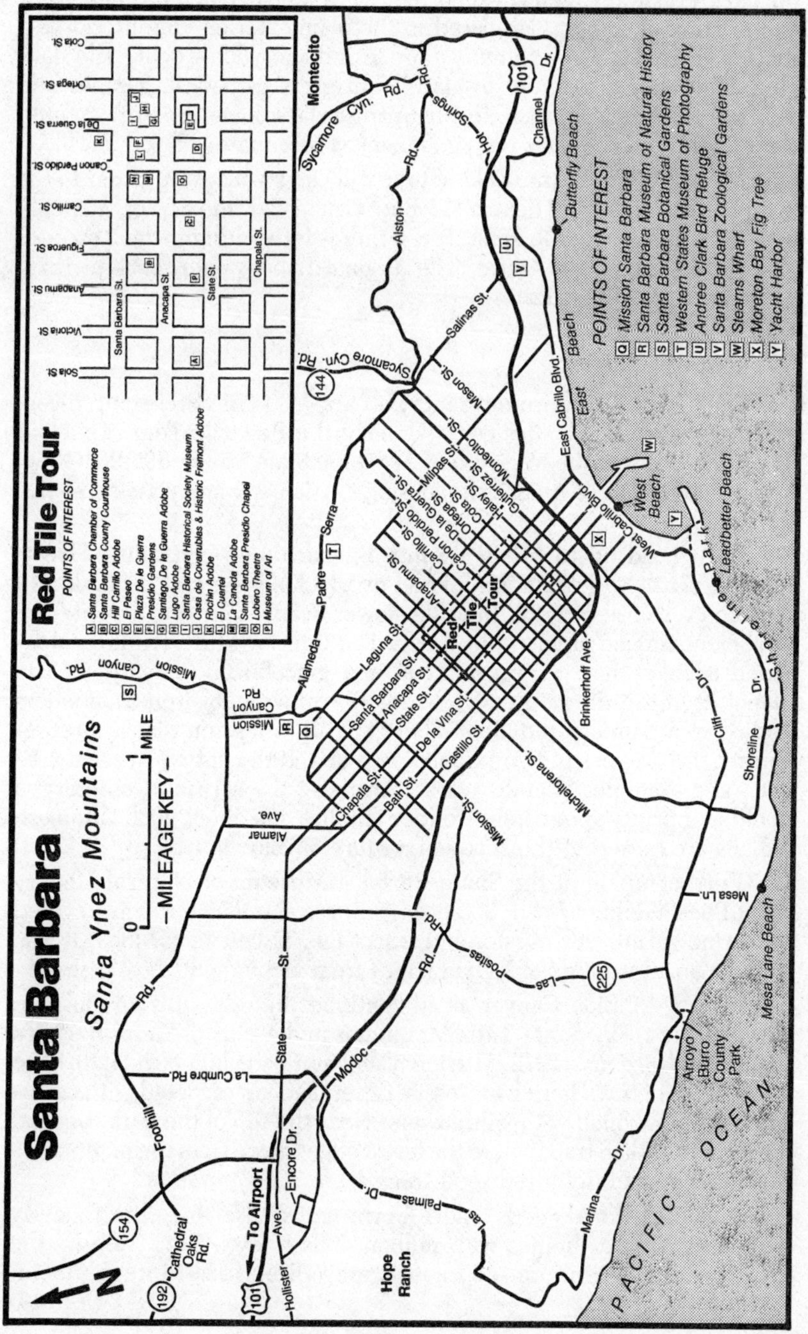
Santa Barbara
Santa Ynez Mountains
0
1
MILE
– MILEAGE KEY –
N
Red Tile Tour
POINTS OF INTEREST
A Santa Barbara Chamber of Commerce
B Santa Barbara County Courthouse
C Hill Carrillo Adobe
D El Paseo
E Plaza De la Guerra
F Presidio Gardens
G Santiago De la Guerra Adobe
H Lugo Adobe
I Santa Barbara Historical Society Museum
J Casa de Covarrubias & Historic Fremont Adobe
K Rochin Adobe
L El Cuartel
M La Caneda Adobe
N Santa Barbara Presidio Chapel
O Lobero Theatre
P Museum of Art
Sola St.
Victoria St.
Anapamu St.
Figueroa St.
Carrillo St.
Canon Perdido St.
De la Guerra St.
Ortega St.
Cota St.
Santa Barbara St.
Anacapa St.
State St.
Chapala St.
Montecito
POINTS OF INTEREST
Q Mission Santa Barbara
R Santa Barbara Museum of Natural History
S Santa Barbara Botanical Gardens
T Western States Museum of Photography
U Andree Clark Bird Refuge
V Santa Barbara Zoological Gardens
W Stearns Wharf
X Moreton Bay Fig Tree
Y Yacht Harbor
PACIFIC OCEAN
Foothill Rd.
Cathedral Oaks Rd.
192
154
101
To Airport
Hollister Ave.
Encore Dr.
Hope Ranch
Las Palmas Dr.
La Cumbre Rd.
State St.
Modoc Rd.
Las Positas Rd.
225
Marina Dr.
Arroyo Burro County Park
Mesa Lane Beach
Mesa Ln.
Cliff Dr.
Shoreline Dr.
Shoreline Park
Leadbetter Beach
West Beach
West Cabrillo Blvd.
East Beach
East Cabrillo Blvd.
Butterfly Beach
Channel Dr.
Alamar Ave.
Mission Canyon Rd.
Alameda Padre Serra
Laguna St.
Santa Barbara St.
Anacapa St.
State St.
De la Vina St.
Castillo St.
Bath St.
Chapala St.
Mission St.
Michelorena St.
Brinkerhoff Ave.
Red Tile Tour
Anapamu St.
Carrillo St.
Canon Perdido St.
De la Guerra St.
Ortega St.
Cota St.
Haley St.
Gutierrez St.
Montecito St.
Milpas St.
Mason St.
Salinas St.
144
Sycamore Cyn. Rd.
Alston Rd.
Hot Springs Rd.
Sycamore Cyn. Rd.

Barbara Presidio Chapel, which re-creates an early Spanish church in its full array of colors. Compared to the plain exterior, the interior is a shock to the eye. Everything is done in red and yellow ochre and dark blue. The altar is painted to simulate a great cathedral. Drapes and columns, difficult to obtain during Spanish days, have been drawn onto the walls. Even the altar railing is painted to imitate colored marble.

The last stop on this walking tour will carry you a step closer to the present. The **Lobero Theatre** (33 East Canon Perdido Street; 805-963-0761) was constructed in 1924. It is a three-tiered design which ascends to a 70-foot high stage house. The original Lobero dates back to 1873, Santa Barbara's first theater.

SCENIC DRIVE

The **Scenic Drive** around Santa Barbara, a 30-mile circle tour, incorporates several of the sites covered along the Red Tile Tour. To avoid repetition begin at the **Museum of Art** (1130 State Street; 805-963-4364) with its collection of American paintings, Asian art, and classical sculpture.

Then head up to **Mission Santa Barbara** (end of Laguna Street; 805-682-4713), which sits on a knoll overlooking the city. Founded in 1786 and restored in 1820, this twin-tower beauty follows a design from an ancient Roman architecture book. The interior courtyard is a colonnaded affair with a central fountain and graceful flower garden. The chapel itself is quite impressive with a row of wrought-iron chandeliers leading to a multicolored altar. There are also museum displays representing the original Indian population, early 19th-century mission artifacts, and examples of crafts works. Also visit the Mission Cemetery, a placid and pretty spot where frontier families and about 4000 Chumash Indians are buried in the shade of a Moreton Bay fig tree.

Further uphill at the **Santa Barbara Museum of Natural History** (2559 Puesta del Sol Road; 805-682-4711) are successive rooms devoted to marine, plant, vertebrate, and insect life. Excellent for kids, it also features small exhibits of Indian tribes from throughout the West.

Nearby Mission Canyon Road continues into the hills for close-up views of the rocky Santa Ynez Mountains and a tour of **Santa Barbara Botanical Gardens** (1212 Mission Canyon Road; 805-682-4726). The three miles of trails here wind past a desert section carpeted with cactus and a meadow filled with wildflowers. Near the top of the park, beyond the ancient Indian trail, where the forest edges down from the mountains, is a stand of cool, lofty redwood trees.

Backtrack to Alameda Padre Serra and cruise this elite roadway past million dollar homes with million dollar views. Then stop by the **Western States Museum of Photography** (Brooks Institute of Photography, 1321 Alameda Padre Serra; 805-965-8664) for a tour of its ever-changing photo exhibits and permanent display of antique cameras.

From Alameda Padre Serra a series of side roads leads through the exclusive bedroom community of **Montecito**. Here a variety of architectural styles combine to create a luxurious neighborhood. After exploring the town's shady groves and manicured lawns, you can pick up **Channel Drive**, a spectacular street which skirts beaches and bluffs as it loops back toward Santa Barbara.

From this curving roadway you'll spy oddly shaped structures offshore. Looking like a line of battleships ready to attack Santa Barbara, they are in fact **oil derricks.** Despite protests from environmentalists and a disastrous 1969 oil spill, these coastal waters have been the site of drilling operations for decades. Those hazy humps further out past the wells are the **Channel Islands.**

The **Andree Clark Bird Refuge** (1400 East Cabrillo Boulevard) is a placid lagoon filled with ducks, geese, and other freshwater fowl. There's a tree-tufted island in the center and a trail around the park. Upstaging all this is the adjacent **Santa Barbara Zoological Gardens** (500 Niños Drive; 805-962-6310; admission) with its miniature train ride and population of monkeys, lions, elephants, and exotic birds.

Cabrillo Boulevard hugs the shore as it tracks past **East Beach,** Santa Barbara's longest, prettiest strand. With its rows of palm trees, grassy acres, and sunbathing crowds, it's an enchanting spot.

For a taste of sea air and salt spray walk out along **Stearns Wharf** (foot of State Street). From the end of this wooden pier you can gaze back at Santa Barbara, realizing how aptly author Richard Henry Dana described the place: "The town is finely situated, with a bay in front, and an amphitheatre of hills behind." Favored by local anglers, the wharf is also noted for the **Sea Center** (211 Stearns Wharf; admission), a marine museum with an aquarium, underwater photographs, and a 37-foot replica of a gray whale and calf.

If you tire of walking, remember that Stearns Wharf is the departure point for the **Santa Barbara Trolley** (805-962-0209), an old-fashioned vehicle which carries visitors along the waterfront, through the downtown area, and out to the mission.

The **Moreton Bay Fig Tree** (Chapala and Moreton streets), another local landmark, is a century-old giant with branches that spread 160 feet. This magnificent specimen stands as the largest tree of its kind in the United States.

Back along the waterfront, Cabrillo Boulevard continues to the **Yacht Harbor** (West Cabrillo Boulevard and Castillo Street) where 1200 pleasure boats, some worth more than homes, lie moored. The walkway leads past yawls, ketches, sloops, and fishing boats to a breakwater.

From here you can survey the fleet and take in the surrounding mountains and ocean.

To continue this seafront excursion, follow Shoreline, Cliff, and Marina drives as they parallel the Pacific, past headlands and beaches, en route to **Hope Ranch.** Santa Barbara is flanked by two posh communities: Montecito in the east and this elite enclave to the west. It's a world of country clubs and cocktail parties, where money and nature meet to create forested estates.

NORTH OF SANTA BARBARA

Route 101 streams northwest past a series of suburban communities, including Goleta and Isla Vista, where the **University of California, Santa Barbara** is located. Cutting a swath between mountains and ocean, the road passes a series of attractive beach parks, then turns inland toward the mountains and interior valleys.

About 35 miles from Santa Barbara Routes 101 and 1 diverge. For a rural drive past white barns and meandering creeks, follow **Route 1.** En route to Lompoc it passes farmlands, pastures, and rolling hills. About five miles south of Lompoc, you can follow **Jalama Road** (★), a country lane which cuts through sharp canyons and graceful valleys on a winding 15-mile course to the ocean, ending at a beach park.

This journey becomes a pilgrimage when Route 1 approaches **La Purisima Mission** (Purisima Road, Lompoc; 805-733-3713). The best-restored of all 21 California missions, this historic site has an eerie way of projecting you back to Spanish days. There's the mayordomo's abode with the table set and a pan on the oven, or the mission store, its barrels overflowing with corn and beans. The entire mission complex, from the sanctified church to the tallow vats where slaughtered cattle were rendered into soap, is re-created. Founded nearby in 1787, the mission was re-established at this site in 1812. Today you can tour the living quarters of priests and soldiers, the workshops where weaving, leather-making, and carpentry were practiced, and the mission's original water system.

In spring and summer the hills around **Lompoc** dazzle with thousands of acres of flowers. The countryside is a rainbow of color throughout the season. Then in fall fields of poppies, nasturtiums, and larkspurs bloom.

SAN LUIS OBISPO AREA

PISMO BEACH

After its lengthy inland course through Lompoc and Guadalupe, Route 1 rejoins Route 101 and returns to the coast at **Pismo Beach.** An unattractive congeries of mobile homes and beach rental stands, this nondescript town has one saving grace—its dunes. They are sand castles in the air, curving, rolling, ever-changing hills of sand. Wave after wave of them parallel the beach, like a crystalline continuation of the ocean.

In fact they comprise the most extensive coastal dunes in California. From Pismo Beach the sand hills run six miles south where they meet the 450-foot-high **Guadalupe dunes** (see the "Beaches & Parks" section of this chapter), forming a unique habitat for wildflowers and shorebirds.

Back in the 1930s and 1940s a group of Bohemians, the "Dunites," occupied this wild terrain. Comprised of nudists, artists, and mystics, the movement believed that the dunes were a center of cosmic energy. Today the area is filled with beachcombers, sunbathers, and off-highway vehicles.

Stop by the **Pismo Beach Chamber of Commerce** (581 Dolliver Street, Pismo Beach; 805-773-2055) for brochures and maps of Pismo Beach, Shell Beach, and Avila Beach, the three seaside communities lining San Luis Obispo Bay. The prettiest of all is **Avila Beach.** Here you can comb a white-sand beach or walk out along three fishing piers. At the far end of town a dramatic headland curves out from the shoreline, creating a crescent-shaped harbor where sailboats bob at their moorings.

There are hot springs in the hills around Avila Beach. **Sycamore Mineral Springs Resort** (1215 Avila Beach Drive, Avila Beach; 805-595-7302) has tapped these local waters and created a lovely spa. There are volleyball courts and a swimming pool here, but the real attractions are the redwood hot tubs. Very private, they are dotted about on a hillside and shaded by oak and sycamore.

From the Pismo Beach–Avila Beach strip, you can buzz into San Luis Obispo on Route 101 or take a quiet country drive into town via **See Canyon Road** (★). The latter begins in Avila Beach and corkscrews up into the hills past apple orchards and horse farms. Along its 13-mile length, half unpaved, you'll encounter mountain meadows and ridge-top vistas. During the fall harvest season you can pick apples at farms along the way.

SAN LUIS OBISPO

San Luis Obispo, a pretty jewel of a town, lies 12 miles from the ocean in the center of an expansive agricultural region. Backdropped by the Santa Lucia Mountains, the town focuses around an old Spanish mission. Cowboys from outlying ranches and students from the nearby campus add to the cultural mix, creating a vital atmosphere that has energized San Luis Obispo's rapid growth.

For a sense of the region's roots, pick up information on the "Path of History" at the **San Luis Obispo Chamber of Commerce** (1039 Chorro Street; 805-543-1323). This self-guided tour begins at **Mission San Luis de Tolosa** (Chorro Street and Mission Plaza; 805-543-6850). Dating to 1772, the old Spanish outpost has been nicely reconstructed, though the complex is not as extensive as La Purisima Mission in Lompoc. There's a museum re-creating the Native American, Spanish, and Mexican eras as well as a pretty church. **Mission Plaza,** fronting the chapel, is a well-landscaped park.

The **County Historical Museum** (696 Monterey Street; 805-543-0638) continues the historic overview with displays from the American period. Across the street at the **San Luis Obispo Art Center** (1010 Broad Street; 805-543-8562) are exhibits of works by local artists.

St. Stephen's Episcopal Church (Nipomo and Pismo streets) is a narrow, lofty, and strikingly attractive chapel. Built in 1867, it was one of California's first Episcopal churches. The **Dallidet Adobe** (Toro Street between Pismo and Pacific streets), constructed by a French vintner in 1853, is another local architectural landmark. A block away and about a century later Frank Lloyd Wright designed the **Kundert Medical Building** (Pacific and Santa Rosa streets).

The **Ah Louis Store** (800 Palm Street) symbolizes the Chinese presence here. A sturdy brick building with wrought-iron shutters and balcony, it dates to 1874 and once served the 2000 Chinese coolies who worked on nearby railroad tunnels.

Around the corner, the **Sauer-Adams Adobe** (964 Chorro Street), covered in clapboard, is an 1860-era house with a second-story balcony. By the turn of the century, Victorian-style homes had become the vogue. Many of San Luis Obispo's finest Victorians are located in the blocks adjacent to where Broad Street intersects with Pismo and Buchon streets.

If you're in town on a Thursday evening, be sure to stop by the **Farmers' Market** (Higuera Street between Osos and Nipomo streets). Farmers from the surrounding area turn out to sell fresh fruits and vegetables. They barbeque ribs, cook sweet corn and fresh fish, then serve them on paper plates to the throngs that turn out weekly. Puppeteers and street dancers perform as the celebration assumes a carnival atmosphere.

To pick your own produce, ask at the Chamber of Commerce about the **farm trails** program. They'll provide information on where to go around town and throughout San Luis Obispo County to gather ripe strawberries, apples, avocados, tomatoes, and dozens of other fruits and vegetables.

MORRO BAY

As Route 1 angles north and west from San Luis Obispo toward the ocean, separating again from Route 101, you'll encounter a procession of nine volcanic peaks. Last in this geologic parade is a 576-foot plug dome called **Morro Rock.** The pride of Morro Bay, it stands like a little Gibraltar, connected to the mainland by a sand isthmus. You can drive out and inspect the brute. Years ago, before conservationists and common sense prevailed, the site was a rock quarry. Today it's a nesting area for peregrine falcons.

All around Morro Bay you'll encounter the same contradiction. The town combines unique natural resources with ugly manmade features. The waterfront is a study in blue-collar architecture with bait-and-tackle shops, plywood restaurants, and slapdash stores everywhere; and dominating the skyline, vying with the great rock itself, are three monstrous concrete smokestacks.

Turn your back on this travesty and you are in a bird sanctuary. Extending for miles out toward Morro Rock is a dramatic **sandspit**, a teeming region of sand dunes and sealife. From town there's a funky sandspit shuttle (699 Embarcadero; 805-772-8085) to boat you across to the dunes. They'll drop you off for as long as you wish to explore the seashore; when you're done, just stand on the tallest dune and wave for a return boat. For something more formal, **Tiger's Folly** (1205 Embarcadero; 805-772-2257) sponsors cruises of the harbor in an old-fashioned paddlewheeler.

Back on terra firma, visit the **Museum of Natural History** (Morro Bay State Park; 805-772-2694) with its displays of local history and wildlife. The museum itself is unimpressive, but it is located at White Point, a rock outcropping in which Indian mortar holes are still evident. From this height there are views of the sandspit, Morro Bay, and Morro Rock. The nearby lagoon, a habitat for 250 migratory and resident bird species, is one of the largest salt marshes in California.

CAMBRIA AND HEARST CASTLE

North from Morro Bay, Route 1 passes the antique village of **Harmony** (population 18), then continues to the seaside town of **Cambria.** Originally settled in the 1860s, Cambria later expanded into a major seaport and whaling center. As the railroad replaced coastal shipping, Cambria declined, only to be resurrected during the past few decades as an artist colony and tourist center. There's even a **Cambria Chamber of Commerce** office (767 Main Street; 805-927-3624).

It's a pretty place, with ridgetop homes, sandy beaches, and rocky coves. But like many of California's small creative communities, Cambria has begun peering too long in the mirror. The architecture along Main Street has assumed a cutesy mock-Tudor look and the place is taking on an air of unreality.

Still, there are many fine artists and several exceptional galleries here. It's a choice place to shop and seek out gourmet food. While you're at it, head up to **Nit Wit Ridge** (Hillcrest Drive just above Cornwall Street). That hodgepodge house on the left, the one decorated with every type of bric-a-brac, is the home of Art Beal, a.k.a. Captain Nit

Wit. He has been working on this folk-art estate, listed in the National Register of Historic Landmarks, since 1928. Then take a ride along **Moonstone Beach Drive,** a lovely oceanfront corridor with vista points and tidepools. It's a marvelous place for beachcombers and daydreamers.

Funny thing about travel, you often end up visiting places in spite of themselves. You realize that as soon as you get back home friends are going to ask if you saw this or that, so your itinerary becomes a combination of the locales you've always longed to experience and the places everyone else says you "must see."

The world-renowned **Hearst Castle** (Route 1, San Simeon; 805-927-4621; admission) is one of the latter. Built by newspaper magnate William Randolph Hearst and designed by architect Julia Morgan, the Hearst San Simeon State Historical Monument includes a main house that sports 37 bedrooms, three guest houses, and part of the old Hearst ranch, which once stretched 40 miles along the coast.

The entire complex took 27 years to build. Back in the 1930s and 1940s, when Hearst resided here and film stars like Charlie Chaplin, Mary Pickford, Clark Gable, and Cary Grant frequented the place, the grounds contained the largest private zoo in the world. Ninety species of wild animals—including lions, tigers, yaks, and camels—roamed about.

An insatiable art collector, Hearst stuffed every building with priceless works. La Casa Grande, the main house, is fronted by two cathedral towers and filled with Renaissance art. To see it is overwhelming. There is no place for the eye to rest. The main sitting room is covered everywhere with tapestries, bas-relief works, 16th-century paintings, Roman columns, and a carved wood ceiling. The walls are fashioned from 500-year-old choir pews, the French fireplace dates back 400 years; there are hand-carved tables and silver candelabra, (I am still describing the same room), overstuffed furniture, and antique statuary. It is the most lavish mismatch in history.

Hearst Castle crosses the line from visual art to visual assault. The parts are exquisite, the whole a travesty. And yet, as I said, you must see the place.

It's so huge that four different two-hour tours are scheduled daily to various parts of the property. Since over one million people a year visit, the guided tours are often booked solid. I recommend that you reserve in advance and plan on taking Tour 1, which covers the ground floor of La Casa Grande, a guest house, the pools, and the gardens. Reservations are made through MISTIX; in California call 800-446-7275; outside the state, 619-452-1950.

Ultimately you'll find that in spite of the pomp and grandiosity, there is a magic about the place. In the early morning, when tour shuttles begin climbing from sea level to the 1600-foot-elevation residence, fog feathers through the surrounding valleys, obscuring everything but the spiked peaks of the Santa Lucia Mountains and the lofty towers of the castle. The entire complex, overbearing as it is, evokes a simpler, more glamorous era, before the Depression and World War II turned the nation's thoughts inward, when without blinking a man could build an outlandish testimonial to himself.

Beyond Hearst Castle Route 1 winds north past tidepools and pocket beaches. There are pretty coves and surf-washed rocks offshore. To leeward the hills give way to mountains as the highway ascends toward the dramatic Big Sur coastline. Over two hundred miles further north sits the city which Hearst made the center of his publishing empire, an oceanfront metropolis called San Francisco.

Shopping

VENTURA SHOPPING

The **Spirit of Haiti Gallery** (1583 Spinnaker Drive, #105), in the Ventura Harbor Village Mall, has a striking collection of colorful paintings from the Caribbean. Evocative and energetic, the works re-create the lush foliage and brilliant hues of the tropics. In addition to oils, there are hand-painted boxes, metal works, and drawings.

SANTA BARBARA SHOPPING

Since Santa Barbara's shops are clustered together, you can easily uncover the town's hottest items and best bargains by concentrating on a few key areas. The prime shopping center lies along State Street, particularly between the 600 and 1300 blocks.

Picadilly Square (813 State Street) is a warehouse-type mall with shops arranged contiguously, separated only by open spaces and low railings. There are boutiques galore here as well as an artisans' loft selling crafts items.

El Paseo (814 State Street), a famous promenade, is one of the most imaginative malls I've ever seen. It consists of several historic adobe houses, dating to the early 19th century, which are combined and converted into a succession of stores. This is a middle- and high-ticket complex: the art galleries, jewelry stores, and designer dress stores number among the best, but there are also curio shops and toy stores.

Pier 1 Imports (928 State Street) looks like a Hong Kong warehouse. It's stuffed to the rafters with wickerware, glassware, scented candles, wood carvings, ethnic rugs, ceramics, and cotton fabrics.

La Arcada (1114 State Street) is another spiffy mall done in Spanish style. The shops here, along the upper lengths of State Street, are more chic and contemporary than elsewhere. **Ghurka HQ.** (1114 State Street) sells leather-trimmed luggage and safari clothing.

A favorite Santa Barbara bookstore is **Earthling Bookshop** (1236 State Street), a spacious store with a friendly staff and tasteful selection of hardbacks and paperbacks.

On the lower end of State Street, **Pacific Travelers' Supply** (529 State Street) carries a complete stock of guidebooks. They also have luggage and travel paraphernalia.

Antiques in Santa Barbara are spelled Brinkerhoff Avenue. This block-long residential street conceals a half-dozen antique shops. Set amid simple clapboard houses is **L. Scott & Co.** (502 Brinkerhoff Avenue), which specializes in folk art, furniture, and gifts. Around the corner at **Redwood Inn Antiques** (124 West Cota Street) there are collectables and vintage clothing. My favorite, **Carl Hightower Galerie & Collective** (528 Brinkerhoff Avenue), is crowded with jewelry, ceramics, and everything else imaginable. (Many of these shops are open only at the end of the week, so it's best to visit on Saturday; next preferable days are Thursday, Friday, and Sunday.)

The corner of State and Ortega streets marks the center for vintage clothing. **Chameleon & Silver Threads Vintage** (706 State Street) blends the contemporary with the antique and promises outfits to suit anyone from Queen Victoria to a rock and roller. **Yellowstone Clothing** (619A State Street) features Hawaiian shirts and other old-time favorites. At **The Street** (21 West Ortega Street) they have great jewelry and men's and women's hats. Also try **The Gypsie's Garden** (35 East Ortega Street) and **Pure Gold** (718 State Street) for everything from early exotic to late lamented.

For over twenty years Santa Barbara County artists and craftspeople have turned out for the **Arts & Crafts Show.** Every Sunday and holiday from 10 a.m. until dusk they line East Cabrillo Avenue. The original artwork for sale includes paintings, graphics, sculptures, and drawings. Among the crafts are macrame, stained glass, woodwork, textiles, weaving, and jewelry. If you are in town on a Sunday make it a point to stop by.

SAN LUIS OBISPO SHOPPING

In this old Spanish town the best stores are located along the blocks surrounding Mission Plaza. Stroll the two blocks along Monterey Street between Osos and Chorro streets, then browse the five-block stretch on Higuera Street from Osos Street to Nipomo Street. These two arteries and the side streets between form the heart of downtown.

The Natural Selection (111 Morro Street) is a unique shop dedicated to nature and science. The posters, books, toys, and greeting cards all follow a similar theme. So if you've been searching everywhere for that moon map, rain gauge, or *Tyrannosaurus rex* T-shirt, look no further.

Renee's (842 Higuera Street) is one of the many San Luis Obispo stores located in historic buildings. In this case the building may be old but the women's fashions are ultra-contemporary (and quite chic).

The Network Mall (778 Higuera Street) is a collection of crafts shops and small stores. Nearby, **Granny's General Store** (1119 Garden Street) resembles a dry goods store around the turn of the century. A good place to pick up simulated antiques or a double-strength bottle of vanilla extract.

Also consider **The Creamery** (Higuera and Nipomo streets), an old dairy plant converted into an ingenious arcade.

CAMBRIA SHOPPING

Located a few miles south of Hearst Castle, this seaside enclave has developed into an artist colony and become an important arts-and-crafts center, with numerous galleries and specialty shops. Several antique shops are also located here; like the crafts stores, they cluster along Main Street and Burton Drive.

Among the foremost galleries is **Seekers** (4090 Burton Drive). It's a glass menagerie inhabited by crystal sculpture, stained-glass windows, and handblown jewelry. There are also handcrafted boxes, hardwood jigsaw puzzles, and ceramic sculptures.

The Soldier Factory (789 Main Street) is a journey back to childhood. Part toy store and part museum, it serves as headquarters for thousands of hand-painted toy soldiers. These antiques are deployed in battle formation, re-enacting clashes from the Civil War and other engagements. Many of the pewter pieces are made in the adjacent "factory" by owner Jack Scruby. His unique shop has been featured in the *Wall Street Journal*.

For a journey into another world visit **Victoriana** (Arlington Street near Main Street). This diminutive store sells miniatures of Victorian house furnishings. Among other things, the owner fabricated the **model Victorian house** (733 Main Street) that adorns the roof of a building around the corner.

Nightlife

VENTURA NIGHTLIFE

Bombay Bar & Grill (143 South California Street; 805-643-4404) offers live entertainment nightly with a musical medley that changes frequently. The South Seas-style bar, with overhead fans and oak-and-mirror decor, features piano plunkers, while the room in back hosts Top-40 live dance bands. Cover.

Over at **Club Soda** (317 East Main Street; 805-652-0100) they painted the walls to resemble a psychedelic nightmare. Then they gave each night a different theme. Maybe you'll walk in on "Waikiki Wednesday" or "Celebrity Night." The video music is strictly deejay format. Cover.

Scene of scenes in the seaside community of Ventura is the **Ventura Terrace Theatre** (26 South Chestnut Street; 805-648-1888), a refurbished movie house. With its intricate gold fixtures, stained-glass windows, and ornamental molding, this 1928 structure has been redone in grand style. The club frequently draws top-name entertainers and offers a cultural mix that includes rock video and dancing. Cover.

Or perhaps you just wanted a comfortable place overlooking the water. That would be **Charlie's Seaside Cafe & Restaurant** (362 California Street; 805-648-6688), where you can enjoy a quiet drink out on the patio or hear local jazz and rock ensembles inside. Cover.

SANTA BARBARA AREA NIGHTLIFE

The Palms (701 Linden Avenue, Carpinteria; 805-684-3811) features local rock bands every Thursday, Friday, and Saturday night. There's a small dancefloor here for footloose revelers.

The State Street strip in downtown Santa Barbara offers several party places. **Gallagher's Bar & Grill** (633 State Street; 805-963-4424), a stylish and popular spot, has live entertainment every night. A couple nights a week are for comedy; the rest of the time there's music ranging from jazz to rock. Up at **Acapulco Restaurant** (1114 State Street; 805-963-3469), in La Arcada mall, you can sip a margarita next to an antique wooden bar or out on the patio. No entertainment, but it's a pretty place to drink.

Eleven Twenty-Nine (1129 State Street, 805-963-7704) is another terrace affair where you can drink outdoors in a garden setting. A jazz duo plays here nightly. In back of this tropical bar sits **Oscar's 1129** (1129 State Street; 805-963-7704), one of Santa Barbara's hottest night spots. Drawing national talent, the nightclub usually has a full calendar of leading jazz and rock bands. Cover. Together with its fellow club, Oscar's 1129 represents *the* place in these parts.

If for no other reason than the view, **Harbor Restaurant** (210 Stearns Wharf; 805-963-3311) is a prime place for the evening. A plate-glass establishment, it sits out on a pier with the city skyline on one side and open ocean on the other. The lounge also features soft music by duos and small ensembles.

Ahzz (27 West Canon Perdido; 805-965-7733) bills itself as a nightclub but looks more like a disco. The decor is contemporary-cum-art-deco with lots of neon and mirrors. The dancefloor downstairs is dominated by a large video screen. The sound is rock, with live bands Friday and Saturday, deejay the rest of the week. Cover weekends.

For sunset views, nothing quite compares to **El Encanto Lounge** (1900 Lasuen Road; 805-687-5000). Located in a posh hotel high in the Santa Barbara hills, it features a split-level terrace overlooking the city and ocean. In the early evening there's a piano bar, then later on a jazz soloist or ensemble strikes up.

Pacific Coast Dance Co. (500 Anacapa Street; 805-966-6411) is a scene-and-a-half. A dancefloor and elevated stage dominate the place. Dancers line the bar, juice bar, and rows of wooden booths. The sound is Top-40 rock and roll, Tuesday through Saturday, and the bands are local. Cover.

Also consider the **Lobero Theatre** (33 East Canon Perdido Street; 805-963-0761), which presents a full schedule of dance, drama, concerts, and lectures.

SAN LUIS OBISPO AREA NIGHTLIFE

Ready for a Western saloon? Stone fireplace, antlers on the wall, etc.? It's called **F. McLintock's Saloon & Dining House** (750 Mattie Road, Shell Beach; 805-773-1892). Unlike its rowdier counterparts, this lounge is low key. The music, seven nights a week, is by solo guitarists playing soft rock and country and western.

The Rose and Crown (1000 Higuera Street, San Luis Obispo; 805-541-1911) is an English pub complete with dart boards and more than a dozen beers on top. The sound is an eclectic blend of deejays and live bands, rock, and jazz. From Wednesday through Sunday it's a good place to dance and drink imported beer.

Over at the **Dark Room** (1037 Monterey Street, San Luis Obispo; 805-543-5131) they host a different band every night. The music is jazz and blues; cover.

Hottest spot in San Luis Obispo is **The Spirit** (1772 Calle Joaquin, San Luis Obispo; 805-544-6060). Perched on a hill outside town and surveying the entire countryside, it draws big-name entertainers. Call first to see who's on tap; cover.

There's a posh piano bar at **The Inn at Morro Bay** (19 Country Club Drive, Morro Bay; 805-772-5651). Appointed with bentwood furniture and pastel panelling, it's a beautiful bar. The most striking feature of all is the view, which extends out across the water to Morro Rock.

Camozzi's Saloon (2262 Main Street, Cambria; 805-927-8941) is a sixty-year-old cowboy bar with longhorns over the bar, wagon wheels on the wall, and a floor that leans worse than a midnight drunk. The place is famous. Besides that, it has a rock band every Friday and Saturday.

For lower-key entertainment try the **Golden Lion Pub** (774 Main Street, Cambria; 805-927-8842). This British bar has a brick fireplace and features piano and organ music on weekends.

CHAPTER SIX
North Central Coast

If the North Central Coast were an oil painting, it would portray a surf-laced shoreline near the bottom of the frame. Pearly beaches and bold promontories would occupy the center, while forested peaks rose in the background. Actually, a mural would be more appropriate to the subject, since the coastline extends 150 miles from Big Sur to San Francisco. The artist would paint two mountain ranges parallel to the shore, then fill the area between with a patchwork of hills, headlands, and farmland.

Even after adding a swath of redwoods along the entire length of the mural, the painter's task would have only begun. The Central Coast will never be captured—on canvas, in print, or in the camera's eye. It is a region of unmatched beauty and extraordinary diversity.

Perhaps the most unique section of this entire stretch of paradise is Big Sur. Extending south of the Monterey Peninsula for 90 miles along the coast, and backdropped by the steep Santa Lucia Mountains, it is one of America's most magnificent natural areas. Only 1500 residents live in this rugged region of bald crags and flower-choked canyons. None but the most adventurous occupy the nearby Ventana Wilderness, which represents the southernmost realm of the coastal redwoods. Once a nesting place for rare California condors, Ventana is still home to wild boar, black bear, and mountain lion.

Beyond Big Sur lies the Monterey Peninsula, a fashionable residential area 125 miles south of San Francisco. Including the towns of Monterey, Pacific Grove, and Carmel, this wealthy enclave is a far cry from bohemian Santa Cruz. If Santa Cruz is an espresso coffee house, Monterey is a gourmet restaurant or designer boutique.

Like every place on the Central Coast, Big Sur, Monterey, and to the north, Santa Cruz, are reached along Route 1, the tortuous coast road that twists past sandy coves and granite cliffs. Paralleling it is Route 101, the inland freeway that leads through the warm, dry agricultural regions of the Salinas Valley.

In the seaside town of Santa Cruz, you'll encounter a former retirement community that has been transformed into a dynamic campus town. When the University of California opened a school here in the 1960s, it created a new role for this ever-changing place. Originally founded as a Spanish mission in 1791, Santa Cruz became a lumber port and manufacturing center when the Americans moved in around 1849. Then in the late 19th century it developed into a tourist resort filled with elaborate Victorian houses.

Due south of San Francisco is Half Moon Bay, a timeless farming and fishing community founded by Italians and Portuguese during the 1860s. The oceanside farms are so bountiful that Half Moon Bay dubs itself the pumpkin capital of the world and nearby Castroville claims to be the artichoke capital. While local farmers grow prize vegetables, commercial fishing boats comb the entire coast for salmon, herring, tuna, anchovies, and cod.

Bordering Half Moon Bay are the Santa Cruz Mountains, accessible along Routes 35 and 9. Unlike the low-lying coastal and inland farming areas, this range measures 3000 feet in elevation and is filled with redwood, Douglas fir, alder, and madrone.

The Esselen Indians who once inhabited Big Sur and its mountains have long since vanished. Together with the Costanoans, who occupied the rest of the Central Coast, the Esselen may have been here for 5000 years. By the time the Europeans happened upon California, about 10,000 Indians lived near the coast between Big Sur and San Francisco. Elk and antelope ranged the region. The Native Americans also hunted sea lions, gathered seaweed, and fed on oysters, abalone, clams, and mussels.

Westerners did not settle Big Sur until after 1850, and Route 1 did not open completely until 1937. During the 1950s, novelist Henry Miller became the focus of an artists' colony here. Jack Kerouac trekked through the area, writing about it in several of his novels. Other Beat poets, lured by Big Sur's dizzying sea cliffs and otherworldly vistas, also cut a path through its hills.

Fully three hundred years before settlers arrived in Big Sur, Monterey was already making history. As early as 1542, Juan Rodriguez Cabrillo, a Portuguese explorer in Spanish employ, set anchor off nearby Pacific Grove. Then in 1602 Sebastian Vizcaino came upon the peninsula again and told a whale of a fish story, grandly exaggerating the size and amenities of Monterey Bay.

His account proved so distorted that Gaspar de Portola, leading an overland expedition in 1769, failed to recognize the harbor. When Father Junipero Serra joined him in a second journey the next year, they realized that this gentle curve was Vizcaino's deep port. Serra established California's second mission in Monterey, then moved it a few miles in 1771 to

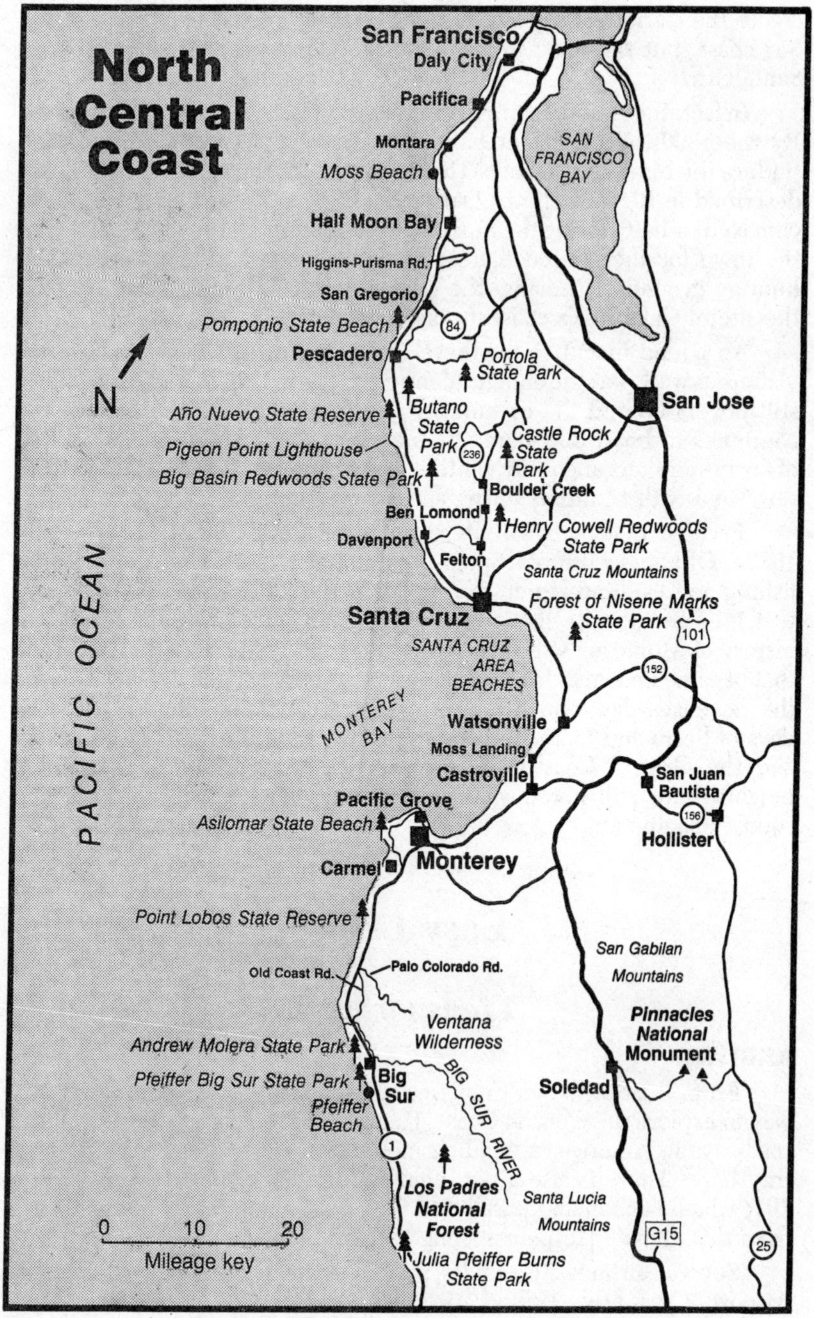
North Central Coast
San Francisco
Daly City
Pacifica
Montara
Moss Beach
Half Moon Bay
Higgins-Purisma Rd.
San Gregorio
Pomponio State Beach
84
Pescadero
Portola State Park
SAN FRANCISCO BAY
San Jose
N
Año Nuevo State Reserve
Butano State Park
Pigeon Point Lighthouse
236
Castle Rock State Park
Big Basin Redwoods State Park
Boulder Creek
Ben Lomond
Henry Cowell Redwoods State Park
Davenport
Felton
Santa Cruz Mountains
PACIFIC OCEAN
Santa Cruz
Forest of Nisene Marks State Park
101
SANTA CRUZ AREA BEACHES
152
MONTEREY BAY
Watsonville
Moss Landing
Castroville
San Juan Bautista
Pacific Grove
156
Asilomar State Beach
Hollister
Carmel
Monterey
Point Lobos State Reserve
San Gabilan Mountains
Old Coast Rd.
Palo Colorado Rd.
Ventana Wilderness
Pinnacles National Monument
Andrew Molera State Park
BIG SUR RIVER
Pfeiffer Big Sur State Park
Big Sur
Soledad
Pfeiffer Beach
1
Los Padres National Forest
Santa Lucia Mountains
0 10 20
Mileage key
G15
25
Julia Pfeiffer Burns State Park

create the Carmel Mission. Neither Serra nor Portola explored the Big Sur coast, but the Spanish were soon building yet another mission in Santa Cruz.

In fact, they found Santa Cruz much easier to control than Monterey. By the 1820s, Yankee merchant ships were plying Monterey waters, trading for hides and tallow. This early American presence, brilliantly described in Richard Henry Dana's classic *Two Years Before the Mast*, climaxed in 1846 during the Mexican War. Commodore John Sloat seized the town for the United States. By 1849, while Big Sur was still the hunting ground of Indians, the adobe town of Monterey had become the site of California's constitutional convention.

An added incentive for these early adventurers, and modern day visitors as well, was the climate along the Central Coast. The temperature still hovers around 67° in summer and 57° during winter; Santa Cruz continues to boast 300 sunny days a year. Explorers once complained of foggy summers and rainy winters, but like today's travelers, they were rewarded with beautiful spring and fall weather.

Perhaps that's why Monterey became a tourist mecca during the 1880s. Of course the old Spanish capital also developed into a major fishing and canning region during the early 20th century. It was then that John Steinbeck, the Salinas-bred writer, added to the already rich history of Monterey with his novels and stories. Much of the landscape that became known as "Steinbeck Country" has changed drastically since the novelist's day, and the entire Central Coast is different from the days of Serra and Sloat. But the most important elements of Monterey and the Central Coast—the foaming ocean, open sky, and wooded heights—are still here, waiting for the traveler with a bold eye and robust imagination.

Easy Living

Transportation

ARRIVAL

From Big Sur to San Francisco, coastal highway **Route 1** is the only way to explore the Central Coast. Happily, it is one of the most beautiful roadways in America, a winding mountain road with etherial views of the shore. There is also a fast, efficient, unimaginative freeway, **Route 101,** which runs inland parallel to the coast. Numerous side roads lead from this highway to points along the Central Coast.

Several airlines fly regular schedules to the Monterey Peninsula Airport. Currently, **United Airlines** (800-241-6522), **American Eagle**

Airlines (800-252-0017), and **WestAir Airlines** (800-421-6522) service this area from San Francisco and other departure points.

For railroad buffs, **Amtrak** (800-872-7245) offers daily service on the "Coast Starlight." The train runs from Seattle to Los Angeles with stops in Oakland and Salinas. Once in Salinas, passengers can transfer to a Greyhound or Monterey–Salinas Transit bus. Both lines provide frequent service to Monterey.

Greyhound Bus Lines (415-433-1500) also has continual service to Santa Cruz and Monterey from San Francisco and Los Angeles.

CAR RENTALS

To rent a car for a trek through the Central Coast region, your best bet is San Francisco. The city offers lower prices and more agencies to choose from.

If flying directly into Monterey, you can rent a car at the airport from **American Auto Rental** (408-649-0200), **Avis Rent A Car** (408-373-3327), **Dollar Rent A Car** (408-373-6121), **Hertz Rent A Car** (408-373-3318), or **National Car Rental** (408-373-4181).

Additional rental agencies are located in town, with prices comparable to those at the airport. **American International Rent A Car** (408-649-0240), **Budget Rent A Car** (408-373-1346), and **Sears Rent A Car** (408-373-1588) are among the best bets.

In the Santa Cruz area check with **Avis Rent A Car** (408-423-1244), **Budget Rent A Car** (408-425-1808), **Hertz Rent A Car** (408-426-3366), **Sears Rent A Car** (408-429-1030), or save money while taking a chance with a "used" vehicle from **Bombs Away** (408-425-1537) or **Rent A Heap Cheap** (408-429-8046).

PUBLIC TRANSPORTATION

From Watsonville, connections can be made to Monterey and Big Sur via the **Monterey–Salinas Transit Company** (408-899-2555). These buses carry passengers to many points of interest including Cannery Row, Point Lobos, and Andrew Molera and Pfeiffer Big Sur State Parks. Buses from Monterey to Big Sur run twice daily from May to September, but only on Saturday during the rest of the year.

From Waddell Creek in northern Santa Cruz County, the **Santa Cruz County Transit System** (408-425-8600) covers Route 1 as far south as Watsonville. (During summer months, shuttle service is provided to the beach from downtown Santa Cruz.) Bus service is also available between Año Nuevo and Santa Cruz. Call for schedules.

Peerless Stages (408-423-1800) connects with Greyhound Bus Lines in San Jose and Oakland and travels to Santa Cruz.

San Mateo County Transit (415-761-7000), or Sam Trans, departing from the Daly City BART station, has local bus service to Pacifica,

Montara, Moss Beach, and Half Moon Bay. The bus runs infrequently, so call for scheduling information. There is limited public transportation between Half Moon Bay and Santa Cruz.

BICYCLING

The Pacific Coast Bikecentennial Route follows Route 1 through the entire Central Coast area. There are camping sites along the way. The ocean views and rolling pastures make this an ideal course to peddle, if you are experienced and careful.

Both Monterey and Santa Cruz have bike paths for beginners and skilled riders alike. Especially good for touring are 17 Mile Drive, the bike trail along the bayshore from Seaside to Marina, and the roads in Point Lobos State Reserve.

For information on bike routes in Monterey, call the **Velo Club Monterey** (408-424-9423) for bike trails and group rides. For scenic and historical bike tours of Monterey, check with **Bay Bikes** (408-646-9090). In Santa Cruz County, call **Santa Cruz County Cycling Club** (408-425-8688).

BIKE RENTALS

For bicycle rentals, try **Bay Bikes** (640 Wave Street, Monterey; 408-646-9090), **Freewheeling Cycles** (188 Webster Street, Monterey; 408-373-3855), **Joselyn's Bicycles** (638 Lighthouse, Monterey; 408-649-8520), **Carmel Cycle Sport** (7150 Carmel Valley Road, Carmel; 408-624-5107), and **Bicycle Center** (1420 Mission Street, Santa Cruz; 408-423-6324).

For scooters check out **Your Scooter Shop** (1204 17th Avenue, Santa Cruz; 408-475-0844).

Hotels

All along the coast from Big Sur to San Francisco are lodging facilities galore. They are concentrated around the seaside communities of Monterey and Santa Cruz, though you'll also find nighttime stopovers on the rural coastline due south of San Francisco.

Prices vary as widely as the styles of accommodations. There are country inns, cottages, a few hostels, and many drab but dependable motels. The choice is a matter of economics and personal taste. Hostels, of course, are the cheapest lodgings and provide good opportunities for meeting people. Country inns create a homey atmosphere. Personally, because this entire stretch fronts the ocean, I think the beach cottages most fully convey the sense of the place. Whatever you choose, try to reserve in advance; the Central Coast is a priceless but poorly kept secret.

BIG SUR HOTELS

Big Sur has long been associated with bohemian values and an easy life style. Today landed gentry and wealthy speculators have taken over many of the old haunts, but a few still remain. One such is **Deetjen's Big Sur Inn** (Route 1, Big Sur; 408-667-2377), a 20-unit slapdash affair where formality is an inconvenience. The place consists of a hodgepodge collection of clapboard buildings. The outer walls are unpainted and the doors have no locks, lending the residence a tumbledown charm. Rooms are roughhewn, poorly insulated, and funky. Throw rugs are scattered about, the furniture is traditional, and local art pieces along the wall serve as decoration. If all this is beginning to discourage you, you're getting older than you think; after all, this offbeat hideaway does possess an enchanting quality. And the prices will return any visitor to those halcyon days of the '60s. There's a single room renting at budget price; doubles begin in the moderate category with shared bath.

If, on the other hand, you spell Big Sur with a capital $, the only roosting place to consider is **Ventana** (Route 1, Big Sur; 408-667-2331). Set along 334 mountainside acres overlooking the Pacific, this fabled resort is the *non plus ultra* of refined rusticity. Buildings are fashioned from raw wood and guest rooms are equipped with tile or marble fireplaces. There are knotty-pine walls, wicker furnishings, and quilt beds. With Japanese hot baths, saunas, two pools, and a sun deck, the place exudes an air of languor. Guests enjoy continental breakfast and afternoon hors d'oeuvres, hike nearby trails, and congratulate themselves for having discovered a secluded resort where doing nothing is a way of life. Ultra-deluxe.

Located within Pfeiffer Big Sur State Park is **Big Sur Lodge** (Route 1, Big Sur; 408-667-2171), a complex containing 61 cottages. The "lodge" represents a full-facility establishment complete with conference center, heated pool, saunas, restaurant, gift shop, grocery, and laundromat. It's very convenient, if undistinguished. The cottages are frame houses with wood-shingle roofs. Simple in design, they rent upwards from the moderate range and are frequently duplex-style. The interiors are pine and feature wall-to-wall carpeting and high beam ceilings; each cottage contains a porch.

Ripplewood Resort (Route 1, Big Sur; 408-667-2242) has 16 cabins ranging in price from moderate to deluxe. The less expensive are small, basic duplex units with knotty-pine walls, gas heaters, and rugs thrown across formica floors. They have baths but lack kitchens. The more expensive units are larger, with kitchens, sitting rooms, and decks, and are located above the river. My advice? Compromise with one of the riverfront cabins. They feature kitchens, decks, and spacious bedrooms yet rent in the moderate range. (No extra charge for the river tumbling past your doorstep.)

For a variety of accommodations, consider **Big Sur Campground and Cabins** (Route 1, Big Sur; 408-667-2322). Set in a redwood grove along the Big Sur River, this 13-acre facility has campsites, tent cabins, and A-frames. Camping out on the grounds costs $14 for two people and includes access to hot showers, laundry, store, basketball and volleyball courts, and a playground. The tent cabins, $30 per night, consist of woodframe skeletons with canvas roofs. They come with beds and bedding and share a bath house. The "cabins" along the river, deluxe-priced, are actually mobile homes, neatly furnished but rather sterile. More intimate are the A-frame cabins, with pine floors, Franklin stoves, and sleeping lofts. They also rent at deluxe prices and, like the mobile homes, include a kitchen and private bath.

South from Big Sur about 25 miles, on the edge of an ocean cliff, sits **Lucia Lodge** (Route 1, Lucia; 408-667-2391). Perched 500 feet above a cobalt blue bay are ten rustic but cozy rooms. Built of knotty pine, furnished with plain, durable pieces, they offer otherworldly views along a curving sweep of shoreline. The accommodations are sufficiently removed from the highway to create a sense of natural living in this extraordinary landscape. An adjacent restaurant and store make it a convenient hideaway. Prices rest in the moderate to deluxe range.

MONTEREY AREA HOTELS

The problem with lodging on the Monterey Peninsula is the same dilemma plaguing much of the world—money. It takes a lot of it to stay here, especially when visiting one of the area's vaunted bed and breakfasts. These country inns are concentrated in Pacific Grove and Carmel, towns neighboring on Monterey.

Monterey does feature a few such inns as well as a string of moderately priced motels. Budget travelers will do well to check into the latter and also to consult several of the Carmel listings below. Monterey's motel row lies along Munras Avenue, a buzzing thoroughfare that leads from downtown to Route 1. Motels are also found along Fremont Street in the adjacent town of Seaside. These are cheaper, drabber, and not as conveniently situated as the Munras hostelries.

Since overnight facilities fill rapidly around Monterey, particularly on weekends and during summer, it's wise to reserve in advance. Two agencies—**Monterey Peninsula Reservations** (800-822-8822) and **Carmel's Tourist Information Service** (408-624-1711) might prove useful in securing that elusive room.

There is also a **YMCA Youth Hostel** on the Monterey Peninsula, though it's a musical chairs affair. The location changes yearly, but during June, July, and August you can count on an American Youth Hostel facility *somewhere* in the region. Lodging runs in the budget category and includes continental breakfast. For information, contact YMCA of Monterey Peninsula, 600 Camino El Estero, Monterey, CA 93940; 408-373-4167.

Among the moderately priced motels lining Munras Avenue, **El Adobe Motel** (936 Munras Avenue, Monterey; 408-372-5409) is closest to downtown Monterey. This 26-unit establishment offers standard motel accommodations. The rooms are clean, carpeted, and comfortable, but far from cozy. They come equipped with television, telephone, table, and desk. There's hokey art on the walls, and the environment generally is safe but sterile. Prices, which include continental breakfast and use of the motel's hot tub, fluctuate within the moderate range between slack season and summer.

You'll find similar quarters at **Monterey Pines Motel** (1288 Munras Avenue, Monterey; 408-375-2168) and **Driftwood Motel** (2362 Fremont Street, Monterey; 408-372-5059).

For good cheer and homespun atmosphere, the **Old Monterey Inn** (500 Martin Street, Monterey; 408-375-8284) provides a final word. Before innkeepers Ann and Gene Swett decided to open their Tudor-style house to guests, they raised six children here. Now they raise rhododendrons and roses in the garden while hosting visitors in their ten-room bed and breakfast. The house rests on a quiet street yet is located within a few blocks of downtown Monterey. Among the trimly appointed rooms are several with tile fireplaces, wicker furnishings, and delicate wallhangings. There are spacious dining and drawing rooms downstairs and the landscaped grounds are studded with oak and redwood. If the ultra-deluxe price proves affordable, you'll find this friendly little inn a perfect spot for an evening fire and glass of sherry.

Merritt House (386 Pacific Street, Monterey; 408-646-9686) is not only an overnight resting place but also a stopping point along Monterey's "Path of History." Part of this 25-room inn rests in a vintage 1830 adobe home. Accommodations in the old house and the adjoining modern quarters are furnished with hardwood period pieces and feature vaulted ceilings, fireplaces, and balconies. The garden abounds with magnolia, fig, pepper, and olive trees. Continental breakfast is served. Located in the downtown district Merritt House prices from deluxe to ultra-deluxe.

Oceanfront on Cannery Row stands the **Spindrift Inn** (652 Cannery Row, Monterey; 408-646-8900), an ultramodern 42-room hotel. Painted in pastel hues, decorated with tile floors and contemporary art, it is the final word in chic surroundings. The lobby is fashionably laid out with skylight and sculptures and there is a rooftop solarium overlooking the waterfront. Guest rooms carry out the award-winning architectural motif with bay windows, hardwood floors, marble fireplaces, and built-in armoires. *La carte, monsieur?* Ultra-deluxe.

Asilomar Conference Center (800 Asilomar Boulevard, Pacific Grove; 408-372-8016) provides one of the area's best housing arrangements. Set in a state park, it's surrounded by 105 acres of sand dunes and pine forests. The beach is a stroll away from any of the center's 28 hotel lodges. There's a dining hall on the premises as well as meeting rooms and recreational facilities. Catering primarily to groups, Asilomar does provide accommodations for independent travelers. Rooms in the "rustic buildings" are small and spartan but adequate. They lack carpeting on the hardwood floors and include little decoration. The "deluxe building" rooms are nicely appointed with wallhangings, study desks, and comfortable furnishings. Accomodations generally price around the moderate range. Fireplaces and kitchenettes are also available for $6 extra for each feature. Every lodge includes a spacious lounge area with stone fireplace. No doubt about it, Asilomar is a splendid place at a relaxing price.

One of Monterey Peninsula's less expensive bed and breakfasts is nearby. **Gosby House Inn** (643 Lighthouse Avenue, Pacific Grove; 408-375-1287), a century-old Victorian mansion, includes 22 refurbished rooms. Each is different, and all have been decorated with special attention to detail. In any one you are liable to discover an antique armoire, brass lighting fixtures, stained glass, a Tiffany lamp, or clawfoot bathtub. They are all small after the Victorian fashion, which sacrifices space for coziness. The afternoon sherry and nightly turn-down service add to the homey feeling. All this warmth is deluxe-priced for a room with shared bath or ultra-deluxe with a private facility.

Green Gables Inn (104 5th Street, Pacific Grove; 408-375-2095) represents one of the region's most impressive bed and breakfasts. The house, a Queen Anne-style Victorian, dates from 1888. Adorned with step-gables, stained glass, and bay windows, it rests in a storybook setting overlooking Monterey Bay. Five bedrooms upstairs and a suite below have been fastidiously decorated with lavish antiques. Most bedrooms share a pair of bathrooms and rent at deluxe price; the suite, with sitting room and private bath, is ultra-deluxe. Set in a town filled with old Victorian homes, this oceanside residence is an ideal representation of Pacific Grove. There are also five separate units in a building adjacent to the main house. These are suites with private bath and fireplace; breakfast and access to the main house are included; ultra-deluxe.

Just down the street stands **Roserox Country Inn** (557 Ocean View Boulevard, Pacific Grove; 408-373-7673), an important contribution to the bed and breakfast scene. Commanding an even finer view, this turn-of-the-century house has a vista sweeping 180° along the ocean. Within its eight guest rooms and four baths are specially selected antiques such as English brass beds and clawfoot tubs. Each room follows a different decorative motif; all have been done with artistry. The public rooms are a bit cramped but the room tabs are competitive for the region (they are deluxe and ultra-deluxe in price, share baths, and feature ocean views). The service is quite good and the mother and two daughters who run this carefully tended establishment are charming.

Carmel River Inn (Route 1 at Carmel River Bridge, Carmel; 408-624-1575), located on the southern outskirts of town, has woodframe cottages priced from moderate to deluxe. Though there's also a motel connected with this 43-unit establishment, the cottages have far greater appeal. The less expensive units are studio-size structures with wall-to-wall carpeting, televisions, and telephones; their interior designer was obviously a capable, if uninspired, individual. (Still, at moderate price we are talking about one of Monterey Peninsula's greatest lodging bargains.) The pricier cottages vary in size and facilities, but may contain extra rooms, a fireplace, or a kitchen.

Carmel's most closely kept secret is a hideaway resort set on 21 acres and overlooking the ocean. Scattered about the tree-shaded grounds at **Mission Ranch** (26270 Dolores Street, Carmel; 408-624-6436) are a dozen 1930s-era cottages with kitchens, a white clapboard bed and breakfast inn, and several century-old structures. There are tennis courts, trim lawns, and ancient cypress trees. With mountains in the background, the views extend across a broad lagoon and out along sandy beachfront. The cottages are simple woodframe affairs, plainly furnished, and decorated with antique photos. The ranch dining room is favored by local people and the cottages are reserved by folks in the know who return year after year. A rare find indeed, with bed and breakfast rooms and motel accommodations at moderate price and cottages in the deluxe range.

The Homestead (Lincoln Street and 8th Avenue, Carmel; 408-624-4119) is also one of the area's better housing arrangements. Set in a maroon house with shiplap siding, it includes 12 rooms starting at moderate price with private bath. This is not a bed and breakfast, so it lacks the community atmosphere of other country inns, though a touch of the intimacy lingers. The rooms are carpeted and equipped with televisions; the furniture is functional more than fashionable. Also available are studio cottages with kitchenettes at moderate cost.

The Pine Inn (Ocean Avenue between Lincoln and Monte Verde streets, Carmel; 408-624-3851) is not only Carmel's oldest hostelry, but also another of the town's more reasonably priced places. This 49-room hotel dates back to 1902 and still possesses the charm that has drawn visitors for decades. The lobby is a fashionable affair with red brocade settees, marble-top tables, and a brick fireplace. Rooms start in the deluxe range. The less expensive accommodations are smaller but do have the antique furnishings, private baths, televisions, and telephones common to all the rooms. Each one has been designed along a different motif, but is likely to feature a brass bed, patterned wallpaper, and ornamental wallhangings. Rather than a country inn, this is a full-service hotel with restaurant and bar downstairs as well as room service for the guests.

Holiday House (Camino Real between Ocean and 7th avenues, Carmel; 408-624-6267), a six-room bed and breakfast several blocks from the beach, has rooms in the deluxe price category. Set in a brown-shingle house, it features a parlor with stone fireplace and a nicely tended garden. The rooms are small, neat, and prim; though attractively furnished, they lack the lavish antiques found in more expensive country inns. The outdoor decoration should adequately substitute—ask for a room with an ocean view.

Highlands Inn (Route 1 about four miles south of Carmel; 408-624-3801) is one of those raw-wood-and-polished-stone places that evoke the muted elegance of the California coast. Ultramodern in execution, it features a stone lodge surrounded by wood shingle buildings. The lodge houses a gourmet restaurant and oceanview lounge while the neighboring structures contain countless guest rooms, each a warren of blond woods and pastel tiles. Most have fireplaces and patios. Parked on a hillside overlooking an awesome sweep of ocean, the inn is the ultimate in Carmel chic with room tabs spelled ultra-deluxe.

Up in Carmel Valley, you might seek lodging at the **Korea Buddhist Sambosa Temple** (28110 Robinson Canyon Road, Carmel Valley; 408-624-3686). This seven-acre Zen retreat hosts guests at budget cost, or invites you to camp on the grounds for a nominal fee. In either case you'll need to bring bedding. The temple, grounds, and kitchen are open to guests. It's a good opportunity for anyone seeking a peaceful, meditative environment.

The ultimate resting place in this corner of the world is the **Tassajara Zen Center.** (For information, contact the Zen Center, 300 Page Street, San Francisco, CA 94102; 415-863-3136.) Set deep in the Santa Lucia Mountains along a meandering country road, Tassajara has been a hot springs resort since the 1880s. Before that its salubrious waters were known to Native Americans and the Spanish. When the Zen Center purchased the place in 1967, they converted it into a meditation center and initiated Japanese-style mineral bathing. There are only a few telephones and electrical outlets in the entire complex, making it ideal for people seeking serenity. Every year from May until September, the Zen Center welcomes day-visitors and overnight guests. The hosts provide three vegetarian meals daily plus lodging in the private rooms and cabins dotted about the grounds. Day-visitors are charged $10 admission, $12 on weekends; lodging facilities begin from $48 per person weekdays and $53 on weekends, meals included; shuttle service into the resort is available. Be sure to make reservations far in advance, since this unique place is very popular.

MONTEREY TO SANTA CRUZ HOTELS

Capitola Venetian Hotel (1500 Wharf Road, Capitola; 408-476-6471) is a mock Italian complex next to Capitola Beach. With its stucco and red tile veneer, ornamental molding, and carved wooden doors, it's a poor cousin to the grand villas of Venice. The 19 guest rooms come equipped with kitchens; many feature sitting rooms adjacent to the bedrooms. There are few wall decorations and the furnishings are plain wooden pieces but the atmosphere is pleasant. Rates drop from deluxe during summer months to moderate throughout the rest of the year.

Harbor Lights Motel (5000 Cliff Drive, Capitola; 408-476-0505), a few steps further uphill from the beach, is similarly laid out but in a more modern fashion. This ten-unit stucco building has rooms with kitchens and ocean views at deluxe rates in summer and moderate to deluxe during other months. The accommodations have shag rugs, hokey wall paintings, and bland furniture. Remember, you're paying for what's outside, not inside.

SANTA CRUZ HOTELS

When seeking overnight accommodations in Santa Cruz, the place to look is near the beach. That is where you'll want to be and, not surprisingly, where you'll find most hotels and motels. The problem during summer months is the cost. In winter you can have a room for a song, but come June the price tags climb. The best bargain in town is **Surfside Apartments** (311 Cliff Street, Santa Cruz; 408-423-5302). This seven-unit establishment contains several cottages and houses clustered around a flower garden. They are truly efficiency units: no television, telephone, parking facilities, or housekeeping services. But they are comfortably furnished, possess a friendly "beach cottage" feel, and feature kitchens. Located two blocks from the Boardwalk, these one-bedroom apartments rent in the moderate range. They are available only in summer and should be reserved far in advance.

Another excellent facility is **Ocean Echo Motel and Cottages** (401 Johans Beach Drive, Santa Cruz; 408-462-4192), located near a quiet neighborhood beach. This clapboard complex sits far from the madding Boardwalk crowd and represents a perfect choice for anyone seeking a Cape Cod-style cottage. The catch is that the place is extremely popular. Many units are rented to permanent residents, and the establishment will book reservations no more than one month in advance. Rooms are moderate in winter, deluxe from April to September; studios and cottages are tabbed deluxe.

It's big, brash, and blocky, but the **Dream Inn** (175 West Cliff Drive; 408-426-4330) is also right on the beach. With pool, jacuzzi, oceanfront restaurants, and lounge, this multitiered establishment extends from a hilltop perch down to a sandy strand. Long on aesthetics it isn't, but for location it can't be topped. The boardwalk and fishing pier are a short stroll away. Guest rooms are trimly done with fabric walls and contemporary furnishings; each sports a private balcony and ocean view. The price tag on all this glamor is deluxe during summer months, and somewhat less for the rest of the year. The question is whether you'll endure the plastic atmosphere for the sake of proximity to the Pacific. It's your call. (Being lazy myself, I'd book reservations in a minute.)

There is also a **Santa Cruz Hostel** (Mission Hill Junior High School, Mission Street, Santa Cruz; 408-423-8304), located some distance from the beach. Open only during summer months, it consists of mattresses on the floor of a junior high school gymnasium. While these may not be the finest accommodations, even by hostel standards, they do include a light breakfast. There are also hot showers, picnic tables, and a common room; bring a sleeping bag, though sheets are available. The nightly fee figures in the budget range; there is also a ten-minute chore; three-night maximum stay.

Country inns are rare in Santa Cruz; this California custom is just catching on here. One recent addition is **Cliff Crest Bed & Breakfast Inn** (407 Cliff Street, Santa Cruz; 408-427-2609), a five-bedroom establishment in an historic 1887 Victorian home. Among the features of the house are an outdoor belvedere, a yard landscaped by the designer of San Francisco's Golden Gate Park, and a solarium illuminated through stained-glass windows. Rooms vary in cost from a small room with private bath to the spacious "Rose Room," but all charges range within the deluxe category. In any case, the decor you're apt to find includes patterned wallpaper, an antique bed, wicker couch, and a tile bath with a clawfoot tub.

An even newer member of this elite club, **Chateau Victorian** (118 First Street, Santa Cruz; 408-458-9458), sits in a vintage home just one block from the Boardwalk. Guests here enjoy two sun decks and a sitting/dining room decorated with antique sideboard and wooden mantel. The entire house has been done by masterful decorators who placed plush carpeting throughout. They also found luxurious armchairs so soft that once settled you may never emerge. The place is chockablock with antiques: canopied beds, oak wardrobes, and so on. Rooms begin at $70 for a small place in the back house with carpet and bay window seat. All rooms have private fireplaces and feature tile baths. Prices in the main house range from deluxe to ultra-deluxe.

Less distinguished, but considerably cheaper, is **American Inn** (645 7th Avenue, Santa Cruz; 408-476-6424), a bed and breakfast across town. The place sits in a two-story stucco house on a busy street several blocks from the beach. It supports ten bedrooms, priced in the budget realm weekdays, moderate weekends; rooms with a kitchen are moderate. The cheaper accommodations share baths; others enjoy private facilities. All are spacious, attractive, and inexpensively furnished. The staff is helpful and friendly, making this place a fortuitous addition to the local housing scene.

Santa Cruz also has a string of neon motels within blocks of the Boardwalk. Count on them to provide small rooms with color television, wall-to-wall carpeting, nicked wooden tables, naugahyde chairs, stall showers, etc.; if they have any decorations at all you'll wish they didn't. But what the hell, for a night or two you can call them home. Their rates will fluctuate wildly depending on the season and tourist flow. Generally they charge budget prices in winter; during summer, prices escalate to the moderate range during the week and deluxe on weekends. The best of the lot is **St. Charles Court** (902 3rd Street, Santa Cruz; 408-423-2091), which has a pool and is spiffier and quieter than the others. Also consider **Big 6 Motel** (335 Riverside Avenue, Santa Cruz; 408-423-1651) and **Villa del Mar Motel** (321 Riverside Avenue, Santa Cruz; 408-423-9449).

SOUTH OF SAN FRANCISCO HOTELS

New Davenport Bed & Breakfast (31 Davenport Avenue, Davenport; 408-425-1818), located near the coast about 12 miles north of Santa Cruz, has a singular appeal. Most rooms here are situated in an historic old house; a few others are in the upstairs of a traditional country store. The staff is congenial and the accommodations mighty comfortable. All rooms have private baths and are imaginatively decorated with watercolors and posters by local artists. In fact, the owners are potters and have adorned many rooms with their handicrafts. You can also look for antique pieces, oak furniture, and wall-to-wall carpeting. Room charges begin in the moderate range.

Comparable to the low-cost lodging at Montara (described below) is **Pigeon Point Lighthouse Hostel** (Route 1, Pescadero; 415-879-0633). It has a similarly dramatic windswept setting above the ocean. The rooms are in several cottages with kitchens, living rooms, and accommodations for couples. Rates, as in other American Youth Hostels, are budget, and a chore is required. Set beneath the nation's tallest lighthouse on a beautiful shoreline, it's a charming place to stay. Reservations strongly recommended.

Among lodgings on this stretch of coastline, **San Benito House** (356 Main Street, Half Moon Bay; 415-726-3425) is a personal favorite. Set in a turn-of-the-century building, it's a 12-room bed and breakfast inn with adjoining bar and restaurant. Rooms with shared bath or with private bath rent for moderate prices. The least expensive accommodations are small but quite nice. One room I saw featured a brass light fixture, hanging plants, quilted beds, framed drawings, and wood furniture. Add a sauna plus a country inn ambience and you have a bargain at the price.

The Cape Cod look has become very popular with establishments in the Half Moon Bay area. One of the foremost, **Pillar Point Inn** (380 Capistrano Road, Princeton; 415-728-7377) is a fully modern bed and breakfast cloaked in 19th-century New England disguise. Overlooking the harbor, this 11-room inn combines video cassettes, televisions, and telephones with traditional amenities like featherbeds, window seats, and fireplaces. Room tabs run in the deluxe and ultra-deluxe ranges and the place possesses an upscale sense of intimacy. Every room boasts a fireplace and private bath, breakfast is a full-course affair, and there's a deck overlooking the waterfront.

For a touch of the truly magnificent, plant yourself a few blocks inland at **Mill Rose Inn** (615 Mill Street, Half Moon Bay; 415-726-9794). This turn-of-the-century home has been decorated by a master of interior design. There are hand-painted wallpapers, European antiques, and colorful tiles throughout. The grounds resemble an English garden and include a kiosk with hot tub and flagstone patio. Each of the six guest rooms is brilliantly appointed; even the least expensive displays an antique armoire, quilt, and marble-top dresser covered with old-style combs and brushes. The sitting room and spacious dining room are equally elegant. One of the finest country inns along the entire Central Coast, it is priced ultra-deluxe.

If there were a hotel located on the site of **Montara Lighthouse Hostel** (Route 1, Box 737, Montara; 415-728-7177), it would easily charge $100 a night. Set on a bluff overlooking the ocean, on one of those dramatic points always reserved for lighthouses, the hostel charges budget prices (and requires a morning chore). The daily fee buys you a bunk in a dorm-style room. There are two kitchens and two common rooms in this old lightkeeper's house.

Restaurants

BIG SUR RESTAURANTS

Most highly recommended of all the Big Sur restaurants is without doubt **Nepenthe** (Route 1, Big Sur; 408-667-2345). Perched on a cliff overlooking the Pacific, this fabled dining spot has plenty of personality. People come across the continent to line its curving bar or dine along the open-air patio. It's a gathering place for locals, tourists, and everyone in between. Surprisingly, the menu is moderately priced. There are sandwiches during lunch. At dinner the menu includes fresh fish, broiled chicken, steak, and other dishes. If you're not hungry, stop in for a drink—the place is a must. (For breakfast or lunch, try the outdoor **Cafe Amphora,** 408-667-2660, next door.)

Ventana Restaurant (Route 1, Big Sur; 408-667-2331), part of the extraordinary complex which includes a prestigious inn, is Big Sur's most elegant dining place. Resting on a hillside overlooking the mountains and sea, it's a perfect spot for a special meal. Enjoy lunch or dinner in the wood-paneled dining room or alfresco along a sweeping veranda. At lunch you'll be served steak and club sandwiches, fresh pasta, trout, eggs Benedict, or calamari. During dinner you can start with oysters on the half shell or steamed artichoke, then proceed to such entrees as roast duckling, rack of lamb, scallops, filet mignon, or fresh fish grilled over oak. Deluxe.

Fernwood (Route 1, Big Sur; 408-667-2422), a combination restaurant-bar-store, has hamburgers, sandwiches, fish and chips, soup, and chili. This local gathering spot is your best bet for a budget-priced lunch or dinner.

For a gourmet dinner at a moderate price, **Glen Oaks Restaurant** (Route 1, Big Sur; 408-667-2623) is the prime location along Big Sur. Bentwood chairs, linen tablecloths, and candlelight create an intimate atmosphere at this small establishment. Add to these a series of attractive watercolors along the walls and a copper sheath fireplace in one corner. The cuisine ranges broadly: there are such pasta dishes as fettucine alfredo and spaghetti with clams, or Chinese-style vegetables with ginger and pineapple, mushroom stroganoff, steak, plus a host of seafood dishes. These last include squid, scallops, and bouillabaise. Glen Oaks also serves Sunday brunch.

For several dozen miles south of Big Sur, restaurants are as rare as snow storms. But in a postage stamp enclave between the postage stamp towns of Gorda and Lucia you will finally stumble upon **Pacific Valley Cafe** (Route 1, Pacific Valley; 805-927-8655). Informal but inviting, this piney wood restaurant serves several egg dishes every morning. At lunch and dinner the menu switches to sandwiches and pizza plus a few special entrees like fresh fish and meat dishes. Budget.

MONTEREY AREA RESTAURANTS

The most economical way to dine in Monterey is by heading downtown and avoiding the tourist traps along the waterfront. One place that should top your itinerary is **Sancho Panza** (590 Calle Principal, Monterey; 408-375-0095). It's a Mexican restaurant housed in an historic adobe that dates from 1841. "Casa Gutierrez" is part of the town's Path of History tour. The low ceiling rests on broad *vegas* characteristic of adobe architecture. It's a small, crowded place that lends an authentic feel for early Spanish life in California. The menu features standard Mexican dishes and is moderately priced.

Franklin Street Bar & Grille (150 West Franklin Street, Monterey; 408-375-1005) is very popular with Monterey folk. A lot of them just come here to drink and carouse. They bend an elbow at the bar and cock an ear to the rock music. Others are here to eat. The reason is quite simple: few tourists wander into this midtown establishment. Pity, because the prices are easy on the purse and the food quite good. The fare's the same at lunch or dinner—steak, calamari, a host of pasta dishes, plus sandwiches, salads, and hamburgers. Moderate.

Over on Municipal Wharf #2, where fishermen rather than tourists still congregate, you'll encounter **The Rogue** (408-372-4586). True to Monterey's maritime tradition the centerpiece of this seafood emporium is a 32-foot fishing boat dating back to 1898. This colorful double ender is a fitting emblem for a moderate-priced fish restaurant that still appeals to local people. The lunch and dinner menus run from fresh sole and snapper to prawns and abalone to pasta dishes. There's a full bar, easy ambience and a view of the fleet.

My favorite Monterey dining place is the **Clock Garden Restaurant** (565 Abrego Street, Monterey; 408-375-6100). Though it's not on the water, it features more fresh fish than Cannery Row ever dreamed of. On an average night they'll have swordfish, fantail prawns, snapper, salmon, and baby clams. Not interested? How about veal piccata, steak topped with pineapple, spare ribs with honey and soy sauce, or chicken with a peach glaze. Prices are moderate if you arrive by 6 p.m. for the early bird specials; otherwise the tab runs a little more. I haven't even mentioned the decor yet. It's Early Hodgepodge. Here a sculpture fashioned of wine bottles, there a collection of antique clocks each set to a different time. Posters, paintings, and pendants round out the ambience. There's a patio outside; they also serve lunch and Sunday brunch; the bar mixes potent drinks—who could ask for more?

Visiting Monterey, it's inevitable that you'll end up in a seafood restaurant along Cannery Row. Touristy as it might be, the lure of a table on the water is irresistible. When the flesh proves weak, the Row has plenty of dining temptations. Among the best is **Steinbeck's Lobster Grotto** (720 Cannery Row, Monterey; 408-373-1884). It's a plate-glass world with a wraparound view of the Pacific. The menu is a surf-and-turf offering with a few fresh catches every day. Open for lunch and dinner, it's moderately tabbed; arrive before 6:30 p.m. and you can enjoy a budget-priced early bird meal.

Also try the **Old Row Cafe** (807 Cannery Row, Monterey; 408-372-7003). Across the street from the waterfront, it's a friendly and unpretentious eatery. The moderately priced breakfast, lunch and dinner menu includes pizza, hamburgers, and sandwiches. The specialty categories are seafood and pasta. The former features cod, prawns, calamari, and cioppino, while the latter ranges from ravioli to fettucine to clam linguini.

Small and personalized with an understated elegance is the most fitting way to describe **Fresh Cream** (Heritage Harbor, Pacific and Scott streets, Monterey; 408-375-9798). Its pastel walls are decorated with

French prints and leaded glass. Service is excellent and the menu, printed daily, numbers among the finest on the Central Coast. Only dinner is served at this gourmet retreat; on a given night you might choose from beef tournedos in Madeira sauce, sautéed veal loin, charred bluefin tuna in sauce *foyot*, roast quail stuffed with truffles, squab, or scallop quenelles. That's not even mentioning the appetizers, which are outstanding, or the desserts, which should be outlawed. Four stars. Ultra-deluxe.

For budget snacks on the beach in Pacific Grove, try the **hot dog stand** in Lover's Point Park (Ocean View Boulevard at the foot of 16th Street). Though it's only open sporadically, the place is something of a local institution.

Nearby at **The Tinnery** (631 Ocean View Boulevard, Pacific Grove; 408-646-1040) you'll find a moderately priced, American-style restaurant serving breakfast, lunch, and dinner. Overlooks the water.

Or step up and over to the **Old Bath House Restaurant** (620 Ocean View Boulevard, Pacific Grove; 408-375-5195), a luxurious building decorated in etched glass and sporting a Victorian-style bar. The Continental cuisine includes pheasant, lamb, lobster, steak, and seafood dishes. Open for dinner only; deluxe.

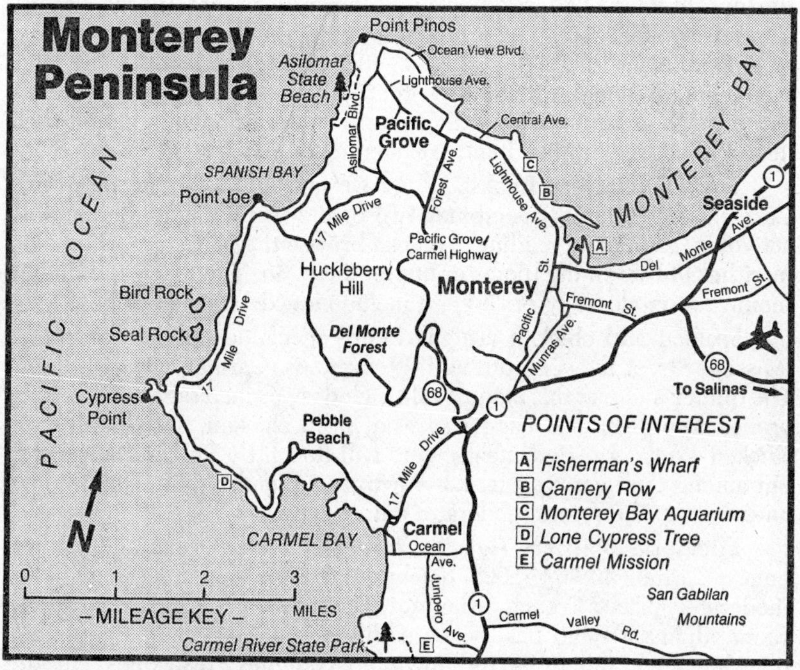

In Carmel, the thing to do is drop by **Tuck Box** (Dolores Street between Ocean and 7th avenues, Carmel; 408-624-6365) for afternoon tea. The establishment sits in a dollhouse-like creation with a swirl roof and curved chimney. The prim and tiny dining room also serves breakfast and lunch. During the noon meal there are omelettes, sandwiches, shrimp salad, and Welsh rarebit. Moderate and sooo quaint!

Then there's **Hog's Breath Inn** (San Carlos between 5th and 6th avenues, Carmel; 408-625-1044), a name so outrageous it begins to have appeal. If owner Clint Eastwood adds a hotel facility, he can call it The Innsomnia. Actually Carmel could use a few more doses of humor like this; the town takes itself so dreadfully seriously. Anyway, back to Hog's Breath. Quite nice, it is laid out in a courtyard arrangement with a flagstone dining patio flanked on one side by a pub and on the other by the dining room. You can eat outdoors or inside next to a stone fireplace. A boar's head adorns one wall and the menu, as you may have guessed, runs heavy on meat. Prices range from moderate to deluxe. Dinner entrees include rack of lamb, pork chops, filet mignon, prime rib, and chicken in whiskey; there is also a catch of the day. Lunch includes sandwiches and omelettes.

Inexpensive restaurants are pretty rare in Carmel, but it's possible to offset the high prices by dining early (from 4 to 6:30 p.m.) at **Scandia Restaurant** (Ocean Avenue between Lincoln and Monte Verde streets, Carmel; 408-624-5659). At a moderate cost, they serve Cornish game hen, Danish meatballs, leg of lamb, filet of sole, and steak. The later dinner menu includes these and other entrees, priced deluxe. There's also a lunch assortment including soups, salads, sandwiches, and such dishes as wiener schnitzel and creamed chicken.

The **Thunderbird Bookshop and Restaurant** (3600 The Barnyard, Carmel; 408-624-9414) combines two of the world's most pleasurable activities, eating and reading. You can browse the bookstore, then dine in either of two dining rooms or out on the patio. The lunch and dinner menus are moderately priced and include a wide array of dishes.

Seafood and chicken are the house specialties at the **Clam Box** (Mission Street between 5th and 6th avenues, Carmel; 408-624-8597). The dinner menu at this modest cafe includes poached salmon casserole, broiled swordfish, sea bass, rock cod, fried chicken, and Polish-style chicken *Wieliczka*. Red meat eaters will find little for the belly here, but among the quasi-vegetarian crowd it's a popular spot. The decor is unassuming, the prices moderate; dinner only.

Patisserie Boissiere (Mission Street between Ocean and 7th avenues, Carmel; 408-624-5008) belongs to that endangered species—the moderately priced French restaurant. The simple French country dining room adjoins a small bakery. In addition to outrageous pastries they offer lunch and dinner entrees including coquilles St. Jacques, chicken

Provençal, beef bourguignon, sole bernaise, and sweetbreads. *Naturalement,* escargots, French onion soup, and pâté are also on the bill of fare. A bargain hunter's delight in dear Carmel.

Shabu Shabu (Mission Street between Ocean and 7th avenues, Carmel; 408-625-2828) is one of the most genuinely Oriental restaurants I've seen anywhere. Decorated in the style of western Japan with wood-frame booths and floor cushions, it features dishes like *yosenabe* and *shabu shabu,* cooked at your table. At lunch and dinner the menu also includes *nikunabe, sashimi,* tempura, and steak cooked on a hibachi. Decorated with pennants and paper lanterns, Shabu Shabu prices deluxe.

Old time Carmel residents will tell you about the **Mission Ranch Dining Room** (26270 Dolores Street, Carmel; 408-624-3824). How it dates back over a century to the days when it was a creamery. Today it's just a warm, homey old building with a stone fireplace plus a view of a sheep pasture and a neighboring ocean. Only dinner is served, a combination of fresh seafood and all-American fare: salmon, swordfish, honey-glazed chicken, that sort of thing. A moderate price for a taste of early Carmel.

Of course the ultimate dining place is **The Covey** at Quail Lodge (8205 Valley Greens Drive, Carmel; 408-624-1581), up in Carmel Valley. Set in one of the region's most prestigious hotels, The Covey is a Continental restaurant with a French emphasis. Richly decorated, it overlooks the lodge's lake and grounds. Deluxe; dinner jackets and reservations, please.

MONTEREY TO SANTA CRUZ RESTAURANTS

On the coastal highway in Moss Landing, try **Skipper's Restaurant** (Route 1 at Moss Landing Bridge; 408-633-4453), or **Genovese's Harbor Inn** (408-724-9371) next door, for good but moderately priced seafood. Both places rest on the water overlooking a pretty harbor and an uncommonly ugly power plant.

For a dining side trip on the road between Monterey and Santa Cruz, turn off to Watsonville. A heterogeneous farm town of 15,000, Watsonville combines bland warehouses with ornate Victorian homes. One of the latter has been transformed into **Mansion House Restaurant** (418 Main Street, Watsonville; 408-724-2495), a favored dining spot. The seafood dishes served here include Nantucket scallops, stuffed sole, and Australian lobster tail; other entrees range from veal *medaillons* to quiche Lorraine. Also open for lunch and Sunday brunch, this century-old establishment has been beautifully refurbished. Deluxe.

Capitola Beach is wall-to-wall with seafood restaurants. They line the strand, each with a different decorative theme but all seeming to merge into a collection of pit stops for hungry beachgoers. If you're expecting me to recommend one you are asking more than mortal man can do. I say when in doubt, guess. So put your money on **Edgewater Seafood Grill** (215 Esplanade, Capitola; 408-475-6215). They offer a dining room above the sand, bar, and a full-bore beef, pasta, and seafood menu. Lunch, dinner, Sunday brunch; moderate.

Better yet, head a few blocks up from the beach to **Trattoria Primizia** (502 Bay Avenue, Capitola; 408-479-1112). It's strongly recommended by friends who come for dinner to dine on *gamberi in cartoccio* (prawns in garlic-dill butter) and *bistecca alla fiorentina* (beef medallions basted in herbs and olive oil). A simple place with magazine racks and white tablecloths, the trattoria also serves pizzas and pasta dishes, all at moderate price.

The Greenhouse Restaurant at the Farm (5555 Soquel Drive, Soquel; 408-476-5613), set amid gardens in a three-acre plot, serves lunch, dinner, and Sunday brunch in an old farm house, a greenhouse, or outside on the patio. Moderately priced, it features mesquite-broiled steaks, fresh seafood, homegrown produce, and a salad bar.

The Santa Cruz area's foremost dining room is actually outside the city in a nearby suburb. True to its name, the multitiered **Shadowbrook Restaurant** (1750 Wharf Road, Capitola; 408-475-1511) sits in a wooded spot through which a creek flows. Food is almost an afterthought at this elaborate affair; upon entering the grounds you descend either via a funicular or a sinuous, fern-draped path. Once in the restaurant, you'll encounter a labyrinth of dining levels and rooms, luxuriously decorated with potted plants, stone fireplaces, and candlelit tables. A mature tree grows through the floor and ceiling of one room; in others, vines climb along the walls. When you finally chart the course to a table, you'll be offered a cuisine including lamb Wellington, salmon filet, scallops tempura, abalone, prime rib, and so on. Definitely a dining experience. Serving dinner and weekend brunch; deluxe.

SANTA CRUZ RESTAURANTS

Most Santa Cruz restaurants can be found near the Boardwalk or Pacific Garden Mall, with a few others scattered around town. Of course, along the Boardwalk the favorite dining style is to eat while you stroll. Stop at **Hodgie's** for a corn dog, Italian sausage sandwich, or french fried zucchini; try a slice from the **Big Slice Pizza Bar**; or pause at the **Sea Beach Grille** for cheeseburgers, baked potatoes, or "chicken nuggets." For dessert there are caramel apples, ice cream, cotton candy, popcorn, and salt water taffy.

If all this proves a bit much, try one of the budget restaurants on Beach Street, across from the Boardwalk. Foremost is **Beach Street Cafe** (399 Beach Street, Santa Cruz; 408-426-7621), an attractive little cranny with white tablecloths and potted plants. Breakfast begins with guacamole omelettes, bagels, croissants, or pancakes. Matter of fact, breakfast continues all day. Try the "Eggs Sardou" (artichoke bottoms with spinach, poached eggs, and Hollandaise sauce) or the "Eggs Beach Street" (for which they replace the spinach with sautéed shrimp). Nearby **El Paisano Tamales** (609 Beach Street, Santa Cruz; 408-426-2382) has the standard selection of tacos, tostadas, enchiladas, and burritos.

Ideal Fish Company (106 Beach Street, Santa Cruz; 408-423-5271) is a tourist trap with tradition. It's been one since 1917. It also has decent food and a knockout view. The place is wedged in a corner between the beach and the pier, which means it looks out on everything, from boardwalk to bounding deep. The specialty is seafood—calamari, sand dabs, oysters, and salmon. Several casseroles, plus a few meat and fowl dishes round out the menu. Most entrees are moderately priced; a few of the more exotic dishes, such as lobster, get expensive. I eat here and like the place, but I always was an easy touch for old establishments and ocean views.

Cozy **Casablanca Restaurant** (101 Main Street, Santa Cruz; 408-426-9063), with its overhead fans and Moroccan flair, is excellent for dinner. The place has a wraparound view of the ocean, not to mention a tony decor. The menu includes such gourmet selections as roast duckling, beef Wellington, spinach fettucine, and filet mignon with brandy. Prices are deluxe, but where else can you sit along a wood-paneled bar gazing at a photo of Bogey?

Among the many places in the Pacific Garden Mall area, my personal favorite is **The Catalyst** (1011 Pacific Avenue, Santa Cruz; 408-423-1338). I don't go there so much to eat as to watch. Not that the food is bad (nor particularly good for that matter), but simply that The Catalyst is a scene. *The* scene in Santa Cruz. At night the place transmogrifies into a club with live music and unfathomable vibrations. By day, it's just itself, a cavernous structure with a glass roof and enough plants to make it an oversized greenhouse. Indeed, some of the clientele seem to have taken root. There's a bar if you're here to people watch. Otherwise meals are cafeteria-style and include a full breakfast menu, deli sandwiches, hamburgers, and a few dinner selections. Budget.

For sandwiches and such, try **Duffy's Deli** (1415 Pacific Avenue, Santa Cruz; 408-425-0499). There are a few tables and chairs scattered about, and a posted menu with a full line of deli products plus a daily dinner special.

It's ironic that an historic spot called **Cooper House Restaurant & Bar** (110 Cooper Street, Santa Cruz; 408-429-5894) is best known for its front-yard patio, but the open-air dining spot is a central attraction on Pacific Garden Mall. The gracious dining room and saloon are almost afterthoughts. But you can dine either indoors or out, selecting from a moderately priced menu which includes oysters, steamed clams, gazpacho, chilled artichoke, guacamole, fruit plate, and sandwiches. Add live music every afternoon and you have one of Santa Cruz's most popular spots.

For Japanese food there's **Benten** (1541 Pacific Avenue, Santa Cruz; 408-425-7079), a comfortable restaurant complete with sushi bar. Open for lunch and dinner, they serve an array of Asian dishes including *yosenabe*, *sashimi*, tempura, teriyaki, and a special plate called *kaki* fry (deep-fried breaded oysters). Understated and reliable; budget.

Covering the rest of the Far Eastern spectrum is **India Joze** (1001 Center Street, Santa Cruz; 408-427-3554) where, depending on the day of the week, they will be serving Indonesian, East Indian, or Mid-East Asian cuisine. On weekends, when the culinary theme is Indonesian, you can dine on red snapper in a Balinese tomato-lime glaze or calamari "wok'd" in hot bean sauce. On Indian night there are *tandoori* chicken and walnut lamb dishes. Stop by for lunch, dinner, or Sunday brunch and you're bound to discover a creative menu at a moderate price. Located in the Santa Cruz Art Center, India Joze is decorated with modern art, illuminated through skylights, and surrounded by pink pastel walls. Don't miss it.

Aldo's Restaurant (616 Atlantic Avenue, Santa Cruz; 408-426-3736), a cafe with patio deck overlooking Santa Cruz Harbor, has seafood dishes and sandwiches. Conveniently located near Seabright Beach, this unassuming place provides moderate-priced breakfast and lunch.

One of the best dining deals anywhere can be found up the hillside on the University of California Santa Cruz campus. The **Whole Earth Restaurant** (Redwood Building, UC Santa Cruz; 408-426-8255) not only serves tasty, nutritious meals, it does so at budget prices. Limited to breakfast and lunch menus during summer, the student-operated restaurant is also open for dinner during the school year. Primarily vegetarian, it features three dinner and lunch specials in addition to the regular array of sandwiches, soups, salads, and juices. On a typical night, one dinner special will be vegetarian, another a chicken or seafood dish. The restaurant itself is neatly tucked into a grove of tall trees and features outdoor dining on a wooden deck. A touch of style at student prices.

SOUTH OF SAN FRANCISCO RESTAURANTS

Several miles north of Santa Cruz, the **New Davenport Restaurant** (Route 1, Davenport; 408-426-4122) offers a countrified atmosphere. It's adjacent to a traditional general store and decorated with colorful wall rugs, handwoven baskets, and fresh flowers. The cuisine at this eatery rambles from *chorizo* and eggs to *tofu* and vegetables to mushroom cheese-melt sandwiches to steamed clams. More ordinary fare—omelettes, hamburgers, steak, and seafood—is also on the agenda. On weekends they feature dinner specials such as salmon, scallops, and chicken. Moderate.

Between Santa Cruz and Half Moon Bay, restaurants are mighty scarce. Practically anything will do along this lonesome stretch; but rather than just anything, you can have **Duarte's Tavern** (202 Stage Road, Pescadero; 415-879-0464). This fifty-year-old restaurant and tavern has earned a reputation all down the coast. The dishes are moderately priced and delicious. There's a menu filled with meat and fish entrees, omelettes, and sandwiches. Personally, I recommend being adventurous by trying the artichoke soup and olallieberry pie.

For contemporary California cuisine in a country inn setting, there's **San Benito Restaurant** (356 Main Street, Half Moon Bay; 415-726-3425). This gourmet restaurant incorporates fresh seafood and produce from the surrounding ocean and farm country; as a result, the dinner menu changes daily. On a typical night you might choose between rack of veal or mesquite-grilled halibut, lingcod or veal-stuffed canneloni. Lunch and brunch are also served; deluxe.

Aficionados of Mexican food often head for **El Perico** (211 San Mateo Road, Half Moon Bay; 415-726-3737). With its antiqued wood panelling and exposed beam ceiling, the place is rusticly fashionable. The menu includes all the south of the border specialties—*chile rellenos,* tostadas, tacos, burritos, *flautas,* enchiladas, and so on, all priced along the border between budget and moderate.

The **Village Green** (89 Avenue Portola, El Granada; 415-726-3690) is another local snuggery. Small and cozy, it's an English-style establishment serving "farmhouse breakfasts," "ploughman's lunches," and afternoon teas. If you're in the mood for scones, English sausage, or a banger and onion sandwich, this is your only chance for many many miles.

If seafood sounds good, **The Fishtrap** (Capistrano Road, Princeton; 415-728-7049) has some of the lowest prices around. Set in a small woodframe building smack on the bay, this unpretentious eatery features several fresh fish dishes daily. They're liable to be serving lingcod, halibut, and swordfish, as well as shellfish, and steak sandwiches, all at moderate prices. Friendly, local, cheap—and highly recommended.

Or try **The Shore Bird** (390 Capistrano Road, Princeton; 415-728-5541), set in a Cape Cod-style building overlooking the water. Open for lunch, dinner, and Sunday brunch, this expansive seafood restaurant features an oyster bar, cocktail lounge, garden patio, and more. Moderate.

For dinner overlooking the ocean, there's nothing quite like **Moss Beach Distillery** (Beach Way and Ocean Boulevard, Moss Beach; 415-728-5595). The place enjoys a colorful history, dating back to Prohibition days, when this area was notorious for supplying booze to thirsty San Francisco. Today it's a quiet plate-glass restaurant with adjoining bar. The deluxe menu includes gulf shrimp, Australian lobster tail, cioppino, steak, and rack of lamb. The bootleggers are long gone, but those splendid sea views will be here forever.

Sharon's Restaurant (8455 Route 1, Montara; 415-728-5600) has an inexpensive menu at its roadside eatery. In addition to soup and sandwiches, the folks serve up several egg dishes, fresh fish, and a few pasta dinners. Good for a quick stop.

For fresh ocean catches, there's a small restaurant just off Route 1 that comes well recommended. **Pacifica Seafood Grotto** (1966 Francisco Boulevard, Pacifica; 415-355-1678), despite the white tablecloths and candles, is a local, moderately priced establishment. Among the entrees are sautéed scallops, a prawn kebab dish, bouillabaise, curried seafood, and abalone. The decor is adequate, if undistinguished, but folks come for the food anyway, not the accouterments.

The Great Outdoors

The Sporting Life

FISHING

The Central Coast is renowned for its open-sea fishing. Charter boats comb the waters for rock cod, salmon, and albacore.

Fishing charters are a specialty at Monterey's Fisherman's Wharf. Contact **Monterey Sport Fishing** (96 Old Fisherman's Wharf #1, Monterey; 408-372-2203) or **Randy's Fishing Trips** (66 Fisherman's Wharf, Monterey; 408-372-7440).

For expeditions from Santa Cruz, call **Tom's Fishermans Supply** (Santa Cruz Yacht Harbor, Santa Cruz; 408-476-2648). For do-it-yourself adventures, nearby **Santa Cruz Boat Rentals** (408-423-1739) provides outboards and fishing gear.

If you want to test your skill further north, contact **Captain John's Fishing Trips** (111 Pillar Point Harbor, Princeton; 415-726-2913) near Half Moon Bay.

WHALE WATCHING AND NATURE CRUISES

To see the whales during their annual migration from December to April, head for whale-watching lookouts at the coast around Cypress Point in Point Lobos State Reserve, Point Pinos in Pacific Grove, Davenport, or Pillar Point in Half Moon Bay. (See the "Whale Watching" section in Chapter Eight.)

If you'd prefer a close look at these migrating mammals and other marine life—sea lions, seals, otters, and sea birds—catch a cruise with **Randy's Fishing Trips** (66 Fisherman's Wharf, Monterey; 408-372-7440),

Sam's Fishing Fleet (84 Fisherman's Wharf, Monterey; 408-372-0577), or **The Sailing Set and Power Boat Company** (413 Lake Avenue, Santa Cruz; 408-475-5411).

SEA KAYAKING

Whether you are young or old, experienced or a novice, the Central Coast awaits discovery by sea kayak. Explore Monterey Bay, Elkhorn Slough or paddle your way along the coastal waters with **Monterey Bay Kayaks** (693 Del Monte Avenue, Monterey; 408-373-5357).

SKIN DIVING

For adventures underwater, contact **Aquarius Dive Shop** (2240 Del Monte Boulevard, Monterey; 408-375-1933), **Adventure Sports** (303 Potrero #15, Santa Cruz; 408-458-3648), or **Ocean Odyssey** (2345 South Rodeo Gulch Road, Santa Cruz; 408-475-3483).

SURFING AND SAILING

Catching a wave when the surf's up near Lighthouse Point north of Santa Cruz is a surfer's dream. Known as "Steamer's Lane," this stretch of coastline hosts many international surfing championships. Surfboards and wet suits (the water is always cold) are available at **Freeline Design** (861 41st Avenue, Santa Cruz; 408-476-2950) or at **O'Neill's Surf Shop** (1149 41st Avenue, Capitola; 408-475-4151).

Or catch the wind on a windsurfing board. Rentals are available at **Santa Cruz Ski Shop** (124 River Street, Santa Cruz; 408-426-6760).

For the traditional sailors in the crowd, contact **Monterey Bay Yacht Center** (Wharf 2, Monterey; 408-375-2002) or **The Sailing Set and Power Boat Company** (413 Lake Avenue, Santa Cruz; 408-475-5411). Both offer sailing lessons and sailboat rentals.

BALLOONING AND HANG GLIDING

If your preference is to soar through the air, hang gliding lessons at Marina Beach are the way to fly. Call **Kitty Hawk Kites** (Reservation Road and Route 1, Monterey; 408-384-2622) for more information. Or, for a hot air balloon ride, try **Monterey Bay Balloon Charters** (360 Paul Avenue, Salinas; 408-422-2556).

HORSEBACK RIDING

Exploring the coast and inland trails astride a galloping horse is one way to enjoy a visit to the Central Coast. There is English-style riding along 34 miles of trails at the **Pebble Beach Equestrian Center** (Portola Road, Pebble Beach; 408-624-2756).

With its four-mile white-sand beach and surrounding farm country, Half Moon Bay is also a choice region for riding. **Friendly Acres Ranch** (2150 Route 1, Half Moon Bay; 415-726-9871), located on the coast, rents horses. They also have pony rides for kids.

GOLF

For golfers, visiting the Monterey Peninsula is tantamount to arriving in heaven. This is home to the annual AT&T at Pebble Beach Pro-Am Championship. Several courses rank among the top in the nation. Most renowned is **Pebble Beach Golf Course** (17 Mile Drive, Pebble Beach; 408-624-3811, ext. 239). Or you might want to tee off at **Spyglass Hill Golf Course** (Stevenson Road, Pebble Beach; 408-624-3811, ext. 239). Be prepared: green fees at these courses are steep!

Also of note are **Old Del Monte Golf Course** (1300 Sylvan Road, Monterey; 408-624-3811) and **Pacific Grove Municipal Links** (77 Asilomar Boulevard, Pacific Grove; 408-375-3456).

Beaches and Parks

BIG SUR BEACHES AND PARKS

Ventana Wilderness—Part of Los Padres National Forest, this magnificent 164,503-acre preserve parallels Route 1 a few miles inland. It covers a broad swath of the Santa Lucia Mountains with elevations ranging from 1200 feet to almost 5000 feet. Within its rugged confines are 237 miles of hiking trails. Together with Pfeiffer Big Sur State Park, this is the southernmost habitat of the Coast redwood; wild boars, black bears, mountain lions, and deer roam its slopes. The most treasured resident was the California condor. These amazing land birds, the largest on the continent, have nine-foot wingspans. They once occupied the most remote regions, but by 1987 all of them had been taken into captivity in an attempt to preserve the species.

Facilities: Ranger stations. For information and permits, write the U.S. Forest Service, Monterey District, 406 South Mildred Avenue, King City, CA 93930, or call 408-385-5434. Restaurants and groceries are located back along Route 1 in Big Sur.

Camping: Permitted in about 55 campsites.

Getting there: From Route 1 in the Big Sur area, the most convenient entry points are at the end of Palo Colorado Road and at Big Sur Ranger Station. The ranger station is just south of Pfeiffer Big Sur State Park and provides maps and permits.

Julia Pfeiffer Burns State Park—This 1800-acre extravaganza extends from the ocean to about 1500 feet elevation and is bisected by Route 1. The central park area sits in a redwood canyon with a stream that feeds through a steep defile into the ocean. Backdropped by sharp hills in a kind of natural amphitheater, it's an enchanting glade. A path leads beneath the highway to a spectacular vista point where McWay

Waterfall plunges into the ocean. Another path, one and eight-tenths miles north of the park entrance, descends from the highway to an isolated beach near Partington Point that has been declared an underwater park.

Facilities: Picnic areas, restrooms; restaurants and groceries about 11 miles away in Big Sur; information, 408-667-2315.

Camping: Permitted at hike-in sites only.

Getting there: Located on Route 1 about 11 miles south of Pfeiffer Big Sur State Park.

Pfeiffer Beach—Of Big Sur's many wonders, this may be the most exotic. It's a sandy beach littered with boulders and bisected by a meandering stream. Behind the strand rise high bluffs which mark the terminus of a narrow gorge. Just offshore loom rock formations into which the sea has carved tunnels and arches. Little wonder poet Robinson Jeffers chose this haunting spot for his orgiastic "Give Your Heart to the Hawks." Since we're dropping names, it's interesting to remember that Richard Burton and Elizabeth Taylor filmed *The Sandpiper* here.

Facilities: Toilets; restaurants and groceries are several miles away in Big Sur.

Getting there: Follow Route 1 for about a mile south past the entrance to Pfeiffer Big Sur State Park. Turn right onto Sycamore Canyon Road, which leads downhill two miles to the beach.

Pfeiffer Big Sur State Park—One of California's southernmost redwood parks, this 821-acre facility is very popular, particularly in summer. With cottages, restaurant, grocery, and gift shop on the premises, it's also quite developed. Nature still retains a toehold in these parts: the Big Sur River overflows with trout and salmon, Pfeiffer Falls tumbles through a fern-banked canyon, and the park serves as the major trailhead leading to Ventana Wilderness.

Facilities: Picnic areas, restrooms, restaurants, groceries; information, 408-667-2315.

Camping: Permitted; reservations are necessary during the summer months.

Getting there: Located along Route 1 in Big Sur.

Andrew Molera State Park—An adventurer's hideaway, this 4800-acre park rises from the sea to a 3455-foot elevation. It features three miles of beach and over 16 miles of hiking trails. The forests range from cottonwood to oak to redwood, while the wildlife includes mule deer, bobcat, harbor seals, sea lions, and gray whales. Big Sur River rumbles through the landscape. The only thing missing is a road: this is a hiker's oasis, its natural areas accessible only by heel and toe. The wilderness rewards are well worth the shoe leather.

Facilities: Toilets. Restaurants and groceries are a few miles away in Big Sur. Information, 408-667-2315.

Camping: Permitted at the walk-in campground about one-quarter-mile from the parking lot; a roving ranger collects $1.00 per person nightly.

Getting there: Located along Route 1 about three miles north of Big Sur.

Garrapata Beach—This broad swath of white sand is particularly favored by local people, some of whom use it as a nude beach. Easily accessible, it's nevertheless off the beaten tourist path, making an ideal hideaway for picnicking and skinny dipping.

Facilities: None; restaurants and groceries are found about eight miles away in Carmel.

Getting there: Located along Route 1 about eight miles south of Carmel. Watch for the curving beach from the highway; stop at the parking lot just north of the Garrapata Creek bridge. From here a path leads down to the beach.

MONTEREY AREA BEACHES AND PARKS

Point Lobos State Reserve—In a region packed with uncommonly beautiful scenery, this park stands forth as something special. A 1225-acre peninsula and underwater preserve, it contains over 300 species of plants and more than 250 species of animals and birds. This is a perfect place to study sea otters, harbor seals, and sea lions. During migrating season in mid-winter and mid-spring, gray whales cruise the coast. Along with Pebble Beach, Point Lobos is the only spot in the world where Monterey cypresses, those ghostly, wind-gnarled coastal trees, still survive. There are 80-foot-high kelp forests offshore, popular with skindivers who know the preserve as one of the most fascinating places on the coast.

Before Westerners arrived, the Indians gathered mussels and abalone here, leaving huge shellmounds. Later Point Lobos was a whaling station, coal mine, and an abalone cannery. Today it's a park intended primarily for nature hikers. You can explore pine forests and cypress groves, a jagged shoreline of granite promontories, and wave-lapped coves. Every tidepool is a miniature aquarium pulsing with color and sea life. The water is clear as sky. Offshore rise sea stacks, their rocky bases ringed with mussels, their domes crowned by sea birds.

Facilities: Picnic areas, restrooms, divers' entranceways; restaurants and groceries are three miles away in Carmel. For information, call 408-624-4909.

Getting there: Located on Route 1 about three miles south of Carmel.

Carmel River State Park—This beach would be more attractive were it not upstaged by Point Lobos, its remarkable neighbor to the south. Nevertheless, there's a sandy beach here as well as a view of the surrounding hills. The chief feature is the bird refuge along the river. The marshes offer willets, sandpipers, pelicans, hawks, and kingfishers, plus an occasional Canadian snow goose.

Facilities: Restrooms; restaurants and groceries are found nearby in Carmel. For information, call 408-649-2836.

Surfing: Good along a lengthy stretch of shoreline.

Getting there: Located at the end of Carmelo Road in Carmel (take Rio Road exit off Route 1).

Asilomar State Beach—This oceanfront facility features over 100 acres of snowy white sand dunes, tidepools, and beach. It's a perfect place for daytripping or collecting driftwood. Since northern and southern currents run together here, the waters are teeming with marine life. If you're into algae, you'll want to know that over 200 species congregate at Asilomar. Another species—*Homo sapiens*—gathers at the park's multifaceted conference center.

Facilities: Restrooms, meeting halls, dining room; overnight accommodations are described in the "Hotels" section in this chapter. Information, 408-372-8016.

Getting there: Located along Sunset Drive in Pacific Grove.

MONTEREY TO SANTA CRUZ BEACHES AND PARKS

Marina State Beach—The tall, fluffy sand dunes at this 131-acre park are unreal. They're part of a giant dune covering 50 square miles throughout the area. There are marvelous views of Monterey here, plus a chance to fish or sunbathe. Very popular with hang gliders.

Facilities: Restrooms; restaurants and groceries are available in the nearby town of Marina. For information, call 408-384-7695.

Surfing: Good beach break in summer, dangerous in winter.

Getting there: Located along Route 1, ten miles north of Monterey.

Salinas River State Beach, Moss Landing State Beach, Zmudowski State Beach—These three state parks are part of a long stretch of sand dunes. They all contain broad beaches and vistas along Monterey Bay. Though relatively uncrowded, their proximity to Moss Landing's smoke-belching power plant is a severe drawback. Quite suitable anywhere else, they can't compete with their neighbors in this land of beautiful beaches.

Facilities: Restrooms are located at Salinas River and Moss Landing; restaurants and groceries are available in Moss Landing. For information, call 408-649-2836.

Surfing: Good near sandbar at Salinas River; at Moss Landing check for surf north of jetty.

Getting there: All three are located off Route 1 within a few miles of Moss Landing.

Sunset State Beach—Over three miles of beach and sand dunes create one of the area's prettiest parks. There are bluffs and meadows behind the beach as well as Monterey pines and cypress trees. This 324-acre park is a popular spot for fishing and clamming. But remember, there's more fog here and further south than in the Santa Cruz area.

Facilities: Picnic areas, restrooms, and showers. Restaurants and groceries are several miles away in Watsonville. For information, call 408-724-1266.

Camping: Permitted in three campgrounds; $12 fee per campsite.

Surfing: Powerful break, exercise caution.

Getting there: Located 16 miles south of Santa Cruz; from Route 1, take the San Andreas Road exit in Rio del Mar and follow it several miles to the park turnoff.

Forest of Nisene Marks State Park—This semi-wilderness expanse, several miles inland, encompasses nearly 10,000 acres. Within its domain are redwood groves, meandering streams, rolling countryside, and dense forest. About 30 miles of hiking trails wind through the preserve. Along them you can explore fossil beds, deserted logger cabins, old trestles, and railroad beds. The park is a welcome complement to the natural features along the coast.

Facilities: None. For information, contact Forest of Nisene Marks State Park, P.O. Box P-1, Felton, CA 95018, or call 408-335-4598. Restaurants and groceries are available several miles away in Aptos.

Getting there: From Route 1 southbound take the Seacliff Beach exit in Aptos, five miles south of Santa Cruz. Take an immediate left on State Park Drive, pass over the highway, and then go right on Soquel Drive. Follow this for a half mile; then head left on Aptos Creek Road. This paved road turns to gravel as it leads into the forest.

Seacliff State Beach—This two-mile strand is very popular. *Too* popular: during summer, RVs park along its entire length and crowds gather on the waterfront. That's because it provides the safest swimming along this section of coast. There are roving lifeguards on duty and a protective headland nearby. The beach also sports a pier favored by anglers. It's a pretty place, but oh so busy.

Facilities: Picnic areas, restrooms, showers; restaurants and groceries are located nearby in Aptos. Information, 408-688-3222.

Camping: Permitted for self-contained vehicles only.

Getting there: Located off Route 1 in Aptos, five miles south of Santa Cruz.

New Brighton State Beach—This sandy crescent adjoins Seacliff Beach and enjoys a wide vista of Monterey Bay. Headlands protect the beach for swimmers; beachcombers frequently find fossils in the cliffs here. Within its mere 94 acres, the park contains hiking trails and a forested bluff.

Facilities: Picnic areas, restrooms, showers, roving lifeguards; restaurants and groceries are nearby in Capitola. For information, call 408-475-4850.

Camping: Permitted in a wooded area inland from the beach.

Surfing: Good for beginners.

Getting there: Located off Route 1 in Capitola, four miles south of Santa Cruz.

Capitola City Beach—Sedimentary cliffs flank a corner of this sand carpet but the rest is heavily developed. Popular with visitors for decades, Capitola is a well-known resort community. Seafood restaurants line its shore and boutiques flourish within blocks of the beach. There's also a fishing pier. A great place for families because of the adjacent facilities, it trades seclusion for service.

Facilities: Restrooms, showers, lifeguards, volleyball; restaurants, groceries.

Fishing: Try the wharf.

Swimming: Since the beach sweeps in from a headland it is well protected for water sports.

Surfing: Winter breaks near the jetty, pier, and river mouth.

Getting there: Located in the center of Capitola.

SANTA CRUZ BEACHES AND PARKS

Moran Lake Beach, Sunny Cove, Lincoln Beach—Located along the southern end of Santa Cruz, these three sandy beaches are in residential areas. As a result, they draw local people, not tourists; they're also more difficult to get to, and, happily, are less crowded. All are backdropped by bluffs. If you want to buck the crowds, they're worth the trouble.

Facilities: Restrooms at Moran Lake Beach and Lincoln Beach; otherwise amenities are scarce. Parking is a problem throughout the area (though Moran Lake Beach has a parking lot); restaurants and groceries are available nearby.

Getting there: All three beaches are located near East Cliff Drive. Moran Lake Beach is near Lake Avenue, Sunny Cove at the end of Johans Beach Drive, and Lincoln Beach sits at the end of 14th Avenue.

Twin Lakes State Beach—Just south of Santa Cruz Harbor is this odd-shaped beach. Smaller than other Santa Cruz beaches to the north, it is also less crowded. The park is 110 acres, with a lagoon behind the beach and a jetty flanking one side. A very pretty spot.

Facilities: Picnic areas, restrooms, lifeguards; restaurants and groceries are available nearby. For information, call 408-688-3241.

Surfing: Sometimes okay in winter or after a storm.

Getting there: Located along East Cliff Drive, south of Santa Cruz Harbor.

Seabright Beach—An important link in Santa Cruz's chain of beaches, this beauty extends from near the Boardwalk to the jetty at Santa Cruz Harbor. It's long, wide, and backdropped by bluffs. The views are as magnificent as from other nearby beaches, and the crowds will be lighter than along the Boardwalk.

Facilities: Restrooms, lifeguard; restaurants and groceries are found nearby. For information, call 408-688-3241.

Getting there: Access to the beach is along East Cliff Drive at the foot of Mott and Cypress avenues, or at the end of Atlantic Avenue.

Santa Cruz Beach—Of the major beaches extending along the Santa Cruz waterfront, this is the most popular, most crowded, and most famous. All for a very simple reason: the Santa Cruz Boardwalk, with its amusement park and restaurants, runs the length of the sand, and the Santa Cruz Municipal Pier anchors one end of the beach. This, then, is the place to come for crowds and excitement.

Facilities: Restrooms, lifeguard, restaurants, and groceries. For rentals of surfboards, boogie boards, wet suits, umbrellas, and beach equipment, contact Santa Cruz Beach Services (206 Municipal Wharf; 408-429-3460).

Surfing: "Steamer Lane" is the Santa Cruz hotspot. A series of reef breaks are located along West Cliff Drive, extending north to Lighthouse Point.

Getting there: Located along Beach Street; access from the Municipal Wharf and along the Boardwalk.

Natural Bridges State Beach—Northernmost of the Santa Cruz beaches, this is a small park with a half-moon-shaped beach. It's quite pretty, though a housing development flanks one side. The central attraction is a sea arch in the offshore rocks. This is also an excellent spot to watch monarch butterflies during their annual winter migration.

Facilities: Picnic areas, restrooms; restaurants and groceries are found in Santa Cruz; information, 408-423-4609.

Surfing: Good winter breaks over an outer reef.

Getting there: Located off Route 1 near the northern edge of Santa Cruz.

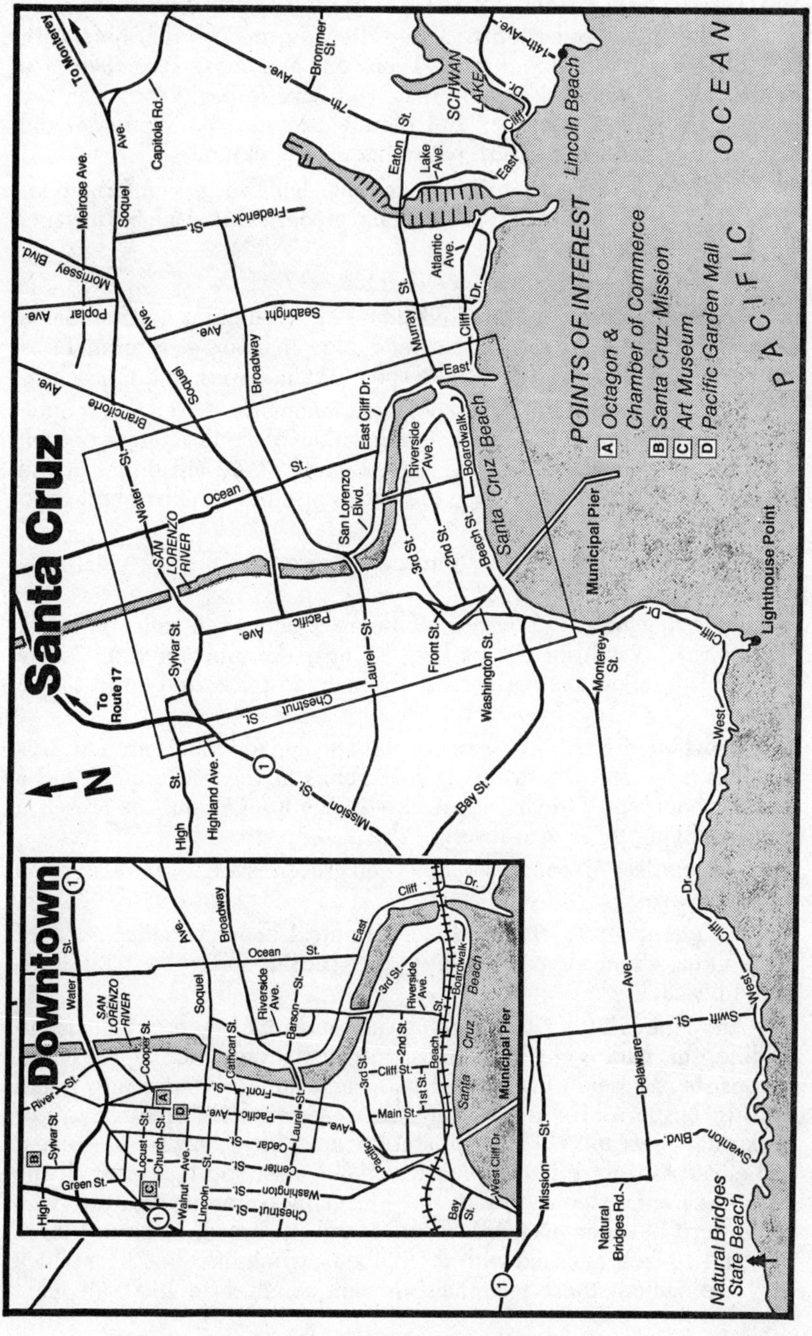
Santa Cruz
Downtown
POINTS OF INTEREST
A Octagon & Chamber of Commerce
B Santa Cruz Mission
C Art Museum
D Pacific Garden Mall
PACIFIC OCEAN
To Monterey
To Route 17
N
Soquel Ave.
Capitola Rd.
Melrose Ave.
Morrissey Blvd.
Poplar Ave.
Branciforte Ave.
7th Ave.
Brommer St.
Frederick St.
Broadway
Seabright Ave.
Water St.
Ocean St.
SAN LORENZO RIVER
Sylvar St.
Pacific Ave.
Chestnut St.
High St.
Highland Ave.
Mission St.
Laurel St.
Bay St.
Washington St.
Front St.
3rd St.
2nd St.
Beach St.
Riverside Ave.
San Lorenzo Blvd.
East Cliff Dr.
Murray St.
Eaton St.
Lake Ave.
Atlantic Ave.
SCHWAN LAKE
14th Ave.
Lincoln Beach
Boardwalk
Santa Cruz Beach
Municipal Pier
Lighthouse Point
Monterey St.
West Cliff Dr.
Delaware Ave.
Swift St.
Swanton Blvd.
Natural Bridges Rd.
Natural Bridges State Beach
River St.
Green St.
Cooper St.
Cathcart St.
Barson St.
Locust St.
Church St.
Walnut Ave.
Lincoln St.
Cedar St.
Center St.
Cliff St.
1st St.
Main St.
West Cliff Dr.

SOUTH OF SAN FRANCISCO BEACHES AND PARKS

Red, White, and Blue Beach—There's a nude beach here with rocky headlands surrounding it. There are also more RVs than at a Fourth of July picnic. Not only that, you have to pay! Of course, the beach does provide facilities and permit camping. But somehow the management takes the nature out of bathing au natural.

Facilities: Picnic areas, restrooms, hot showers; information, 408-423-6332; admission. Restaurants and groceries are available in Santa Cruz, seven miles away.

Camping: Permitted; fee charged.

Getting there: Located off Route 1, seven miles north of Santa Cruz. Watch for the red, white, and blue mailbox at Scaroni Road intersection; follow Scaroni Road a short distance west to the beach.

Bonny Doon Beach—This spot ranks among the most popular nude beaches in California. Known up and down the coast, the compact beach is protected on either flank by rugged cliffs. There are dunes at the south end of the beach, caves to the north, plus bevies of barebottomed bathers in between.

Facilities: None; restaurants and groceries are a few miles away in Davenport.

Getting there: Located off Route 1 about ten miles north of Santa Cruz. Watch for the parking lot near the junction with Bonny Doon Road; follow the path across the railroad tracks and down to the beach.

Greyhound Rock—One of the most secluded strands around, this beach is a beauty. There are startling cliffs in the background and a gigantic boulder—Greyhound Rock—in the foreground; the area is a favorite among those who love to fish.

Facilities: None; restaurants and groceries are seven miles away in Davenport.

Getting there: Located along Route 1 about 19 miles north of Santa Cruz. From the parking lot at the roadside follow the path down to the beach.

Año Nuevo State Reserve—Awesome in its beauty, abundant in wildlife, this park is one of the most spectacular on the California coast. It consists of a peninsula heaped with sand dunes. A miniature island lies just offshore. There are tidepools to search and a nature trail for exploring. Seals and sea lions inhabit the area; loons, eagles, pheasants, and albatrosses have been spied here. But most spectacular of all the denizens are the elephant seals, those loveably grotesque creatures who come here between December and March to breed. Reaching three tons and 16 feet, adorned with the bulbous, trunk-like snouts for which they are named, these mammals are unique. Back in 1800, elephant seals numbered in the hundreds of thousands; by the end of the century, they were practically extinct; it's only recently that they have achieved a comeback. During breeding season the bulls stage bloody battles and collect large harems, creating a spectacle that has unfortunately drawn crowds.

Facilities: Toilets. During breeding season, rangers lead two-and-a-half-hour tours which must be booked in advance (information, 415-879-0227). Otherwise, the reserve is closed to the public throughout the breeding season; during the rest of the year the park is open, but the elephant seals are not in residence. Restaurants and groceries are ten miles away in Davenport.

Surfing: Summer breaks off north end of beach.

Getting there: Located off Route 1 about 22 miles north of Santa Cruz.

Butano State Park—This inland park, several miles from the coast, provides a welcome counterpoint to the beach parks. About 2200 acres, it features a deep redwood forest, including stands of virgin timber. Hiking trails traverse the territory. Not so well-known as other nearby redwood parks, Butano suffers less human traffic.

Facilities: Picnic areas, restrooms; restaurants and groceries are several miles away in Pescadero.

Camping: Permitted in several sites, including a hike-in campground set in a redwood forest.

Getting there: Located 27 miles north of Santa Cruz. On Route 1, go two miles south of Pigeon Point Lighthouse; take Gazos Creek Road, and then Cloverdale Road, both dirt roads, about four miles to the park. Or from Pescadero you can follow the paved portion of Cloverdale Road south for five miles.

Bean Hollow State Beach—The small sandy beach here is bounded by rocks, so sunbathers go elsewhere while tidepool watchers drop by. Particularly interesting is nearby **Pebble Beach,** a coarse-grain strand studded with jasper, serpentine, agates, and carnelians. The stones originate from a quartz reef offshore and attract rockhounds by the pack.

Facilities: Picnic area, restrooms; restaurants and groceries are located several miles away in Pescadero.

Getting there: Located along Route 1 about 17 miles south of Half Moon Bay; Pebble Beach is about a mile north of Bean Hollow.

Pescadero State Beach—Backed by sand dunes and saltwater ponds, this lovely park also features a wide beach. There are tidepools to the south and a wildlife preserve across the highway. Steelhead run annually in the streams here, while deer, blue herons, and egrets inhabit the nearby marshland.

Facilities: Toilets, trails; restaurants and groceries are found in nearby Pescadero.

Getting there: Located on Route 1 about 15 miles south of Half Moon Bay.

Pomponio State Beach—Less appealing than neighboring San Gregorio State Beach, this park has a white-sand beach that's traversed periodically by a creek. There are headlands on either side of the beach.

Facilities: Picnic areas, restrooms; restaurants and groceries are 13 miles away in Half Moon Bay.

Getting there: Located on Route 1 about 13 miles south of Half Moon Bay.

San Gregorio State Beach—There is a white-sand beach here framed by sedimentary cliffs and cut by a small creek. Star of the show, though, is the nearby **nude beach** (★) (admission), reputedly the first beach of its type in California. Among the nicest of the state's nude beaches, it features a narrow sand corridor shielded by high bluffs.

Facilities: Picnic area, toilets at the state beach, no facilities at the nude beach. Restaurants and groceries are 11 miles away in Half Moon Bay.

Getting there: Located along Route 1 about 11 miles south of Half Moon Bay. Entrance to the nude beach is several hundred yards north of the state beach entrance.

Half Moon Bay State Beach—Despite a four-mile-long sand beach, this park receives only a guarded recommendation. Half Moon Bay is a working harbor, so the beach lacks the seclusion and natural qualities of other strands along the coast. Of course, with civilization so near at hand, the facilities here are more complete than elsewhere. Also, the park is a three-part affair: you can choose Francis Beach, Venice Beach, or Dunes Beach. Personally, I pick the last.

Facilities: Restrooms available at all three parks; picnic areas at Francis Beach; restaurants and groceries are located nearby in Half Moon Bay. Information, 415-726-6238.

Camping: Permitted at Francis Beach; $10 fee per campsite.

Surfing: Sandy beach break at Francis Beach and below Half Moon Bay jetty.

Getting there: All three park segments are located along Route 1 in Half Moon Bay.

Moss Beach or James V. Fitzgerald Marine Reserve—Boasting the best facilities among the beaches in the area, this park also has a sandy beach and excellent tidepools. It's a great place to while away the hours watching crabs, sea urchins, and anemones. Since there are houses nearby, this is more of a family beach than the freewheeling areas to the immediate north and south.

Facilities: Restrooms, picnic area, and hiking trails; information center, 415-728-3584; restaurants and groceries are available nearby in Moss Beach.

Getting there: Located off Route 1 in Moss Beach about ten miles south of Pacifica.

Montara State Beach—A half-mile-long sand swath, this area is popular with horseback riders. Nude sunbathers congregate near the north end of the beach, while volleyball players and frisbee throwers can be found everywhere. Backdropped by a rocky bluff, it's a very pretty place.

Facilities: Toilets. Restaurants and groceries are located nearby in Montara.

Surfing: Small swells are ridable.

Getting there: Located along Route 1 eight miles south of Pacifica. There is a trail leading to the beach from Route 1 and 2nd Street in Montara.

Edun Cove or Gray Whale State Beach—This white-sand crescent is a popular nude beach. Tucked discreetly beneath steep cliffs, it is also a beautiful spot.

Facilities: Toilets; restaurants and groceries are located several miles away in Montara and Pacifica. Information, 415-728-5336.

Getting there: Located along Route 1 five miles south of Pacifica. Watch for the parking lot (fee charged) on the east side of the highway. Cautiously cross the highway and proceed down the staircase to the beach.

Hiking

To fully capture the beauty and serenity of the region's woodlands, chaparral country, and beaches, explore its hiking trails. The Santa Lucia and Santa Cruz mountains offer several hundred miles of trails through fir, madrone, and redwood forests. Getting lost, so to speak, among these stands of ancient trees is a splendid way to vacation. Or hike the inland hills with their caves and rock spires. Down at the sea's edge you'll discover more caves, as well as tidepools, sand dunes, and a world of marine life. Any of these environments will reveal the Central Coast as it's been since time immemorial.

VENTANA WILDERNESS TRAILS

Over 150,000 acres of rugged mountain terrain comprise the Ventana Wilderness of Los Padres National Forest. About 200 miles of hiking trails make it easy to explore the Santa Lucia Mountains while escaping the trappings of civilization. There are three coastal entrances to the preserve—Big Sur Station, Bottchers Gap Station, and Nacimiento Station.

Bottchers Gap–Devils Peak Trail (4 miles) is a steep hike through coniferous forests to spectacular vistas overlooking the northern section of the Ventana Wilderness.

Kirk Creek–Vicente Flat Trail (6 miles) loops from Nacimiento Station along ridgelines that afford mountain views.

Pine Ridge Trail (40.7 miles) begins in Pfeiffer Big Sur State Parkand carries two miles to the park boundary before heading into the Ventana Wilderness. First stop is Ventana Camp, near the Big Sur River. Then the trail leads past several campgrounds to China Camp and loops back to Big Sur Station.

POINT LOBOS STATE RESERVE TRAILS

One of California's most beautiful spots is the six-mile shoreline at Point Lobos State Reserve. The park is laced with trails leading to tidepools, sandy coves, and whale-watching vistas.

Cypress Grove Trail (.8 mile), one of the most popular (and populated) in the park, leads through a stand of Monterey cypress trees and offers cliff-top views of the ocean.

Bird Island Trail (.8 mile) takes you through coastal shrubbery to two exquisite white-sand beaches—China Cove and Gibson Beach. The path also overlooks Bird Island, a refuge for cormorants and brown pelicans.

Pine Ridge Trail (.7 mile), beginning near Piney Woods, goes inland through forests of Monterey pines and Coast live oak. Deer, squirrel, and such birds as pygmy nuthatches and chestnut-backed chickadees make this a tranquil nature hike.

South Shore Trail (1 mile), an oceanside walk between Sea Lion Point and the Bird Rock parking area, allows close looks at tidepool life and shore birds. You can also play amateur geologist, examining multicolored patterns in sedimentary rocks.

AÑO NUEVO STATE RESERVE TRAILS

If you have an urge to see elephant seals breeding, take the three-mile guided walk led by park rangers. To protect these mammoth mammals, the preserve is open during breeding season only to those on the guided tours. They are scheduled from December through March and require reservations; call 415-879-0227. To explore this area after mating season, you can hike on your own past sand dunes, tidepools, and sea caves. Follow **Año Nuevo Trail** (2 miles), beginning at the west end of the parking lot, to Año Nuevo Point.

Travelers' Tracks

Sightseeing

A tour of the Central Coast could prove to be a long-term commitment. There's a lot of countryside and shoreline to see.

South of Monterey rises the Big Sur district where the Santa Lucia Mountains encounter the Pacific. Backed by the challenging Ventana Wilderness, this region is marked by sharp coastal cliffs and unbelievable scenery. Though it's hard to conceive, Big Sur may be even more beautiful than the other sections of the Central Coast.

Coastal Route 1 leads to the Monterey Peninsula, a posh resort region centered in the towns of Monterey, Pacific Grove, and Carmel. Most famous is Monterey, the old Spanish mission town built of adobe. Pacific Grove, which grew up in the 19th century, is Victorian in style, while Carmel features a melange of architectural modes.

Further up the coast rests the seaside community of Santa Cruz, a campus town with an old-fashioned boardwalk and amusement park. Between here and San Francisco are rolling farmlands where giant pumpkins grow to the edge of the sea.

BIG SUR

From Hearst Castle in Southern California, the highway hugs the coastline as it snakes north toward Big Sur. Like Route 1 north of San Francisco, this is one of America's great stretches of roadway. Situated between the Santa Lucia Mountains and the Pacific, Route 1 courses about 30 miles from Big Sur to Carmel, then spirals further north along the coast toward San Francisco.

Each turnout en route provides another glimpse into a magic-lantern world. Here the glass pictures a beach crusted with rocks, there a wave-wracked cliff or pocket of tidepools. The canyons are narrow and precipitous, while the headlands are so close to the surf they seem like beached whales. Trees are broken and blasted before the wind. The houses, though millionaire affairs, appear inconsequential against the backdrop of ocean and stone.

Big Sur, a rural community of about 1500 people, stretches the length of the six-mile-long Big Sur River Valley. Lacking a town center, it consists of houses and a few stores dotted along the Big Sur River. The place received its name from early Spanish settlers, who called the wilderness south of Carmel *El Pais Grande del Sur,* "the big country to the south."

Later it became a rural retreat and artists' colony. Henry Miller lived here from 1947 until 1964, writing *Big Sur and the Oranges of*

Hieronymus Bosch, Plexus, and *Nexus* during his residence. Today the artists are being displaced by soaring land values, while the region is gaining increased popularity among visitors. It's not difficult to understand why as you cruise along its knife-edge cliffs and timbered mountainsides.

There's not much to the **Henry Miller Memorial Library** (Route 1 about a mile south of Ventana Inn; 408-667-2574), but somehow the unassuming nature of the place befits its candid subject. Occupying a small woodframe house, the museum contains volumes from the novelist's library as well as his evocative artworks.

For an incredible side trip, you can follow **Coast Road** (★) for about 11 miles up into the Santa Lucia Mountains. Climbing along narrow ledges, then corkscrewing deep into overgrown canyons, the road carries past exquisite views of forests and mountain ridges. There are hawk's-eye vistas of the Pacific, the rolling Big Sur countryside, and Pico Blanco, a 3709-foot lime-rich peak. This is the old coast road, the principal thoroughfare before Route 1 was completed in the 1930s. Take heed: it is so curvy it makes Route 1 seem a desert straightaway; it is also entirely unpaved, narrow, rutted, and impassable in wet weather. But oh those views! Coast Road begins at Andrew Molera State Park and rejoins Route 1 at Bixby Bridge.

If instead of detouring you stay on Route 1, it will pass a lengthy beach leading to **Point Sur Light Station.** Set on a volcanic headland, this solitary sentinel dates back to 1889. Further on at **Little Sur Beach** you'll encounter a sandy crescent bounded by a shallow lagoon. There are dunes and lofty hills all around, as well as shorebirds. Then the road climbs along **Hurricane Point,** a promontory blessed with sweeping views and cursed by lashing winds.

Route 1 traverses **Bixby Creek Bridge,** which stretches from one cliff to another across an infernal chasm. Local legend cites it incorrectly as the world's longest concrete arch span. With fluted hills in the background and a fluffy beach below, it may, however, be the world's prettiest.

For an intriguing excursion into those hills, head about three miles up **Palo Colorado Road** (★), which intersects with Route 1 a couple of miles south of Garrapata Creek. Though paved, this country road is one lane. The corridor tunnels through an arcade of redwoods past log cabins and rustic homes. If you're feeling adventurous, follow the twisting eight-mile road to its terminus at Los Padres National Forest.

At **Soberanes Point,** eight miles south of Carmel, hiking trails lead out along the headlands. Here you can stand on a rock shelf directly above the ocean and gaze back at the encroaching hills.

MONTEREY AREA

Over three million visitors tour the Monterey Peninsula every year. Little wonder. Its rocky coast fringed with cypress forests, its hills dotted with palatial homes—the area is unusually beautiful. The peninsula also serves as a gateway to the tumbling region of Big Sur.

For a tour of Monterey Peninsula, begin in Monterey itself. Here are historic homes, an old Spanish presidio, Fisherman's Wharf, and Cannery Row. Pacific Grove next door is a quiet town with an invitingly undeveloped waterfront. Paths lead for miles along this rock-crusted shore. Carmel is a former artists' colony transformed into a shoppers' paradise, but retaining much of its early charm.

MONTEREY'S PATH OF HISTORY

History in Monterey is a precious commodity which in most cases has been carefully preserved. Ancient adobe houses and Spanish-style buildings are so commonplace that some have been converted into shops and restaurants. Others are museums or points of interest that can be seen on a walking tour along the **Path of History.** This "Path," carrying through the center of Monterey, measures over two miles if walked in its entirety.

The best place to begin is the **Custom House** at Custom House Plaza across from Fisherman's Wharf. California's earliest public building, the structure dates back to 1827. It was here in 1846 that Commodore Sloat raised the American flag, claiming California for the United States. Today the stone and adobe building houses displays re-creating Monterey's history as a major Pacific seaport. Together with some of the other important landmarks along the Path of History, it is part of Monterey State Historic Park (information, 408-649-7118; one admission covers all points in the park).

Across the plaza rises **Pacific House,** a two-story balconied adobe with a luxurious courtyard. Constructed in 1847, it was used over the years to house everything from military supplies to a tavern to a courtroom and church. The exhibits inside trace California's history from Native American days through the advent of Spanish settlers and American pioneers. Next door at **California Heritage Guides** (10 Custom House Plaza; 408-373-6454), there are maps, brochures, and guided tours available.

Just behind Pacific House sits **Casa del Oro** (Olivier and Scott streets), a tiny white adobe which served as Monterey's general store during the 1850s. Today it houses the **Boston Store** (408-649-3364), a shop selling early American items.

California's First Theater, a block up the street (Scott and Pacific streets), certainly qualifies as a living museum. Not only are there illustrations from its days as a pre-Gold Rush entertainment center, but the place is still used to stage theatrical performances. Wander this clapboard and adobe building and you'll encounter almost a century-and-a-half of Monterey's dramatic tradition.

A left on Pacific leads to **Casa Soberanes** (336 Pacific Street), a Monterey-style house with red tile roof and second-story balcony. Completed around 1830, this impressive structure originally housed the commander of the Spanish Presidio. Part of the Monterey State Historic Park, it features guided tours on the hour.

Casa Serrano (412 Pacific Street), built in 1843, contains wrought-iron decorations over its narrow windows. Once home to a blind Spanish teacher, it is now open for touring only on weekends.

Nearby spreads **Friendly Plaza,** a tree-shaded park which serves as a focus for several important places. The **Monterey Peninsula Museum of Art** (559 Pacific Street; 408-372-7591) features works by local artists as well as special exhibits. Pierce Street, running along the upper edge of the plaza, contains a string of historic 19th-century homes. **Colton Hall** is an imposing two-story stone structure with white pillars and classical portico. Site of California's 1849 constitutional convention, it displays memorabilia from that critical event. Given its unique architecture and lovely setting, it's one of Monterey's prettiest buildings. The squat **Old Jail** next door, fashioned from granite, with wrought-iron bars across the windows, dates back to the same era. It creates a startling contrast to its stately neighbor. **Casa Gutierrez** (across the street) was built by a cavalryman with 15 children. That was back in 1841; today the old adobe is a restaurant.

After exploring the plaza, turn left into Madison Street from Pacific Street, then left again along Calle Principal to the **Allen Knight Maritime Museum** (550 Calle Principal) with its model ships and old nautical photographs. Two 19th-century adobes are located next to the museum. Then you'll encounter one of the town's most famous homes, the **Larkin House** (Calle Principal and Jefferson Street). Designed in 1835 by Thomas Larkin, this elegant edifice represents a prototype of Monterey-style architecture. Combining New England and Spanish principles, it's a two-story adobe house with ground floor verandah and second-story balcony. Today the antique home is a house-museum filled with period pieces that provide a glimpse into early American life on the West Coast. The house is especially important historically since its owner was the United States Consul to California and a key player in the American takeover.

A right on Jefferson Street and another quick right on Polk Street takes you past a cluster of revered houses. **Casa Amesti** (516 Polk Street; 408-372-8173), dating from 1824, is presently a private club open to the public only on weekends. The **Cooper-Molera Adobe** across the road (Polk and Munras streets) is a sprawling affair currently being restored

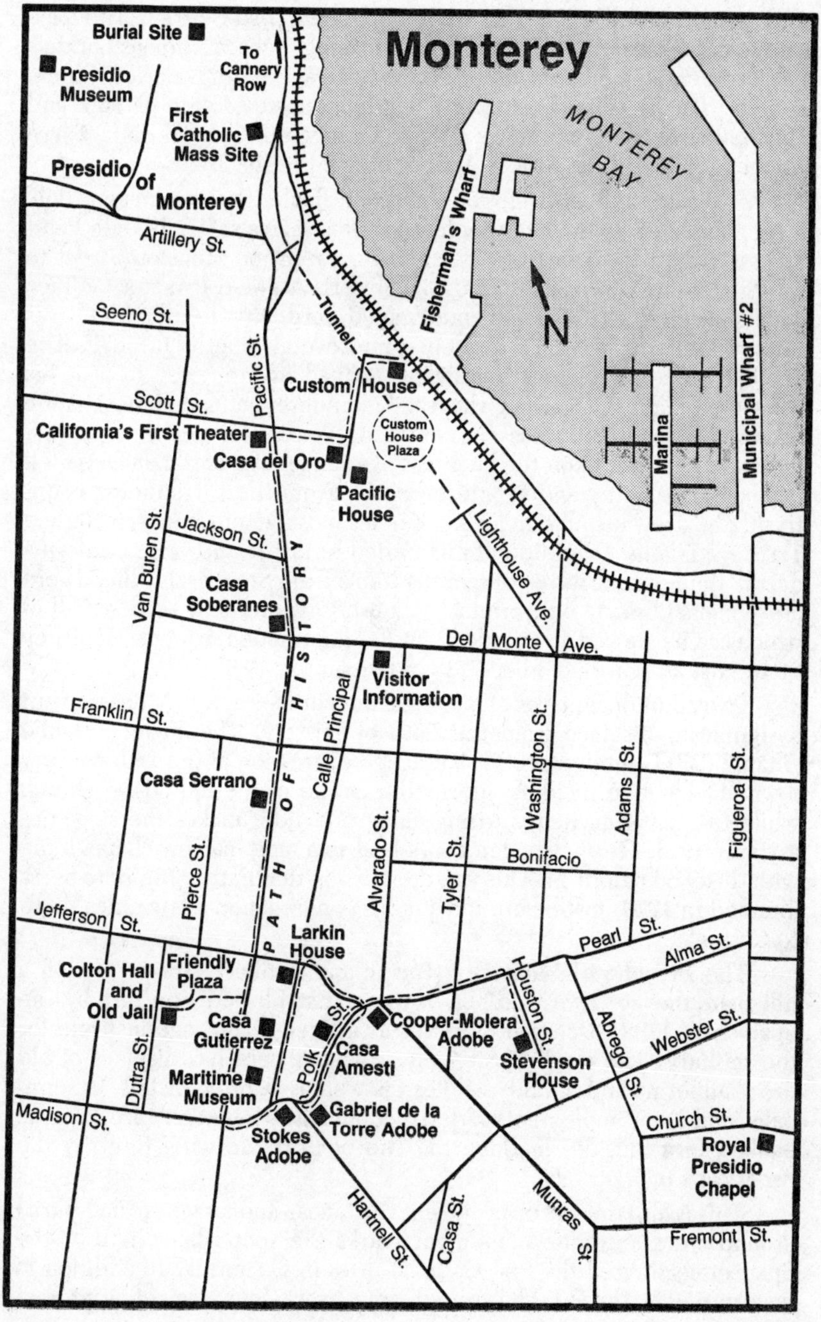
Monterey
Burial Site
Presidio Museum
To Cannery Row
First Catholic Mass Site
Presidio of Monterey
Artillery St.
MONTEREY BAY
Fisherman's Wharf
N
Tunnel
Seeno St.
Pacific St.
Custom House
Custom House Plaza
Scott St.
California's First Theater
Casa del Oro
Pacific House
Marina
Municipal Wharf #2
Lighthouse Ave.
Jackson St.
Van Buren St.
Casa Soberanes
PATH OF HISTORY
Del Monte Ave.
Visitor Information
Calle Principal
Franklin St.
Casa Serrano
Washington St.
Adams St.
Figueroa St.
Alvarado St.
Tyler St.
Bonifacio
Pierce St.
Jefferson St.
Larkin House
Pearl St.
Alma St.
Colton Hall and Old Jail
Friendly Plaza
Houston St.
Casa Gutierrez
Polk St.
Cooper-Molera Adobe
Casa Amesti
Stevenson House
Abrego St.
Webster St.
Dutra St.
Maritime Museum
Madison St.
Stokes Adobe
Gabriel de la Torre Adobe
Church St.
Royal Presidio Chapel
Hartnell St.
Casa St.
Munras St.
Fremont St.

as an important museum, part of the Monterey Historic Park. The massive structure, over two decades in the making, housed Thomas Larkin's half-brother, a merchant who sailed the waters of South America, China, and the Pacific isles. Facing one another on either side of Polk and Hartnell streets are two more vintage homes, the **Gabriel de la Torre Adobe,** 1836, and the **Stokes Adobe,** erected in the 1840s.

If you are still with me for the grand finale, backtrack along Polk Street one block to the five-way intersection, take a soft right onto Pearl Street, walk a few short blocks, then turn right on Houston Street to the **Stevenson House** (530 Houston Street). A grand two-story edifice with shuttered windows and landscaped yard, this former hotel was Robert Louis Stevenson's residence for several months in 1879. The Scottish writer, vivacious but sickly, arrived in Monterey to visit his wife-to-be Fanny Osbourne. The fragile wanderer had sailed the Atlantic and traveled overland across the continent. Writing for local newspapers, depending in part upon the kindness of strangers for sustenance, he fell in love with Fanny and Monterey both. From the surrounding countryside he drew inspiration for some of his most famous books, including *Treasure Island*. In addition to its period furniture and early California decor, the house features numerous items from Stevenson's life. There are personal belongings, original manuscripts, and first editions, all of which can be viewed on a guided tour (for information, contact Monterey State Historic Park, 408-649-7118; admission).

Two additional places of historical note are located in Monterey but a significant distance from the Path of History. The **Royal Presidio Chapel** (550 Church Street) is a graceful expression of the 18th-century town. Decorative molding adorns the facade of the old adobe church while the towering belfry, rising along one side, makes the structure asymmetrical. Heavy wooden doors lead to a long, narrow chapel hung with dusty oil paintings. This was the mission that Father Junipero Serra founded in 1770, just before moving his congregation a few miles south to Carmel.

The **Presidio of Monterey** (Pacific and Artillery streets) sits on a hill near the northwest corner of town. Established as a fort by the Spanish in 1792, it currently serves as a foreign language institute for the military. The small U.S. Army Museum here has displays of old dress uniforms and cavalry saddles, as well as swords, pistols, cannonballs, and other implements of destruction. Elsewhere there are cannons banked in a hillside, marking the site of Fort Mervine, built by the Americans in 1846.

This is also the site of an ancient Costanoan Indian village and burial ground. And a granite monument marks the spot where in 1602 the Spanish celebrated the first Catholic mass in California. In addition to historic points, the Presidio grounds enjoy marvelous views of Monterey.

You can look down upon the town, then scan along the bay's curving horizon.

FISHERMAN'S WHARF

Strangely, Monterey, which elsewhere demonstrates special care in preserving its heritage, has let its wharves and piers fall prey to tinsel-minded developers. **Municipal Wharf #2** (foot of Figueroa Street), a welcome exception, is all that remains from the heyday of Monterey's fishing fleet. Here broad-hulled boats still beat at their moorings, while landlubbing anglers cast from pierside. Gulls perch along the handrails, sea lions bark from beneath the pilings, and pelicans work the waterfront. On one side is the dilapidated warehouse of a long-defunct freezer company. At the end of the dock, fish companies still operate. It's a primal place of cranes and pulleys, forklifts and conveyor belts. There are ice boxes and old packing crates scattered hither-thither, exuding the romance and stench of the industry.

Then there is the parody, much better known than the original. **Fisherman's Wharf,** like its San Francisco namesake, has been transmogrified into what the travel industry thinks tourists think a fishing pier should look like. Something was lost in the translation. Few fishing boats operate from the wharf these days; several charter companies sponsor tours and whale-watching expeditions. Otherwise the waterfront haven is just one more mall, a macadam corridor lined on either side with shops. There are ersatz art galleries, shops vending candy apples and personalized mugs, plus a school of seafood restaurants. A few outdoor fish markets still sell live crabs, lobsters, and squid, but the symbol of the place is the hurdy-gurdy man with performing monkey who greets you at the entrance.

Actually this is only the most recent in the wharf's long series of role changes. The dock was built in 1846 to serve cargo schooners dealing in hides. Within a decade the whaling industry took it over, followed finally by Italian fishermen catching salmon, cod, and mackerel. During the Cannery Row era of the '30s, the sardine industry played a vital part in the life of the wharf. Today all that has given way to a bizarre form of public nostalgia.

CANNERY ROW

The same visionary appears responsible for the resurrection of **Cannery Row.** Made famous by John Steinbeck's feisty novels *Cannery Row* and *Sweet Thursday,* this oceanfront strip has been transformed into a neighborhood of wax museums and dainty antique shops. As Steinbeck remarked upon returning to the old sardine canning center, "They fish for tourists now."

Cannery Row of yore was an unappealing collection of corrugated warehouses, dilapidated stores, seedy hotels, and gaudy whorehouses.

There were about 18 canneries, 100 fishing boats, and 4000 workers populating the place. The odor was horrible, but for several decades the sardine industry breathed life into the Monterey economy. The business died just before *Cannery Row* was published in 1945.

Before the entire oceanfront strip was developed in the early 1980s, you could still capture a sense of the old Cannery Row. A few weather-beaten factories remained. Rust stained their ribbed sides, windows were punched, and roofs had settled to an inward curve. In places, the stone pilings of old loading docks still stood, haunted by seagulls. Now only tourists and memories remain.

At the other end of the Row, Steinbeck aficionados will find a few literary settings. La Ida Cafe has given way to **Kalisa's** (851 Cannery Row), but retains the same tumbledown appearance; Wing Chong Market is now the **Alicia's Antiques** (835 Cannery Row), and the building that housed **Doc Rickett's Marine Lab** stands at 800 Cannery Row.

In the middle you'll encounter the scene of the malling of Cannery Row. Old warehouses have been renovated into shopping centers, new buildings have risen, and the entire area has experienced a face lift. Brightest tooth in the new smile is the **Edgewater Packing Company** (Cannery Row and Prescott Avenue), a miniature amusement park with a hand-carved carousel.

The latest addition is the **Monterey Bay Aquarium** (Cannery Row and David Avenue; 408-649-6466; admission), a state-of-the-art museum that re-creates the natural habitat of local sea life. Monterey Bay is one of the world's biggest submarine canyons, deeper than the Grand Canyon. At the aquarium you'll encounter about 100 display tanks representing the wealth of underwater life that inhabits this mineral-rich valley. For instance, the Monterey Bay Tank, a 90-foot-long glass enclosure, portrays the local submarine world complete with sharks, brilliant reef fish, and creosote-oozing pilings. Another aquarium contains amature kelp forest crowded with fish. Together the many displays and exhibitions make it one of the world's great aquariums.

PACIFIC GROVE

Projecting out from the northern tip of Monterey Peninsula is the diminutive town of **Pacific Grove.** Covering just 1700 acres, it is reached from Monterey along Lighthouse Avenue. Better yet, pick up Ocean View Boulevard near Cannery Row and follow as it winds along Pacific Grove's surf-washed shores.

Costanoan Indians once dove for abalone in these waters. By the 19th century, Pacific Grove had become a religious retreat. Methodist Episcopal ministers pitched a tent city and decreed that "bathing suits shall be provided with double crotches or with skirts of ample size to cover the buttocks." The town was dry until 1969. Given the fish canneries in Monterey and teetotalers in this nearby town, local folks called the area "Carmel-by-the-Sea, Monterey-by-the-Smell, and Pacific Grove-by-God."

Today Pacific Grove is a sleepy residential area decorated with Victorians, brown-shingle houses, and clapboard ocean cottages. The waterfront drive goes past rocky beaches to **Point Pinos Lighthouse.** When this beacon first flashed in 1855, it burned sperm oil. Little has changed except the introduction of electricity; this is the only early lighthouse along the entire California coast to be preserved in its original condition.

Sunset Drive continues along the sea to **Asilomar State Park.** Here sand dunes mantled with ice plant front a wave-lashed shore. There are tidepools galore, plus beaches for picnics, and trails leading through the dunes.

Pacific Grove's major claim to fame lies in two areas several blocks inland: around George Washington Park on Melrose Street and in a grove at 1073 Lighthouse Avenue. This otherwise unassuming municipality is "Butterfly Town, U.S.A." Every November, brilliant orange-and-black **monarch butterflies** migrate here, remaining until March. Some arrive from several hundred miles away to breed amid the cypress and oak trees. At night they cling to one another, curtaining the branches in clusters that sometimes number over a thousand. Then, at first light, they come to life, fluttering around the groves in a frenzy of wings and color.

Also of interest are the **Pacific Grove Museum of Natural History** (Central and Forest avenues; 408-372-4212), an excellent small museum; the **ivy-cloaked cottage** at 147 11th Street (not open to the public) where John Steinbeck lived and wrote *Tortilla Flat, In Dubious Battle,* and *Of Mice and Men*; plus **Gosby House Inn** (643 Lighthouse Avenue) and the **Hart Mansion** (now the Maison Bergerac Restaurant) next door, two elaborate old Victorian houses.

17 MILE DRIVE

From Pacific Grove, **17 Mile Drive** leads to Pebble Beach, one of America's most lavish communities. This place is so exclusive that the rich charge $5 to anyone wishing to drive around admiring their homes. No wonder they're rich.

Galling as the gate fee might be, this is an extraordinary region that must not be missed. The road winds through pine groves down to a wind-combed beach. There are miles of rolling dunes tufted with sea vegetation. (The oceanfront can be as cool and damp as it is beautiful, so carry a sweater or jacket, or better yet, both.)

Among the first spots you'll encounter is **Spanish Bay,** where Juan Gaspar de Portola camped during his 1769 expedition up the California coast. (The picnic area here is a choice place to spread a feast.) At **Point Joe,** converging ocean currents create a wild frothing sea that has drawn several ships to their doom.

Seal and Bird Rocks, true to their nomenclature, are carpeted with sea lions, harbor and leopard seals, cormorants, and gulls. Throughout this thriving 17 Mile Drive area are black-tail deer, pelicans, sooty shearwaters, sea otters, and, during migration periods, California gray whales.

There are crescent beaches and granite headlands as well as vista points for scanning the coast. You'll also pass the **Lone Cypress,** the solitary tree on a rocky point that has become as symbolic of Northern California as perhaps the Golden Gate Bridge. Monterey cypresses such as this one grow nowhere in the world but along Carmel Bay.

The **private homes** en route are mansions, exquisite affairs fashioned from marble and fine hardwoods. Some appear like stone fortresses, others seem made solely of glass. They range from American Colonial to futuristic and were designed by noted architects like Bernard Maybeck, Julia Morgan, and Willis Polk.

This is also home to several of the world's most renowned **golf courses**—Pebble Beach, Spyglass Hill, and Cypress Point—where the AT&T at Pebble Beach Pro-Am Tournament takes place each year. More than the designer homes and their celebrity residents, these courses have made Pebble Beach a place fabled for wealth and beauty.

The best part of the drive lies along the coast between the Pacific Grove and Carmel gates. Along the backside of 17 Mile Drive, where it loops up into Del Monte Forest, there are marvelous views of Monterey Bay and the San Gabilan Mountains. Here also is **Huckleberry Hill,** a forest of Monterey and Bishop pine freckled with bushes.

CARMEL

The first law of real estate should be this: The best land is always occupied by the military, bohemians, or the rich. Think about it. The principle holds for many of the world's prettiest spots.

Generally the military arrives first, on an exploratory mission or as an occupying force. It takes strategic ground, which happens to be the beaches, headlands, and mountaintops. The bohemians select beautiful locales because they possess good taste. When the rich discover where the artists have settled, they start moving in, driving up the rents, and forcing the displaced bohemians to discover new homes, which will then be taken by another wave of the wealthy.

The Monterey Peninsula is no exception. In Carmel the military established an early beachhead when Spanish soldiers occupied a barracks in the old Catholic mission. Later the bohemians arrived in numbers. Poet George Sterling came in 1905, followed by Mary Austin, the novelist. Eventually such luminaries as Upton Sinclair, Lincoln Steffens, and Sinclair Lewis, writers all, settled for varying periods. Jack London and Ambrose Bierce visited. Later, photographers Ansel Adams and Edward Weston relocated here.

The figure most closely associated with this "seacoast of Bohemia" was Robinson Jeffers, a poet who came seeking solitude in 1914. Quarrying rock from the shoreline, he built the Tor House and Hawk Tower, where he lived and wrote haunting poems and epics about the coast.

Then like death and tax collectors, the rich inevitably moved in. As John Steinbeck noted when he later returned to this artists' colony, "If Carmel's founders should return, they could not afford to live there. . . .They would instantly be picked up as suspicious characters and deported over the city line."

It's doubtful many would want to remain anyway. Today Carmel is so cute it cloys. The tiny town is cluttered with over four dozen inns, about six dozen restaurants, and more than 150 shops. Ocean Avenue, the main street, is wall-to-wall with merchants. Shopping malls have replaced artist garrets, and there are traffic jams where there was once solitude.

Typifying the town is the **Tuck Box,** a gingerbread-style building on Dolores Street between Ocean and 7th avenues (there are no street numbers in Carmel), or the fairy tale-like **Hansel-and-Gretel cottages** on Torres Street between 5th and 6th avenues.

Still, reasons remain to visit Carmel, which is reached from Monterey via Route 1 or from the Carmel gate along 17 Mile Drive. The window shopping is good and several galleries are outstanding. Some of the town's quaint characteristics have appeal. There are no traffic lights or parking meters, and at night few street lights. Drive around the side streets and you will encounter an architectural mixture of log cabins, adobe structures, board-and-batten cottages, and Spanish villas.

A secret that local residents have long withheld from visitors is **Mission Trail Park** (★). No signs will direct you here, so watch for an entrance at the corner of Mountain View and Crespi avenues. Within this forest preserve are miles of hiking trails. They wind across foot bridges, through redwood groves, and past meadows of wildflowers en route to Carmel Mission. There are ocean vistas, deer grazing the hillsides, and an arboretum seeded with native California plants.

Carmel's most alluring feature is the one which early drew the bohemians—the Pacific. At the foot of Ocean Avenue rests Carmel Beach, a snowy strand shadowed by cypress trees. From here, Scenic Road hugs the coast, winding above rocky outcroppings.

Just before the intersection with Stewart Way, gaze uphill toward those two stone edifices. Robinson Jeffers' **Tor House** and **Hawk Tower**

(Text continued on page 316.)

The Coast By Train

America's railroads are associated more with interior valleys and broad plains than open ocean. But two trains, the "San Diegan" from San Diego to Los Angeles, and the "Coast Starlight," which continues from Los Angeles en route to Seattle, parallel the coast, passing areas inaccessible by automobile. With their dining cars, sleeping compartments, and observation cars, they are a flash from the American past, part of **Amtrak's** (800-872-7245) 24,000 miles of track, final vestige of the nation's once-proud rail system.

In the course of its three-hour route the "San Diegan" travels for an hour along the shore, taking in the sights from Del Mar to Dana Point. It rumbles past Los Penasquitos Marsh Natural Preserve, a nesting place for migratory birds, then rims a series of lofty sea cliffs, which fall away to reveal narrow bands of sandy beach. There are four other marshes and lagoons en route, representing some of California's most vital wetlands.

Along the way lies one of the nation's major centers for cut flowers and ornamental plants. Then further north Camp Pendleton, a Marine base and site of frequent military manuevers, stretches along 17 miles of prime coastline. Another unsettling sight, the San Onofre nuclear power plant, flashes by before the train enters San Clemente, home to President Richard Nixon during his ill-fated administration. From here the "San Diegan" turns inland to the old mission town of San Juan Capistrano and cuts through the heart of Orange County.

Picking up the baton in Los Angeles, the "Coast Starlight" continues north past ticky-tack homes, those proverbial houses on the other side of the tracks, and squat, blocky office buildings stained with graffiti. It arrives at the ocean in Oxnard and parallels the Pacific, shuttling past stretches of open water populated with surfers and occasional fishermen. From here north the tracks hone a fine line along sharp rockfaces. Farm houses flit by on one side, while looming offshore are oil rigs and the Channel Islands.

The mission towns of Ventura and Santa Barbara are stations on the itinerary. Then the train crosses high trestles and climbs above the shore toward Point Concepcion. This is California's geographic turning point, where the coast veers sharply right and the beaches, which earlier pointed south, turn to face the west.

Beyond the lighthouses at Point Concepcion and Point Arguello rise the missile silos of Vandenberg Air Force Base. This is the western spaceport for the Space Shuttle, whose launch pads and support building rest along the tracks. It is also headquarters for a Strategic Air Command launch site complete with satellite stations and Minuteman missiles. The entire area, otherwise closed to the public, is open to view from the "Coast Starlight."

Grand finale to the coast portion of the journey are the Nipomo Dunes, massive, wind-shaved sand hills that shadow the shore for more than 20 miles. At Pismo Beach, known for the beds of Pismo clams within its sands, the "Coast Starlight" turns inland, trading the wide Pacific for California's broad, fertile Central Valley.

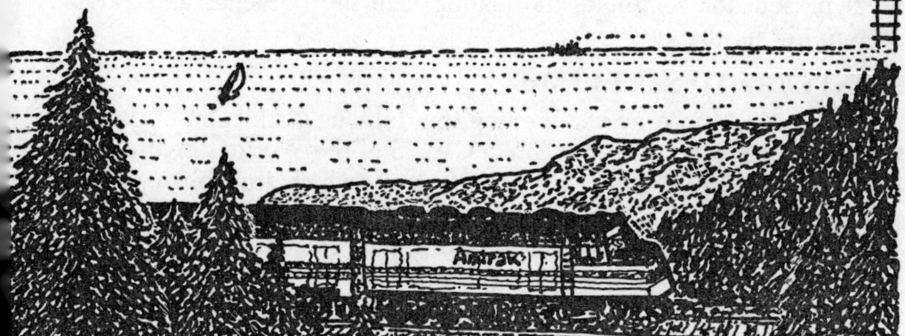

seem drawn from another place and time, perhaps a Scottish headland in the 19th century. In fact, the poet modeled the house after an English-style home and built the three-story garret in the fashion of an Irish tower. Completed during the 1920s, the structures are granite and include porthole windows that Jeffers salvaged from a shipwreck. Tours of the house and tower are conducted on Friday and Saturday by reservation (information, 408-624-1813; admission).

Just beyond stretches **Carmel River State Beach,** a sandy corridor at the foot of Carmel Bay. For further information, see the "Beaches and Parks" section in this chapter.

Even for the non-religious, a visit to **Carmel Mission** (located on Rio Road just off Route 1; information, 408-624-3600) becomes a pilgrimage. If the holiness holds no appeal, there's the aesthetic sense of the place. Dating back to 1771, its Old World beauty captivates and confounds. The courtyards are alive with flowers and birds. The adobe buildings surrounding have been dusted with time—their eaves are hunchbacked, the tile roofs coated in moss.

Established by Father Junipero Serra, this mission is one of California's most remarkable. The basilica is a vaulted-ceiling affair adorned with old oil paintings and wooden statues of Christ; its walls are lime plaster made from burnt seashells. The exterior is topped with a Moorish tower and four bells.

Junipero Serra lies buried on the grounds, his grave dramatically marked with a stone sarcophagus. There are also museum rooms demonstrating early California life—a kitchen with stone hearth and rudimentary tools, the state's first library (complete with waterstained bibles), and the cell where Father Serra died, its bed a slab of wood with a single blanket and no mattress. Close by, in the cemetery beside the basilica, several thousand Indians are also buried.

Just three miles south of Carmel lies **Point Lobos State Reserve,** an incomparable natural area of rocky headlands and placid coves. The park features hillside crow's nests from which to gaze out along Carmel Bay. This region, also rich in wildlife and underwater life, should not be bypassed; for complete information, see the "Beaches and Parks" section in this chapter.

MONTEREY TO SANTA CRUZ

North of Monterey you'll enjoy the dubious distinction of passing through Castroville, the "Artichoke Capital of the World." Before that, however, lie Seaside, Sand City, and Marina—which probably represent the sand capitals of the world. The entire area rests on a sand dune which measures up to 300 feet in depth, and extends ten miles along the coast and as much as eight miles inland. From here you can trace a course into Monterey along wind-tilled rows of sand.

Route 1 next traverses Moss Landing, a weather-beaten fishing harbor. With its one-lane bridge, bright-painted boats, and unpainted fish market, the town has a warm personality. There is one eyesore, however, a huge power plant with twin smokestacks that stand out like two sentinels of an occupying army. Otherwise the place is enchanting, particularly nearby **Elkhorn Slough,** a 1240-acre world of salt marshes and tidal flats preserved in part through the beneficent actions of the San Francisco-based Nature Conservancy. Within this delicate environment live some 100 species of waterfowl, about 50 land-bound species (among them golden eagles), as well as harbor seals, muskrats, oysters, and clams. For the visitor center, follow Dolan Road for three miles, go left on Elkhorn Road, and proceed two more miles.

From the coast highway, Beach Street leads east into Watsonville. Central to the surrounding farm community, Watsonville is the world's strawberry-growing capital. It's also rich in **Victorian houses,** which you can tour with a printed guide available from the Chamber of Commerce (444 Main Street; 408-724-3849).

Or you can follow Beach Street west to the ocean. The entire stretch of coastline hereabouts is flanked by high sand dunes, a wild and exotic counterpoint to the furrowed fields nearby.

For a rural side trip that will carry you past miles of farmland before rejoining Route 1 in Rio del Mar, follow San Andreas Road north from Beach Road. It courses past rich agricultural land, then tunnels through forest. Intricately tilled fields roll down to the sea and edge up to the foot of the mountains. This Pajaro Valley area counts its wealth in strawberries, apples, flowers, and mushrooms.

From Rio del Mar, Route 1 courses north to Aptos, a bedroom community with sparkling beaches, and Capitola, a town known for its pretty beach and September Begonia Festival.

SANTA CRUZ

Santa Cruz is a playground. It enjoys spectacular white-sand beaches, entertaining nightlife, and an old-style boardwalk amusement park. The city faces south, providing the best weather along the Central Coast. Arts and crafts flourish here, and vintage houses adorn the area.

WATERFRONT AND BOARDWALK

Route 1, California's magnificent coastal highway, runs slightly inland in Santa Cruz, which means it's time to find a different waterfront drive. Not to worry, the best way to begin exploring the place is at the north end of town around **Natural Bridges State Beach.** All but one of the sea arches here have collapsed, leading local wags to dub the spot "Fallen Arches." A pretty spot for a picnic, it's the place to pick up West Cliff Drive, which sweeps the Santa Cruz waterfront.

The shoreline is a honeycomb of tiny coves, sea arches, and pocket beaches. From **Lighthouse Point** on a clear day, the entire 40-mile curve of Monterey Bay silhouettes the skyline. Even in foggy weather, sea lions cavort on the rocks offshore, while surfers ride the challenging "Steamer Lane" breaks. Testament to their talent is the tiny **Surfing Museum** (West Cliff Drive and Lighthouse Point; 408-429-3429) situated in the lighthouse. Here vintage photos and antique boards re-create the history of the Hawaiian sport that landed on the shores of Santa Cruz early in the century.

Beach Street continues this coast-hugging route to **Santa Cruz Municipal Pier,** a half-mile-long wharf lined with bait shops, restaurants, and fishing charters. Those early morning folks with the sun-furrowed faces are either fishing or crabbing. They are here everyday with lawn chairs and tackle boxes. When reality overcomes optimism, they have been known to duck into nearby fresh fish stores for the day's catch. The pier is a perfect place to promenade, soak up sun, and seek out local color. It also provides a peaceful counterpoint to the next attraction.

Santa Cruz Beach Boardwalk (400 Beach Street; 408-423-5590) is Northern California's answer to Coney Island. Pride of the city, it dates back to 1907 and sports several old-fashioned rides. The Cocoanut Grove Ballroom (408-423-2053) here hosted Big Band greats like Benny Goodman and the Dorsey brothers, and still sponsors musical performances. But the Boardwalk remains first and foremost an amusement park. The penny arcade features vintage machines as well as modernistic video games. You'll find shooting galleries and candy stalls, coin-operated fortune tellers and do-it-yourself photo machines. Shops sell everything from baubles to bikinis. Then there are the ultimate entertainments: a slow-circling ferris wheel with chairs suspended high above the beach; the antique merry-go-round, a whirl of mirrors and flashing color; a funicular whose brightly painted cars reflect the sun; rides with names that instantaneously evoke childhood memories—tilt-a-whirl, haunted castle, bumper cars; and that soaring symbol of amusement parks everywhere, the roller coaster.

ARCHITECTURAL TOURS

The playground for shoppers sits several blocks inland along Pacific Avenue. **Pacific Garden Mall** is a tree-lined promenade stretching from Cathcart to Water streets. Amid its magnolias and azaleas is every shop under the sun (and a few left perennially in the fog). The entire mall is a study in urban landscaping and planning, beautifully executed.

Like many California college towns, Santa Cruz supports its share of lost souls. Along the Pacific Avenue strip looms the darker side of the playground. The burnouts congregating here are like kids left entangled in the monkey bars long after the others have gone home. They are the people who flunked the electric-kool-aid-acid test, drop-outs from the psychedelic revolution with minds in a cosmic web and bodies here on earth.

Walking distance from the mall are several places that merit short visits. The **Octagon** (118 Cooper Street) dates back over a century and houses the Santa Cruz County Historical Museum within its eight brick walls; **Santa Cruz Mission** (126 High Street; 408-426-5686), a reduced-scale replica of the 1793 structure, pales by comparison with the missions in Carmel and San Juan Bautista; the **Art Museum of Santa Cruz County** (224 Church Street; 408-429-3420) features permanent and rotating exhibits of traditional and modern art.

The nearby Chamber of Commerce (105 Cooper Street; 408-423-1111) is a helpful information center; among the brochures available here is one describing **architectural tours** of the city. Santa Cruz's rich history has left a legacy of elegant Victorian houses. The Chamber of Commerce divides them into four walking tours, each about 20 minutes long. The Beach Hill tour, not far from the Boardwalk, leads past a gem-like home at **1005 Third Street,** counterpoint to the multilevel confection with Queen Anne turret at **311 Main Street.** Near Pacific Garden Mall, the Laurel Area walking tour includes the Civil War-era **Calvary Epsicopal Church** (532 Center Street), with its clapboard siding and shingle roof, and the **200 block of Walnut Avenue,** which is practically wall-to-wall Victorians. Another tour goes several blocks along **Ocean View Avenue** past a series of stately 19th-century mansions. The Mission Hill tour, near the Santa Cruz Mission, begins at the white-painted brick **Holy Cross Roman Catholic Church** (126 High Street). The steeple of this 1889 Gothic Revival beauty is a landmark for miles around. Nearby **Francisco Alviza House** (109 Sylvar Steet), vintage 1850s, is the oldest home in town. Around the corner, the **200 block of Mission Street** displays several houses built shortly afterwards; the nearby **W. W. Reynolds House** (123 Green Street) was an Episcopal Church in 1850.

SANTA CRUZ CAMPUS

From this last Victorian cluster, High Street leads to the **University of California Santa Cruz** campus (408-429-0111). Turn right at Glenn Coolidge Drive and you'll find an information booth dispensing maps, brochures, and words of wisdom. Those stone ruins and sunbleached buildings nearby are the remains of the old Cowell ranch and limestone quarry from which the campus' 2000 acres were drawn.

No ivory tower ever enjoyed the view that U.C. Santa Cruz commands of Monterey Bay. Set on a hillside, with redwood forest and range land all around, the campus possesses incredible beauty. The university itself is divided into eight colleges, insular and self-defined, each marked by a different architectural style. Of particular interest are the organic farm which supplies food for the campus, and the arboretum with its Mediterranean garden and outstanding collection of Australian and South African plants. But the best way to see this campus is simply to wander: walk the fields, trek its redwood groves, and explore the different colleges that make it one of the West's most progressive institutions.

SOUTH OF SAN FRANCISCO

North from Santa Cruz, Route 1 streams past bold headlands and magnificent seascapes. There are excellent beaches to explore and marvelous vista points along the way.

Miles of sand dunes border **Año Nuevo State Reserve,** an enchanting park containing an offshore island where three-ton elephant seals breed in winter. With its tidepools, exotic bird population, sea lions, and harbor seals, the reserve is a natural playground. The Ohlone Indians highly valued the region for its abundant fish and shellfish population. It was here they experienced their first contact with whites in 1769 when Juan Gaspar de Portola trekked through en route to his discovery of San Francisco Bay. (For further information on this area, see the "Beaches and Parks" section in this chapter.)

Further north rises **Pigeon Point Lighthouse,** a 115-foot sentinel that's one of the nation's tallest lighthouses. The point gained a nasty reputation during the 19th century when one ship after another smashed on the rocks. The lighthouse went up in 1871, and originally contained a 1000-piece lens. Doubling as a youth hostel, it now warns sailors while welcoming travelers.

Pescadero represents a timeworn town hidden a short way from Route 1. It's a woodframe hamlet of front-porch rocking chairs and white steeple churches. The name translates as "fisherman," but the Portuguese and Italian residents are farmers, planting artichokes, Brussels sprouts, beans, and lettuce in the patchwork fields surrounding the town.

Also a short distance from the highway, you'll encounter **San Gregorio,** another weather-beaten little town. Once a resort area, today it reveals a quaint collection of sagging roofs and unpainted barns. Be sure to drop by **Peterson and Alsford General Merchandise,** a classic general store that's been around almost a century.

Half Moon Bay is what happens when the farm meets the sea. It's a hybrid town, half landlubber and half old-salt. They are as likely to sell artichokes here as fresh fish. The town was named for its crescent beach, but thinks of itself as the pumpkin capital of the world. At times the furrowed fields seem a geometric continuation of ocean waves, as if the sea lapped across the land and became frozen there. It is Half Moon Bay's peculiar schizophrenia, a double identity that lends an undeniable flair to the community.

On the southern outskirts of Half Moon Bay, watch for **Higgins Purisima Road** (★), a country lane that curves for eight miles into the

Santa Cruz Mountains, returning to Route 1. This scenic loop passes old farmhouses and sloping pastures, redwood-forested hills and mountain meadows. Immediately upon entering this bumpy road, you'll spy a stately old New England-style house set in a plowed field. That will be the **James Johnston House,** a saltbox structure with sloping roof and white clapboard facade. Dating back to 1853 and built by an original 49er, it is the oldest house along this section of coastline.

In Moss Beach a four-mile-long white-sand beach is backdropped by neatly tilled farmlands. Near the village of Montara, you'll pass an old lighthouse whose utility buildings have been converted to a youth hostel.

This placid landscape soon gives way to some of California's most unpredictable countryside. As the road rises above a swirling coastline you'll be entering a geologic hotspot. The San Andreas fault, villain of the 1906 earthquake, heads back into shore near Pacifica. As the road cuts will reveal, the sedimentary rock along this area has been twisted and warped into bizarre shapes. At **Devil's Slide,** several miles south of Pacifica, unstable hillsides periodically collapse into the sea.

Now that I have totally terrified you, I should add that this is an area not to be missed. Drive carefully and you'll be safe to enjoy the outstanding ocean vistas revealed at every hairpin turn in this winding roadway. Rocky cliffs, pocket beaches, and erupting surf open to view There are sea stacks offshore and, in winter, gray whales cruise the coast.

The road north to San Francisco leads through one of America's ugliest towns. In fact, **Daly City** is the perfect counterpoint to the bay city: it is as hideous as San Francisco is splendid. If Tony Bennett left his heart in San Francisco, he must have discarded a gall bladder in Daly City. This town was memorialized in Malvina Reynold's song, "Little Boxes," which describes its "ticky tacky" houses and over-developed hillsides.

Shopping

BIG SUR AND MONTEREY AREA SHOPPING

Set in a circular wooden structure resembling an oversized wine cask is one of Big Sur's best known art centers. The **Coast Gallery** (Route 1, Big Sur; 408-667-2301) is justifiably famous for its displays of arts and crafts by local artists. There are lithographs by novelist Henry Miller as well as paintings, sculptures, ceramics, woodwork, and blown glass by Northern California craftspeople. An adjoining shop features a wide selection of Miller's books.

In Monterey, there are stores throughout the downtown area and malls galore over on **Cannery Row.** Every year another shopping complex seems to rise along the Row. Already the area features cheese and wine stores, clothiers, antique shops, a fudge factory, and a gourmet supply store. There's also a collector's comic book store, the inevitable T-shirt shop, knickknack stores, and galleries selling artworks that are like Muzak on canvas.

The main area for window browsing in Pacific Grove can be found along Lighthouse Avenue. Just above this busy thoroughfare, on 17th Street, artisans have renovated a row of small beach cottages. In each is a creatively named shop. There's **Reincarnation Antique Clothing** (214 17th Street) selling used clothing and old knickknacks, **The Two of Us** (230 17th Street) with antiques, and **Past and Presents** (226 17th Street), which features knickknacks and antiques.

In Carmel, shopping seems to be the raison d'être. If ever an entire town was dressed to look like a boutique, this is the one. Its shops are stylish and expensive.

The major shopping strip is along Ocean Avenue between Mission and Monte Verde streets, but the best stores generally are situated on the side streets. The **Doud Craft Studios** (San Carlos between Ocean and 7th avenues) is a mall featuring artisan shops. Here you'll find leather merchants, potters, jewelers, a metalsmith, and woodworker.

Most of the artists who made Carmel famous have long since departed, but the city still maintains a wealth of art galleries. While many are not even worth browsing, others are outstanding. The **Carmel Bay Gallery** (Lincoln Street between Ocean and 7th avenues) features posters by contemporary artists, while the **Pasquale Ianetti Art Gallery** (Mission Street and 6th Avenue) contains works by the great masters. And the **Carmel Art Association Galleries** (Dolores Street and 6th Avenue), owned and operated by artists, offers paintings and sculpture by local figures.

Carmel is recognized as an international center for photographers. Two of the nation's most famous—Ansel Adams and Edward Weston—lived here. The **Weston Gallery** (6th Avenue near Dolores Street) displays prints by both men. At **Photography West Gallery** (Dolores Street between Ocean and 7th avenues) these photographers are represented, as well as Imogen Cunningham, Henri Cartier-Bresson, and Brett Weston.

Carmel's prettiest shopping plaza is **The Barnyard** (Route 1 and Carmel Valley Road), an innovative mall housing dozens of shops. Set amid flowering gardens is a series of raw wood structures reminiscent of old farm buildings. Browse the boutiques and gift shops, then follow those brick pathways to the **Thunderbird Bookshop & Restaurant** (408-624-1803). With a marvelous collection of hardbacks, paperbacks, and children's books, it is one of the finest bookstores along the Central Coast. Better still, they have an adjoining restaurant.

SANTA CRUZ SHOPPING

The central shopping district in Santa Cruz is along Pacific Garden Mall, a six-block strip of Pacific Avenue converted to a promenade. The section is neatly landscaped with flowering shrubs and potted trees. The sidewalks, widened for window browsers, nevertheless overflow with people.

To see the area, it's best to begin at Cathcart Street, walk up oneside of the outdoor mall, and return along the other. (Numbers listed are street numbers for Pacific Avenue.) Of particular interest is **Pacific Garden Import** (1110) with Asian rugs, handwoven baskets, and colorful wallhangings. **Artisan's Cooperative** (1364) deals in fine handcrafts and gift items by local artists. They feature outstanding pottery, woodwork, glassware, and wall rugs.

Before turning around at Mission Street, walk over to the **Santa Cruz Art Center** (1001 Center Street). Here is more merchandise fashioned by area craftspeople. There are galleries, gift stores, plus arts and crafts shops. Also, many artisans' studios are located at the center, making it a gathering place for craftspeople as well as a clearinghouse for their wares.

Another short jog from Pacific Avenue places you in **Galleria Santa Cruz** (Front and Cooper streets), one of the town's most modern malls. There are three tiers of shops comprising this stucco-and-brick enclave.

Proceeding down the other side of Pacific, you'll immediately happen upon **Bookshop Santa Cruz** (1547), the finest among this college town's many wonderful bookstores.

Nightlife

Along the Central Coast, night owls roost predominately around Monterey and Santa Cruz. A few local taverns provide diversions along the rural stretches of the coastline, but the main action happens in the tourist-haven-by-the-wharf, Monterey, and the campus-town-by-the-sea, Santa Cruz.

BIG SUR NIGHTLIFE

In Big Sur the lights go out early. There is one place, **River Inn** (Route 1, Big Sur; 408-667-2237), a wood-paneled bar overlooking the Big Sur River, that keeps a candle burning. During the week the bar is open until the wee hours; on weekends a rock band cranks up and draws the locals in for a little action.

MONTEREY AREA NIGHTLIFE

There's live deejay music and disco dancing in downtown Monterey at **Footloose** (180 Franklin Street, Monterey; 408-373-4566). The place draws a teenage crowd. Cover.

The classiest spot around is **The Club** (321-D Alvarado Street, Monterey; 408-646-9244). Entertainment here changes nightly, so it's advisable to check what's on tap. One evening they'll offer comedy, another evening will include rock video, a disc jockey spinning platters, or a band playing Top 40. Once a week The Club spotlights nationally known entertainers. Cover and minimum charges vary from show to show.

There are also several nightspots over by Cannery Row. **Kalisa's** (851 Cannery Row, Monterey; 408-372-8512), a funky club in a building that dates to the Steinbeck era, offers impromptu entertainment nightly.

Doc Rickett's Lab (95 Prescott Avenue, Monterey; 408-649-4241) has dancing to Top-40 rock and country and western bands.

If you'd prefer a quiet corner overlooking the ocean, consider **Mark Thomas Outrigger** (700 Cannery Row, Monterey; 408-372-8543). This watering hole enjoys a plate-glass window on the world.

The Tinnery (631 Ocean View Boulevard, Pacific Grove; 408-646-1040), an attractive complex on the waterfront in Pacific Grove, spotlights local entertainers every night, usually a duo or trio playing contemporary music.

For the warm conviviality of an English pub consider the **Adobe Inn** (Dolores Street and 8th Avenue, Carmel; 408-625-1750). Another restaurant-cum-bar is **The Forge in the Forest** (Junipero Street and 5th Avenue, Carmel; 408-624-2233) with its copper walls, hand-carved bar and open fire.

Possibly the prettiest place you'll ever indulge in the spirits is the **Sunset Lounge** at Highlands Inn (Route 1 about four miles south of Carmel; 408-624-3801). An entire wall of this leather-armchair-and-marble-table establishment is plate glass. And the picture on the other side of those panes is classic Carmel—rocky shoreline fringed with cypress trees and lashed by passionate waves. If that's not entertainment enough, there's a piano bar during the week and dancing to a combo on weekends.

SANTA CRUZ NIGHTLIFE

South of Santa Cruz, several of the restaurant lounges lining Capitola's waterfront provide nightly entertainment. Over at **Edgewater Seafood Grill** (215 Esplanade, Capitola; 408-475-6215) the deejay cranks up the victrola and let's fly with rock and roll dance music. Weekend cover. A few doors down at **Zelda's** (203 Esplanade, Capitola; 408-475-4900) there's live music ranging from salsa to rock nightly.

For mellow piano bar music, try **Shadowbrook Restaurant** (1750 Wharf Road, Capitola; 408-475-1511). Its candlelit ambience and luxurious surroundings create a soft sense of well being, like brandy and a blazing fire.

For rock and roll sounds, folks hereabouts head out to **O. T. Price's Music Hall** (3660 Soquel Drive, Soquel; 408-476-3939) in nearby Soquel. There's dancing to live music every night, though it's on weekends that the place kicks loose. Cover charge.

In Santa Cruz, **The Catalyst** (1011 Pacific Avenue, Santa Cruz; 408-423-1336) is the common denominator. A popular restaurant and hangout by day, it becomes a favored entertainment spot at night. There's live music most weekday evenings in the Atrium, where local groups perform. But on weekends the heavyweights swing into town and The Catalyst lines up big rock performers. Free during the week; cover on weekends.

The Crow's Nest (2218 East Cliff Drive, Santa Cruz; 408-476-4560) offers eclectic entertainment. On a given night they will be headlining a jazz, country and western, or soft rock band. Ocean view; cover.

Further north, there's jazz every Sunday afternoon and classical music on Friday night at the **Bach Dancing and Dynamite Society** (307 Mirada Road, Miramar; 415-726-4143). Situated beachfront off Route 1 about two miles north of the Route 92 intersection, it's renowned for quality sounds.

CHAPTER SEVEN

San Francisco

It is a city poised at the end of the continent, civilization's last fling before the land plunges into the Pacific. Perhaps this is why visitors demand something memorable from San Francisco. People expect the city to resonate along a personal wavelength, speak to them, fulfill some ineffable desire at the center of the soul.

There is a terrible beauty at the edge of America: the dream begins here, or ends. The Golden Gate Bridge, that arching portal to infinite horizons, is also a suicide gangplank for hundreds of ill-starred dreamers. Throughout American history, those who crossed the country in search of destiny ultimately found it here or turned back to the continent and their own past.

Yet San Francisco is only a city, a steel-and-glass metropolis mounted on a series of hills. With a population of about 750,000, it covers 47 square miles at the tip of a peninsula bounded by the Pacific Ocean and San Francisco Bay. An international port and gateway to Asia, San Francisco supports a multicultural population with large concentrations of Chinese, Hispanics, Blacks, Italians, Filipinos, and Japanese. Adding to the cosmopolitan atmosphere is a gay population constituting perhaps 15 percent of the city's residents.

The myth of San Francisco originates not only from its geography, but its history as well. If, as early Christians believed, the world was created in 4004 B.C., then the history of San Francisco began on January 28, 1848. That day a hired hand named James Marshall discovered gold in California. Year One is 1849, a time etched in the psyche of an entire nation. The people swept along by the mania of that momentous time have been known forever since as "49ers." They crossed the Rockies in covered wagons, trekked the jungles of Panama, and challenged the treacherous seas around Cape Horn, all because of a shiny yellow metal.

Gold in California was the quintessence of the American Dream. San Francisco became the center of that dream. The peaceful hamlet

(Text continued on page 330.)

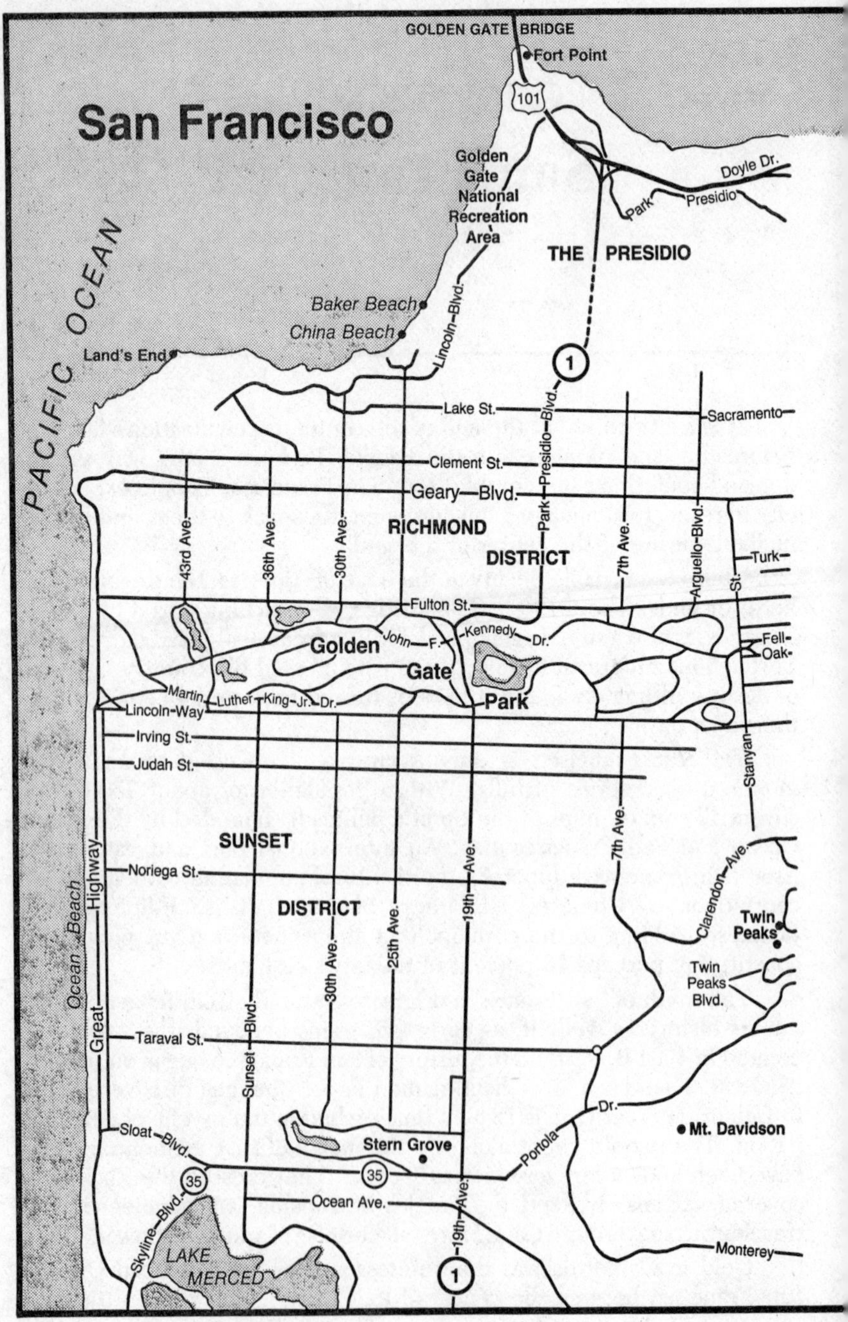
San Francisco
GOLDEN GATE BRIDGE
Fort Point
101
PACIFIC OCEAN
Golden Gate National Recreation Area
THE PRESIDIO
Doyle Dr.
Park
Presidio
Baker Beach
China Beach
Lincoln Blvd.
Land's End
1
Lake St.
Sacramento
Park Presidio Blvd.
Clement St.
Geary Blvd.
RICHMOND
DISTRICT
43rd Ave.
36th Ave.
30th Ave.
7th Ave.
Arguello Blvd.
Turk
St.
Fulton St.
John F. Kennedy Dr.
Fell
Oak
Golden
Gate
Park
Martin Luther King Jr. Dr.
Lincoln Way
Irving St.
Judah St.
Stanyan
SUNSET
DISTRICT
Noriega St.
19th Ave.
25th Ave.
30th Ave.
7th Ave.
Clarendon Ave.
Twin Peaks
Twin Peaks Blvd.
Ocean Beach
Great Highway
Taraval St.
Sunset Blvd.
Portola Dr.
Mt. Davidson
Sloat Blvd.
Stern Grove
35
35
Ocean Ave.
19th Ave.
Skyline Blvd.
LAKE MERCED
1
Monterey

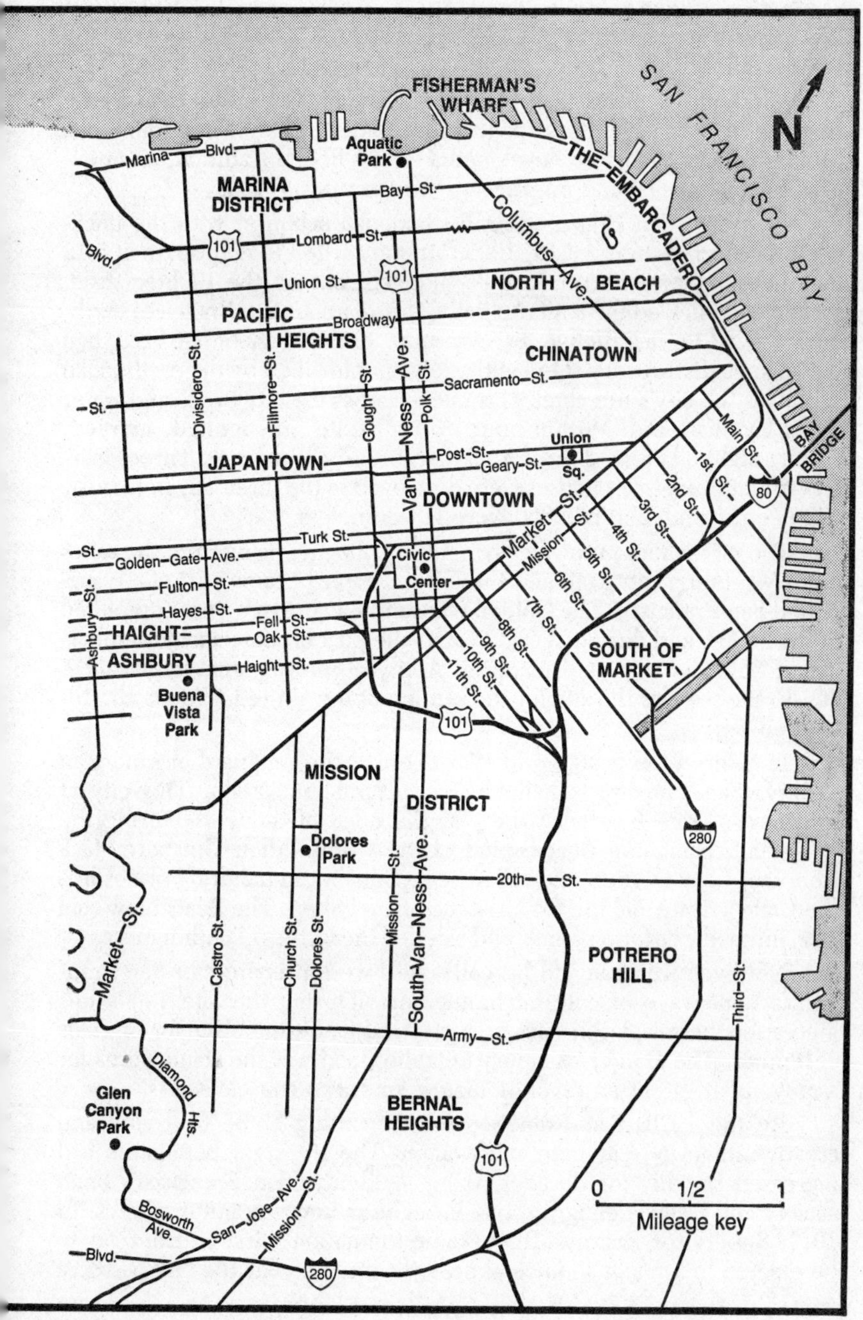

FISHERMAN'S WHARF
Aquatic Park
SAN FRANCISCO BAY
N
THE EMBARCADERO
Marina Blvd.
MARINA DISTRICT
Bay St.
Columbus Ave.
Blvd.
101
Lombard St.
101
Union St.
NORTH BEACH
PACIFIC HEIGHTS
Broadway
CHINATOWN
Divisidero St.
Fillmore St.
Gough St.
Van Ness Ave.
Polk St.
Sacramento St.
St.
Main St.
Union Sq.
BAY BRIDGE
1st St.
JAPANTOWN
Post St.
Geary St.
2nd St.
80
DOWNTOWN
Market St.
3rd St.
Turk St.
St.
Mission St.
4th St.
Golden Gate Ave.
Civic Center
5th St.
Fulton St.
6th St.
Ashbury St.
Hayes St.
7th St.
HAIGHT-
Fell St.
Oak St.
8th St.
ASHBURY
Haight St.
9th St.
10th St.
11th St.
SOUTH OF MARKET
Buena Vista Park
101
MISSION
DISTRICT
Dolores Park
280
20th St.
Market St.
Castro St.
Church St.
Dolores St.
Mission St.
South Van Ness Ave.
POTRERO HILL
Third St.
Army St.
Diamond Hts.
Glen Canyon Park
BERNAL HEIGHTS
101
0
1/2
1
Mileage key
Bosworth Ave.
San Jose Ave.
Mission St.
Blvd.
280

was transmogrified into a hellbent city, a place to make the Wild West look tame. Its population exploded from 900 to 25,000 in two years; by 1890 it numbered 300,000.

Amid all the chaos, San Francisco grew into an international city. Because of its multicultural population, and in spite of periodic racial problems, San Francisco developed a strong liberal tradition, an openness to the unusual and unexpected, which prevails today.

Of course San Francisco's most famous encounter with the unexpected occurred on April 18, 1906. Dream turned to nightmare at 5:12 that morning as a horrendous earthquake, 8.3 on the Richter scale, rocked and buckled the land. Actually, the infamous San Francisco earthquake owed its destructive ferocity more to the subsequent fires than the seismic disturbance. One of the few people killed by the earthquake itself was the city's fire chief. Gas mains across the city broke and water pipes lay shattered. Within hours, 50 separate fires ignited, merged, and by nightfall created firestorms that tore across the city. Three-quarters of San Francisco's houses were destroyed in the three-day holocaust, 452 people died, and 250,000 were left homeless.

The city whose municipal symbol is a phoenix rising from the ashes quickly rebuilt. City Hall and the Civic Center became part of a resurrected San Francisco. The Golden Gate and Bay bridges were completed in the 1930s, and during World War II the port became a major embarkation point for men and materiel. A city of international importance, San Francisco was the site for the signing of the United Nations charter in June 1945.

It entered the post-World War II era at the vanguard of American society. San Francisco's hallmark is cultural innovation. This city at continent's edge boasts a society at the edge of thought. During the 1950s it became the Beat capital of the world. Allen Ginsberg, Jack Kerouac, Gary Snyder, and other Beat poets began haunting places like the Caffe Trieste and the Co-Existence Bagel Shop. The Beats blew cool jazz, intoned free form poems, and extolled the virtues of nothingness.

Not even Kerouac and his colleagues were prepared for San Francisco's next wave of cultural immigrants. During the late 1960s this mecca for the misplaced became a mystical gathering place for myriads of hippies. The Haight–Ashbury neighborhood was the staging area for a movement intent on revolutionizing American consciousness.

By the 1970s San Francisco was becoming home to a vital and creative minority, gay men and women. The city's gay population had increased steadily for decades; then, suddenly, San Francisco's open society and freewheeling lifestyle brought an amazing influx of gays. In 1977, Supervisor Harvey Milk became the nation's first outfront gay to be elected to a major municipal post. That same year the city passed a landmark gay rights ordinance. With an advancing population which today numbers perhaps 100,000, gays became a powerful social and political force.

Throughout the 1980s, San Francisco has retained a gay supervisor whose constituency represents an integral part of the city's life. Today the gay population leads the fight against a terrible AIDS epidemic which has devastated its ranks.

A multicultural society from its early days, San Francisco remains a city at the edge, open to experiment and experience. The city does sometimes seem to contain as many cults as people, but it also boasts more than its share of artists.

There are also problems: during the last few decades, San Francisco's skyline has been Manhattanized, crowded with clusters of dark skyscrapers. At the same time, the city has allowed its port to shrivel. Most cargo ships travel across the Bay to Oakland, while San Francisco's once great waterfront is being converted into gourmet restaurants and chic shopping malls. It is a city in love with itself, trading the mundane business of shipping for the glamorous, profitable tourist industry.

Rudyard Kipling once called the place "a mad city—inhabited for the most part by perfectly insane people." William Saroyan saw it as "a city that invites the heart to come to life. . .an experiment in living." The two thoughts do not contradict: San Francisco is madly beautiful, a marvelous and zany place. Its contribution to the world is its lifestyle.

The people who gravitate here become models—some exemplary, others tragic—for their entire generation. Every decade San Francisco moves further out along the edge, maintaining a tradition for the avant-garde and iconoclastic that dates back to the 49ers. The city is a jigsaw puzzle that will never be completed. Its residents, and those who come to love the place, are parts from that puzzle, pieces which never quite fit, but rather stand out, unique edges exposed, from all the rest.

Easy Living

Transportation

ARRIVAL

The major highways leading into San Francisco are **Route 1**, the picturesque coastal road, **Route 101**, California's main north-south thoroughfare, and **Route 80**, the transcontinental highway that originates on the East Coast.

BY AIR

San Francisco International Airport, better known as SFO, sits 15 miles south of downtown San Francisco off Routes 101 and 280. A major destination from all points of the globe, the airport is always bustling.

Most domestic airlines fly into SFO, including **Alaska Airlines** (800-426-0333), **American Airlines** (800-433-7300), **Braniff Airlines** (800-272-6433), **Continental Airlines** (800-525-0280), **Delta Air Lines** (800-221-1212), **Eastern Airlines** (800-327-8376), **Hawaiian Airlines** (800-367-5320), **Horizon Airlines** (800-547-9308), **Northwest Orient Airlines** (800-225-2525), **Pan American World Airways** (800-221-1111), **Piedmont Airlines** (800-251-5720), **Pacific Southwest Airlines** (800-435-9772), **Southwest Airlines** (415-885-1221), **Trans World Airlines** (800-221-2000), **United Airlines** (800-241-6522), **USAir** (800-428-4322), and **WestAir Airlines** (800-225-9993).

International carriers are also prominent: **Air Canada** (800-422-6232), **British Airways** (800-247-9297), **CAAC** (415-392-2156), **China Airlines** (800-227-5118), **Canadian Airlines International** (800-426-7000), **Japan Airlines** (800-525-3663), **Lufthansa German Airlines** (800-645-3880), **Mexicana Airlines** (800-531-7921), **Philippine Airlines** (800-435-9725), **Qantas Airways** (800-227-4500), **Singapore Airlines** (800-742-3333) and **TACA International Airlines** (800-535-8780) have regular flights into San Francisco's airport.

To travel from the airport to downtown San Francisco, there's a **San Francisco Airporter** (415-877-0345) bus service that runs every 15 to 30 minutes. Or you can catch a **San Mateo County Transit**, or Sam-Trans, bus (415-761-7000) to the Transbay Terminal (425 Mission Street) or transfer in Daly City to **BART** (415-788-2278) transfer points. Taxi and limousine service are also available, or try **Lorrie's Taxi** (415-626-2113), which provides economical door-to-door service.

BY BUS

Both **Greyhound Bus Lines** (415-433-1500) and **Trailways** (415-982-6400) service San Francisco from around the country. The Greyhound terminal is located at 7th and Market streets; Trailways arrives at the Transbay Terminal.

Also consider the **Green Tortoise** (Box 24459, San Francisco, CA 94124; 415-821-0803), a New Age company with a fleet of funky buses. Each is equipped with sleeping platforms allowing travelers to rest as they cross the country. The buses stop at interesting sightseeing points en route. The Green Tortoise, an endangered species from the '60s, travels to and from the East Coast, Seattle, Los Angeles, and elsewhere. It provides a mode of transportation as well as an experience in group living.

BY TRAIN

For those who prefer to travel by rail, **Amtrak** (800-872-7245) offers three trains daily to the Bay Area—the "Coast Starlight," "San Francisco Zephyr," and "San Joaquin." These trains arrive and depart the Oakland train station, with connecting bus service to San Francisco's Transbay Terminal.

CAR RENTALS

The easiest way to explore San Francisco is by foot or public transportation. Driving in San Francisco can be a nightmare. Parking spaces are rare, parking lots expensive. Then there are the hills, which require you to navigate along dizzying inclines while dodging cable cars, trollies, pedestrians, and double-parked vehicles. The streets of San Francisco make Mr. Toad's wild ride look tame. But if you decide to rent a car, most major rental agencies have franchises at the airport. These include **Avis Rent A Car** (415-877-678), **Budget Rent A Car** (415-877-4477), **Dollar Rent A Car** (415-952-6200), **Hertz Rent A Car** (415-877-1600), **National Car Rental** (415-877-4745), as well as **Sears Rent A Car** (415-877-4477).

For less expensive but also less convenient service, try the agencies that are located outside the airport and provide pick-up service: **American International Rent A Car** (415-347-4711), **Flat Rate Rent A Car** (415-583-9232), and **Rent A Wreck** (415-776-8700).

To rent a car in downtown San Francisco, check the yellow pages and shop around. Prices vary significantly.

PUBLIC TRANSPORTATION

San Francisco is a city where public transit works. To get anywhere in the city, call **San Francisco Muni** (415-673-6864) and an operator will direct you to the appropriate mode of public transportation.

Over 70 bus lines travel around, about, and through the city. Trolley buses, street cars, light-rail subways, and cable cars also crisscross San Francisco. Most lines operate daily (with a modified schedule on weekends and holidays). Free transfers allow a 90-minute stopover or connection to another line. Exact fares are required. For complete information on the Muni system, obtain a copy of the "Ride the Muni" map from the Visitors Center (900 Market Street; 415-974-6900) or at local bookstores.

Unlike San Francisco's classic cable cars, the **Bay Area Rapid Transit System** (415-788-2278), or BART, operates streamlined cars that zip beneath city streets. This space-age system travels from Downtown to the Mission District, Glen Park, and Daly City. It also crosses San Francisco Bay to Oakland, Berkeley, and other parts of the East Bay. Trains run every 10 or 20 minutes depending on the time of day.

CABLE CARS

Cable cars, those clanging symbols of San Francisco, are *the* way to see this city of perpendicular hills. The 112-year-old system covers a ten-mile section of downtown San Francisco.

The cable car was invented in 1873 by Andrew Hallidie and works via an underground cable which travels continuously at a speed of nine-and-a-half miles per hour. Three of the system's original twelve lines still operate year-round. The Powell–Mason and Powell–Hyde cars travel from the Downtown district to Fisherman's Wharf; the California Street line runs east to west and passes through Chinatown and Nob Hill.

TAXIS

Taxicabs are plentiful in San Francisco, but flagging them down is a trick—it's best to call by phone. The main companies include **DeSoto Cab Company** (415-673-1414), **Luxor Cabs** (415-282-4141), **Veteran's Cab** (415-552-1300), and **Yellow Cab** (415-626-2345).

BICYCLING

San Francisco is not a city designed for cyclers. Some of the hills are almost too steep to walk and downtown traffic can be gruelling. There are places, however, which are easy to ride and beautiful as well.

Golden Gate Park, the Golden Gate Promenade, and Lake Merced all have excellent bike routes (see the "Sightseeing" section of this chapter for information on attractions in these areas).

Among the city's most dramatic rides is the bicyclists' sidewalk on the Golden Gate Bridge. Or, if you're less adventurous, the Sunset Bikeway begins at Lake Merced Boulevard, then carries through a residential area and past views of the ocean to the Polo Field in Golden Gate Park.

For information and a guide to San Francisco bike routes, contact **CALTRANS** (P.O. Box 3366, Rincon Annex, San Francisco, CA 94119; 415-557-1840).

BIKE RENTALS

To rent a bike in San Francisco, contact **Lincoln Cyclery** (772 Stanyan Street; 415-221-2415), located adjacent to Golden Gate Park, or **Park Avenue Cyclery** (1269 9th Avenue; 415-665-1394).

WALKING TOURS

San Francisco is a city made for walkers. Appropriately, it offers a number of walking tours which explore various neighborhoods and historical spots.

Chinese Heritage Walks, conducted by the Chinese Culture Center (750 Kearny Street; 415-986-1822; fee) reveals the true Chinatown. There is also a **Culinary Walk** which visits markets and herb shops, then stops for lunch in a *dim sum* restaurant.

The **Dashiell Hammett Walking Tour** (537 Jones Street; 415-564-7021; fee) is a three-mile search for the old haunts of the mystery writer and his fictional sleuth, Sam Spade.

Hotels

Variety in hotel accommodations is one thing San Francisco does not lack. The place is chockablock with facilities, ranging from scruffy Tenderloin digs to world-famous hostelries. Everyone from budget traveler to big spender seems to find a niche.

The greatest concentration of hotels occurs in the Downtown area around Union Square. This central location is a good choice if you seek to be in the midst of the action. Those interested in a slower, more subdued atmosphere can check in to one of the city's bed and breakfast inns or a neighborhood hotel. Whichever you choose, it's a good idea to reserve a room well in advance; this is a popular city where space is at a premium.

DOWNTOWN HOTELS

Downtown Budget Hotels: Some of the finest budget accommodations are found at two sister facilities, **Windsor Hotel** (238 Eddy Street; 415-885-0101) and **Olympic Hotel** (140 Mason Street; 415-982-5010), located in the Tenderloin district. The Windsor is a 105-room affair with an attractive lobby and friendly staff. The place is wildly decorated—the room I saw had a checkered rug, flower upholstered chair, and a bed with a patterned spread. Hardly anything matched. But what the heck, the place was clean, pleasant enough, and quite comfy. There were rooms without bath and others with both a bathroom and television. You can expect more of the same at the Olympic Hotel where singles and doubles are available with or without private bath. The rooms here are slightly smaller than at the Windsor. My preference is for the Windsor; in a pinch either will do quite nicely.

To my mind the best hotel bargain of all is found at the **Adelaide Inn** (5 Adelaide Place; 415-885-9658). Billed as "San Francisco's unique European pensione," it is an 18-room, family-operated establishment. There is a small lobby plus a coffee room and kitchen for the guests. The atmosphere is congenial and the room prices are friendly to the pocketbook. Rooms are small, tidy, and plainly furnished; each is equipped with a sink and television; bathrooms are shared. Most important, the inn is located in a prime downtown location, not in the Tenderloin.

Downtown Moderately Priced Hotels: In my opinion the best hotel buys in San Francisco are the middle range accommodations. These usually offer good location, comfortable surroundings, and reasonable service at a cost that does not leave your pocketbook empty. Happily, the city possesses a substantial number of these facilities, the best of which are listed below.

European elegance at low cost: that's what the **Beresford Hotel** (635 Sutter Street; 415-673-9900) has offered its clientele for years. You'll sense a touch of class immediately upon treading the lobby's red carpet and settling into a plump armchair. There's an historical flair about the place, highpointed by the adjoining White Horse Tavern and Restaurant, with its olde England ambience. Upstairs the rooms are outstanding—shag carpets, wooden headboards, original paintings, comfortable furnishings, and a marble-top vanity in the bathroom. All this, just two blocks from Union Square. If you can beat it, let me know how.

The **Beresford Arms** (701 Post Street; 415-673-2600) is a sister hotel to the Beresford in more than name. Featuring a similar antique lobby, the Beresford Arms has gracefully decorated its public area with a crystal chandelier, leather-tooled tables, stuffed armchairs, and an old grandfather clock. Casting that same European aura, rooms often feature mahogany dressers and headboards as well as the expected amenities like wall-to-wall carpeting, tile tubs, and spacious closets. All at the same prices as the Beresford.

For a stay of any length in San Francisco, the **Hotel Mark Twain** (345 Taylor Street; 415-673-2332) is an excellent choice. Named after that incorrigible storyteller whose early writing career began in California, the hotel celebrates Mark Twain with period photos in the lobby. There's also a stylish old Twain Saloon as well as a collection of riverboat memorabilia. Samuel Clemens was born too early to enjoy a rest here, but another great American stayed at the hotel. The Billie Holiday Suite has been furnished in 1940s period pieces and decorated with photos of the legendary blues singer. That facility rents for ultra-deluxe prices, but standard rooms begin in the moderate range. For that, you get a comfortable, neatly furnished room with plush carpeting, radio, color television, and remodeled bathroom.

Downtown Deluxe Hotels: If your wallet is willing, the city's deluxe hotels are waiting. Among them are several that I suggest you consider.

The **Hotel Bedford** (761 Post Street; 415-673-6040) is a European-style hostelry. The lobby here is a fresh, bright place hung with crystal and dotted about with potted plants. Upstairs the private rooms possess an air of artistry with their gallery prints, floral drapes, and white furniture. These brilliantly coordinated accommodations rent for deluxe prices.

Another upscale establishment is the **Hotel Union Square** (114 Powell Street; 415-397-3000). Built early in the century to accommodate visitors to the Panama–Pacific International Exposition, this 120-plus room hotel was refurbished several years ago. Mystery writer Dashiell Hammett and playwright Lillian Hellman, who once frequented the place, might recognize it even today. The lobby still possesses an art deco ambience with its mosaic murals and soft persimmon coloring. The old speakeasy, reputed to have included a secret "chute entrance" from Ellis Street, has become a cabaret. Walls upstairs have been sandblasted to expose original brick and the rooms have been exquisitely decorated in quiet hues and floral prints.

When a travel writer is reduced to writing about a hotel's hallways, the establishment is either problematic or exceptional. Corridors at **The Inn at Union Square** (44 Post Street; 415-397-3510) are fashionably done along their entire length with mirrors and brass wall sconces, and most rooms leading off the halls are equipped with a brass lion-head door knocker. All that brass is a polisher's nightmare, but adds immeasurably to the charm of this pocket hotel. The entire inn numbers only 30 rooms, so intimacy is a primary consideration here. There is a small lobby on each floor where continental breakfast and afternoon tea are served. Rooms are plush and cozy with quilted bedspreads, wooden headboards, and antique Georgian furnishings. In sum, a marvelous establishment, one of the city's finest bed and breakfasts.

Downtown Ultra-Deluxe Hotels: San Francisco is renowned for its world-class hotels, most of which lie concentrated near Union Square or on Nob Hill. Among them are two, one in the theater district off Union Square and the other on the side of Nob Hill, which I think stand out from the rest.

Personalized service and beautiful surroundings are taken for granted at the **Four Seasons Clift Hotel** (495 Geary Street; 415-775-4700). This grand old building, dating to 1916 and rising 17 stories above the city, has a spacious lobby and over 300 rooms. The lobby is a study in marble, redwood paneling, and crystal chandeliers, and the guest accommodations are furnished with select hardwood pieces and finely decorated.

There's a similar emphasis on style and service at the **Stanford Court Hotel** (905 California Street; 415-989-3500). Dating to the same period as the Clift, its hallmark is the *porte cochere,* illuminated through a leaded-glass dome. The 402 guest rooms combine antiques and modern pieces to create a singular effect. There are several restaurants, shops, and lounges, plus and excellent staff. Five stars.

EMBARCADERO HOTELS

San Francisco's waterfront offers one budget hotel, the **Embarcadero YMCA** (166 Embarcadero; 415-392-2191), which represents the most attractive of all the Ys in the city. The lobby is done in tile and the athletic facilities (free to guests) include a sauna, pool, gymnasium, weight room, racquetball court, and sundeck. Rooms in this sprawling facility are quite small and plainly furnished, though they are a step above other YMCAs. All rooms share a bath. Situated near the waterfront, though in a heavily commercial area, the building fronts a freeway, so ask for a room in back.

FISHERMAN'S WHARF HOTELS

Fisherman's Wharf contains more hotels than fishermen. All the facilities here are overpriced and undernourished. I'm only going to mention two, since I think you'll do much better financially and experience San Francisco more fully in a downtown or neighborhood hotel.

The first is **The Wharf Inn** (2601 Mason Street; 415-673-7411), a place best described as nondescript. This 51-room motel is a squat three-story affair with shiny green doors and blue trim. The moderate-size rooms have modern though unimaginative decor. They're carpeted wall-to-wall and feature standard amenities like television, radio, and tile bathroom with stall shower. The ambience is one of naugahyde and simulated wood; the place is clean and bright, offering the same type of facility you could have downtown for moderate cost. Here doubles begin in the deluxe category. This, after all, is Fisherman's Wharf. In an area of pricey hotels, The Wharf Inn has the best rates around.

Sheraton at Fisherman's Wharf (2500 Mason Street; 415-362-5500) offers the best accommodations among the deluxe hotels. Singles at this sprawling 525-room facility begin in the deluxe to ultra-deluxe range. That buys a spacious room tastefully furnished in Sheraton fashion, plus room service and nightly turndown service. The hotel has other alluring features like a brick-paved entranceway, liveried doormen, swimming pool, and attractive gift shops.

NORTH BEACH HOTELS

As a nighttime visit to North Beach will clearly indicate, this neighborhood was not made for sleeping. The "love acts" and encounter parlors along Broadway draw rude, boisterous crowds until the wee hours.

But if noise and neon have a soporific effect upon you, or if you have some bizzare and arcane need to know what sleeping on the old Barbary Coast was like, check out **Hotel Europa** (310 Columbus Avenue; 415-391-5779). The price is certainly right: budget rates for a clean, carpeted room and shared bath.

Or better yet, retreat a little further from Broadway to **Millefiori Inn** (444 Columbus Avenue; 415-433-9111), a subdued bed and breakfast hotel that will cause you quickly to forget the garish side of North Beach. To be safe though, ask for a quiet room in back rather than one along Columbus Avenue. You'll be ushered into one of the hotel's 15 small, cozy rooms. From the porcelain chandeliers to the oak night tables, they have all been decorated with loving care. Each room reflects a unique flower motif and features an antique wardrobe and tile bathroom. The continental breakfast and smiles from the staff are free with the asking price; standard doubles begin at moderate cost, suites run in the deluxe range. Highly recommended.

MARINA DISTRICT HOTELS

"Ours is an attempt to return to the original B & B concept popularized in Britain: a modest room at a practical price." At **Edward II Inn** (3155 Scott Street; 415-921-9776) the proprietors have fully realized their motto. Taking the old Hotel Edward, which provided accommodations for the nearby Panama–Pacific International Exposition of 1915, they transformed it into the 33-room Edward II. In the process they provided an opportunity for guests to enjoy bed and breakfast luxury at boarding house cost (doubles with or without bath price in the moderate range). The room I saw was English in decor and included such features as quilted bedspread and a dresser with beveled mirror; the bathroom was tiled and trimmed in wood. While I highly recommend this facility, I also advise that you ask for a room in back, away from noisy Lombard Street.

Marina Inn Bed and Breakfast (3110 Octavia Street; 415-928-1000) is a perfect example of a lodging place which in any other era would simply be a hotel. It's a four-story Victorian apartment house built in 1924 that has been converted into a 40-room facility. Given the current "B & B" craze, the owners chose to serve a continental breakfast, provide afternoon sherry, and call it a bed and breakfast. Despite its location on Lombard Street, the inn has great appeal. The rooms are decorated in American country style with pine furniture, poster beds, and patterned wallpaper; many feature bay windows and all of them (returning to the hotel theme) have televisions and telephones. Moderate.

Among the many motels lining Lombard Street, only the **Marina Motel** (2576 Lombard Street; 415-921-9406) seems to possess character; others are part of the mondo condo world. The Marina is located near a noisy thoroughfare, but most rooms are set back off the street. This 45-unit motel resembles a white adobe structure with the rooms surrounding a courtyard. Accommodations run in the budget category and are clean and tidy, though rather drab in decor.

SAN FRANCISCO'S OUTBACK HOTELS

Say the word "hostel" and the first pictures to come to mind are spartan accommodations and shabby surroundings. At **San Francisco International Hostel** (Fort Mason, Building 240, Bay and Franklin streets; 415-771-7277) that simply is not the case. Set in Fort Mason, an old military base that is now part of a magnificent national park, the hostel overlooks San Francisco Bay. In addition to eye-boggling views, the facility is within walking distance of the Marina district and Fisherman's Wharf. The hostel itself is contained in a Civil War-era barracks and features a living room, kitchen, and laundry. The rooms, carpeted and quite clean, are dorm-style with two to five bunk beds in each. The catch to this otherwise excellent accommodation is that you can't use your room or the hostel between 10 a.m. and 4:30 p.m. Open to men, women, and children. Children half price. Budget.

If you're seeking a hotel near the ocean, removed from the hubbub of downtown San Francisco, consider **Seal Rock Inn** (545 Point Lobos Avenue; 415-752-8000). Perched on a bluff overlooking the Pacific, it's located just outside the Golden Gate National Recreation Area, a stone-skip away from Ocean Beach and Golden Gate Park. This 27-room facility is reasonably priced, with rooms tabbed in the moderate range. The accommodations are very spacious, easily sleeping four people. Furnishings and decor are unimaginative but quite comfortable; the rooms are carpeted wall-to-wall and equipped with televisions and telephones. Also, a godsend in this region of frequent fog, some rooms have fireplaces. These are a little extra, as are rooms featuring mini-kitchenettes and ocean views.

Restaurants

San Francisco is a gourmet's city. The place sports about 2500 restaurants ranging from hot dog counters to world-class establishments. Touring these urban dining rooms, we'll start in the Downtown district, describing restaurants in the Tenderloin, near Union Square, and around the Financial District. Then we'll continue to Fisherman's Wharf, Chinatown, North Beach, and finally to the Pacific side of San Francisco. *Bon appetit!*

DOWNTOWN RESTAURANTS

Squid's (96 McAllister Street; 415-861-0100) is the new wave answer to dining. The art deco interior, done in pink and black, is dotted about with expressionistic prints. There are neon lights at every booth. The menu, printed in pink, boasts steak, fresh fish, sandwiches, and true to its name, a host of calamari dishes. Worth the plunge, this imaginative restaurant is moderately priced.

What can you say about a cozy restaurant that's always packed with diners? In the case of **Nhu's Vietnamese Cuisine** (581 Eddy Street; 415-474-6487), you can say it passes the ultimate test of ethnic restaurants by attracting ethnics. Not only Vietnamese are drawn to this unassuming cafe; the menu offers something for everyone. There are steamed rice dishes with spicy chicken, Vietnamese pork kebab, or lemon-grass beef, plus beefball soup, sautéed vegetables, imperial rolls, chicken salad, and prawns. All are budget priced.

Whoever coined the slogan "Eat at Joe's" surely had San Francisco in mind. The city sports a dizzying number of restaurants named after the omnipresent Joseph. But down along Taylor Street rests the **Original Joe's** (144 Taylor Street; 415-775-4877). It's one of those cafes where the waiters don tuxes and the prices never compete with the quality of the food. A San Francisco institution for fifty years, Original Joe's features a steak-and-chop menu which also includes Italian and fresh seafood dinners. Open for any meal; moderate.

Whether they are hungry or not, Dashiell Hammett fans always track down **John's Grill** (63 Ellis Street; 415-986-3274). It's the restaurant that detective Sam Spade popped into during a tense scene in *The Maltese Falcon*. Today the wood-paneled walls, adorned with memorabilia and old photos, still breathe of bygone eras. Waiters dress formally, the bartender gossips about local politicians, and the customers sink onto bar stools. The menu features broiler and seafood dishes priced moderately. A touch of nostalgia costs more, pal: that would be one of the chops, baked potato, and sliced tomato platters Spade wolfed down on that fateful day.

Along the waterfront south of the Bay Bridge, where longshoremen work aboard tankers and freighters, you'll come upon **Mission Rock Resort** (817 China Basin; 415-621-5538). A blue-collar restaurant with a deck overlooking the harbor, it's open for breakfast, lunch, and Sunday brunch. The snack bar cooks burgers and dogs while the restaurant upstairs has an assortment of seafood dishes. Funky but dependable; budget.

The spot in San Francisco for Sunday brunch is **Lehr's Greenhouse** (740 Sutter Street; 415-474-6478). First of all, there's the decor—a combination of California and Hawaii, with ferns, spider plants, and other botanical wonders hanging everywhere. Then there are the tables, laden with smoked cod, lox, pickled herring, caviar, fresh fruit, egg dishes, crepes, sausages, roast chicken, and on, and on. This tropical wonderland has a lunch menu including crepes, Hawaiian chicken, shrimp creole, and steak, and a dinner menu with fish and meat dishes. The price tag on this bountiful spread is moderate.

Carlos Goldstein's Tijuana Taco Stand (52 Belden Place; 415-781-9171) provides a welcome relief to the formal air of the Financial District.

This freewheeling restaurant offers almost everything—take-out food, alfresco dining, a bar, and a canvas-roofed dining room. The interior features Mexican memorabilia; reward posters and Pancho Villa portraits decorate the walls. The cuisine is Jalisco-style and includes *flautas*, enchiladas, burritos, tostadas, and egg dishes. A great spot for carousing, it's moderately priced.

Tadich Grill (240 California Street; 415-391-2373) means wood-paneled walls, tile floor, and art deco light fixtures. It also means a counter running the length of the grill, white-linen-covered tables, and wooden booths. The history of the place is so rich it consumes the first page of the menu. It all began during that gilded year, 1849, and has continued as a businessperson's restaurant in the heart of the Financial District. A new menu is printed daily, though on any given day, lunch and dinner remain the same. The specialty is seafood (sole, salmon, snapper, swordfish, shrimp, and scallops), but charcoal-broiled steak, chops, and chicken are also available. Proud in tradition and cuisine, this San Francisco institution remains topflight all the way. Moderate to deluxe in price.

San Francisco's modern version of camp is **Fog City Diner** (1300 Battery Street; 415-982-2000). It is the most upscale diner you've ever seen. Check out the exterior with its art deco curves, neon lights, and checkerboard tile. Then step into a wood and brass paneled restaurant that has the feel of a club car on the Orient Express. Featuring California cuisine, the menu changes seasonally, though on a given day it will be the same for both lunch and dinner. The season I was there they were offering "small plates" of garlic custard with mushrooms, *quesadilla* with hazelnuts, crabcakes, and sweetbread fritters. The "large plates" included dry-aged New York steak, grilled sausages and polenta, grilled poussin, lamb chops with mint pesto, and calf's liver. Everything is a la carte, including the "housemade ketchup" and Fog City T-shirts. What can I tell you except to book a reservation well in advance; no breakfast; moderate to deluxe.

Across the street at **Samantha's** (1265 Battery Street; 415-986-0100) you can dine on Southern cuisine. Fronting the fountain at Levi Plaza, this fashionable spot offers private dark-wood booths and upholstered banquettes. The lunch and dinner menus range from Creole cassoulet with duck, blackened filet mignon, and spicy Mississippi catfish to "drunken shrimp" (cooked in beer), bourbon glazed porkchops, and eggplant stuffed with shrimp. All this at a moderate tab. No breakfast.

Have lunch during the week at **Square One** (190 Pacific Street; 415-788-1110) and you'll mix with business people from the nearby Financial District. In the evening the crowd is more varied. One constant is the menu; while it changes daily, there's little difference on a particular day between lunch and dinner. The cuisine is international, with an

SAN FRANSISCO

DINER

SEARS FINE FOODS

439 POWELL

BETWEEN SUTTER &

POST

462739

Telephone:

---

you are applying, this post is
of the Rehabilitation of Offenders
75. Applicants are, therefore,
nvictions which for other purposes

r, if you are in doubt as to the
queries on a separate sheet which

emphasis on Mediterranean dishes: *fusilli* with *pancetta*, chicken in Moroccan marinade. Pork in clam sauce, baked sea bass with tomatoes and cream, just your average everyday gourmet cuisine. The focus is on fresh food, including pasta, mustard, mayonnaise, ice cream, and baked bread, all prepared on the premises. No breakfast; deluxe.

Speaking of high-priced dining places, San Francisco offers several European-style gourmet restaurants. Most are located in major hotels and feature exquisite surroundings as well as fine cuisine. Others are dotted about town in small, intimate locales. The tab at these exclusive addresses is in the ultra-deluxe range. Dishes are often a la carte, and a full-course dinner prices in the stratosphere. Two of the very best are listed below. Remember, they serve dinner only, require guests to be well-dressed, and recommend advance reservations.

Donatello (501 Post Street; 415-441-7182) has written the final word on fine Italian cuisine. An intimate restaurant with two small dining areas and a marble bar, it specializes in regional dishes from Northern Italy. The menu, which is continuously being transformed, might begin with sautéed mushrooms or ravioli stuffed with lobster and scallops, then shift during the main course to salmon in black olive sauce, filet of beef with three different peppers, and quail stuffed with bacon and sausage. The real allure is the fixed-price dinner, which includes four courses, each served with a different Italian wine.

Another small and romantic dining room, **Masa's** (648 Bush Street; 415-989-7154), is my favorite San Francisco restaurant. Elite yet understated, the decor is a mix of brass sconces, potted plants, caneback chairs, and dark trim. What makes Masa's famous, however, is not the dining room but the kitchen. Changing daily, the contemporary French menu might include sweetbreads in crayfish sauce, lamb with green peppercorns, veal *medaillons* garnished with wild mushrooms, lobster with shrimp quenelles, and breast of muscovy duck. There are soufflés, sorbets, and mousses for dessert. But inventorying the menu can never do justice to this splendid place. You have to experience it yourself.

FISHERMAN'S WHARF RESTAURANTS

Dining at Fisherman's Wharf usually means spending money at Fisherman's Wharf. The neighborhood's restaurants are overpriced and over-touristed. If you look hard enough, however, it's possible to find a good meal at a fair price in a fashionable restaurant. Of course, the easiest way to dine is right on the street, at one of the **seafood cocktail stands** along Jefferson Street. An old wharf tradition, these curbside vendors began years ago feeding bay fishermen. Today they provide visitors an opportunity to sample local catches like crab, shrimp, and calamari.

Another San Francisco favorite, sourdough bread, can be tasted at **Boudin Bakery** (156 Jefferson Street; 415-928-1849). A pungent French bread particularly popular in seafood restaurants, sourdough is the staff of life in these parts. Boudin Bakery, founded in 1849, has had plenty of time to fit its recipe perfectly to the local palate.

Situated between the Wharf and North Beach, **Cafe Francisco** (2161 Powell Street; 415-397-8010) enjoys the best of both worlds—it's strolling distance from the water and possesses a bohemian flair. A great place for light and inexpensive meals, this trendy cafe serves salads and sandwiches for lunch. Breakfast at the espresso bar ranges from a continental repast to bacon and eggs. Decorated with gallery prints, it attracts a local crowd.

The **Eagle Cafe** (Pier 39; 415-433-3689) is another old-timer. It's so much a part of San Francisco that plans to tear the place down a few years ago occasioned a public outcry. Instead of flattening the old wood-frame building, they lifted it—lock, stock, and memories—and moved it to the second floor of the Pier 39 shopping mall. Today it looks like an ostrich at a beauty pageant, a plain cafe surrounded by glittering tourist shops. It's also one of the only reasons I'd bother visiting Pier 39. Unlike its fashionable neighbors, the Eagle has soul. The walls are covered with faded black-and-white photographs, Eagle baseball caps, and other memorabilia. Actually, the bar is more popular than the restaurant. Who wants to eat when they can drink to old San Francisco? The bar is open all day and into the night, while the restaurant serves only breakfast and lunch. All-American cuisine, budget-priced.

Would you believe a hidden restaurant in tourist-mobbed Fisherman's Wharf? **Scoma's** (Pier 47 near the foot of Jones Street; 415-771-4383) is the place. Seafood is the password to this chummy restaurant. There's *cioppino alla pescatore*, a Sicilian-style broth; *calamone alla anna*, squid prepared "in a totally different manner;" or just plain old sole, snapper, shrimp, or scallops. There's lobster tail, too, and Dungeness crab. Lunch or dinner features the same menu with prices swimming in moderate waters. For the sights, sounds, and seafood of the San Francisco waterfront, Scoma's is the catch of the day.

For spicy food from the subcontinent, everyone's choice is **Gaylord India Restaurant** (900 North Point Street; 415-771-8822). From its corner roost in Ghirardelli Square, this fashionable dining emporium enjoys a startling view of San Francisco Bay. It also hosts an extensive menu that varies from Tandoori chicken and spiced lamb to meatless entrees such as eggplant baked in a clay oven, creamed lentils, or spiced cauliflower and potatoes. With its unusual artwork, Asian statuary, and potted plants, Gaylord creates a warm ambience into which it introduces a deliciously tangy cuisine. Open for lunch and dinner; priced moderately.

El Tapatio (475 Francisco Street; 415-981-3018) evokes old Mexico. The high-ceilinged interior has been decorated with sombreros, serapes, and Spanish murals. The menu features everything from enchiladas and burritos to tostadas and *flautas*. There's a cantina upstairs plus a series of Mexican wallhangings. If that's not enough, the staff exudes goodwill and warmth from south of the border. Moderate.

Il Giglio (545 Francisco Street; 415-441-1040) is a high-heeled hole-in-the-wall, a small but fashionable restaurant serving Italian and American dishes. The interior is pink, as in pink napkins, pink wallpaper, and pink carnations. Add gold leaf mirrors, crystal chandeliers with matching wall sconces, and it seems like there's no place for the eye to rest. Except, of course, the menu: there you can focus on *saltimbocca alla romana*, roast chicken, beef tournedos, sweetbreads, or a New York cut. Evening meals include vegetables, a shrimp dish, *tortellini*, and asparagus; lunch features an abbreviated version of the dinner menu. Excellent cuisine and service; deluxe.

There's a cute row of three-story Victorians near Fisherman's Wharf that houses **El Meson** (1333 Columbus Avenue; 415-928-2279). Serving Spanish cuisine (dinner only), this garden-like dining room is extremely inviting. Surrounded by wrought-iron balconies and Spanish murals, it's illuminated by skylight and decorated with streamers. There are dishes like *calamares rebozados* (breaded squid), *pollo al chilindron* (chicken sautéed with ham, mushrooms, and pimentos), as well as *paella* (a mixed bag of chicken, seafood, shellfish, and vegetables). For food, wine, and *música de España*, El Meson can't be matched; moderate.

CHINATOWN RESTAURANTS

The *New Yorker* once called **Hunan Restaurant** (853 Kearny Street; 415-788-2234) "the best Chinese restaurant in the world." Those are pretty big words, hard to substantiate this side of Peking. But it's certainly one of the best San Francisco has to offer. Understand now, we're talking cuisine, not ambience. The atmosphere at Hunan is characterized by noise and crowds; there are red cushion stools lining the counter and a few bare tables along the wall. But the food will transport you to another land entirely. It's hot, spicy, and delicious. Sit at the counter and you can watch masterful chefs working the woks, preparing pungent sauces, and serving up bean curds with pickled vegetables, Hunan scallops, and a host of other delectables. A cultural and culinary experience well worth the moderate price of admission.

Vegetarians prefer **Lotus Garden** (532 Grant Avenue; 415-397-0707), a lovely restaurant that includes a Taoist temple on its upper floor. With oriental murals and ornamented altars, the temple provides a calming retreat from bustling Chinatown. The restaurant itself is equally mellow. In addition to standard Chinese vegetarian fare, it serves up exotic dishes like sweet corn and snow fungus soup, plus bitter melon with sliced gluten puff.

Among budget restaurants, **Sam Wo** (813 Washington Street; 415-982-0596) is a San Francisco classic. Dining in this jook house is a rare adventure. The entrance is also the kitchen, and the kitchen is just a corridor filled with pots, stovepipes, cooks, and steamy smells. Sam Wo's menu is extensive and the food is quite good for the price.

For luxurious dining in the heart of Chinatown, no place matches the **Empress of China** (838 Grant Avenue; 415-434-1345). Set on the top floor of the China Trade Center, with nothing between you and heaven, it is a culinary temple. Dining rooms are adorned with carved antiques and the waitresses are clad in embroidered silk. Lunch at this roof garden restaurant begins with appetizers like rice wafer shrimps and barbequed quail, then graduates to lichee chicken and Manchurian beef. Dinner is the true extravagance. The menu includes a royal variety of chicken, duck, lamb, shellfish, pork, and beef dishes. There are also unique selections like hundred blossom lamb, prepared with sweet and sour ginger; lobster *see jup* in black bean sauce; and phoenix dragon, a medley of shrimp, chicken, and onions sautéed in wine. Deluxe.

Of course, the ultimate Chinatown experience is to dine *dim sum* style. Rather than choosing from a menu, you select dishes from trundle carts laden with steaming delicacies. A never-ending convoy of waitresses wheels past your table, offering plates piled with won tons, pork tidbits, and Chinese meatballs. It's up to you to create a meal (traditionally breakfast or lunch) from this succession of finger-size morsels.

Many *dim sum* establishments are cavernous restaurants, sparsely decorated like cafeterias. But each has a particular personality and generates warmth from the crowds passing through. Don't be fooled by the neon facades, for an Asian adventure waits within these dining palaces. You should be careful about prices, however: most *dim sum* courses cost only a dollar or two, but it's easy to lose count as you devour dish after dish. Figure that the restaurants noted below will be moderate in price, unless you become a *dim sum* addict.

My favorite *dim sum* restaurant is tucked away in an alley above Grant Avenue. Personalized but unpretentious, **Hang Ah Tea House** (1 Hang Ah Street; 415-982-5686) is a rare find. Enter the foyer, lined on either side with water-stained photos of Miss Chinatown, and it's obvious you've arrived at a singular spot. That old phone booth on your left lacks only one thing—a telephone. Step down to the semi-subterranean dining room with its private booths and mismatched decor. Serving a full Mandarin cuisine as well as *dim sum* portions, it warrants an exploratory mission into the alleys of Chinatown.

Tung Fong (808 Pacific Street; 415-362-7115), one of the city's best *dim sum* dining rooms, is a small restaurant decorated with Asian wallhangings and incongruous chandeliers. In addition to *dim sum* service at lunch and dinner, they offer such standard dishes as chow mein, won tons, and boiled noodles, plus delicacies like spiced duck feet, intestine, and beef tripe. Of special interest are the desserts—water chestnut cake, lotus seed buns, Chinese pickled greens, and coconut juice cake.

NORTH BEACH RESTAURANTS

If a poll were conducted asking San Franciscans their favorite restaurant, **Little Joe's and Baby Joe's** (523 Broadway; 415-982-7639) would win forks down. Not only is the food outstanding, it's prepared before your eyes by some of the city's great showmen. Working a row of oversized frying pans, these jugglers rarely touch a spatula. Rather, with a snap of the wrist, they flip sizzling veal, steak, or calamari skyward, then nonchalantly catch it on the way down. Open for lunch and dinner, this moderately priced restaurant also serves delicious lamb, roast chicken, and sausage dishes, each accompanied by pasta and fried vegetables. Very crowded, especially on weekends.

The best pizza in town is served at **Tommaso's Neapolitan Restaurant** (1042 Kearny Street; 415-398-9696) where the chefs bake in an oak-fired oven. The creations they prepare have resulted in this tiny restaurant being written up in national magazines. As soon as you walk in you'll realize it's the food, not the surroundings, that draws the attention. Entering the place is like stepping down into a grotto. The walls are lined with booths and covered by murals; it's dark, steamy, and filled with inviting smells. Filmmaker Francis Ford Coppola drops by occasionally, as should every pizza and pasta lover. Moderate.

At least once during a North Beach visit, you should dine at a family-style Italian restaurant. Dotted all around the neighborhood, these moderately priced establishments have a local flavor unmatched by the area's chic new restaurants. A good choice is **Capp's Corner** (1600 Powell Street; 415-989-2589), a local landmark adorned with celebrity photos, more celebrity photos, and a few photos of celebrities. The prix-fixé lunch and dinner includes soup, salad, pasta, entree, and dessert—more food than anyone could consume in a day, much less a sitting. Among the entrees are veal, steak, short ribs, lamb shanks, roast beef, and other choices.

If there is any place in San Francisco that elevates dining to the level of high adventure, it is **Caffe Sport** (574 Green Street; 415-981-1251). First, the place introduces itself a block before you arrive; if you're not buried beneath the waves of garlic it wafts along Green Street, you'll be visually assaulted by the garish orange facade. Once inside, you'll discover a baroque nightmare; the place is chockablock with bric-a-brac—faded photos, tacky candelabra, antiques circa 1972, and tables with fishtanks as centerpieces. Besides that, it's hot, steamy, unbeliev-

(Text continued on page 350.)

Clement Street Restaurants

For any city in the country, there's a rule of thumb to good eating: to dine where the locals dine, go where the locals live. In San Francisco that means Clement Street. Paralleling Golden Gate Park and the Presidio and set midway between the two, this friendly street is the center of a multicultural neighborhood. Irish, Russians, Chinese, Japanese, Jews, and others have called the district home for varying periods of time.

The result is a marvelous mix of ethnic restaurants. Stroll Clement Street, from 1st to 12th Avenue or 19th to 26th Avenue, and encounter Italian, Danish, Thai, and Indonesian restaurants. There are Irish bars, French patisseries, bistros, health food stores, open-air vegetable stands, and numerous Asian dining places.

The only difficulty you'll encounter is deciding on a particular place. I have a few suggestions, but if they don't fit your fancy, you'll doubtless find a dozen places that do.

There's an outstanding Vietnamese restaurant just off Clement. **Golden Turtle** (308 5th Avenue; 415-221-5285) might well be the best in the city. With dinners priced painlessly in the moderate range, this cozy eatery specializes in charcoal-broiled marinated beef. Other delicacies include steamed rock cod, Saigon chicken marinated in coconut milk, and a host of appetizer and dessert finger foods. There's a comfortable atmosphere here with potted plants all around and a rose at each table. *Très bien!*

In addition to all the other ethnic groups around Clement, there are the city's Russians. Foremost among their eating places is the **Russian Renaissance Restaurant** (5241 Geary Boulevard; 415-752- 8558), which claims to have "brought to the United States artistic ideas and old world culinary craftsmanship." Among the handcrafted products filling the dinner plate are chicken Kiev, skewered lamb, *shashlik karsky* (marinated rack of

lamb), *podjarka* (milk-fed veal served flambé style), and filet mignon in mushroom wine sauce. For dessert there is *plombir* (Russian ice cream) and baked apples. Moderate.

The next hardest thing to choosing a restaurant on Clement is selecting a Chinese restaurant. One of the very finest is the **Ocean Restaurant** (726 Clement Street; 415-221-3351), an unpretentious family-style establishment. Moderate in price, the Ocean features a catalog-size menu with an array of beef, fowl, seafood, vegetarian, and pork dishes. A great place for fresh oysters and squid, this outstanding eatery also offers less adventurous dishes like roast duck, snow pea beef, or pork spareribs. Among the specialties are delicacies prepared in clay pots.

Take an ornate interior, decorate it with gilded mirrors and bas-relief. Add elaborate chandeliers, place straight-back chairs at the tables, and you have a touch of Spain. That's **Alejandro's** (1840 Clement Street; 415-668-1184). This intriguing restaurant also captures the taste and flavor of Iberia. There's trout prepared with serrano ham, rabbit in peanut sauce, and spiced shellfish. The *carne, pescado, y ave* dishes price near the top of the moderate range, with a few less expensive enchilada plates from Spain's old colony, Mexico. Fiesta time is only in the evening; no lunch served. But those dinners are huge; if there are three in your party, order two meals; there will be plenty left over.

Chandeliers in a hamburger joint? **Bill's Place** (2315 Clement Street; 415-221-5262) ain't just any hamburger joint! Many San Franciscans insist it's a hamburger palace, the best in the city. There's the Dwight Chapin burger (remember Watergate?) with cheese, sprouts, and bacon; the Letterman burger; the Red Skelton burger (garnished like a clown); and so on. If you want to be gauche, you can order a sandwich or hot dog instead. And if you'd rather forego the counter or table service out front, there's an open-air patio in back. Bill's is the place for fast food with a flair. Moderate.

ably crowded, and the waiters are rude. What more can I say, except that you'll love the place. Known for its pasta, this is also *the* spot for Italian-style seafood. They prepare calamari several different ways, and do magical things with lobster, crab, scallops, prawns, and clams. Deluxe.

Why anyone would want to dine in a place frequented by writers is beyond me, but if the spirit moves you, and your stomach agrees, head over to the **Washington Square Bar & Grill** (1707 Powell Street; 415-982-8123). This literary gathering spot is often elbow-to-elbow with such questionable characters as local novelists, newspaper reporters, and aspiring word merchants. They come to gossip and to engage in that vaunted avocation of scribblers everywhere, the imbibing of spirits. Occasionally they wander from the brass-rail bar to the dining area, where the lunch and dinner menu changes daily. The focus here is on pasta, veal, and seafood dishes and the price tab fits a deluxe budget. It's actually an excellent restaurant, and an even better place to drink.

For traditional Basque cuisine, consider **Des Alpes Restaurant** (732 Broadway; 415-391-4249). An oilcloth restaurant with a small bar out front, it serves full-course dinners at moderate prices. Selections are limited to a few entrees each night, so call ahead for the day's menu. On a typical evening, they'll be serving chicken with rice, roast lamb, sliced beef, or roast pork; dinner also includes soup, salad, coffee, and dessert. A good spot for a family-style meal.

The **Shadows Restaurant** (1349 Montgomery Street; 415-982-5536) is a high-heeled French restaurant perched atop Telegraph Hill. Claiming to be "a very famous restaurant since 1932," it's set in a cozy brick building above North Beach. The bay views are well worth the price of admission and the continental dinners are outstanding. Choose from a dozen selections including breast of duck, beef tournedos, veal *medaillons*, coquilles St. Jacques, steamed red fish, saddle of lamb, and filet of sole. There is a stunning decor highlighted by glass light fixtures, antiqued chairs, and pink tablecloths. Dinner only; deluxe.

The heart of North Beach beats in its cafes. Gathering places for local Italians, the neighborhood's coffee houses are also literary scenes. Step into any of the numerous cafes dotting the district and you're liable to hear an elderly Italian singing opera or see an aspiring writer with notebook in one hand and espresso cup in the other.

The best North Beach breakfasts are the continental-style meals served in these cafes. But any time of day or night, you can order a croissant and cappucchino, lean back, and take in the human scenery. Foremost among these people-watching posts is **Caffe Trieste** (601 Vallejo Street; 415-392-6739), the old Beatnik rendezvous. Other prime locations include **Caffe Roma** (414 Columbus Avenue; 415-391-8584), **Caffe Puccini** (411 Columbus Avenue; 415-989-7033), and the **Bohemian Cigar Store** (566 Columbus Avenue; 415-362-0536).

MARINA DISTRICT RESTAURANTS

Over on Chestnut Street, a few blocks from San Francisco Bay, you'll find **Judy's Restaurant** (2268 Chestnut Street; 415-922-4588). As the local crowds flowing in here everyday attest, it's an excellent dining choice. Judy's is small, intimate, and decorated with wicker lamps, antique furnishings, and potted plants. There's a balcony level where you can enjoy a lunch menu that features sandwiches and specials like sautéed fish and chicken piccata. Judy also offers breakfast and Sunday champagne brunch. No dinner served; moderate.

For inexpensive Asian food, try **Rama Thai** (3242 Scott Street; 415-922-1599). At lunch they feature sautéed vegetables, chicken curry, Bangkok shrimp, or fishball and pork. The dinner menu expands to include fried oysters with bean sprouts, beef in chili sauce, ginger chicken, pork spareribs with beancake, and seafood stew. With wood-paneled walls and paintings depicting Asian scenes, it's a comfortable, moderately priced little place.

In the realm of Japanese restaurants, **Kichihei** (2084 Chestnut Street; 415-929-1670) holds the status of shogun. This traditional dining room offers a sushi bar, Japanese garden, and series of Japanese tables. The cuisine varies from tempura, teriyaki, and *sashimi* to iron-pot dishes like *udonsuki* (a combination of fish, shellfish, vegetables, and chicken served in a bubbling broth); dinner only; moderate.

Comparable in class, but serving Italian food, is **Ristorante Parma** (3314 Steiner Street; 415-567-0500) just a block away. A tiny place with mirror walls and leatherette banquettes, it serves popular Southern European dishes nightly. Offerings range from eggplant scallopine, stuffed veal, and saltimbocca to prawns in garlic and lemon-butter sauce or baked petrale. For dessert the specialty is zabaglione, one of the most evil dishes ever devised; dinner only; moderate.

If it's Eastern European cuisine you're seeking, there's **Vlasta's** (2420 Lombard Street; 415-931-7533), a Czechoslovakian restaurant serving sauerbraten, schnitzel, goulash, and beef stroganoff. Other entrees include veal roast in champagne, stuffed cabbage, sweetbreads, and the house specialty—roast ducking with dumplings and red cabbage. For good food in a warm family environment it's hard to match this Old World establishment; dinner only; moderate.

The all-American eatery hereabouts is **Mel's Drive In** (2165 Lombard Street; 415-921-3039), a classic '50s-style joint with push-button jukeboxes and posters of vintage cars. I don't have to tell you we're talking hamburgers, hot dogs, and chili here. If you're looking for something more substantial, how about meat loaf, fish and chips, or a "ground round plate." And don't forget a side of "lumpy mashed potatoes" or "wet fries" (with gravy). Good luck. Moderate.

One of San Francisco's finest seafood restaurants, **Scott's** (2400 Lombard Street; 415-563-8988) should rank high on your dining itinerary. With an oak-paneled bar, white tablecloths, and softly lit interior, it provides an inviting atmosphere. The food is simply outstanding. You can sample cracked crab, cioppino, poached salmon, fried calamari, or fisherman's stew. At lunch, the regulars include "soup, steamers, and salads," plus fresh fish dishes. Scott's also serves meat entrees, but to order steak here is to miss the point. Deluxe.

San Francisco's most popular vegetarian restaurant is incongruously situated in an old waterfront warehouse. With pipes exposed and a metal superstructure supporting the roof, **Greens at Fort Mason** (Fort Mason, Building A; 415-771-6222) possesses the aura of an airplane hangar. But this outstanding eatery, run by the Zen Center, has been deftly furnished with burlwood tables, and there's a view of the Golden Gate out those warehouse windows. The lunch menu includes vegetable brochettes fired over mesquite charcoal, pita bread stuffed with hummus, grilled *tofu*, soups, and various specials. Dinner menu is a la carte Tuesday through Thursday, pre-set on Friday and Saturday. The menu changes daily: a typical multicourse repast would be *fugasse* with red onions, Tunisian salad, eggplant soup, Gruyère tart, lettuce salad, tea, and dessert. Deluxe in price.

SAN FRANCISCO'S OUTBACK RESTAURANTS

Try as you might to escape the trodden paths, some places in the world are simply inevitable. Such a one is the Cliff House, an historic structure at the edge of the sea which is positively inundated with tourists. Since there's little else out on the city's ocean side, you'll have to consider one of the three restaurants here. Downstairs at the **Seafood & Beverage Co.** (1090 Point Lobos Avenue; 415-386-3330) you'll find a trim restaurant overlooking Seal Rocks and serving lunches and dinners of steak, poultry, and seafood; also Sunday brunch; moderate. **Upstairs At The Cliff House** (415-387-5847) offers the same view in a cafe setting. The breakfast and lunch menu boasts 45 kinds of omelettes as well as soups and sandwiches. At dinner there are pasta dishes, several seafood selections, and a few chicken or veal entrees. Moderate.

For a tad less expensive meal, head uphill a few steps to **Louis'** (902 Point Lobos Avenue; 415-387-6330), a cliffside cafe that's been family-owned since 1937. Dinner, appropriately, is family-style, served with soup, salad, potatoes, vegetable, coffee, and dessert. Entrees include roast beef, prawns, scallops, and veal cutlet. Breakfast and lunch are similar all-American affairs. Add a postcard view of the Sutro Baths and Seal Rocks and you have one hell of a budget-priced bargain.

The Beach House (4621 Lincoln Way; 415-681-9333) is not really on the water, but once you step into this cozy restaurant ocean views will seem irrelevant anyway. The interior features a comfortable country-style decor with dried wildflower bouquets, decorative dishes, and an antique sideboard. Come prepared to like seafood. The menu is divided into about a dozen categories, all hailing from the ocean. There's sole, snapper, swordfish, calamari, crab, clams, and so on. Moderate.

Out in San Francisco's southwest corner, in Harding Park on the shores of Lake Merced, you'll discover a spiffy budget-priced dining room, **The Boathouse Restaurant** (1 Harding Park Road; 415-681-2727). With pretty views and white table cloths, it offers a lunch and dinner menu of steak, seafood, sandwiches, and salad. The theme here is sports and they take their themes seriously. Waiters wear striped referee shirts, corridor walls are lined with photos of local athletes, and every corner (as in all four) has a television to keep you posted on the latest scores. If you're out here to begin with, its probably to go golfing, boating, hiking, or hang gliding, so the athletic ambience shouldn't bother you. Weekend brunch.

The Great Outdoors

The Sporting Life

FISHING

If you hanker to spend a day deep-sea fishing for rock cod, bass, or salmon, check out **Muni Bait Shop** (North Point and Polk streets; 415-673-9815), **Sport Fishing Center** (561 Prentiss; 415-285-2000), **Miss Farallones** (Fisherman's Wharf; 415-352-5708), or **Quite A Lady** (2331 44th Avenue; 415-821-3838). Bring a lunch and dress warmly.

SAILING

Some of the world's most challenging sailing can be found on San Francisco Bay. To charter boats and captains, contact **Sail Tours of San Francisco** (Pier 39; 415-456-1144), **A Day on the Bay** (San Francisco Marina; 415-922-0227), or **Pacific Marine Yacht Charters** (St. Francis Yacht Harbor; 415-388-3400).

KITE FLYING

San Francisco has been called the "city of kites." Ocean breezes, mild weather, and lots of open space create perfect conditions for kite flying. Nearly every day, brightly colored streamers litter the sky, swooping and soaring. Popular kite-flying spots include the Marina Green, Golden Gate Park's Polo Field, Lake Merced, and Fort Funston. (See the "Sightseeing" section in this chapter for directions.)

Local kite stores sell exotic designs ranging from traditional box kites to tandems, octagons, hexagons, and silk dragons. Try **The Kite Shop** (Ghirardelli Square, 900 North Point Street; 415-673-4559) or **Kitemakers of San Francisco** (Pier 39; 415-956-3181) for your flyer.

HANG GLIDING

If you'd prefer to soar the skies yourself, try hang gliding. For lessons, call **Chandelle Hang Gliding Center** (488 Manor Plaza, Pacifica; 415-359-6800). There are hang gliding sites at Fort Funston (Skyline Boulevard at the far end of Ocean Beach) and Westlake (just south of Fort Funston). If you're not ready to test those wings, you'll find it's fun just watching.

GOLF

For the earthbound, golf can be a heavenly sport in San Francisco. Several courses are worth checking out, including **Glen Eagles International Golf Club** (2100 Sunnyvale Avenue; 415-587-2425), **Golden Gate Park Golf Course** (415-751-8987), a short but tricky nine-hole course, and **Harding Park Golf Course** (Harding Park Road; 415-664-4690), considered to be one of the finest public courses in the country.

ROLLER SKATING

When Sunday rolls around, several hundred folks are apt to don roller skates and careen along the sidewalks and streets of Golden Gate Park. It's great exercise, and a lot of fun to boot. Rentals are available outside the park around Haight and Stanyan streets.

JOGGING

In a city of steep hills, where walking provides more than enough exercise, jogging is nevertheless a favorite pastime. There are actually places to run where the terrain is fairly level and the scenery spectacular. Most popular are the Golden Gate Bridge, the Presidio Highlands, Glen Canyon Park Trail, Ocean Beach, Golden Gate Park, and Angel Island. (See the "Sightseeing" section in this chapter for locations.)

Parcourses, combining aerobic exercises with short jogs, are located at Justin Herman Park (the foot of Market Street near the Ferry Building), Marina Green (along Marina Boulevard near the foot of Fillmore Street), Mountain Lake Park (Lake Street between 8th and Funston avenues), and the Polo Field in Golden Gate Park.

SWIMMING

Although the air temperature remains moderate all year, the ocean and bay around San Francisco stay cold. If you're ready to brave the Arctic current, join the hearty swimmers who make the plunge regularly at Aquatic Park. Many of these brave souls belong to either the **Dolphin Club** (502 Jefferson Street; 415-441-9329) or the **South End Rowing Club**

(500 Jefferson Street; 415-441-9523). Both clubs are open to the public (on alternating days) and provide saunas and showers for a small fee.

Beaches and Parks

For information on the city's beaches and parks, consult the "Sightseeing" section in this chapter, or check the index for listings on specific parks. Of particular interest are Aquatic Park, Buena Vista Park, Golden Gate National Recreation Area, Baker Beach, China Beach, Land's End Beach, Ocean Beach, Fort Funston, Lake Merced-Harding Park, and Golden Gate Park.

Hiking

For information on walking tours in the city, consult the "Transportation" or "Sightseeing" sections in this chapter.

Travelers' Tracks

Sightseeing

There are lessons, the chroniclers tell us, to be learned from history. Take, for instance, San Francisco.

Sir Francis Drake, the great explorer-cum-pirate, sailed past the place in 1579. Obsessed with dreams of gold, he missed the Golden Gate. It was two centuries later that a rival band of Spaniards finally discovered one of the world's most magnificent harbors. For two hundred years, San Francisco lay hidden behind mist and Indian legend.

Today much of the city still remains hidden. Tourists trace a course around the fringes, never discovering the heart. Yet the soul of the place is right here—along the waterfront, amid the vegetable stalls of Chinatown, on the wooden sidewalks of Telegraph Hill.

For the imaginative traveler, sightseeing San Francisco means experiencing traditional tourist spots, then carrying their exploration a step further. It is the added step that will introduce you to native San Francisco.

This is a city fronting an extraordinary bay on one side and open ocean on the other. It's a patchwork city where ethnic neighborhoods—Japanese, Italian, Chinese, Russian, Spanish—spread quilt-like across curving hills. Most important, San Francisco is a walker's city, a compact metropolis where a brief stroll transports you from the markets of Asia to the cafes of Europe.

After you've explored the center of the city, head off to "San Francisco's Outback," a broad green belt looping half-way round the city's circumference. Here the Golden Gate National Recreation Area, the Presidio, and Golden Gate Park provide miles of open space for exploration.

DOWNTOWN

Visit any city in the world and the sightseeing tour will begin in a vital but nebulous area called "Downtown." San Francisco is no different. Here, Downtown is spelled **Union Square** (Geary and Stockton streets), a tree-dotted plot in the heart of the city's hotel and shopping district. Lofty buildings bordering the area house major department stores while the network of surrounding streets features many of the city's poshest shops and plushest hotels.

Union Square's most intriguing role is as San Francisco's free-form entertainment center. On any day you may see a brass band high-stepping through, a school choir singing the world's praises, or a gathering of motley but talented musicians passing the hat for bus fare home. Union Square is a scene—where the rich and powerful come to view the merely talented, where bums sometimes seem as plentiful as pigeons.

Cable cars from the nearby turnaround station at Powell and Market streets clang past en route to Nob Hill and Fisherman's Wharf. So pull up a patch of lawn and watch the world work through its paces, or just browse the Square's hedgerows and flower gardens.

Then you can head off toward the city's high voltage Financial District. Appropriately enough, the route to this pinstriped realm leads down **Maiden Lane**, headiest of the city's high-heeled shopping areas. Back in Barbary Coast days, when San Francisco was a dirty word, this two-block-long alleyway was wall-to-wall with bawdy houses. But today it's been transformed from red light district to ultra chic mall. Of particular interest among the galleries and boutiques lining this pedestrian-only thoroughfare is the building at **140 Maiden Lane**. Designed by Frank Lloyd Wright in 1948, its circular interior stairway and other unique elements foreshadow the motifs he later used for the famous Guggenheim Museum.

CIVIC CENTER

With its bird-whitened statues and gray-columned buildings, the Civic Center is the domain of powerbrokers and political leaders; ironically, its grassy plots and park benches also make it the haunt of the city's derelicts and layabouts. As you pass the reflecting pool and formal gardens, then ascend the steps of **City Hall** (Polk and Grove streets), you'll see how both halves live.

Modeled after the national capitol, this granite and marble edifice sports a dome that is actually higher than the one in Washington. The rotunda is a dizzying sandstone and marble affair encrusted with statuary and encircled by a wrought-iron balcony. French Renaissance in style,

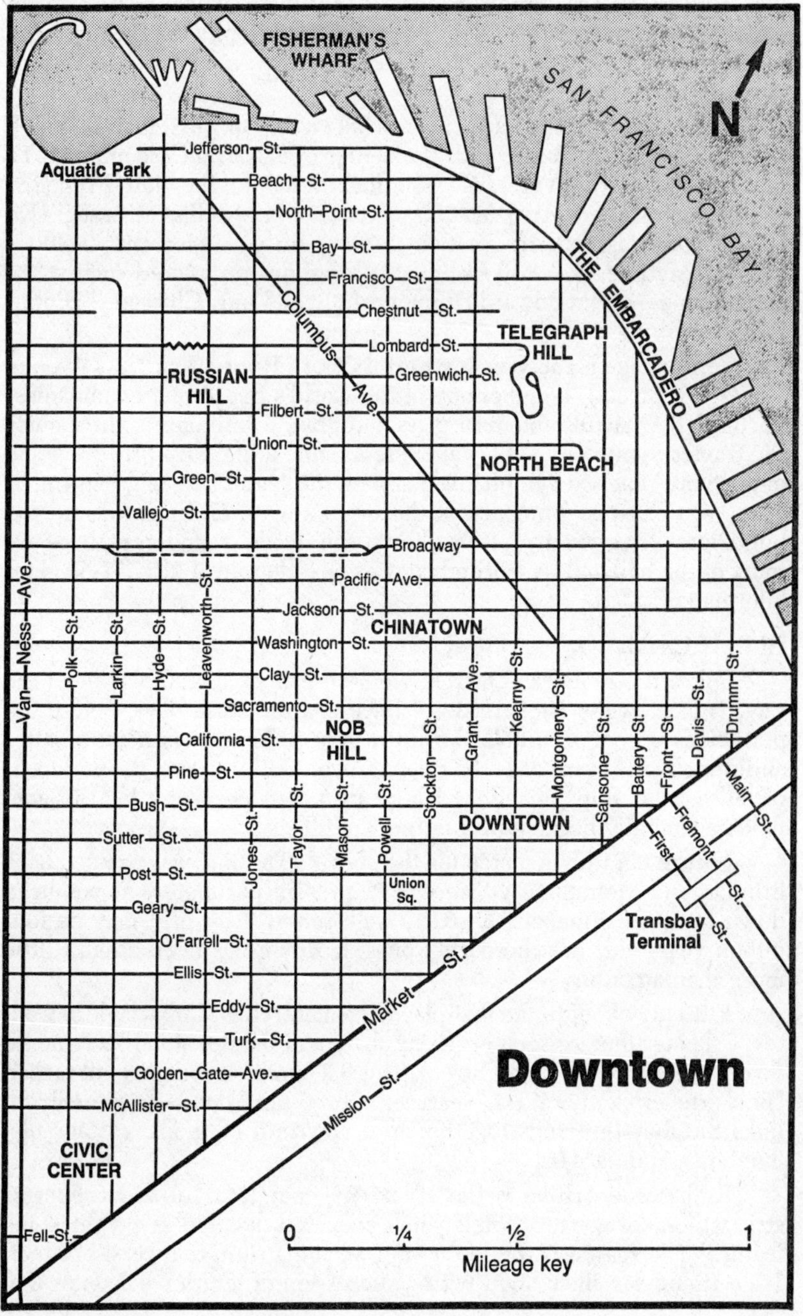
FISHERMAN'S WHARF
SAN FRANCISCO BAY
N
Aquatic Park
THE EMBARCADERO
TELEGRAPH HILL
RUSSIAN HILL
NORTH BEACH
CHINATOWN
NOB HILL
DOWNTOWN
Union Sq.
Transbay Terminal
CIVIC CENTER
Downtown
Jefferson St.
Beach St.
North Point St.
Bay St.
Francisco St.
Chestnut St.
Lombard St.
Greenwich St.
Filbert St.
Union St.
Green St.
Vallejo St.
Broadway
Pacific Ave.
Jackson St.
Washington St.
Clay St.
Sacramento St.
California St.
Pine St.
Bush St.
Sutter St.
Post St.
Geary St.
O'Farrell St.
Ellis St.
Eddy St.
Turk St.
Golden Gate Ave.
McAllister St.
Fell St.
Columbus Ave.
Van Ness Ave.
Polk St.
Larkin St.
Hyde St.
Leavenworth St.
Jones St.
Taylor St.
Mason St.
Powell St.
Stockton St.
Grant Ave.
Kearny St.
Montgomery St.
Sansome St.
Battery St.
Front St.
Davis St.
Drumm St.
Main St.
Fremont St.
First St.
Market St.
Mission St.
0
1/4
1/2
1
Mileage key

City Hall is the centerpiece of the Civic Center, which in turn is the ultimate expression of the "City Beautiful" philosophy that inspired the rebuilders of post-earthquake San Francisco to design one of the country's most splendid civic centers.

As you step out the back of City Hall on to Van Ness Avenue, you'll be standing face to facade with the center of San Francisco culture. To the right rises the Veterans' Building, home to the **San Francisco Museum of Modern Art** (Van Ness Avenue and McAllister Street, 415-863-8800; admission). In addition to a superb collection that includes Picasso, Matisse, and Pollock, the museum has premiered such visual extravaganzas as the Edward Hopper exhibit and Judy Chicago's "Dinner Party" exhibit.

Centerstage is the **War Memorial Opera House** (Van Ness Avenue and Grove Street), home of one of the world's finest opera companies. To the left, that ultramodern glass-and-granite building is the **Louise M. Davies Symphony Hall** (Van Ness Avenue and Grove Street), home of the San Francisco Symphony. Through the semi-circle of green-tinted glass, you can peer into one of the city's newest and most glamorous buildings. Or if you'd prefer to be on the inside gazing out, there are tours of the hall and its cultural cousins next door (call 415-552-8338 for information).

EMBARCADERO

Below the Financial District, where the city's skyscrapers meet the Bay, is located the Embarcadero. Back in Gold Rush days, before the pernicious advent of landfill, the entire area sat beneath fathoms of water and went by the name of Yerba Buena Cove. Matter of fact, the hundreds of tall-masted ships abandoned here by crews deserting for the gold fields eventually became part of the landfill.

Nature is rarely a match for the shovel. The Bay was pressed back from around Montgomery Street to its present perimeter. As you head down from the Financial District, walk softly; the world may be four billion years old, but the earth you're treading has been around little more than a century.

Fittingly enough, the first place encountered is **Embarcadero Center**, a skein of four skyscrapers rising sharp and slender along Sacramento Street to the foot of Market Street. This $300 million complex, oft tagged "Rockerfeller Center West," features a three-tiered pedestrian mall that links the four buildings together in a labyrinth of shops, restaurants, fountains, and gardens.

Embarcadero Five is the **Hyatt Regency** (Market and California streets), one of the few hotels you'll ever find detailed as a sightseeing feature. The reason is the lobby, a towering atrium that rises 170 feet. It's a triangular affair lined with a succession of interior balconies that rise to a skylighted roof. Along one side, plants cascade in a twenty-story hanging garden, while another wall is designed in a zigzag shape which gives the sensation of being inside a pyramid. With fountains and flowering plants all about, glass capsule elevators scaling the walls, tropical birds racketing from their perches, and sunflecks splashing in through the roof, the place surely is a 21st-century pyramid.

Speaking of the future, that blocky complex of cement pipes from which water pours in every direction is not an erector set run amok. It's **Vaillancourt Fountain**, situated smack in the Hyatt's front yard. The patchwork of grass and pavement surrounding is **Justin Herman Plaza**, perfect place for a promenade or picnic. Craft vendors with engraved brass belt buckles, silver jewelry, and beanbag chairs have made the plaza their storefront.

Just across the road, where Market Street encounters the Embarcadero, rises San Francisco's answer to the Statue of Liberty. Or what *was* the city's answer at the turn of the century, when the clock tower of the **Ferry Building** was as well-known a landmark as the Golden Gate Bridge is today. Back then there were no bridges, and 100,000 ferryboat commuters a day poured through the portals of the world's second busiest passenger terminal. Built in 1896, the old landmark is making a comeback. Sleek, jet-powered ferries stream into refashioned slips, and plans are afloat to space age the entire complex with the help of noted architect I. M. Pei.

You might want to walk the ramp that leads up to the **World Trade Center** (Embarcadero at the foot of Market Street) here. It's lined with Covarrubias' murals that were preserved from the 1939 Golden Gate International Exposition. They look like those maps in your old sixth grade social studies book; one vividly depicts "the people of the Pacific" with aborigines sprouting up from the Australian land mass and seraped Indians guarding the South American coast.

Stretching from either side of the Ferry Building are the rows of shipping piers that once made San Francisco a fabulous harbor. Today much of the commerce has sailed across the Bay to the Port of Oakland. To recapture San Francisco's maritime era, head north on Embarcadero from the Ferry Building along the odd-numbered piers. The city looms to your left and the Bay heaves and glistens before you. This is a world of seaweed and fog horns where proverbial old salts still ply their trade. Blunt-nosed tugboats tie up next to rusting relics from Guadalcanal. There are modern jet ferries, displaying the latest aeronautical curves and appearing ready at any moment to depart from the water for open sky. The old, big-girthed ferries have been stripped of barnacles, painted nursery colors, and leased out as office space; they are floating condominiums.

Along this parade of piers you'll see cavernous concrete wharves astir with forklifts and dockhands. Locomotives shunt with a clatter, trucks jockey for an inside post, and container cranes sweep the air. Other piers have fallen into desuetude, rustcaked wharves propped on water-rotted pilings. The only common denominators in this odd arithmetic progression of piers are the seagulls and pelicans whitening the pylons.

Across from Pier 23, **Levi's Plaza** (1155 Battery Street) features a grassy park ideal for picnicking; just beyond Pier 35 there's a waterfront park with a wonderful vantage for spying on the ships that sail the Bay.

Follow the promenade that leads around the Bay side of Pier 39. You'll have a bay window on the waterfront with a vista sweeping from the Golden Gate to Mt. Tamalpais, Alcatraz, Treasure Island, and beyond. **Pier 39** (Embarcadero and Beach Street) itself is an elaborately laid-out shopping mall catering primarily to tourists who spill over from neighboring Fisherman's Wharf. With its carnival atmosphere and overpriced shops, Pier 39 is a perfect prelude to the arena you are about to enter—Fisherman's Wharf.

Nearby Pier 41 is the departure point for the Red and White Fleet (415-546-2810), which sponsors Bay cruises, Alcatraz tours, and ferry service to Angel Island, Sausalito, and Tiburon. The trip to **Alcatraz** is highlighted with a National Park Service tour of the infamous prison. Originally a fort and later a military prison, Alcatraz gained renown as "The Rock" when it became a maximum security prison in 1934. Al Capone, "Machine Gun" Kelly, and Robert "Birdman of Alcatraz" Stroud were among its notorious inmates. On the tour, you'll enter the bowels of the prison, walk the dank corridors, and experience the cage-like cells in which America's most desperate criminals were kept.

The prison closed in 1963; then in 1969 a group of Native Americans occupied the island for almost two years, claiming it as Indian territory. Today Alcatraz is part of the Golden Gate National Recreation Area.

A cruise to **Angel Island** is a different adventure entirely. Unlike "The Rock," this star-shaped island is covered with forest and rolling hills. During previous incarnations it has served as a military installation, quarantine station, immigration center, and prisoner of war camp. Today, the largest island in San Francisco Bay is a lacework of hiking trails and flowering meadows. You can trek six miles around the island or climb to the top for 360° views of the Bay Area. Deer graze throughout the area and there are picnic areas galore. It's a perfect spot for a day in the sun.

FISHERMAN'S WHARF

Places have a way of becoming parodies of themselves—particularly if they possess a personal resonance and beauty or have some unique feature to lend the landscape. People, it seems, have an unquenchable need to change them.

Such is the fate of Fisherman's Wharf. Back in the 19th century, a proud fishing fleet berthed in these waters and the shoreline was a quiltwork of brick factories, metal canning sheds, and woodframe warehouses. Genoese fishermen with rope-muscled arms set out in triangular-sailed *feluccas* that were a joke to the west wind. They had captured the waterfront from the Chinese and would be supplanted in turn by Sicilians. They caught sand dabs, sea bass, rock cod, bay shrimp, king salmon, and Dungeness crab. Salt caked their hands, wind and sun gullied their faces.

Today the woodplanked waterfront named for their occupation is hardly a place for fishermen. It has become "Tourist's Wharf," a bizarre assemblage of shopping malls and penny arcades that make Disneyland look like the real world. The old waterfront is an amusement park with a wax gallery, a Ripley's museum, helicopter rides, and trinket shops. The architecture subscribes to that modern school which makes everything look like what it's not—there's pseudo-Mission, ready-made antique Victorian, and simulated falsefront.

But salt still stirs the air here and fog fingers through the Bay. There are sights to visit along "the Wharf." It's a matter of recapturing the past while avoiding the plastic-coated present. To do that you need to follow a basic law of the sea—hug the shoreline.

From Pier 39 it's a short stroll to Pier 43, where the **Balclutha** (415-982-1886; admission) lies berthed. A three-masted merchant ship built in Scotland in 1866, the *Balclutha* measures 301 feet. This steel-hulled craft sailed around Cape Horn 17 times in her youth. She loaded rice in Rangoon, guano in Callao, and wool in New Zealand. Today the old ship's cargo consists of a below-deck maritime museum and a hold full of memories.

Pier 45 is a working wharf, bleached with bird dung and frequented by fishing boats. From here it's a short jog to the docks on Jefferson Street, between Jones and Taylor streets. The remnants of San Francisco's fishing fleet lies gunnel to gunnel here. The *Nicky-D, Saint Teresa, Lindy Sue, Santa Anna,* and an admiralty of others cast off every morning around 4 a.m. to return in late afternoon. With their brightly painted hulls, Christmas tree rigging, and roughhewn crews, they carry the odor and clamor of the sea.

Fish Alley is another nostalgic nook. Just duck into the narrow corridor next to Castagnola's Restaurant on Jefferson Street and walk out towards Scoma's Restaurant. Those corrugated metal sheds lining the docks are fishpacking operations. The fleet deposits its daily catch here to be processed for delivery to restaurants and markets. This is an area of piers and pilings, hooks and hawsers, flotsam and fish scales, where you pay a price to recapture the past: as you work further into this network of docks, approaching nearer and nearer the old salty truths, you'll also be overwhelmed by the moldering stench of the sea.

For a breather, it's not far to the Hyde Street Pier, where history is less offensive to the nose. Docked along the length of this wharf are the **Historic Ships** (415-556-6435). Part of the National Maritime Museum, they include a wood-hulled, three-masted schooner, *C. A. Thayer*, that once toted lumber along the California coast. You can also board the *Eureka*, an 1890 ferryboat which worked the San Francisco–Tiburon run for almost thirty years. To walk this pier is to stride back to San Francisco's waterfront at the turn of the century. Salt-bitten lifeboats, corroded anchors, and old coal engines are scattered hither-thither. The *Eppleton Hall* is an old paddlewheeler and the *Alma* a "scow schooner" with a flat bottom and square beam.

Together with the nearby **Maritime Museum** (Beach and Polk streets; 415-556-2904), it's enough to make a sailor of you. The museum, in case you mistook it for a ferryboat run aground, is actually an art deco building designed to resemble a ship. Onboard there's a weird collection of body parts from old ships plus a maritime library and a magnificent photo collection.

All these nautical showpieces are anchored in **Aquatic Park**, which sports a lovely lawn that rolls down to one of the Bay's few sandy beaches. A melange of sounds and spectacles, the park has a *bocci* ball court where you'll encounter old Italian men exchanging stories and curiously eyeing the tourists. There are street vendors galore. If that's not enough, you can watch the Powell and Hyde Street cable cars being turned around for their steep climb back up Nob Hill. Or catch an eye-boggling glimpse of San Francisco Bay. Alcatraz lies anchored offshore, backdropped by one of the prettiest panoramas in this part of the world.

CHINATOWN

In appropriately dramatic fashion, you enter Chinatown through an arching gateway bedecked with dragons. Stone lions guard either side of this portal at Grant Avenue and Bush Street.

Climb the steps, proceed up Grant Avenue, and enter the heart of San Francisco's most densely populated neighborhood. Home to 25,000 of the city's 70,000 Chinese, this enclave has been an Asian stronghold since the 1850s.

To stroll the eight-block length of Chinatown's **Grant Avenue** is to walk along San Francisco's oldest street. Today it's an ultramodern thoroughfare lined with Chinese arts and crafts shops, restaurants, and Asian markets. It's also one of the most crowded streets you'll ever squeeze your way through. Immortalized in a song from the musical *Flower Drum Song*, Grant Avenue, San Francisco, California, U.S.A., is a commotion, clatter, a clash of cultures. At any moment, a rickety truck may pull up beside you, heave open its doors, and reveal its contents—a cargo of chinaware, fresh produce, or perhaps flattened pig carcasses. Elderly Chinese men lean along doorways smoking fat cigars, and Chinatown's younger generation sets off down the street clad in designer jeans.

At the corner of California Street, where cable cars clang across Grant Avenue, rises the lovely brick structure of **Old St. Mary's Church.** Dating to 1854, this splendid cathedral was originally built of stone quarried in China. Just across the way in **St. Mary's Square**, there's a statue of the father of the Chinese Republic, Dr. Sun Yat Sen, crafted by San Francisco's foremost sculptor, Beniamino Bufano. You might take a hint from the crowds of businesspeople from the nearby financial center who bring their picnic lunches to this tree-shaded plaza.

Next you'll encounter **Nam Kue School** (755 Sacramento Street). With a red iron fence, golden doors, and pagoda-like facade, it's an architectural beauty ironically backdropped by a glass-and-concrete skyscraper.

As you walk along Grant Avenue, with its swirling roof lines and flashing signs, peek down **Commercial Way.** This curious brick-paved street permits a glimpse into "hidden" Chinatown. Lined with everything from a noodle company to a ginseng shop, this tightly packed street also houses the **Mow Lee Company** (774 Commercial Way), Chinatown's second oldest establishment.

Down another alley adjacent to Grant Avenue, Adler Place, you'll happen upon a hole-in-the-wall museum that will open wide your perspective on Chinatown's history. The **Chinese Historical Society of America** (17 Adler Place; 415-391-1188) graphically presents the history of San Francisco's Chinese population. In the museum you'll find a magnificent collection of photographs and artifacts re-creating the Chinese experience from the days of pig-tailed "coolies" to the recent advent of ethnic consciousness. Small in size but wide in scope, the museum is a two-room treasure house with a helpful and congenial staff.

After you've immersed yourself in Chinese history, head down to **Portsmouth Square** (Kearny and Washington streets) for a lesson in the history of all San Francisco. Formerly the city's central plaza, it was here in 1846 that Yankees first raised the Stars and Stripes. Two years later, the California gold discovery was announced to the world from this square. Rudyard Kipling, Jack London, and Robert Louis Stevenson once wandered the grounds. At one corner of the park you'll find the bronze statue of a galleon celebrating the ocean-going Stevenson. Today this gracious park is a gathering place for old Chinese men playing *mah jongg* and practicing *tai chi.* From the center of the plaza, a walkway arches directly into the **Chinese Cultural Center** (750 Kearny Street; 415-986-1822), with its theater and displays of Asian art.

Now that you've experienced the traditional tour, you might want to explore the hidden heart of Chinatown. First take a stroll along **Stockton Street**, which runs parallel to, and one block above, Grant Avenue. It is here, not along touristy Grant Avenue, that the Chinese shop.

The street vibrates with the crazy commotion of Chinatown. Open stalls tumbling with vegetables cover the sidewalk, and crates of fresh fish are stacked along the curb. Through this maze of merchandise, shoppers press past one another. In store windows hang Peking ducks, and on the counters are displayed pigs' heads and snapping turtles. Rare herbs, healing teas, and chrysanthemum crystals crowd the shelves.

The local community's artwork is displayed in a fantastic **mural** that covers a half-block between Pacific and Jackson streets.

To further explore the interior life of Chinatown, turn down Sacramento Street from Stockton Street, then take a quick left into Hang Ah Street. This is the first in a series of alleyways leading for three blocks from Sacramento Street to Jackson Street. When you get to the end of each block, simply jog over to the next alley.

A universe unto themselves, these **alleyways of Chinatown** (★) are where the secret business of the community goes on, as it has for over a century. Each door is a barrier beyond which you can hear the rattle of *mah jongg* tiles and the sounds of women bent to their tasks in laundries and sewing factories.

Along Hang Ah Street, timeworn buildings are draped with fire escapes and colored with the images of fading signs. As you cross Clay Street, at the end of Hang Ah Street, be sure to press your nose against the glass at **Grand Century Enterprise** (858 Clay Street). Here the ginseng and other precious roots sell for as much as $80 an ounce. A few doors down at **Tin Shung Trading Company** (852 Clay Street) you can purchase dried lizards. According to the lad at the counter, they are pressed on sticks and served with soup.

The next alley, **Spofford Lane**, is a corridor of painted doorways and brick facades humming with the strains of Chinese melodies. It ends at Washington Street where you can zigzag over to **Ross Alley**. This is the home of the **Golden Gate Fortune Cookie Factory** (56 Ross Alley). At this small family establishment you can watch your fortune being made.

The last segment in this intriguing tour will take you back to **Waverly Place**, a two-block stretch leading from Washington Street to Sacramento Street. Readers of Dashiell Hammett's mystery story, "Dead Yellow Women," will recall this spot. It's an enchanting thoroughfare, more alley than street. At first glance, the wrought-iron balconies draped along either side of Waverly evoke images of New Orleans. But not even the French Quarter can boast the beauty contained in those Chinese cornices and pagoda swirl roof lines.

Prize jewel in this architectural crown is **Tin Hou Temple** (125 Waverly Place). Here Buddhists and Taoists worship in a tiny temple overhung with fiery red lanterns. There are statues portraying battlefields and country landscapes; incense smolders from several altars. From the pictures along the wall, Buddha smiles out upon the believers. They in turn gaze down from the balcony onto Chinatown's most magical street.

Just uphill from Chinatown stands the **Cable Car Barn** (1201 Mason Street; 415-474-1887), a brick goliath which houses the city's cable cars. The museum here provides a great opportunity to see how these wood-and-steel masterpieces operate. From the viewing room you can see cars shuttling in and out of the barn. The system's powerhouse, repair, and storage facilities are here, as are the 14-foot diameter sheaves which neatly wind the cable into figure-eight patterns. The museum also has on display three antique cable cars, including the first one ever built.

NORTH BEACH

Introductions to places should be made gradually, so the visitor comes slowly but certainly to know and love the area. In touring North Beach, that is no longer possible, because the logical spot to begin a tour is the corner of Broadway and Montgomery streets, at night when the neon arabesque of Broadway is in full glare.

Broadway, you see, has become San Francisco's answer to Times Square, a tawdry avenue that traffics in sex. Lined bumper to bumper with strip joints, belly dance clubs, transsexual revues, massage parlors, peekaramas, and X, Y, Z-rated theaters, it's a present-day Barbary Coast.

At night, when the neon facades cast a surreal glow across the cityscape, the hawkers swoop down upon unknowing tourists, luring them with a crooked finger and husky bark into topless dives. All this sexual teasing climaxes at Broadway and Columbus Avenue. Nested on the corner is **The Condor**, "where it all began." According to the bronze plaque which the local historic commission (undoubtedly in one of its wilder moments) placed on the building, The Condor is "the birthplace of the world's first topless and bottomless entertainment."

Now that you've dispensed with North Beach's sex scene, your love affair with the neighborhood can begin. Start at **City Lights Bookstore** (261 Columbus Avenue; 415-362-8193). Established in 1953 by poet Lawrence Ferlinghetti, City Lights is the old hangout of the Beat poets. Back in the heady days of the '50s, a host of "angels"—Allen Ginsberg, Jack Kerouac, Gary Snyder, and Neal Cassady among them—haunted its book-lined rooms and creaking staircase. Today the place remains a vital cultural scene and gathering point. Be sure to check out the paintings and old photos as well as the window display. Thirty years after the Beats, the inventory here still represents a who's who in avant-garde literature. **Vesuvio's** bar next door (255 Columbus Avenue; 415-362-3370) was another hallowed Bohemian retreat. Then head up nearby Grant

Avenue to the **Caffe Trieste** (415-392-6739), at the corner of Vallejo Street. With its water-spotted photos and funky espresso bar, the place has changed little since the days when bearded bards discussed cool jazz and Eisenhower politics.

You're on "upper Grant," heart of the old Beat stomping grounds and still a major artery in the city's Italian enclave. Chinatown is at your back now, several blocks behind, but you'll see from the Oriental script adorning many shops that the Asian neighborhood is sprawling into the Italian. Still remaining, however, are the cafes and delicatessens that have lent this area its Mediterranean flair since the Italians moved in during the late 19th-century.

Beyond Filbert Street, as Grant Avenue continues along the side of Telegraph Hill, the shops give way to Italian residences and Victorian houses. When you arrive at Lombard Street, look to your left and you'll see the sinuous reason why Lombard is labeled "The Crookedest Street in the World." Then turn right as Lombard carries you up to the breeze-battered vistas of Telegraph Hill.

Named for the semaphore station located on its height during the 1850s, **Telegraph Hill** was a Bohemian haunt during the 1920s and 1930s. Money moved the artists out; today, this hillside real estate is about the most desirable, and most expensive, in the city.

Poking through the top of Telegraph Hill is the 210-foot-high **Coit Tower** (admission). Built in 1934, this fluted structure was named for Lillie Hitchcock Coit, a bizarre character who chased fire engines and became a fire company mascot during the 1850s. Lillie's love for firemen gave rise to stories that the phallic tower was modeled after a fire hose nozzle. Architectural critics scoff at the notion. Some of the nation's most outstanding **WPA murals** decorate the tower interior. Done as frescoes by New Deal artists, they sensitively depict the lives of California laborers. Upstaging these marvelous artworks is the view from the summit. All San Francisco spreads before you.

Having taken in the view, it's time to weave your way through the hidden crannies of the city. Unlike Coit Tower, there will be no elevator to assist on the way down, but then again there won't be any tourists either.

After exiting Coit Tower, turn right, cross the street, and make your way down the brick-lined staircase. In the middle of San Francisco, with wharves and factories far below, you have just entered a countrified environment. Ferns and ivy riot on either side of the **Greenwich Steps** (★), while vines and conifers climb overhead.

At the bottom of the steps, turn right, walk a short distance along Montgomery Street, then head left down the **Filbert Steps** (★). The art deco apartment house on the corner (1360 Montgomery Street) was featured in one of Humphrey Bogart's great but unheralded movies, *Dark Passage.* Festooned with flowers and sprinkled with baby tears, the steps carry you into a fantasy realm inhabited by stray cats and framed with clapboard houses. Among the older homes are several that date to the 1870s; if you follow the Napier Lane Boardwalk that extends from the steps, there are falsefront buildings from which sailors reportedly once were shanghaied.

Retracing your tracks back up the steps, then descending the other side of Filbert Street, you'll arrive at **Washington Square** (Filbert and Stockton streets) the heart of North Beach. Nestled between Russian and Telegraph hills, this is the gathering place for San Francisco's "Little Italy." In the square, old Italian men and women seek out wooden benches where they can watch the "young people" carrying on. From the surrounding delis and cafes you might put together a picnic lunch, plant yourself on the lawn, and catch this daily parade.

Sitting amidst this garden setting, it's hard to imagine that the square was a tent city back in 1906. The great earthquake and fire totally devastated North Beach, and the park became a refuge for hundreds of homeless.

St. Peter & Paul Catholic Church (Filbert and Stockton streets) anchors one side of the square. Its twin steeples dominate the North Beach skyline. The facade is unforgettable, an ornate affair upon which eagles rest in the company of angels. The interior is a wilderness of vaulting arches hung with lamps and decorated in gilt bas-relief. Tourists proclaim its beauty. For my taste, the place is overdone; it drips with architectural jewelry. Everything is decoration, an artistic happening; there is no tranquility, no silent spot for the eye to rest.

North Beach Museum, housed inside Eureka Federal Savings (1435 Stockton), presents a history in black-and-white. There are sepia photos of Sicilian fishermen, pictures of the terrible quake, and other images of the people who make this neighborhood such an intriguing place to visit.

SAN FRANCISCO'S OUTBACK

THE PRESIDIO

Are you ready for this? I'm now going to propose that you sightsee on an Army base. Of course, this is not just any military installation.

It happens to be the Presidio, 1500 acres of undulating hills sprinkled with acacia, madrone, pine, and redwood trees. You'll find this island of green in the northern section of the city, slightly inland from the Golden Gate National Recreation Area. In addition to being the city's largest wooded expanse, the Presidio constitutes the oldest active military base in the country. The place is a National Historic Landmark; it was established by the Spanish in 1776 and taken over by the United States in 1846. Civil War troops trained here and the Sixth Army still headquarters on the grounds, but the area has the feel of a country retreat. Hiking trails snake through the property and there are expansive Bay views that would gladden the eye of any sentry.

Best way to explore the Presidio is by stopping first at the **Army Museum** (Funston Avenue near Lincoln Boulevard; 415-561-4115). This three-story museum was originally a hospital, built in 1857. Faced with pillars and protected by a collection of antique cannons, it's still an imposing sight. The displays inside consist primarily of military uniforms and weapons. (Maps of the reservation are available from the Presidio Public Affairs Office, Building 37; 415-561-3870).

The nearby **Officers' Club** (Moraga Avenue), a tile-roof, Spanish-style structure, includes part of the original 1776 Presidio, one of the first buildings ever constructed in San Francisco. The **National Cemetery** (Lincoln Boulevard), with rows of tombstones on a grassy knoll overlooking the Golden Gate Bridge, is San Francisco's salute to the nation's war dead.

The remainder of our Presidio tour is of a more natural bent. There's **El Polin Spring** (end of MacArthur Avenue) where, as the brass plaque proclaims, "the early Spanish garrison attained its water supply." History has rarely been made in a more beautiful spot. The spring is set in a lovely park surrounded by hills upon which eucalyptus trees battle with conifers for strategic ground. Hiking trails lead down and outward from this enchanted glade.

The battle lines are drawn at **Lover's Lane**. March, or even stroll, along this narrow pathway, and review these armies of nature. On one side, standing sentinel straight, outthrust arms shading the lane, are the eucalyptus. Mustered along the other front, clad in darker uniforms, seeming to retreat before the wind, are the conifer trees. Forgetting for a moment these silly games soldiers play, look around. You are standing in an awesome and spectacular spot, one of the last forests in San Francisco.

Mountain Lake Park (Lake Street between 8th and Funston avenues), stationed along the Presidio's southern flank, is another idyllic locale. With its grassy meadows and wooded walkways, it's a great place to picnic or stroll. The lake itself, a favorite watering hole among ducks visiting from out of town, is skirted with tule reeds and overhung with willows.

The base's prettiest walk is actually in civilian territory along the **Presidio Wall** bordering Lyon Street. Starting at the Lombard Street Gate, where two cannons guard the fort's eastern entrance, walk uphill along Lyon Street. That wall of urbanity to the left is the city's chic Union Street district, breeding place for fern bars and antique stores.

To the right, beyond the Presidio's stone enclosure, are the tumbling hills and towering trees of the old garrison.

After several blocks, Lyon ceases to be a street and becomes a staircase. The most arduous and rewarding part of the trek begins; you can follow this stairway to heaven, which happens to be Broadway, two heart-pounding blocks above you. Ascend and the city falls away—the Palace of Fine Arts, Alcatraz, the Marina, all become landing points for your vision. Closer to hand are the houses of San Francisco's posh Pacific Heights district, stately structures looming several stories and sprawling across the landscape. When you reach the stone steps at the top of Broadway, they will still rise above, potent and pretentious, hard contrast to the Presidio's leafy acres.

GOLDEN GATE NATIONAL RECREATION AREA

One of San Francisco's most spectacular regions belongs to us all. The Golden Gate National Recreation Area, a 35,000-acre metropolitan park, draws about twenty million visitors annually.

A place of natural beauty and historic importance, this magnificent park stretches north from San Francisco throughout much of the Bay Area. In the city itself, the Golden Gate National Recreation Area forms a narrow band around the waterfront. It follows the shoreline of the Bay from Aquatic Park to Fort Mason to the Golden Gate Bridge. On the ocean side it encompasses Land's End, an exotic and untouched preserve, as well as the city's finest beaches.

Ironically, this natural wonderland begins alongside the city's most overdeveloped area—Fisherman's Wharf. Matter of fact, Hyde Street Pier and Aquatic Park, described in the Fisherman's Wharf sightseeing section in this chapter, are actually part of the national park.

The most serene way to escape the plastic fantastic world of the wharf is via the **Golden Gate Promenade**. This three-and-a-half-mile walk will carry you across a swath of heaven that extends from Aquatic Park to the shadows of the Golden Gate Bridge.

Just start in the park and make the short jaunt to the **Municipal Pier**. This hook-shaped cement walkway curls several hundred yards into the Bay. As you follow its curving length a 360° view unfolds—from the Golden Gate to the Bay Bridge, from Mt. Tamalpais to Alcatraz to downtown San Francisco. The pier harbors fisherfolk and seagulls, crab-netters and joggers; few tourists seem to make it out here.

From the pier it's uphill and downstairs to **Fort Mason Center** (Marina Boulevard and Buchanan Street; 415-441-5705), a complex of old wharves and tile-roof warehouses that was once a major military embarkation point. Fort Mason today is the cultural heart of avant-garde San Francisco. About twelve years ago the warehouses were recycled into offices; over 50 non-profit organizations subsequently set up shop.

Nearly all the arts and crafts are represented—several theater groups are home here; there is an on-going series of workshops in dance, creative writing, painting, weaving, printing, sculpture, music, and so on. A number of environmental organizations, including Greenpeace, also have offices in the center. As one brochure describes, "You can see a play, stroll through a museum or gallery, learn how to make poetry films, study yoga, attend a computer seminar, or find out about the rich maritime lore of San Francisco."

Museo Italo Americano (Building C; 415-673-2200) presents samplings of Italian artistry. The museum is dedicated to displaying the works of Italian-American artists. The permanent collection features the work of several artists, some of whom have made San Francisco their home for years. There are also temporary exhibits ranging from 1930s photos of Italy to a display of contemporary Italian cinematographers like Francis Ford Coppola, Dino deLaurentiis, Michael Cimino, and Martin Scorcese.

Other ethnic groups are represented at the **Mexican Museum** (Building D; 415-441-0404), with its displays of Pre-Columbian art, and the **San Francisco African-American Historical & Cultural Society** (Building C; 415-441-0640), which collects African artifacts as well as the memorabilia of Blacks in the United States.

Permanently docked at one end of Fort Mason is the **S.S. Jeremiah O'Brien**, the only one of 2751 World War II Liberty Ships to remain in original condition. A beamy hulk, the *Jeremiah O'Brien* numbers among its combat ribbons the D-Day invasion of Normandy. Visitors are welcome to walk the decks of the old tub, explore the sailors' quarters, and descend into the depths of the engine room. They can also listen to an excellent audio tape which features the voices of the men and women who built the Liberty Ships.

Having been fully versed in the arts, environment, and World War II history, continue on the shoreline to the **Marina**, along Marina Boulevard. (The remainder of the tour can be completed by car, though walking is definitely the aesthete's and athlete's way.) Some of this sailor-city's spiffiest yachts are docked along the esplanade.

Nearby **Marina Green**, a stretch of park paralleling the Bay, is a landlubber's haven. Bicyclers, joggers, jugglers, soccer players, touch football aficionados, sunbathers, and a world of others inhabit it. The park's most interesting denizens are the kite-fliers who fill the blue with a rainbow of soaring colors.

Continue on past a line-up of luxury toys—boats with names like *Haiku, Sea Lover, Valhalla,* and *Windfall.* When you arrive at the far end of that small green rectangle of park, you'll have to pay special attention to your navigator; you're on Marina Boulevard at the corner of Yacht Road; if going by car, proceed directly ahead through the U.S.

Army gate and follow Mason Street, Crissy Field Avenue, and Lincoln Boulevard, paralleling the water, to Fort Point; if on foot, turn right onto Yacht Road, then left at the waterfront, and follow the shoreline toward the Golden Gate Bridge.

Before doing either, you have an alluring detour in store. Turn left at Yacht Road, cross Marina Boulevard, and proceed to that magnificent Beaux Art monument looming before you. It's the **Palace of Fine Arts,** a domed edifice built of arches and shadows. Adorned with molded urns and bas-relief figures, it represents the only surviving structure from the 1915 Panama–Pacific International Exposition. Happily, it borders on a sun-shivered pond. The pond in its turn is peopled by mallards and swans, as well as pintails and canvasbacks from out of town. Together, the pool, the pillars, and surrounding park make this one of the city's loveliest spots for sitting and sunning.

Or, if education is on your mind, note that one wing of the Palace houses the **Exploratorium** (Marina Boulevard and Lyon Street; 415-563-3200; admission). This "hands-on" museum, with imaginative exhibits demonstrating the principles of optics, sound, animal behavior, etc., was deemed "the best science museum in the world" by *Scientific American*. It's an intriguing place with displays that include a "distorted room" lacking right angles and an illusionary mirror into which you seemingly pass.

But enough for detours; we were embarked on a long march to the bridge. If you cheated and drove, you're already at Fort Point, and we'll catch up with you later; otherwise you're on foot, with the Bay at your side and the Golden Gate dead ahead. This is a land where freighters talk to foghorns, and sloops scud along soundlessly. The waterfront is a sandy beach, a rockpile in seeming upheaval, then beach again, sand dunes, and occasional shade trees. That wooded grove rising to your left is the Presidio; those bald-domed hills across the Bay to the right are the Marin Headlands, and the sharp-rising buildings poking at your back are part of the San Francisco skyline. You'll pass a Coast Guard Station and a fishing pier before arriving at the red brick fort that snuggles in the arch of the Golden Gate Bridge.

Modeled on Fort Sumter and completed around the time Confederate forces opened fire on that hapless garrison, **Fort Point** (end of Marine Drive) represents the only brick fort west of the Mississippi. With its collection of cannons and Civil War-era exhibits, it's of interest to history buffs. Also, if you follow the spiral granite staircase to the roof, you'll stand directly beneath the Golden Gate Bridge and command a sentinel's view out into the Pacific.

From Fort Point, a footpath leads up to the observation area astride the **Golden Gate Bridge**; if driving, take Lincoln Boulevard to the vista point. By whichever route, you will arrive at "The Bridge at the End of the Continent." Aesthetically, it is considered one of the world's most beautiful spans, a medley of splayed cable and steel struts. Statistically, it represents one of the longest suspension bridges anywhere—6450 feet of suspended concrete and steel, with twin towers the height of 65-story buildings, and cables that support 200 million pounds. It is San Francisco's emblem, an engineering wonder that has come to represent an entire metropolis.

If you're game, you can walk across, venturing along a dizzying sidewalk out to one of the most magnificent views you'll ever experience. The Bay from this height is a toy model built to scale; beyond the bridge, San Francisco and Marin, slender arms of land, open onto the boundless Pacific.

The Golden Gate Promenade ends at the bridge, but Lincoln Boulevard continues along the cliffs that mark the ocean side of San Francisco. There are **vista points** overlooking the Pacific and affording startling views back toward the bridge. After about a mile you'll reach **Baker Beach** (off Lincoln Boulevard on Gibson Road), a wide corridor of white sand. Ideal for picnicking and sunbathing, this lovely beach is a favorite among San Franciscans. Adventurers can follow this strand, and the other smaller beaches with which it connects, on a fascinating walk back almost all the way to the Golden Gate Bridge. With the sea unfolding on one side and rocky crags rising along the other, it's definitely worth a little sand in the shoes. As a final reward, there's a **nude beach** (★) just outside the bridge.

Lincoln Boulevard transforms into El Camino del Mar which winds through Sea Cliff, one of San Francisco's most affluent residential neighborhoods. This exclusive area has something to offer the visitor in addition to its scenic residences—namely **China Beach** (formerly known as James Phelan Beach). More secluded than Baker, this pocket beach is backdropped by a rocky bluff atop which stand the luxurious plate-window homes of Sea Cliff. Named for the Chinese fishermen who camped here in the 19th century, the beach has a dilapidated beach house. (To get there, turn right on 25th Avenue, left on Sea Cliff Avenue, then follow until it dead ends.)

Continuing on El Camino del Mar as it sweeps above the ocean, you'll come upon San Francisco's prettiest museum. With its color naded courtyard and arching entranceway, the **Palace of the Legion of Honor** (Legion of Honor Drive in Lincoln Park; 415-750-3659; admission) is modeled after a gallery in Paris. Appropriately, it specializes in French art and culture. The exhibits trace France's aesthetic achievements from the religious art of the Middle Ages to Renaissance painting, the Baroque and Rococo periods, and the Impressionists of the 19th and 20th centuries.

After you've drunk in the splendid view of city and Bay from the museum grounds, head downhill on 34th Avenue past the golf course, turn right on Geary Boulevard, which becomes Point Lobos Avenue, then turn right on to El Camino del Mar and follow it to the end. (Yes, this is the same street you were on earlier; no, I'm not leading you in circles. It seems that years ago landslides collapsed the midriff of this highway, leaving among the survivors two dead-end streets known forever by the same name.)

This is **Land's End** (★), a thumb-like appendage of real estate which San Francisco seems to have stolen from the sea. It is the nearest you will ever approach to experiencing San Francisco as the Costanoan Indians knew it. Hike the trails which honeycomb the hillsides hereabout and you'll enter a wild, tumbling region where winds twist cypress trees into the contours of the earth. The rocks offshore are inhabited by slithering sea creatures. The air is loud with the unceasing lash of wave against shoreline. Land's End is San Francisco's grand finale—a line of cliffs poised at the sea's edge and threatening imminently to slide into eternity.

From the parking lot at the end of El Camino del Mar, go to the right along the path. Walk several hundred yards until you cross a wood-plank footbridge, then follow one of the narrow paths leading down to the water. That dirty blonde swath of sand is a popular **nude beach** (★), perfectly situated here in San Francisco's most natural region.

(While hiking the footpaths, beware! Land's End is plagued by landslides and foolish hikers. Stay on the trails. Exercise caution and this exotic area will reward you with eye-boggling views of Marin's wind-chiseled coast.)

Continuing down Point Lobos Avenue, at the corner where the road turns to parallel the Pacific, rest the ruins of the **Sutro Baths**. From the configuration of the stones, it's a simple trick to envision the foundation of Adolf Sutro's folly; more difficult for the mind's eye is to picture the multitiered confection that the San Francisco philanthropist built upon it in 1896. Sprawling across three oceanfront acres, Sutro's baths could have washed the entire city. There were actually six baths, Olympian in size, as well as three restaurants and 500 dressing rooms—all contained beneath a stained-glass dome.

Towering above them was the Cliff House, a Gothic castle which survived the earthquake only to be consumed by fire the next year. Following several reincarnations, the **Cliff House** (1066 Point Lobos Avenue) today is a rather bland structure housing several restaurants and tourist shops. Most important among its features are the National Park Service information office (415-556-8642) and the view. From this crow's nest you can gaze out over a sweeping expanse of ocean. Just offshore the **Seal Rocks** lie anchored. Those barking beasts sunning themselves on the rock islands might look like giant sea slugs, but they are sea lions, San Francisco's wild mascots.

Below the Cliff House, extending to the very end of vision, is the Great Highway. The salt-and-pepper beach beside it is **Ocean Beach**, a slender ribbon of sand that decorates three miles of San Francisco's western perimeter. Remember, this is San Francisco—land of fog, mist, and west winds—beachwear here more often consists of sweaters than swimsuits. The water, sweeping down from the Arctic, is too cold for mere mortals; only surfers and polar bear swimmers brave it. Nevertheless, to walk this strand is to trek the border of eternity. The Indians called San Francisco's ocean the "sundown sea." If you'll take the time some late afternoon, you'll see that the fiery orb still settles nightly just offshore.

Fort Funston (Skyline Boulevard, at the far end of Ocean Beach) is the prettiest stretch to stroll. The fort itself is little more than a sequence of rusting gun emplacements, but there is a half-mile nature trail here that winds along cliffs overlooking the sea. It's a windblown region of dune grass and leathery succulent plants, with views that span San Francisco and alight on the shore of Marin. Hang gliders dust the cliffs of Fort Funston, adding another dramatic element to this spectacle of sun and wind.

Across the highway lies **Lake Merced Harding Park** (Skyline and Lake Merced boulevards), a U-shaped reservoir which has the unusual distinction of once having been salt water. Bounded by golf links and hiking trails, it provides a pretty spot to picnic. If you decide to pass up the hang gliding at Fort Funston, you might rent a rowboat or sailboat at the clubhouse here and try a less nerve-jangling sport.

Heading back along the Great Highway, you'll encounter the **San Francisco Zoo** (Great Highway and Sloat Boulevard; 415-661-4844; admission). With over 100 endangered species, plus an excellent gorilla habitat and Primate Discovery Center, it's a great place to visit.

GOLDEN GATE PARK

It is the Central Park of the West. Or perhaps we should say that Central Park is New York's answer to Golden Gate Park. It extends from the Haight–Ashbury neighborhood, across nearly half the width of San Francisco, all the way to the ocean. With its folded hills and sloping meadows, its lakes and museums, Golden Gate is everyone's favorite park.

Once a region of worthless sand dunes, the park today encompasses over 1000 acres of gardens, lawns, and forests. The transformation from wasteland to wonderland came about during the late-19th and early-20th centuries through the efforts of a mastermind named John McLaren. A gardener by trade, this Scotsman could rightly be called an architect of the earth. Within his lifetime he oversaw the creation of the world's largest human-made park.

What he wrought was a place that has something to suit everyone: there are tennis courts; lawn bowling greens; hiking trails; byways for bicyclers, rollerskaters, skateboarders, even unicyclers; a nine-hole golf course; archery field; flycasting pools; playgrounds; fields for soccer and football; riding stables; even checker pavilions. Facilities for renting bicycles and skates are located just outside the park along Haight and Stanyan streets.

Or, if you'd prefer not to lift a finger, you can always pull up a shade tree and watch the parade. The best day to visit Golden Gate Park is Sunday when many of the roads are closed to cars but open to skaters, jugglers, bicyclers, troubadors, mimes, skateboarders, impromptu theater groups, sun worshippers, and anyone else who feels inspired.

Touring the park should be done on another day, when you can drive freely through the grounds. There are two roads spanning the length of the park. Each begins near Stanyan Street on the east side of Golden Gate Park and runs about four miles westward to the Pacific. The best way to see this area is to travel out along John F. Kennedy Drive and back by Martin Luther King, Jr. Drive, detouring down the side roads that lead into the heart of the park.

The first stop along John F. Kennedy Drive lies immediately after the entrance. That red-tile building overgrown in ivy is **McLaren Lodge** (415-750-3659), park headquarters and home base for maps, brochures, pamphlets, and information.

The startling glass palace nearby is the **Conservatory.** Built in 1879 and Victorian in style, it houses a plant kingdom ruled by stately palm trees and peopled with fingertip flowers, pendent ferns, and courtly orchids.

You'll find the kingdom's colonies spread throughout the park, but one of particular import is **Rhododendron Dell**, just down the street. A lacework of trails threads through this 20-acre garden; if you're visiting in early spring, when the rose-hued bushes are blooming, the dell is a concert of colors.

Just beyond this garden beats the cultural heart of Golden Gate Park. Located around a tree-studded concourse are the De Young Museum, Academy of Sciences, and Japanese Tea Garden. The **M. H. De Young Memorial Museum** (415-750-3659; admission), the city's finest, houses an impressive collection. Western art exhibits trace the course of European art from Greek and Roman times through the Renaissance to the modern era. There's also an intriguing display of works from Africa and Oceania. The *pièce de résistance* of this entire complex is the **Asian Art Museum** (415-668-8921; admission) adjacent to the De Young. Featuring major pieces from China, Tibet, Japan, Korea, Iran, Syria, and throughout the continent, this superlative facility was the first museum in the country devoted exclusively to Asian art. Some of the exhibits date back 6000 years.

It takes a facility like the **California Academy of Sciences** (415-750-7145; admission) to even compete with a place like the De Young Museum. Here you'll find a planetarium where the stars rise all day, an array of African animals grouped in jungle settings, and a "roundabout" aquarium in which you stand at the center of a circular glass tank while creatures of the deep swim around you. A tremendous place for kids, this natural history museum also features numerous "hands-on" exhibits.

If you're like me, it won't be more than an hour or two before museum fatigue sets in and dinosaur vertebrae start looking like rock formations. It's time for the **Japanese Tea Garden** (admission). Here you can rest your heavy eyes on carp-filled ponds and handwrought gateways. There are arch footbridges, cherry trees, bonsai gardens, and, of course, a tea house where Japanese women serve jasmine tea and cookies.

All these cultural gathering places cluster around a **Music Concourse** where concerts regularly are staged. The concourse is also a departure point for horse-and-buggy rides (for information call 415-761-8272). With turn-of-the-century carriages, and drivers attired in formal livery, they provide a marvelous way to see the park.

Otherwise, by car or foot, you can get back on John F. Kennedy Drive and resume your self-guided tour by continuing to **Stow Lake.** This is a donut-shaped body of water with an island as the hole in the middle. From the island's crest you can gaze across San Francisco from Bay to ocean. Or, if an uphill is not in your day's itinerary, there's a footpath around the island perimeter that passes an ornate Chinese pagoda. There are also rowboats, pedalboats, and electric motorboats for rent, and a small snack bar.

Next along John F. Kennedy Drive you'll pass **Rainbow Falls**. That monument at the top, from which this cascade appears to spill, is **Prayer-book Cross**, modeled after an old Celtic cross.

This is followed close on by a chain of meadows, a kind of rolling green counterpoint to the chain of lakes which lie ahead. **Speedway Meadow** and **Lindley Meadow** offer barbecue pits and picnic tables; both are fabulous areas for sunbathing.

Spreckels Lake is home to ducks, seagulls, and model sailboats; across the road are the **Golden Gate Park Stables** (John F. Kennedy Drive and 36th Avenue; 415-668-7360), where you can take riding lessons. Nearby is the **Buffalo Paddock**, where the great beasts still roam, though within the confines of a barbed wire fence.

Immediately beyond is the **Chain of Lakes**, a string of three reservoirs stretching the width of the park, perpendicular to John F. Kennedy Drive. Framed by eucalyptus trees, they offer hiking paths around each shoreline. As you circumnavigate these baby lakes, you'll notice they are freckled with miniature islands. Each lake possesses a singular personality: North Lake is remarkable for its hip-deep swamp cypress; Middle Lake features an island tufted with willows; and South Lake, tiniest of the triplets, sprouts bamboo along its shore.

If these ponds be babies, the great mother of them all rests nearby. Where the road meets the Pacific you'll come upon the **Dutch Windmill**, a regal structure built in 1903. With its wooden struts and scale-like shingles, it stares into the face of the sea's inevitable west winds. The Dutchman's cousin, **Murphy Windmill**, an orphan with broken arms, lives several hundred yards down the coast.

From here at continent's edge, it's a four-mile trip back through the park along Martin Luther King, Jr. Drive. After picking it up at Murphy Windmill, you'll find that this softly curving road passes lakes and forests, meadows and playgrounds. More important, it borders **Strybing Arboretum** (415-661-1316), a place specially made for garden lovers. Strybing is a world within itself, a 70-acre flower quilt stitched together by pathways. Over 5000 species peacefully coexist here—dwarf conifers and sprawling magnolias, as well as plants from Asia, the Andes, Australia, and America. There is a "redwood trail" devoted to native California plants, a "garden of fragrance" redolent of flowers, and a Japanese strolling garden. It's a kind of park within a park, a glorious finale for your visit to this park within a city.

Shopping

Shopping is really a form of consumer sightseeing. Many folks would rather browse store windows than museum showcases. A city reveals itself by the styles of its stores, so a sharpwitted traveler can gain a real sense of place by exploring commercial districts.

In San Francisco you should come away with a sense of the cosmopolitan. This Pacific coast city wears Asian and New York designs with equal comfort. Its downtown center includes many of New York's famed department stores, while the city's ethnic neighborhoods support mom 'n' pop shops of various nationalities.

DOWNTOWN SHOPPING

Union Square quite simply is *the* center for shopping in San Francisco. First of all, this grass-and-hedgerow park (located between Post and Geary, Stockton and Powell streets) is surrounded by department stores: **I. Magnin** and **Macy's** along one border, **Sak's Fifth Avenue** guarding another. **Neiman-Marcus**, the Texas-bred emporium, claims one corner; an elite men's clothing shop named **Bullock & Jones** is also situated in this well-heeled neighborhood.

Of course, that's just on the square. Beyond the plaza are scads of stores. Along Stockton, one of the streets radiating out from the square, stands **Grodin's**, an excellent spot to shop for men's wear.

Then if you follow Post, another bordering street, there's **Gumps** (250 Post Street), which features fine imported decorations for home and body. If you get bored looking through the antiques, china pieces, and oriental art, you can always adjourn to the Jade or Crystal room.

The streets all around host a further array of stores. You'll encounter jewelers, dress designers, boutiques, furniture stores, tailor shops, and more. So take a gander—there's everything out there from the unexpected to the bizarre.

Braunstein/Quay Gallery (250 Sutter Street) is an outstanding place to view the work of local artists. As the catalog claims, owner Ruth Braunstein "embodies the brash, irreverent, and irrepressible energy of the San Francisco art world." This contemporary gallery also exhibits works from other parts of the world.

Tillman Place Bookshop (8 Tillman Place) is a postage stamp-size store tucked into an alleyway. Within, however, you'll find a tasteful collection of coffee-table books, paperback classics, travel guides, and a selection of color prints, all contained in a Victorian setting.

For toys, there's no place like **FAO Schwartz** (180 Post Street). A branch of New York's famous Fifth Avenue emporium, it includes two huge floors dripping with spectacular kites, oversized tinkertoys, and monstrous stuffed animals. There's everything from designer doll dresses to the latest computer toys. A wonderland for all ages.

The **Galleria** (50 Post Street) is a glass-domed promenade lined with fashionable shops. A center for well-heeled crowds from the Financial district, the mall showcases designer fashions and elegant gifts.

When looking for maps and travel guides, it's hard to top **Thomas Brothers Maps** (550 Jackson Street). This company actually produces many of the maps it sells and has gained renown for its excellent city maps.

Most of these shops are located along the eastern flank of Union Square. There are also countless stores on the other side. The **500 and 600 blocks of Sutter Street**, for instance, contain a covey of art galleries.

Harold's Books & Cards (599 Post Street) is a shop specializing in "hometown newspapers." There are dailies from all over the world. For homesick travelers, or those just interested in a little local news, it's a godsend.

Shoppers along the Embarcadero head for either of two places—Embarcadero Center or Pier 39. Preferable by far is **Embarcadero**

Center (Sacramento Street near the foot of Market Street), a vaulting glass-and-concrete "town" inhabited by stores and restaurants. This multifaceted mall consists of the lower three levels of four consecutive skyscrapers. You pass from one building to the next along corridors that open onto a galaxy of shops. Verily, what Disneyland is for kids, Embarcadero Center is to shoppers. The place possesses positively everything. There are bookstores, bakeries, jewelry stores, gift bazaars, newsstands, and camera shops. There's even a "general store," plus dozens of restaurants, cocktail lounges, and espresso bars, a luggage shop, a store devoted entirely to nature, and on and on and on in labyrinthine fashion.

Though its wooden boardwalks and clapboard buildings look promising, **Pier 39** (Embarcadero and Beach Street) proves hardly the place for bargains or antiques. It's a haven for tourists and features gift stores that range from cutesy card shops to places selling ceramic unicorns. There are restaurants and stores galore, plus an amusement arcade. Kids often enjoy the carnival atmosphere here. On a given day there might be jugglers, clowns, or other entertainers performing free for the public.

FISHERMAN'S WHARF SHOPPING

Fisherman's Wharf is a shopper's paradise . . . if you know what you're doing. If not, it's a fool's paradise. This heavily touristed district houses a mazelike collection of shops, malls, arcades, and galleries. Most of them specialize in high-priced junk. How someone can arrive in the world's most splendid city and carry away some trashy trinket to commemorate their visit is beyond me. But they do. Since you're certainly not the type searching out an "I Got Crabs at Fisherman's Wharf" T-shirt, the best course is to go where the natives shop.

For locally crafted goods, be sure to watch for the **street vendor stalls**. Located along Beach Street between Hyde and Larkin, and on side streets throughout the area, they offer hand-fashioned wares with homemade price tags. You'll find jewelry, leather belts, statuary, framed photos of the bay city, tie-dye shirts, kites, and anything else the local imagination can conjure.

Before people buy anything in the City, they go to **Cost Plus** and see if it's there. If so, it's cheaper; if not, maybe they don't really need it. An enormous, multibuilding complex, Cost Plus sprawls across several blocks of Fisherman's Wharf. Start at the main building at 2552 Taylor Street for jewelry, ceramics, wallhangings, and a host of other items. Then wander around the other brickfront buildings that comprise this amazing place. There are temple rubbings from Thailand, amber jewelry from Egypt, Indian mirrorcloths, scenic San Francisco posters, ceramics, brassware, household furnishings, clothes, gourmet foods, etc. Everything under the sun, at prices to brighten your day.

Another popular spot among San Franciscans is the old brick canning factory on Jefferson and Leavenworth streets. Thanks to innovative architects, **The Cannery** has been transformed into a tri-level mall dotted with interesting shops. The central plaza, with its olive trees and potted flowers, contains picnic tables and a snack kiosk. Among the dozens of shops are many selling handcrafted originals.

The chocoholics who don't know will be delighted to discover that the home of Ghirardelli chocolate, **Ghirardelli Square** (900 North Point Street), has been converted into yet another shopping complex. This early 20th-century factory is another example of old industrial architecture being turned to contemporary uses. Around the factory's antique chocolate making machines is located a myriad of shops varying from designer outlets to sundry stores. There are also import stores, boutiques, and so on.

So there you have the secret of shopping Fisherman's Wharf: simply ignore everything else and beeline between the street vendors, Cost Plus, The Cannery, and that brick-red chocolate factory.

CHINATOWN SHOPPING

Shopping in Chinatown brings you into immediate contact with both the common and the unique. If you can slip past the souvenir shops, many of which specialize in American-made "Chinese products," you'll eventually discover the real thing—Chinese arts and crafts as well as Asian antiques.

Grant Avenue is the neighborhood's shopping center, but local Chinese favor Stockton Street. My advice is to browse both streets as well as the side streets between. Some of the city's best bargains are right here in Chinatown.

The soul of the place resides somewhere between the Hong Kong souvenirs and the antique tapestries. While there is a lot of gimcrackery sold here, many specialty shops provide a sense of the richness of Chinese arts and crafts. Slip into one of the district's silk stores to admire the kimonos, or drop by a tea shop and sample one of the hundreds of varieties of teas.

NORTH BEACH SHOPPING

Shopping in North Beach is a grand escapade. As you browse the storefronts here, do like the Sicilians and keep an eye out for Italian treasures. Like the hand-painted ceramics and colorful wallhangings still brightening many a home in old Italia.

For the mod mob, there are slick boutiques and avant-garde novelty shops. To start, why not choose a place that stocks both the traditional and the avant-garde—**City Lights Bookstore** (261 Columbus Avenue). Within the hallowed confines of this oddly shaped store is a treasure trove of magazines on arts and politics, plus books on everything from nirvana to the here and now.

Gourmet Guides (1767 Stockton Street) is one of those rare and wondrous creatures, a bookstore devoted to travel books. Piled in hodgepodge fashion, stack on stack, are travelogues, guides, and cookbooks. You almost need a map to find your way through this literary labyrinth, but once you gain your bearings, you'll discover a world for the adventurer and armchair traveler alike.

Biordi Italian Imports (412 Columbus Avenue) provides the Italian answer to gourmet living. Specializing in kitchen goods, the place is loaded with Italian imports. There are hand-painted pitchers from Florence, Venetian blown-glass pieces, and noodle makers. To decorate the kitchen, Biordi's has baroque chandeliers, wall mirrors framed in ceramic fruit, and other high-kitsch items. Walking through this singular shop is like browsing an Italian crafts fair.

Head over to **Postermat** (401 Columbus Avenue) for movie posters, art prints, and novelty cards. Owner Ben Friedman's store has become a San Francisco institution and a great place to shop for wallhangings and knickknacks. Of particular interest is Friedman's outstanding collection of posters from the old Fillmore and Avalon ballrooms. Incorporating psychedelic and collage art at its finest, these posters are 1960s-era collector items.

No North Beach shopping spree would be complete without a visit to **A. Cavalli & Co.** (1441 Stockton Street). Operating since 1880, this family business caters to all sorts of local needs. They offer an assortment of Italian cookbooks as well as records and tapes ranging from Pavarotti to Italian new wave. Cavalli's also stocks Italian travel posters, Puccini opera prints, Italian movies on cassette, and magazines from Rome.

Nightlife

Since its rowdy Gold Rush days, San Francisco has been renowned as a wide-open town, hard-drinking and easygoing. Today there are over 2000 places around the city to order a drink, including saloons, restaurants, cabarets, boats, private clubs, and even a couple hospitals. There's a bar for every mood and each occasion.

North Beach, the old Beatnik quarter, is the area for slumming. It's door-to-door with local bars and nightclubs, not to mention the topless and bottomless joints lining Broadway. The city's Downtown and Nob Hill districts are the best places to seek out quiet piano bars, while Union Street is known for its swinging singles spots. The gay bars congregate along Castro Street, Polk Street, and South of Market, with others in the Hayes Valley and Haight–Ashbury neighborhoods; lesbian bars are located around Valencia Street.

Known for its distinct rock 'n' roll and new wave sounds, the city is a prime place for live entertainment. There are music clubs and cabarets in almost every neighborhood, plus several outstanding comedy clubs. Both traditional and avant-garde theater flourish here, concentrated around Geary Street in the Downtown district. San Francisco is also rich culturally in its opera, symphony, and ballet, located in the Civic Center area. Since tickets to major theatrical and other cultural events are expensive, consider buying day-of-performance tickets from **San Francisco Ticket Box Office Service** (STBS) on Stockton Street between Post and Geary streets (415-433-7827). Open from noon until just before showtime, they sell tickets at half-price.

The Convention and Visitor's Bureau sponsors an event hotline, **Dial-an-Event** (415-391-2000), with information on theater, sports, and other activities in the city. Check the **Michelob Jazz Line** (415-769-4818) for local jazz events and KMEL's **Concert Connection** (415-397-0106) for music events and happenings at clubs throughout the area.

When looking for nightlife, the location is never as important as the type of entertainment, so the listings below are organized by category rather than neighborhood. It's also advisable to consult the "Datebook," commonly called the "pink section," in the Sunday *San Francisco Examiner and Chronicle* for current shows and performers. However you decide to spend the evening, you'll find plenty of possibilities in this city by the bay.

BARS

THE BEST BARS

Waterfront bars are generally attractively appointed and expensive. Not so **Mission Rock Resort** (817 China Basin; 415-621-5538). True, it *is* on San Francisco Bay, but in the South of Market neighborhood, where the specialties are shipyards and factories rather than scenic views. The crowd at the bar is lively, the sundeck warm and inviting, and the drinks are priced to fit small pockets. This is what bars were like back when San Francisco was a sailor's city.

Vesuvio Cafe (255 Columbus Avenue; 415-362-3370) hasn't changed much since the Beat poets haunted the place during the days of Eisenhower. Kerouac, Ginsberg, Corso, and the crew spent their nights here and their days next door at City Lights Books. It's still a major North Beach scene, rich in soul and history.

To step uptown, just walk down the hill to the **San Francisco Brewing Company** (155 Columbus Avenue; 415-434-3344). Built the year after the earthquake, it's a mahogany-paneled beauty with glass lamps and punkah wallah fans. Legend tells that Jack Dempsey once worked here as a bouncer. Today it's the only pub in San Francisco that brews its own beer on the premises.

It's hard to escape tourists along the San Francisco waterfront. Best bet is **Peer Inn** (Bay Street and Embarcadero; 415-788-1411), a bubble-top bar near Pier 33. Passenger liners still embark from a nearby wharf, adding local color to this neighborhood lounge.

The **Eagle Cafe** (Pier 39; 415-433-3689), perched beside Fisherman's Wharf, appears like some strange bird which has landed in the wrong roost. All around lies touristville, polished and preening, while the Eagle remains old and crusty, filled with waterfront characters. Old photos and baseball caps adorn the walls, and in the air hang memories fifty years old.

Buena Vista Cafe (2765 Hyde Street; 415-474-5044), situated near Fisherman's Wharf, is popular with local folks and tourists alike. There's a fine old bar and friendly atmosphere, and the place claims to have introduced America to the Irish coffee.

SINGLES BARS

Shortly after quitting time, the singles scene centers around the Financial District, then moves west across the city as the night progresses. The best evening spots are **Channel's** (1 Embarcadero Center; 415-956-8768) and **The Holding Company** (2 Embarcadero Center; 415-986-0797). Both are crowded with young professionals on the make.

Most popular, crowded, and famous of all the swingles bars is **Perry's** (1944 Union Street; 415-922-9022). It's a meat market for the over-thirty set. Appropriately, there's a sporting theme to the decor. On weekends, the place is more crowded than a stadium on Super Bowl Sunday.

In fact, the only place that's more crowded is **Pierce Street Annex** (3138 Fillmore Street; 415-567-1400). A throbbing, dimly lit nightspot, it is pick-up central.

The prize for San Francisco's archetypal fern bar goes to **Lord Jim's** (1500 Broadway; 415-928-3015), where you'll find hanging plants and Tiffany lamps, as well as mirrors decorated with whiskey advertisements.

PIANO BARS

Without doubt the city's finest bar pianist is a facile-fingered gentleman named Peter Mintun. He works the ivory nightly at the fashionable **L'Etoile Restaurant** (1075 California Street; 415-771-1529) on Nob Hill. The sounds will be Porter and Gershwin, the crowd elegant, and the drinks expensive. Dress code.

Another favored relaxing place for the rich is the **Redwood Room** (Geary and Taylor streets; 415-775-4700) in the Clift Hotel. With art-deco lamps, marble tables, and burnished redwood paneling, it is nothing less than sumptuous. As at Peter Mintun's playground, men will feel more comfortable wearing coats and ties, women dresses.

VIEW BARS

If San Francisco tourists were given an association test and asked the first thing that came to mind when a "bar with a view" was mentioned, about 101 out of every 100 would list **The Top of the Mark** (California and Mason streets; 415-392-3434). With good reason: from its roosting place in Nob Hill's Mark Hopkins Hotel, this venerable lounge enjoys extraordinary vistas of the bay and beyond. Dress code.

Another favorite is the **Carnelian Room** (555 California Street; 415-433-7500) atop the Bank of America in the city's Financial District. Perched on the 52nd floor, this luxurious lounge has the best views of all, sweeping from little old San Francisco Bay out across the boundless deep. Dress code.

Way across town, where San Francisco meets the Pacific, there's **Phineas T. Barnacle** (1090 Point Lobos Avenue; 415-386-7630). Set in the Cliff House, it's heavily touristed and rather pricey, but the views are unmatched. Seal Rocks stand sentinel offshore, with barking denizens who can be heard even over the din of drinkers.

DANCEHALLS AND DISCOS

Located atop the St. Francis Hotel, **Oz** (335 Powell Street; 415-397-7000) is favored by many for its disco dancing. The place is nicely appointed with marble bar and draws a well-heeled crowd. In addition to disco, the sounds include new wave and rock. The visual display is provided by video and fiber optics. Cover; dress code.

City Nights (715 Harrison Street; 415-546-7774) is the last word in elegance. In addition to a spacious dancefloor, they occassionally feature live entertainment. But generally the music is deejay-style. There is a cover charge.

The Oasis (278 11th Street; 415-621-8119), another South of Market nightspot, headlines bands on Wednesday and Friday and deejay music during the rest of the week. Restaurant and swimming pool. Swimming pool? Cover.

Hottest of all the city's dancehalls is the **I-Beam** (1748 Haight Street; 415-668-6006). With new wave bands wailing into the wee hours, it draws both straight and gay crowds. This cavernous club also features other varieties of rock 'n' roll.

NIGHTCLUBS AND CABARETS

San Francisco has always been a great place for music. Back in the '50s, numerous folk music groups started here. Then in the '60s, rock bands like the Jefferson Airplane, Grateful Dead, and Big Brother and the Holding Company created a distinctive San Francisco sound.

Today several clubs headline nationally known bands. **Wolfgang's** (901 Columbus Avenue; 415-474-2995), owned by rock impresario Bill

Graham, brings in top groups from around the country. Graham produces other shows regularly throughout the Bay Area.

The Stone (412 Broadway; 415-391-8282) also showcases hot groups, mixing rock with blues and jazz.

Over at the **Great American Music Hall** (859 O'Farrell Street; 415-885-0750), a vintage 1907 building has been splendidly converted to a nightclub featuring a variety of entertainers. Included in the lineup are musical greats like Sarah Vaughan.

For jazz, definitely check out **Milestone** (376 5th Street; 415-777-9997), a club in the South of Market neighborhood; and **Kimball's** (300 Grove Street; 415-861-5555), which features jazz combos every weekend. Cover at both clubs.

Pier 23 (Embarcadero and Pier 23; 415-362-5125) is a funky roadhouse that happens to sit next to the San Francisco waterfront. The sounds emanating from this saloon are pure Dixieland, and the vibrations are those of San Francisco before the age of skyscrapers and condominiums. Highly recommended to those searching for the simple rhythms of life.

The **Plush Room** (940 Sutter Street; 415-885-6800) in the York Hotel caters to an upscale clientele and draws big name cabaret acts. It's a lovely setting. Cover.

There are also two theater clubs worthy of note. **Finocchio's** (506 Broadway; 415-982-9388) features a succession of screamingly outrageous female impersonators. The costuming is colorful and the acts very bitchy. Cover.

Club Fugazi (678 Green Street; 415-421-4222) features an equally outlandish musical revue, *Beach Blanket Babylon*, which has been running for years. The scores and choreography are good, but the costumes are great. The hats—elaborate, multilayered confections—make Carmen Miranda's adornments look like Easter bonnets. Cover.

COMEDY CLUBS

Three clubs regularly spotlight San Francisco's collection of characters as well as other comedians. The **Holy City Zoo** (408 Clement Street; 415-386-4242) launched Robin "Mork" Williams into orbit and continues to showcase rising stars. The **Punch Line** (444 Battery Street; 415-397-7573) books a wide variety of acts from around the country. **The Other Cafe** (100 Carl Street; 415-681-0748), a neighborhood club, draws many talented performers.

THEATER

The "On Broadway" theater scene in San Francisco is on Geary Street, near Union Square; while the "Off Broadway," or avant-garde drama, is scattered around the city. The **American Conservatory Theatre**

(415 Geary Street; 415-673-6440), or ACT, is the biggest show in town. It's also the nation's largest resident company. The repertory is traditional and ranges from Shakespeare to French comedy to 20th-century drama.

The **Curran Theater** (445 Geary Street; 415-673-4400) brings Broadway musicals to town. **Golden Gate Theater** (25 Taylor Street; 415-474-3800) also attracts major shows and national companies. Built in 1922, the theater is a grand affair with marble floors, rococo ceilings, and a Wurlitzer organ. Among the city's other playhouses are **Marine's Memorial Theater** (609 Sutter Street; 415-771-6900), **Theater on the Square** (450 Post Street; 415-433-9500), and the **Orpheum Theater** (1192 Market Street; 415-474-3800).

It's the city's smaller companies and local playwrights, however, that make San Francisco a national center for drama. The **Magic Theater** (Fort Mason, Building D; 415-441-8822) has produced several plays by Pulitzer Prize-winning dramatist Sam Shepard. The **San Francisco Mime Troupe** (855 Treat Avenue; 415-285-1717) has performed political satires in the city's parks for a quarter of a century. **Pickle Family Circus** (400 Missouri Street; 415-826-0747), a delightful collection of acrobats, jugglers, and other performers, also tours the area.

Among the bay city's important experimental theater groups are the **Eureka Theater** (2730 16th Street; 415-558-9898), **Theater Artaud** (450 Florida Street; 415-621-7797), **Asian American Theater Company** (1881 Bush Street; 415-346-8922), **Julian Theater** (953 De Haro Street; 415-647-8098), and the **One-Act Theater** (430 Mason Street; 415-421-6162).

OPERA, SYMPHONY, AND DANCE

San Francisco takes nothing quite so seriously as its opera. The **San Francisco Opera** (War Memorial Opera House, Van Ness Avenue and Grove Street; 415-864-3330) is world class in stature. The international season begins in mid-September and runs for 13 weeks. There is also a spring and summer **Pocket Opera** at the Waterfront Theater (900 North Point Street; 415-398-2220) with many performances in English.

The **San Francisco Symphony** (Davies Hall, Van Ness Avenue and Grove Street; 415-431-5400) stands nearly as tall on the world stage. The season extends from September until May, with a series of special concerts during the summer.

The **San Francisco Ballet** (War Memorial Opera House, Van Ness Avenue and Grove Street; 415-621-3838), performing for a half-century, is the nation's oldest permanent ballet, and one of the finest.

Also consider one of the city's many outstanding dance companies. Featuring modern and experimental dance, they include the **Margaret Jenkins Dance Company** (3153 17th Street; 415-863-1173), **Oberlin**

Dance Collective (3153 17th Street; 415-863-6606), and the **San Francisco Moving Company** (223 Mississippi Street; 415-861-5797).

THE GAY SCENE

One example of San Francisco's wide-open tradition is the presence of almost 200 gay bars in the city. There's everything here from rock clubs to piano bars to stylish cabarets.

Over in the Polk Street neighborhood, the **Polk Gulch Saloon** (1100 Polk Street; 415-771-2022) starts early and parties late. The **Cinch Saloon** (1723 Polk Street; 415-776-4162) is a Western-style bar complete with wagon wheels and old-time motif. Nicest of all the neighborhood bars, however, is **Kimo's** (1351 Polk Street; 415-885-4535). With mirrors and potted palms all around, it's a comfortable atmosphere. Another nicely appointed rendezvous is the oak-and-brass **Giraffe** (1131 Polk Street; 415-474-1702).

There are a dozen or so bars in the Castro Street area, many open from early morning until the wee hours. Among the nicest is **Twin Peaks** (401 Castro Street; 415-864-9470) with its overhead fans and mirrored bar.

The finest drinking place in the entire Castro sits upstairs at **Cafe San Marcos** (2367 Market Street; 415-861-3846). It's a glass-and-mirror affair with high-tech furnishings and track lighting.

South of Market, you'll find **The Stud** (399 9th Street; 415-863-6623), everybody's favorite gay bar. Everybody in this case includes aging hippies, multihued punks, curious straights, and even a gay or two, all packed elbow to armpit into this pulsing club. Anyone who isn't at The Stud is probably dancing at **Hamburger Mary's Organic Grill** (1582 Folsom Street; 415-626-5767), another omni-sexual hangout.

San Francisco's lesbian bars are located not only around Valencia Street, but in other parts of the city as well. Foremost is **Amelia's** (647 Valencia Street; 415-552-7788), featuring a jukebox and small dancefloor downstairs and a full-bore dancehall upstairs, complete with deejays, mirrored walls, and flashing lights.

Baybrick Inn (1190 Folsom Street, 415-552-1121) is another hot spot, featuring a lounge and cabaret. There's deejay dancing as well as live entertainment. Over in the Haight–Ashbury neighborhood, **Maud's** (937 Cole Street; 415-731-6119) draws young feminists who come to dance and shoot pool. **Peg's Place** (4737 Geary Boulevard; 415-668-5050) features deejay music and live entertainment and is very popular with professional women. Cover.

CHAPTER EIGHT

North Coast

When visitors to San Francisco seek a rural retreat, paradise is never far away. It sits just across the Golden Gate Bridge along a coastline stretching almost 400 miles to the Oregon border. Scenically, the North Coast compares in beauty with any spot on earth.

There are the folded hills and curving beaches of Point Reyes, Sonoma's craggy coast and old Russian fort, plus Mendocino with its vintage towns and spuming shoreline. To the far north lies Redwood Country, silent domain of the world's tallest living things.

Along the entire seaboard are fewer than a dozen towns with populations over 600 people. Traffic lights are almost as rare as unicorns. Civilization appears in the form of fishing villages and logging towns. Matter of fact, a lot of the prime real estate is saved forever from developers' heavy hands. California's Coastal Commission serves as a watchdog agency protecting the environment.

Much of the coast is also preserved in public playgrounds. Strung like pearls along the Pacific are a series of federal parks—the Golden Gate National Recreation Area, Point Reyes National Seashore, and Redwood National Park.

The main highway through this idyllic domain is Route 1. A sinuous road, it snakes along the waterfront, providing the slowest, most scenic route. Paralleling this road and following an inland course is Route 101. This superhighway streaks from San Francisco to Oregon. It is fast, efficient, and boring. In the town of Leggett, Route 1 merges into Route 101, which continues north through Redwood Country.

Route 1 runs through San Francisco into Marin County, passing Sausalito before it branches from Route 101. While the eastern sector of Marin, along San Francisco Bay, is a suburban sprawl, the western region consists of rolling ranch land. Muir Woods is here, featuring 1000-year-old redwoods growing within commuting distance of the city. There is Mt. Tamalpais, a 2600-foot "sleeping maiden" whose recumbent figure has been the subject of numerous poems.

(Text continued on page 392.)

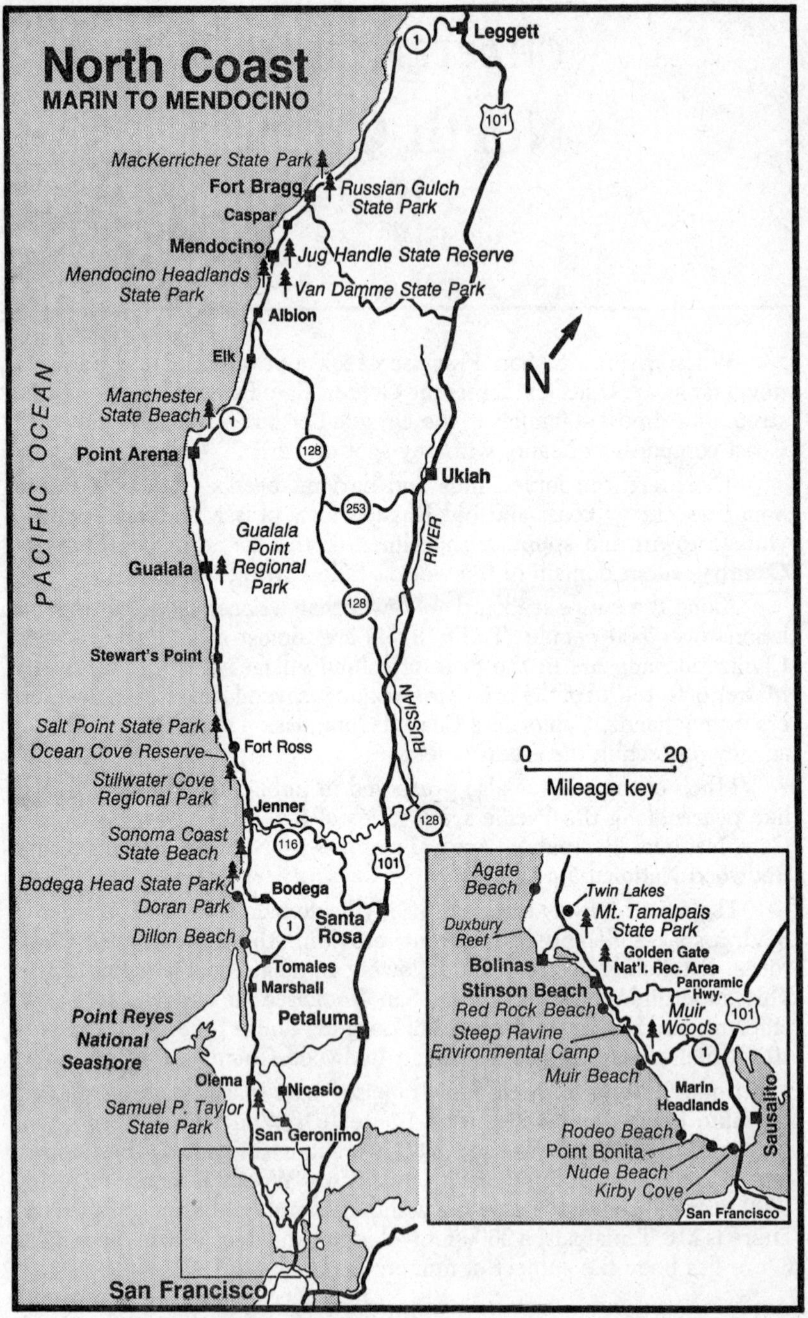
North Coast
MARIN TO MENDOCINO
Leggett
1
101
MacKerricher State Park
Fort Bragg
Russian Gulch State Park
Caspar
Mendocino
Jug Handle State Reserve
Mendocino Headlands State Park
Van Damme State Park
Albion
Elk
N
PACIFIC OCEAN
Manchester State Beach
Point Arena
128
Ukiah
253
Gualala Point Regional Park
Gualala
RIVER
Stewart's Point
RUSSIAN
Salt Point State Park
Ocean Cove Reserve
Fort Ross
0 20
Mileage key
Stillwater Cove Regional Park
Jenner
Sonoma Coast State Beach
116
Bodega Head State Park
Bodega
Doran Park
Santa Rosa
Dillon Beach
Tomales
Marshall
Point Reyes National Seashore
Petaluma
Olema
Nicasio
Samuel P. Taylor State Park
San Geronimo
San Francisco
Agate Beach
Twin Lakes
Mt. Tamalpais State Park
Duxbury Reef
Bolinas
Golden Gate Nat'l. Rec. Area
Stinson Beach
Panoramic Hwy.
Red Rock Beach
Muir Woods
Steep Ravine Environmental Camp
Muir Beach
Marin Headlands
Sausalito
Rodeo Beach
Point Bonita
Nude Beach
Kirby Cove
San Francisco

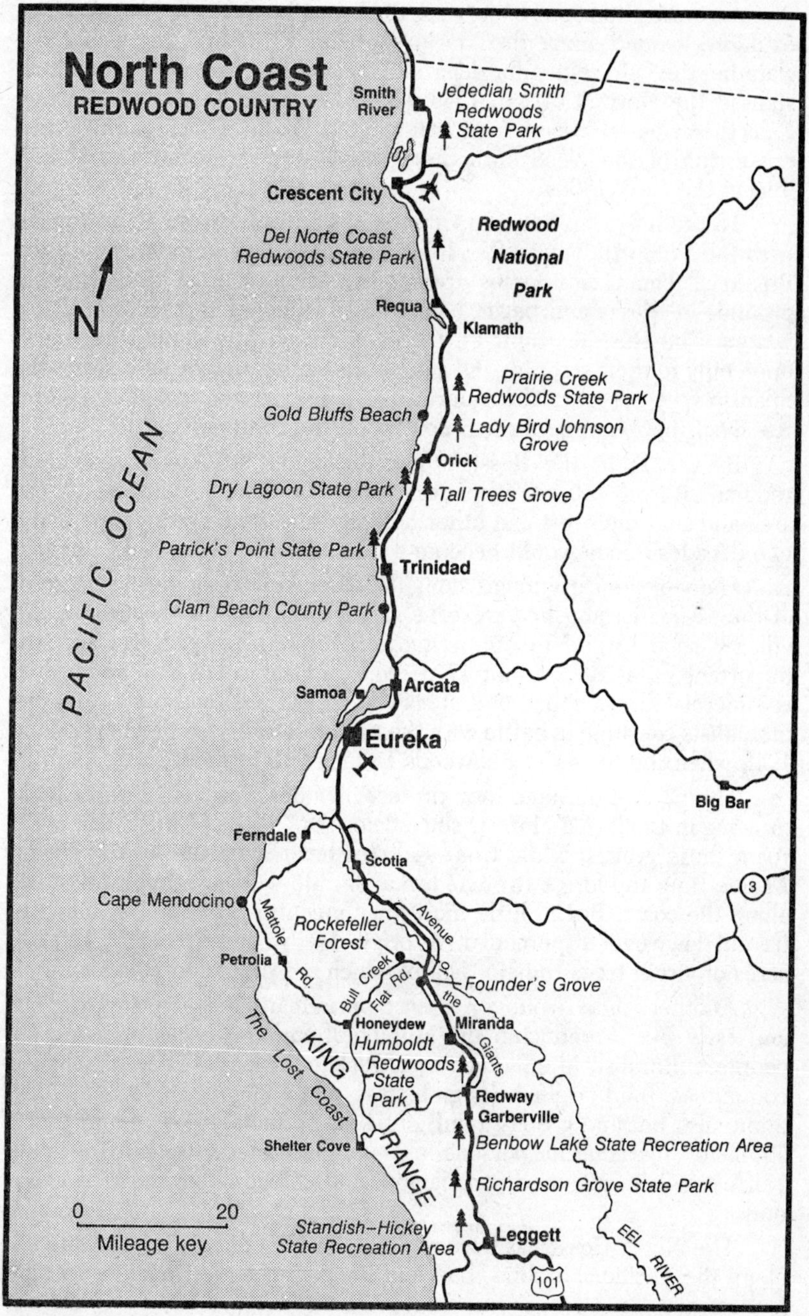
North Coast
REDWOOD COUNTRY
N
PACIFIC OCEAN
Smith River
Jedediah Smith Redwoods State Park
Crescent City
Redwood National Park
Del Norte Coast Redwoods State Park
Requa
Klamath
Prairie Creek Redwoods State Park
Gold Bluffs Beach
Lady Bird Johnson Grove
Orick
Dry Lagoon State Park
Tall Trees Grove
Patrick's Point State Park
Trinidad
Clam Beach County Park
Samoa
Arcata
Eureka
Big Bar
Ferndale
Scotia
3
Cape Mendocino
Mattole Rd.
Rockefeller Forest
Avenue of the Giants
Petrolia
Bull Creek Flat Rd.
Founder's Grove
Honeydew
Miranda
Humboldt Redwoods State Park
The Lost Coast
KING RANGE
Redway
Garberville
Shelter Cove
Benbow Lake State Recreation Area
Richardson Grove State Park
0
20
Mileage key
Standish-Hickey State Recreation Area
Leggett
101
EEL RIVER

According to some historians, Sir Francis Drake, the Renaissance explorer, landed along the Marin shore in 1579, building a fort and claiming the wild region for dear old England. The Portuguese had first sighted the North Coast in 1543 when they espied Cape Mendocino. Back then Coastal Miwok Indians inhabited Marin, enjoying undisputed possession of the place until the Spanish settled the interior valleys during the early 1800s.

To the north, in Sonoma County, the Miwok shared their domain with the Pomo Indians. After 1812 they were also dividing it with the Russians. The Czar's forces arrived in California from their hunting grounds in Alaska and began taking large numbers of otters from local waters. The Russians built Fort Ross and soon proclaimed the region open only to their shipping. Of course, these imperial designs made the Spanish very nervous. The American response was to proclaim the Monroe Doctrine, warning foreign powers off the continent.

By the 1830s the Russians had decimated the otter population, reducing it from 150,000 to less than 100. They soon lost interest in the area and sold their fort and other holdings to John Sutter, whose name two decades hence would become synonymous with the Gold Rush.

Many of the early towns along the coast were born during the days of the 49ers. Established to serve as pack stations for the mines, the villages soon turned to lumbering and fishing. Today these are still important industries. About 17 percent of California's land consists of commercial forest, much of it along the coastal redwood belt. Environmentalists continue to battle with the timber interests as they have since 1918 when the Save-the-Redwoods League was formed.

The natural heritage they protect includes trees which have been growing in California's forests since before the birth of Christ. Elk herds roam these groves, while trout and steelhead swim the nearby rivers. At one time the forest stretched in a 30-mile-wide swath for 450 miles along the coast. But in little more than a century the lumber industry has cut down over 90 percent of the original redwoods. Presently, 155,000 acres of virgin trees remain, half of which are protected in parks.

Another, much younger, cash crop is marijuana. During the '60s and early '70s, Mendocino and Humboldt counties became meccas for counterculturalists intent on getting "back to the land." They established communes, built original-design houses, and plunged into local politics. Some also became green-thumb outlaws, perfecting potent and exotic strains of *sinsemilla* for personal use and black-market sale. They made Northern California marijuana famous and helped boom the local economy.

The North Coast has become home to the country inn as well. All along the Pacific shoreline, bed and breakfasts serve travelers seeking informal ana relaxing accommodations. Local artisans have also proliferated while small shops have opened to sell their crafts.

The great lure for travelers is still the environment. This coastal shelf, tucked between the Coast Ranges and the Pacific, has mountains and rivers, forests and ocean. Once the habitat of Yuki, Athabascan, Wiyot, Yurok, and Tolowa Indians, it remains an adventureland for imaginative travelers. Winters are damp, mornings and evenings sometimes foggy, but the weather overall is temperate. It's a place where you can fish for salmon, go crabbing, and scan the sea for migrating whales. Or simply ease back and enjoy scenery that never stops.

Easy Living

Transportation

ARRIVAL

When traveling by car you can choose between coastal **Route 1** or inland **Route 101**. For those flying, **United Airlines** (800-241-6522) and **WestAir Airlines** (800-241-6522) service the North Coast area. Departing from San Francisco, both stop in Eureka/Arcata; the latter also serves Crescent City.

Greyhound Bus Lines (707-442-0370) travels the entire stretch of Route 101 between San Francisco and Oregon, including the main route through Redwood Country.

CAR RENTALS

It's advisable to rent an auto in San Francisco rather than along the North Coast. There are more rental agencies available and prices are lower. Along lengthy stretches of the coast, car rental companies simply do not exist. There are a few in Mill Valley, Fort Bragg, Eureka, Arcata, Orick, and Crescent City. When they can be found, they are generally in the yellow pages.

PUBLIC TRANSPORTATION

Golden Gate Transit (415-332-6600) has service between San Francisco and Sausalito, then beyond to Point Reyes National Seashore. It also covers Route 101 from San Francisco to Santa Rosa. From Santa Rosa you can pick up coastal connections on **Mendocino Transit Authority** (707-884-3723), which travels Route 1 from Jenner to Point Arena. (There is only one bus a day each way.)

Also, Greyhound runs a bus along Route 128 that follows the coast road between Albion and Fort Bragg. **Mendocino Stage** (707-964-0167), a local line, serves Mendocino and Fort Bragg.

Public transportation from San Francisco to Marin can become a sightseeing adventure when you book passage on a **Golden Gate Transit** (415-453-2100) ferry boat. Cruises to Sausalito and Larkspur from the Ferry Building in San Francisco are crowded with commuters and vacationers alike. The **Red and White Fleet** (415-546-2800) also operates ferries from San Francisco to Sausalito and Tiburon.

BICYCLING

Two-wheeling north of San Francisco is an invigorating sport. Not only is the scenery magnificent, but the accommodations aren't bad either. Many state and national parks sponsor "Bikecentennial" campgrounds where cyclists and hikers can stay for a nominal fee.

In Marin, the Sausalito Bikeway carries along the shoreline past marshes and houseboats. Another bikeway in Tiburon offers spectacular views of Sausalito and San Francisco.

Route 1, the coast road, offers a chance to pedal past a spectacular shoreline of hidden coves, broad beaches, and sheer headlands. Unfortunately, the highway is narrow and winding, and therefore recommended for experienced cyclists only.

Point Reyes National Seashore features miles of bicycling, particularly along Bear Valley Trail. Other popular areas further north include the towns of Mendocino and Ferndale, where level terrain and beautiful landscape combine to create a cyclist's paradise.

For extraordinary bicycle tours, contact **Backroads Bicycle Touring Company** (415-895-1783). This group has various tours through California, designed for beginning, intermediate, and advanced peddlers.

RENTALS

The place to call in south Marin is **Ken's Bike & Sport** (94 Main Street, Tiburon; 415-435-1683).

Point Reyes Bikes (11431 Route 1, Point Reyes Station; 415-663-1768), near Point Reyes National Seashore, and **Mendocino Cyclery** (45040 Main Street, Mendocino; 707-937-4744) also rent bicycles.

Hotels

The best things in life may be free, but beauty has its price on the North Coast, at least where lodging is concerned. The bed and breakfast revolution has swept the area and country inns are proliferating. They are homey, historic, and expensive. There are few ways to better experience this seaside than snuggling in an old country house. Unfortunately, finding a bed and breakfast at a budget price is a trick worthy of any magician.

If you can afford it, don't hesitate. Sitting before a dancing fire while fog curls along the cliffs marks one of the great joys of California life. Should the overhead be too high, you can seek out less expensive lodging in nearby motels and hostels. I've tried to provide possibilities covering a range of prices; since the North Coast is so extensive, however, facilities are listed geographically from south to north rather than by price.

MARIN COAST HOTELS

One of the top resting places in the bayside town of Sausalito is the **Sausalito Hotel** (16 El Portal, Sausalito; 415-332-4155), a 15-room bed and breakfast near the waterfront. Accommodations range from moderate for a small room with shared bath to ultra-deluxe for the Marques of Queensbury room. The last contains furniture once owned by Ulysses S. Grant. All the rooms are beautifully decorated with antiques: clawfoot tubs, brass lamps, extravagant chandeliers, and mahogany wardrobes are some of the elegant accouterments here. Add a congenial staff and you've got a place second only to home.

The nearby **Casa Madrona Hotel** (801 Bridgeway, Sausalito; 415-332-0502) features a modern complex of rooms attached to a 19th-century landmark house. You'll find this two-part structure on a Sausalito hillside overlooking San Francisco Bay. Rooms, beginning at deluxe price and ending in the ultra-deluxe range, have a personal feel and individual names. The modest "Honeywood" is decorated with blond wood and enjoys a garden view, while the "Mariner Room" is done in redwood and looks out on the harbor. There are also three private cottages available in this 35-room bed and breakfast.

Golden Gate Hostel (Fort Barry, Building 941; 415-331-2777) is located in the spectacular Marin Headlands section of the Golden Gate National Recreation Area. Housed in an historic woodframe building, this hostel's dormitory-style accommodations go for low budget prices. There are kitchen facilities available, a game room, and living room. Like most hostels it is closed during the day; you're permitted access only at night and in the morning. Reservations are advised during the summer.

Green Gulch Farm (Route 1 near Muir Beach; 415-383-3134), a Zen retreat and organic farm, offers a guest residence program. Located on a 115-acre spread in a lovely valley, it's a restful and enchanting stop. Enroll in the Buddhist Retreat Program, stay three to five days, and you will pay budget rates, with meals included. The schedule involves meditation, chanting and bowing, plus light work. Or you can simply rent a room by the night (at moderate cost; plus $5 per meal). With nearby hiking trails and beaches, it's a unique place.

Most folks grumble when the fog sits heavy along the coast. At **The Pelican Inn** (Route 1, Muir Beach; 415-383-6000), guests consider fog part of the ambience. Damp air and chill winds add a final element to the old-English atmosphere at this seven-chamber bed and breakfast. Set in a Tudor-style building near Muir Beach, The Pelican Inn re-creates 16th-century England. There's a pub downstairs with a dart board on one wall and a fox hunting scene facing on another. The dining room serves country fare like meat pies, prime rib, and bangers. Upstairs the bedrooms complete the theme. The room I saw contained time-honored furnishings, a wooden chest that looked to have barely survived its Atlantic crossing, and several other antiques. The bed was canopied and the walls adorned with period prints. Highly recommended; reserve well in advance; deluxe.

Location, they say, is the key to real estate. That would make **Sandpiper Motel** (1 Marine Way, Stinson Beach; 415-868-1632) prime property: the place is a short stroll from Stinson Beach, close enough to hear the surf wash the sand. Architecturally, however, the property is no palace. You can rent a sterile, uninspiring room with a mini-kitchenette in the new section for a moderate price. The place will be clean, carpeted, and cluttered with naugahyde furniture. Better yet, take a room in one of the old, funky duplex "cottages." These woodframe affairs have sloping floors and rattling refrigerators (moderate cost with kitchen), but they are roomier and possess a more natural feel. Either way, you can always escape to the beach.

Motel Baulines (41 Wharf Road, Bolinas; 415-868-1311) is one of the cheapest deals around. Located in the rustic town of Bolinas with easy access to the beach, this six-unit facility has rooms at budget prices. Accommodations are clean but spartan: white walls with a few decorations, a table here, a desk there, etc. There is wall-to-wall carpeting and a beamed ceiling but no radio, television, telephones or other newfangled inventions.

There's also **Grand Hotel** (15 Brighton Avenue, Bolinas (415-868-1757), a tiny two-unit business where a room with shared bath and kitchen rents in the budget range. The proprietor also serves as a referral service for other places in town, so check with him about local accommodations.

Within Point Reyes National Seashore, consider the **American Youth Hostel** (Limantour Road, Point Reyes National Seashore; Box 247, Point Reyes Station, CA 94956; 415-669-7414), providing low-rent lodging. In addition to dormitory-style accommodations, the hostel has a patio, ranch-style kitchen, and a living room with fireplace. Perfect for explorers, it is situated near several hiking trails. Budget.

Nearby in Inverness there's a moderately priced place, **Inverness Motel** (12718 Sir Francis Drake Boulevard, Inverness; 415-669-1081), commanding a location along Tomales Bay that would be the envy of many well-heeled hostelries. Unfortunately the architect who designed it faced the rooms toward the road, not the water. You can crane your head out the bathroom window for a slice of that million-dollar view, or suggest that the management lift the establishment from its foundation and turn it 180°. Or decide to pay a moderate rate and forego a view. After all, you will get a color television in a small room with wall-to-wall carpeting. And a chance to play amateur architect for an evening.

As country living goes, it's darn near impossible to find a place as pretty and restful as Point Reyes. People with wander in their hearts and wonder in their minds have been drawn here for years. Not surprisingly, country inns sprang up to cater to star-struck explorers and imaginative travelers. A half-dozen of these small bed and breakfasts, dotted in towns around Point Reyes National Seashore, have joined together to form an information service, **The Inns of Point Reyes** (P.O. Box 145, Inverness, CA 94937; 415-663-1420). Contact them for a descriptive brochure.

Foremost among this bed and breakfast confederacy is **Blackthorne Inn** (266 Vallejo Avenue, Inverness; 415-663-8621), an architectural extravaganza set in a forest of oak, bay trees, and Douglas fir. The four-level house is expressive of the flamboyant "woodbutcher's art" building style popular in the 1970s. Using recycled materials and heavy doses of imagination, the builders created a maze of skylights, bay windows, and french doors, capped by an octagonal tower. A spiral staircase corkscrews up through this multitiered affair to the top deck, where both a hot tub and cold tub are available to guests. There are five bedrooms, all sharing baths and ranging in price between the deluxe and ultra-deluxe categories. Each has been personalized; the most outstanding is the "Eagle's Nest," occupying the glass-encircled octagon at the very top of this Aquarian wedding cake.

Another favorite bed and breakfast lies along the flagstone path at **Ten Inverness Way** (10 Inverness Way, Inverness; 415-669-1648). The place is filled with pleasant surprises, like fruit trees and flowers in the yard, a player piano, and a warm living room with stone fireplace. The four bedrooms are small but cozy, carpeted wall-to-wall and imaginatively decorated with hand-fashioned quilts. All have private baths and rent in the deluxe range. It's a short stroll from the house to the shops and restaurants of Inverness.

In the town of Tomales consider **Byron Randall's Guest House** (25 Valley Street, Tomales; 707-878-9992). It's an old Victorian offering spacious rooms with shared bath at moderate cost. Casual is the password in these parts. There's a sign outside with instructions on how to check yourself in and out if no one is around. Similarly, the rooms are furnished in an imaginatively slapdash fashion and the entire house is decorated with original paintings. That, you see, is because this bed and breakfast doubles as an art gallery. Why not? It also boasts a kitchen, library, and living room for guest use, farmland out back, and a local population of robins, owls, crickets, and bullfrogs. Personally I rate this place with a sky full of stars.

SONOMA AND MENDOCINO COAST HOTELS

In the town of Jenner, where the Russian River meets the Pacific, there are several guest facilities. Least expensive among them is **Lazy River Motel** (Route 1, Jenner; 707-865-2409), a ramshackle brown-shingle building poised above the river. Rooms in this five-unit establishment are carpeted and adequately, if inelegantly, furnished; they range in the moderate price bracket. Try for one with a river view.

A prime Jenner resting spot is **Murphy's Jenner by the Sea** (Route 1, Jenner; 707-865-2377), a bed and breakfast overlooking the river. Several buildings comprise Murphy's spread: you can rent a room, a suite, even a house. Prices start in the moderate range. One of the less expensive accommodations, the personalized "Gull Room," features a quilted bed, old oak wardrobe, and a deck overlooking the river. The "Captain's Cabin," a higher-priced suite, adds features like a hand-carved headboard, living room with a wood stove and antique rocker, and a loft for extra guests. All this includes breakfast in the lodge's fine dining room, an exposed-beam affair with potted plants and yet another river view.

Several lodges along the California coast reflect in their architecture the raw energy and naked beauty of the surrounding sea. Such a one is **Timber Cove Inn** (21780 North Route 1; 15 miles north of Jenner; 707-847-3231). Elemental in style, it is a labyrinth of unfinished woods and bald rocks. The heavy timber lobby is dominated by a walk-in stone fireplace and sits astride a Japanese pond. The 47 guest rooms are finished in redwood with beams and columns exposed. Many are decorated with Ansel Adams prints and Dorothy Bowman serigraphs. Furniture is fashioned from redwood burls and a Japanese motif is reflected in the hot tubs. A bit too stark and unfinished for my taste, the guest rooms nevertheless afford marvelous views of the mountains and open sea. Many have decks, fireplaces, and hot tubs. Timber Cove, fittingly, rests on a cliff directly above the ocean. Restaurant and lounge; deluxe to ultra-deluxe.

A fair bargain can be found along the coast at **Fort Ross Lodge** (20705 Route 1, Jenner; 707-847-3333), three miles north of the old Russian fort. Situated on a hillside overlooking the ocean, this 16-unit establishment consists of a cluster of woodframe buildings. The rooms, priced moderately, have ocean views; the ceilings are knotty pine, floors are carpeted wall-to-wall, and the stylized decor consists of woven baskets hung along the walls. There are televisions and private baths in all rooms, plus a community sauna and hot tub.

About 16 miles north of Jenner, set on a plateau above the ocean, is **Stillwater Cove Ranch** (Route 1, Jenner; 707-847-3227). Formerly a boys' school, this complex of buildings has been transformed into a restful retreat. Rooms start in the budget range and for a moderate price tag you can rent a cottage with fireplace! Even the dairy barn can accommodate guests: it's been converted to a bunkhouse. Set on lovely grounds and populated with peacocks, Stillwater Cove is certainly worth checking in to.

Mar Vista Cottages (35101 Route 1, Gualala; 707-884-3522) is a community of 12 separate cottages scattered around eight acres of ocean-view property. Each is an old woodframe affair with a sitting room and kitchen as well as a bedroom. Several are equipped with decks, fireplaces, or wood stoves; all price in the moderate category. A soaking tub and barbeque facility on the property are surrounded by trees; a long path leads to the beach.

Built in 1903, the **Gualala Hotel** (Route 1, Gualala; 707-884-3441) is a massive two-story structure. It's an old clapboard affair, fully refurbished, that includes a bar and dining room. The 19 rooms upstairs are rather small, and rent in the moderate price range. The wallpaper decor and old-time flourishes give the place a comfy traditional feel, making it a rare find on the North Coast.

A short distance north of Gualala's hotel, but a long step up in price, is the **Old Milano Hotel** (38300 Route 1, Gualala; 707-884-3256). Dating from 1905, it is one of those very special places that people return to year after year. The two-story shiplap house rises between a delicately tended garden and the sea. Anchored just offshore is Castle Rock, a dramatic sea stack. But this palls in comparison to the interior. Each of the six bedrooms upstairs has been furnished and decorated with luxurious antiques: oil paintings, brass lamps, quilts, oak headboards, and plump armchairs. The "wine parlor" downstairs features a stone fireplace and the music room is decorated with William Morris designs. Little wonder the house is registered as an historic place. Rooms at this bed and breakfast inn range upward from the deluxe category; there's also a cottage available, as well as an old caboose converted into living quarters.

Country inns of this genre are quite frequent further north. Near the town of Mendocino there are numerous bed and breakfasts, some outstanding. The seaside towns of Elk, Albion, Little River, Mendocino, and Fort Bragg each house several. Prices are generally high, but for intimacy and personal care, Northern California's inns are unparalleled.

Among the more renowned is **Harbor House** (Route 1, Elk; 707-877-3203). Set on a rise overlooking the ocean, the house is built entirely of redwood. The living room alone, with its unique fireplace and exposed-beam ceiling, is an architectural feat. The house was modeled on a design exhibited at San Francisco's 1915 Panama–Pacific Exposition. Of the ten bedrooms and cottages, several have Franklin stoves and patterned wallpaper as well as antique appointments. Rates are ultra-deluxe, but include breakfast and dinner.

Heritage House (Route 1, Little River; 707-937-5885) was constructed in 1877 and reflects the New England architecture popular then in Northern California. Baby Face Nelson is reputed to have hidden in the old farmhouse which today serves as the inn's reception and dining area. Most guests are housed in nearby cottages which, like the hideout itself, overlook a rocky cove. Rates are set at the ultra-deluxe mark, including breakfast and dinner.

The New England-style farmhouse that has become **Glendeven** (Route 1, Little River; 707-937-0083) dates even farther back, to 1867. The theme is country living, with a meadow out back and dramatic headlands nearby. The sitting room is an intimate affair with a baby grand piano and comfortable armchairs set before a brick fireplace. In the rooms you're apt to find a bed with wooden headboard, an antique wardrobe, and ferns hanging from the ceiling. Glendeven is as charming and intimate as a country inn can be. Rooms price in the deluxe neighborhood, with light breakfast.

The **Little River Inn** (7751 North Route 1, Little River; 707-937-5942), centered in a quaint 1850s-era house, has expanded into a mini-resort with 55 units, a restaurant, tennis courts, lounge, and an 18-hole golf course. Intimacy was lost along the way, but a host of facilities were added. Rooms at the inn proper, decorated in early-California fashion, are moderately priced. There is also a tastefully done motel wing (moderate) as well as a series of cottages, deluxe-priced. The cottages are panelled in wood, furnished in hardwood, and decorated with watercolors. Like most of the other accommodations, they afford grand ocean views.

Less expensive accommodations can be found at the **Mendocino Hotel** (45080 Main Street, Mendocino; 707-937-0511). Set in a falsefront building which dates to 1878, the 52-room hotel building has quarters with shared bath at moderate cost (deluxe in summer). It's a wonderful place, larger than other nearby country inns, with a wood-paneled lobby, full dining room, and living quarters adorned with antiques. Rooms in the garden cottages out back range upward from deluxe price (ultra-deluxe in summer).

The queen of Mendocino is the **MacCallum House** (45020 Albion Street, Mendocino; 707-937-0289), a Gingerbread Victorian built in 1882. The place is a treasure trove of antique furnishings, knickknacks, and other memorabilia. Many of the rooms are individually decorated with canopied beds, rocking chairs, quilts, and wood stoves. Positively everything—the carriage house, barn, greenhouse, gazebo, even the water tower—has been converted into a guest room. Rates on these tastefully rendered rooms start in the moderate category with shared bath, or deluxe with a private privy. The inn serves a continental breakfast.

If location, location, location are the three most important features of real estate, then **Sea Rock Bed & Breakfast Inn** (11101 North Lansing Street, Mendocino; 707-937-5517) poses a triple threat. This 18-unit facility faces the open ocean and offers marvelous views of the waves crashing along Mendocino's vaunted coastline. The guest quarters are tiny clapboard cottages perched on a bluff. Priced in the moderate and deluxe range, these are adequately furnished and equipped with wood burning stoves. The primary appeal is the view, which guests can enjoy from their cottages or a grassy courtyard.

Also consider **Mendocino Village Inn** (44860 Main Street, Mendocino; 707-937-0246), a vintage 1882 house that has two attic rooms, one with a sea view, in the moderate price range. A white shingle-and-clapboard building with mansard roof, the place offers more spacious accommodations with private baths at moderate prices. In a land of pricey hotels, this represents a rare discovery. So does the nearby **Sea Gull Inn** (Lansing and Ukiah streets, Mendocino; 707-937-5204), which has rooms with ocean views at moderate cost. At that price you'll be in the heart of Mendocino in a small hostelry which features an adjoining restaurant.

Seclusion par excellence is found three miles outside Mendocino in a redwood forest. Here **Ames Lodge** (★) (42287 Little Lake Road, Mendocino; 707-937-0811), a raw wood retreat originally planned as a hideaway for writers and musicians, offers commodious accommodations at budget and moderate prices. Built in 1967, this laid-back lodge displays the A-frame and plate-glass style of the era. The decor is understated but appealing (this is the only bed and breakfast you'll ever find that is proud about its lack of antiques). There's a vaulted-ceiling living room with tile fireplace and eight acres of forest. Trails from the lodge lead to a pygmy forest and nearby river. A perfect place to commune with nature. Families welcome.

The **Orca Inn** (31502 Route 1, Fort Bragg; 707-964-5585), a cluster of farmhouses on a bluff directly above the ocean, sits on an 835-acre ranch that extends for a mile along the shore. This unique enclave, ten miles north of Fort Bragg, features a country inn with two moderate-priced rooms. Each is attractively decorated with flower wallpaper, potted plants, and wrought-iron beds. Guests share a homey sun porch and living room with the owners and have access to the kitchen. But the overriding attraction here is the colony of three cottages, each priced moderate. These include a three-bedroom farmhouse, two-bedroom cottage, and a modern studio-style house. All have kitchens and are amply furnished and well decorated. Children under 12 stay for free, over 12 for $10 each, making it ideal for families.

One rule of thumb along the Mendocino Coast—if it's a lodging place it's inevitably a bed and breakfast. That includes the **Cobweb Palace** (38921 Route 1, Westport; 707-964-5588), an 1890-vintage hotel that has been converted by two partners into a country inn with six guest rooms. The ambience is Mendocino-rustic with sloping floors, bland furniture, and bright (too bright) decor. But the vibes are friendly and guests share a sitting room, dining room, and bar. Besides that, the place sits across the street from the ocean with a path that leads down to a sandy beach. Another plus is the rate schedule, which stands in the moderate range for all rooms, including two with private baths and ocean views.

REDWOOD COUNTRY HOTELS

One of Northern California's finest old lodges is the imposing, Tudor-style **Benbow Inn** (445 Lake Benbow Drive, Garberville; 707-923-2124). Located astride a shimmering lake, this regal retreat is bounded by lawns, gardens, and umbrella-tabled patios. The structure itself is a bold three-story manor in the English country tradition. The lobby, paneled in carved wood and adorned by ornamental molding, is a sumptuous sitting area with a grand fireplace. Jigsaw puzzles lie scattered on the clawfoot tables and rocking horses decorate the room. The dining area and lounge are equally elegant. Guest quarters, pegged in the moderate and deluxe price categories, offer such flourishes as quilted beds with wooden headboards, hand-painted doors, marble topped nightstands, period wallprints, and complimentary sherry. Visitors also enjoy tea and scones in the afternoon and evening hors d'oeuvres. Add to this the adjoining lake with its fishing and boating and you have one fine facility.

The cheapest lodging I've found in the southern redwoods area is **Johnston's Motel** (839 Redwood Drive, Garberville; 707-923-3327). Unlike the region's big tag caravansaries, this ten-unit facility has rooms at budget prices. Don't expect a lot of shine. The plain rooms lack any decoration along the cinderblock walls, display scarred furniture, and are small. But they do have wall-to-wall carpeting and stall showers.

Not that I have anything against Johnston's; it's just that Garberville is not my idea of paradise. For a few well-spent dollars more you can rent a room in any of several motels along redwood-lined Avenue of the Giants. **Miranda Gardens Resort** (Avenue of the Giants, Miranda; 707-943-3011) is a good choice. This 16-unit motel has rooms with kitchens and fully equipped cabins at moderate cost. The place features a heated swimming pool, shuffleboard, playground, and market. The facilities are tucked into a redwood grove and the rooms are paneled entirely in redwood.

The predominant business in Redwood Country is the lumber industry, which casts a lengthy shadow in surrounding towns like Scotia. Here the 1920s-era **Scotia Inn** (Main and Mill streets, Scotia; 707-764-5683) lavishly displays the region's product in a redwood-paneled lobby. Antique furnishings decorate this sprawling hotel, which boasts a fashionable restaurant and lounge. The guest rooms, reasonably tabbed in the moderate to deluxe range, are furnished in oak and adorned with armoires, brass lamps, and silk wallpaper. The bathrooms, not to be upstaged, boast brass fixtures, clawfoot tubs, and medicine cabinets of carved wood. A gem.

Way out in Shelter Cove, at the southern end of California's remote Lost Coast, there's the **Beachcomber Inn** (★) (Beachcomber Drive, Shelter Cove; 707-986-7733). A rare find, this three-unit house rests on a bluff overlooking the ocean. The rooms are stylishly furnished and appointed in ultramodern fashion. Two come with kitchens and wood-burning stoves; all seem to be lovingly cared for. Considering that the price tag on this luxury is moderate and that Shelter Cove is one of the coast's most secluded hideaways, the Beachcomber Inn is well worth the effort.

To get away from it all, head further out along the Lost Coast, where the 4000-foot King Range has created a shoreline wilderness. Amenities are rare in these parts but you will find a collection of clapboard cottages back up in the mountains. **Mattole River Resort** (★) (42354 Mattole Road, Honeydew; 707-629-3445) offers full-facility cottages complete with kitchenettes. Each is plain but comfortably furnished and features a sitting room as well as a bedroom. This rustic colony sits amid shade trees and is backdropped by forested hills. Budget.

The cheapest lodging of all is in the neon motels along Route 101 on the outskirts of Eureka. Many advertise room rates on highway signs along the southern entrance to town. **Surf Motel** (2411 Broadway, Eureka; 707-443-4660) is typical. Rooms here are priced in the budget range. These small bland rooms lack wall decorations over the simulated-wood panelling, and feature naugahyde furniture, stall showers, etc. But they are clean, carpeted, and equipped with color televisions.

For country inn sensibility in an urban environment, **Old Town Bed & Breakfast Inn** (1521 3rd Street, Eureka; 707-445-3951) comes highly recommended. Just a couple blocks from Eureka's fabled Carson Mansion, this five-bedroom house dates from 1871. It's a Greek revival structure with a winding staircase and a wealth of antiques. Plushly carpeted and adorned with patterned wallpaper, the house has been beautifully redecorated. Room prices, still competitive for an inn of this sort, range in the moderate category. The price of admission includes evening wine and hors d'oeuvres and a full country-style breakfast.

Another of Eureka's spectacular bed and breakfast inns is **Carter House** (1033 3rd Street, Eureka; 707-445-1390), one of the finest Victorians I've ever seen. This grand old three-story house is painted in light hues and decorated with contemporary art work, lending an airy quality seldom found in vintage homes. The place, quite simply, is beautiful: light streams through bay windows; Oriental rugs are scattered across hardwood floors; there are sumptuous sitting rooms, and oak banisters that seemingly climb forever. In the seven guest rooms are antique nightstands and armoires, beds with bold wooden headboards, ceramic pieces, and knickknacks. Style is the password to this retreat (and a moderate to deluxe tab the price of admission).

For traditional and stylish lodging, also consider **Eureka Inn** (7th and F streets, Eureka; 707-442-6441). Set in an imposing Tudor gabled building near Eureka's Old Town section, it provides excellent accommodations. There's a wood-beamed lobby with large fireplace and comfortable sitting area, a pool, jacuzzi and sauna, plus a cafe, gourmet restaurant, and piano bar. Built in 1922 and registered as a National Historic Landmark, this huge hotel has 110 guest rooms. These are well-appointed and attractively decorated; priced in the deluxe category.

For an extra dash of history in your nightly brew, there is **Shaw House Inn** (703 Main Street, Ferndale; 707-786-9958) in nearby Ferndale. It's only fitting to this bed and breakfast that Ferndale is an island in time where the Victorian era still obtains. The Shaw House, it seems, is the oldest home in town. A Carpenter Gothic creation, it was modeled on Hawthorne's *House of the Seven Gables*. A library, parlor, dining room, and deck are available to guests, and a full breakfast is served every morning. The owner, a former antique dealer, has furnished each room with antiques, many from her private collection. Ironically, the only negative feature here is the owner herself. In each of the three encounters my wife and I have had with her she has been incredibly rude. Rooms with shared or half baths are moderate in price.

Also outside Eureka in the town of Arcata, **Arcata Crew House Hostel** (1390 I Street, Arcata; 707-822-9995) provides lodging at budget prices. One of the more commodious hostels, it has several private and double rooms; no room contains more than four sleepers. Varying from similar setups, the Crew House permits couples to stay together. Situated in two adjacent houses, the place features a wood-paneled living room with brick fireplace, dining room, yard, and kitchen. Open only in summer (June through August).

True to its name, the **Plough and Stars Country Inn** (1800 27th Street, Arcata; 707-822-8236) is set in an 1860s-era farmhouse and surrounded by tilled fields. Located outside Arcata, this five-room bed and breakfast offers guests three sitting rooms and two acres on which to roam. The place has an easy, homey feel about it. Each room is trimly decorated and furnished with basic accouterments. Accommodations with shared or private baths are moderately priced.

You will be hard pressed anywhere along the coast to find a view more alluring than that of **Trinidad Bed & Breakfast** (Edwards and Trinity streets, Trinidad; 707-677-0840). This New England-style shingle house, set in a tiny coastal town, looks across Trinidad Bay, past fishing boats and sea rocks, seals and sandy beaches, to tree-covered headlands. The country-style rooms are equipped with standard furnishings and painted nursery colors. There are two fireplaces and a dining room for guests to share. Rooms with shared baths are moderate in price (deluxe during summer). Of the four guest rooms, two enjoy private baths, one has a kitchen.

Farther north in Crescent City, along the scimitar strand that gave the town its name, is **Crescent Beach Motel** (1455 Route 101, Crescent City; 707-464-5436). A 23-unit establishment, it has plate-glass views of the ocean at budget rates. Rooms are small, unimaginatively furnished in naugahyde, and lack any decoration. They do have carpets, televisions, and those oh so priceless sea vistas.

Restaurants

MARIN COAST RESTAURANTS

From the Marin Headlands region, the nearest restaurants are in the bayside town of Sausalito. Then, progressing north, you'll find dining spots scattered throughout the towns and villages along the coast.

In Sausalito, you'll know the bill of fare by the name—**Hamburgers** (737 Bridgeway, Sausalito; 415-332-9471); and you can tell the quality of the food by the line outside. Local folks and out-of-towners alike jam this postage-stamp-sized eatery. They come not only for charcoal-broiled burgers, but bratwurst, Italian sausage, and foot-long hotdogs as well. It's tough securing a table, but you can always pull up a bench in the park across the street.

Better yet, head to **Zack's By the Bay**, (Bridgeway and Turney Street, Sausalito; 415-332-9779) where you can enjoy a charbroiled burger on a patio overlooking the water. Prices are slightly higher at this local gathering place, but those bayside tables are worth the monetary outlay. In addition to sandwiches, breakfast items, and several dinner entrees, Zack's features a full bar. Budget to moderate.

Sausalito sports many seafood restaurants, most of which are overpriced and few of which are good. So it's best to steer a course for **Seven Seas** (682 Bridgeway, Sausalito; 415-332-1304). It lacks the view of the splashy establishments, but does feature an open-air patio in back. The menu includes scallops, Alaskan king crab, salmon, and other entrees, priced moderately. Landlubbers can choose from several meat platters; at lunch sandwiches are served; also open for breakfast.

If you long for a sea vista and an eyeful of San Francisco skyline, try **Horizons** (558 Bridgeway, Sausalito; 415-331-3232). Housed in the turn-of-the-century San Francisco Yacht Club, this spiffy seafood restaurant has a wall of windows for those inside looking out, and a porch for those who want to be outside looking further. Then, of course, there's the food: shellfish and other aquatic fare, with chicken and steak dishes added for good measure. Some beautiful carpentry went into the design of this place. There's also a popular bar here, making it a choice spot to drink as well as eat. Moderate to deluxe.

Stinson Beach sports several restaurants; my favorite is the **Sand Dollar Restaurant** (3466 Route 1, Stinson Beach; 415-868-0434), with facilities for dining indoors or on the patio. At lunch this informal eatery serves hamburgers and sandwiches. At dinner there are fried prawns, scallops, and fresh fish dishes; they also serve meat dishes like broiled lamb chops, beef *medaillons*, and porterhouse steak. With oilcloths on the table and random artwork on the wall, it is a local gathering point.

Over in Bolinas the **Wild Rose Cafe** (11 Wharf Road, Bolinas; 415-868-9969) serves breakfast, lunch, and dinner. At breakfast, choose from among several omelettes plus such dishes as eggs Benedict and eggs Blackstone; lunch features burgers and sandwiches; dinner involves a half-dozen entrees including streak, prawns, fish, chicken, and a vegetable dish. Price-wise, dinner is the best bargain (served only in summer). Breakfasts are tabbed a bit high, but overall this cozy country restaurant is moderately priced.

A bit less formal is **The Shop** (46 Wharf Road, Bolinas; 415-868-9984) down the street. Here you can pull up a table or counter space and order from a soup, salad, and sandwich menu. With its dark pine walls and rustic decor, this cafe has a singular air. A good spot for a light meal.

The Grey Whale (12781 Sir Francis Drake Boulevard, Inverness; 415-669-1244), a woodframe cafe in the center of tiny Inverness, serves delicious pizza and bakery goods as well as soups and salads. With its overhead fans and espresso machine, the place has a touch of city style in a country setting. A good place for lunch or light dinner.

Nearby **Inverness Inn Restaurant** (Sir Francis Drake Boulevard, Inverness; 415-669-1109) has a wider array of dishes. The lunch menu features soups, sandwiches, omelettes, and several Mexican dishes. At dinner there are oysters from local beds, chicken and prawn dishes, and fresh fish; all dinners are priced in the moderate range.

Small as Inverness may be, it supports a noticeable Czech community which is evident in places like **Manka's Czech Restaurant** (30 Callendar Way, Inverness; 707-669-1034). With its open fireplace and ethnic decor, this white-tablecloth dining room prepares Eastern European breakfasts and dinners. Morning dishes include *ceske palacinky* (crepes filled with raspberry preserves) and an egg dish called *vajicka*. At night you can munch on herring or sausage appetizers, then dig into a plate of *teleci na paprice* (veal in garlic, paprika, and sour cream), *veprovy gulas* (pork goulash) or *pecena kachna* (duckling with caraway sauce). Deluxe.

The Station House Cafe (Main Street, Point Reyes Station; 415-663-1515) comes highly recommended by several local residents. There is a down-home feel to this wood-paneled restaurant. Maybe it's the artwork along the walls. Regardless, it's really the food that draws folks from the surrounding countryside. The dinner menu includes fresh oysters, plus chicken, steak, and fish dishes. There are also daily chef's specials, such as grilled salmon or chicken breast on spinach julienne. Dinners are served with soup or salad, and a basket of piping hot popovers. The Station House also features a complete breakfast menu; at lunch time there are light crepe and seafood dishes, plus sandwiches and salads. Moderate to deluxe.

SONOMA AND MENDOCINO COAST RESTAURANTS

The businesses listed below represent the best restaurants, in terms of cuisine and cost, I found on that long stretch of coastline from Bodega Bay to Leggett. Sometimes the distance between dining spots may prove too great for your appetite. In that case, remember towns like Bodega Bay, Fort Ross, Casper, and Westport have roadside cafes. It's just that none seemed particularly worthy of note. Should hunger call, however, don't feel limited to my subjective selections.

Up in Jenner the best bet for an economical meal is **Bridgehaven Restaurant** (Route 1, Jenner; 707-865-2095), a comfortable place with plate-glass views of the Russian River. The many breakfast selections, hamburgers, and club sandwiches are the budget-minded diner's wisest choice. Lunch entrees like fettucine alfredo and shrimp creole price in the moderate category. But dinners—including oysters, prawns, prime rib, and pork chops—rise quickly into the deluxe range.

For the *best* meal hereabouts (or for that matter, anywhere about), head for **River's End Restaurant** (Route 1, Jenner; 707-865-2484). Situated at that momentous crossroad of the Russian River and Pacific Ocean (and commanding a view of both), this outstanding little place is a restaurant with imagination. How else do you explain a dinner menu that ranges from *medaillons* of venison to crisped duckling to coconut-fried shrimp; or breakfast fare that includes German glazed apple pancakes and *gravlax* with shrimp and capers? Not to mention good service and a selection of aperitifs. River's End is a great place for ocean lovers and culinary adventurers. Deluxe in quality and price.

Salt Point Lodge (23255 Route 1, Jenner; 707-847-3234), 17 miles north of Jenner, features a small restaurant serving breakfast, lunch, and dinner at moderate prices. The menu relies heavily on seafood—halibut, oysters, scallops—but also includes chicken, steak, and lamb dishes. At lunch, enjoy a variety of salads, sandwiches, or seafood selections.

The 80-year-old **Gualala Hotel** (Route 1, Gualala; 707-884-3441) has an attractive dining room with a moderate–deluxe menu that varies from country fried chicken to breaded oysters. Stops along the way include snapper, ravioli, and rib-eye steak. Lunch is served and you can also stop for a hearty breakfast featuring omelettes. What makes dining here really special is the old hotel with its big front porch and antique decor.

Okay, so **St. Orres** (36601 Route 1, Gualala; 707-884-3303) is yet another California cuisine restaurant. But it's the only one you'll see that looks more like it should be in Russia than along the California coast. With its dizzying spires this elegant structure evokes images of Moscow and old St. Petersburg. Serving dinner and Sunday brunch, the kitchen provides an everchanging menu of fresh game and fish dishes. The fixed-price menu will include hot and chilled soups, poached salmon, beef filets, rack of lamb, and several seasonal specialties. Even if you're not interested in dining, it might be worth a stop to view this architectural extravaganza. Deluxe.

The Upstairs Cafe (245 Main Street, Point Arena; 707-882-2600) serves tasty homemade cuisine at breakfast and lunch. Morning fare includes buckwheat pancakes, *huevos rancheros*, and cheese omelettes; at lunchtime there are tostadas, burritos, sautéed *tofu*, and a hot sandwich dish, all at budget prices.

For more traditional dishes try the **Point Arena Cafe** (Main Street, Point Arena; 707-882-2069), a small restaurant nearby. Pull up a table or a chair at the counter and order from an all-American, budget-priced menu.

The **Roadhouse Cafe** (6061 South Route 1, Elk; 707-877-3285) serves breakfast and lunch at budget to moderate prices. Meals are a standard offering of egg dishes and pancakes, hamburgers, and sandwiches.

The **Albion River Inn** (3790 North Route 1, Albion; 707-937-4044), set high on a hillside above the Albion River and the ocean, is a plate-glass dining spot serving California cuisine. The pasta, seafood, vegetables, and herbs are all fresh. Open only for dinner, it provides a menu of lingcod, red snapper, and petrale sole as well as steaks, veal, and chicken dishes. Priced in the moderate to deluxe range, it specializes in otherworldly ocean views.

For budget-priced Mexican meals stop by **Original Chubbs Cafe** (7675 North Route 1, Little River; 707-937-1404). It's a small shingle house with an oceanview deck. Here are burritos, tostadas, tacos, *quesadillas,* and hamburgers as well as daily specials. No breakfast served.

I'm told that the **Little River Restaurant** (7750 North Route 1, Little River; 707-937-4945) is an absolute must. It's only open Thursday through Sunday, just for dinner, and has but a half-dozen tables. The California cuisine includes appetizers of smoked albacore and steamed mussels. For entrees there are roast duck with apricot-vermouth sauce, leg of lamb smeared with apple brandy and garlic, quail in a hazelnut-port sauce, and roasted pork loin flavored with red chiles and currants. Deluxe.

In Mendocino moderate prices went out when the flood of tourists came in. Over at **The Sea Gull** (Lansing and Ukiah streets, Mendocino; 707-937-2100) you can still order solid meals at reasonable prices. The menu is a standard blend of fresh seafood, meat, and poultry dishes. At lunch there are soups, sandwiches, and assorted entrees, and during breakfast you'll find a variety of omelettes. With a knotty-pine interior and musical instruments as decor The Sea Gull is unique and inviting.

The best place for a light meal in Mendocino is **Main Street Delicatessen** (Main Street, Mendocino; 707-937-5031). An informal establishment, it's largely self-service. The substantial breakfast menu starts the day, and a selection of deli-style sandwiches is featured later on. Definitely budget.

For complete multicourse meals, **Papa Luigi's Wellspring Restaurant** (955 Ukiah Street, Mendocino; 707-937-4567) offers one of Mendocino's most reasonably priced menus. Dinner features several Italian and international meals, including Indonesian *tempe* sautéed with vegetables and coconut milk, fresh pasta, stuffed clams, and veal dishes. There's also salmon, a catch of the day prepared in any of three ways, and a stir-fry vegetable dish. At a moderate price no less! The restaurant itself is simple and rustic in decor, with knotty-pine panelling, weavings on the walls, and a proliferation of potted plants. It's also open for lunch. All in all an enticing establishment.

Mendocino's best known dining room is well deserving of its renown. **Cafe Beaujolais** (961 Ukiah Street, Mendocino; 707-937-5614), situated in a small antique house on the edge of town, serves designer dishes. Breakfast and lunch alone are culinary occasions with the afternoon menu including spicy ground lamb sandwiches, baked polenta with meat sauce and cheese, cold poached seafood, and Thai short ribs. Dinner is less predictable given the ever-changing menu. Perhaps they'll be serving warm duck salad and rabbit soup with entrees like sautéed trout with Szechuan peppercorns, leg of lamb stuffed with garlic, and steamed salmon with chervil beurre blanc sauce. Or you might order a fixed-price dinner with oysters in duck sauce, baked goat cheese, roast leg of lamb, and coconut ice cream sundae. Excellent cuisine; deluxe.

Fort Bragg's favorite dining spot is easy to remember—**The Restaurant** (418 North Main Street, Fort Bragg; 707-964-9800). Despite the name, this is no generic eating place but a creative kitchen serving excellent dinners. It's decorated with dozens of paintings by contemporary artists, lending a sense of the avant garde to this informal establishment. Serving lunch, dinner, and Sunday brunch, The Restaurant offers entrees like sautéed prawns with shallots, blackened rockfish, lamb chops in parmesan crust, chicken cutlet with chile butter and lime, and asparagus quiche. Deluxe.

REDWOOD COUNTRY RESTAURANTS

Personally, my favorite dining place in these parts is the **Benbow Inn** (445 Lake Benbow Drive, Garberville; 707-923-2124). This Tudor lodge serves meals in a glorious wood-paneled dining room that will make you feel as though you're feasting at the estate of a British baron. The sideboards are carved wood with marble tops and the multi-pane windows look out upon landscaped gardens. Every evening the bill of fare includes prawns sautéed in apples and cucumbers, sweetbreads flambéed in cognac, and steak in roquefort sauce. There is also salmon, duck, curried chicken, and trout almondine. Deluxe.

In the southern redwoods region you'll be hard pressed to find a better moderate-priced restaurant than **Woodrose Cafe** (911 Redwood Drive, Garberville; 707-923-3191). T'aint much on looks—just a counter, a few tables and chairs, and a small patio out back. But the kitchen folk cook up some potent concoctions. That's why the place draws locals in droves. The night I was there the dinner menu was a study in fish, chicken, and vegetarian cuisine. There was fresh seafood, pasta marinara, chicken piccata, pasta al pesto, and a host of other dishes. Breakfast and lunch looked equally inviting. The Woodrose Cafe is a good reason to visit otherwise drab Garberville.

Proceeding north along the Avenue of the Giants, you'll encounter cafes in tiny towns like Miranda, Myers Flat, Weott, and Pepperwood. Most are tourist-oriented businesses, undistinguished and slightly overpriced, but adequate as way stations.

For a touch of good taste in the heart of Redwood Country try the **Scotia Inn** (Main and Mill streets, Scotia; 707-764-5683). The dining room of this revered old hotel is trimly paneled in polished redwood, furnished with captain's chairs, and illuminated by brass chandeliers. Serving dinner only, it features a menu with butterflied prawns, snapper almondine, oysters, duck à l'orange, chicken teriyaki, prime rib, steak, and veal dishes. Deluxe.

Marina Restaurant (Shelter Cove; 707-986-7432) is just your standard nondescript cafe—vinyl tables, naugahyde booths, simulated wood paneling. Likewise, the menu is a moderately priced mix of fresh fish, fried chicken, barbequed ribs, steak, scallops, shrimp, and other all-American fare. The reason you'll be intensely interested in this common cafe is that it represents one of the few restaurants along the 80-mile stretch of shoreline solitude known as California's Lost Coast. Moreover, it's located on a sea bluff directly above the fishing fleet on Shelter Cove. The views extend along miles of mountainous coastline.

The historic Old Town section of Eureka, a rebuilt neighborhood of stately Victorians, supports several good restaurants. **The Sandwich Factory** (317 3rd Street, Eureka; 707-443-3622) has a sandwich menu worthy of any delicatessen. There are also soups, salads, and a few Greek dishes at this laid-back dining spot.

Down the street at **Tomaso's Tomato Pies** (216 E Street, Eureka; 707-445-0100) they serve pizzas as well as spinach pie, sausage sandwiches, and pizza burgers. That's at lunch. Come dinner they add calzone, lasagna, ravioli, canneloni, and a host of other Italian dishes. Excellent food at moderate prices.

For Asian fare there's **Samurai Japanese Cuisine** (621 5th Street, Eureka; 707-442-6802), a simple dining room appointed with bamboo screens and colorful cloth paintings. It's dinner only, folks, with a menu that includes standard sukiyaki, tempura, and teriyaki dishes, plus a "Shogun's Feast" that features marinated shrimp and beef. Moderate.

When the evening calls for intimate dining in a small gourmet restaurant, consider **Ramone's Opera Alley Cafe** (409 Opera Alley, Eureka; 707-444-3339). This white-tablecloth dining room, with simple country decor, serves sophisticated dishes like roquefort shrimp, ginger-mustard scallops, chicken Greco (with feta cheese and Greek olives), veal with prosciutto and steak *au poivre*. At lunch there are stuffed croissants, salads, and a few charcoal-broiled dishes. Deluxe.

For a seafood dinner overlooking Humboldt Bay, one place stands above anything else. **Lazio's** (foot of C Street, Eureka; 707-442-5772), a sprawling restaurant, has been a Eureka institution for years. Priced in the deluxe category, it features crab legs, shrimp, scallops, and oysters prepared in a variety of ways. There's also breaded halibut, broiled salmon, and grilled rex sole. The meat menu is limited to steak and chicken. But when in Rome. . .do as Italian fishing families like the Lazios do.

For a dining experience lumberjack-style, there's **Samoa Cookhouse** (Samoa Road, Samoa; 707-442-1659) just outside Eureka. A local lumber company has opened its chow house to the public, serving three meals daily. Just join the crowd piling into this unassuming eatery, sit down at a school cafeteria-style table and dig in. You'll be served redwood-size portions of soup, salad, meat, potatoes, vegetables, and dessert—you can even ask for seconds. Ask for water and they'll plunk down a pitcher, order coffee and someone will bring a pot. It's noisy, crowded, hectic, and great fun. Moderate prices, with reduced rates for children.

Paradise Ridge Cafe (942 G Street, Arcata; 707-826-1394), an Arcata spot popular with students from nearby Humboldt State, has a diverse menu that ranges in price from moderate to deluxe. On the lighter end of the scale are burgers, sandwiches, and several Mexican and fettucine meals. At the other end are the steak and prawn dishes. With its potted plants (including a banana tree!) and overhead fans, the place does have a touch of its namesake. What sold me was not only the tasty food but the fact that the cafe has that greatest of human inventions—an espresso machine. And uses it with facility!

The **Seascape Restaurant** (Trinidad Pier, Trinidad; 707-677-3762) is small and unassuming. There are little more than a dozen tables and booths at this seafood dining room. But the walls of plate glass gaze out upon a rocky headland and expansive bay. Situated at the foot of Trinidad Pier, the local eating spot overlooks the town's tiny fishing fleet. The dishes, many drawn from surrounding waters, include halibut, rock cod, salmon, clams, and lobster. Landlubbers dine on tournedos, broiled chicken, and filet mignon. Lunch and breakfast menus are equally inviting. Moderate.

From Trinidad to the Oregon border the countryside is sparsely populated. Crescent City is the only town of real size, but you'll find nondescript cafes in such places as Orick, Klamath, and Smith River.

Crescent City—like the entire North Coast—is seafood country. Best place around is **Harbor View Grotto** (155 Citizen's Dock Road, Crescent City; 707-464-3815), a family restaurant with an ocean view. Moderately priced, this plate-glass eatery features a long inventory of ocean dishes—whole clams, fried prawns or oysters, scallops, red snapper, salmon, cod, halibut, trout, and so on, not to mention the seafood salads and shrimp cocktails. There are also a few meat dishes plus an assortment of sandwiches. Worth a stop.

The Great Outdoors

The Sporting Life

FISHING

All along the coast, charter boats depart daily to fish for salmon, Pacific snapper, or whatever else is running. If you hanker to try your luck, contact **Caruso's Sportfishing and Seafood** (Harbor Drive, Sausalito; 415-332-1015), **Loch Lomond Live Bait House** (Loch Lomond Marina, San Rafael; 415-456-0321), **Bodega Bay Sportfishing** (Bodega

Whale Watching

It is the world's longest mammal migration: 6000 miles along the Pacific coast from the Bering Sea to Baja California, then back again. The creatures making the journey measure 50 feet and weigh 40 tons. During the entire course of their incredible voyage they neither eat nor sleep.

Every year from mid-December through early February, the California gray whale cruises southward along the California coast. Traveling in "pods" numbering three to five, these magnificent creatures hug the shoreline en route to their breeding grounds.

Since the whales use local coves and promontories to navigate, they are easy to spot from land. Just watch for the rolling hump, the slapping tail, or a lofty spout of spuming water. Sometimes these huge creatures will breach, leaping 30 feet above the surface, then crashing back with a thunderous splash.

Several outfits sponsor whale-watching cruises: these include **Oceanic Society Expeditions** (415-474-3385) in San Francisco, **New Sea Angler & Jaws** (Box 1148, Bodega Bay; 707-875-3495), and **King Salmon Charters** (5333 Herrick Road, Eureka; 707-442-3474). For information elsewhere consult the "Sporting Life" sections.

California gray whales live to 40 or 50 years and have a world population numbering about 17,000. Their only enemies are killer whales and humans. They mate during the southern migration one year, then give birth at the end of the following year's migration. The calves, born in the warm, shallow waters of Baja, weigh a ton and measure about 16 feet. By the time they are weaned seven months later, the young are already 26 feet long.

Blue whales, humpback whales, dolphins, and porpoises also sometimes visit the coast. Gray whales can be seen again from March through mid-May, though further from shore, during their return migration north. So keep an eye sharply peeled: that rocky headland on which you are standing may be a crow's nest in disguise.

Bay; 707-875-3344), **Noyo Fishing Center** (32450 North Harbor Drive, Fort Bragg; 707-964-7609), **King Salmon Charters** (5333 Herrick Avenue, Eureka; 707-442-3474), or **Sailfish** (Eureka; 707-442-6682).

HORSEBACK AND LLAMA RIDING

There are few prettier places to ride than Point Reyes National Seashore, where you can canter through rolling ranch country and out along sharp sea cliffs. **Bear Valley Stables** (Bear Valley Road, Inverness; 415-663-1570) conducts mounted tours of this extraordinary area.

Further north there are opportunities to ride at **Lazy L Ranch** (2969 Fickle Hill Road, Arcata; 707-822-6736).

For a unique pack trip on the back of a llama, contact **Mama's Llamas** (P.O. Box 655, El Dorado, CA 95623; 916-622-2566), which conducts tours of Point Reyes and other areas, or **Lost Coast Llama Caravans** (77321 Usal Road, Whitethorn, CA 95489), which explores the Lost Coast region.

RIVER EXPLORING

Try the **Electric Rafting Company** (P.O. Box 3456, Eureka; 707-445-3456) for trips down the Salmon and Klamath rivers.

WINDSURFING

The surf may not be up on San Francisco Bay, but the wind almost always is! For sailboard rentals, try **Battens & Boards** (Bridgeway and Pine Street, Sausalito; 415-332-0212) and **Sausalito Sailboards** (1505 Bridgeway, Sausalito; 415-331-9463).

TENNIS

The Bay Area is the third most active region in the nation for tennis. Cities all around the Bay have public courts, many lighted for night play. For information in Sausalito, call 415-332-4520.

Beaches and Parks

MARIN COAST BEACHES AND PARKS

MARIN HEADLANDS AREA BEACHES AND PARKS

Kirby Cove—This pocket beach, located at the end of a one-mile trail, nestles in the shadow of the Golden Gate Bridge. The views from beachside are unreal: gaze up at the bridge's steel lacework or out across the gaping mouth of the Gate. When the fog's away, it's a sunbather's paradise; regardless of the weather, this cove is favored by those who like to fish.

Facilities: Picnic area, toilets; restaurants and groceries are available several miles away in Sausalito.

Getting there: The beach is located in the Marin Headlands section of the Golden Gate National Recreation Area. Take the first exit, Alexander Avenue, after crossing the Golden Gate Bridge. Then take an immediate left, following the sign back toward San Francisco. Next, bear right at the signs for Forts Baker, Barry, and Cronkhite. Follow the road three-tenths of a mile to a turnout where a sign will mark the trailhead.

Nude Beach (★)—This is a long, narrow corridor of sand tucked under the Marin Headlands. With steep hills behind and a grand view of the Golden Gate in front, it's a perfect place for naturists and nature lovers alike. It cannot be found on maps or atlases, but local folks and savvy travelers know it well (some call it "Black Sands," others "Upper Fisherman's Beach").

Facilities: Restaurants and groceries are located several miles away in Sausalito.

Getting there: This beach is located in the Marin Headlands section of the Golden Gate National Recreation Area. Follow the directions to Kirby Cove trailhead (see listing above). Continue on the paved road (Conzelman Road) for two-and-a-third miles. Shortly after passing the steep downhill section of this road, you'll see a parking lot on the left with a trailhead. Follow the trail to the beach.

Rodeo Beach—A broad sandy beach, this place is magnificent not only for the surrounding hillsides and nearby cliffs, but also for the quiescent lagoon at its back. It boasts a miniature island offshore, named appropriately for the creatures that turned its surface white—Bird Island. Given its proximity to San Francisco, Rodeo Beach is a favorite among the natives.

Facilities: Restrooms; information center, 415-331-1541. Restaurants and groceries are several miles away in Sausalito.

Camping: Not permitted. There is, however, a hostel nearby (see "Hotels" section in this chapter).

Getting there: The beach is located in the Marin Headlands section of the Golden Gate National Recreation Area. After crossing Golden Gate Bridge on Route 101, take the first exit, Alexander Avenue. Follow the signs through the tunnel to Golden Gate National Recreation Area. Continue along Bunker Road to Rodeo Beach.

MARIN HEADLANDS TO POINT REYES BEACHES AND PARKS

Muir Woods National Monument—If it weren't for the crowds, this redwood preserve would rank little short of majestic. Designated a national treasure by President Theodore Roosevelt in 1908, it features stately groves of tall timber. For a complete description, consult the "Sightseeing" section in this chapter.

Facilities: Snack bar, giftshop, restrooms; six miles of hiking trails; information center, 415-388-2595.

Getting there: Located off Route 1 on Panoramic Highway about 17 miles north of San Francisco.

Mt. Tamalpais State Park—Spectacularly situated between Mt. Tamalpais and the ocean, this 6000-acre park offers everything from mountaintop views to a rocky coastline. Thirty miles of hiking trails wind past stands of cypress, Douglas fir, Monterey pine, and California laurel. The countryside draws nature lovers and sightseers alike.

Facilities: Picnic areas, restrooms, refreshment stand, and a ranger station are located in various parts of the park. At **West Point Inn** (100 Panoramic Highway, Mill Valley; 415-388-9955) there are rooms and cabins available; kitchen facilities. Located along a trail, the inn provides a marvelous retreat. $15 per person nightly; bring a sleeping bag and food. No heat or electricity; very rustic.

Camping: Permitted at Pantoll Park Headquarters (415-388-2070); facilities in this well-shaded spot include picnic areas, restrooms, running water; seven-day limit; reservations through Ticketron. There's also camping at Shansky Backpack Camp, located along the Pacific Coast Trail, two miles south of park headquarters. Picnic tables, pit toilet, no running water; $10 nightly; seven-day limit. The newest and most attractive campsite is Steep Ravine Environmental Camp (see listing below).

Getting there: Follow Route 1 north through Mill Valley; turn right on Panoramic Highway, which runs along the park border.

Muir Beach—Because of its proximity to San Francisco, this spot is a favorite among local people. Located at the foot of a coastal valley, Muir forms a semicircular cove. There's a sandy beach and ample opportunity for picnicking.

Facilities: Picnic area, restrooms. Restaurants and groceries are located several miles away.

Getting there: Located on Route 1, about 16 miles north of San Francisco.

Steep Ravine Environmental Camp—Set on a shelf above the ocean, this outstanding site is bounded on the other side by sharp slopes. Contained within Mt. Tamalpais State Park, it features a small beach and dramatic sea vista. This is a good place for nature study.

Facilities: Cabins, campsites. Restaurants and groceries are located one mile away in Stinson Beach.

Camping: Permitted in campsites and cabins; 916-323-2988 for reservations and information. Tent sites $6 per night; cabins $15.

Getting there: Located along a dirt road off Route 1 about one mile south of Stinson Beach.

Red Rock Beach (★)—One of the area's most popular nude beaches, this pocket beach is wall-to-wall with local folks on sunny weekends. Well protected along its flank by steep hillsides, Red Rock is an ideal sunbathers' retreat.

Facilities: None. Restaurants and groceries are located one mile away in Stinson Beach.

Getting there: Part of Mt. Tamalpais State Park, Red Rock is located off Route 1 about one mile south of Stinson Beach. Watch for a large (often crowded) parking lot on the seaward side of the highway. Follow the steep trail down to the beach.

Stinson Beach Park—One of Northern California's finest beaches, this broad, sandy corridor curves for three miles. Backdropped by rolling hills, Stinson also borders beautiful Bolinas Lagoon. Besides being a sunbather's haven, it's a great place for beachcombers and birdwatchers. To escape the crowds congregating here weekends, stroll up to the north end of the beach. You'll find a narrow sand spit looking out on Bolinas. You still won't have the beach entirely to yourself, but a place this beautiful is worth sharing.

Facilities: Picnic areas, snack bar, restrooms. Lifeguards in summer (because of currents from Bolinas Lagoon, the water here is a little warmer than elsewhere); if you dare swim anywhere along the North Coast, it might as well be here.

Getting there: Located along Route 1 in the town of Stinson Beach, 23 miles north of San Francisco.

Bolinas Beach—Beginning near Bolinas Lagoon and curving around the town perimeter, this salt-and-pepper beach provides ample opportunity for walking. A steep bluff borders the beach. In the narrow mouth of the lagoon you can often see harbor seals and waterfowl.

Facilities: None, but the town of Bolinas is within walking distance.

Getting there: Located at the end of Wharf Road in Bolinas.

Agate Beach and Duxbury Reef—A prime area for beachcombers, Agate Beach is rich in found objects (and objects waiting to be found). At low tide, Duxbury Reef to the south is equally outstanding for tidepool gazing. Both are highly recommended for adventurers, daydreamers, and amateur biologists.

Facilities: None, but downtown Bolinas is nearby.

Getting there: From Olema–Bolinas Road in Bolinas, go up the hill on Mesa Road, left on Overlook Drive, and right on Elm Avenue. Follow Elm Avenue to the parking lot at the end; take the path down to the ocean.

Twin Lakes (★)—Favored by swimmers and nude sunbathers, these miniature lakes offer a variation from nearby ocean beaches. Both are fringed with grassland and bounded by forest, making them idyllic spots within easy reach of the highway.

Facilities: None. Restaurants and groceries are several miles away in Bolinas.

Getting there: On Route 1 go three-and-a-half miles north of the Bolinas turnoff (at the foot of Bolinas Lagoon). You'll see a shallow parking lot on the right side of the highway. A dirt road leads uphill several hundred yards to the lakes. Take the first left fork to one lake; take the first right fork to the larger, more attractive lake.

Samuel P. Taylor State Park—Located several miles inland, this facility provides an opportunity to experience the coastal interior. The place is heavily wooded and offers 2600 acres to roam. In addition to the campgrounds, there are hiking trails and swimming holes.

Facilities: Picnic areas, restrooms, showers; information, 415-488-9897. Restaurants and groceries located nearby in several small towns.

Camping: Permitted.

Getting there: Located on Sir Francis Drake Highway, east of Route 1 and five miles from Olema.

POINT REYES BEACHES AND PARKS

Point Reyes National Seashore—One of the great natural features of Northern California, this 65,000-acre park contains everything from wind-blown beaches to dense pine forests. No traveler should miss it. For a full description, consult the "Sightseeing" section in this chapter. However, some of the many features within this gigantic park are described below, as are the independent parks surrounding Point Reyes National Seashore.

Facilities: Picnic areas, restrooms, and miles of hiking trails; information center, 415-663-1092. Restaurants and groceries are located in the nearby towns of Inverness and Point Reyes Station.

Camping: You may camp in any of four sites, all accessible only by hiking trails. Sky Camp sits on the side of Mt. Wittenberg, commanding stunning views of Drake's Bay. Coast Camp rests on a bluff above a pretty beach. Glen Camp lies in a forested valley. Wildcat Camp nestles in a meadow near the beach. Each camp is equipped with toilets, water, and picnic areas. Wood fires are not allowed; plan to bring alternate campfire materials. Camping is free, but permits are required. They can be obtained at Bear Valley Visitor Center (Point Reyes, CA 94956; 415-663-1092). You are limited to one night in each campsite and a total of four nights in the park. Nearby **Bear Valley Stables** (Bear Valley Road, Inverness; 415-663-1570), a private enterprise, sometimes permits campers to bivouac in a back pasture. Facilities are limited to a bathroom; $10 nightly per car.

Getting there: Located off Route 1 about 40 miles north of San Francisco.

Limantour Beach—This white-sand beach is actually a spit, a narrow peninsula pressed between Drake's Bay and an estuary. It's an exotic area of sand dunes and sea breezes. Ideal for exploring, the region shelters over 350 bird species. There's good (but cold) swimming and fishing seaside; in the estuary behind the beach you can search for clams and shrimp, as well as seals and stingrays.

Facilities: Toilets. Restaurants and groceries are located nearby in Inverness.

Camping: None, but the American Youth Hostel (see "Hotels" section in this chapter) is located on the road to Limantour.

Getting there: Once in Point Reyes National Seashore, follow Limantour Road to the end.

Tomales Bay State Park—This delightful park, which abuts on Point Reyes National Seashore, provides a warm, sunny alternative to Point Reyes' frequent fog. The water, too, is warmer here in Tomales Bay, making it a great place for swimming, as well as fishing, boating, and clamming. Rimming the park are several sandy coves; most accessible of these is Heart's Desire Beach, flanked by bluffs and featuring nearby picnic areas. From Heart's Desire a half-mile trail goes northwest to Indian Beach, a long stretch of white sand fringed by trees. Hiking trails around the park lead to other secluded beaches, excellent for picnics and day hikes.

Facilities: Picnic areas, restrooms; information, 415-669-1140. Restaurants and groceries can be found four miles away in Inverness.

Camping: For backpackers and bicyclists; $1 fee.

Getting there: From Route 1 in Olema take Sir Francis Drake Boulevard to Point Reyes National Seashore. Then follow Pierce Point Road to the park.

Shell Beach—Actually part of Tomales Bay State Park, this pocket beach is several miles from the park entrance. As a result, it is often uncrowded. A patch of white sand bordered by steep hills, Shell Beach is ideal for swimming and picnicking.

Facilities: None. Restaurants and groceries are two miles away in Inverness.

Getting there: Once in Point Reyes National Seashore, take Sir Francis Drake Boulevard one mile past Inverness, then turn right at Camino del Mar. The trailhead is located at the end of this street; follow the trail three-tenths of a mile down to the beach.

Marshall Beach (★)—This secluded beach on Tomales Bay is a wonderful place to swim and sunbathe, often in complete privacy. The beach is a lengthy strip of white sand fringed by cypress trees.

Facilities: Toilets. Restaurants and groceries are eight miles away (over hiking trail and roads) in Inverness.

Getting there: Once in Point Reyes National Seashore, take Pierce Point Road. Immediately after passing the entrance to Tomales Bay State Park, turn right onto the paved road. This road travels uphill, turns to gravel and goes two-and-six-tenths miles to a gate. From the gate you hike one-and-a-half miles along the road/trail to the beach.

Abbotts Lagoon—Because of its rich waterfowl population and beautiful surrounding dunes, this is a favorite place among hikers. From the lagoon it's an easy jaunt over the dunes to Point Reyes Beach.

Facilities: Toilets. Restaurants and groceries are six miles away in Inverness.

Getting there: Once in Point Reyes National Seashore, take Pierce Point Road. The trailhead is located along the roadside, two miles past the turnoff for Tomales Bay State Park; follow the trail one mile to the lagoon.

Kehoe Beach—Bounded by cliffs, this strand is actually the northern end of ten-mile-long Point Reyes Beach. It's a lovely place, covered with wildflowers in spring and boasting a small lagoon. The isolation makes it a great spot for explorers.

Facilities: Toilets at the trailhead. Restaurants and groceries are eight miles away in Inverness.

Getting there: Once in Point Reyes National Seashore, take Pierce Point Road. The trailhead is along the roadside four miles past the turnoff for Tomales Bay State Park; follow the trail a half-mile to the beach.

McClure's Beach—Of the many beautiful beaches in Point Reyes National Seashore, this is by far my favorite. It is a white-sand beach protected by granite cliffs which stand like bookends on either flank. Tidepool watching is great sport here; if you arrive during low tide it's possible to skirt the cliffs along the south end and explore a pocket beach next door. But don't let a waxing tide catch you sleeping! Swimming is dangerous here; surf fishing, birdwatching, and driftwood gathering more than make up for it. Quite simply, places like this are the reason folks visit Northern California.

Facilities: Toilets at the trailhead. Restaurants and groceries are 12 miles away in Inverness.

Getting there: Located in Point Reyes National Seashore at the end of Pierce Point Road. A steep trail leads a half-mile down to the beach.

Point Reyes Beach—It will become wonderfully evident why this is nicknamed "Ten Mile Beach" when you cast eyes on this endless sand swath. A great place for whale watching, beachcombing, and fishing, this is not the spot for swimming. Sharks, riptides, and unusual wave patterns make even wading inadvisable. Also the heavy winds along this coastline would chill any swimmer's plans. But that does not detract from the wild beauty of the place, or the fact you can jog for miles along this strand.

Facilities: Restrooms. Restaurants and groceries are located nine miles away in Inverness.

Getting there: Located off Sir Francis Drake Boulevard about 14 miles from park headquarters.

Drake's Beach—Edged by cliffs, this crescent beach looks out upon the tip of Point Reyes. Since it's well protected by Drake's Bay, this is a good swimming spot. It also provides interesting hikes along the base of the cliffs to the inlet at Drake's Estero.

Facilities: Picnic tables, restrooms; snack bar. Restaurants and groceries are ten miles away in Inverness.

Getting there: Located off Sir Francis Drake Boulevard 15 miles from park headquarters.

Olema Ranch Campground—This roadside camping park, catering primarily to trailers, also has facilities for tent campers. The price however, ain't cheap—$12.50 for a tent and two people. That will buy a plot of ground in a grassy area. You won't have a sense of wilderness amid the Winnebagos here, but the place is strategically situated along Route 1 near the turnoff for Point Reyes National Seashore.

Facilities: Picnic areas, restrooms, showers, laundromat. Restaurants nearby; information, 415-663-8001.

Getting there: Located at 10155 Route 1 in Olema.

SONOMA AND MENDOCINO COAST BEACHES AND PARKS

OLEMA TO BODEGA BAY BEACHES AND PARKS

Dillon Beach—Located at the mouth of Tomales Bay, this beach is popular with boaters and clammers. The surrounding hills are covered with resort cottages, but there are open areas and dunes to explore.

Facilities: Picnic areas, restrooms, grocery; boat rentals; fishing charters; $3 day-use fee.

Camping: At nearby Lawson's Landing (707-878-2443); $7.50 per night. Take note: this campground hosts hundreds of trailers.

Getting there: From Route 1 in Tomales take Dillon Beach Road west for four miles.

Doran Park—This peninsular park is situated on a sand spit between Bodega Bay and the ocean. With a broad sand beach and good facilities, it's an excellent spot for daytrippers and campers alike. You can explore the tidal flats or fish up on the jetty.

Facilities: Picnic areas, restrooms, showers; restaurants and groceries are nearby in Bodega Bay; $2 day-use fee; information, 707-875-3540.

Camping: In attractive areas near the bay or along the beach; $2 per person a night for walk-in campsites or $9 per vehicle for improved vehicle sites.

Getting there: Located off Route 1 in Bodega Bay.

Bodega Head State Park—There are pocket beaches here dramatically backdropped by granite cliffs. A good place to picnic and explore, this is also a favored whale-watching site.

Facilities: None; there are picnic areas, restrooms, and showers in nearby Westside Park.

Getting there: Located off Route 1 in Bodega Bay along Bay Flat Road.

BODEGA BAY TO FORT BRAGG BEACHES AND PARKS

Sonoma Coast State Beach—This magnificent park extends for 13 miles between Bodega Head and the Russian River. It consists of a number of beaches separated by steep headlands; all are within easy hiking distance of Route 1. The beaches range from sweeping strands to pocket coves and abound with waterfowl and shorebirds, clams, and abalone. The park headquarters and information center is located at Salmon Creek Beach, where endless sand dunes backdrop a broad beach. Schoolhouse Beach is a particularly pretty pocket cove bounded by rocky cliffs; Portuguese Beach boasts a wide swath of sand; Blind Beach is rather secluded with a sea arch offshore; and Goat Rock Beach faces the town of Jenner and is decorated with offshore rocks. Pick your poison—hiking, tidepooling, birdwatching, camping, picnicking, fishing—and you'll find it waiting along this rugged and hauntingly beautiful coastline.

Facilities: Bodega Dunes, Salmon Creek Beach, Schoolhouse Beach, Portuguese Beach, and Wright's Beach have restrooms; Bodega Dunes and Wright's Beach also feature picnic areas. All beaches are within a half-dozen miles of restaurants and groceries either in Bodega Bay or Jenner. Information, 707-865-2391.

Camping: Bodega Dunes, at the southern end of the park, has a lovely campground with sites tucked between grass-tufted dunes. Wright's Beach, in the park's northern half, offers an equally nice spot for campers on a beach framed by hills.

Getting there: Located along Route 1 between Bodega Bay and Jenner.

Fort Ross Reef Campground—Set on a bluff overlooking the ocean, this facility is beautifully located and features a redwood grove. At one time it was a private park, but the state took it over. The result is a public facility with spectacular surroundings and gorgeous views.

Facilities: Picnic areas, restrooms; restaurants and groceries eight miles away in Jenner; $3 day-use fee; information, 707-865-2391.

Camping: Permitted; $6 per night.

Getting there: Located at 18000 Route 1, eight miles north of Jenner; watch for a cluster of red barns on the west side of the highway.

Stillwater Cove Regional Park—Situated amid pine trees on a hillside above the ocean, this is a small park with access to a beach.

Facilities: Picnic areas, restrooms, showers; restaurants and groceries are located within a few miles. Day-use fee. Information, 707-847-3245.

Camping: Permitted; $9 per night.

Getting there: Located on Route 1, about 16 miles north of Jenner.

Ocean Cove Reserve—This privately owned campground has sites on a bluff above a rocky shoreline. The scenery is mighty attractive, and the campsites are well-removed from the road.

Facilities: Information, Ocean Cove Store (23125 Route 1, Jenner; 707-847-3422). Grocery nearby.

Camping: Permitted; $5 minimum a night per campsite.

Getting there: Located on Route 1 about 17 miles north of Jenner.

Salt Point State Park—Extending from the ocean to over 1000 feet elevation, this 4300-acre spread includes coastline, forests, and open range land. Along the shore are weird honeycomb formations called tafoni, caused by sea erosion on coastal sandstone. Up amid the stands of Douglas fir and Bishop pine there's a pygmy forest, where unfavorable soil conditions have caused fully mature redwoods to reach only a few feet in height. Blacktail deer, wild pig, and bobcat roam the area. Miles of hiking trails lace the park, including one through a rhododendron reserve.

Facilities: Picnic areas, restrooms; restaurants and groceries are available within a few miles. Information, 707-847-3221.

Camping: Permitted; $10 per night.

Getting there: Located on Route 1 about 18 miles north of Jenner.

Gualala Point Regional Park—Located where the Gualala River meets the ocean, this charming place has everything from sandy beach to redwood groves.

Facilities: Information center, 707-785-2377; picnic areas, restrooms; restaurants and groceries are located in nearby Gualala.

Camping: Permitted; $9 per night.

Getting there: Located along Route 1 due south of Gualala.

Manchester State Beach—This wild, windswept beach extends for miles along the Mendocino coast. Piled deep with driftwood, it's excellent for beachcombing and hiking.

Facilities: Information center, 707-937-5804; picnic areas, restrooms; restaurants and groceries are about eight miles away in Point Arena.

Camping: Permitted in an area that is neatly tucked behind sand dunes, away from prevailing winds; $6 per night fee.

Getting there: Located along Route 1 about eight miles north of Point Arena.

Van Damme State Park—Extending from the beach to an interior forest, this 2069-acre park has several interesting features: a "pygmy forest" where poor soil results in fully mature pine trees reaching heights of only six inches to eight feet; a "fern canyon" smothered in different species of ferns; and a "cabbage patch" filled with that fetid critter with elephant ear leaves—skunk cabbage. This park is also laced with hiking trails and offers excellent beachcombing opportunities.

Facilities: Information center, 707-937-5804; picnic areas, restrooms, showers.

Camping: Permitted.

Getting there: Located on Route 1 about 30 miles north of Point Arena.

Mendocino Headlands and **Big River Beach State Parks**—These adjoining parks form the seaside border of the town of Mendocino. And quite a border it is. The white-sand beaches are only part of the natural splendor. There are also wave tunnels, tidepools, sea arches, lagoons, and 360° vistas that sweep from the surf-trimmed shore to the prim villagescape of Mendocino.

Facilities: None. Private canoe rental nearby; restaurants and groceries in Mendocino.

Getting there: Located in the town of Mendocino.

Russian Gulch State Park—Set in a narrow valley with a well-protected beach, this park has numerous features. There are marvelous views from the craggy headlands, redwood groves, a waterfall, and a blowhole that rarely blows. Rainbow and steelhead trout inhabit the creek while hawks and ravens circle the forest. The park is also conveniently close to Mendocino.

Facilities: Picnic areas, restrooms, showers; restaurants and groceries are about one mile away in Mendocino; information, 707-937-5804.

Camping: Permitted in 28 sites located in a wooded area near the beach.

Getting there: Located along Route 1 just north of Mendocino.

MacKerricher State Park—Another of the region's outstanding parks, this facility features a crescent of sandy beach, dunes, headlands, a lake, forest, and wetlands. Harbor seals inhabit the rocks offshore and over 90 bird species frequent the area.

Facilities: Picnic areas, restrooms, showers; restaurants and groceries are available three miles away in Fort Bragg; information, 707-937-5804.

Camping: Permitted in 140 sites. You will have to carry in or boil your drinking water.

Getting there: Located along Route 1 about three miles north of Fort Bragg.

REDWOOD COUNTRY BEACHES AND PARKS

LEGGETT TO EUREKA BEACHES AND PARKS

The "Lost Coast" (★)—California's coastal Route 1 is one of the greatest highways in America. Beginning at the Mexican border, it sweeps north through Big Sur, Carmel, San Francisco, and Mendocino, past ocean scenery indescribably beautiful. Then it disappears. At the foot of Redwood Country, Route 1 quits the coast and turns into Route 101.

The region it never reaches is California's fabled "Lost Coast." Here the King Range, with its sliding talus and impassable cliffs, shoots 4087 feet up from the ocean in less than three miles. No road could ever rest along its shoulder. The place has been left primitive, given over to mink, deer, river otter, and black bear; rare bald eagles and peregrine falcons work its slopes.

The range extends about 35 miles. Along the shore is a wilderness beach from which seals, sea lions, and porpoises, as well as gray and killer whales, can be seen. There's also an abandoned lighthouse and the skeletons of ships wrecked on the rocks.

Most of the region is now protected as the King Range Conservation Area. Two major trails traverse it: King Crest Trail, which climbs the main coastal ridge for 16 miles, with views of the ocean and Eel River Valley; and the five-mile-long Chemise Mountain trail. Both ascend the summit of King Peak. There is also hiking along the wilderness beach.

One of the wettest areas along the Pacific Coast, King Range receives about 100 inches of rain annually. The precipitation is particularly heavy from October to April. Summer carries cool coastal fog and some rain. Weather permitting, it's a fascinating region to explore—wild and virgin, with the shellmounds of Indians who inhabited the area over a century ago still scattered on the beach.

Facilities: Motels, restaurants, groceries, and boat rentals are available in Shelter Cove, at the south end of the Conservation Area. For information, contact the District Manager, U.S. Bureau of Land Management, 555 Leslie Street, Ukiah, CA 95482; 707-462-3873.

Camping: Four sites with tables, grills, toilets, and water are available in the southern sector of the Conservation Area. Other specific sites throughout the region are open for primitive camping.

Getting there: From Garberville on Route 101, a road leads to nearby Redway and then southwest to Shelter Cove. Midway along this road another road forks northwest, paralleling the Conservation Area, to Ettersberg and Honeydew.

Standish-Hickey State Recreation Area—Near the southern edge of Redwood Country, this 1000-acre park primarily consists of second-growth trees. The single exception is a 1200-year-old giant named after the Mayflower pilgrim, Captain Miles Standish. The forest here also has Douglas fir, oak, and maple trees. The south fork of the Eel River courses through the area, providing swimming holes and fishing spots.

Facilities: Picnic areas, restrooms, showers. Restaurants and groceries are two miles away in Leggett; information, 707-925-6482.

Camping: Permitted in several areas; $10 per night.

Getting there: Located along Route 101 two miles north of Leggett.

Richardson Grove State Park—The first of the virgin redwood parks, this 1000-acre facility features a grove of goliaths. For some bizarre reason the highway builders chose to put the main road through the heart of the forest. This means you won't miss the redwoods, but to really appreciate them you'll have to disappear down one of the numerous hiking trails that loop through the grove. The south fork of the Eel River flows through the park, providing swimming and trout fishing opportunities.

Facilities: Information center, 707-247-3318; grocery, snack bar, gift shop, picnic areas, restrooms, showers.

Camping: Permitted.

Getting there: Located on Route 101 about 18 miles north of Leggett.

Benbow Lake State Recreation Area—One of the less desirable parks in the area, this facility fronts the Eel River near the dam that creates Benbow Lake. Route 101 streams through the center of the park, disrupting an otherwise idyllic scene. Nevertheless, there's good swimming and fishing in the river-lake.

Facilities: Picnic areas, restrooms, showers; groceries and restaurants are available in nearby towns.

Camping: Permitted in sites along the river.

Getting there: Located on Route 101 about 23 miles north of Leggett.

Humboldt Redwoods State Park—One of the state's great parks, it is set within a 20-million-year-old forest. The park is a tribute to early conservationists who battled lumber interests in an effort to save the area's extraordinary trees. Today 51 miles of hiking trails lead through redwood groves and along the Eel River. Within the park's 40-mile length there are also ample opportunities for swimming, biking, or tree gazing.

Facilities: Information center, 707-946-2311; picnic areas, restrooms, showers; restaurants and groceries are located in small towns within the park.

Camping: Permitted in three different campsites (one in winter); there are also six hike-in camps.

Getting there: Located along the Avenue of the Giants between Garberville and Eureka.

EUREKA TO OREGON BEACHES AND PARKS

Clam Beach County Park—There's a broad expanse of beach here with good views of surrounding headlands, but this place is best known for its clams. Low tides and early mornings bring local people out to dig for razor clams, sweet and fleshy mollusks that can be baked, sautéed, or eaten raw. If interested, you'll need a state license.

Facilities: Toilets; restaurants and groceries are available several miles away in Trinidad. Information, 707-445-7652.

Camping: Permitted; $5 overnight parking fee; one-night limit.

Getting there: Located along Route 101 about 15 miles north of Eureka.

Patrick's Point State Park—This 625-acre park is particularly known for Agate Beach, a long crescent backdropped by wooded headlands. Here it's possible to gather not only driftwood but semi-precious agate, jasper, and black jade. There are tidepools to explore, sea lions and seals offshore, and several miles of hiking trails.

Facilities: Information center, 707-677-3570; museum, picnic areas, restrooms, showers; restaurants and groceries are available several miles away in Trinidad.

Camping: Permitted in three campgrounds.

Getting there: Located off Route 101 about 25 miles north of Eureka.

Humboldt Lagoon State Park—A 1036-acre facility, this beach park can be reached from the road in two places. The main entrance leads to a sandy beach tucked between rocky outcroppings and heaped with driftwood. Behind the beach an old lagoon has slowly transformed into a salt marsh. The northern entrance leads to the campground and a sandy beach backed by a beautiful (and wet!) lagoon. Add the two areas together and you come up with a splendid park.

Facilities: Toilets; restaurants and groceries four miles away in Orick. Information, 707-488-5435.

Camping: At Stone Lagoon primitive campground; $6 nightly fee.

Getting there: Located off Route 101 about 31 miles north of Eureka; the campground is just north of the main entrance.

Redwood National Park—Actually three parks in one, this 106,000-acre giant encompasses Prairie Creek Redwoods, Del Norte Coast Redwoods, and Jedediah Smith Redwoods State Parks. Together they stretch over 40 miles along the coast from Orick to the Crescent City region. Within that span, one of California's wettest areas (80 inches of rain yearly in Del Norte), are hidden beaches, ocean cliffs, deep redwood forests, and mile on mile of hiking trails.

Along the coast are wind-scoured bluffs and gently sloping hills. The beaches range from sandy to rocky; because of the rugged terrain in certain areas, some are inaccessible. In addition to beaches, many streams—including Prairie Creek, Redwood Creek, and the Smith River—traverse this series of parks.

Hikers and redwood lovers will find that several spectacular groves lie adjacent to Routes 101 and 199. Others can be reached along uncrowded trails. Tan oak and madrone grow around the redwoods, while further inland there are Jeffrey pine and Douglas fir.

Bird watchers will encounter mallards, hawks, owl, grouse, quail, and great blue herons. The mammal population ranges from shrews and moles to rabbit and beaver to mule deer and an occasional bear. Along the coast live river otters and harbor seals.

These and other features make the parks a natural for swimming, fishing, canoeing, and kayaking.

Facilities: Information centers, picnic areas, restrooms, and showers; restaurants and groceries are located in the small towns throughout the park. Park headquarters is at 1111 2nd Street, Crescent City; 707-464-6101.

Camping: Permitted in four widely scattered sites; state park regulations prevail.

Getting there: Located along Route 101 between Orick and Crescent City; Jedediah Smith Redwoods State Park is along Route 199 north of Crescent City.

Hiking

To call California's North Coast a hiker's paradise is an understatement. After all, in San Francisco and north of the city is the Golden Gate National Recreation Area. Together with continuous county, state, and national parks it offers over 100,000 acres to be explored.

Within this ambit are trails ranging from trifling nature loops to tough mountain paths. The land varies from tidal areas and seacliffs to ranch country and scenic mountains. In the far north are the giant redwood forests, located within national parks and featuring networks of hiking trails.

MARIN HEADLANDS TRAILS

The Marin Headlands (information, 415-331-1540), a region of bold bluffs and broad seascapes, contains a few hiking paths in its otherwise unpredictable landscape.

Kirby Cove Trail (1 mile) leads from Conzelman Road down to a narrow beach. The views of San Francisco en route and the caves along the beach's east end provide a lot of adventure for a short hike.

Wolf Ridge Loop (5 miles) begins at Rodeo Beach, follows the Pacific Coast Trail and Wolf Ridge Trail, then returns along Miwok Trail. It ascends from a shoreline environment to heights with sweeping views of both San Francisco and Mt. Tamalpais.

Tennessee Valley Trail (2 miles) winds along the valley floor en route to a small beach and cove. The trailhead sits off Route 1 at the end of Tennessee Valley Road.

MT. TAMALPAIS STATE PARK AND MUIR WOODS TRAILS

About 30 miles of trails loop through Mt. Tamalpais State Park (415-388-2070). These link to a 200-mile network of hiking paths through Muir Woods National Monument (415-388-2595) and Golden Gate National Recreation Area. Explorers are rewarded with a diverse terrain, startling views of the entire Bay Area, and a chance to hike within commuting distance of San Francisco.

Most trails begin at Pantoll Park Headquarters. Here you can pick up trail maps and descriptions from which to devise your own combination loop trails, or consult with the rangers in planning anything from an easy jaunt to a rugged trek.

Dipsea Trail (6.8 miles) is a favorite path beginning in Mill Valley and heading along rolling hills, past sea vistas, then ending near Stinson Beach. The easiest way to pick up the trail is in Muir Woods, about a mile from the Mill Valley trailhead.

Similarly, **Matt Davis Trail** (3.5 miles) descends 1200 feet from Pantoll Park Headquarters to Stinson Beach. Along the way are deep woods and windswept knolls, plus views of San Francisco and Point Reyes.

Steep Ravine Trail (2 miles), true to its name, angles sharply downward from Pantoll Park Headquarters through a redwood-studded canyon, then joins the Dipsea Trail.

Redwood Creek Nature Trail (2.5 miles) is a paved loop through several remarkable redwood stands. A favorite with tourists, this trail begins near Muir Woods park headquarters and is often crowded. So it's best hiked either early or late in the day.

There are numerous other trails which combined form interesting loop hikes. For instance, from Bootjack Camp in Mt. Tamalpais State Park, you can follow **Bootjack Trail** down a steep canyon of redwood and Douglas fir to Muir Woods, then take **Ben Johnson Trail** back up to Pantoll Park Headquarters. From there it's a half-mile walk back to Bootjack. This 4.2-mile circle tour carries through relatively isolated sections of Muir Woods.

For a little shorter (3.5 mile) circular trek to the top of Mt. Tamalpais, begin at Mountain Home, an inn located along Panoramic Highway. Follow **Throckmorton Trail** as it ascends the mountain, then turn left on **Old Railroad Grade.** This will lead to West Point Inn, a cozy lodging place for hikers. From here you climb to the road that goes to East Peak, one of Mt. Tamalpais' three summits. Heading down along **Fern Creek Trail,** you'll encounter Old Railroad Grade once more. En route are flowering meadows, madrone stands, chaparral-cloaked hillsides, and mountaintop views.

POINT REYES NATIONAL SEASHORE TRAILS

Within its spectacular 65,000-acre domain, this park contains over 100 miles of hiking trails plus four hike-in campsites. The trails form a latticework across forests, ranch lands, and secluded beaches and along sea cliffs, brackish inlets, and freshwater lakes. Almost 200 bird species inhabit the preserve. Black-tailed deer, Euro-Asian fallow deer, and spotted axis deer abound. You might also encounter raccoons, weasels, rabbits, badgers, bobcats, even a skunk or two.

Most trailheads begin near Bear Valley Visitor Center (415-663-1092), Palomarin, Five Brooks, or Estero. For maps and information check with the rangers at the visitor center.

Earthquake Trail (.7 mile) begins from the visitor center and leads along the epicenter of the 1906 earthquake. The ground here shifted over 15 feet during that terrible upheaval.

Nearby **Woodpecker Trail** (.7 mile) is a self-guiding trail with markers explaining the natural environment. The annotated path leads to a horse "museum" set in a barn.

Bear Valley Trail (4.4 miles), also beginning near the visitor center, courses through range land and wooded valley to cliffs overlooking the ocean. The park's most popular trail, it is level and may unfortunately be crowded with hikers and bicyclists.

Coast Trail (13.3 miles) runs between Palomarin (near Bolinas) and Limantour Beach. Hugging the shoreline en route, this splendid trail leads past four freshwater lakes and two camping areas, then turns inland to the American Youth Hostel.

Olema Valley Trail (5 miles) parallels Route 1 as it tracks a course along the infamous San Andreas Fault. Originating from Five Brooks, it alternates between glades and forest while beating a level path to Dogtown.

Estero Trail (4.6 miles) shadows the shoreline of Drake's Estero and provides opportunities to view local waterfowl as well as harbor seals, sea lions, and bat rays.

HUMBOLDT REDWOODS STATE PARK TRAILS

There are more than 100 miles of hiking and riding paths within this forest preserve. Many lead through dense redwood stands, others meander along the Eel River, and some lead to the park's six hike-in camps. For information, call 707-946-2311.

Founders Grove Nature Trail (.5 mile) tunnels through a virgin redwood forest that once boasted the world's tallest tree. Though a storm significantly shortened the 364-foot giant, it left standing a cluster of equally impressive neighbors.

Rockefeller Loop Trail (.5 mile) ducks into a magnificent grove that includes a 359-foot redwood.

There are also longer trails leading deep into the forest and to the top of 3379-foot Grasshopper Peak.

REDWOOD NATIONAL PARK TRAILS

Comprised of three distinct state parks and extending for miles along California's northwestern corner, this diverse enclave offers adventure aplenty to daytrippers and mountaineers alike. There are over 150 miles of trails threading the parks, leading through dense redwood groves, along open beaches, and atop wind-buffeted bluffs. For information, call 707-464-6101.

PRAIRIE CREEK REDWOODS STATE PARK

Redwood Creek Trail (8.2 miles) leads from a trailhead two miles north of Orick to Tall Trees Grove, home of the world's tallest living things. There is backcountry camping en route; permits available at the trailhead.

Tall Trees Trail (1.3 miles) provides a shorter route to the same destination. A shuttle service (fare) runs from the Orick ranger station (707-488-3461) to the trailhead.

Lady Bird Johnson Grove Nature Loop Trail (1 mile) follows an old logging trail through virgin redwood country.

Little Creek Trail (.3 mile) cuts through a blowdown region; in places the path passes beneath fallen redwoods.

James Irvine Trail (4.2 miles) goes from the Prairie Creek visitor center along a redwood ridge to Fern Canyon. For a longer loop (10.3 miles), hike south on Gold Bluffs Beach, then pick up Miner's Ridge Trail. This last trail follows a corduroy logging road used early in the century.

Fern Canyon Trail (.7 mile) courses along a gulch dripping with vegetation, up to an abandoned mining area.

Beach Trail (3 miles) begins at Fern Canyon and parallels Gold Bluffs Beach.

Boat Creek Trail (2 miles) diverges from Beach Trail and alternates between thick redwood forest and sweeping ocean views.

West Ridge Trail (5 miles) traces a sharp ridgetop through virgin forest.

Revelation Trail (.3 mile), a marvelous innovation, contains handrails and braille guidebooks for the blind. For those of us gifted with sight, it provides a fuller understanding of the scents, sounds, and textures of a redwood forest.

Cathedral Trees Trail (1.5 miles) heads along streams and meadows to elk country.

Brown Creek Trail (1.2 miles), reputedly one of the park's prettiest hikes, leads along streams and through old redwood stands.

DEL NORTE COAST REDWOODS STATE PARK

Coastal Trail (4 miles), located south of the state park, begins at Klamath River Overlook. In addition to ocean vistas, it offers a walk through a spruce and alder forest, plus glimpses of sea lions, whales, and numerous birds.

Yurok Loop Trail (1 mile), with its berry patches and wildflowers, begins near the terminus of Coastal Trail.

Enderts Beach Trail (.6 mile), south of Crescent City, features tidepools, seaside strolling, and primitive camping. It also offers access to **Last Chance Trail** (6 miles), an old roadway which cuts through forests of redwood, alder, and spruce, and features glorious ocean views.

Damnation Creek Trail (2.5 miles), an ancient Yurok Indian path, winds down from Route 101 to a hidden cove and beach.

Hobbs Wall Trail (3.8 miles) leads through a former lumberjacking region.

Alder Basin Trail (1 mile) meanders along a stream through stands of willow, maple, and alder.

JEDEDIAH SMITH REDWOODS STATE PARK

Stout Grove Trail (1 mile) highlights several spots along its short course: a 340-foot redwood tree, swimming and fishing holes, plus rhododendron regions.

Hiouchi Trail (2 miles), with its huckleberries, trilliums, and rhododendrons, is equally impressive. This nature trail goes right through a burned-out redwood; it also affords scenic vistas along the Smith River.

Hatton Trail (.3 mile) tours a virgin redwood grove.

Nickerson Ranch Trail (.8 mile) leads through a corridor of ferns and redwoods to an orchard that represents the lone remnant of an old ranch.

Old Stage Road (.5 mile), now overgrown with salmonberries, was once a vital stagecoach route.

Travelers' Tracks

Sightseeing

Sightseeing the North Coast is adventure on a grand scale. This enchanting region offers some of the most outstanding scenery in the world. In Marin County, just north of San Francisco, are bold headlands, broad beaches, and lofty redwoods. The Golden Gate National Recreation Area and Point Reyes National Seashore are outdoor preserves rarely equaled for breadth and beauty.

Then coastal highway Route 1 twists through Sonoma County to an old Russian fort and continues north into Mendocino County. En route are cliffside vista points and rugged shorelines. There are antique towns dating back to the mid-19th century.

Finally Route 1 merges into Route 101 and enters Redwood Country. Here several national parks preserve towering groves of age-old trees. There are also Victorian towns like Eureka and Ferndale. It's along and winding road from San Francisco to the Oregon border, one with frequent surprises and few disappointments.

MARIN COAST

MARIN HEADLANDS

An exploration of the northern coast begins immediately upon crossing the Golden Gate Bridge on Route 101. There's a **vista point** at the far end of the bridge affording marvelous views back toward San Francisco and out upon the Bay. (If some of your party want to start off with an exhilarating walk across the bridge, drop them at the vista point on the city side and pick them up here a little later.)

Once across the bridge, take the first exit, Alexander Avenue; then take an immediate left, following the sign back toward San Francisco. Next, bear right at the sign for Forts Baker, Barry, and Cronkhite.

For what is literally a **bird's eye view** of the Golden Gate Bridge, go three-tenths of a mile uphill and stop at the first turnout on the left. From here it's a short stroll out and up, past deserted battery fortifications, to a 360° view point sweeping the Pacific and Bay alike. You'll practically be standing on the bridge, with cars careening below and the tops of the twin towers vaulting above you.

Continue along Conzelman Road and you will pass a series of increasingly spectacular views of San Francisco. Ahead the road will fall away to reveal a tumbling peninsula, furrowed with hills and marked at its distant tip by a lighthouse. That is **Point Bonita,** a salient far outside the Golden Gate. After proceeding to the point, you can peer back through the interstices of the bridge to the city or turn away from civilization and gaze out on a wind-tousled ocean.

Nature writes in big letters around these parts. You're in the **Marin Headlands** section of **Golden Gate National Recreation Area,** an otherworldly realm of spuming surf, knife-edge cliffs, and chaparral-coated hillsides. From Point Bonita the road leads down to Bunker Road; a left turn here will carry you to the Ranger Station (415-331-1540), with maps and information about the area.

Walk along **Rodeo Beach,** a sandy corridor separating the Pacific from a tule-fringed lagoon awhirr with waterfowl. Miles of hiking trails lace up into the hills (see the "Hiking" section in this chapter). At the far end of the beach you can trek along the cliffs and watch the sea batter the continent.

At the nearby **California Marine Mammal Center** (415-331-7325) are seals and sea lions who have been found injured or orphaned in the ocean and brought here to recuperate. Center workers conduct rescue operations along 900 miles of coastline, returning the animals to the wild after they have gained sufficient strength.

SAUSALITO

From the Marin Headlands Route 101 carries through Sausalito, where sightseeing begins on Bridgeway, a sinuous road paralleling the waterfront. I won't even begin to describe the views of Belvedere, Angel Island, and Alcatraz along this esplanade. Suffice it to say that the Sausalito waterfront offers the single element missing from every vista in San Francisco—a full-frame view of the city itself.

Sausalito is a shopper's town: galleries, boutiques, and antique stores line Bridgeway, and in several cases have begun creeping uphill along side streets. **Plaza Vina del Mar** (Bridgeway and El Portal), with its elephant statues and dramatic fountain, is a grassy oasis in the midst of the commerce. Several strides seaward of this tree-thatched spot lies **Gabrielson Park**, where you can settle on a bench or plot of grass at water's edge.

Then continue along the piers past chic yachts, delicate sloops, and rows of millionaires' motorboats. To get an idea of the inland pond where the rich sail these toys, check out the U.S. Army Corps of Engineers **Bay Model** (2100 Bridgeway; 415-332-3870). Built to scale and housed in a two-acre warehouse, this hydraulic model of San Francisco Bay is used to simulate currents and tidal flows. You can watch the tide surge through the Golden Gate, swirl around Alcatraz, and rise steadily along the Berkeley shore. The tidal cycle of an entire day takes 14 minutes as you witness the natural process from a simulated height of 12,000 feet.

Over in Tiburon, I heartily recommend the quarter-mile self-guided tour through the **Richardson Bay Wildlife Sanctuary** (376 Greenwood Beach Road; 415-388-2524; admission). It will provide an inkling of what Marin was like before the invention of cars and condominiums. Several hundred bird species inhabit this 900-acre preserve; during winter months sea lions and harbor seals rest along the shore. You can wander through dells and woodlands, past salt marshes and tidepools. Also contained on the property is **Lyford House**, a magnificent Victorian which commands a strategic spot on the shore of Richardson Bay.

SAUSALITO TO POINT REYES

From Sausalito follow Route 101 north a few miles, then pick up Route 1. You'll be on the northern leg of one of the most beautiful roads in America. With its wooded sanctuaries and ocean vistas, Route 1 is for many people synonymous with California.

When Route 1 forks after several miles, turn right on Panoramic Highway toward Muir Woods and Mt. Tamalpais; the left fork leads to Stinson Beach, but that comes later. It's uphill and then down to **Muir Woods** (415-388-2595), a 550-acre park inhabited by *Sequoia sempervirens*, the coast redwood. Though these forest giants have been known to live over two millenia, most enjoy a mere four- to eight-century existence. In Muir Woods they reach 240 feet, while further up the coast they top 350 feet (with roots that go no deeper than six feet!).

Facts can't convey the feelings inspired by these trees. You have to move among them, walk through Muir's Cathedral Grove where redwoods form a lofty arcade above the narrow trail. It's a forest primeval, casting the deepest, most restful shade imaginable. Muir Woods has the double-edged quality of being the redwood forest nearest to San Francisco. It can be horribly crowded. Since silence and solitude are vital to experiencing a redwood forest, plan to visit early or late in the day, and allow time to hike the more remote of the park's six miles of trails.

Back up on Panoramic Highway, the road continues through Mt. Tamalpais State Park en route to **Mt. Tamalpais'** 2571-foot peak. Mt. Tam, as it is affectionately known, represents one of the Bay Area's most prominent landmarks. Rising dramatically between the Pacific and the Bay, the site was sacred to Indians. Even today some people see in the sloping silhouette of the mountain the sleeping figure of an Indian maiden. So tread lightly up the short trail that leads to the summit. You'll be rewarded with a full circle view that sweeps across the Bay, along San Francisco's miniature skyline, and out across the Pacific. Contrary to rumor, on a clear day you cannot see forever, but you can see north toward Redwood Country and east to the Sierras.

Then continue on Panoramic Highway as it corkscrews down to Stinson Beach. Better yet, take the longer but more spectacular route to Stinson: backtrack along Panoramic to where the fork originally separated from Route 1 (Shoreline Highway). Turn right and head north on Route 1.

Shortly, a turnoff will lead down to **Green Gulch Farm** (415-383-3134), a 115-acre Zen retreat tucked serenely in a coastal valley. Residents here follow a rigorous program of work and meditation. There is a temple on the grounds and guests are welcome to tour the organic farm. Sunday is the best day to visit since a special guest program is offered then.

It's not far to **Muir Beach** where you'll find a crescent-shaped cove with sandy beach. Though swimming is not permitted, this is a good spot for picnicking. About a mile further up the road, follow the "vista point" sign to **Muir Beach Overlook.** Here you can walk out along a narrow ridge for a view extending from Bolinas to the coastline south of San Francisco. It's an outstanding place for whale watching in winter. Matter of fact, this lookout is so well-placed it became a site for World War II gun batteries, whose rusty skeletons remain.

You have entered a realm that might well be called the Land of a Thousand Views. Until the road descends to the flat expanse of Stinson Beach, it follows a tortuous route poised on the edge of oblivion. Below, precipitous cliffs dive to the sea, while above the road, rock walls edge upward toward Mt. Tamalpais. Around every curve another scene opens to view. Before you, Bolinas is a sweep of land, an arm extended seaward.

Behind, the San Francisco skyline falls away into the past. If God built highways, they'd look like this.

Stinson Beach, that broad sandy hook at the bottom of the mountain, is one of Northern California's finest strands. Anglers haunt the rocks along one end in pursuit of plenny and lingcod, while birdwatchers are on the lookout for sandpipers, shearwaters, and swallows. Everyone else comes for sand, surf, and all that glorious sun.

Birdwatchers also flock to **Audubon Canyon Ranch** (415-383-1644), located astride Route 1 on Bolinas Lagoon. Open only weekends and holidays, the ranch includes four canyons, famed as rookeries for egrets and herons. From the hiking trails here you can see up to 90 bird species as well as gray fox, deer, badgers, and bobcats.

Bolinas Lagoon is also a bird sanctuary. Great egrets, ducks, and great blue herons make this one of their migratory stops. A colony of harbor seals lives here permanently and is joined in summer by migrating seals from San Francisco.

To reach the next point of interest you'll have to pay close attention. That's because you're approaching **Bolinas,** subject of a book called *The Town That Saved Itself,* a place I prefer to call "The Town That Loves Itself." To get there from Route 1, watch for the crossroad at the foot of the lagoon; go left, then quickly left again and follow the road along the other side of the lagoon; take another left at the end of the road.

There should be signs to direct you. But there probably won't be. Not because the state neglected them or highway workers forgot to put them up. It seems that local residents subscribe to the self-serving philosophy that since Bolinas is beautiful and they got there first, they should keep everyone else out. They tear down road signs and discourage visitors. The rest of Northern California is fair game, they seem to say, as long as Bolinas is left as some sort of human preserve.

The place they are attempting to hide is a delightful little town which rises from an S-shaped beach to form a lofty mesa. There are country roads along the bluff that overhangs the beach.

Whether you stroll the beach or hike the highlands, you'll discover in the houses here a wild architectural array. There are domes, glass boxes, curved-roof creations, huts, ranch houses, and stately brown-shingle designs.

Bolinas, abutting on the Point Reyes National Seashore, is also a gateway to the natural world. Follow Mesa Road for several miles outside town and you'll encounter the **Point Reyes Bird Observatory,** where a research station studies a bird population of over 350 species.

On the way back to town take a right on Overlook Drive, then a right on Elm Avenue; follow it to the parking lot at road's end. Hiking trails lead down a sharp 160-foot cliff to **Duxbury Reef,** a mile-long shale reef. Tidepool-watching is great sport here at low tide: starfish, periwinkles, abalone, limpets, and a host of other clinging creatures inhabit the marine preserve. Back in 1971 a huge oil spill endangered this spectacular area, but volunteers from all around the state worked day and night to save the reef and its tenacious inhabitants. Just north of this rocky preserve is **Agate Beach**, an ideal spot to collect agates, driftwood, and glass balls.

Back on Route 1, continue north through Olema Valley, a peaceful region of horse ranches fringed by forest. Peaceful, that is, until you realize that the **San Andreas Fault**, the global suture that shook San Francisco back in 1906, cuts through the valley. Matter of fact, the highway you are traveling parallels the fault line. During the great quake, houses collapsed, trees were uprooted, and fences decided to mark new boundaries.

As you turn off Route 1 onto Sir Francis Drake Boulevard headed for the Point Reyes Peninsula, you'll be passing from the North American Plate, one of the six tectonic plates on which the entire earth's surface rides, to the Pacific Plate, which extends across the ocean. It is the pressure formed by the collision of these two great land masses that causes earthquakes. No sign will notify you as you cross this troubled geologic border, no guide will direct you along the rift zone. If you're like the people who live hereabouts, within 15 minutes of crossing over you'll have forgotten the fault exists. Especially when you see what is served on the Pacific Plate.

POINT REYES NATIONAL SEASHORE

Point Reyes National Seashore is without doubt one of the finest seaside parks on any of the world's six plates. It is a realm of sand dunes and endless beaches, Scottish moors and grassy hillsides, salt marshes and pine forests. Bobcats, mountain lions, fox, and elk inhabit its wrinkled terrain, while harbor seals and gray whales cruise its ragged shoreline. It supports dairies and cattle ranches.

The first stage in exploring this multifeatured preserve involves a stop at the **Bear Valley Visitor Center** (415-663-1092). Here you can obtain maps, information, and camping permits. A short hike from the center will lead you to a **Miwok Indian Village**, where the round-domed shelters of the area's early inhabitants have been re-created.

Like the information center, most points of interest lie along Sir Francis Drake Boulevard, which rolls for miles through the park. It will carry you past the tiny town of **Inverness**, with its country inns and ridgetop houses, then out along **Tomales Bay.** Like the Golden Gate, this finger-shaped inlet is a drowned river valley.

Deeper in the park, a side road twists up to **Mount Vision Overlook,** where vista points sweep the peninsula. At **Johnson's Oyster Farm**

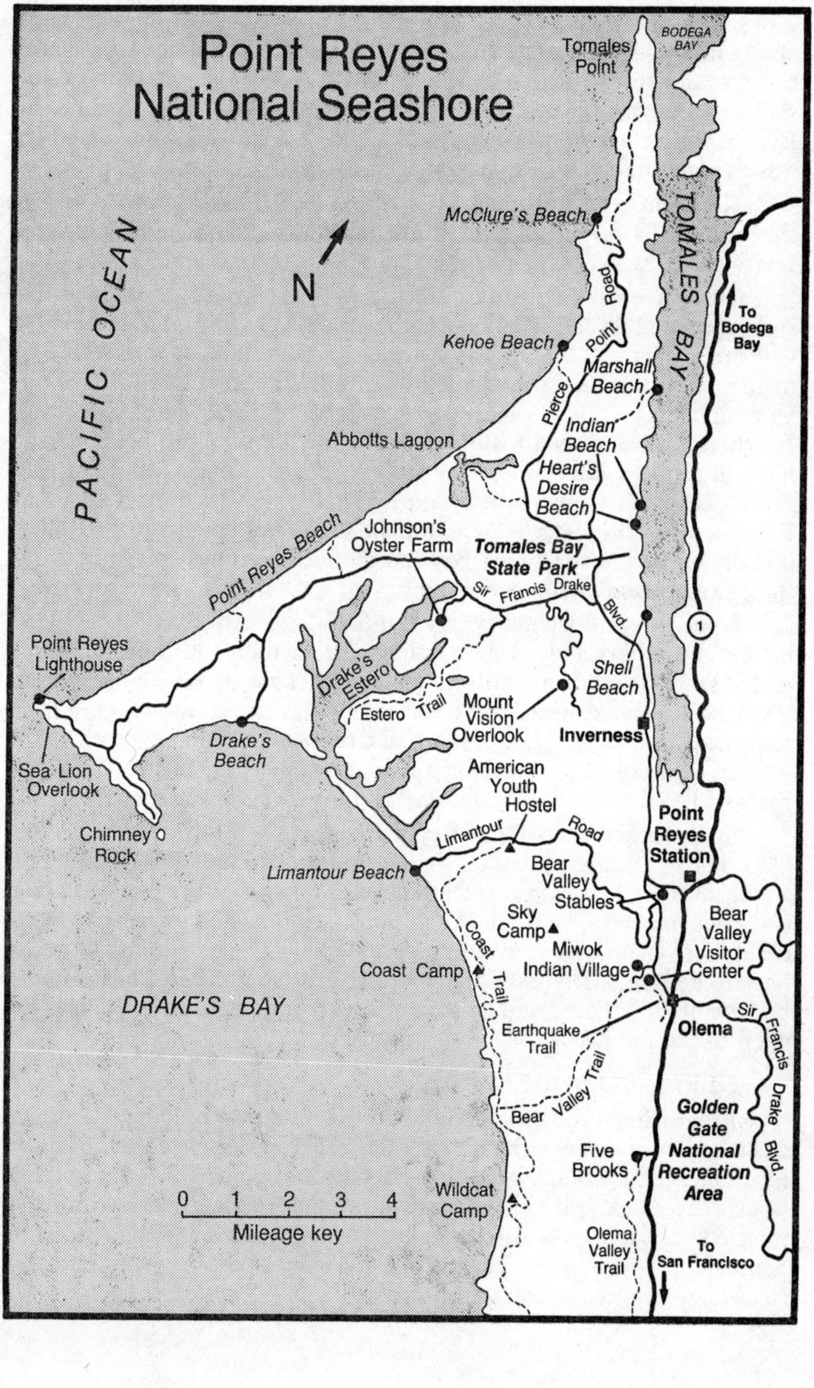
Point Reyes
National Seashore
PACIFIC OCEAN
N
Tomales Point
BODEGA BAY
TOMALES BAY
McClure's Beach
Pierce Point Road
Kehoe Beach
Marshall Beach
To Bodega Bay
Indian Beach
Abbotts Lagoon
Heart's Desire Beach
Point Reyes Beach
Johnson's Oyster Farm
Tomales Bay State Park
Sir Francis Drake Blvd.
1
Point Reyes Lighthouse
Drake's Estero
Estero Trail
Mount Vision Overlook
Shell Beach
Inverness
Drake's Beach
Sea Lion Overlook
American Youth Hostel
Chimney Rock
Limantour Road
Point Reyes Station
Limantour Beach
Bear Valley Stables
Sky Camp
Bear Valley Visitor Center
Coast Trail
Miwok Indian Village
Coast Camp
DRAKE'S BAY
Olema
Sir Francis Drake Blvd.
Earthquake Trail
Bear Valley Trail
Golden Gate National Recreation Area
Five Brooks
Wildcat Camp
0 1 2 3 4
Mileage key
Olema Valley Trail
To San Francisco

(415-669-1149), along another side road, workers harvest the rich beds of an estuary. The farm is a conglomeration of slapdash buildings, house trailers, and rusty machines. The shoreline is heaped over with oyster shells and the air is filled with pungent odors. Raw oysters are for sale. Even if you detest them, you might want to visit anyway. After all, when was the last time you saw an oyster farm?

The main road continues over folded hills that fall away to reveal sharp bluffs. Farm animals graze through fields smothered in wildflowers. There are ocean vistas stretching along miles of headland.

On **Drake's Beach** you can picnic and beachcomb. Or gaze at the surrounding cliffs and wonder whether they truly resemble the White Cliffs of Dover. In that question resides a story told by one school of historians and vehemently denied by others. It seems that in 1579 the English explorer Sir Francis Drake anchored somewhere along the Northern California coast. But where? Some claim he cast anchor right here in Drake's Bay, others say Bolinas Lagoon, even San Francisco Bay. A brass plate, purportedly left by Drake, was discovered near San Francisco Bay in 1936; later it was believed that the plate had been initially located near Drake's Bay and then inadvertently moved; finally the plate was deemed a counterfeit.

Point Reyes Beach, a windy ten-mile-long strip, is an ideal place for beachcombers and whale-watchers. From there, it's not far to the end of Point Reyes' hammerhead peninsula. At one tip is **Chimney Rock,** a sea stack formed when the ocean eroded away the intervening land mass, leaving this islet just offshore. On the way to Chimney Rock you'll pass an **overlook** that's ideal for watching sea lions; then from Chimney Rock, if the day is clear, you'll see all the way to San Francisco.

At the other tip is **Point Reyes Lighthouse,** a century-old beacon placed at the foggiest point on the entire Pacific coast. The treacherous waters offshore have witnessed numerous shipwrecks, the first occurring way back in 1595. The original lighthouse, constructed to prevent these calamities, incorporated over a thousand pieces of crystal in its intricate lens. A modern beacon eventually replaced this multifaceted instrument, but the old lighthouse and an accompanying information center are still open to the public.

OLEMA TO BODEGA BAY

From Olema you can continue north on Route 1 or follow a looping 25-mile detour through **the region's pastoral interior** (★). On the latter, Sir Francis Drake Boulevard leads east past bald-domed hills and isolated farms. Livestock graze at the roadside while overhead hawks work the range. Grassland gives way to dense forest as you enter the realms of **Samuel P. Taylor State Park.** Then the road opens again to reveal a succession of tiny, woodframe towns.

At San Geronimo, turn left on Nicasio Valley Road. This carries further into the pastoral region of west Marin, which varies so dramatically from the county's eastside suburban enclaves. Indeed, the inland valleys are reminiscent more of the Old West than the busy Bay Area. At the Nicasio Reservoir, turn left onto Point Reyes–Petaluma Road and follow it to Sir Francis Drake Boulevard, closing the circle of this rural tour.

From Olema, Route 1 continues north along Tomales Bay, the lovely fjord-shaped inlet. Salt marshes stretch along one side of the road; on the other are rumpled hills tufted with grass. The waterfront village of Marshall consists of fishing boats moored offshore and woodframe houses anchored firmly onshore. Then the road turns inland to Tomales, another falsefront town with clapboard church and country homes. It continues past paint-peeled barns and open pastureland before turning seaward at Bodega Bay.

SONOMA AND MENDOCINO COASTS

BODEGA BAY TO THE LOST COAST

The fishing village of Bodega Bay might look vaguely familiar, for it was the setting of Alfred Hitchcock's eerie film *The Birds*. It's questionable whether any cast members remain among the population of snowy egrets, brown pelicans, and blue herons, but the Bay still supports a variety of winged creatures.

Here, at **Lucas Wharf** (Route 1 and Smith Brothers Lane, Bodega Bay) and elsewhere along this working waterfront, you can watch fishermen setting off into the fog every morning and hauling in their catch later in the day.

To the north lies the Sonoma Coast, a beautiful and still lightly developed area. Placid range land extends inward while along the shoreline, surf boils against angular cliffs. Far below are pocket beaches and coves; offshore rise dozens of tiny rock islands, or sea stacks. The coast teems with fish—salmon and steelhead, as well as crabs, clams, and abalone. Rip currents, sneaker waves, and the coldest waters this side of the Arctic make swimming inadvisable. But the landscape is wide open for exploration, enchanting and exotic.

For another **rustic detour** (★), you can follow Coleman Valley Road when it departs from Route 1 north of Bodega Bay. A rolling country road, it weaves through farmland and offers great views of ocean and mountains. About ten miles out it leads to the forest-rimmed village of Occidental.

Or, when Route 1 winds down to the woodframe town of Jenner (population 170, elevation 19), where the broad Russian River meets the ocean, you can take Route 116 up the river valley to the fabled **Russian River** resort area and winegrowing region.

The Russians for whom the river is named were explorers and trappers sailing down the Pacific coast from Russian outposts in Alaska. They came in search of sea otters and in hope of opening trade routes with the early Spanish settlers. In 1812 these bold outlanders went so far as to build **Fort Ross,** a wooden fortress overlooking the sea.

The old Russian stronghold, 13 miles north of Jenner, is today a state historic park (information, 707-847-3286; admission). Touring the reconstructed fort you'll encounter a museum, an old Russian Orthodox chapel, a stockade built of hand-tooled redwood, and an octagonal blockhouse. Together they provide an insight into an unusual chapter in California history.

From Jenner north through Fort Ross and beyond, Route 1 winds high above the coast. Every curve exposes another awesome view of adze-like cliffs slicing into the sea. Driving this corkscrew route can jangle the nerves, but the vistas are soothing to the soul. With the exception of scattered villages, the coastline remains undeveloped. You'll pass sunbleached wooden buildings in the old town of Stewart Point. Then the road courses through **Sea Ranch,** a development bitterly opposed by environmentalists, which nevertheless displays imaginative contemporary-design houses set against a stark sea.

Just north of Point Arena a side road from Route 1 leads out to **Point Arena Lighthouse** (707-882-2777; admission). The original lighthouse, built in 1870, was destroyed in the 1906 San Francisco earthquake, which struck Point Arena even more fiercely than the bay city. The present beacon, rebuilt shortly afterwards, rises 115 feet from a narrow peninsula. The lighthouse is open for tours. The views, by definition, are outstanding.

In Mendocino County, the highway passes through tiny seaside villages. Elk, Albion, and Little River gaze down on the ocean from rocky heights. The coastline is an intaglio of river valleys, pocket beaches, and narrow coves. Forested ridges, soft and green in appearance, fall away into dizzying cliffs.

The houses which stand amid this continental turmoil resemble Maine saltboxes and Cape Cod cottages. In the town of **Mendocino,** which sits on a headland above the sea, you'll discover New England incarnate. Settled in 1852, the town was built largely by Yankees who decorated their village with wooden towers, Victorian homes, and a Gothic Revival Presbyterian church. The town, originally a vital lumber port, has become an artists' colony. With a shoreline honeycombed by beaches and a villagescape capped with a white church steeple, Mendocino is a mighty pretty corner of the continent.

Mendocino Headlands State Park, located atop a sea cliff, offers unmatched views of the town's tumultuous shoreline. From the bluffs you can gaze down at placid tidepools and wave-carved grottoes. Headquarters for the park is the historic **Ford House** (Main Street, Mendocino; 707-937-5397), an 1854 home with a small museum and visitor center.

The best way to experience this antique town is by stopping at the **Kelley House Museum** (45007 Albion Street; 707-937-5791). Set in a vintage home dating from 1861, the museum serves as an historical society and unofficial chamber of commerce. Pick up a walking tour guide here and you can wander past Mendocino's intriguing locales. The **Chinese Temple** (Albion Street) is a 19th-century cottage converted into a religious shrine; nearby **MacCallum House** (Albion Street), a gingerbread Victorian, has been reborn as an inn and restaurant. Another building of note is the **Masonic Hall** (Ukiah Street), an 1865 structure adorned with a cupola. Then after meandering the side streets, stop at the **Mendocino Art Center** (45200 Little Lake Street; 707-937-5818). Here exhibits by painters, potters, photographers, textile workers, and others will give an idea of the tremendous talent contained in tiny Mendocino.

North of town, on the way to Fort Bragg, stop at **Jug Handle State Reserve** (along Route 1 about one mile north of Caspar; 707-937-5804). Here you can climb an ecological stairway which ascends a series of marine terraces. On the various levels you'll encounter the varied coast, dune, and ridge environments that form the area's diverse eco-system.

For a thoroughly delightful stroll to the sea, meander through the **Mendocino Coast Botanical Gardens** (18220 Route 1, Fort Bragg; 707-964-4352; admission). This coastal preserve, with two miles of luxuriant pathways, is "a garden for all seasons" with something always in bloom. The unique Northern California coastal climate is conducive to heathers, perennials, succulents, and rhododendrons, which grow in colorful profusion here. Trails lead past gardens of ivy, ferns, and drawf conifers to a coastal bluff with vistas up and down the rugged shoreline.

Near the center of Fort Bragg you can board the **Skunk train** for a half- or full-day ride aboard a diesel-powered railroad. Dating from 1885, the Skunk was originally a logging train; today it also carries passengers along a 40-mile route through mountains and redwoods to the inland town of Willits. For information, contact California Western Railroad (707-964-6371) in Fort Bragg.

North of Fort Bragg, Route 1 runs past miles of sand dunes and traverses several small towns. Then, after having followed the coast all the way from Southern California, it abruptly turns inland. The reason is the mysterious Lost Coast of California. Due north, where no highway could possibly run, the King Range vaults out of the sea, rising over 4000 feet in less than three miles. It is a wilderness inhabited by black bears and bald eagles, with an abandoned lighthouse and a solitary beach piled with ancient Indian shellmounds (see the "Sightseeing" section below and the "Beaches and Parks" section in this chapter).

REDWOOD COUNTRY

FROM LEGGETT TO EUREKA

Near the nondescript town of Leggett, Route 1 joins Route 101. Logging trucks, those belching beasts that bear down upon you without mercy, become more frequent. You are entering **Redwood Country**.

This is the habitat of *Sequoia sempervirens*, the coastal redwood, a tree whose ancestors date to the age of dinosaurs and which happens to be the world's tallest living thing. These "ambassadors from another time," as John Steinbeck called them, inhabit a 30-mile-wide coastal fog belt stretching 450 miles from the Monterey area north to Oregon. Redwoods live five to eight centuries, though some have survived over two millenia, while reaching heights over 350 feet and diameters greater than 20 feet.

There is a sense of solitude here uncapturable anywhere else. The trees form a cathedral overhead, casting a deep shade across the forest floor. Solitary sun shafts, almost palpable, cut through the grove; along the roof of the forest, pieces of light jump across the treetops, poised to fall like rain. Ferns and a few small animals are all that survive here. The silence and stillness are either transcendent or terrifying. It's like being at sea in a small boat.

The Redwood Highway, Route 101, leads north to the tallest, most dense stands of *Sequoia sempervirens*. At **Richardson Grove State Park** the road barrels through the very center of a magnificent grove. A short nature trail leads through this virgin timber, though the proximity of the road makes communing with nature seem a bit ludicrous.

North of Garberville, follow the **Avenue of the Giants**, a 33-mile alternative route which parallels Route 101. This two-lane road winds along the Eel River south fork, tunneling through dense redwood groves. Much of the road is encompassed by **Humboldt Redwoods State Park**, a 50,000-acre preserve with some of the finest forest land found anywhere. Park headquarters contains a visitor center (707-946-2311).

Further along is **Founder's Grove**, where a nature trail loops through a redwood stand. The forest is dedicated to early Save-the-Redwoods League leaders who were instrumental in preserving thousands of redwood acres, particularly in this park. Nearby **Rockefeller Forest** has another short loop trail leading to a 359-foot goliath, the tallest tree in the area. Avenue of the Giants continues through towns that are little more than way stations and then rejoins Route 101, which leads north to Eureka.

There are alternate routes to Eureka, however, leading along the perimeter of California's **Lost Coast** (★) region. From Route 101 near Redway take Briceland Thorne Road, which turns into Shelter Cove Road as it winds through the King Range.

Shelter Cove is a tiny bay neatly folded between sea cliffs and headlands. A point of embarkation for people exploring the Lost Coast, it has a few stores, restaurants, and hotels. Stock up here: the rest of this backcountry jaunt promises little more than a couple stores.

Outside Shelter Cove you can pick up Kings Peak Road or Ettersburg–Honeydew Road, which connect with Wilder Ridge Road and lead to the general store town of **Honeydew.** This is a prime marijuana growing region and a colony of hippies is bound to be sitting on the stoop swapping tales.

Mattole Road heads northeast, meandering along the Mattole River, to another forest hamlet, **Petrolia.** Nestled in a river valley and marked by a white-steeple church, the town is a scene straight from a Norman Rockwell painting. Hawks glide overhead. Old men rock on their front porches. The fire tower houses a red bell.

Next, Mattole Road ascends a succession of plateaus to a ranch land of unpainted barns and broad shade trees, then noses down to the coastline and parallels the waves for perhaps five miles. Here the setting is Scottish. Hillsides are grazed by herds of sheep and covered with tenacious grasses that shake in the sea wind. The gray-sand beach is covered with driftwood. Along the horizon peaks rise in jagged motions, seemingly thrust upward by the lash of the surf.

It's not far to **Cape Mendocino**, most westerly point in the contiguous United States. Here you'll have broad views of the ocean, including the menacing shoals where countless ships have been slapped to timber. Next, the road curves up through forest and sheep-grazing lands before rolling down to the gentle pastureland near the unique town of Ferndale.

A Victorian-style hamlet set in the Eel River valley, **Ferndale** is so perfectly refurbished it seems unreal. Main Street and nearby thoroughfares are lined with Gothic Revival, Queen Anne, Eastlake, and Italianate-style Victorians, brightly painted and blooming with pride. The best way to see the town is by stopping first at the **Ferndale Museum** (515 Shaw Avenue; 707-786-4466; admission). Here is an ever-changing collection of antiques and memorabilia from the region, plus an old blacksmith shop. There are also maps available for self-guided walking tours of this historic community. It's an architectural wonder that shouldn't be missed. (From Ferndale it's five miles to Route 101 and another ten to Eureka; if you can't take the aforementioned "alternate route," plan to make a side trip from Eureka to Ferndale.)

EUREKA

Eureka's 25,000 inhabitants make it the largest town on the Northern California coast. Founded in 1850, the town's first industry was mining; the name "Eureka!" came from an old gold mining exclamation meaning "I found it."

Today fishing and lumbering have replaced more romantic occupations, but much of the region's history is captured in points of interest. Stop at the Chamber of Commerce (2112 Broadway; 707-442-3738) on the way into town for maps, brochures, and information. This group also organizes five-hour tours which take in most of the town's highlights.

Make certain to ask for the architectural tour map. Eureka has over 100 glorious **Victorian homes** ranging from understated designs to the outlandish **Carson Mansion** (2nd and M streets), a multilayered confection that makes other Gothic architecture seem tame. It was built in the 1880s by William Carson, a wealthy lumber merchant with the same need for ostentation that afflicted the robber barons on San Francisco's Nob Hill.

Of a more subdued nature are the **covered bridges** (★) on the southern outskirts of town. To reach them from Route 101, take Elk River Road two miles to Bertas Road or three miles to Zanes Road (there is a wooden span covering both). You'll enter a picture of red barns and green pasture framed by cool, lofty forest. The bridges, crossing a small river, evoke Vermont winters and New Hampshire sleigh rides.

Fort Humboldt (3431 Fort Avenue; 707-445-6567) is also stationed at this end of town. Built in the early 1850s to help settlers war against indigenous tribes of Yurok, Hoopa, and Mattole Indians, it has been partially restored. Rather than re-creating army life (experienced here by a hard-drinking young officer named Ulysses S. Grant), the historic park displays early logging traditions. There's a drafty logger's cabin, a small lumber industry museum, and a couple of remarkable old steam engines.

Nearby **Sequoia Park** (W Street between Glatt and Madrone streets) provides a nifty retreat from urban life. Tucked into its 52-acre preserve is a petting zoo, picnic area, playground, and a thick stand of redwoods.

Then head to **Old Town**, Eureka's answer to the nation's gentrification craze. This neighborhood was formerly the local bowery; the term "skid row" reputedly originated right here. It derived from the bums residing beside the nearby "skid trails," along which redwood logs were transported to the waterfront. Now the ghetto is gilded: old Victorians, woodframe warehouses, brick buildings, and clapboard houses have been rebuilt and painted striking colors. Stylish shops have sprung up and restaurants have opened.

At the foot of C Street in Old Town, where the bowery meets the bay, the **Humboldt Bay Harbor Cruise** (707-445-1910) departs. For several well-invested dollars, you'll sail past an egret rookery, oyster beds, pelican roosts, ugly pulp mills, and the town's flashy new marina.

Last, but in my heart first, is **Clarke Museum** (240 E Street; 707-443-1947) with its outstanding collection of Native American artifacts. Here are ornate baskets, feather regalia, fur quivers, beaded moccasins, war clubs, and a dugout redwood canoe. It provides a unique insight into this splendid Humboldt Bay region before the age of gold pans and axe handles.

EUREKA TO OREGON

Heading north from Eureka there are two towns worth noting. **Arcata**, home of Humboldt State University, is a student town with an outstanding collection of old Victorians. For a self-guided architectural tour, obtain a map at the Chamber of Commerce (1062 G Street; 707-822-3619).

Trinidad, one of the area's oldest towns, perches above a small port. Sea stacks and sailboats lie anchored offshore, watched over by a miniature lighthouse. For a tour of the pocket beaches and rocky shores lining this beautiful waterfront, take a three-mile trip south from town along Scenic Drive.

Next is **Redwood National Park**, fitting finale to this lengthy coastal journey. Park of parks, it's a necklace strung for over 40 miles along the coast. Among its gems are secluded beaches, elk herds, and the world's tallest tree.

First link in the chain is the **ranger station** at Orick (707-488-3461). In addition to information, there is a shuttle service (fare) here for the trailhead to **Tall Trees Grove**. A one-and-three-tenths-mile hike leads to a redwood stand boasting the tallest of all California's redwoods, including a 367-foot giant. There are also horseback rides from Orick (Lane's Pack Station; 707-488-5225) leading through the park's stately groves. **Lady Bird Johnson Grove**, located off Bald Hill Road on a one-mile trail, represents another magnificent cluster of ancient trees.

Another side road, Davison Road (day-use fee), leads along remote **Gold Bluffs Beach** six miles to **Fern Canyon**. Here angular walls 50 feet high are covered with rioting vegetation.

Redwood National Park consists of three state parks—Prairie Creek, Del Norte, and Jedediah Smith. Just before the main entrance to the first you'll pass **Madison Grant Forest Elk Refuge**, where herds of Roosevelt elk graze across open meadows. Immediately past the entrance, Cal Barrel Road, another short detour, courses through dense redwood forest.

Also plan to turn off onto **Coastal Drive**, a gravel road paralleling Route 101. Its numerous turnouts expose extraordinary ocean vistas. The road snakes high above the coast before emptying onto the main highway near the mouth of the Klamath River.

The Del Norte section of the park reveals more startling seaviews en route to Crescent City, where the main **park headquarters** is located (1111 2nd Street; 707-464-6101). There is travel information aplenty here and at the Chamber of Commerce building across the street (Front Street; 707-464-3174).

Route 101 north to Route 199 leads to the park's Jedediah Smith section with its mountain vistas and thick redwood groves. The Smith River, rich in salmon and steelhead, threads through the region. Either highway will carry you further north to Oregon.

Shopping

The best shopping spot in all Marin County is the town of Sausalito. Here you can stroll the waterfront along Bridgeway and its side streets, visiting gourmet shops, boutiques, and antique stores. One of the Bay Area's wealthiest towns, Sausalito sports few bargains, but it does host an assortment of elegant shops.

California Visions (21 Princess Street) displays a variety of natural crystal pieces. They also feature handcrafted jewelry and numerous other items. The nearby **High As A Kite** shop (34 Princess Street) is fun to walk through, even if you are afraid of heights.

Several shops in the mini-mall at 660 Bridgeway are also worth a browse. Glass menagerie lovers will peek into the **Crystal Dolphin**. And style-savvy women will check out **Kolonaki** with its designer line of cotton resort wear. For souvenir items and Asian bric-a-brac, there's **Takahashi** (668 Bridgeway).

Of the several art shops lining Sausalito's streets, **Shelby Galleries** (673 Bridgeway) displays the most interesting collection. Rather than tourist landscapes, the shop specializes in quality art and features several renowned painters.

The downtown facility most crowded with shops and shoppers is **Village Fair** (777 Bridgeway), a multilevel mall boasting forty-three stores. Here are leather shops, jewelers, clothing stores, confectioners, notion shops, crafts galleries, ceramic shops, and so on.

Past Sausalito, the shopping scene along the North Coast is concentrated in a few towns. There are small shops scattered about in rural areas, but the best selection of arts and crafts is located around Point Reyes, Mendocino, and Eureka.

During the '60s and '70s many talented people, caught up in the "back to the land" movement, migrated to the state's northern counties. Here they developed their skills and further refined their art. As a result, crafts like pottery, woodworking, weaving, stained glass manufacturing, jewelry, and fashion designing have flourished.

Stinson Beach Books (Route 1, Stinson Beach) may be located in a small town, but it handles a large variety of books. Compressed within the confines of the place is an array of travel books, best sellers, novels, how-to handbooks, etc. It's a great place to stop before that long, languorous day at the beach.

For an idea of the local art scene, you should certainly stop by **Bolinas Gallery** (48 Wharf Road, Bolinas). Judy Molyneaux has stocked it with an impressive selection of her work.

Just north of the Bolinas turnoff on Route 1 there are signs for **Dogtown Pottery.** Follow the bumpy road down to this informal establishment and you'll find a building full of ceramics. Combining fine designs and glazes, this gallery features an assortment of decorative and functional items. The folks who run the place are trusting souls: if they're not present to serve you, they ask that you simply write a check and leave it for them. (Oh that all the world worked in such ways.)

For an idea of the early California art scene, consider **Carrell Gallery** (11315 Route 1, Point Reyes Station). Here are oil paintings and other pieces by 19th- and early 20th-century West Coast artists. The gallery also carries French and American bronze sculptures.

Beverly's Life Masks (11431 Route 1 #3, Point Reyes Station) is an unusual shop where ceramicist Beverly Toyu molds "life masks" from clients' faces and fashions handsome pottery as well. Nearby **Gallery Route One** (11431 Route 1, Point Reyes Station) spotlights paintings by contemporary artists.

Shaker Shops West (5 Inverness Way, Inverness) is a marvelous store specializing in reproductions of Shaker arts and crafts, particularly furniture. In addition to rag rugs, candlesticks, and woven baskets, there are beautifully handcrafted boxes. The early American household items range from cross-stitch needlepoint to wall clocks. Touring the store is like visiting a mini-museum dedicated to this rare American community.

Farther up the coast, in the New England-style town of Mendocino, you'll discover a shopper's paradise. Prices are quite dear, but the window browsing is unparalleled. Housed in the town's old Victorians and Cape Cod cottages are a plethora of shops. There are stores specializing in soap, seashells, candles, and T-shirts; not to mention bookstores, potters, jewelers, art galleries, and antique shops galore. Most are located along the woodframe Main Street, but also search out the side streets and passageways in this vintage town.

Particularly noteworthy among the galleries are **Gallery Fair** (Kasten and Ukiah streets) and **Highlight Gallery** (45052 Main Street), with their displays of modern art, jewelry, and woodwork, and the **Mendocino Art Center** (45200 Little Lake Street), which has numerous crafts studios as well as an art gallery.

Then in Ferndale, a picturesque Victorian town south of Eureka, there's another covey of intriguing shops. The community has attracted a number of artisans, many of whom display their wares in the 19th-

and early 20th-century stores lining Main Street. There are shops selling woodstoves, stained glass, and kinetic sculptures; others deal in ironwork, used books, handknits, and rag rugs. There are even stores specializing in "paper treasures," boots and saddles, dolls, and "nostalgic gifts." All are contained along a three-block section that more resembles a living museum than a downtown shopping district.

Eureka, too, has been gentrified. Most of the refurbishing has occurred in Old Town, where stately Victorians, falsefront stores, and tumbledown buildings have been transformed into sparkling shops. Window browse down 2nd and 3rd streets from C Street to H Street and you're bound to find several inviting establishments. Of particular interest are **Imperiale Place** (320 2nd Street), a multilevel mall, and **Humboldt Cultural Center** (422 1st Street), an art gallery housed in an 1870s mercantile store.

Nightlife

Now don't misunderstand—California's northern coast and redwood region are wild and provocative places. It's just that the word "wild" up here is taken in the literal sense, as in wilderness and wildlife. Somehow the urban meaning of crazy nights and endless parties was never fully translated in these parts.

There are small bars and local gathering places along the coast, but few sophisticated nightspots. To give you a general idea of the scene, such as it is, I've listed a few suggestions. It's also a good idea to ask around town about special events and favored hangouts. You might just get lucky.

The window simply reads "Bar"; the address is 757 Bridgeway in Sausalito; and the place is famous. Famous for its name, the **no name** (415-332-1392), and because it's a favored hangout among young swingers and old salts alike. With an antique bar, piano, and open-air patio, it's a congenial spot to bend an elbow.

When the sun goes down in Bolinas, you are left with several options. Sleep, read, curl up with a loved one, fade into unrelieved boredom, or head for **Smiley's Schooner Saloon** (41 Wharf Road, Bolinas; 415-868-1311). Since local folks often follow the latter course, you're liable to find them parka-to-parka along the bar. They come to shoot pool, poke the juke box, and admire the lavish wood panel bar. Smiley's, after all, is the only show in town.

Local folks in Point Reyes Station ease up to a similar wooden bar at **Western Saloon** (Route 1, Point Reyes Station; 415-663-1661) practically every night of the week. But on every other Friday, when the place features dancing 'til the wee hours, the biggest crowds of all arrive.

The **Sea Gull Cellar Bar** (Lansing and Ukiah streets, Mendocino; 707-937-2100), which naturally is on the second floor, has various ensembles performing Thursday, Friday, and Saturday nights. The sound may be rock, jazz fusion, solo guitar, or country. A kind of musical potluck.

Or enjoy a quiet drink at the **Mendocino Hotel** (45080 Main Street, Mendocino; 707-937-0511). Here you can relax at a Victorian-style lounge or in an enclosed garden patio.

There's music seven nights a week at the **Caspar Inn** (Caspar Road, Caspar; 707-964-5565). This down-home bar room spotlights local bands as well as groups from outside the area. Hit it on the right night and the joint will be rocking.

The **Benbow Inn** (445 Lake Benbow Drive, Garberville; 707-923-2124) features a fine old lounge with carved walls and an ornate fireplace. A pianist plays every evening, adding to the intimacy.

For a quiet drink in a traditional setting consider the **Scotia Inn** (Main and Mill streets, Scotia; 707-764-5683). This old country hotel sports a comfortable lounge; on weekends a solo musician performs.

The swing scene in Eureka centers around **Old Town Bar & Grill** (327 2nd Street, Eureka; 707-445-2971), which presents live music several nights a week. Located in the gentrified Old Town district, it consists of an old warehouse beautifully refurbished with brick walls and redwood panelling. Cover charge.

The Ritz Club (240 F Street, Eureka; 707-445-5850) is an art deco jewel with etched-glass adornments and colored-glass mirrors. Here you can relax over a tall cool one while admiring the architecture.

There's rock, blues, and reggae live at **Jambalaya** (915 H Street, Arcata; 707-822-4766). This college town bar has a dancefloor and down-home crowd. The bands are local and the scene is loose. Cover.

Index

Abbreviations used for area names are:

(LA) Los Angeles County; (NC) North Coast; (NCC) North Central Coast; (OC) Orange Coast; (SCC) South Central Coast; (SD) San Diego County; (SF) San Francisco.

Note: Hotel and restaurant names are not indexed; names of beaches, parks, and major sightseeing spots are.

Leslie Henriques

About the Author

Ray Riegert is the author of five travel books, including *Hidden San Francisco and Northern California*. His most popular work, *Hidden Hawaii*, has won the coveted Lowell Thomas Travel Journalism Award for Best Guidebook. In addition to his role as publisher of Ulysses Press, he writes for Fodor's Travel Guides, the San Francisco *Examiner & Chronicle* and *Travel & Leisure*. Ray is a member of the society of American Travel Writers and writes a weekly travel column for a Gannett chain newspaper. Currently working on a new book, *Hidden Los Angeles and Southern California*, he lives in the San Francisco Bay Area with his wife, travel photographer Leslie Henriques, and their son Keith and daughter Alice.

About the Illustrator

The son of Japanese parents who emigrated to California, Victor Ichioka holds a master's degree in painting from the University of California. He has illustrated a book of Jamaican short stories as well as books on flyfishing and restaurants. Spending his spare time painting and combing the coast, Victor lives in Berkeley, California with his wife Marilyn and their children, Sarah and Michael.